Mathematics of Investment

Mathematics
of Investment
FIFTH EDITION

William L. Hart
University of Minnesota

D. C. HEATH AND COMPANY
Lexington, Massachusetts Toronto London

Published simultaneously in Canada.

Printed in the United States of America.

International Standard Book Number: 0-669-93690-1

Library of Congress Catalog Card Number: 74-10021

Preface

This text is designed, first, to provide a brief first course in the theory and applications of interest and annuities certain, considerably simplified by special devices and elimination of outdated content. The short course would be based on the first six chapters without omissions, where all annuity problems come under the *simple case.** Also, in Chapters 1–6, computational difficulties are minimized by the nature of the content and special care in selection of the data for the problems. These six chapters culminate in a comprehensive miscellaneous review exercise of about 100 problems. Thus, Chapters 1–6 may be considered as a relatively brief book with attained objectives, within the text as a whole. The content of this rounded unit facilitates a course of moderate extent including all topics of the mathematics of finance appropriate for the general student in a college of business administration, and especially for those students who will major in accounting and the theory of investments. The content also would be highly desirable in the training of prelegal students. In fact, the subject matter of the brief course would be very useful to the general student in his personal business affairs in later life.

Three chapters are provided for expansion in varying amounts, if desired, of the short course which has been described. Chapter 7 presents a unique treatment of the general case for annuities certain with a first part of reasonable simplicity, and the remainder† of more difficult type. Chapters 8 and 9 offer an introduction to the mathematics of life annuities and life insurance, with corresponding applications. The theory in these expansion Chapters 7–9 is not particularly difficult, although it is at a higher level than most of Chapters 1–6. For the student who studies Chapters 7–9, the major difficulty is likely to be the added complexity of the computation involved in solving problems in the exercises. However, if this situation is faced properly,‡ the complete content of Chapters 7–9 rounds out a thorough and interesting introduction to the mathematics

---

*Use of the *interest rate per conversion period* rather than the *nominal rate* as the fundamental interest variable, and recognition of the *interest period* rather than a *year* as the natural time unit in formulas, was initiated in the subject by the author in the second edition of this text. At the same time, he named a situation as a *simple case* for an annuity problem if the payment interval of the annuity is the same as the conversion period of the rate of compound interest. Fortunately, this case embraces almost all applications of annuities certain in business practice. Exceptions to this statement occur mainly in advanced actuarial science, or in connection with business contracts of a type where, perhaps by accident, conditions are stated which prevent application of the simple case in legal litigation.

†This content, and various other items throughout the text and its exercises, are earmarked with a black star ★ to show that the subject matter may be omitted without disturbing the continuity of the remainder of the text.

‡A modern computer would be the ideal aid, but this assistance cannot be anticipated as commonly available. Otherwise, logarithmic computation would suffice, with

of investment as it occurs in current business and investment affairs, and in the vast activities of life insurance companies.

The Tables

This text includes the complete *Tables for Mathematics of Investment*, in a *Fifth Edition*, by the author. These tables have been altered from their Fourth Edition as follows. The Commissioners' Standard Ordinary Mortality Table of 1941 (CSO Table), and the corresponding table of commutation columns at 2½% interest, of the Society of Actuaries, have been removed. Instead, the Fifth Edition includes the CSO Table of 1958, and a table of the corresponding commutation columns at 3% interest, of the Society of Actuaries, which now are standard in insurance practice. The interest tables go far beyond what might be expected as tables for student use in a text on the mathematics of investment. The Tables were designed to be sufficient for all normal needs of a student in a college of business administration in his later courses in investment theory or general economics, banking, bond practices, and particularly in accounting courses. Also, it is expected that a practicing accountant, real estate or investment broker, and many employees in banks, would find that the Tables are sufficient for most of the needs where interest tables are required. In addition to the interest and annuity tables, provided for thirty-two interest rates,* the Tables include complete five-place and six-place tables of logarithms, and a useful extract of a seven-place table, to increase accuracy in computation of $(1 + i)^n$ or $(1 + i)^{-n}$.

The Auxiliary Topics

In three brief chapters, not considered as content to be taught as part of the usual course, the text includes topics which would be desirable for reference at various places, if a student should wish a quick review of background content. The topics in Chapters 10 and 12 are treated very briefly. Chapter 11, concerning ordinary computation and logarithms, is presented in a very complete form.

Special Features

In common with previous editions of this text, there is heavy emphasis on *verbal problems* with a distinctly practical flavor, rather than merely

---

the aid of both five-place and six-place logarithms, and an extract of a seven-place table of logarithms in the tables.
*See Introduction for the Tables in this text.

on mechanical drill problems. This edition adds to the emphasis on what might be labeled as *consumer education* not only in the discussion in the text, but also in problems. There is distinct encouragement for the use of *time diagrams,* which emphasize the fundamental fact that the mathematics of finance deals with *"dated values."* Answers for the odd-numbered problems are included in the text. A separate *Manual for the Instructor,** including answers for even-numbered problems, has been prepared by the author. This manual includes suggestions for motivation in connection with the content; sometimes a background for the methods; reasons for omitting certain content; suggestions about solutions of the more difficult problems; and sample examinations which are pertinent at various places in the course.

The author takes pleasure in thanking the numerous teachers of former editions of this text who have sent to him comments and suggestions about the content. Included in this group, thanks are extended to various teachers in the Philippines and in India where special editions of this book are in use.

The author also wishes to express his appreciation of the cooperation and assistance he has received in connection with the preparation of this Fifth Edition from the staff of D. C. Heath and Company.

William L. Hart
La Jolla, California

*Furnished free to the instructor.

Contents

7/ General Annuity Formulas   176

8/ Life Annuities   189

9/ Life Insurance   210

Auxiliary Topics

10/ Certain Basic Topics   227

List of Tables at End of Text

> **Compound Interest And**
> **Annuity Tables For The Interest Rates**
>
> $\frac{1}{4}\%$, $\frac{7}{24}\%$, $\frac{1}{3}\%$, $\frac{3}{8}\%$, $\frac{5}{12}\%$, $\frac{1}{2}\%$, $\frac{7}{12}\%$, $\frac{5}{8}\%$, $\frac{3}{4}\%$, $\frac{7}{8}\%$, 1%,
> $1\frac{1}{8}\%$, $1\frac{1}{4}\%$, $1\frac{3}{8}\%$, $1\frac{1}{2}\%$, $1\frac{5}{8}\%$, $1\frac{3}{4}\%$, 2%, $2\frac{1}{4}\%$, $2\frac{1}{2}\%$, $2\frac{3}{4}\%$,
> 3%, $3\frac{1}{4}\%$, $3\frac{1}{2}\%$, 4%, $4\frac{1}{2}\%$, 5%, $5\frac{1}{2}\%$, 6%, $6\frac{1}{2}\%$, 7%, 8%

Selected Actuarial Tables

1/ Simple Interest

1. Interest

Suppose that an investor lends money to a debtor. Then the latter must pay back the money originally borrowed, and also an additional sum called *interest*. From the investor's standpoint, interest is income from invested capital. From the debtor's viewpoint, interest is money paid for the use of money.

NOTE 1. Whenever we use a number symbol for a concrete quantity, in accordance with common practice the symbol will represent the *measure* of the quantity in terms of an appropriate unit. Thus, if it is known that the money unit is $1, we may say "*let P represent the capital*," meaning that it is $P. However, if we wish to emphasize the money unit, we might say "*let $P represent the capital*." Our equations involve the *numbers* representing the measures of whatever concrete quantities are involved. Our unit for money will be $1.

In the description of interest, we shall have occasion to use the language of percentage at various places. Recall that the symbol % is read *percent* and means $\frac{1}{100}$. Thus, if h is a number, then $h\%$ means $h(.01)$. Any number expression is unaltered in value if it is multiplied by 100 and then has the symbol % written at the right.

ILLUSTRATION 1.   We have $3\% = 3(.01) = .03$. To change 1.35 to percent form, we write $1.35 = (1.35)(100)\% = 135\%$.

The capital originally invested in a transaction is called the **principal**. At any time after the investment of the principal, the sum of the principal and the interest due is called the **amount.*** For any specified time unit (which sometimes will *not* be one year), *the ratio of the interest earned in one time unit to the*

---

* On account of the technical meaning assigned to "*amount*," other words such as *sum* should be used when possible instead of *amount* where it might be met colloquially.

principal is called the **interest rate**. If r is this rate, and P is the principal, then

$$r = \frac{\text{interest on } P \text{ per unit time}}{P}; \tag{1}$$

$$(\text{interest on } P \text{ per unit time}) = Pr. \tag{2}$$

All forms of interest have the common property that the interest on P is equal to P times the interest on $1. Hence, in (1), the numerator is P times the interest on $1. Thus.

$$r = \frac{P \cdot (\text{interest on \$1 for one unit of time})}{P}, \; or$$

$$r = (\text{interest on \$1 for one unit of time}).$$

In other words, r is *the measure in dollars* of the interest on $1 for one time unit.

ILLUSTRATION 2.   If $1000 earns $36.60 interest in one year, then (1) gives $r = (36.60/1000) = .0366 = 3.66\%$.

ILLUSTRATION 3.   If the interest rate is $5\frac{1}{2}\%$ per year and $P = \$1000$, then $r = .055$ and, from (2), the interest for 1 year is $1000(.055) = \$55$.

2.   Simple Interest

Hereafter, our time unit will be one year, unless otherwise specified. Suppose, now, that a principal P is invested at the rate r for t years. If it is agreed that the interest on P for t years will be t *times the interest on $P for one year*, then it is said that simple interest is being charged. Thus, at simple interest, the interest is computed on the original principal during the whole time, at the stated interest rate. In this chapter, the word *interest* will refer to *simple interest*, unless otherwise stated.

Let F be the final amount resulting from the investment of P for t years at the rate r, and let I be the interest due at the end of t years. Then,

$$F = P + I. \tag{1}$$

The interest on P for one year is Pr; hence the simple interest for t years is Prt:

$$I = Prt. \tag{2}$$

From (2), $$P + I = P + Prt = P(1 + rt), \; or$$

$$F = P(1 + rt). \tag{3}$$

To compute simple interest, we use $I = Prt$, where r is the rate expressed as a decimal and t is the time expressed in years. If the time is expressed in months, we express it in years, assuming that a year consists of 12 equal months. If the time is given in days, say D days, two varieties of simple interest are in use: **ordinary interest**, where the year is taken as 360 days; **exact interest**, where the year is taken as 365 days. Thus, when the term of investment is D days, (2) gives the following results:

$$\text{\textbf{Exact interest} } \textit{for D days:} \qquad t = \frac{D}{365}; \qquad I = Pr\frac{D}{365}. \qquad (4)$$

$$\text{\textbf{Ordinary interest} } \textit{for D days:} \quad t = \frac{D}{360}; \qquad I = Pr\frac{D}{360}. \qquad (5)$$

Example 1. Find the ordinary and the exact interest at 5% on $5000 and the corresponding amounts at the end of 59 days.

SOLUTION. We employ $I = Prt$ with $t = 59/360$ for the ordinary interest and $t = 59/365$ for the exact interest. Then we use $F = P + I$.

Ord. int.: $\qquad\qquad I = 5000(.05)\frac{59}{360} = \$40.97; \qquad F = \$5040.97.$

Exact int.: $\qquad\qquad I = 5000(.05)\frac{59}{365} = \$40.41; \qquad F = \$5040.41.$

COMMENT. In computation, avoid inexact divisions as long as possible. In fractions, be alert to divide out common factors. Thus,

$$\frac{5000(.05)59}{365} = \frac{50(59)}{73} = \frac{2950}{73} = 40.41, \qquad (6)$$

where we divided to three decimal places before rounding off to 40.41. In (6), instead of dividing, we may use Table XVII to obtain the reciprocal of 73, and then multiply, if we desire to avoid division, as follows.

$$\frac{2950}{73} = 2950\left(\frac{1}{73}\right) = 2950(.013699) = \$40.41.$$

In Example 1, we illustrated the fact that *ordinary* interest for D days is *greater* than *exact* interest for D days. This is due to the fact that the denominator 365 in (4) is larger than 360 in (5).

The use of simple interest usually is restricted to business transactions where the time involved is at most one year. However, simple interest may be involved, with periodic payments at short intervals, in the discharge of debts extending over more than one year.

3. Calculation of the Time Between Dates

In computing interest, we include the last day but not the first day in counting the time between two dates. Sometimes the time between two dates is counted under the assumption that each month has 30 days; we shall call the result the *approximate time*. Usually it is less than the actual time.

Example 1. Find the actual and the approximate time between June 30, 1975, and February 23, 1976.

SOLUTION. 1. To find the *actual time*, use Table IV, and count from January 1, 1975. February 23 is the 54th day of 1976; since $365 + 54 = 419$, we proceed as follows:

Feb. 23, 1976:   419th *day, counting from* Jan. 1, 1975;
June 30, 1975:   181st *day, counting from* Jan. 1, 1975.

Time between dates is $\overline{238}$ days.   (*Subtracting*)

2. To find the *approximate time*, first express Feb. 23, 1976, on the basis of months starting from Jan. 1, 1975. The time is $[7(30) + 23]$ days, or 233 days, which is less than the actual time.

	Year	Mo.	Days	Year	Mo.	Days	Year	Mo.	Days
Feb. 23, 1976	1976 :	2	: 23	1975 :	14	: 23	1975 :	13	: 53
June 30, 1975							1975 :	6	: 30
Elapsed time							0 :	7	: 23

Summary

In finding simple interest between two dates, we have four types of interest available:

  I. *Ordinary interest for the actual number of days.*

 II. *Exact interest for the actual number of days.*

III. *Ordinary interest for the approximate number of days.*

IV. *Exact interest for the approximate number of days.*

Usually, Method I is the most favorable for the creditor, because the actual time usually is greater than the approximate time, and ordinary interest is greater than the exact interest for the same time. Suppose that plain arithmetic is to be used in computing interest, without reference to any interest table. Then ordinary interest may offer a numerical convenience because 360 has considerably more integral factors than 365. Method I is called the **Banker's Rule** and is used widely in business practice where simple interest is charged.

ILLUSTRATION 1. At 8%, the interest on $1000 from June 30, 1975, to February 23, 1976, could be computed in the following ways. We use the results in Example 1.

Ord. int., actual time: $I = 1000(.08)\frac{238}{360}.$

Exact int., actual time: $\qquad$ $I = 1000(.08)\frac{238}{365}.$

Ord. int., approximate time: $\qquad$ $I = 1000(.08)\frac{233}{360}.$

Exact int., approximate time: $\qquad$ $I = 1000(.08)\frac{233}{365}.$

Hereafter, unless otherwise specified, if the time for computation of simple interest is given in days directly, or in days between two dates, we agree to use the Banker's Rule, Method I above. Although this usually is the most favorable of Methods I–IV for the creditor, a borrower has no justification for resenting use of Method I if he is told in advance that it is the lender's method for charging interest.

4. Six Percent Method for Computing Interest

From $I = Prt$, the ordinary interest at 6% on P is as follows:

for 60 *days,* $I = P(.06)(\frac{1}{6}) = .01P;$ $\quad$ *for* 6 *days,* $I = P(.06)\frac{1}{60} = .001P.$ $\quad$ (1)

We can obtain $.01P$ and $.001P$ by moving the decimal point in P two places and three places to the left, respectively. Thus, we arrive at the following method, which sometimes is convenient when r is related simply to 6%.

Summary

The 6% method for ordinary interest on \$P for D days at a rate r:

Express D as the sum of simple multiples of 60 and 6.

By use of (1), find the ordinary interest at 6% for each of the parts of D days, and add, to obtain the interest at 6% for D days.

Add, or subtract, convenient fractional parts of the interest at 6% in order to obtain the interest at the rate r.

Example 1. Find the ordinary interest on \$1389.20 for 143 days at 4.5%.

SOLUTION. $143 = 120 + 20 + 3 = 2(60) + \frac{1}{3}(60) + \frac{1}{2}(6).$

$\qquad$ \$13.892 is interest at 6% for 60 days.

$\qquad$ \$27.784 is interest at 6% for 120 days. $\quad$ (2×60 days)
$\qquad$ 4.631 is interest at 6% for 20 days. $\quad$ ($\frac{1}{3} \times 60$ days)
$\qquad$ .695 is interest at 6% for 3 days. $\quad$ ($\frac{1}{2} \times 6$ days)

(*Add*) $\quad$ \$33.110 is interest at 6% for 143 days.
$\qquad$ 8.278 is interest at $1\frac{1}{2}$% for 143 days. $\quad$ ($\frac{1}{4}$ of 6%)

(*Subtract*) $\quad$ \$24.832 is interest at $4\frac{1}{2}$% for 143 days.

Exercise 1

Find the ordinary interest and the amount.

1. On $5000 at 6% for 216 days.   **2.** On $7200 at 4% for 300 days.
3. On $8000 at .045 for 93 days.   **4.** On $6000 at .035 for 180 days.

Find the exact interest and the amount.

5. On $3000 at 4% for 146 days.   **6.** On $10,950 at 5% for 75 days.
7. On $2500 at .055 for 27 days.   **8.** On $5570 at $3\frac{1}{2}$% for 219 days.

Find the actual and the approximate time between the dates.

9. April 24 and October 23, 1975.   **10.** March 15 and August 22, 1976.

Find the interest in each problem hereafter by the Banker's Rule if the time is described by given dates.

11. The interest at 7% on $20,400 from March 1 to November 1, 1978, and the amount due.
12. The interest at 8% and the final amount due if $12,000 is invested from August 17 to December 7 of 1977.
13. Mr. Hargraves borrows $5000 from Mr. Jerico on October 1 of 1976 and promises to pay the principal and simple interest at 9% to discharge the debt on June 28 of 1977. What amount does Mr. Hargraves pay?

Find the ordinary interest by the 6% method.

14. On $2850 for 170 days at .06.   **15.** On $563.40 for 196 days at .06.
16. On $4918 for 134 days at .07.   **17.** On $1321 for 139 days at .05.
18. On $9830 for 143 days at .045.   **19.** On $2385 for 624 days at .075.

5. Accumulation and Discount at Simple Interest

If a sufficient number of the variables P, I, F, r, and t are given, the others can be found by use of

$$F = P + I; \quad I = Prt; \quad F = P(1 + rt). \tag{1}$$

In financial transactions involving money due on different dates, every sum of money which is mentioned should be thought of *with an attached date*. That is, the mathematics of investment deals with **dated values**. This is one of the most important facts to be emphasized in the text. On the time scale in Figure 1, where O represents the initial date, called the *present*, the point M represents the end of t years. The letter T indicates that the line is a *time scale*. We place P at O and F at M. When P and F are related by (1), P and F are equivalent sums of money. We call P the **present value** of the future **amount** F. With investment at simple interest at the rate r, P grows or *accumulates* to the value F at the end of t years.

Figure 1

Example 1. Accumulate $2000 for 3 years at 7% simple interest.

SOLUTION. 1. *Data:* $P = 2000;$ $r = .07;$ $t = 3.$

2. From $I = Prt,$ $I = 2000(.07)(3) = \$420.$

From $F = P + I,$ $F = 2000 + 420 = \$2420.$

Example 2. If $1000 accumulates to $1250 when invested at simple interest for 3 years, find the interest rate.

SOLUTION. 1. *Data:* $P = \$1000;$ $F = \$1250;$ $t = 3.$

2. From $F = P + I,$ $I = 1250 - 1000 = 250.$

From $I = Prt,$ $250 = 1000r(3);$ $r = \frac{250}{3000} = .08\frac{1}{3} = 8\frac{1}{3}\%.$

Example 3. If *money is worth** $7\frac{1}{2}\%$ simple interest, find the present value of $1100 which is due at the end of $2\frac{1}{2}$ years.

SOLUTION. 1. *Data:* $F = 1100;$ $r = .075;$ $t = \frac{5}{2}.$ The data are indicated on the time scale in Figure 2. We wish to find $P.$

2. From $F = P(1 + rt),$

$$P\left[1 + \frac{5}{2}(.075)\right] = 1100; \qquad P\left(\frac{2 + .375}{2}\right) = 1100; \qquad (2)$$

$$P = \frac{2200}{2.375} = \frac{2,200,000}{2375} = \frac{88,000}{95} = \frac{17,600}{19} = \$926.32. \qquad (3)$$

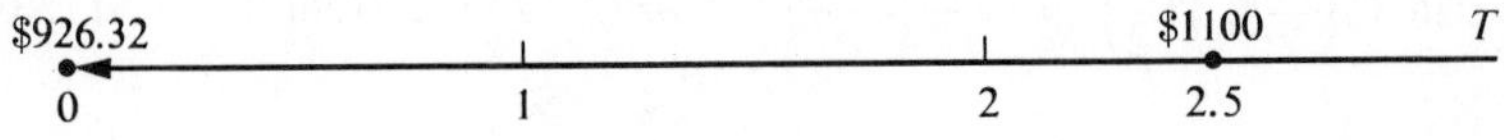

Figure 2

COMMENT. Notice that, in (2), we performed *multiplications* and *additions* first, since they are exact operations, and then solved for $P.$ In (3), we multiplied the numerator and denominator by 1000 to eliminate the decimal point, and divided both numerator and denominator by 25, and then by 5. Finally, we divided by 19. We could have used the reciprocal Table XVII if desired to obtain $(1/19) = .052632,$ and then multiplied by 17,600. However, this method would have left the cents in doubt in the result. To simplify the unavoidable arithmetic in this chapter, it is wise to remain alert to the possibility of dividing out common

* This means that money *can be invested at the given rate.*

factors from the numerator and denominator of any fraction. In any division, as in (3), round off the result to the nearest cent. Also, delay any inexact division as long as possible.

To discount $\$F$ for t years means to find the *present value* $\$P$ of $\$F$ on a day which is t years before $\$F$ is due. The difference between the future value $\$F$ and its present value $\$P$ is called **the discount** on $\$F$. That is, the discount on F is $(F - P)$. Since $F = P + I$, then $I = F - P$. Hence, the symbol I has been given two useful names:

$$I = \begin{cases} \text{the interest on the present value } P; \\ \text{the discount on the amount } F. \end{cases} \qquad (4)$$

Sometimes we call P *the discounted value of F.* The relation between P, F, and t is illustrated on the time scale in Figure 3.

Figure 3

ILLUSTRATION 1. In Example 3, we *discounted* $\$1100$ for $2\frac{1}{2}$ years at $7\frac{1}{2}\%$ simple interest, and found the *present value* $P = \$926.32$. *The discount* on $\$1100$ was

$$I = discount = 1100 - 926.32 = \$173.68.$$

Also, $\$173.68$ is the *interest* on $\$926.32$ for $2\frac{1}{2}$ years at $7\frac{1}{2}\%$. To check the preceding statement, and thus also to verify the result in Example 3, we use $I = Prt$ with $P = 926.32$:

$$I = 926.32\left(\frac{15}{2}\%\right)\left(\frac{5}{2}\right) = \frac{9.2632(75)}{4}, \qquad or \qquad I = 2.3158(75) = \$173.68.$$

Summary

When money is worth the rate r, simple interest:

I. **To accumulate** *a principal P for t years, use* $I = Prt$ *and* $F = P + I$.

II. **To discount** *an amount F for t years, substitute the given values of F, r, and t in* $F = P(1 + rt)$ *and solve for P.*

We have introduced the word *discount* first as a *verb* and, second, as a *noun.* As a verb, *to discount* an amount F means to find a present value. As a noun, *the discount* on F means the difference $I = F - P$.

In commercial transactions, the word *discount* frequently refers to a reduction in the cost of a bill of goods in return for prompt payment in place of an allowable deferred payment. Such a use of *discount* is consistent with that introduced before in this section. Hence we may phrase various commercial problems involving discount in terms of the symbols of simple interest. The trade discount offered in a transaction frequently is described as a percentage of the face value of a bill.

Example 4. A merchant buys a bill of goods requiring the payment of $1500 at the end of 180 days. He is offered a 5% discount for cash in 30 days. What is the highest rate at which he could afford to borrow money in order to take advantage of the discount?

SOLUTION. 1. *Cash in 30 days* means payment at the end of 30 days. The discount offered is 5% of $1500, or $75. $1500 − $75 = $1425.

2. *Options:* $1500 at the end of 180 days, or $1425 at the end of 30 days. The time between the optional dates is 150 days.

3. The highest rate at which he can afford to borrow is the rate r at which $1425 is the present value of $1500 due in 150 days: $t = \frac{5}{12}$; $P = \$1425$; $F = \$1500$.

4. Hence, $I = \$75$ and, from $I = Prt$,

$$75 = 1425r\left(\frac{5}{12}\right); \qquad 75(12) = 5(1425)r; \qquad r = \frac{12}{95} = .126.$$

NOTE 1. If a trade discount in the sale of goods involves no time element permitting future payment, then no investment problem arises.

Exercise 2

Compute any unknown interest rate correct to tenths of 1%.

1. Accumulate $1000 for 3 years at 7% simple interest.
2. Accumulate $2000 for 7 months at 8% simple interest.
3. Accumulate $1500 from January 15 to October 2, 1975, at 9% simple interest. Use the 6% method.
4. Accumulate $1200 from August 14, 1976, to February 17, 1977, at $7\frac{1}{2}$% simple interest.
5. If money is worth 5% simple interest, find the present value of $1300 due at the end of 6 years. Check by accumulating the result for 6 years.
6. Discount $2000 for 8 months at 9% simple interest. What is the discount?
7. Discount $1650 for 4 months at 6% simple interest. What is the discount?
8. Find the present value of $2000 due at the end of 6 months if money is worth 8% simple interest. Check the result by accumulating.

9. Find the discount, if $2500 is discounted for 9 months at 10% simple interest.

10. At what simple interest rate is $420 the interest for $2\frac{1}{2}$ years on $1200?

Equations (1) of simple interest on page 6 involve $\{F, P, I, r, t\}$. In each of the following problems, find the values of those of the preceding variables whose values are not given.

11. $F = 3900; P = 3750;$ time is 120 days.

12. $P = 625; I = 140; r = .08.$

13. $F = 1525; r = 6\%;$ time is 2 years and 9 months.

14. $F = 729; P = 720;$ time is 3 months.

15. Roberts agreed to pay Hansen $2500 at the end of 5 years. What should Roberts pay today to cancel this debt if Hansen agrees that money is worth (a) 4% simple interest; (b) 6% simple interest? Which rate is the better for Roberts; for Hansen?

16. A debtor owes $2200 due at the end of 2 years. He asks his creditors for the privilege of paying the debt immediately. At what simple interest rate, 5% or 6%, would the creditor prefer to compute the required present value, and how much would he gain by the better choice?

17. If you lend a man $1000, to be repaid together with simple interest at the end of 2 years, which of the rates, 7% or 9%, would you prefer to specify? What added profit would you gain by the better choice?

18. A $100 United States Savings bond of the variety sold in 1974 cost the purchaser $75 in return for $100 payable at the end of 5 years. At what rate would the purchaser gain simple interest over the 5 years?

In each of the following problems, draw a time scale and locate the data on it in order to determine the time element in the problem.

19. Crawford buys a bill of goods from a merchant who asks $1250 at the end of 60 days (*cash in 60 days*). Crawford wishes to pay immediately and the merchant offers to compute the cash price on the assumption that money is worth 8% simple interest. Find the cash price today.

20. In buying a television set, I am offered the options of paying $250 cash or $270 at the end of 90 days. At what rate am I paying simple interest if I agree to pay at the end of 90 days?

21. A bill for a motor boat specifies the cost as $1200 due at the end of 100 days but offers a 4% discount for cash in 30 days. What is the highest rate, simple interest, at which the buyer can afford to borrow money in order to take advantage of the discount?

22. The terms of a bill are net cash (*face value*) in 100 days or 3% discount for cash in 40 days. At what rate is interest earned if the buyer takes the discount? (Let the face be $100.)

23. The terms of a bill are net cash in 150 days, with a 6% discount for payment within 30 days. Find the highest rate, simple interest, at which the buyer can afford to borrow in order to take advantage of the discount.

6. Simple Discount

In dealing with F, P, and I, we have talked of I as either the *interest* on P or the *discount on F*. In considering I as the interest on P, we use $I = Prt$, expressing *I as a percentage of the principal P*. In considering I as the *discount on F*, it sometimes is convenient to have an expression for *I as a percentage of F*. This leads to the introduction of a discount rate, which will occupy a position in *discount* problems similar to that filled by an interest rate in *accumulation* problems.

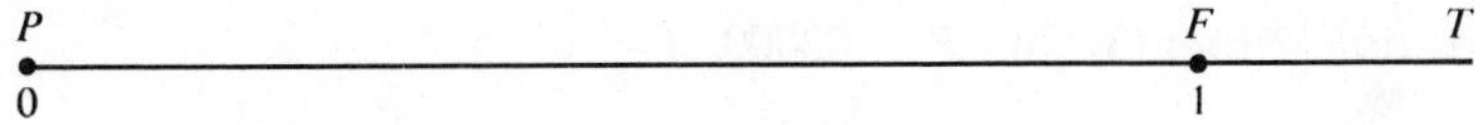

Figure 4

In the time diagram in Figure 4, F is due at the end of one year, P is the present value of F, and the discount on F for one year is I. Then the discount rate d is defined by

$$d = \frac{\text{discount on } F \text{ for one year}}{F};$$

$$(\text{discount for one year}) = Fd.$$

ILLUSTRATION 1.   If \$57 is the discount on \$1000 which is due at the end of one year, then the discount rate is 57/1000, or $d = .057$.

If an amount F is due at the end of t years then, by definition, the *simple discount* on F is t times the discount for one year, or $t(Fd)$. Therefore, since I represents the discount on F,

$$I = Fdt. \tag{1}$$

Since $P + I = F$,

$$P = F - I. \tag{2}$$

From (1), $F - I = F - Fdt = F(1 - dt)$, and hence

$$P = F(1 - dt). \tag{3}$$

If the time is given in days, we may use either *exact* or *ordinary* simple discount, according as we take the year equal to 365 or to 360 days in finding the value of t. Any brief method for computing simple interest applies also to the computation of simple discount. Thus, we may use the 6% method for computing simple discount. In this book, in simple discount problems where the time is given in days, use *ordinary* simple discount unless otherwise directed, and compute the *actual* time between dates. Usually, we assume that $t \le 1$ in (1)–(3). The preceding agreements correspond to business practice in essentially all situations where (1)–(3) are used.

Example 1. At 6% simple discount, find the present value of $300 which is due at the end of 90 days. What is the discount on the $300?

SOLUTION. From (1) and (2) with $F = \$300$, $t = \frac{1}{4}$, and $d = .06$,

$$I = 300(.06)(\tfrac{1}{4}) = \$4.50; \qquad P = 300 - 4.50 = \$295.50.$$

Thus, the discount for 90 days at 6% is $4.50.

Example 2. Find the amount due at the end of 15 months whose present value is $2000 at 5% simple discount.

SOLUTION. From (3) with $P = \$2000$, $d = .05$, and $t = \frac{5}{4}$,

$$2000 = F\left[1 - .05\left(\frac{5}{4}\right)\right]; \qquad 2000 = F\left(\frac{4 - .25}{4}\right).$$

Multiply by 4: $\qquad\qquad 8000 = F(3.75); \qquad F = \$2133.33.$

The remainder of this section is devoted to emphasizing the difference between simple interest and simple discount. Whether we are dealing with simple interest or with simple discount, *to discount F* means *to find its present value* on some day before F is due.

To discount F for t years,

at **simple discount**, *rate d, use $I = Fdt$ and then $P = F - I$*;

at **simple interest**, *rate r, use $F = P(1 + rt)$ to find P.*

Example 3. Discount $1000 for 9 months and find the discount (*a*) at 8% simple interest; (*b*) at 8% simple discount.

SOLUTION. We desire the present value of $1000 due in 9 months.

(*a*) At simple interest with $\{F = 1000, r = .08, t = \frac{3}{4}\}$, by use of the equation $F = P(1 + rt)$ we obtain

$$1000 = P[1 + (.08)(\tfrac{3}{4})]; \qquad P(1.06) = 1000;$$

$$P = \frac{1000}{1.06} = \frac{50,000}{53} = \$943.40.$$

(*b*) At simple discount with $\{F = 1000, d = .08, t = \frac{3}{4}\}$, by use of the equations $I = Fdt$ and $P = F - I$, we find

$$I = 1000(.08)(\tfrac{3}{4}) = \$60.00; \qquad P = 1000 - 60 = \$940.00.$$

Thus, use of simple discount at the rate $d = .08$ does not yield the same result as simple interest at the rate $r = .08$.

In considering an amount $\$F$ due on a given date, we shall say that a simple interest rate r and a simple discount rate d are *equivalent* if the present value of

F at simple discount, with the rate d, is the same as the present value of F at simple interest, at the rate r.

Example 4. What simple interest rate is equivalent to the simple discount rate 6% in discounting an amount for (*a*) 3 months; (*b*) 6 months?

SOLUTION. (*a*) With $\{F = \$1000, d = .06, t = \frac{1}{4}\}$, from $I = Fdt$ we obtain

$$I = 1000(.06)(\tfrac{1}{4}) = \$15; \qquad P = F - I = \$985.$$

To obtain the equivalent interest rate r, we have $\{P = 985, F = 1000, I = 15, t = \frac{1}{4}\}$. Then, from $I = Prt$,

$$15 = 985r\left(\frac{1}{4}\right); \qquad r = \frac{60}{985} = \frac{12}{197} = .0609.$$

Hence, simple interest at the rate 6.09% is equivalent to simple discount at the rate 6% in *discounting* money for 3 months. Equally well, we may say that the preceding rates are equivalent in *accumulating* money for 3 months.

(*b*) The student may verify, as in (*a*), that the simple interest rate 6.19% is equivalent to the simple discount rate 6% in a transaction with length 6 months.

In Example 4, we illustrated the fact that, if use of simple interest at a rate r is equivalent to use of simple discount at a rate d in borrowing or lending money for a given time, then $r > d$. On account of lack of extensive applications in business affairs, we shall not emphasize the subject of equivalent rates r and d.

7. Current Use of Simple Discount

In business affairs, including consumer debts due to purchases not for cash, an enormous number of loans, or deferred payment agreements equivalent to loans, extend for relatively short periods of time. Some of these loans involve periodic payments, and will be considered later in the text. Another type involves a single payment at the maturity date of the loan. That variety is appropriate for consideration in this chapter, and is equivalent to the type of debt represented by a promissory note, as treated in the next section. In the United States, in all cases where a debtor pays for the use of money, the creditor now is subject to the "*Truth in Lending Act*"* passed by the Congress of the United States in 1968. This law requires a creditor to state the rate at which *simple interest* is being charged in any period of time. *Previously* with many loans, the charge for the debtor was described as "*interest payable in advance*." For instance, with interest payable in advance at the rate 6%, suppose that a man borrows $\$1000$ payable at the end of one year. The interest in advance is $\$60$; he receives $(1000 - 60)$ or $\$940$, and pays back $\$1000$ at the end of one

---

* Abbreviated hereafter as the "*T.L. Act.*"

year. In other words, the borrower pays *simple discount* at the rate $d = .06$. By the method of Example 4 of Section 6, the equivalent *simple interest rate* is $r = 6/94$, or $r = 6.38\%$, for a one-year loan. It is no longer legal to specify "*interest in advance*, without telling the equivalent interest rate."

The elimination of all references to "*interest payable in advance*" has greatly decreased the importance of simple discount. Hence we shall restrict the extent of our attention to equations (1)–(3) of Section 6.

NOTE 1.   In the large transactions in the world of finance involving Treasury bills of the Treasury of the United States, it is customary to state *prices** on the basis of a *rate of simple discount*, as illustrated in the next example. A Treasury bill is simply a promissory note of the Treasury promising to pay the face value of the note on a certain date without interest. At any given time, billions of dollars worth of Treasury bills are outstanding in the hands of banks, brokerage firms, individuals or institutions, pensions funds, and corporations, both domestic and foreign. The minimum face value of a Treasury bill in 1974 was $10,000. Most of the bills are redeemable in 13 or 26 weeks from the dates of their sale by the Treasury. Occasionally it sells bills with longer lives.

Example 1.   On March 1, 1974, Treasury bills due in 90 days were quoted for sale at a discount rate of $7\frac{1}{2}\%$. If an investor bought one of the bills on March 1 and held the bill until the maturity date, at what rate did he obtain simple interest on his investment?

SOLUTION.   1. Let the face value of the bill be $10,000. The investor pays the present value, at the simple discount rate $7\frac{1}{2}\%$, of $10,000 due at the end of 90 days. We have $\{F = 10,000, d = .075, t = \frac{1}{4}\}$. From Section 6,

$$(\text{the discount}) = I = 10,000(.075)(\tfrac{1}{4}) = \$187.50;$$

$$(\text{price paid}) = P = F - I = 10,000 - 187.50 = \$9812.50.$$

2. To obtain the interest rate, we have $\{P = 9812.50, I = 187.50, t = \frac{1}{4}\}$. From $I = Prt$,

$$187.50 = 9812.50r\left(\frac{1}{4}\right); \qquad r = \frac{4(187.50)}{9812.50} = \frac{4(1875)}{98,125}.$$

Divide both numerator and denominator by 5, four times in succession, and finally compute the fraction:

$$r = \frac{4(375)}{19,625} = \frac{4(75)}{3925} = \frac{4(15)}{785} = \frac{12}{157} \doteq .0764.$$

Hence, the investor obtained simple interest at the rate 7.64%, approximately. Notice that we used "$\doteq$" for "*approximately equals.*"

---

* The T.L. Act applies only to *loans*. It does *not* outlaw use of simple discount in the selling of any "*promise to pay.*"

In Example 1, the seller specified simple discount at $7\frac{1}{2}\%$ for the sale. In doing this he did not violate the T.L. Act. No money was loaned. Use of a discount rate applied to the face value was merely a convenient way of specifying the selling price of a valuable object.

Exercise 3

If a given rate is labeled as d, it is a discount rate.

1. If $F = \$3000$, $d = .07$, and $t = \frac{3}{4}$, find I and P.
2. Find the present value of $2000 due at the end of 8 months if the discount rate is .06. What is the discount?
3. Find the ordinary simple discount for 150 days at 4% on $3000. What is its present value?
4. Discount $5000 for 3 months at 7%.
5. If $1200 is due on September 25, 1976, find the present value on June 27, 1976, if the discount rate is 7%.
6. If $P = \$1000$, $d = .04$, and $t = \frac{3}{2}$, find F.
7. Find the amount due at the end of 8 months whose present value is $8000 (a) when the discount rate is 9%; (b) when the interest rate is 9%.
8. Find the discount rate if $700 is the present value of $750 which is due at the end of 4 months.
9. If $1190 is the present value of $1250 which is due at the end of 9 months, find (a) the discount rate; (b) the interest rate.
10. If $2400 is the present value of $2500 which is due at the end of 9 months, find (a) the interest rate; (b) the discount rate.
11. Discount $2080 for 8 months at (a) 6% simple interest; (b) 6% simple discount.
12. Find the amount due at the end of 6 months whose present value is $1930 at (a) 7% simple interest; (b) 7% simple discount.
13. Suppose that $1000 is due at the end of six months, and that it is discounted to the present date at 8% simple discount. Find the equivalent simple interest rate r, that is, the rate r which would produce the same present value at simple interest.
14. Repeat Problem 13 if $1000 is due at the end of 8 months and the simple discount rate is 9%.
15. Find the simple discount rate which is equivalent to the simple interest rate 5% in accumulating or discounting money for 6 months. (Let $P = \$1000$ and first find F.)
16. Repeat Problem 15 if $r = .09$ and the time element is 8 months.
17. On March 8, 1974, Treasury bills due in 90 days were quoted at the discount rate 7.68%. If a bill was bought by an investor and held to its maturity date, at what rate did the investment yield simple interest? (Use 360 days in a year.)

8. Discounting Promissory Notes

A promissory note, of the type considered in this section, is a promise to pay a single stipulated sum of money, which we call the **maturity value**, on the **maturity date** of the note.

ILLUSTRATION 1. The following note was **drawn** (written) by Smith to the order of Jones. The note's **term** is 180 days and **face** is $5000. The note falls due 180 days after June 1; from Table IV we find that the maturity value, $5175, is due on November 28, as indicated in Figure 5. Jones has the right to sell his ownership of the note to any other person. If Jones sells to a banker *B* on July 31, 1975, the sale is accomplished by Jones *endorsing* the note (that is, *writing on it*) as follows:

July 31, 1975.   *Pay to the order of B.*   (*Signed*) H. W. Jones

It would be said that *B discounts the note*, because he pays Jones the present value, at a certain discount rate, on July 31 of $5175 due on November 28.

$5000   *Los Angeles, California,   June 1*, 19<u>75</u>

_____*One hundred eighty days*_____after date, for value received, the

undersigned promises to pay in lawful money of the United States of

America to the order of _____*H. W. Jones*_____the principal sum of

_____*five thousand and no/100*_____dollars

with interest from date at the rate of ____7%____ per year, computed on

the basis of a three hundred sixty (360) day year and actual days elapsed,

payable when the principal is due.

Payable in_____*Los Angeles*_____   (Signed)_____*A. M. Smith*

Figure 5

The preceding note duplicates the actual language in regard to interest of the standard promissory note of a certain prominent bank. Observe the care exercised in clearly describing any interest to be paid. The Banker's Rule is specified for use.

The time from the day a note is *bought* (or is *discounted*) to the maturity date is called the **term of the discount**. In Illustration 1, the term is 120 days, as indicated in Figure 5. The discounting of a note almost always involves a term less than one year. In such a case, in finding either the maturity date or the term of the discount, the actual number of days between dates is used. Also, ordinary interest or discount is used for any actual time in days.

Summary

To discount a promissory note at the discount rate d:
Compute the maturity value F and the maturity date.
Find the term of the discount; let this time be t years.
Discount F for t years by use of $I = Fdt$, to find $P = F - I$.

Example 1. If a banker B discounts the note of Illustration 1 on July 31 at the discount rate 8%, find Jones' proceeds from the sale.

SOLUTION. 1. The maturity value is $5175, due November 28, and the time from July 31 to November 28 is 120 days, as in Figure 5. B will pay to Jones the present value of $5175 due in 120 days, as computed by use of the discount rate $d = .08$:

2. *Data for discounting:* $F = \$5175; \quad d = .08; \quad t = \frac{1}{3}.$

$I = 5175(.08)(\frac{1}{3}) = \$138.00; \quad P = 5175 - 138.00 = \$5037.00 = proceeds.$

The security behind a note is increased each time a temporary owner sells the note. Thus, for the note in Illustration 1, after Jones sold the note to bank *B*, then Smith is supposed to make the maturity payment to *B*. However, if Smith fails to pay, then *B* can require Jones, the original owner, to pay the maturity value. Each temporary owner in turn becomes responsible for the payment involved.

ILLUSTRATION 2. Suppose that H. M. Roberts obtains a loan of $10,000 for 90 days from the University National Bank of St. Paul, Minnesota, with interest specified at the rate 8%. The interest to maturity will be $200. Assume that, for convenience, the bank prefers to have Roberts sign a note of the following variety which does not bear interest. The bank computes the interest, adds it to the sum which is borrowed, and specifies the result as the face of the note, which also is its maturity value. Such a note concentrates all of the computation on the day the note was drawn. Roberts does not pay the interest in advance. He receives only $10,000 and pays the interest as usual in the maturity payment.

$10,200   *St. Paul, Minnesota, August 1,* 19*76*

   Ninety days after date, for value received, the undersigned promises to

pay to the   *University National Bank of St. Paul, Minnesota*   ,

    Ten thousand, two hundred, and no/100 . . . . dollars

This sum includes all interest due on a loan of   *ten thousand and no/100*

dollars made on   *August 1, 1976*   , to the undersigned.

Payable in   *St. Paul, Minnesota*   (Signed)   *H. W. Roberts*

Promissory notes arise in various forms in essentially every variety of business affairs where one individual or company enters a transaction requiring a future payment or payments to another individual or company. The note involved may be an invoice or bill specifying the amount and required date for a payment. Other evidences of payments to be made may be in the forms of so-called *trade acceptances.* In the study of accounting, a comprehensive investigation is made of all written forms of evidence of indebtedness.

Exercise 4

1. On July 1, 1975, the note of Illustration 1 on page 16 is sold by Jones to a bank *B* whose discount rate is $9\frac{1}{2}\%$. Find the proceeds of the sale which Jones receives.
2. On September 12, 1976, Gibson draws a note to the order of Johnson, promising to pay $600 without interest at the end of 4 months. Find the proceeds for Johnson if the note is discounted for him at 9% on October 14, 1976, by the Commercial National Bank. Since the time is stated in months, the note matures on January 12, 1977. The term of the discount is the actual number of days between October 14, 1976, and January 12, 1977.
3. On July 15, 1977, Saunders draws a note promising to pay Tilden $2000, together with interest from date at 7%, 150 days later. A banker discounts, this note for Tilden at 9% on August 14, 1977. Find (*a*) the maturity date and maturity value; (*b*) the proceeds received by Tilden on August 14.

Find the proceeds from the sale of the promissory note corresponding to the data.

4. Face $1440; dated 5/15/76; due in 120 days; bears interest at $8\frac{1}{2}\%$; discounted for sale on 6/14/76 at the discount rate $7\frac{1}{2}\%$.

5. Face $1200; dated 4/10/75; does not bear interest; due in 150 days; discounted at the rate $8\frac{1}{2}\%$ on 7/9/75.

6. Face $3000; dated 4/20/77; due in 180 days; bears interest at 7%; discounted at 9% on 7/19/77.

7. Face $2000; dated 7/16/75; due in 3 months; bears interest at 8%; discounted on 9/1/75 at 9%.

8. Face $1500; dated 3/25/76; due in 200 days; bears interest at $6\frac{1}{2}\%$; sold at a discount rate of 8% on 5/14/76.

9. Jefferson owes Robinson $3000 due now. In payment, Jefferson draws a 75-day note to the order of Robinson with a face value not bearing interest. Robinson intends to sell the note immediately to a bank B whose discount rate is 8%. What should be the face of the note in order that Robinson will obtain $3000 from its sale to B?

10. A 4-month note whose face is $5000 bears interest at 9%. The note is discounted 60 days before maturity at a bank whose discount rate is 8%. Find the proceeds.

2 / Compound Interest

9. Terminology for Compound Interest

If, at stated intervals during the term of an investment, the interest due is added to the principal and thereafter earns interest, the sum by which the original principal has increased by the end of the term of the investment is called *compound interest*. At any date, the total amount due, which consists of the original principal plus the compound interest, is called the **compound amount**. We speak of interest being *compounded* or *converted* into principal. The time between successive conversions of interest into principal is called the **conversion period**.

Example 1. Find the compound amount and the compound interest at the end of one year if $100 is invested at 8% compounded quarterly.

SOLUTION. 1. The conversion period is 3 months. Interest is earned at the rate 8% per year during each period, or at the rate 2% *per period*, on all principal on hand at the beginning of the period.

At end of 3 mo. $2.000 interest is due;   *new principal is* $102.000.
At end of 6 mo. $2.040 interest is due;   *new principal is* $104.040.
At end of 9 mo. $2.081 interest is due;   *new principal is* $106.121.
At end of 1 yr. $2.122 interest is due;   *new principal is* $108.243.

2. The compound interest earned in 1 year is $8.243. The average rate per year at which interest is earned on the original principal during the year is

$$\frac{8.243}{100} = .08243 \quad or \quad 8.243\%.$$

10. Compound Interest Formula

Let the interest rate per conversion period be i, expressed as a decimal. Let P be the original principal and let F be the final compound amount to which P accumulates by the end of n periods. Then we shall prove that

$$F = P(1 + i)^n. \tag{1}$$

20

PROOF.   1. The original principal invested is $P.$

The interest due at the end of 1 conversion period is $Pi.$

The new principal at the end of 1 period is $P + Pi = P(1 + i).$

2. The interest due at the end of 2 periods is $iP(1 + i).$

The new principal at the end of 2 periods is

$$P(1 + i) + iP(1 + i) = P(1 + i)(1 + i) = P(1 + i)^2.$$

3. Similarly, by the end of any conversion period the principal which was on hand at the beginning of the period will be multiplied by $(1 + i)$. Thus, at the end of 3 periods the new principal will be $(1 + i)$ times the principal on hand at the end of 2 periods:

$$[P(1 + i)^2](1 + i) \quad or \quad P(1 + i)^3.$$

By the end of n periods the original principal P will have been multiplied by n factors $(1 + i)$ or by $(1 + i)^n$. Hence, the compound amount at the end of n periods is $P(1 + i)^n$, as in (1).

ILLUSTRATION 1. If \$100 is invested for 10 years at 6% compounded quarterly, then

$$i = \tfrac{1}{4}(.06) = .015, \quad n = 4(10) = 40, \quad and \quad F = 100(1 + .015)^{40}.$$

We shall say that P, due now, and F, due at the end of n periods, are **equivalent values** when money is worth the rate i per period, if P and F satisfy (1). We call P the **present value** of F. The sums P and F, due as stated, are equally desirable because P grows to the value F by the end of n periods. If I is the compound interest earned by P in n periods, then

$$I = F - P. \tag{2}$$

To accumulate a principal P for n conversion periods means to find the compound amount F resulting at the end of n periods if P is invested at the specified interest rate. The **accumulation problem** is solved by use of (1).

Extensive tables are available giving values of $(1 + i)^n$ for use with (1). Table V provides values of $(1 + i)^n$ for thirty-two common values of i.

Example 1.   Accumulate \$3000 for $9\tfrac{1}{4}$ years at 6% compounded quarterly, and find the compound interest which is earned.

SOLUTION.   1. The number of conversion periods is $n = 4(9\tfrac{1}{4}) = 37$ and $i = .015$. From (1), the compound amount is

$$F = 3000(1.015)^{37} = 3000(1.73477663) = \$5204.33. \qquad \text{(Table V)}$$

2. The compound interest earned is $\quad 5204.33 - 3000 = \$2204.33.$

Example 2. Find the amount due at the end of $10\frac{1}{4}$ years if $1000 is invested at 5% compounded monthly.

SOLUTION. Since .05/12 is an endless decimal, we *do not divide*; the rate per period is $i = \frac{5}{12}\%$ and $n = 12(10\frac{1}{4}) = 123$. Hence, the amount is

$$F = 1000\left(1 + \frac{.05}{12}\right)^{123} = 1000(1.66768302) = \$1667.68. \qquad \text{(Table V)}$$

Also we could write $F = (1 + \frac{5}{12}\%)^{123}$ above.

For any values of n and i, the value of $(1 + i)^n$ could be computed exactly by use of the binomial expansion, as given in Chapter 12. This method will be requested for a small value of n in a problem of the next exercise. The method would be impractical for construction of a table such as Table V. For any n and i, by use of logarithms we could compute $(1 + i)^n$ approximately to a limited number of decimal places, where the number would depend on the number of decimal places in the logarithms being employed. The methods just mentioned are completely out of date. The entries in any table such as Table V, if prepared currently, would be determined by use of a modern electronic computer. By this means, any value of $(1 + i)^n$ can be found rapidly with accuracy to as many decimal places as a problem in practice might require. The tables in this text are exceptionally extensive. However, even if tables are available for a great many more interest rates,* cases will arise in practice where $(1 + i)^n$ must be obtained for an unlisted value of i, or n. Thus, it might be desired to obtain $(1 + i)^n$ for $i = .08137$ and $n = 56$. In such a case, the desired value would be obtained by use of an electronic computer on the basis of laws of exponents.

On account of the numerical complication involved in use of logarithms or the binomial theorem to compute values of $(1 + i)^n$, and other related functions which we shall employ, no problems requiring elaborate use of such methods will appear in the illustrative examples or in routine problems in the exercises. Only in a very few problems will it be found necessary to use methods where the interest tables do not apply.

ILLUSTRATION 2. By use of multiplication (on a computer if many decimal places are desired), $(1 + i)^n$ may be found relatively conveniently for any value of n greater than the limit in Table V, with the aid of a law of exponents. Thus, to obtain $(1.005)^{300}$, we could proceed as follows:

$$(1.005)^{300} = (1.005)^{250}(1.005)^{50}. \qquad (3)$$

Each power on the right can be taken from Table V. Then, by multiplication on a computer of suitable type, $(1.005)^{300}$ could be obtained with as high accuracy as is found in the entries in Table V. With only four significant digits desired in

* For instance, as in the *Financial Compound Interest and Annuity Tables*, current edition; Financial Publishing Company, publishers, Boston.

the result, which is designed merely to illustrate the available method, from (3) and Table V we obtain

$$(1.005)^{300} = (3.4795)(1.2832) = 4.465.$$

Exercise 5

Solve by the method of Example 1 on page 20.

1. Find the compound interest earned if $1000 is invested for 1 year at 6% compounded quarterly.
2. Find the compound interest and the amount if $1000 is invested for $1\frac{1}{2}$ years at 4% compounded quarterly.

By use of Table V, find the amount and the compound interest due at the end of the time if the money is invested at the given rate.

3. $2000; 12 years at 8% compounded quarterly.
4. $1000; 14 years and 6 months at 9% compounded semiannually.
5. $1500; $4\frac{1}{2}$ years at $6\frac{1}{2}$% compounded semiannually.
6. $3000; $5\frac{1}{4}$ years at 9% compounded monthly.
7. $1000; 10 years at $4\frac{1}{2}$% compounded monthly.
8. $500; 11 years and 3 months at 5% compounded quarterly.
9. $750; $8\frac{1}{2}$ years at $7\frac{1}{2}$% compounded monthly.
10. Find the compound interest due at the end of 7 years if $1000 is invested at 8% compounded semiannually.
11. Accumulate $1200 for 4 years at 7% compounded annually.
12. Accumulate $2000 for 18 years at 9% compounded semiannually.
13. Find the compound interest earned by the end of 20 years and 7 months if $2000 is invested at 7% compounded monthly.
14. Accumulate $1500 for 7 years at 9% compounded quarterly.
15. Accumulate $100 for 50 years (a) at 6% compounded annually; (b) at 6% simple interest.
16. Mr. Jones owes me $2000 due now. He offers to pay the principal plus accumulated simple interest at the rate 5% at the end of 3 years. I insist on charging 5% compounded quarterly. How much more do I receive at the end of 3 years as compared to his offer?
17. Compute $(1.03)^3$ by use of the definition of an exponent.
18. Find the amount due at the end of one year if $1000 is invested at (a) 7% simple interest; (b) 7% compounded semiannually; quarterly; monthly.
19. If $1 is invested at the rate j compounded m times per year, find the compound amount at the end of (a) one year; (b) k years. Prove that, if the results of (a) and (b) are G and F respectively, then $F = G^k$.
20. By use of Table V and $(1.02)^{m+n} = (1.02)^m(1.02)^n$, calculate $(1.02)^{120}$ by multiplication without logarithms correct to four significant digits.

21. On a single xy-coordinate plane with the x-axis horizontal, and with x on the interval $\{0 \le x \le 20\}$, draw a graph of each of the following equations:

$$y = 100(1 + .05x); \qquad y = 100(1.05)^x.$$

The equation at the left gives the amount $\$y$ at the end of x years if $\$100$ is invested at 5% simple interest. The equation at the right gives the compound amount at the end of x years if $\$100$ is invested at 5% compounded annually. First make up a table of a few solutions (x, y) for each equation as a basis for the graph. Obtain pairs (x, y) for the equation of compound interest by using values of x in Table V. Comparison of these graphs will indicate the effect of compound interest as compared to simple interest. Use a whole sheet of cross-section paper.

22. Let $y = 100(1 + i)^x$, and write this equation for each of the following values of i: $\{.01, .05, .08\}$. For each equation, by use of Table V, make up a table of a few solutions (x, y) with x on the interval $\{0 \le x \le 20\}$. In one xy-plane, on a whole sheet of coordinate paper, draw a graph of each equation to obtain, graphically, an impression of the effect on the compound amount of an increase in the interest rate.

23. If $\$1000$ is invested now, find the amount at the end of 15 years if interest is at the rate $\{.04, m = 1\}$ for the first 5 years, and thereafter is at the rate $\{.08, m = 2\}$.

★24. Verify the value of $(1 + .02)^{20}$ to four decimal places by use of I–IV about the binomial expansion on page 274. Use only as many terms as are necessary to obtain the requested accuracy.

11. The Discount Problem

To discount an amount F for n conversion periods means to find its present value P on a day which is n periods before F is due. If we let I be *the discount* on F, then $I = F - P$. For convenience in solving discount problems, we alter $F = P(1 + i)^n$ by solving for P:

$$P = \frac{F}{(1 + i)^n} = F\frac{1}{(1 + i)^n}; \tag{1}$$

$$P = F(1 + i)^{-n}. \tag{2}$$

Values of $(1 + i)^{-n}$ are given in Table VI. Each entry in this table is the value of a certain quotient.

ILLUSTRATION 1. From Table VI,

$$\frac{1}{(1.02)^9} = (1.02)^{-9} = .83675527.$$

This could be computed *inconveniently* by use of Table V and division:

$$\frac{1}{(1.02)^9} = \frac{1}{1.19509257} = .83675527.$$

The use of Table VI eliminates the division indicated above.

Example 1. If money can be invested at 4% compounded semiannually, find the present value of $1000 due at the end of $4\frac{1}{2}$ years.

SOLUTION. By use of (2) with $F = \$1000$, $i = .02$, and $n = 9$,

$$P = 1000(1.02)^{-9} = 1000(.83675527) = \$836.76. \qquad \text{(Table VI)}$$

Example 2. Discount $1000 for 10 years at 5% compounded annually and find the discount.

SOLUTION. We desire the unknown present value P if $F = \$1000$, $i = .05$, and $n = 10$. From (2) and Table VI,

$$P = 1000(1.05)^{-10} = 1000(.61391325) = \$613.91.$$

The discount on the $1000 is $I = 1000 - 613.91$, or $I = \$386.09$.

In Example 2 we might say that the *compound discount* is $386.09, to emphasize that we are dealing with discount under investment at compound interest, as contrasted with discount in a transaction where the methods of simple interest or of simple discount are employed. Hereafter in this book, the unqualified phrase *to discount* will mean *to discount at compound interest* and *the discount* will refer to *the discount at compound interest*.

Since we use $F = P(1 + i)^n$ to *accumulate* P and $P = F(1 + i)^{-n}$ to *discount* a future value F, it is customary to call $(1 + i)^n$ the **accumulation factor** and $(1 + i)^{-n}$ the **discount factor**. We multiply a principal P by the proper accumulation factor to find the compound amount. We multiply a future value F by the proper discount factor to discount F.

NOTE 1. Sometimes v is used to denote the discount factor for one period, or $v = (1 + i)^{-1}$. Then, in (2), $P = Fv^n$.

Exercise 6

1. Verify the entry for $(1.02)^{-4}$ in Table VI by using Table V and completing the division to four decimal places: $(1.02)^{-4} = 1/(1.02)^4$.
2. Find the present value of $6000 due at the end of 8 years, if money can be invested at 7% compounded monthly.

Find the present value on January 1, 1975, *of the sum which is due on the specified date, if money can be invested at the given rate.*

3. $1000 due on January 1, 1984; 5% compounded monthly.

4. $5000 due on July 1, 1980; 9% compounded quarterly.

5. $10,000 due on January 1, 1982; 5.5% compounded semiannually.

6. $10,000 due on January 1, 1983; 7% compounded annually.

7. Discount $500 for 15 years at 7% compounded monthly.

8. Discount $2500 for $15\frac{1}{2}$ years at $6\frac{1}{2}\%$ compounded quarterly. What is the discount?

9. At the birth of a child, what sum should his father invest in order to provide the child with $5000 at age 21 if the money earns 5% compounded quarterly?

10. To provide for the purchase of an automobile worth $5000 as a gift to a son when he graduates from college 4 years from now, how much should his father invest today at 6% compounded semiannually?

11. How much must a man 35 years of age deposit in a savings account today, in a bank paying $4\frac{1}{2}\%$ compounded quarterly, in order to have $25,000 in the account 25 years from now?

12. If money is worth $7\frac{1}{2}\%$ compounded monthly, find the discount if $3000 is discounted for 12 years.

13. I owe $6250 which is due without interest at the end of $3\frac{1}{2}$ years. What sum should my creditor be willing to accept now in place of the future payment if he is able to invest money at 5% compounded quarterly?

14. If money is worth 5% compounded annually, find the present value of $1000 which is due at the end of (*a*) 25 years; (*b*) 50 years. State an inference about the change in a present value resulting from an increase in the length of time for which a sum is discounted.

15. Discount $1000 for 20 years (*a*) at 5% compounded annually; (*b*) at 7% compounded annually. State an inference about the change in a present value resulting from an increase in the interest rate.

16. Suppose that money can be invested at 4% compounded annually. (*a*) Accumulate $1000 for 25 years. (*b*) Discount the result of (*a*) for 10 years. (*c*) Accumulate $1000 for 15 years. Compare (*b*) and (*c*).

17. Suppose that money can be invested at 4% simple interest. (*a*) Accumulate $1000 for 25 years. (*b*) Discount the result of (*a*) for 10 years. (*c*) Accumulate $1000 for 15 years.

NOTE 1.   The results of (*b*) and (*c*) in Problem 17 are *not the same*. In other words, the convenient property of compound interest illustrated in Problem 16, and proved in Problem 18, does *not* hold for simple interest.

18. Prove that, if *P* is accumulated for *k* conversion periods at the rate *i* per period, and if the result then is discounted for *h* periods, the final value is equal to the result if *P* is accumulated for (*k* − *h*) periods.

19. Discount $1000 for 15 years (*a*) at 5% compounded annually; (*b*) at 5% simple interest.

20. By use of Table VI and $(1.03)^{-(m+n)} = (1.03)^{-m}(1.03)^{-n}$, calculate $(1.03)^{-150}$ by multiplication without logarithms correct to three significant digits. Thus, by multiplication on a suitable computer, we may obtain $(1 + i)^n$ and

$(1 + i)^{-n}$ for as large an integer n as needed, for any rate i used in Tables V and VI.

12. Nominal and Effective Rates

The rate percent quoted in describing a variety of compound interest is called the *nominal rate*. As a standard abbreviation, sometimes we shall use j for the nominal rate and m for the number of times per year that this rate is compounded, where we assume that m is an integer.

ILLUSTRATION 1. To indicate that the rate is 8% compounded quarterly, we may write that the rate is $\{.08, m = 4\}$. The nominal rate here is 8% and the rate per conversion is $.08/4$ or $.02$.

If a principal P is invested at a nominal rate j compounded *more* than once per year, the interest earned by the end of one year is *greater* than Pj.

ILLUSTRATION 2. If \$1 is invested at 8% compounded quarterly, the amount F and interest I at the end of one year are

$$F = (1.02)^4 = \$1.08243; \qquad I = \$.08243.$$

The interest I is 8.243% of the original principal \$1, and is the same as that obtained if \$1 is invested for one year at 8.243% compounded *annually*.

With a given nominal rate j compounded m times per year, we define the corresponding **effective rate** to be *that rate w which, if compounded* **annually**, *is equivalent to the given rate*. That is,

$$w = \frac{interest\ earned\ in\ one\ year}{principal\ invested\ at\ the\ beginning\ of\ the\ year}. \tag{1}$$

Or, with the principal in (1) equal to \$1,

$$w = \left\{ \begin{array}{l} \textbf{int. in dollars for 1 year on \$1 at the} \\ \textbf{rate } j \textbf{ compounded } m \textbf{ times per year.} \end{array} \right\} \tag{2}$$

Investment at the effective rate w compounded *annually* yields the same interest at the end of the year, and hence at the end of any number* of years, as investment at the rate j compounded m times per year. If $m = 1$, then both j and w are compounded annually and hence $w = j$, because they yield the same interest at the end of each year.

ILLUSTRATION 3. In Illustration 2, with interest at the rate 8% compounded quarterly, the effective rate is $w = 8.243\%$, which is greater than the nominal rate because *interest on interest* at the nominal rate 8% is earned during three conversion periods of the year.

---

* At present, this *number* is a *positive integer*. Later, we shall interpret the statement with "*number*" meaning *any positive number*.

ILLUSTRATION 4. To state that *the effective rate of interest is* 5%, or that interest is at the rate 5% *effective*, is equivalent to saying that principal accumulates at the rate 5% compounded *annually*.

To obtain a relation between j, m, and w, we determine an expression for the right-hand side of (2). If \$1 is invested at the rate j compounded m times per year, the amount F and interest I at the end of one year are found by use of $F = P(1 + i)^n$ with $P = \$1$, $i = j/m$, and $n = m$:

$$F = \left(1 + \frac{j}{m}\right)^m; \quad I = \left(1 + \frac{j}{m}\right)^m - 1. \tag{3}$$

From (2) and (3), $\qquad w = \left(1 + \dfrac{j}{m}\right)^m - 1$, *or*

$$1 + w = \left(1 + \frac{j}{m}\right)^m. \tag{4}$$

If desired, (4) may be rewritten in the form

$$1 + w = (1 + i)^m, \tag{5}$$

where i is the rate per conversion period, or $i = j/m$.

ILLUSTRATION 5. To find the effective rate corresponding to 5% compounded quarterly, substitute $j = .05$ and $m = 4$ in (4):

$$1 + w = (1.0125)^4 = 1.05094534; \quad w = .05094534. \quad \text{(Table V)}$$

Example 1. What rate converted monthly yields the effective rate 5%?

SOLUTION. 1. Place $w = .05$ and $m = 12$ in (4):

$$\left(1 + \frac{j}{12}\right)^{12} = 1.05. \tag{6}$$

2. Recall (4) on page 238. From (6), we see that $(1 + \frac{1}{12}j)$ is the 12th root of 1.05. Also, by the definition of a rational exponent on page 239, we may write $\sqrt[12]{1.05}$ as $(1.05)^{1/12}$. Hence, on taking the 12th root of both sides of (6), we obtain

$$1 + \frac{j}{12} = \sqrt[12]{1.05}, \quad or \quad \frac{j}{12} = (1.05)^{1/12} - 1;$$

$$j = 12[(1.05)^{1/12} - 1]. \tag{7}$$

3. The value of $(1.05)^{1/12}$ is found in Table XIV for $i = .05$ and $p = 12$. Hence, from (7),

$$j = 12(1.00407412 - 1), \quad or \quad j \doteq .04888944. \tag{8}$$

The last two decimal places are unreliable because of the multiplication by 12 in (8). Hence, we state that interest at the nominal rate 4.8889%, approximately, compounded monthly, yields the effective rate 5%.

ILLUSTRATION 6. For instruction, the preceding solution was given in considerable detail. Similar problems should be solved briefly. Thus, to obtain the nominal rate j which, if compounded quarterly, will yield the effective rate 6%, substitute $w = .06$ and $m = 4$ in (4) to obtain

$$\left(1 + \frac{j}{4}\right)^4 = 1.06; \qquad 1 + \frac{j}{4} = (1.06)^{1/4};$$

$$j = 4[(1.06)^{1/4} - 1] = 4(1.01467385 - 1) \doteq .058695. \qquad \text{(Table XIV)}$$

Example 2. Obtain the nominal rate j which, if compounded p times per year, will yield the effective rate i.

SOLUTION. With $w = i$ and $m = p$ in (4), we obtain

$$\left(1 + \frac{j}{p}\right)^p = 1 + i; \qquad 1 + \frac{j}{p} = \sqrt[p]{1 + i} = (1 + i)^{1/p}.$$

Hence, $$j = p[(1 + i)^{1/p} - 1]. \qquad (9)$$

The result in (9) is represented by $\{j_p \text{ at } i\}$ in Table XIII, and in later parts of the text. The result in (7) could be read directly from Table XIII as $\{j_{12} \text{ at } .05\} = .04888949$. For acquaintance with the fundamental result (4), in the next exercise the solutions of some problems will be requested by the method of Example 1 without use of Table XIII.

Hereafter, any interest rate which is mentioned will be a *nominal* rate unless otherwise described. If no statement is made as to the length of the conversion period, it should be assumed that interest is compounded *annually*.

ILLUSTRATION 7. A statement that money *is worth* 4% means that interest is at the rate 4% compounded *annually*.

To compare different varieties of compound interest we compare their corresponding effective rates.

Example 3. Which method is the better, to invest at 5% compounded monthly or at 5.5% compounded semiannually?

SOLUTION. First we ask for the effective rates. By use of (4):

At $\{.05, m = 12\}$, $\quad w = \left(1 + \frac{.05}{12}\right)^{12} - 1 = 1.05116190 - 1 = .05116190.$

At $\{.055, m = 2\}$, $\quad w = (1.0275)^2 - 1 = 1.05575625 - 1 = .05575625.$

Since .0512 is less than .0558, $\{5.5\%, m = 2\}$ is the better.

13. Effect of Frequency of Conversion

When a nominal rate j is compounded annually, the effective rate w is equal to j as an immediate consequence of the definition of w. If the number, m, of conversions per year of the rate j increases, the corresponding effective rate increases, but essentially reaches an upper bound when $m = 365$. If $j = .06$, the effective rates for different values of m are as follows:

$m =$	1	2	4	12	52	365
$w =$	.06000	.06090	.06136	.06168	.06180	.06183

In recent years, savings and loan associations have been limited by law in regard to the maximum interest rates which may be offered depositors on ordinary "*passbook accounts*," which are similar to savings accounts at a bank, and on other means for investment as offered by the associations. However, the legal limitations place no restrictions on *the number of times per year that any specified interest rate may be compounded*. Hence, to encourage investors to place money at interest in an association at a legally limited rate, it has become a widespread custom for the association to pay interest *compounded daily*. Early in the year 1974, a certain savings and loan company in California was offering interest at nominal rates ranging from $5\frac{1}{4}\%$ to $7\frac{1}{2}\%$ compounded daily on various types of passbook accounts and long-term deposits. The corresponding effective rates ranged from 5.39% to 7.79%. If, instead of being compounded daily, the nominal rates had been compounded only quarterly, the corresponding effective rates would have ranged from 5.35% to 7.71%. For instance, on $1000 invested for just one year, at the nominal rate $5\frac{1}{4}\%$, daily compounding results in $53.90 interest, and quarterly compounding gives $53.50 interest at the end of one year. Hence, with investments of moderate size, daily compounding creates a superficial impression of extremely generous interest which is not borne out by the actual facts. On investments of large size, the effect of daily compounding would be more appreciable, but still not large relative to the total amount involved.

★14. The Number e and Interest Compounded Continuously

In the advanced theory of logarithms, and their applications in calculus, the following important number e arises:

$$e = \lim_{h \to 0} (1 + h)^{1/h} = 2.71828\cdots. \tag{1}$$

In (1), the arrow "$\to$" is read *approaches*; then (1) is read "*e is equal to the limit as h approaches zero of* $(1 + h)^{1/h}$, *is equal to*, and so on." The decimal on the right in (1) is endless and nonrepeating. Hence, e is an irrational number.

Now consider the relation

$$1 + w = \left(1 + \frac{j}{m}\right)^m \tag{2}$$

between the effective rate w and the nominal rate j when it is compounded m times per year. From (2), if $m \to \infty$, by laws of exponents we obtain:

$$1 + w = \lim_{m \to \infty} \left(1 + \frac{j}{m}\right)^m = \lim_{m \to \infty} \left[\left(1 + \frac{j}{m}\right)^{m/j}\right]^j = \left[\lim_{m \to \infty} \left(1 + \frac{j}{m}\right)^{m/j}\right]^j. \quad (3)$$

In (3), we read "$m \to \infty$" as "m *approaches infinity*," which means that "m *grows large without bound*." In (3), let $h = j/m$. Then $h \to 0$ when $m \to \infty$, and (3) becomes

$$1 + w = \left(\lim_{h \to 0} (1 + h)^{1/h}\right)^j = e^j, \quad (4)$$

because of (1). We refer to w in (4) as the *effective rate corresponding to the nominal rate j when it is "compounded continuously*," which is our interpretation of the condition "$m \to \infty$." The following table of values of e^j for certain values of j gives $(1 + w)$, and then w in (5) below, as the effective rate for j when interest is compounded *continuously*.

$$1 + w = e^j. \quad (5)$$

$j =$	.05	.06	.07	.075	.08
$e^j =$	1.05127	1.06184	1.07251	1.07788	1.08328
$w =$	.05127	.06184	.07251	.07788	.08328

Recall the effective rate .06183 when $j = .06$ and $m = 365$ (compounding daily) in the table in Section 13. Notice how slightly the effective rate is increased (to .06184) when interest is compounded continuously. Similarly, each of the effective rates in the preceding table differs only slightly, in the fifth decimal place, from the corresponding effective rate when interest is compounded daily. That is, practically the whole effect of compounding interest *continuously* is created by merely compounding interest *daily*. Even if interest is compounded only *quarterly*, the effect is practically the same for an investment of moderate size as if interest were compounded daily or continuously.

Exercise 7

When necessary, employ Table XIV to avoid the use of logarithms.

1. Find the effective rate corresponding to the rate 5% compounded (*a*) annually; (*b*) semiannually; (*c*) quarterly; (*d*) monthly.
2. Find the effective rate if the nominal rate 4% is converted (*a*) annually; (*b*) semiannually; (*c*) quarterly; (*d*) monthly.

3. When interest is compounded quarterly find the effective rate if the nominal rate is (a) 3%; (b) 6%; (c) 8%; (d) 9%.
4. If interest is converted quarterly find the nominal rate if the effective rate is 4%.
5. What nominal rate compounded semiannually will yield the effective rate 6%?
6. If interest is converted monthly find the nominal rate which will yield the given effective rate: (a) $3\frac{1}{2}$%; (b) 6%; (c) 7%.
7. If interest is compounded quarterly find the nominal rate when the effective rate is (a) 3%; (b) 4%; (c) 7%.
8. Which yields more interest, $\{2\frac{3}{4}\%, m = 2\}$ or $\{2\frac{1}{2}\%, m = 4\}$?
9. Should I invest in bonds yielding 6% compounded annually, or in a savings and loan association paying 6% converted quarterly?
10. Instead of buying bonds which yield 5% effective, at what rate compounded quarterly could I just as well invest my money?
11. If my savings account yields $4\frac{1}{2}$% compounded semiannually, should I change my investment to bonds yielding 4.6% effective?
12. If my money is invested in bonds yielding $6\frac{1}{2}$% compounded semiannually, should I change to an investment yielding 6.7% effective?

★*Compute by use of 5-place or 6-place logarithms, as directed by the instructor, and check with Table* XIV.

13. $\sqrt{1.05}$.   14. $\sqrt[12]{1.03}$.   15. $(1.06)^{1/3}$.   16. $(1.02)^{1/4}$

HINT: Since $\sqrt{1.05} = (1.05)^{1/2}$, then $\log \sqrt{1.05} = \frac{1}{2} \log 1.05$, etc.

15. Equivalent Rates

The notion of equivalent methods of investment was used in Chapter 1 for the restricted types of data considered there. At this place we discuss the notion more generally. Two methods for investing money for a specified time, k years, will be called *equivalent* in case a principal of $1 (and hence *any* principal P) accumulates to the *same amount* F by the end of k years under each of the methods. The rates of interest or discount involved in the methods will be called *equivalent rates*. Clearly, if each of two methods is equivalent to a third, the first two are equivalent to each other. When simple interest or simple discount is involved, the sizes of equivalent rates *depend on the length of the investment*.

ILLUSTRATION 1.   In Example 4 on page 13, we saw that simple discount at the rate 6% is equivalent to simple interest at the rate 6.19% in a 6-month transaction, and to 6.09% in a 3-month transaction.

If two varieties of *compound* interest are involved, the length of the time of an investment is of *no importance* in considering the equivalence of the two rates. For, if the two varieties give equal compound amounts on $1 at the end of *one* year, then, proceeding year by year, the varieties will give equal amounts on $1 at the end of *any* number of years. Hence, in describing equivalent compound interest rates, we refer to an investment of a specified principal for just *one* year.

Two varieties of compound interest are equivalent in case the investment of $1 under each of the methods gives the same compound interest at the end of one year or, in other words, if the effective rates for the two varieties are equal.

Example 1. What nominal rate compounded quarterly is equivalent to 5% compounded semiannually?

SOLUTION. 1. Let j be the unknown nominal rate, with $m = 4$. Let w be the effective rate, which is the same for each method.

2. From (4) on page 28,

at $\{.05, m = 2\}$, $\qquad\qquad\qquad\qquad\qquad\qquad 1 + w = (1.025)^2;$

at the unknown rate $\{j, m = 4\}$, $\qquad\qquad\qquad 1 + w = \left(1 + \dfrac{j}{4}\right)^4.$

3. Hence, $\qquad\qquad\qquad\qquad\qquad \left(1 + \dfrac{j}{4}\right)^4 = (1.025)^2. \qquad\qquad (1)$

4. Extract the 4th root on each side in (1):

$$1 + \frac{j}{4} = \sqrt[4]{(1.025)^2} = [(1.025)^2]^{1/4} = 1.025^{2(1/4)}, \ or$$

$$1 + \frac{j}{4} = 1.025^{1/2} = 1.01242284. \qquad\qquad \text{(Table XIV)}$$

5. Hence,

$$\frac{j}{4} = .01242284, \quad or \quad j = 4(.01242284).$$

Thus, $j = 4.969136\%$; the last figure is in doubt, because of multiplication by 4.

Example 2. What nominal rate compounded quarterly is equivalent to 7% compounded monthly?

SOLUTION. 1. Let j be the unknown nominal rate, with $m = 4$. Let w be the effective rate, which is the same for $\{.07, m = 12\}$ as for $\{j, m = 4\}$. From (4) on page 28,

$$1 + w = (1 + \tfrac{7}{12}\%)^{12}; \qquad 1 + w = (1 + \tfrac{1}{4}j)^4.$$

Hence $\qquad\qquad\qquad (1 + \tfrac{1}{4}j)^4 = (1 + \tfrac{7}{12}\%)^{12} \qquad\qquad\qquad\qquad (2)$

2. Recall that $\sqrt[4]{H} = H^{1/4}$. Take the 4th root of each side in (2) and apply a law of exponents:

$$\sqrt[4]{(1 + \tfrac{1}{4}j)^4} = \sqrt[4]{(1 + \tfrac{7}{12}\%)^{12}} = (1 + \tfrac{7}{12}\%)^{12 \cdot (1/4)}; \qquad (3)$$

$$1 + \tfrac{1}{4}j = (1 + \tfrac{7}{12}\%)^3 = 1.01760228. \qquad\qquad \text{(Table V)}$$

Hence, $\qquad \tfrac{1}{4}j = .01760228, \quad or \quad j \doteq .0704091 = 7.04091\%.$

Example 3. What simple interest rate is equivalent to 7% compounded semiannually if money is invested for 3 years?

SOLUTION. 1. Let r be the unknown rate for simple interest. If $\$P$ is invested for 3 years at this rate, the amount due at the end of the time is $F_1 = P(1 + 3r)$. At $\{7\%, m = 2\}$, the amount F_2 at the end of 3 years is $F_2 = P(1.035)^6$. The two methods are equivalent when and only when $F_1 = F_2$, or

$$P(1 + 3r) = P(1.035)^6, \quad or \quad 1 + 3r = (1.035)^6. \qquad (4)$$

2. By use of Table V, from (4) we obtain

$$3r = 1.22925533 - 1 = .22925533.$$

Hence, $\qquad\qquad r = .07641844, \quad or \quad r \doteq 7.642\%.$

★*Example 4.* What nominal rate, compounded semiannually, is equivalent to investing a principal $\$P$ at the simple interest rate 7%, with a single payment to be made to the investor at the end of 4 years?

SOLUTION. 1. Let j be the unknown nominal rate. If $\$P$ is invested at $\{j, m = 2\}$, the amount $\$F$ at the end of 4 years is $F = P(1 + \frac{1}{2}j)^8$. At 7% simple interest, the amount F_1 at the end of 4 years is $F_1 = P(1 + .28)$.

2. The two methods of investment are equivalent if and only if $F = F_1$, or

$$P(1 + \tfrac{1}{2}j)^8 = P(1.28), \quad or \quad (1 + \tfrac{1}{2}j)^8 = 1.28. \qquad (5)$$

Take the 8th root of both sides in (5):

$$1 + \tfrac{1}{2}j = \sqrt[8]{1.28}.$$

3. By use of Table I, $\quad \log 1.28 = 0.10721$

$$\log \sqrt[8]{1.28} = \tfrac{1}{8}(0.10721) = 0.01340.$$

Hence, $\qquad\qquad \sqrt[8]{1.28} = 1.0313 = 1 + \tfrac{1}{2}j; \quad j \doteq .063.$

By use of Table II, we could have obtained j to four decimal places.

Exercise 8

Use Table V or Table XIV when possible to avoid use of logarithms. Any problem requiring use of Table I (or Table II if desired) is marked with a black star.

1. Find the nominal rate which if compounded semiannually is equivalent to 6% compounded quarterly.
2. What rate converted quarterly is equivalent to $\{.05, m = 12\}$?
3. What rate compounded quarterly is equivalent to $\{.03, m = 2\}$?

4. What rate converted monthly is equivalent to $\{.05, m = 2\}$?

5. What rate compounded semiannually is equivalent to 8% compounded quarterly?

6. What rate compounded monthly is equivalent to 7% compounded quarterly?

7. What rate compounded quarterly is equivalent to $\{.04, m = 12\}$?

8. What simple interest rate is equivalent to 7% compounded semiannually in case a man borrows $5000 with the agreement to pay the principal plus the accumulated interest at the end of 4 years?

9. A man borrows $5000 and promises to pay the compound amount at 9% compounded quarterly at the end of 6 years. At what simple interest rate could he just as well borrow, with the agreement to make a single payment including all interest at the end of 6 years?

10. What simple interest rate is equivalent to $\{.07, m = 4\}$, if a man borrows money and agrees to pay a single sum at the end of (*a*) three years; (*b*) five years?

★11. A man borrows $5000 with the agreement to pay the principal and all accumulated simple interest at the rate 8% at the end of 4 years. (*a*) At what nominal rate compounded quarterly could he just as well pay compound interest? (*b*) If the final single payment is due at the end of 2 years, repeat the solution.

★12. A man borrows $10,000 with the creditor agreeing that interest at the nominal rate 6% will be converted into principal only once in each two years. Find the effective rate. (Invest for just two years.)

16. Compound Interest for n Periods, n Not an Integer

The definition of compound interest at the beginning of this chapter has no meaning unless the term of the investment is a whole number of interest periods. Hence, up to this point, in use of $F = P(1 + i)^n$ we always have assumed that n is an *integer*. For certain theoretical purposes concerning annuities, as met briefly late in this text, we shall agree that, even when n is *not* an integer, the compound amount $\$F$ resulting from the investment of $\$P$ for n interest periods is given by $F = P(1 + i)^n$. We shall refer to this result as the *theoretical compound amount* when n is *not* an integer, and similarly shall call $P = F(1 + i)^{-n}$ the *theoretical present value* of F. We shall not be interested in computing theoretical amounts or present values, with n not an integer, at any place in this text.

ILLUSTRATION 1.   If $1000 is invested for 2 years and 8 months at 8% compounded semiannually, the number of interest periods is $2(2\frac{2}{3}) = 5\frac{1}{3} = 16/3$. The theoretical compound amount at the end of the specified time is $F = 1000(1.04)^{16/3}$.

On rare occasions, the buying or selling of a promissory note or some other financial transaction might require the accumulation of a principal, or the discounting of some amount for n interest periods where n is not an integer. In any such case, it is likely that the people engaged in the transaction would agree to use whichever of the following methods for accumulating and discounting would apply. We shall refer to these procedures as *approximate methods*, in contrast to the method called *theoretical* in Illustration 1.

Approximate accumulation *of a principal $\$P$ at compound interest for a time which is not a whole number of interest periods:*

Find the compound amount on $\$P$ at the end of the last whole interest period contained in the given time, to obtain an amount F_1 on that date.

Accumulate F_1 for the remaining time at **simple interest** *at the given nominal rate.*

Approximate discounting *of an amount $\$F$ due at the end of a time which is not a whole number of interest periods.*

Discount $\$F$ for the smallest number of whole periods containing the given time; this produces the discounted value $\$P_1$ of $\$F$ at a date D_1 before the actual present day D_0.

Accumulate $\$P_1$ from day D_1 to the present day D_0 at **simple interest** *at the given nominal rate.*

Example 1. By the approximate method, find the compound amount at the end of 2 years and 8 months if $1000 is invested at 8% compounded semi-annually.

SOLUTION. 1. On the time scale in Figure 6, D represents the present date; S is the end of 2 years and 8 months; R is the end of 2 years and 6 months, the end of the last interest period contained in the given time.

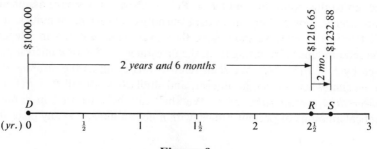

Figure 6

2. First accumulate $1000 for $2\frac{1}{2}$ years, to date R, which gives

$$F_1 = 1000(1.04)^5 = \$1216.653.$$

3. The remaining time is 2 months; accumulate F_1 for 2 months at 8% simple interest. The interest is

$$I = 1216.653(.08)(\tfrac{1}{6}) = \$16.222.$$

Hence, the approximate amount F at the end of 2 years and 8 months, at point S, is

$$F = 1216.653 + 16.222 = \$1232.88.$$

In Illustration 1, if we had computed the result we would have found that it is close to the approximate value F just obtained. We shall not verify this fact.

Example 2. By the approximate method, discount $1000 for 1 year and 8 months at 6% compounded semiannually.

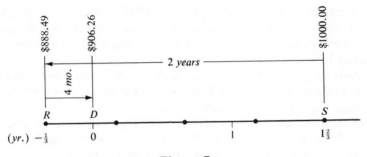

Figure 7

SOLUTION. 1. On the time scale in Figure 7, D represents the present date and S is the end of 1 year and 8 months. The beginnings of interest periods, *counting back from S*, are marked by dots on the time scale. The nearest beginning of an interest period occurring before D is R which is at -4 months on the time scale. First we shall discount $1000 to R, 4 months before D. Then we shall accumulate the result P_1 from R to D at simple interest.

2. The discounted value at R is

$$P_1 = 1000(1.03)^{-4} = \$888.487.$$

The time from R to D is 4 months. Simple interest on P_1 from R to D at 6% is

$$I = 888.487(.06)(\tfrac{1}{3}) = \$17.76974.$$

The approximate present value at D is

$$P_0 = 888.487 + 17.770 = \$906.26.$$

Exercise 9

In each problem, first construct a time scale as in preceding examples to clarify the solution. Use the approximate methods for accumulating or discounting.

1. Find the compound amount if $1000 is invested for 2 years and 7 months at 6% compounded quarterly.
2. Accumulate $2000 for 4 years and 8 months at 5% compounded semi-annually.
3. Accumulate $3000 for 5 years and 10 months at 8% compounded annually.
4. Discount $2500 for 8 years and 7 months with interest at 6% compounded semiannually.
5. If money is worth 7% compounded annually, find the present value of $2000 due at the end of 5 years and 4 months.
6. If money is worth .045 compounded quarterly, find the present value of $1000 due at the end of 7 years and 10 months.
7. Find the amount if $1250 is invested for 7 years and 5 months at $5\frac{1}{2}\%$ compounded quarterly.
8. On December 1, 1975, Jefferson borrows $1000 and agrees to pay the compound amount on the day he settles the account. If interest is at the rate $6\frac{1}{2}\%$ compounded quarterly, how much must he pay to discharge the debt on August 1, 1978?
9. Roberts owes Jones $2000 due on March 1, 1979. What will Jones accept from Roberts on January 1, 1977 to cancel the debt, if it is agreed that money is worth 5% compounded semiannually?
10. Webster owes $1000 due on May 1, 1978. The creditor allows Webster to pay off the debt on March 1, 1975, under the assumption that money is worth 7% compounded quarterly. What does he pay?

With the theoretical compound amount and present value defined by the formulas $F = P(1 + i)^n$ and $P = F(1 + i)^{-n}$ even when n is not an integer, only write an expression for the present value or amount specified in the problem. If this theoretical amount or present value were computed, it would be found to be close to the value obtained by the corresponding approximate method used previously.

11. The theoretical compound amount in Example 1, page 36.
12. The theoretical present value in Example 2, page 37.
13–17. The theoretical amount or present value in Problems 1–5, respectively.

17. Linear Interpolation

A linear function f of a variable x is of the form $f(x) = mx + b$, where m and b are constants with $m \neq 0$. Let $y = mx + b$. The graph of f is the graph of the equation $y = mx + b$, which is a *line*. This fact is discussed in Chapter 10.

ILLUSTRATION 1. In Figure 8, line L is the graph of the linear function $f(x) = \frac{1}{2}x + 1$, or of the equation $y = \frac{1}{2}x + 1$.

In Figure 8, let us refer to L as if it is the graph of *any* linear function $f(x) = mx + b$. Suppose that $x_1 < x_2$ and that x_0 is such that $x_1 < x_0 < x_2$, or x_0 is *between* x_1 and x_2. In Figure 8 we have the following values of line segments.

$$\overline{CM} = \overline{AP} = x_2 - x_1; \qquad \overline{CS} = \overline{AB} = x_0 - x_1;$$

$$\overline{SR} = \overline{BR} - \overline{BS} = \overline{BR} - \overline{AC} = f(x_0) - f(x_1).$$

$$\overline{MN} = \overline{PN} - \overline{PM} = \overline{PN} - \overline{AC} = f(x_2) - f(x_1).$$

From the similar $\triangle$'s CSR and CMN,

$$\frac{\overline{SR}}{\overline{CS}} = \frac{\overline{MN}}{\overline{CM}}, \qquad or \qquad \frac{f(x_0) - f(x_1)}{x_0 - x_1} = \frac{f(x_2) - f(x_1)}{x_2 - x_1}. \tag{1}$$

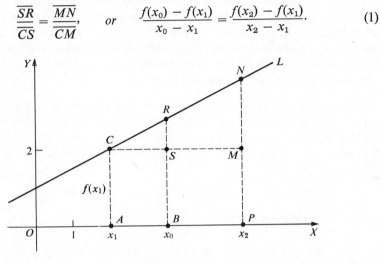

Figure 8

Each of the equal fractions in (1) is called the *slope* of the line L. In (1), suppose that $\{x_1, x_0, x_2, f(x_1), f(x_2)\}$ are given numbers. Then $f(x_0)$ can be obtained by use of (1). Or, if $\{x_1, x_2, f(x_1), f(x_1), f(x_0)\}$ are known, then x_0 can be found from (1); this is the principal case in which we shall be interested. For this purpose, in (1), multiply both sides by $(x_0 - x_1)$, and divide both sides by $[f(x_2) - f(x_1)]$, to obtain

$$\frac{x_0 - x_1}{x_2 - x_1} = \frac{f(x_0) - f(x_1)}{f(x_2) - f(x_1)}. \tag{2}$$

The result (2) can be recalled by reference to the following table of values of $f(x)$, where vertical arrows represent differences.

x	$f(x)$
x_1	$f(x_1)$
x_0	$f(x_0)$
x_2	$f(x_2)$

$(x_2 - x_1)$ $(x_0 - x_1)$ $[f(x_0) - f(x_1)]$ $[f(x_2) - f(x_1)]$

$$\tag{3}$$

Assume, now, that a function $f(x)$ is *not* linear, but that x_1 and x_2 are so close in values that the graph of $y = f(x)$ is *approximately a straight line* when x is on the interval from x_1 to x_2. Then we may use (2) to find x_0 or $f(x_0)$, approximately, when all other numbers in the equation are known. The resulting process in use of (2) is called **linear interpolation**. The name is appropriate. Thus, in finding x_0 from (2), we obtain an *intermediate value* of the variable x by use of values of x_1 and x_2 on either side, and the corresponding values of $f(x)$.

Linear interpolation is particularly useful when values of $f(x)$ are given in a table. Thus, linear interpolation is used with a table of logarithms, as on page 261. We shall use linear interpolation also with each of Tables V–IX in this text, where use with Table V appears in the next section. For future use with tables of values of a function, we summarize (2) as follows.

$$\left\{ \begin{array}{l} \textit{Suppose that values of a function } f(x) \textit{ are listed for values of } x \textit{ spaced} \\ \textit{at some regular interval. Then we assume that, for small changes in } x \\ \textit{from any listed value, the ratio of changes in the values of } x \textit{ is approxi-} \\ \textit{mately equal to the ratio of the corresponding changes in the values of} \\ f(x). \end{array} \right\} \quad (4)$$

18. Interpolation Methods

An unknown interest rate can be found with sufficient accuracy for most purposes by interpolation in Table V.

Example 1. If interest is compounded quarterly, find the nominal rate at which $2350 accumulates to $3500 at the end of $4\frac{3}{4}$ years.

SOLUTION. 1. Let i be the rate per conversion period. The nominal rate will be $4i$. From $F = P(1 + i)^n$ with $F = \$3500$, $P = \$2350$, and $n = 19$,

$$3500 = 2350(1 + i)^{19}; \qquad (1 + i)^{19} = \frac{3500}{2350} = 1.4894.$$

In the *row* for $n = 19$ in Table V, we find $(1.02)^{19} = 1.4568$, which is *less* than 1.4894, and $(1.0225)^{19} = 1.5262$, which is *greater* than 1.4894. Hence, i is between 2% and $2\frac{1}{4}$%. In reaching this decision, we say that we have **bracketed** the unknown rate i between the two nearest rates in the table.

2. In finding i by interpolation, i plays the role taken by x in Section 17, and $f(i) = (1 + i)^{19}$, with $f(i) = 1.4894$ and i unknown. In the following interpolation table, we have

$$i - 2\% = d; \qquad 2\tfrac{1}{4}\% - 2\% = \tfrac{1}{4}\%;$$

$$f(i) - f(2\%) = 1.4894 - 1.4568 = .0326;$$

$$f(2\tfrac{1}{4}\%) - f(2\%) = 1.5262 - 1.4568 = .0694.$$

We assume that the graph of $y = f(i)$ is well approximated by a straight line when i is on the interval from $i = 2\%$ to $i = 2\frac{1}{4}\%$. Then, by (4) on page 40, and by reference to the following interpolation table, we obtain the results below.

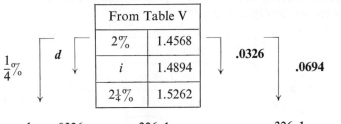

From Table V	
2%	1.4568
i	1.4894
$2\frac{1}{4}\%$	1.5262

$$\frac{d}{\frac{1}{4}\%} = \frac{.0326}{.0694}; \qquad d = \frac{326}{694}\cdot\frac{1}{4}\%; \qquad i = 2\% + \frac{326}{694}\cdot\frac{1}{4}\%; \tag{1}$$

$$(nominal\ rate) = 4i = 8\% + \frac{326}{694}\% = 8.47\%. \tag{2}$$

It would waste time to compute $i = 2.117\%$ in (1).

COMMENT. Experience shows that interest rates per period determined as in Example 1 usually are in error by not more than $\frac{1}{30}$ of the difference between the table rates used. Results obtained by interpolation should be computed to one more than the number of places which are expected to be accurate. When interpolating in Table V, it was sufficient to use only four decimal places of the entries, because the use of more places could not increase the accuracy of the method.

Suppose that a problem such as Example 1 arises in a situation in business affairs where the interest rate is desired with exceptional accuracy. Then, the result of Example 1 could be taken as a first approximation to the final answer. On this basis, if the accountant involved knew calculus, he could use a method called **Newton's Method** to obtain a much better approximation. Or, if the accountant had access to a modern computer, he could compute $(1 + i)^{19}$ for two values of i, say $i = 2.116\%$ and $i = 2.118\%$, bracketing the unknown rate which we realize is near 2.117%. Then, by interpolation between the new values thus obtained for $(1 + i)^{19}$, a better approximation could be found for i. This process could be continued to as great an extent as needed for the required final accuracy.

Example 2. How long will it take $5250 to accumulate to $7375 if invested at 6% compounded quarterly?

SOLUTION. Let n be the necessary number of interest periods.

$$7375 = 5250(1.015)^n; \qquad (1.015)^n = \frac{7375}{5250} = 1.4048. \tag{3}$$

In the column for $1\frac{1}{2}\%$ in Table V, we find that 1.4048 is between the entries for $n = 22$ and $n = 23$. Hence, the value of n satisfying (3) lies between 22 and 23. The entries for $n = 22$ and $n = 23$, and the value 1.4048 for the unknown value of n are listed in the following table. With $d = n - 22$, the ratio $d/1$ is assumed to be equal to the ratio of corresponding differences on the right. We obtain the following results, by (4) on page 40:

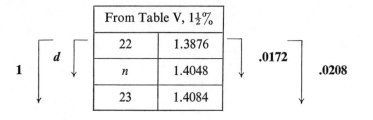

$$1.4048 - 1.3876 = .0172; \qquad 1.4084 - 1.3876 = .0208.$$

$$\frac{d}{1} = \frac{.0172}{.0208}, \qquad or \qquad d = \frac{172}{208} = .827. \tag{4}$$

Hence, $\qquad\qquad n = 22 + d = 22.827, \text{ periods of 3 months;}$

$$(time\ in\ years) = \tfrac{1}{4}(22.827) = 5.71\ years.$$

Less conveniently, we could have used the equation $5250 = 7375(1.015)^{-n}$, and then have interpolated in Table VI.

By a logarithmic method, a more exact solution of (3) is $n = 22.831$. However, an exact solution would have little use, whereas the approximate solution has the following interesting property:

*With accuracy which is limited only by the number of decimal places available in Table V, the value of n obtained by interpolation is the **exact solution** of the given problem with the understanding that simple interest is to be used for any time less than an interest period, as in Section 16.*

In Example 2, this property is a consequence of the following fact. In using linear interpolation leading to (4), we assumed that $(1.015)^n$ grew from $(1.015)^{22}$ to $(1.015)^{22}(1.015)$ so that the graph of $(1.015)^n$ over the interval $22 \le n \le 23$ is a *straight line*. That is, with n on this interval *we acted as if* $(1.015)^n = (1.015)^{22}(1 + .015t)$, for $0 \le t \le 1$. This means that we acted as if the increase was at *simple interest* on the interval $\{22 \le n \le 23\}$. The following computation verifies the preceding discussion for the data and result in Example 2.

Amount at end of 22 periods is $\qquad\qquad 5250(1.015)^{22} = \$7284.71.$

Simple interest for .827 period is $\qquad .827(.015)(7284.7) = \$90.37.$

Amount at end of 22.827 periods is $\qquad 7284.71 + 90.37 = \$7375.08.$

We would have had *exactly* $7375, to the nearest cent, if the entries from Table V and the interpolation had been carried to three more places.

Exercise 10

Solve each problem by interpolation in Table V.

1. At what rate compounded annually will $2500 accumulate to $4000 in 16 years?
2. How long will it take $800 to accumulate to $3300 at 4% compounded annually? Check the result as for Example 2 in Section 18.
3. When is $3000 due if its present value is $2400 when money is worth 5%?
4. Find the effective rate of interest in case $4000 is the present value of $6500 which is due at the end of 12 years.
5. $1200 accumulates to $5600 if invested at $\{.05, m = 2\}$. Find the term of the investment.
6. $3000 is the present value of $6100 due at the end of 15 years if interest is compounded semiannually. Find the nominal rate.
7. $2650 is the compound amount if $2000 is invested for 4 years and 9 months with interest compounded quarterly. Find the nominal rate.
8. The amount is $3120 if $1200 is invested at $\{.045, m = 4\}$. Find the term of the investment.
9. An investment of $5000 increases to $8800 if invested for $8\frac{1}{2}$ years, with interest compounded monthly. Find the nominal rate.
10. A $100 United States Savings bond of the variety sold in 1956 cost $75 and promised a payment of $100 to the buyer 10 years after the date of purchase. In 1974, with the same cost, the bond promised payment of $100 to the buyer 5 years after the date of purchase. For each of the bonds, find the effective rate yielded to the buyer. (The interest rate was increased later on the bonds sold in 1956.)
11. A promissory note requires Harrison to pay $6250 at the end of 2 years and 9 months. The creditor allows him to discharge the debt by paying $5720 now. Find the rate compounded quarterly at which the creditor discounted the debt.
12. At the time of the transaction in Problem 11, the market rate for safe investment for the time involved was $\{7\%, m = 4\}$. Why did the creditor specify the low rate found in Problem 11?
13. Roberts receives a loan of $2000, with interest at $6\frac{1}{2}\%$ compounded quarterly. He promises to pay his creditor in full on the day when $3000 will be due. Find when Roberts pays, with the method of Section 16 used.

NOTE 1. The following method gives approximately the time necessary for money to double itself at compound interest: (*a*) *Divide .693 by the rate per interest period*; (*b*) *add .35 to the preceding result to obtain the time in conversion periods.* The error in this result generally is less than a few hundredths of a period. A proof of the rule requires use of calculus, and is omitted. By use of this rule in Problem 14 we find

$$n = \frac{.693}{.025} + .35 = 28.07.$$

14. How long will it take for money to double itself if it is invested at 5% compounded semiannually? Solve by interpolation.
15. By use of the preceding Note 1, find how long it takes for money to double itself at each of the following rates: $\{.06, m = 2\}; \{.04, m = 4\}; \{.05, m = 1\}; \{.07, m = 4\}; \{.08, m = 1\}.$
16. By use of the results in Problem 15, find how long it takes for money to quadruple itself at each of the rates in Problem 15.

★19. Logarithmic Methods

In modern government or business affairs, particularly as they arise in banks, brokerage firms, and large corporations, any problem similar to one of the following illustrative examples would be solved by use of an electronic computer. With that method involved, the results would be obtained with almost unlimited accuracy. Hence, the following logarithmic methods should be viewed as available for obtaining approximate results on those rare occasions when more accurate methods are not available. Examples 1 and 2 are concerned with accumulating or discounting money at an interest rate per period not found in any table of values of $(1 + i)^n$. Examples 3 and 4 deal with problems of types solved by interpolation in the preceding section.

Example 1. Compute $F = 5000(1.0187)^{40}$.

SOLUTION. To increase the final accuracy, *we use Table* III *first* to obtain log 1.0187 to *seven* decimal places.

$$\log 1.0187 = 0.0080463 \qquad \text{(Table III)}$$

$$\log (1.0187)^{40} = 40 \log 1.0187 = 0.321852$$
$$\log 5000 = 3.698970 \qquad \text{(Table II)}$$
$$\text{(Add)} \quad \log F = 4.020822; \qquad F = \$10,491. \qquad \text{(Table II)}$$

There was no object in interpolating for six digits in finding F from Table II, because multiplication of log 1.0187 by 40 causes log F to be unreliable in the 6th decimal place and possibly unreliable in the 5th decimal place.

Example 2. If interest is at the rate 3.74% compounded semiannually, find the present value of $350.75 due at the end of $6\frac{1}{2}$ years.

SOLUTION. We have $i = .0187$ and $n = 13$:

$$P = 350.75(1.0187)^{-13} = \frac{350.75}{(1.0187)^{13}}.$$

	log 350.75 = 2.544998	(Table II)
13 log 1.0187 =	13(.0080463) = 0.104602	(Table III)
(Subtract) log P = 2.440396.	P = \$275.67.	(Table II)

In the interpolation for P in Table II, we met a tabular difference 158 and partial difference 117; $\frac{117}{158} = .7\,+$, to the nearest tenth, and this gives the answer to the nearest cent. Use of five-place logarithms would leave the cents in doubt.

Example 3. Find the nominal rate, converted quarterly, at which \$2350 accumulates to \$2750 at the end of $4\frac{3}{4}$ years.

SOLUTION. Let i be the unknown period rate; the nominal rate is $4i$.

$$2750 = 2350(1 + i)^{19}; \qquad (1 + i)^{19} = \frac{2750}{2350}.$$

We extract 19th roots and employ Table II.

$$1 + i = \left(\frac{2750}{2350}\right)^{1/19}. \qquad \begin{array}{l} \log 2750 = 3.439333 \\ \log 2350 = 3.371068 \end{array}$$

$$\text{(Subtract)} \ \log \text{quot.} = 0.068265$$

$$\tfrac{1}{19} \log \text{quot.} = 0.003593 = \log(1 + i).$$

From Table II: $\quad \log 1.00800 = .003461 \rceil\ 132 \rceil$
$\qquad\qquad\qquad \log(1 + i) = .003593\ \downarrow \qquad\quad 430 \qquad \frac{132}{430} = .31-.$
From Table II: $\quad \log 1.00900 = .003891 \qquad\qquad\downarrow$

Therefore, $1 + i = 1.00831$; $i = .00831$. The nominal rate is $4i = .0332$.

Example 4. By use of Table I, find how long it will take for \$3500 to accumulate to \$4708 if invested at 8% compounded quarterly.

SOLUTION. Let n be the necessary number of conversion periods.

$$4708 = 3500(1.02)^n; \qquad (1.02)^n = \frac{4708}{3500}. \qquad \therefore\ n \log 1.02 = \log \frac{4708}{3500}.$$

$$\begin{array}{l} \log 4708 = 3.67284 \\ \log 3500 = 3.54407 \end{array} \qquad\qquad \log 1.02 = 0.0086002$$

$$\log \text{quot.} = 0.12877. \qquad\qquad \therefore\ n(0.0086002) = .12877.$$

$$n = \frac{12877}{860.02}. \qquad\qquad \begin{array}{l} \log 12877 = 4.10982 \\ \log 860.02 = 2.93451 \end{array}$$

$$\text{(Subtract)} \ \log n = 1.17531$$

The time is $n = 14.973$ periods of 3 months, or 3.743 years. In this problem, we have solved an exponential equation for n by first taking the logarithm of both sides. However, the discussion following Example 2 of Section 18 shows that the preceding logarithmic solution has no merit compared to a solution by interpolation.

★Exercise 11

The instructor may direct use of either Table I *or Table* II, *except where otherwise specified.*

Use a logarithmic method in each problem. Employ Table III *first when the value of* $(1 + i)^n$ *or* $(1 + i)^{-n}$ *is involved for a given i.*

1. Compute $(1.0225)^{50}$ by using Table III first and then Table I (or, Table II); compute $(1.0225)^{50}$ by use of Table I alone (or, Table II alone). Compare with Table V.
2. Accumulate $1850 for $4\frac{1}{2}$ years at $\{.064, m = 4\}$.
3. Discount $2500 for $8\frac{1}{2}$ years at $\{7.8\%, m = 2\}$.
4. If $1500 is the present value of $3125 due at the end of 6 years, find the rate at which interest is compounded quarterly.

Find the effective rate correct to .01%, *for the given nominal rate. Use Table* III *first, and then Table* II.

5. 4.8% compounded quarterly.   6. 7.2% compounded semiannually.

Find the time by solving an exponential equation logarithmically. Use Table III *at the start.*

7. If interest is at the rate 4% compounded semiannually, find how long it will take for $1350 to accumulate to $3250.
8. How long will it take for money to double itself at $\{.055, m = 2\}$?

20. Values of Obligations and their Comparison

We suppose that all money mentioned is invested at compound interest at some rate i per conversion period. Then, the desirability of a sum of money depends on when we shall receive it. We emphasize again the fact that the mathematics of investment thus deals primarily with *dated values*. If a sum P is due on one date and F is due n interest periods later, we refer to these sums as *equivalent values* in case $F = P(1 + i)^n$.

The objective of this section is to emphasize the preceding remarks about dated values, and how we may compare them. These features are fundamental in almost all later content of the mathematics of finance. It is admitted that the illustrative examples, with minor exceptions, cannot be labeled as real applications in business affairs. The problems present simple situations to emphasize the principles involved. On account of the preceding attitude, it would be a waste of time to obtain the numerical results with a high degree of accuracy, for instance to the nearest cent in each case. Although answers to the illustrative examples are given to the nearest cent, it will be recommended that results for problems in the next exercise should be computed only to a very limited number of significant figures. In the typical problem, an answer correct to the nearest $10 would assure the student that he has correctly appreciated the essential objective of the example.

A promise to pay a specified sum of money on a designated date will be referred to as a *financial obligation*. For concreteness, we may think of any obligation as written in the form of a promissory note. The simplest type of obligation is illustrated by the following note.

NOTE I. Jones *promises to pay* $1000 *to* Smith *or order* three years after January 1, 1977, *without interest*.

This note requires the payment of the *maturity value* $1000 on the *maturity date*, January 1, 1980. Smith may sell his right to the final payment and any buyer may resell the note.

At a stipulated rate of interest, the value of an obligation *before* its maturity date is obtained by *discounting* the maturity value to the date of sale.

Example 1. Note I is sold by Smith to Hansen on January 1, 1978. If money is worth 7% compounded quarterly in this transaction, what does Hansen pay?

SOLUTION. The note promises $1000 on January 1, 1980. On January 1, 1978, Hansen discounts $1000 for 2 years and pays

$$1000(1.0175)^{-8} \quad or \quad \$870.41. \tag{1}$$

The value of an obligation n interest periods *after* the maturity date is obtained by *accumulating* the maturity value for n periods at the stipulated interest rate.

Example 2. If Jones arranges not to pay Note I until five years after it is due, what must he pay then if money is worth 7% compounded quarterly?

SOLUTION. Jones pays the compound amount at the end of 5 years, or

$$1000(1.0175)^{20} \quad or \quad \$1414.78. \tag{2}$$

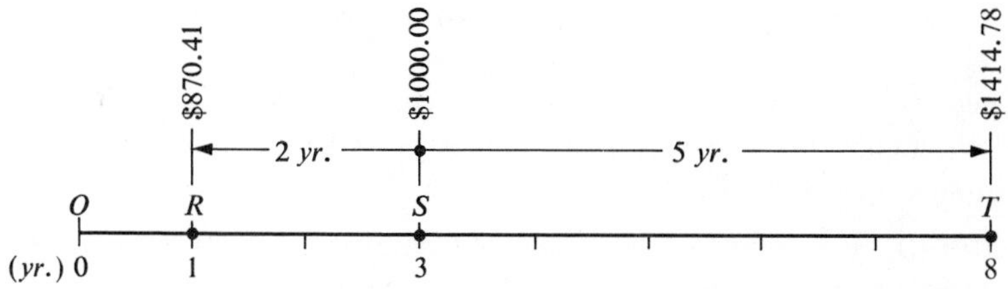

Figure 9

COMMENT. In Figure 9, point O represents January 1, 1977. Note I is an obligation to pay $1000 at date S. We obtained the *equivalent value* or, for short, the *value*, of this obligation at R in Example and at T in Example 2. At each point on the time scale the obligation has a definite value obtainable by accumulating or discounting $1000 for the proper time. *Each of these values is equivalent to any one of the other values.* Thus, if $870.41 is accumulated for 7 years, from R to T, the result is $1414.78; this can be verified without computation by use of (1), (2), and a law of exponents:

$$870.41(1.0175)^{28} = 1000(1.0175)^{-8}(1.0175)^{28} = 1000(1.0175)^{20}.$$

The face of the following interest-bearing obligation is $1000; the maturity value is $1000 (1.015)^{15} = \$1250.23$. The note promises $1250.23 on the maturity date, October 1, 1978, indicated in Figure 10. The face value is of no importance after the maturity value is found.

NOTE II.   Three years and nine months *after* January 1, 1975, Jones *promises to pay to* Smith *or order* $1000 plus accumulated interest from this date *at the rate* 6% compounded quarterly.

Example 3.   Smith sells Note II to Roberts on January 1, 1976. What does Roberts pay, if he is willing to discount at 7% compounded quarterly?

SOLUTION.   The time from 1/1/1976 to the maturity date, 10/1/1978 is 11 interest periods. The maturity value is $1000(1.015)^{15}$, or $1250.23. Hence, the value on 1/1/1976 is obtained by discounting $1250.23 for 11 periods, as seen in Figure 10:

Roberts pays $1250.23(1.0175)^{-11} = \$1033.03.$

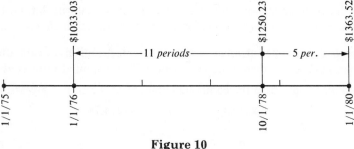

Figure 10

Example 4.   Jones will not pay Note II when due. What should he pay to cancel the debt on January 1, 1980, if it is agreed that money is worth 7% compounded quarterly after 10/1/1978.

SOLUTION.   The time from the maturity date to 1/1/1980 is $1\frac{1}{4}$ years or 5 interest periods. We accumulate $1250.23 for 5 periods:

Jones will pay $1250.23(1.0175)^{5} = \$1363.52.$

To compare two obligations due on *different* dates, the values of the obligations must be compared on some *common date*, which we shall call the **comparison date**.

Example 5. If money is worth 5% compounded annually, which of the following obligations (*a*) and (*b*) is the more valuable?

(*a*) $1100 *due at the end of one year (that is, due without interest).*

(*b*) $1000 *due at the end of four years with accumulated interest from today at the rate 6% compounded semiannually.*

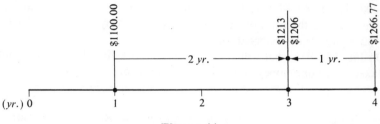

Figure 11

SOLUTION. Compare values at the end of 3 years. Hence, at the rate $\{.05, m = 1\}$, accumulate the maturity value of (*a*) for 2 years and discount the maturity value of (*b*) for 1 year, as indicated in Figure 11. Since $1213 is greater

	Maturity Value	Maturity Date	Value at End of 3 Years
(*a*)	$1100	*end of* 1 *year*	$1100 (1.05)^2 = \$1213$
(*b*)	$1000 (1.03)^8 = \$1266.77$	*end of* 4 *years*	$1267 (1.05)^{-1} = \$1206$

than $1206, (*a*) is the more valuable. The same conclusion would be reached if any other comparison date were used. This is true because the values of the obligations on any date can be obtained by accumulating or discounting the values found at the end of 3 years. In the solution, the end of 4 years would have been a more convenient comparison date; the end of 3 years was used for illustrative purposes.

Exercise 12

Obtain individual terms leading to the results correct only to the nearest $1, *or nearest* $10, *as permitted by the instructor.**

1. Roberts borrows a certain sum of money from Hartman on June 1, 1974, and signs a note promising to pay him a total of $10,000 at the end of 5

---

* If results are accepted to the nearest $10, then the student might prefer to perform the computation by use of plain arithmetic, if no computing device is available. If results are desired correct to the nearest $1, computation by use of just five-place logarithms would be satisfactory.

years. Hartman sells this promissory note to Jones on June 1, 1977. If Jones insists on discounting the note at 4% compounded quarterly, what will he pay for the note?

2. In regard to the promissory note of Problem 1, Roberts gets permission to delay his payment until June 1, 1981, under the assumption that money is worth {4%, $m = 4$} after the note matures. What final payment is Roberts required to make?

3. $2000 is due on May 1, 1979. If money is worth 5% compounded semiannually, find the value of this obligation (a) on May 1, 1975; (b) on May 1, 1982 if payment is deferred until then.

4. On July 15, 1976 what will Johnson receive on selling the following note to Baker, to whom money is worth 4% compounded semiannually?

> July 15, 1975
>
> Three years *from date* I *promise to pay to* Raymond Johnson *or order* $2000 *with accumulated interest from date at* 3% compounded semiannually. (*Signed*) Herbert Carlson

5. If you insist on discounting at 3% compounded quarterly, what would you pay for the note of Problem 4 on October 15, 1976?

6. $2500 was borrowed on May 15, 1974, it was to be repaid on August 15, 1977, with accumulated interest at 4% compounded quarterly. No payment will be made until August 15, 1980. What is due then if the creditor demands that interest shall be at the rate 5% compounded semiannually after August 15, 1977?

7. If money is worth {$4\frac{1}{2}$%, $m = 2$}, which obligation is the more valuable: (a) $700 due at the end of 2 years, or (b) $750 due at the end of 3 years?

8. If money is worth {5%, $m = 2$}, determine which of the following obligations is the more valuable: (a) $500 due at end of 4 years with accumulated interest from today at {.06, $m = 2$}, or (b) $700 due at the end of 5 years.

9. If money is worth {7%, $m = 2$}, which obligation is the more valuable: (a) $3000 due at the end of 3 years with accumulated interest from today at {8%, $m = 2$}; (b) $3800 due without interest at the end of 4 years?

10. Suppose that money is worth 4% *simple interest* and consider the following obligations: (a) $1160 due at the end of 4 years; (b) $1240 due at the end of 6 years. Find the present values of the obligations and, also, their values at the end of 6 years.

NOTE. In Problem 10, the present values are equal but the values at the end of 6 years are unequal. This proves that, if money is invested at simple interest, two obligations may have *equal* values on one date but *unequal* values on other dates. In contrast, at compound interest, if two obligations have equal values on one comparison date, the obligations have equal values on *all other dates*. This accounts for the fundamental role of compound interest in the mathematics of finance.

21. Equations of Value

An *equation of value* is an equation stating that the sum of the values, on a certain comparison date, of one set of obligations is equal to the sum of the values of another set on this date. The concept of an equation of value is basic in future chapters. The objective of this section is similar to that of Section 20. The fundamental principle, and not the numerical work involved, is of main importance. It is admitted that the illustrative problems, and those in the exercises, are not typical of actual business situations. The data are chosen to provide convenient practice in writing equations of value.

Example 1. Jones owes his creditor (*a*) $1000 due without interest at the end of 10 years, and (*b*) $3000 due at the end of 4 years with accumulated interest from today at 4% compounded annually. Jones will discharge his obligations by two equal payments at the ends of the 3rd and 6th years. If the creditor states that money is worth 6% compounded semiannually, find the new payments.

SOLUTION.　1. Let $x represent each of the new payments.

Old Obligations		New Obligations	
Maturity Value	*Due After*	*Maturity Value*	*Due After*
(*a*) $1000	10 years	$x	3 years
(*b*) $3000 $(1.04)^4$	4 years	$x	6 years

2. *Equation of value with the end of 4 years as a comparison date.* Observe Figure 12. In the right-hand member we *accumulate* the first $x payment for 1 year and *discount* the second $x for 2 years. In the left-hand member we discount (*a*) for 6 years and take the maturity value of (*b*) unchanged.

$$1000(1.03)^{-12} + 3000(1.04)^4 = x(1.03)^2 + x(1.03)^{-4}; \qquad (1)$$

$$4210.96 = x(1.06090) + x(.888487) = x(1.94939); \qquad \text{(Tables V, VI)}$$

$$x = \frac{4210.96}{1.94939} \doteq \$2160.$$

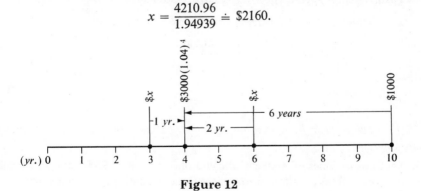

Figure 12

COMMENT. The end of 4 years was the most convenient comparison date on account of (*b*). To appreciate this, consider the following equation in which the comparison date is the end of 6 years. The arithmetic for (2) would be more complicated than for (1).

$$1000(1.03)^{-8} + 3000(1.04)^4(1.03)^4 = x(1.03)^6 + x. \qquad (2)$$

Observe that (2) can be obtained by multiplying both sides of (1) by $(1.03)^4$, because each term in (1) must be accumulated for 2 years or 4 interest periods in changing to the date for (2). Hence, (1) and (2) are *equivalent equations* and therefore are satisfied by the same value of x. The equivalence of the equations of value corresponding to different comparison dates shows that *the choice of the comparison date does not affect the result* when we are using an equation of value to find unknown payments.

Example 2. W borrowed $2000 from Y on June 1, 1975, and $500 on June 1, 1977, agreeing that money is worth 5% compounded annually. W paid $500 on June 1, 1978, $400 on June 1, 1979, and $700 on June 1, 1980. What additional sum should W pay on June 1, 1983, to discharge all remaining liability?

SOLUTION. Let x be the final payment on June 1, 1983. On any comparison date, the value of the set of sums *paid* should equal the value of the set *received*. Hence, we write an equation of value with June 1, 1983, as the comparison date.

Received	Paid
$2000 on June 1, 1975	$500 on June 1, 1978
$500 on June 1, 1977	$400 on June 1, 1979
	$700 on June 1, 1980
	$x on June 1, 1983

$$2000(1.05)^8 + 500(1.05)^6 = 500(1.05)^5 + 400(1.05)^4 + 700(1.05)^3 + x.$$

$$x = 2000(1.05)^8 + 500(1.05)^6 - 500(1.05)^5 - 400(1.05)^4 - 700(1.05)^3.$$

$$x \doteq \$1690.$$

Exercise 13

Solve each problem by writing an equation of value. Also, draw a preliminary time diagram.

1. Smith owes Jones $500 due at the end of 3 years and $2000 due at the end of 7 years. Smith is allowed to replace these obligations by a single payment at the end of 5 years. If money is worth $4\frac{1}{2}\%$, (*a*) write equations of value for

finding the new payment $x with the comparison dates chosen as the present, the end of 4 years, and the end of 7 years, respectively, but *do not solve* these equations. (*b*) Solve by use of the end of 5 years as the comparison date.

2. If money is worth $5\frac{1}{2}\%$ compounded semiannually, find the single payment at the end of 4 years which could replace the following obligations.

I. $800 *due at the end of 3 years.*

II. $600 *due at the end of 6 years.*

Use the end of 4 years as a comparison date.

3. Solve for *x*, as a fraction: $7530 = x(1.03)^2 + x(1.03)^{-4} + x.$

4. Marston buys a house worth $45,000 cash. He pays $5000 immediately, $5000 at the end of 2 years, $8000 at the end of 4 years, and a final payment at the end of 7 years. Find the final payment if money is worth 8%.

In those remaining problems where two parts (a) and (b) are involved, only write the equations of value for (a), unless directed by the instructor to do part (b) also. In (b), if done, obtain the results correct only to the nearest $10 to minimize the computation.

5. Money is worth 3%, and we desire to replace obligations I and II of Problem 2 by two equal payments at the ends of the 4th and 8th years. (*a*) Write equations of value for finding the new payments with the comparison dates chosen as the present, the end of 3 years, and the end of 5 years, respectively, but *do not solve* these equations. (*b*) Find the unknown payments by use of a more convenient comparison date.

6. Hansen receives a loan of $4000 from Kelly today and will receive $6000 more at the end of 2 years. Hansen will pay $200 at the end of 3 years, $3000 at the end of 5 years, and a final payment at the end of 6 years. If money is worth 4%, (*a*) write an equation for the final payment, using the end of 5 years as a comparison date, but *do not solve* the equation; (*b*) find the payment, using a convenient comparison date.

7. Money is worth 6% compounded semiannually, and we decide to replace the following obligations by a single payment at the end of 4 years.

I. $500 *due at the end of 2 years without interest.*

II. $1500 *due at the end of 7 years with accumulated interest from today at 5% converted annually.*

(*a*) Write an equation for finding the unknown payment by use of the end of 6 years as a comparison date but *do not solve* this equation.

(*b*) Solve by use of the end of 7 years as the comparison date.

8. Money is worth 6% and we desire to discharge obligations (I) and (II) of Problem 7 by two equal payments at the ends of the 5th and 8th years. (*a*) Write an equation for finding the payments by use of the end of 5 years as the comparison date, but *do not solve* the equation. (*b*) Find the payments by use of a more convenient comparison date.

9. Walden owes Martin the following obligations.

    I. $1000 *due at the end of* 4 *years.*

    II. $2000 *due at the end of* 6 *years with accumulated interest from today at the rate* 4% *effective.*

Walden will be allowed to replace his total obligation by a payment of $1500 at the end of 3 years and a second payment at the end of 5 years, with money worth 5%. (*a*) Write an equation for finding the payment using the end of 4 years as a comparison date, but *do not solve* the equation. (*b*) Find the unknown payment.

10. Walden wishes to replace the obligations of Problem 9 by a first payment at the end of 2 years and twice as much at the end of 8 years, with money worth $3\frac{1}{2}$%. (*a*) Write equations of value for finding the payments with the ends of 2, 6, and 8 years as comparison dates but *do not solve* the equations. (*b*) Find the payments.

11. Stevens owes Bradshaw $2500 due without interest at the end of $4\frac{1}{2}$ years. Stevens will replace this obligation by a payment of $500 at the end of 2 years and two equal payments at the ends of 3 and 6 years. Find each of these payments to the nearest $10 if money is worth 4% compounded quarterly.

12. If money is worth 5%, when is $1500 due if its value is equal to that of $1750 due at the end of 5 years? Use the present as the comparison date; then interpolate.

Exercise 14 | Review of Chapters 1 and 2

1. Find the ordinary and the exact simple interest on $1578 at 6% from March 3 to November 27 of any year.

2. If money can be invested at 7% simple interest, find the present value of $2000 which is due at the end of 240 days. Recall that ordinary interest is to be used unless otherwise requested.

3. Find the discount if $2000 is discounted for six months at (*a*) 8% simple interest; (*b*) 8% simple discount; (*c*) 8% compounded quarterly.

4. Find the nominal rate which will yield the effective rate 7% if interest is compounded (*a*) annually; (*b*) quarterly; (*c*) semiannually; (*d*) monthly. Use Table XIV. Check by reference to Table XIII.

5. I owe $10,000 due at the end of 3 years without interest. What should my creditor be willing to accept today if he discounts at (*a*) 7% simple interest; (*b*) 7% compounded annually; (*c*) 7% simple discount?

6. Find the compound interest due at the end of 5 years and 9 months if $10,000 is invested at $\{.05, m = 12\}$.

7. Find the effective rate if the nominal rate 7% is compounded (a) annually; (b) semiannually; (c) monthly; (d) quarterly.

8. A merchant is offered a 5% discount for immediate payment of a bill which is due in 90 days. What is the largest simple interest rate at which he could accord to borrow in order to pay cash?

9. A merchant owes $6000 due immediately. For what face sum should he make out a 90-day noninterest-bearing note so that his creditor may realize $6000 on it if a bank discounts the note immediately at 8%?

10. On June 1, 1975, Thompson signs the following note: "*At the end of* 180 *days, I promise to pay to Richards, or order,* $1000 *together with simple interest from date at the rate* 7%." On July 16, 1975, Richards sells this note to a bank whose discount rate is 9%. Find Richards' proceeds.

11. Find the nominal rate which, if compounded semiannually, is equivalent to $\{7\%, m = 12\}$.

12. Find the nominal rate which, if compounded quarterly, is equivalent to 8% compounded semiannually.

13. A debtor owes Ryan the following sums, due without interest: $1000 due at the end of 2 years and $2000 due at the end of 5 years. What equivalent single payment would Ryan be willing to accept at the end of 4 years, if money is worth $\{8\%, m = 4\}$ to him? Draw a time diagram.

14. What simple interest rate would be equivalent to charging 8% compounded semiannually, if I lend Jeffrey $2000 with the agreement that he will pay a single sum of money to me at the end of 3 years?

15. Find the nominal rate if interest is compounded semiannually and if a principal of $3000 grows to $5000 by the end of 8 years. Use interpolation.

16. Find the compound amount at the end of 9 years and 8 months if $5000 is invested at $\{5\%, m = 2\}$, by the approximate method.

NOTE 1. Outside of the field of interest theory, if it is said that a certain quantity *increases at the rate i per year*, it is meant that the quantity increases just as a principal grows when invested at compound interest at the rate i compounded annually.

17. If the daily gasoline consumption is to increase at the rate 7% per year, find when the daily consumption will be double what it is now, (a) by interpolation; (b) by an approximate rule.

18. Which of the following obligations (a) and (b) is the more valuable, and by how large an amount, if money can be invested at $\{.06, m = 1\}$?

(a) $2000 due without interest at the end of 4 years.

(b) $1660 due at the end of 2 years with accumulated interest at 4% compounded annually.

19. If $4000 is invested at the rate $\{.08, m = 2\}$, when will the compound amount be $7000? Solve the interpolation. Also verify, approximately to the nearest dollar, that the result is correct if the amount is computed by the approximate method involving simple interest for part of an interest period.

20. Warren owes Humphrey $2000 due without interest at the end of 2 years, and $1000 due with accumulated interest at $\{.05, m = 2\}$ at the end of 3 years. Warren paid Humphrey $1500 at the end of one year. Money now is worth $\{.08, m = 4\}$. What additional equal payments at the ends of $3\frac{1}{2}$ and 5 years would cancel Warren's remaining liability? Only write equations of value for finding the payments with the comparison dates (a) the end of 3 years; (b) the end of 5 years. Do NOT solve the equations.

21. If $1000 is invested now, obtain an expression (but do not compute it) for the amount at the end of 25 years if interest is at $\{5\%, m = 1\}$ for the first 15 years and at $\{7\%, m = 1\}$ for the last 10 years.

22. Find an expression for the present value of $2500 due at the end of 15 years, if money is worth 4% until the end of 7 years, and 5% thereafter. Do NOT compute the expression.

23. Sullivan borrows $2000 and agrees to pay the principal and accumulated simple interest at the rate 6% at the end of 3 years. Find the equivalent nominal rate compounded semiannually at which Sullivan could have borrowed.

3/ The Simple Case for Annuities

22. Terminology for Annuities

An **annuity** is a sequence of periodic payments, which we shall suppose of equal size unless otherwise specified. An *annuity certain* is one whose payments extend over a fixed term of years. A *contingent annuity* is one whose payments extend over a period of time whose length cannot be foretold accurately. Until otherwise specified, we shall deal entirely with annuities certain; the word *annuity* always will refer to an *annuity certain*. Contingent annuities will be met in the study of life annuities and life insurance in this text.

ILLUSTRATION 1. The equal monthly payments made in purchasing a house on the installment plan form an annuity certain. The equal sums paid as premiums on a life insurance policy form a contingent annuity, because the payments end at the death of the insured person, an uncertain date.

The time between successive payment dates of an annuity is called the **payment interval**. For many purposes, it is convenient to think of each payment belonging to the interval which *precedes* it, rather than to the interval which *follows* it. Hence, the unqualified word *annuity*, or sometimes for emphasis the words **ordinary annuity**, always will refer to a sequence of periodic payments which are thought of as occurring at the ends of corresponding payment intervals. The time from the beginning of the first payment interval to the end of the last one is called the **term** of the annuity. Unless otherwise specified, the term of any annuity is presumed to begin *immediately*. The first payment is due *one payment interval after the beginning of the term*; the last payment is due *at the end of the term*.

ILLUSTRATION 2. A sequence of payments of $50 each, due at the end of each month for the next 15 years, forms an annuity whose payment interval is

57

1 month and whose term is 15 years. The term begins immediately (1 month before the first payment) and ends at the close of 15 years.

23. Present Value and Amount of an Annuity

At a specified rate of interest, the *present value* of an annuity is the *sum of the present values of the payments*. **The present value of an annuity is the value of the annuity at the beginning of its term.** The *amount* of an annuity is the *sum of the compound amounts on hand at the end of the term if each payment accumulates until then from the date when it was due.* Briefly, **the amount of an annuity is the value of the annuity at the end of its term.** Very appropriately, the amount of an annuity sometimes is called the **accumulation** of the annuity. Usually we shall employ A to represent the present value and S for the amount of an annuity.

ILLUSTRATION 1.   Consider an annuity of $100 payable annually for 5 years. If interest is at the rate 4% compounded annually, we obtain the present value A of this annuity by adding the terms at the left and the amount S by adding the terms at the right in Figure 13. Or, we obtain A and S by adding columns in the following table. The amounts and present values for the payments were computed by use of $F = P(1 + i)^n$ and $P = F(1 + i)^{-n}$. Since A and S are equivalent values five years apart, as seen in Figure 13, we should have $S = A(1.04)^5$. By use of Table V, we verify that

$$445.182(1.04)^5 = 445.182(1.21665290) = 541.632. \tag{1}$$

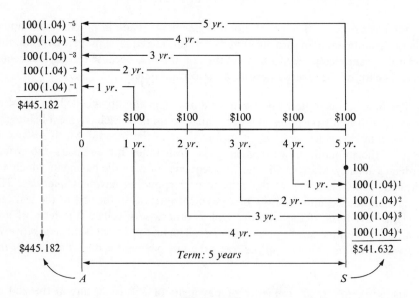

Figure 13

The present value of an annuity is met in *amortization* problems; the first letter, *A*, of amortization gives justification for the use of *A* for the *present value* of an annuity. Similarly, *S* for the amount makes contact with *sinking fund* problems, where amounts of annuities are applied.

Payment of $100 Due at End of	Present Value of Payment	Compound Amount at End of Term if Payment Is Left to Accumulate at Interest
1 year	$100(1.04)^{-1} =$ 96.15385	$100(1.04)^{4} =$ 116.98586
2 years	$100(1.04)^{-2} =$ 92.45562	$100(1.04)^{3} =$ 112.48640
3 years	$100(1.04)^{-3} =$ 88.89964	$100(1.04)^{2} =$ 108.16000
4 years	$100(1.04)^{-4} =$ 85.48042	$100(1.04)^{1} =$ 104.00000
5 years	$100(1.04)^{-5} =$ 82.19271	$100 =$ 100.00000
	(*Add*) $A = \$445.18224$	(*Add*) $S = \$541.63226$

The present value *A* of an annuity is the sum of the discounted values of the payments of the annuity at *the beginning of its term*. The amount *S* of the annuity is the sum of the accumulated values of the same payments *at the end of the term*. Hence, *A* due at the *beginning* of the term has the same value as *S* due at the *end* of the term. That is, *A* is the present value obtained by discounting *S*, or *S* is the amount obtained by accumulating *A* for the length of the term of the annuity at compound interest. If the term of an annuity is *n* interest periods, and if *i* is the interest rate per conversion period, then *A* and *S* satisfy the usual relation between equivalent values as given by the equation of compound interest:

$$S = A(1 + i)^{n}, \quad or \quad A = S(1 + i)^{-n}. \tag{2}$$

This relation between *A* and *S* will be very useful later, and was met in (1).

ILLUSTRATION 2.   From Illustration 1, $445.182 is the sum of the *present values* of the annuity payments. Hence, formation of a fund by investment of $445.182 at 4% should provide for the annuity payments, with the fund exactly exhausted by the final payment, as verified in the following table. The headings are labeled as if the fund becomes a *debt* where the borrower *obtains* $445.182 and discharges his liability as to *principal and interest* by making the annuity payments. In such a case the *creditor* permissibly may think of *compound interest*, seeing $445.182 as the sum of present values of the payments, as in Illustration 1. The *debtor* might think only of the elementary necessity of *paying interest as due*, and (in most cases) *might not even understand the compound interest attitude of Illustration* 1, which will give us future formulas.

Year	Debtor Liability at Beginning of Year	Interest at 4% Due at End of Year	Debtor Liability at End of Year	Payment at End of Year
1	$445.182	$17.807	$462.989	$100
2	362.989	14.520	377.509	100
3	277.509	11.100	288.609	100
4	188.609	7.544	196.153	100
5	96.153	3.846	99.999	100

Let a fund be formed by depositing the payments of an annuity as they fall due and allowing them to accumulate at compound interest. Then, by definition, the *amount* of the annuity is the sum which will be in the fund at the end of the term of the annuity.

ILLUSTRATION 3. The following table shows the growth of a fund formed by investing the payments of the annuity of Illustration 1. The final amount is seen to be *S* of Illustration 1.

At End of	Int. Due	Payment to Fund	In Fund
1st year	0	$100	$100.000
2nd year	$ 4.000	100	204.000
3rd year	8.160	100	312.160
4th year	12.486	100	424.646
5th year	16.986	100	$S =$ 541.632

Exercise 15

1. If money can be invested at 5% compounded semiannually, construct tables like those of Illustrations 1, 2, and 3 of Section 23 for an annuity of $100 payable at the end of each 6 months for 3 years.

24. Geometric Progressions for *A* and *S*

Example 1. If money is worth $\{.04, m = 2\}$ find the present value and the amount of an annuity of $50 paid at the end of each 6 months for 20 years.

SOLUTION. 1. *To find S.* Each payment must be accumulated to the end of the annuity's term, the end of 20 years. The last payment is due then and hence is taken *unchanged*. We accumulate the next to the last payment for 6 months, or 1 period; the 2nd from the last payment, due at the end of 19 years, for 2 periods; the 1st, due at the end of 6 months, for $19\frac{1}{2}$ years or 39 periods; the 2nd for 38 periods, from the end of 1 year to the end of 20 years; and so on, as shown in Figure 14. Each amount was found by use of $F = P(1 + i)^n$ with $P = 50$ and $i = .02$. The amount S is the sum of the items at the right in Figure 14.

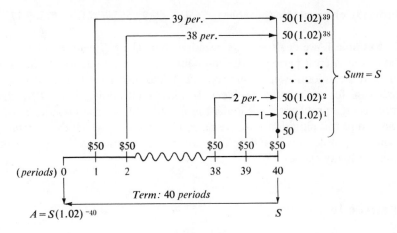

Figure 14

2. From Figure 14, we obtain

$$S = 50 + 50(1.02) + 50(1.02)^2 + \cdots + 50(1.02)^{38} + 50(1.02)^{39};$$

$$S = 50[1 + (1.02) + (1.02)^2 + \cdots + (1.02)^{38} + (1.02)^{39}]. \tag{1}$$

For the geometric progression within brackets in (1), we have

$$(\textit{first term}) = b = 1; \quad \textit{ratio} = u = 1.02; \quad (\textit{last term}) = l = (1.02)^{39};$$

$$ul = (1.02)(1.02)^{39} = (1.02)^{40} \quad \textit{and} \quad u - 1 = .02.$$

By use of (7) on page 273,

$$S = 50 \frac{ul - b}{u - 1} = 50 \frac{(1.02)^{40} - 1}{.02}. \tag{2}$$

3. *To find the present value A.* The term of the annuity is 20 years; hence, if S is discounted for 20 years, or 40 periods, as indicated in Figure 14, we obtain A. That is, from (2) on page 59, $A = S(1.02)^{-40}$, or

$$A = 50\left[\frac{(1.02)^{40} - 1}{.02}\right](1.02)^{-40}; \quad A = 50 \frac{1 - (1.02)^{-40}}{.02}, \tag{3}$$

where we used $$(1.02)^{40}(1.02)^{-40} = (1.02)^0 = 1.$$

We could obtain (3) also by writing the progression whose sum is A,

$$A = 50[(1.02)^{-40} + (1.02)^{-39} + \cdots + (1.02)^{-2} + (1.02)^{-1}], \tag{4}$$

and then applying (7) of page 273, with $u = 1.02$.

ILLUSTRATION 1. From (2), as a special case of the formula heading Table VII, with $i = 2\%$ and $n = 40$, on page 95 of the tables,

$$S = 50(60.40198318) = \$3020.10.$$

From (3), on page 115 in the tables, $\quad A = 50(27.35547924) = \$1367.77.$

In Example 1, we dealt with an annuity where the payment interval was the same as the interest period of the compound interest rate at which the present value and the amount were being computed. We shall refer to such data as the *simple case* for an annuity problem. In almost all applications of annuities, fortunately the problems come under the simple case. We shall restrict all of our discussion to this situation until we reach Chapter 7, in which the general case for annuity problems is included. This case may be considered as supplementary content in many classes.

Exercise 16

By the method of the preceding Example 1, *find the present value and the amount of each annuity. After obtaining expressions for A and S, compute them by use of Tables* VII *and* VIII.

Prob.	Term	Payment Interval	Each Payment	Interest Rate
1.	4 yr.	1 yr.	$200	.06, $m = 1$
2.	2 yr.	6 mo.	50	.05, $m = 2$
3.	8 yr.	3 mo.	100	.06, $m = 4$
4.	12 yr.	3 mo.	25	.04, $m = 4$
5.	$15\frac{1}{2}$ yr.	1 mo.	25	.06, $m = 12$

6. Compute $\dfrac{(1.02)^{60} - 1}{.02}$ by use of Table V. Check by use of Table VII.

7. Compute $\dfrac{1 - (1.02)^{-60}}{.02}$ by use of Table VI. Check by use of Table VIII.

25.   Formulas for the Simple Case

Until specified otherwise, for each annuity which we consider, **the payment interval will be the same as the interest period involved.** We first consider a special case of later data.

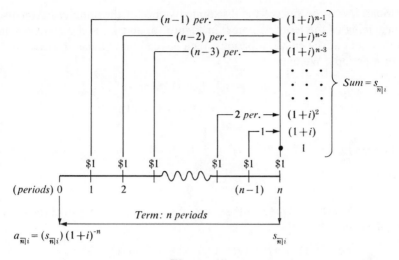

Figure 15

Problem. *To obtain the present value and the amount of an annuity of $1 payable at the end of each interest period for n periods, if i is the interest rate per period.*

SOLUTION.   1. Let * $a_{\overline{n}|i}$ and $s_{\overline{n}|i}$ be the present value and the amount, respectively, of the annuity. First, we shall obtain $s_{\overline{n}|i}$. It is equal to *the sum of the accumulated values of the payments at the end of n interest periods,* the end of the term. Thus, in finding $s_{\overline{n}|i}$, the last $1 payment, due at the end of n periods, is taken unchanged. We accumulate the next to the last payment for 1 period; the 2nd from the last for 2 periods; the 1st for $(n - 1)$ periods; the 2nd for $(n - 2)$ periods, and so on. These compound amounts are obtained by use of $F = P(1 + i)^k$ with $P = 1$, and are seen at the right in Figure 15, which shows payment dates and times to the end of the annuity's term. From Figure 15 and the definition of the amount of an annuity,

$$s_{\overline{n}|i} = 1 + (1 + i) + \cdots + (1 + i)^{n-2} + (1 + i)^{n-1}. \tag{1}$$

The right-hand member in (1) is the sum of a geometric progression of n terms for which

$$(first\ term) = b = 1;\quad ratio = u = 1 + i;\quad (last\ term) = l = (1 + i)^{n-1};$$

$$ul = (1 + i)(1 + i)^{n-1} = (1 + i)^n \quad and \quad u - 1 = i.$$

Hence, on employing the formula $(ul - b)/(u - 1)$, we obtain

$$s_{\overline{n}|i} = \frac{(1 + i)^n - 1}{i}. \tag{2}$$

* We read "$a_{\overline{n}|i}$" as "*a angle n at i*," and $s_{\overline{n}|i}$ similarly.

2. Since $a_{\overline{n}|i}$ is the sum of the discounted values of the annuity payments at the beginning of the term, at time 0 in Figure 15, and $s_{\overline{n}|i}$ is the corresponding sum of values at the end of n periods, then $a_{\overline{n}|i}$ can be obtained by discounting $s_{\overline{n}|i}$ for n periods. We have

$$a_{\overline{n}|i} = (s_{\overline{n}|i})(1 + i)^{-n}, \text{ or} \tag{3}$$

from (2),
$$a_{\overline{n}|i} = \left[\frac{(1 + i)^n - 1}{i}\right](1 + i)^{-n}. \tag{4}$$

Since $(1 + i)^n(1 + i)^{-n} = (1 + i)^0 = 1$, from (4) we obtain

$$a_{\overline{n}|i} = \frac{1 - (1 + i)^{-n}}{i}. \tag{5}$$

NOTE 1.   We can derive (5) without use of $s_{\overline{n}|i}$. By the definition of the present value of an annuity,

$$a_{\overline{n}|i} = (1 + i)^{-n} + (1 + i)^{-n+1} + \cdots + (1 + i)^{-1}. \tag{6}$$

The common ratio of the geometric progression at the right in (6) is $(1 + i)$. Then, by use of the formula for the sum of the progression on page 273, from (6) we obtain the right-hand side of (5). The student may verify this in the next exercise.

ILLUSTRATION 1. $s_{\overline{25}|.02}$ is read "*s angle* 25 at 2%." From (2),

$$s_{\overline{25}|.02} = \frac{(1.02)^{25} - 1}{.02} = 32.03029972. \qquad \text{(Table VII)}$$

Summary

For an annuity problem in which **the interest period is the same as the payment interval** *and the data are as follows:*

R *is the periodic payment of the annuity.*
n *is the length of the term, expressed in interest periods, or*
n *is the number of payments of the annuity.*
i *is the interest rate per conversion period.*

The present value A and amount S of the annuity are given by

$$A = Ra_{\overline{n}|i}; \quad S = Rs_{\overline{n}|i}, \tag{7}$$

where $a_{\overline{n}|i}$ *and* $s_{\overline{n}|i}$ *are defined by*

$$a_{\overline{n}|i} = \frac{1 - (1 + i)^{-n}}{i} \quad s_{\overline{n}|i} = \frac{(1 + i)^n - 1}{i}. \tag{8}$$

Example 1.   If money is worth 6% compounded quarterly, find the present value and the amount of an annuity paying \$150 quarterly for $15\frac{1}{2}$ years.

SOLUTION.   Use (7) with $R = \$150$, $i = .015$, and $n = 62$.

$Amount \ = 150s_{\overline{62}|.015} = 150(101.13773956) = \$15,170.66.$　　　(Table VII)

$(Pr.\ val.) = 150a_{\overline{62}|.015} = 150(40.18080408) \ = \$6027.12.$　　　(Table VIII)

Example 2. The buyer of a farm pays $4200 cash and promises to pay $800 at the end of each 6 months for 7 years. If money is worth 8% compounded semiannually, find the equivalent cash price for the farm.

SOLUTION.   The cash price is the sum of the present values of all of the payments, which consist of $4200 cash and an annuity of 14 payments.

$$(Cash\ price) = 4200 + 800a_{\overline{14}|.04} = \$12,650.50.$$

Any annuity problem to which the preceding Summary applies is called a problem of the **simple case**.

Exercise 17

1. If money is worth 4%, find the present value and the amount of an annuity of $1000 payable annually for 25 years.
2. If money is worth $4\frac{1}{2}\%$, find the present value and the amount of an annuity of $2000 payable annually for 30 years.
3. Find the present value and the amount of an annuity of $75 payable monthly for 20 years if money is worth 5% compounded monthly.

Find the present value and the amount of the annuity at the specified interest rate.

4. $500 quarterly for 22 years and 9 months; at $\{.07,\ m = 4\}$.
5. $500 at the end of each 6 months for 17 years; at $\{.055,\ m = 2\}$.
6. $100 monthly for 14 years; at $\{.04,\ m = 12\}$.
7. $200 quarterly for $19\frac{1}{4}$ years; at $\{.045,\ m = 4\}$.
8. $1000 semiannually for $8\frac{1}{2}$ years; at $\{.07,\ m = 2\}$.
9. $200 monthly for 11 years and 5 months; at $\{.035,\ m = 12\}$.

10. The purchaser of a farm will pay $8000 cash and $1000 at the end of each 6 months for 10 years to discharge all principal and interest at the rate 9% compounded semiannually. Find the equivalent all cash price for the farm.
11. At the end of each year for 8 years, a corporation will deposit $12,500 in a depreciation fund to provide for replacement of machinery at the end of 8 years. If the fund accumulates at 8% effective, how much is in it (*a*) just after the last deposit; (*b*) just after the 5th deposit?
12. If I deposit $50 in an account with a savings and loan association at the end of each month, and if the association accumulates the fund at $\{.05,\ m = 12\}$, how much is to my credit just after my 180th deposit?

13. A man will deposit with a trust company a sum just sufficient to provide his family with an annuity of $750 per month for 15 years. How much does he deposit if the fund accumulates at $\{4\frac{1}{2}\%, m = 12\}$?

14. At the end of each month, a father will deposit $100 in an account invested at $\{.05, m = 12\}$ with a savings and loan association to provide a fund for the college education of his son. How much will be in the account at the end of 10 years?

15. A bond with face value $10,000 will pay interest at 5% on the face value at the end of each six months for the next 15 years. At the end of that time the face value will be paid to the owner of the bond. Find the price which an investor should be willing to pay for the bond today if he wishes the equivalent of 6% compounded semiannually on all of his investments.

16. In obtaining a loan, Hansen has agreed to pay $150 at the end of each month for 30 months. Just after he makes his 14th payment, he asks for the privilege of making an immediate cash payment to discharge his remaining indebtedness. The creditor allows him to do this under the assumption that money is worth 4% compounded monthly. (*a*) How much does Hansen pay to discharge his debt? (*b*) The debt was originally contracted with the payments to include interest at the rate 7% compounded monthly. How much did the creditor gain by specifying 4% instead of 7% for closing the transaction?

17. Find the amount of an annuity whose present value is $2500 and term is 7 years, if money is worth $\{.065, m = 4\}$. (No data are given which permit finding the periodic payment.)

18. Find the present value of an annuity whose amount is $6000 and term is 8 years, if money is worth 5%.

19. Examine Table VII and decide how $s_{\overline{n}|i}$ is affected if n is held fast, and i is changed from a given value i_0 to a greater value. Examine Table VIII and answer the same question about $a_{\overline{n}|i}$. Why are these facts true?

26. Valuation of a Contract Involving an Annuity

From an investor's standpoint on any date, the value of a financial contract promising various payments is given by the following equation of value:

$$\textbf{(value of contract)} = \textbf{(present value of its future payments)}, \tag{1}$$

where present values are computed at the investor's interest rate.

If a debtor is discharging a debt by a sequence of payments,* then on any date let us speak of the present value of his unpaid installments as his *remaining liability*. This liability can be thought of as a sum of money which, if paid on the

---

* In such a case, we shall assume that, on any date, the creditor is willing to accept the present value of future payments at the original interest rate, instead of requiring the payments to be delayed to the dates specified in the contract. In actual practice, the creditor might *not* be willing to do this.

specified date, would satisfactorily close the transaction from the standpoint of the creditor:

$$(\text{remaining liability}) = (\text{present value of unpaid installments}). \qquad (2)$$

The *cash value* of a piece of property is the sum of the present values of all payments which the purchaser will make to the seller.

Example 1. In purchasing a house, a man pays $8000 cash and, in addition, agrees to pay $1500 at the end of each 6 months for 10 years, to discharge all requirements for payment of principal and interest at the rate 8% compounded semiannually. (*a*) Find the all cash price of the house. (*b*) Just after the buyer pays his sixth installment of $1500, what is his remaining liability?

SOLUTION.   1. The $1500 payments form an ordinary annuity of 20 payments whose present value must be added to the cash payment to find the equivalent cash price. Hence, by use of Table VIII,

$$\text{cash price} = 8000 + 1500a_{\overline{20}|.04}$$

$$= 8000 + 20,385.49 = \$28,385.49.$$

2. Just after the 6th installment is paid, the remaining payments form an annuity of 14 payments. Hence,

$$(\text{remaining liability}) = 1500a_{\overline{14}|.04} = \$15,844.68.$$

Example 2. Suppose that the buyer in Example 1 made the cash payment but failed to pay any of the installments. Then, two years after buying the house, he offers to discharge his accumulated liability because of the payments not made, plus his liability for the future payments, by making a single payment immediately. If the creditor allows this privilege with money considered as worth $\{.08, m = 2\}$, how much should the buyer pay?

SOLUTION.   He should pay the accumulated value of the first four unpaid installments, or the amount of the annuity which they form, plus the present value of the future payments. If P is the required single payment, then

$$P = 1500s_{\overline{4}|.04} + 1500a_{\overline{16}|.04}, \; or$$

$$P = 1500(4.24646400 + 11.65229561) = \$23,848.14.$$

NOTE 1.   In applications of $a_{\overline{n}|i}$ and $s_{\overline{n}|i}$ in the business world, it is inevitable that cases will arise where the available tables will not apply. This situation is more likely to be due to an unusual interest rate per period than lack of an extensive range for values of n in the tables. Without considering the cause, suppose that $a_{\overline{n}|i}$ and/or $s_{\overline{n}|i}$ are needed for n and i where the available tables do not apply. Observe (8) on page 64. If $(1 + i)^n$ is computed first (probably on an electronic computer) then $s_{\overline{n}|i}$ can be calculated easily. If $a_{\overline{n}|i}$ also is needed, first the reciprocal of $(1 + i)^n$ would be computed to obtain $(1 + i)^{-n} = 1/(1 + i)^n$. Then $a_{\overline{n}|i}$ is obtainable easily. Thus, to compute $a_{\overline{67}|.0316}$ and $s_{\overline{67}|.0316}$, first we would compute $(1.0316)^{67}$, and then proceed as just outlined. Consideration of such unusual cases is outside the scope of this course.

Exercise 18

1. The buyer of a house will pay $7500 cash and $1000 at the end of each 3 months for 12 years. If money is worth 9% compounded quarterly, find (a) the cash value of the house; (b) the remaining liability of the debtor just after he pays his 10th installment of $1000; (c) his remaining liability just before he pays the 10th installment.
2. The buyer of a farm pays $9000 cash, and promises to pay $800 at the end of each 3 months for 8 years. If money is worth 7% compounded quarterly, find (a) the cash value of the farm; (b) the sum which the purchaser should pay at the end of 3 years, in addition to the payment due then, in order to cancel his remaining liability.
3. In return for a loan, with money worth 7% compounded semiannually, a man promises to pay $600 at the end of each 6 months for 8 years. (a) Find the sum which he borrows. (b) Find his remaining liability just after his 6th payment; (c) just before his 9th payment.
4. Suppose that the debtor in Problem 3 failed to make his first 6 payments when they were due. What should he pay to his creditor at the end of $3\frac{1}{2}$ years to cancel his accumulated liability?
5. Suppose that the debtor of Problem 3 pays nothing until the end of 3 years. What should he pay then to cancel the debt completely?
6. Suppose that the purchaser of the farm in Problem 2 failed to pay any of the $800 installments when they were due. What should he pay at the end of 5 years to cancel his debt?
7. The purchaser of a farm made a cash payment and also promised to pay $400 at the end of each 3 months for 8 years. He failed to make the first 7 payments of $400 each. At the end of 2 years he desires to complete the purchase of the farm by making a single payment. How much should he pay if money is worth 9% compounded quarterly?
8. In return for a loan with interest at 5.5% compounded quarterly, a debtor agrees to pay $250 at the end of each 3 months for 9 years. (a) Find the sum borrowed. (b) How much must the debtor pay to complete payment of the debt just after his 15th payment has been made?
9. On January 1, 1970 the McKnight Company agreed to pay Roberts $250 at the end of each month for 4 years in return for a loan. Nothing was paid until January 1, 1976. What should be paid then if Roberts stipulates that money was worth 6% compounded monthly up to January 1, 1974 and 9% compounded monthly thereafter?
10. A $1000 bond promises coupon payments of $40 (called *interest*) at the end of each 6 months for 25 years, and a final additional payment of $1000 at

the end of 25 years. How much is the bond worth today, to an investor who considers money worth 9% compounded semiannually.

11. A $1000 bond promises coupon payments of $35 at the end of each 6 months for 20 years, and a final redemption payment of $1050 at the end of 20 years. What would an investor be willing to pay for this bond if he considers money worth 8% compounded semiannually?

27. Solution for an Unknown Periodic Payment

We shall prove that

$$\frac{1}{s_{\overline{n}|i}} = \frac{1}{a_{\overline{n}|i}} - i \quad or \quad \frac{1}{s_{\overline{n}|i}} + i = \frac{1}{a_{\overline{n}|i}}. \tag{1}$$

PROOF. 1. Recall that the reciprocal of any fraction is the fraction *inverted*. Hence, by use of the formula for $s_{\overline{n}|i}$ in (8) on page 64,

$$\frac{1}{s_{\overline{n}|i}} + i = \frac{i}{(1 + i)^n - 1} + i \tag{2}$$

$$= \frac{i}{(1 + i)^n - 1} + \frac{i[(1 + i)^n - 1]}{(1 + i)^n - 1}. \tag{3}$$

$$\frac{1}{s_{\overline{n}|i}} + i = \frac{i + i(1 + i)^n - i}{(1 + i)^n - 1} = \frac{i(1 + i)^n}{(1 + i)^n - 1}. \tag{4}$$

2. By use of the formula for $a_{\overline{n}|i}$ in (8) on page 64,

$$\frac{1}{a_{\overline{n}|i}} = \frac{i}{1 - (1 + i)^{-n}} = \frac{(1 + i)^n}{(1 + i)^n}\left[\frac{i}{1 - (1 + i)^{-n}}\right]. \tag{5}$$

where we insert the factor $(1 + i)^n$ in the numerator and denominator.

Since $\qquad (1 + i)^n(1 + i)^{-n} = (1 + i)^0 = 1,$

from (5) we obtain

$$\frac{1}{a_{\overline{n}|i}} = \frac{i(1 + i)^n}{(1 + i)^n - 1}. \tag{6}$$

From (4) and (6) it is seen that (1) is true.

The first equation in (1) is important because, by means of it, we are able to use Table IX to obtain values of $\dfrac{1}{s_{\overline{n}|i}}$ as well as $\dfrac{1}{a_{\overline{n}|i}}$. We shall use Table IX in obtaining an unknown periodic payment for an annuity.

ILLUSTRATION 1. From Table IX, $\dfrac{1}{a_{\overline{15}|.05}} = .09634229$. From (1),

$$\frac{1}{s_{\overline{15}|.05}} = \frac{1}{a_{\overline{15}|.05}} - .05 = .09634229 - .05 = .04634229.$$

Example 1. A man borrows $5000 and agrees to cancel his debt by paying equal sums at the end of each 3 months for $20\frac{1}{2}$ years. Find his quarterly payment if interest is at the rate 5% compounded quarterly.

SOLUTION. Let R be the unknown quarterly payment. The payments form an annuity whose present value is $5000. Hence, from $A = Ra_{\overline{n}|i}$ with $A = \$5000$, $n = 82$, and $i = .0125$, and Table IX,

$$Ra_{\overline{82}|.0125} = 5000; \qquad R = \frac{5000}{a_{\overline{82}|.0125}}.$$

$$R = 5000\left(\frac{1}{a_{\overline{82}|.0125}}\right) = 5000(.01956437) = \$97.82.$$

Example 2. If interest is at the rate 8% compounded semiannually, what sum must be invested at the end of each 6 months to accumulate a fund of $10,000 at the end of 8 years?

SOLUTION. Let R be the unknown semiannual deposit for the fund. The periodic payments form an annuity whose amount is $10,000. From $Rs_{\overline{n}|i} = S$,

$$Rs_{\overline{16}|} = 10,000; \qquad R = \frac{10,000}{s_{\overline{16}|}} = 10,000\left(\frac{1}{s_{\overline{16}|}}\right).$$

From Table IX, at 4%, $\qquad \dfrac{1}{s_{\overline{16}|}} = .08582000 - .04 = .04582000.$

Hence, $\qquad\qquad R = 10,000(.04582000) = \$458.20.$

NOTE 1. The student should realize that the equations $5000 = Ra_{\overline{82}|}$ in Example 1 and $10,000 = Rs_{\overline{16}|}$ in Example 2 are *equations of value*, with the comparison date at zero time in Example 1, and at the end of 8 years in Example 2. **Wherever we use the formulas $A = Ra_{\overline{n}|i}$ and $S = Rs_{\overline{n}|i}$ we are using equations of value.**

Exercise 19

Find the unknown annuity payment for the data.

1. Annual payments for 20 years; present value $5000; at $\{.03, m = 1\}$.
2. Semiannual payments; for 15 years; amount $4000; at $\{.06, m = 2\}$.
3. Quarterly payments for $9\frac{1}{2}$ years; amount $3000; at $\{.04, m = 4\}$.
4. Monthly payments for $6\frac{3}{4}$ years; present value $2000; at $\{.03, m = 12\}$.
5. Monthly payments for $7\frac{1}{2}$ years; amount $6000; at $\{.05, m = 12\}$.

6. On retirement at age 65, a man finds that his share of a pension fund is

$25,000. If the fund is invested at 4% compounded quarterly, what pension payment would it give to the man (or his heirs) at the end of each 3 months for the next 20 years?

7. In order to have a building fund of $100,000 available at the end of 10 years, a church congregation will invest equal sums at the end of each 3 months at 5% compounded quarterly. Find the quarterly investment.

8. A man borrows $5000 and agrees to discharge his liability as to principal and interest by paying equal sums at the end of each 6 months for 8 years. If money is worth $6\frac{1}{2}$% compounded semiannually, find his semiannual payment.

9. An insurance policy pays $20,000 at the death of a man, and is left invested with the insurance company at 3% compounded quarterly. What payment would this provide at the end of each 3 months for the next 15 years for the man's family?

10. In order to provide for the purchase of a new piece of production machinery, costing $250,000, at the end of 9 years, what sum should a company deposit in a fund at the end of each 6 months for the 9 years, if the money is invested at 7% compounded semiannually?

11. In purchasing a house worth $30,000 cash, a man pays $10,000 cash and agrees to make equal payments at the end of each 3 months for 12 years, to discharge all principal and interest at 8% compounded quarterly. Find his periodic payment.

12. On discharge from the armed forces, a young man finds that he has cash resources of $6000. He places this in a savings account yielding 5% compounded quarterly, from which he will withdraw equal sums at the end of each 3 months during 4 years of college study. How much does he withdraw quarterly if the fund is exactly exhausted by the withdrawal at the end of 4 years?

13. What annuity payable monthly for 7 years can be purchased for $6500 if money is worth 7% compounded monthly?

14. A man promised to pay $1500 at the end of each year. If money is worth 6% compounded monthly, what payment at the end of each month would be equally satisfactory?

15. A man promised to pay $2000 at the beginning of each year. What payment at the end of each 3 months would be equally satisfactory if money is worth 5% compounded quarterly?

16. Find the annuity, with quarterly payments for 10 years, which can be purchased for $20,000 if money is worth $6\frac{1}{2}$% compounded quarterly.

17. In purchasing a house, a man agrees to pay $750 at the end of each 3 months. If money is worth 9% compounded monthly, what payment at the end of each month would be equally satisfactory?

18. A certain annuity pays $100 at the end of each interest period. Without using a table, find the rate of interest per period if the present value of the annuity is $7800 and the amount is $13,000.

28. Interpolation for an Unknown Rate or Time

Example 1. At what nominal rate compounded quarterly is $7150 the present value of an annuity of $220 payable quarterly for $12\frac{1}{2}$ years?

SOLUTION. 1. Let i be the unknown rate per interest period. From the equation $A = Ra_{\overline{n}|i}$ with $A = \$7150$, $n = 50$, and $R = \$220$,

$$220a_{\overline{50}|i} = 7150; \qquad a_{\overline{50}|i} = \frac{7150}{220} = 32.500. \tag{1}$$

2. In the row for $n = 50$ in Table VIII, the values of $a_{\overline{n}|}$ for $i = 1\frac{3}{4}\%$ and $i = 2\%$ bracket 32.500, as in the table below. Hence, i in (1) lies between $1\frac{3}{4}\%$ and 2%. We assume that i is the same fraction of the way from $1\frac{3}{4}\%$ to 2% as 32.5000 is of the way from 33.141 to 31.424, giving (2) below, by linear interpolation.

Table VIII, $n = 50$	
$1\frac{3}{4}\%$	33.141
i	32.500
2%	31.424

d bracket: $\frac{1}{4}\%$ .641   1.717

$$33.141 - 32.500 = .641; \qquad 33.141 - 31.424 = 1.717.$$

$$\frac{d}{\frac{1}{4}\%} = \frac{641}{1717} \quad \text{or} \quad d = \frac{641}{1717}\left(\frac{1}{4}\%\right); \tag{2}$$

$$i = 1\frac{3}{4}\% + \frac{641}{1717}\left(\frac{1}{4}\%\right). \quad \left(i = 1\frac{3}{4}\% + .093\% = 1.843\%\right) \tag{3}$$

Nominal rate is $4i = 7\% + \frac{641}{1717}\% = 7\% + .37\% = 7.37\%$.

Notice that the arithmetic within the parentheses in (3) was *unnecessary*, because eventually we desire *not i*, but $4i$.

Experience shows it is safe to assume that a value of i found by interpolation as in Example 1 is in error by not more than 1/30 of the difference of the table rates used in the interpolation, and usually is subject to much less than this error. Thus, $i = .01843$ is in error by not more than $\frac{1}{30}(.0025)$ or .0001, and the error in $4i$ is at most .0004. If Example 1 arose in practical affairs, and if i were desired with high accuracy, first we would obtain $i = .01843$ as above. By computing devices, we would compute $a_{\overline{50}|i}$ first for $i = .0184$, and also for some close neighboring value, say .0185, to *bracket* $a_{\overline{50}|i} = 32.500$. Then, i would be determined by interpolation again, between .0184 and .0185, and so on, with any assigned degree of accuracy.

Example 2. If $175 is deposited in a fund at the end of each 3 months, when will the fund first amount to at least $7500 if the money accumulates at 6% compounded quarterly?

SOLUTION. Use $S = Rs_{\overline{n}|i}$ with $S = \$7500$, $R = \$175$, and $i = .015$:

$$7500 = 175s_{\overline{n}|.015}; \quad s_{\overline{n}|.015} = \frac{7500}{175} = 42.857. \tag{4}$$

In the column in Table VII for $i = .015$, we find the following entries:

$$s_{\overline{33}|.015} = 42.299, \text{ which is } less \text{ than } 42.857;$$

$$s_{\overline{34}|.015} = 43.933, \text{ which is } greater \text{ than } 42.857.$$

Hence, the fund will be *less* than $7500 just after the 33rd payment, and *greater* than $7500 just after the 34th payment. Thus, the fund will first amount to *at least* $7500 at the end of 34 periods, or $8\frac{1}{2}$ years.

COMMENT. A detailed solution of $s_{\overline{n}|.015} = 42.857$ by interpolation in Table VII would give $n = 33.34$. We have not assigned any meaning to an annuity whose term is not an integral number of payment intervals and hence we have no simple interpretation to give to the final decimal ".34" in $n = 33.34$. Our solution of Example 2 demands knowledge merely of the fact that (4) requires n to be larger than 33, but smaller than 34. It would be a waste of energy to obtain the solution by interpolation, $n = 33.34$, or to solve for n even more exactly.

Example 3. A man borrows $8000, with interest at the rate .06, compounded semiannually. He agrees to pay $500 at the end of each 6 months until a final payment date when less than the regular installment closes the transaction. How long must he pay?

SOLUTION. From $A = Ra_{\overline{n}|i}$ with $A = \$8000$, $i = .03$, and $R = \$500$,

$$8000 = 500a_{\overline{n}|.03}; \quad a_{\overline{n}|.03} = 16.$$

In the column in Table VIII for $i = .03$, we find

$$a_{\overline{22}|.03} = 15.937, \text{ which is } less \text{ than } 16;$$

$$a_{\overline{23}|.03} = 16.444, \text{ which is } greater \text{ than } 16.$$

Hence, the present value of 22 payments of $500 each is *less* than $8000, and the present value of 23 payments of $500 each is *greater* than $8000. Therefore the debtor must pay 22 semiannual payments of $500 and *an additional sum, less than* $500, at the end of 23 periods. The determination of the exact size of such a concluding payment will be considered in a later chapter dealing with amortization of debts.

Exercise 20

Find any unknown nominal rate by interpolation, to hundredths of 1%.

1. A contract calls for the payment of $1200 at the end of each year for 15 years. At what interest rate compounded annually would this agreement be equivalent to a cash payment of $11,400?
2. At the end of each 6 months, $300 is deposited in a fund. At what interest rate compounded semiannually does the fund accumulate if it contains $8700 just after the 21st deposit?
3. A man will pay $500 at the end of each 3 months for 17 years to discharge a loan of $22, 935. At what interest rate converted quarterly do the payments discharge all of his liability as to principal and interest?
4. A man borrowed $24,200. To discharge this debt, principal and interest included, he promised to pay $1000 at the end of each 3 months for 7 years and 6 months. At what interest rate compounded quarterly is interest involved?
5. In purchasing a house, a man makes a cash payment, and takes out a mortgage for $10,000 on which he agrees to pay $200 at the end of each month for 5 years in paying all principal and interest. At what interest rate compounded monthly was interest charged on the mortgage?
6. The cash value of a farm is $15,000. A purchaser pays $3000 cash and agrees to pay $750 at the end of each 6 months as long as necessary, with a smaller payment 6 months after the last regular payment. If money is worth .065 compounded semiannually, when will he make the last $750 payment?
7. A corporation will invest $5000 in a depreciation fund at the end of each 6 months to accumulate $100,000 to initiate a plant overhaul. If the fund is invested at .065 compounded semiannually, on what semiannual date will the fund contain at least $100,000?
8. At what interest rate compounded quarterly will $7500 purchase an annuity of $300 payable quarterly for 7 years and 3 months?
9. At the end of each 3 months, a man will place $300 in a savings account which accumulates at 5% compounded quarterly. On what date will the fund first make it possible for him to buy a Cadillac for $9000?

29. A Useful Attitude About A and S for an Annuity

When we refer to a sequence of equal periodic payments simply as an *annuity*, or for emphasis as an *ordinary annuity*, we think of each payment as belonging to the *preceding payment interval*. Then the term of the annuity is said to begin *one interval before the first payment*, and to end *on the day of the last payment*, as in Figure 16 where black dots indicate payment dates. Since the beginning of the term frequently will *not* be the actual present date, it is useful to emphasize the following facts, where the somewhat deceptive "*present value*" for A and "*amount*" for S are replaced simply by *dated values*.

$$A = Ra_{\overline{n}|i} \quad gives \quad \left\{ \begin{array}{l} \textit{the } \textbf{VALUE } \textit{of a sequence of n payments of } \$R \\ \textit{each } \textbf{one period before the 1st payment.} \end{array} \right\} \quad (1)$$

$$S = Rs_{\overline{n}|i} \quad gives \quad \left\{ \begin{array}{l} \textit{the } \textbf{VALUE } \textit{of a sequence of n payments of } \$R \\ \textit{each } \textbf{on the day of the last payment.} \end{array} \right\} \quad (2)$$

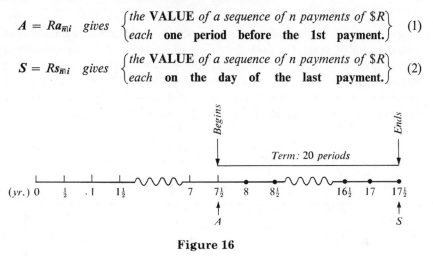

Figure 16

ILLUSTRATION 1.   Consider a sequence of 20 semiannual payments of $100 each where the first occurs at the end of 8 years, and hence the last occurs at the end of $17\frac{1}{2}$ years, as shown by black dots in Figure 16. If we think of these payments as forming an ordinary annuity, the term begins 6 months before the first payment, at the end of $7\frac{1}{2}$ years, and ends on the day of the last payment. If interest is at the rate $\{.04, m = 2\}$, the VALUE of the annuity at the end of $7\frac{1}{2}$ years is $A = 100a_{\overline{20}|.02}$, and of $17\frac{1}{2}$ years is $S = 100s_{\overline{20}|.02}$.

30.   Annuities Due

Frequently, when a sequence of equal periodic payments is met in practice, the first payment is due *immediately*. It is customary to introduce a special name, as follows, to emphasize the preceding feature.

An **annuity due** is an annuity whose first payment occurs *immediately*, on a day to be called the *present*. When we refer to a sequence of payments as an *annuity due*, we agree to think of each payment as *belonging to the following payment interval*, and to refer to the payments as made at the *beginnings* of payment intervals.

The **term** of an annuity due is defined as the time from the beginning of the 1st payment interval to the end of the last one. Hence, the 1st payment occurs at the beginning of the term, and it ends one payment interval after the last payment. The present value of an annuity due, or its **VALUE** *on the day of the 1st payment*, is the sum of the present values of the payments. The amount of an annuity due, or its **VALUE** *at the end of the term*, is the sum of the accumulated values of the payments at the end of the term.

Example 1. If money is worth 4% compounded semiannually, find the present value and the amount of an annuity due paying $50 semiannually for a term of $3\frac{1}{2}$ years.

SOLUTION.   1. *Description of payments.* $50 is payable at the beginning of each 6 months for $3\frac{1}{2}$ years. Or, since the *end* of an interval is the same instant as the *beginning of the next interval*, the annuity due consists of $50 *cash* plus an *ordinary* annuity of $50 payable at the *end* of each 6 months for 3 years. In Figure 17, the point 0 marks the present and there are black dots at the payment dates. The first payment date is circled to suggest the method of Step 2 below.

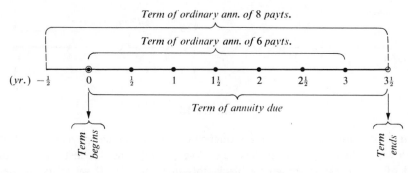

Figure 17

2. The present value A of the annuity due can be found by adding the first payment, which occurs at time 0, to the present value of the last 6 payments, which form an *ordinary* annuity whose term commences at time 0. Hence,

$$A = (\text{1st payt.}) + (\text{pr. val. of last 6 payts.});$$

$$A = 50 + 50a_{\overline{6}|.02} = 50 + 280.07 = \$330.07.$$

3. The amount S of the annuity due is the sum of the accumulated values of its 7 payments at the end of $3\frac{1}{2}$ years, the end of the term. Now, *imagine* an 8th payment of $50 *artificially inserted* at the end of $3\frac{1}{2}$ years, shown by an open circle in Figure 17. Then, the *actual* payments together with the *fictitious* 8th payment form an *ordinary* annuity of 8 payments, whose term begins $\frac{1}{2}$ year *before* time 0 and *ends at the end of* $3\frac{1}{2}$ *years.* The amount of this ordinary annuity, or $50s_{\overline{8}|.02}$, is the sum of the accumulated values of the 8 payments on the day of the last payment, which is the end of $3\frac{1}{2}$ years. Hence, on writing an equation of value with the end of $3\frac{1}{2}$ years as the comparison date, we obtain

$$S = (\text{accumulated val. of 8 payts.}) - (\text{val. of the fictitious payt.});$$

$$S = 50s_{\overline{8}|.02} - 50 = 429.15 - 50 = \$379.15.$$

NOTE 1.   In actuarial science, the symbols $\ddot{a}_{\overline{n}|i}$ and $\ddot{s}_{\overline{n}|i}$ are used to represent the present value and amount, respectively, of an annuity due as described in the Summary, with $R = 1$. Thus, $\ddot{a}_{\overline{n}|i} = 1 + a_{\overline{n-1}|i}$ and $\ddot{s}_{\overline{n}|i} = s_{\overline{n+1}|i} - 1$. We shall not use these new symbols.

Summary

Let $\$\ddot{A}$ and $\$\ddot{S}$ be the present value and the amount, respectively, of an annuity due of n payments of $\$R$ each, and let i be the interest rate per conversion period, which is the same as the payment interval.

I. *To find $\ddot{A}$, add the first payment to the present value of the ordinary annuity formed by the last $(n - 1)$ payments:*

$$\ddot{A} = \text{(1st payt.)} + \text{(pr. val. of remaining payts.)}; \tag{1}$$

$$\ddot{A} = R + Ra_{\overline{n-1}|i}. \tag{2}$$

II. *To find $\ddot{S}$, imagine an additional payment of $\$R$ at the end of n periods, to create an ordinary annuity of $(n + 1)$ payments. Then,*

$$\ddot{S} = [\text{value of annuity of } (n + 1) \text{ payts. on last payt. date}] - R;$$

$$\ddot{S} = Rs_{\overline{n+1}|i} - R. \tag{3}$$

Example 2. A man agrees to make equal payments at the beginning of each 6 months for 10 years to discharge a debt of $5000, due now. If money is worth 8% compounded semiannually, find the semiannual payment.

SOLUTION. Let $\$R$ be the payment. The payments form an annuity due of 20 payments whose present value is $5000. From (1) and Table VIII,

$$5000 = R + Ra_{\overline{19}|.04} = R + R(13.1339);$$

$$5000 = R(1 + 13.1339); \qquad 5000 = 14.1339R; \qquad R = \$354.$$

Example 3. To accumulate a fund of $8000 at the end of 10 years, a man will make equal annual deposits in the fund at the beginning of each year. How much should he deposit annually if the fund is invested at 5% compounded annually?

SOLUTION. 1. Think of a fictitious 11th deposit of $\$R$ at the end of 10 years. The 11 deposits (including the fictitious deposit) form an annuity whose term ends at the end of 10 years, and the amount of this annuity is $Rs_{\overline{11}|.05}$. To obtain the value of the 10 actual payments, subtract the fictitious payment of $\$R$ at the end of 10 years.

2. The equation of value at the end of 10 years for the fund is

$$Rs_{\overline{11}|.05} - R = 8000; \qquad R(s_{\overline{11}|.05} - 1) = 8000; \tag{4}$$

$$R = \frac{8000}{s_{\overline{11}|.05} - 1} = \frac{8000}{14.206787 - 1} = \$606.$$

In the preceding solution, the reasoning leading to (3) was repeated for a special case. The student is advised to employ such reasoning in future problems instead of using (3) without thought as a readymade formula.

Exercise 21

Draw a time diagram for each problem and specify clearly the comparison date on which the final equation of value is written, even though some formula might be applied mechanically to obtain the solution.

Find the present value and the amount of the annuity due at the specified interest rate.

1. Payments of $250 will occur at the beginning of each year for 18 years; at $\{.04, m = 1\}$.
2. Payments of $500 will be made at the beginning of each month for $7\frac{1}{2}$ years; at $\{.05, m = 12\}$.
3. Payments of $300 will be made at the beginning of each 3 months for 4 years; at $\{.065, m = 4\}$.

4. If money is worth 5% compounded monthly, find the present value and the amount of an annuity due of $100 payable monthly for 7 years.
5. In purchasing a farm, a man made a cash payment six months ago. He also agrees to pay $500 at the beginning of each 3 months for 8 years starting today, when he takes possession. If these payments include all interest at 7% compounded quarterly, find the present value of his quarterly payments, when he takes possession.
6. A college student is granted a fellowship which will pay $250 at the beginning of each month for 4 years. If money is worth 5% compounded monthly, find the present value of the fellowship.
7. If $100 is deposited in a fund at the beginning of each 3 months for 8 years, and the money is invested at 5% compounded quarterly, how much is in the fund (*a*) at the end of $7\frac{3}{4}$ years just after the payment due then is made; (*b*) at the end of 8 years?
8. A man is promised a pension of $250 at the beginning of each month for 15 years. If money is worth 5% compounded monthly, find the present value of this pension, if it is assumed that the man will live to receive all payments.
9. To discharge a debt, with interest at 7% compounded monthly, Robertson agrees to pay $200 at the beginning of each month for 6 years. (*a*) Find the original size of the debt. Find the remaining liability of Robertson (*b*) just after he makes his 5th payment; (*c*) just before he makes his 10th payment.
10. A fund to replace a deteriorating machine will be formed by depositing $2000 in the fund at the beginning of each 6 months for 7 years. If the fund

accumulates at 7% compounded semiannually, how much is in it: (*a*) at the end of 7 years; (*b*) just after the 8th deposit; (*c*) just after the last deposit?

11. A debtor agrees to pay $500 at the beginning of each 3 months for 6 years. If money is worth $6\frac{1}{2}\%$ compound quarterly, find (*a*) the present value of his debt, before he makes a payment; (*b*) his outstanding liability just before his 15th payment; (*c*) just after the 15th payment.

12. What equal payments at the beginning of each year for 12 years will discharge a debt of $9000, due now, if money is worth 8%?

13. A man agrees to make equal payments at the beginning of each 6 months for 10 years, to pay all interest and principal in purchasing a farm worth $25,000 cash. If money is worth 7% compounded semiannually, find the semiannual payment.

14. At retirement, a man finds that his share of a pension fund is $25,000. What payment will this provide at the beginning of each month for 20 years, for him or his estate, if the fund is invested at 5% compounded monthly?

15. What equal deposits should be placed in a fund at the beginning of each year for 12 years in order to have $20,000 in the fund at the end of 12 years, if the money accumulates at 5%?

16. To create an endowment of $1,000,000 at the end of 8 years for a hospital, each of 10 men agrees to deposit equal payments in a fund at the beginning of each month for the 8 years. Find the monthly payment for each man if the money is invested at $3\frac{1}{2}\%$ compounded monthly.

17. A debtor, who receives a loan of $30,000, agrees to deposit equal sums at the beginning of each 3 months for 10 years with a trust company, in order to pay the principal at the end of 10 years. If the fund earns 3% compounded quarterly, find the periodic deposit.

18. It was agreed to pay $30 at the beginning of each month for 15 years. If money is worth 4.5% compounded monthly, what equivalent payment would be acceptable (*a*) at the beginning of each year; (*b*) at the end of each year?

Solve for any unknown interest rate by interpolation.

19. At what interest rate compounded annually will payments of $500 at the beginning of each year for 12 years discharge a debt of $4300?

20. Find the rate at which interest is compounded semiannually if payments of $800 at the beginning of each 6 months for 10 years are sufficient to discharge a debt of $12,000.

21. If payments of $200 at the beginning of each 3 months for 4 years are sufficient to accumulate a fund of $3575 at the end of 4 years, find the rate at which interest is compounded quarterly.

22. A contract calls for the payment of $3000 at the beginning of each year for the next 10 years, and $1000 at the beginning of each year for the following 5 years. Find the present value of the payments if money is worth 8%.

(Think of one annuity due of $2000 per year and one of $1000 per year.)

31. Deferred Annuities

A *deferred annuity* is an annuity whose term does not begin until the expiration of a specified time. To say that an annuity is *deferred* for a certain time means that *the term of the annuity commences at the end of this time.* The present value of a deferred annuity is the sum of the present values of the payments.

Example 1. If money is worth 5% compounded semiannually, find the present value of a sequence of 12 semiannual payments of $50 each, the first of which is due at the end of $4\frac{1}{2}$ years.

SOLUTION.   1. The payment dates for the deferred annuity are indicated by black dots in Figure 18. The term of the annuity commences 6 months before the 1st payment date, or at the end of 4 years. The term is 12 payment intervals, or 6 years, and hence ends at the end of 10 years.

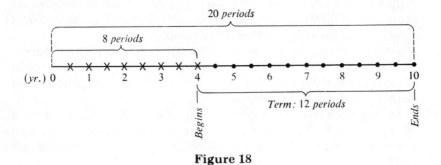

Figure 18

2. *Insert fictitious payments.* Imagine additional payments of $50 each at the end of each 6 months during the first 4 years (shown by crosses in Figure 18). Then, these 8 fictitious payments together with the 12 actual payments make up an annuity of 20 payments whose terms begin now, at 0 in Figure 18. The 8 fictitious payments *separately* form an annuity whose term begins now, and whose present value must be *deducted* from the present value of the 20 payments. Let A be the present value of the deferred annuity.

$$A = (pr.\ val.\ of\ 20\ payts.) - (pr.\ val.\ of\ first\ 8\ payts.); \qquad (1)$$

$$A = 50a_{\overline{20}|} - 50a_{\overline{8}|} = 50(a_{\overline{20}|} - a_{\overline{8}|}); \qquad (at\ 2\frac{1}{2}\%)$$

$$A = 50(15.58916229 - 7.17013717) = \$420.95. \qquad (Table\ VIII)$$

Summary

To obtain the present value A of a deferred annuity whose term is n interest periods and is deferred h periods, with $R as the periodic payment and i as the interest rate per period.

I. *Imagine additional payments of $R at the end of each period for the first h periods, as well as during the actual term.*

II. *Then, A is equal to the present value of all payments, imaginary and actual, minus the present value of the imaginary payments:*

$$A = \left\{ \begin{array}{l} \text{[pres. val. of annuity with term } (h + n) \text{ periods]} \\ - \text{(pres. val. of annuity with term } h \text{ periods);} \end{array} \right. \tag{2}$$

(pr. val. of deferred annuity) $\qquad\qquad A = Ra_{\overline{n+h}|i} - Ra_{\overline{h}|i}.$ $\qquad$ (3)

Example 2. A man borrows $30,000, with interest at the rate 6% compounded semiannually. He agrees to discharge his obligation by paying a sequence of 8 equal semiannual payments, the first being due at the end of $5\frac{1}{2}$ years. Find the semiannual payment.

SOLUTION 1. Let $R be the semiannual payment. Insert imaginary payments of $R each at the end of each 6 months for 5 years. The debt $30,000 is a value at time 0, the present. The equation of value for solving the problem will be written at time 0.

2. The imaginary payments, and the deferred annuity formed by the actual payments, together form an ordinary annuity of 18 payments. With the comparison date as time 0, the present,

$$30,000 = (\textit{pr. val. of } 18 \textit{ paymts.}) - (\textit{pr. val. } 10 \textit{ imag. paymts.});$$

$$30,000 = Ra_{\overline{18}|} - Ra_{\overline{10}|} = R(a_{\overline{18}|} - a_{\overline{10}|}); \qquad (at\ 3\%)$$

$$30,000 = R(13.75351 - 8.53020) = R(5.22331);$$

$$R = \frac{30,000}{5.22331} = \$5743.48.$$

The amount of a deferred annuity is defined as the sum of the accumulated values of the payments at the *end of the term*, and thus is *the same as the amount of the ordinary annuity* whose term is deferred. Hence, no new problem arises in connection with the amount of a deferred annuity.

NOTE 1. In the notation of actuarial science, $_h|a_{\overline{n}|}$ represents the present value of a deferred annuity of $1 payable at the end of each interest period for n periods, if the term is deferred h periods. From (3), with $R = 1$,

$$_h|a_{\overline{n}|i} = a_{\overline{n+h}|i} - a_{\overline{h}|i}.$$

We shall not have occasion to use this symbol.

Exercise 22

For each problem, draw a time diagram illustrating the data and the solution.
Find the present value of the deferred annuity which is described, at the specified interest rate.

1. $200 payable annually for 8 years, with the first payment at the end of 10 years; at $(.05, m = 1)$.
2. $100 payable semiannually for $4\frac{1}{2}$ years, with the term of the annuity deferred 5 years; at $(.065, m = 2)$.
3. $75 payable quarterly for 7 years, with the term of the annuity deferred for 6 years; at $(.06, m = 4)$.
4. A sequence of annual payments of $1000 each, with the first one due at the end of 8 years and the last at the end of 29 years; money is worth 5%.
5. A sequence of 8 annual payments of $750 each, with the first payment due at the beginning of the 6th year; money is worth 6%. (The beginning of year 6 is the end of year 5.)
6. A sequence of quarterly payments of $500 each, with the first payment due at the end of 5 years and the last at the end of 18 years; money is worth $6\frac{1}{2}\%$ compounded quarterly.
7. A man, now 60 years old, will receive a pension of $300 per month for 15 years, with the 1st payment to occur one month after his 65th birthday. If money is worth 5% compounded monthly, find the present value of the pension, assuming that he will die just after age 80.
8. A purchaser of a farm pays $8000 cash and also agrees to pay a sequence of 12 semiannual payments of $750 each, the first due at the end of $2\frac{1}{2}$ years. If money is worth 7% compounded semiannually, find the cash value of the farm.
9. A farm is offered for sale for $22,500 cash, or $7500 cash and a sequence of 5 annual payments of $4000 each, the first due at the end of 3 years. If money is worth 7%, which purchase agreement is the better?
10. An investment in an oil field will yield no operating profit until the end of 4 years, when the investor will receive $20,000. After that, he will receive $20,000 at the end of each year for 15 more years. Find the present value of this income if money is worth 6%.
11. A mine will yield an annual operating profit of $150,000 starting with a return at the end of 5 years, and ending with profit at the end of 20 years, when the mine becomes worthless. What is the value of this mine to an investor to whom money is worth 5%?
12. A debtor owes $10,000 due now. He agrees to pay a sequence of 9 equal annual payments, the first due at the end of 3 years, to discharge the debt with interest at 6.5% compounded annually. Find the payment.
13. A house costs $25,000 cash. A purchaser will pay $5000 cash and a sequence of 8 equal annual payments, the first due at the end of 3 years. If money is worth 7%, find the annual payment.

14. A man, in starting a business, obtains a loan of $20,000 with interest at 9% compounded semiannually. He will discharge his debt by a sequence of equal semiannual payments, the first due at the end of 4 years and the last at the end of 10 years. Find the periodic payment.

15. The United States makes a loan of $10,000,000 for industrial development to a country under an aid program, with an agreement that interest is at 6% compounded annually. The country will discharge its obligation by a sequence of 20 annual payments, the first due at the end of 10 years. Find the required payment.

16. A manufacturer borrows $50,000 with interest at 9% compounded monthly, and agrees to discharge the loan by a sequence of equal payments at the beginning of each month for 5 years, with the first payment at the beginning of the 4th year. Find the periodic payment.

17. A man agrees to make $5000 payments at the ends of the first 5 years, $4000 at the ends of the next 5 years, and $3000 at the ends of the next 5 years. If money is worth 4%, find the present value of this agreement.

★18. A man borrows $9200. To discharge all principal and interest obligations, he agrees to pay a sequence of 6 equal annual payments of $2000 each, the first due at the end of 4 years. By interpolation, find the rate at which interest is compounded annually.

32. Value of an Annuity on an Arbitrary Date

Recall (1) and (2) on page 75. We emphasized the flexibility of referring to $Ra_{\overline{n}|i}$ as the VALUE of a sequence of n payments of $R each *on a day which is one period before the first payment*. Similarly, $Rs_{\overline{n}|i}$ is the VALUE of the payments *on the day of the last payment*. In order to obtain the value of the sequence of payments on an *arbitrary date*, first we may use $Ra_{\overline{n}|i}$ or $Rs_{\overline{n}|i}$ on an appropriate date; then we accumulate or discount the result to the arbitrary date involved in the application.

Example 1. A sequence of 5 semiannual payments of $50 each will start with a payment at the end of $2\frac{1}{2}$ years. If money is worth 8% compounded semiannually, find the sum of the values of these payments at the end of (a) 2 years; (b) $4\frac{1}{2}$ years; (c) 6 years. (d) Find the actual present value of the payments.

SOLUTION. 1. The payment dates are shown by black dots in Figure 19. The payments form an ordinary annuity whose term begins at the end of 2 years and ends at the end of $4\frac{1}{2}$ years. Hence, $Ra_{\overline{n}|i}$ gives the value of the payments at the end of 2 years and $Rs_{\overline{n}|i}$ gives the value at the end of $4\frac{1}{2}$ years.

2. Value at the end of 2 years is $\qquad$ $50a_{\overline{5}|.04} = \$223.$

3. Value at the end of $4\frac{1}{2}$ years is $\qquad$ $50s_{\overline{5}|.04} = \$271.$

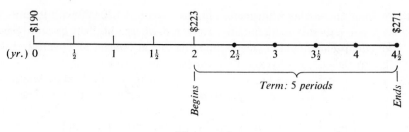

Figure 19

4. To find the actual present value, discount the result of Step 2 for 2 years or the result of Step 3 for $4\frac{1}{2}$ years:

$$(actual\ present\ value) = 50(a_{\overline{5}|.04})(1.04)^{-4} = \$190;\ or \tag{1}$$

$$(actual\ present\ value) = 50(s_{\overline{5}|.04})(1.04)^{-9} = \$190.$$

5. To find the value of the annuity at the end of 6 years, accumulate the result of Step 2 for 4 years, or the result of Step 3 for $1\frac{1}{2}$ years:

$$val.\ at\ end\ 6\ yr.\ is\ 50(a_{\overline{5}|.04})(1.04)^8 = (223)(1.3686) = \$305;$$

$$val.\ at\ end\ 6\ yr.\ is\ 50(s_{\overline{5}|.04})(1.04)^3 = (271)(1.1249) = \$305.$$

In finding the result in (1), we illustrated a new method for obtaining the present value of a deferred annuity. However, *the method presented before in Section 31 is more simple.* The method of Example 1 sometimes is useful in writing equations of value where annuities are involved. A method similar to that of Example 1 would apply in finding the present value or the amount of an annuity due. However, the resulting numerical details would be more complicated than those met with the previous methods of Section 30 for annuities due.

Example 2. In financing a new shopping center, the owner receives a loan of \$20,000 at the beginning of each six months for four years. He agrees to pay all accumulated liability, with interest at the rate $\{8\%, m = 2\}$, by a single payment at the end of 6 years. Find his payment.

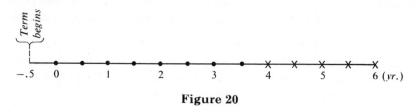

Figure 20

SOLUTION. 1. The loans are indicated by black dots in Figure 20. Consider five fictitious payments of \$20,000 inserted semiannually, starting with one at the end of four years. These payments are indicated by crosses in Figure 20. The actual loans plus the fictitious payments form an annuity whose term begins 6 months before the present and ends at the end of 6 years. Thus, the term is 13 periods.

2. Let $L be the liability of the debtor at the end of 6 years. Then, L is equal to the amount of the annuity formed by the actual and the fictitious payments, *minus* the amount of the annuity formed by the fictitious payments:

$$L = 20{,}000s_{\overline{13}|.04} - 20{,}000s_{\overline{5}|.04};$$

$$L = 20{,}000(16.62683768 - 5.41632256) = \$224{,}210.$$

In writing an equation of value involving an annuity, either the *beginning* or the *end* of the term of the annuity is a useful *comparison date*.

Example 3. In order to have $10,000 in a fund at the end of 9 years, $2000 is deposited now and equal payments will be added to the fund at the ends of 3, 4, 5, and 6 years. Find these annual payments if the fund accumulates at 4%.

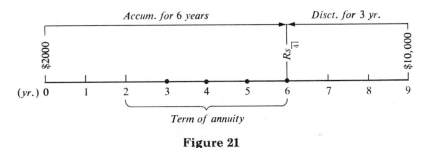

Figure 21

SOLUTION. The annual payments of $R each form an annuity whose term begins at the end of 2 years and ends at the end of 6 years, as indicated in Figure 21. Equivalent sums of money are shown in the following table.

Paid into Fund	Final Fund
$2000 *at the present date.*	$10,000 *at the end of 9 yr.*
$R *at the ends of 3, 4, 5, and 6 yr.*	

To write an equation of value at the end of 6 years, we discount $10,000 for 3 years, accumulate $2000 for 6 years, and obtain the value of the annuity at the end of its term by use of $Rs_{\overline{n}|i}$.

$$2000(1.04)^6 + Rs_{\overline{4}|.04} = 10{,}000(1.04)^{-3};$$

$$Rs_{\overline{4}|.04} = 10{,}000(1.04)^{-3} - 2000(1.04)^6; \qquad R = \$1498.$$

★33. A New Derivation of the Annuity Formulas

Inspection of formulas (8) for $a_{\overline{n}|i}$ and $s_{\overline{n}|i}$ on page 64 verifies the following statements, which give a clue to a neat method for deriving the formulas for $a_{\overline{n}|}$ and $s_{\overline{n}|}$.

$s_{\overline{n}|i}$ is the quotient obtained by dividing the compound interest on \$1 for n interest periods by the interest rate per period.

$a_{\overline{n}|i}$ is the quotient obtained by dividing the discount on \$1, due at the end of n interest periods, by the interest rate per period.

PROOF OF THE FORMULA FOR $a_{\overline{n}|}$. Suppose that a principal of \$1 is on hand now. If it is invested at the rate i per interest period, then $i \times \$1$ or \$$i$ is due as interest at the end of each period. Therefore, \$1 on hand now will provide for an *annuity* of \$$i$ per interest period and also will provide \$1 intact at the end of n periods. We recall that

$$(\text{present value of } \$1 \text{ due at the end of n periods}) = (1 + i)^{-n}; \qquad (1)$$

$$(\text{present value of annuity of } \$i \text{ per period for n periods}) = ia_{\overline{n}|}. \qquad (2)$$

Hence, \$1 on hand now is the sum of (1) and (2):

$$1 = (1 + i)^{-n} + ia_{\overline{n}|}; \qquad ia_{\overline{n}|} = 1 - (1 + i)^{-n}; \qquad (3)$$

Divide by i:
$$a_{\overline{n}|} = \frac{1 - (1 + i)^{-n}}{i}. \qquad (4)$$

NOTE 1. The last equation in (3) states that the *discount* on \$1 which is due at the ends of n periods, or $1 - (1 + i)^{-n}$, is the present value of the annuity of \$$i$ per period for n periods.

PROOF OF THE FORMULA FOR $s_{\overline{n}|}$. If \$1 is invested now at compound interest at the rate i per conversion period, the original principal itself provides \$$i$ interest at the end of each period. This annuity of \$$i$ per period accumulates at compound interest, and the final compound amount at the end of n periods can be looked at as follows:

$$(\text{comp. amt. on } \$1) = \$1 + (\text{amt. of an annuity of } \$i \text{ per period}). \qquad (5)$$

Or,
$$(1 + i)^n = 1 + is_{\overline{n}|}; \qquad is_{\overline{n}|} = (1 + i)^n - 1; \qquad (6)$$

Divide by i:
$$s_{\overline{n}|} = \frac{(1 + i)^n - 1}{i}.$$

NOTE 2. The last equation in (6) states that the *compound interest*, $(1+i)^n - 1$, on \$1 is the amount of the annuity created by the interest payments \$$i$ on the original principal, \$1.

Exercise 23

For each problem in the exercise, draw a time diagram showing the payment dates, and the beginning and the end of the term of any ordinary annuity involved.

In Problems 1 and 2, write an expression for each specified value in terms of $a_{\overline{n}|i}$ and then $s_{\overline{n}|i}$. Do NOT compute the expressions unless directed to do so by the instructor.

1. A sequence of 8 annual $100 payments starts with one 5 years from now, and money is worth 5%. The value of the annuity is desired on the following dates: (a) end of 4 years; (b) end of 12 years; (c) end of 18 years; (d) now.

2. An annuity of $75 payable quarterly for 8 years is deferred 5 years, and money is worth 4% compounded quarterly. The value of the annuity is desired on the following dates: (a) end of 5 years; (b) end of 17 years; (c) end of 13 years; (d) now.

3. How much will be in a fund at the end of 20 years if $1000 is deposited in it at the end of each 6 months for the first 12 years, and if the fund accumulates at 3% compounded semiannually? (Insert fictitious payments.)

4. Solve Problem 3 if the deposits occur at the beginning of each 6 months for the first 12 years.

5. In starting a business venture, the owner is granted a loan of $1000 at the beginning of each 3 months for 4 years. He agrees that money is worth 7% compounded quarterly, and that he will discharge all accumulated liability by a single payment at the end of 5 years. What must he pay?

6. A man becomes temporarily disabled and, for 3 years, is unable to pay $150 due at the end of each month on his contract for the purchase of his home. His creditor agrees to allow him to make only the regular monthly payments during the 4th and 5th years, plus a single payment at the end of 5 years to discharge the accumulated liability from the first 3 years. If money is worth 5% compounded monthly, find the single payment.

7. Given that the present value of $10,000 due at the end of $37\frac{1}{2}$ years is $1551.48 when money is worth 5% compounded quarterly, find $a_{\overline{150}|.0125}$ without using logarithms.

8. Given that the compound amount on $1000 at the end of 75 years will be $4448.42 if interest is at the rate 2% compounded semiannually, find $s_{\overline{150}|.01}$ without using logarithms.

In the remaining problems, find each result only to the nearest $10 if desired.

9. A fund for replacement of machinery in a plant must contain $30,000 at the end of 9 years. If the fund is invested at 3.5% compounded semiannually, what equal deposits should be placed in the fund at the end of each 6 months just for the first 4 years?

10. In Problem 9, if equal deposits are to be placed in the fund at the beginning of each 6 months just for the first 5 years, find the periodic deposit.

★11. A house costs $40,000 cash. A purchaser will pay $9000 cash, $6000 at the end of 2 years, and a sequence of 6 equal annual payments starting with one at the end of 4 years, to discharge all liability as to principal and interest at .07 compounded annually. Find the annual payment which must be made for 6 years. (Write an equation of value.)

★12. In order to provide $6000 as the cash payment on a new home at the end of 4 years, a man invests $1000 in a fund today and will add equal deposits at the end of each 3 months for the next 2 years. If the fund accumulates at $5\frac{1}{2}\%$ compounded quarterly, find his quarterly deposit.

★13. Deposits of $1000 are placed in a fund at the end of each year for 12 years. How much is in the fund at the end of 12 years if it accumulates at 5% for the first 8 years, and at 6% for the last 4 years?

★14. A man owes $1000 due at the end of 6 years, and wishes to pay off the debt in full immediately. What should he pay if his creditor will discount the debt with money worth 5% during the first 2 years and 3% during the last 4 years?

NOTE 1. A sequence of periodic payments is called an **increasing annuity** if each payment, after the first, exceeds the preceding payment by a fixed sum. The annuity is called a **decreasing annuity** if each payment, except the last, exceeds the next payment by a fixed sum.

★15. By use of (8) on page 64, prove that, if i is the interest rate per period,

$$a_{\overline{1}|} + a_{\overline{2}|} + \cdots + a_{\overline{n-1}|} + a_{\overline{n}|} = \frac{n - a_{\overline{n}|}}{i}.$$

$$s_{\overline{1}|} + s_{\overline{2}|} + \cdots + s_{\overline{n-1}|} + s_{\overline{n}|} = \frac{(1 + i)s_{\overline{n}|} - n}{i}.$$

★16. Consider a decreasing annuity with payments nW, $(n - 1)W$, $(n - 2)W$, ..., $3W$, $2W$, and W at the ends of the first n interest periods, with i as the rate per period. Prove that the present value, A, of these payments is given by

$$A = W\frac{n - a_{\overline{n}|i}}{i}.$$

HINT. Superimpose the following ordinary annuities: W per period for n periods; W per period for $(n - 1)$ periods, and so on; W per period for 2 periods; W per period for just 1 period. Use Problem 15. The amount of the decreasing annuity could be obtained by accumulating A for n periods.

★17. Consider an increasing annuity paying, W, $2W$,..., nW at the ends of 1, 2,..., n interest periods, respectively. Prove that, if i is the interest rate per period, the sum of the compound amounts on these payments at the end of n periods is given by

$$S = W \frac{(1 + i)s_{\overline{n}i} - n}{i}.$$

The present value, A, of this increasing annuity is found by discounting the amount for n periods: $A = S(1 + i)^{-n}$.

★18. Jones borrows $5000 from Smith and signs a contract to pay, at the end of each month as long as necessary, $100 of the principal and interest at the rate 6% on all principal outstanding during the month. Just after the 10th monthly payment on the debt, Smith sells his ownership of the contract to Roberts. What does Roberts pay to Smith if money is worth 7% compounded monthly in this transaction? Use Problem 16.

★19. The purchase contract for a house worth $42,000 cash specifies that the buyer will pay $12,000 cash and, at the end of each 3 months as long as necessary, $1500 of the principal and interest at the rate 8% on all principal outstanding during the 3 months. At the end of 2 years, the contract for the future payments is sold by the original owner to a new investor to whom money is worth $\{9\%, m = 4\}$. What does he pay?

Exercise 24 | Review of Chapter 3

1. A man agrees to pay $300 at the end of each month for 20 years, in purchasing a house. (a) Find the present value of this agreement if money is worth 7% compounded monthly. (b) Find the debtor's remaining liability at the beginning of the 7th year.

2. A man borrows $10,000, and agrees to discharge his liability by making equal payments at the end of each 3 months for 8 years. Find the periodic payment if money is worth 4.5% compounded quarterly.

3. In order to accumulate a fund of $15,000 by the end of 8 years, what equal deposits should be placed in the fund at the end of each 6 months if interest is at 5% compounded semiannually?

4. If $250 will be placed in a fund at the end of each 3 months for 6 years, and if the fund accumulates at $5\frac{1}{2}\%$ compounded quarterly, how much will be in the fund just after (a) the 15th deposit; (b) the final deposit?

5. On retirement, a workman finds that his company pension calls for payments of $300 to him (or to his estate if he dies) at the beginning of each month for 20 years. Find the present value of this pension at 5% compounded monthly.

6. If money is worth 7% compounded quarterly, what equal payments at the beginning of each 3 months for 7 years will discharge a debt of $8000 due now?

7. A man now aged 55 is promised a pension of $500 at the end of each 3 months for 20 years, payable to him, or to his estate if he dies, with the first payment due 3 months after he is 60 years old. Find the present worth of this promise at 4% compounded quarterly.

8. On Nelson's 60th birthday, he creates a trust fund of $30,000 to pay to him, or his estate if he dies, a sequence of 15 annual payments, the first due on his 65th birthday. If the fund earns 5% compounded annually, find the annual payment.

9. Given that $(1.03)^{140} = 62.691904$ and $(1.03)^{-140} = .01595102$, compute $a_{\overline{140}|.03}$ and $s_{\overline{140}|.03}$.

10. By use of geometric progressions, derive the usual algebraic expressions for the present value and the amount of an annuity of $50 payable quarterly for 5 years, if money is worth 6% compounded quarterly.

11. Under a factory savings plan, a workman deposits $25 at the beginning of each month for 4 years, and the management guarantees accumulation at 6% compounded monthly. How much stands to the workman's credit at the end of 4 years?

12. If money is worth 5% compounded monthly, and if $2000 is the amount of an annuity whose term is 5 years, find the present value of the annuity.

13. If $500 is placed in a fund at the end of each 3 months, and the fund is invested at 6% compounded quarterly, on what date will the fund first contain at least $9000 just after a deposit is made?

14. An endowment fund of $200,000 is invested at 5% compounded annually, and is designed to pay out $20,000 for college scholarships at the end of each year, until a final date when only a smaller sum will be available. Find the date on which this event will occur.

15. At what nominal rate compounded quarterly will payments of $800 at the end of each 3 months for 5 years discharge all liability for a debtor who borrows $14,000 today? Find the rate by interpolation.

16. In order to create a fund for factory repair to contain $25,000 at the end of 6 years, what deposits should be placed in the fund if it is invested at $3\frac{1}{2}$% compounded semiannually and the deposits will be made (a) at the end of each 6 months for 6 years; (b) at the beginning of each 6 months for 6 years?

17. Suppose that United States social security taxes for a man will amount to $600 at the end of each year of his working life of 40 years. If these

payments were to accumulate at compound interest, how large a pension payable at the end of each year for 25 years would the resulting fund provide, if all money is invested at 4%?

18. In order to make possible a required payment of $6000 at the end of 5 years, a man will create a fund by investing $1000 now, and adding to it equal deposits at the end of each year for 5 years. Find the annual deposit if the fund is invested at $4\frac{1}{2}\%$ effective.

19. What equal annual deposits should be placed in a fund at the end of each year for 6 years, in order to have $10,000 at the end of 9 years, if the fund is invested at 5%?

20. A corporation obtains a loan of $200,000, with interest at 8% compounded semiannually. The loan agreement calls for a payment of $25,000 at the end of 3 years, and a sequence of 6 equal semiannual payments, the first due at the end of $4\frac{1}{2}$ years, to discharge all liability as to principal and interest. Find the semiannual payment.

★21. By use of the expressions for $a_{\overline{n}|}$ and $s_{\overline{n}|}$, derive the following formulas, where h and k are positive integers, and i is the interest rate per period.

$$a_{\overline{k}|} + a_{\overline{2k}|} + \cdots + a_{\overline{hk}|} = \frac{1}{i}\left[h - \frac{a_{\overline{hk}|}}{s_{\overline{k}|}}\right].$$

$$s_{\overline{k}|} + s_{\overline{2k}|} + \cdots + s_{\overline{hk}|} = \frac{1}{i}\left[(1 + i)^k \frac{s_{\overline{hk}|}}{s_{\overline{k}|}} - h\right].$$

4/ Extinction of Debts by Periodic Payments

34. Amortization of a Debt

In current language, the *amortization* of a debt means the extinction of the debt by any satisfactory set of payments. In this chapter, however, when we say that a debt is **amortized**, we shall mean, usually, that *all liabilities as to principal and interest are discharged by a sequence of equal payments* due at the ends of equal intervals of time. In such a case, the payments form an annuity whose present value is the original principal of the debt.

Example 1. A man borrows $15,000 with the agreement that money is worth 5% compounded annually. The debt is to be paid, interest included, by equal installments at the end of each year for 5 years. Find the annual payment and construct an amortization schedule.

SOLUTION. 1. Let R be the unknown installment. Then

$$Ra_{\overline{5}|.05} = 15{,}000; \qquad R = 15{,}000\,\frac{1}{a_{\overline{5}|}} = \$3464.622. \qquad \text{(Table IX)}$$

2. The following table shows the outstanding principal at each payment date, and was constructed one row at a time. Thus, at the end of 1 year, the interest due is $15{,}000(.05) = \$750$; the principal repaid is

$$3464.622 - 750 = \$2714.622;$$

the remaining indebtedness is

$$15{,}000 - 2714.622 = \$12{,}285.378; \dots$$

A check on the arithmetic is that the first and the last items in the row for the 5th year should be equal. Interest payments *decrease*, whereas the payments of principal *increase*, during the transaction.

Amortization Schedule

Year	Outstanding Principal at Beginning of Year	Interest at 5% Due at End of Year	Total Payment at End of Year	For Repayment of Principal at End of Year
1	$15,000.000	$ 750.000	$ 3464.622	$ 2714.622
2	12,285.378	614.269	3464.622	2850.353
3	9,435.025	471.751	3464.622	2992.871
4	6,442.154	322.108	3464.622	3142.514
5	3,299.640	164.982	3464.622	3299.640
Totals		$2323.110	$17,323.110	$15,000.000

The preceding table verifies that the solution of Example 1, $3464.62, also is the solution of the following problem in which *there is no necessity for thinking of the notion of compound interest.*

Example 2. What equal payments at the end of each year for 5 years will be sufficient to **pay the principal and interest** on a debt of $15,000 if interest at the rate 5% is **payable** at the end of each year on all principal outstanding during the year?

The connection between Examples 1 and 2 could have been foreseen without numerical verification. For, if a sequence of payments satisfies a creditor who invests all of his money at 5% *compounded* annually, then the payments automatically *provide 5% interest at the end of each year* on all principal outstanding during the year. In a problem like Example 2, where interest is specified to be **payable periodically**, we obtain the solution by attacking an *equivalent* problem where interest is said to be **compounded**.

With any method of discharging a debt, **the outstanding liability at any date is the present value of all payments which remain to be made**. This use of the *future history* of the debt will be referred to as the **prospective method** for evaluating a remaining liability.

Example 3. In Example 1, without using the schedule, find the outstanding liability at the beginning of the 3rd year.

SOLUTION. The outstanding liability is the present value of the payments still to be made. These form an annuity payable for 3 years.

Outstanding liability: $3464.622a_{\overline{3}|.05} = \$9435.03.$

The following Summary describes how any single row in an amortization schedule may be computed without making up the complete table. This possibility is very important in business applications where the table might be extensive.

Summary

Computation of the interest and the principal included in any amortization payment:

I. *Find the outstanding principal just after the preceding payment.*

II. *Compute interest for one interval on the principal just obtained in order to find the interest paid on the next date.*

III. *Subtract the interest found in Step 2 from the periodic amortization payment to find the principal repaid.*

Example 4. Without using the schedule in Example 1, find what interest and what principal will be paid on the 4th payment date.

SOLUTION. The 4th payment provides interest on the principal outstanding just after the 3rd payment.

Outst. princ. just after 3rd *payt. is* $3464.622a_{\overline{21}|.05} = \$6442.15.$

Int. on $\$6442.15$ *for* 1 *yr. at* 5% *is* $\$322.11$, *included in* 4th *payt.*

The principal repaid is $3464.62 - 322.11 = \$3142.51.$

Example 5. A man owes $10,000, with interest at 6% payable semi-annually. What equal payments at the beginning of each 6 months for 8 years will discharge his debt?

SOLUTION. If $\$R$ is the semiannual payment, then $10,000 = R + Ra_{\overline{15}|.03}$;

$$10,000 = R(12.93794); \qquad R = \frac{10,000}{12.93794} = \$772.92.$$

Example 6. A debt for purchase of household furniture will be discharged, principal and interest included at 12% payable monthly, by payments of $100 at the end of each month for two years. (*a*) Find the original debt. (*b*) How much of the fifth payment is interest and how much is payment of principal? (*c*) What principal remains unpaid just after the fifth monthly payment?

SOLUTION. 1. Original debt is $\quad A = 100a_{\overline{24}|.01} = \$2124.34.$

2. The 5th payment includes interest on the principal, A_4, still unpaid just after the 4th payment of $100, where

$$A_4 = 100a_{\overline{20}|.01} = \$1804.555.$$

The 5th payment includes interest for one month on A_4:

$$(\textit{interest in } 5\text{th } \textit{payment}) = 1804.555(.01) = \$18.046.$$

The principal repaid by the 5th payment is

$$100 - 18.046 = \$81.954.$$

Remaining principal unpaid after 5th payment:

$$A_5 = \$1804.555 - 81.954 = \$1722.60.$$

The repayment of debts by periodic installments, usually equal, is the common practice in many branches of business, including the enormous number of transactions where consumers rather than corporations are the debtors. The Federal Truth in Lending Act of 1968 now requires the creditor to inform the debtor about the rate at which interest is being paid in the case of each partial payment. Also, income tax regulations permit an individual to claim a deduction against his income to reduce his tax for all interest which he pays. Thus, when a person is paying off a mortgage on a home by periodic installments, it is essential that the creditor should state how much of each payment is interest and how much is a repayment of principal. A debtor would be acting well within his legal rights if he should request his creditor to provide an amortization schedule, as just discussed, to be the basis for clarifying the manner in which the debt is discharged. Every creditor with a careful accounting system has on hand, or easily could construct, an amortization schedule for any debt. It is recommended that each student studying this text, even if he does not become an accountant, should demand, or construct for himself, an amortization schedule to apply in the case of any debt which he may contract later. On account of the importance thus ascribed to amortization schedules, they will be emphasized in future exercises, even though considerable routine arithmetic is involved in the process. If any corporation is discharging a debt by peridic payments, it is certain that the accounting department of the corporation would prepare the equivalent of an amortization schedule for the debt.

35. Proof of $A = Ra_{\overline{n}|i}$ Without Mention of Compound Interest

In the preceding section, reasoning was presented to show that interest can be referred to as *payable* rather than *compounded*, in obtaining $A = Ra_{\overline{n}|i}$. The argument in Section 34 was verbal. In this section, the same objective is attained analytically. The basis for $A = Ra_{\overline{n}|i}$ in the phraseology of compound interest would be thoroughly confusing to the average person, who thinks in the language of "*interest payable*." The following proof should increase the confidence of the student in any future statements about $A = Ra_{\overline{n}|i}$ to an indvidual who is not familiar with compound interest. We shall prove that $\{A, R, n, i\}$ in (2) below satisfy

$$A = Ra_{\overline{n}|i}. \tag{1}$$

$$\left\{ \begin{array}{l} A \text{ loan of } \$A \text{ is to be discharged by payments of } \$R \text{ at the end} \\ \text{of each period for } n \text{ periods, with these payments including all} \\ \text{interest, at the rate } i \text{ per period, } \textbf{payable} \text{ at the end of each} \\ \text{period on the unpaid principal at the beginning of the period.} \end{array} \right\} \tag{2}$$

PROOF.   1. The original principal of the debt is A. At the end of one interest period, the principal plus the interest due is $(A + Ai)$ or $A(1 + i)$. After the first payment of $\$R$ is made, the remaining liability of the debtor is

$$A_1 = A(1 + i) - R. \tag{3}$$

2. At the end of two periods, the debtor's liability is

$$A_1(1 + i) \quad or \quad A(1 + i)^2 - R(1 + i). \tag{4}$$

Just after the debtor makes his second payment of $\$R$, his remaining liability A_2 is given by

$$A_2 = A_1(1 + i) - R, \quad or \quad A_2 = A(1 + i)^2 - R[1 + (1 + i)]. \tag{5}$$

3. The student may verify that, just after the debtor makes his third payment of $\$R$, the remaining liability A_3 is given by

$$A_3 = A(1 + i)^3 - R[1 + (1 + i) + (1 + i)^2]. \tag{6}$$

Similarly, just after the nth payment of $\$R$, the debtor's remaining liability is $\$0$, and

$$0 = A(1 + i)^n - R[1 + (1 + i) + (1 + i)^2 + \cdots + (1 + i)^{n-1}]. \tag{7}$$

4. From (1) on page 63, it is seen that the sum within brackets in (7) is $s_{\overline{n}|i}$. Hence, from (7)

$$A(1 + i)^n = Rs_{\overline{n}|i}; \quad A = R\frac{1}{(1 + i)^n} s_{\overline{n}|i} = R(1 + i)^{-n}s_{\overline{n}|i}. \tag{8}$$

From (3) on page 64, recall that $a_{\overline{n}|i} = (1 + i)^{-n}s_{\overline{n}|i}$. Then, by use of (8), $A = Ra_{\overline{n}|i}$, which we desired to prove. Also, observe that *no mention of compound interest occurred in the proof.*

Exercise 25

Do not make up an amortization schedule unless it is requested. In any schedule, calculate each entry correct to three decimal places by plain arithmetic.

1. A debt of $\$5000$ with interest at 6% payable semiannually is to be amortized by equal payments at the end of each 6 months for 3 years. Find the periodic payment and construct the amortization schedule, with entries in the final row accurate to the nearest cent.

2. A debt, $\$A$, will be discharged, principal and interest included at 7% payable annually, by payments of $\$1000$ at the end of each year for five years. (*a*) Find the original debt. (*b*) Make up an amortization schedule for the debt. (*c*) Without using the schedule, find the principal remaining unpaid just after the 3rd payment of $\$1000$, and check with the schedule.

3. A debt, $\$A$, will be discharged, principal and interest included at 6%

payable annually, by payments of $2000 at the end of each year for 10 years. (a) Find the original debt. (b) Make up the first three rows of an amortization schedule for the debt. (c) Without use of the schedule, find the remaining liability of the debtor just after his 3rd payment of $2000, and check with the schedule.

4. In purchasing a new automobile, a man makes a cash payment, and also signs a promissory note agreeing to pay the remainder of the cost, principal and interest included at 12% payable monthly, by payments of $100 at the end of each month for 30 months. (a) Find the original debt on the date of purchase. (b) How much of the 6th monthly payment is interest and how much is repayment of the principal of the debt? (The rate 12% was approximately the rate charged by many banks on new car loans in 1974.)

5. In the purchase of a color television set, a buyer pays $200 cash. He will discharge the balance, principal and interest included at 18% payable monthly on the unpaid balance, by payments of $75 at the end of each month for a year. (a) Find the cash value of the television set. (b) How much of the 4th monthly payment is interest and how much is a repayment of the principal of the debt? (The rate 18% was customary on consumer purchases in 1974.)

6. In making a purchase of furniture, a man agrees to pay $200 at the end of each month for 6 months. If these payments include interest at 18% payable monthly on the unpaid balance, (a) find the original cash value of the furniture; (b) obtain the total amount of interest paid in discharging the debt; (c) how much of the 4th payment is interest and how much is a repayment of principal?

7. A man deposits $10,000 with a savings and loan association which pays 5% interest annually. The fund is to provide equal payments at the end of each year for 6 years. (a) Find the annual payment. (b) Calculate the first two rows of an amortization schedule showing the annual reductions in the fund.

8. A debt is being discharged, principal and interest included at 8% payable quarterly, by payments of $1200 at the end of each 3 months. On a certain payment date, just after the regular payment is made, the remaining liability of the debtor is $9850.78. How much principal remains unpaid just after the next payment of $1200?

9. A debt is being discharged, principal and interest at 7% payable annually included, by payments of $2500 at the end of each year. On a certain payment date, just after the regular payment is made, the remaining liability of the debtor is $15,880.46. How much principal remains unpaid 2 years later just after the regular payment is made? (Make up two rows of an amortization schedule.)

10. A man will discharge a debt, principal and interest included at 6% payable annually, by paying $1500 at the end of each year for 9 years. Without making up an amortization schedule, find how much of his 5th payment is interest and how much is a repayment of principal.

11. A man will discharge a debt, principal and interest included at 8% payable semiannually, by paying $1000 at the end of each 6 months for 7 years. Without making up an amortization schedule, find how much interest and how much principal is paid on the 5th payment date.

12. In buying a house, a man makes a cash payment and agrees to pay $1000 at the end of each 6 months for 11 years, where the payments include all interest at 8% payable semiannually. (a) What was the original unpaid principal when he took possession of the house? (b) What part of his 7th payment of $1000 was interest?

13. A man owes $12,000 today and agrees to discharge the debt by equal payments at the beginning of each 3 months for 8 years, where these payments include all interest at 8% payable quarterly. Find the quarterly payment.

14. A man purchases a factory with the cash value $75,000. He pays $35,000 cash and agrees to make a sequence of 12 equal annual payments, the first due at the end of 4 years. If interest is at 6% compounded annually, find the periodic payment.

15. An endowment insurance policy, on maturing, gives the option of a cash payment of $22,000, or $2000 at the end of each 6 months for 6 years. What interest rate is used by the insurance company?

16. A debt of $40,000 will be discharged, interest included, by payments of $2250 at the beginning of each 3 months for 5 years. At what rate is interest payable quarterly?

17. A farm is worth $18,000 cash. The purchaser will pay $3000 cash, $3000 at the end of 1 year, $7000 at the end of 4 years, and a final payment at the end of 6 years, to discharge all liability with interest at 6% effective. Find the necessary final payment.

18. To discharge a debt of $20,000 with interest at 5% compounded semi-annually, the debtor will pay $9000 at the end of 4 years and equal payments at the end of each 6 months for 6 years after that date. Find the semi-annual payment. (Write an equation of value.)

36. Amortization, with an Irregular Final Payment

If a loan of A is made, with a round sum R specified arbitraily as the periodic payment which will discharge the debt over a period of time, it is almost certain that the final payment will be less than R.

Example 1. A debt of $8800, with interest at 5% payable semiannually, will be discharged by payments of $1200 at the end of each 6 months as long as necessary, with a final payment 6 months after the last $1200 is paid. Find when the final payment is due.

SOLUTION. 1. If n payments of $1200 each would satisfy the creditor, then

$$1200a_{\overline{n}|.025} = 8800; \qquad a_{\overline{n}|.025} = 7.333. \qquad (1)$$

2. From Table VIII at $2\frac{1}{2}\%$:

$a_{\overline{8}|} = 7.17$, which is <7.333; hence, *more than 8 payments of* $1200 *each will be needed.*

$a_{\overline{9}|} = 7.97$, which is >7.333; hence, 9 payments of $1200 each would be *more* than is demanded by the creditor.

3. From Step 2, it follows that the debtor should pay 8 installments of $1200 each and a *smaller* payment at the end of 9 periods. The following schedule shows that the final payment is $244.57.

Amortization Schedule

Payment Interval	Outstanding Principal at Beginning of Interval	Interest Due at End of Interval	Total Payment at End of Interval	Principal Repaid at End of Interval
1	$8800.000	$ 220.000	$1200.000	$ 980.000
2	7820.000	195.500	1200.000	1004.500
3	6815.500	170.388	1200.000	1029.612
4	5785.888	144.647	1200.000	1055.353
5	4730.535	118.263	1200.000	1081.737
6	3648.798	91.220	1200.000	1108.780
7	2540.018	63.500	1200.000	1136.500
8	1403.518	35.088	1200.000	1164.912
9	238.606	5.965	244.571	238.606
Totals		$1044.571	$9844.571	$8800.000

In a problem like Example 1, suppose that the table and the final payment have not been computed. Then, to find the outstanding principal *just after any particular payment*, it is useless to state that the outstanding liability is the present value of all *future* payments, because they are not completely known. That is, the *prospective* method of Section 34 on page 93 does not apply. Hence, we use the *past history* of the transaction to obtain the desired result. This so-called **retrospective method** is as follows:

Summary

To find the outstanding principal just after any particular payment, when periodic payments of $R *each are amortizing a debt with original principal* $A, *write an equation of value on the date of the payment involved, stating that*

(outst. princ.) = (accum. val. of $A) − (accum. val. of past payts.) (2)

With (2) employed to find any outstanding principal, then we may use the Summary on page 94 to find the principal and interest paid on any date.

Example 2. For the debt in Example 1, without making up the amortization schedule, (*a*) find the outstanding principal just after the 5th payment; (*b*) find the principal and interest paid on the 6th payment date; (*c*) find the final payment and when it is due.

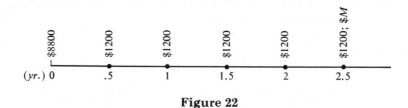

Figure 22

SOLUTION.   1. Let $M be the outstanding principal, or remaining liability, of the debtor just after his 5th payment of $1200. The time scale in Figure 22 indicates the dates of the original debt, the five payments, and $M. Then, at $\{.05, m = 2\}$, $8800 at time 0 has the same value as $M at the end of 5 periods, with payments of $1200 at the end of each period for 5 periods, as shown in the following table for the data. On the basis of (2), we write an equation of value at the end of 5 periods. The accumulated value of the $1200 payments is the amount of the annuity which they form. Thus, we obtain

Original Debt	Equivalent Payments
$8800 *due at the beginning of the transaction.*	1. *$M due at the end of* 2½ *years.* 2. *Payments of* $1200 *due at the end of each 6 months for* 2½ *years.*

$$8800(1.025)^5 = M + 1200s_{\overline{5}|.025};$$

$$M = 8800(1.025)^5 - 1200s_{\overline{5}|.025} = 9956.39 - 6307.59 = \$3648.80. \quad (3)$$

2. Refer to the Summary on page 94. On the 6th payment date, the interest due is interest for one period on $M, from (3). The principal paid is the balance of the $1200 payment:

$$(int. due) = 3648.80(.025) = \$91.22; (princ. paid) = 1200 - 91.22 = \$1108.78.$$

Thus, we have computed the 6th row in the schedule for Example 1, without computing the whole table.

3. *To find the final payment* $H, first we ask when it is due, and consider $1200a_{\overline{n}|.025} = 8800$, as in Example 1. The last $1200 payment will be made at

the end of 8 periods; the final payment H will be made at the end of 9 periods. Now, we think of forming the *last row* in the schedule as seen in Example 1 (without having made up the other rows). As in Step 1 of this Solution, let M be the outstanding principal just after the 8th payment. On writing an equation of value just after the 8th payment, we obtain

$$M = 8800(1.025)^8 - 1200s_{\overline{8}|.025} = \$238.61.$$

Hence, at the end of 9 periods,

$$(int. \ due) = 238.61(.025) = \$5.96; \qquad H = 238.61 + 5.96 = \$244.57.$$

Summary

To find the final payment when a debt of A is to be discharged, principal and interest included, by equal payments of specified size R at the end of each interest period as long as necessary:

I. *From $A = Ra_{\overline{n}i}$ where n is unknown, by mere inspection of Table VIII find when the last regular payment of R is due, and when the final smaller payment should be made.*

II. *Find the outstanding principal just after the last regular payment of R.*

III. *Add interest for one payment interval to the result of Step II in order to determine the final smaller payment.*

NOTE 1.   Another solution for H in Example 3 is as follows:

Compute the *excess* payment on the 9th payment date if $1200 is paid then. The excess is

$$1200s_{\overline{9}|.025} - 8800(1.025)^9 = \$955.43.$$

Subtract the result of Step I from $1200 in order to find H:

$$H = 1200 - 955.43 = \$244.57.$$

★37.   A Property of Interpolation for n in $A = Ra_{\overline{n}i}$

The following procedure for obtaining a final irregular amortization payment may be preferred, and is proved later in this section. The method yields the exact* result, with accuracy limited only by the number of decimal places in the entries of Table VIII.

* Hence, for a second time in this text, we meet an interpolation method yielding the *exact* result for a problem. The first case occurred on page 42. This emphasises the fact that an interpolation method does not always give results subject to a certain amount of error.

Summary

Interpolation method for obtaining any final irregular amortization payment when $\{A, R, i\}$ *are given and n is unknown in* $A = Ra_{\overline{n}|i}$:

I. *Obtain* $a_{\overline{n}|i} = W$, *where* $W = A/R$.

II. *Act* **AS IF** $a_{\overline{n}|i}$ *is defined for* **ALL VALUES*** *of n. Solve* $W = a_{\overline{n}|i}$ *by interpolation in Table* VIII *to obtain* $n = k + h$, *where k is an integer and* $0 < h < 1$.

III. *The final payment* H *is due at the end of* $(k + 1)$ *periods, and* $H = \$hR$.

Example 1. Find the final payment H in Example 1 of Section 36 by interpolation.

SOLUTION. 1. We have $\qquad a_{\overline{n}|.025} = 7.333333$.

The following data are from Table VIII.

	n	$a_{\overline{n}|.025}$
	8	7.170137
	n	7.333333
	9	7.970866

(with bracket annotations: h and 1 on the left; $.163196$ and $.800729$ on the right)

2. By linear interpolation, $\qquad \dfrac{h}{1} = \dfrac{163{,}196}{800{,}729} = .203809$.

Hence, $n = 8.203809$. The last regular payment of \$1200 is made at the end of 8 periods. The final payment is

$$\$H = \$1200h = \$(1200)(.203809) = \$244.57.$$

In order to prove the fact stated in the preceding summary, we shall need an expression for $(a_{\overline{k+1}|i} - a_{\overline{k}|i})$, obtained as follows. From (6) on page 64,

$$a_{\overline{k}|i} = (1 + i)^{-1} + (1 + i)^{-2} + \cdots + (1 + i)^{-k};$$

$$a_{\overline{k+1}|i} = (1 + i)^{-1} + (1 + i)^{-2} + \cdots + (1 + i)^{-k} + (1 + i)^{-(k+1)}.$$

Hence, $\qquad a_{\overline{k+1}|i} - a_{\overline{k}|i} = (1 + i)^{-(k+1)}.$ \hfill (1)

We have not given any meaning to $a_{\overline{n}|i}$ when n is *not* an integer. However, assume that $\{R, A, i\}$ are known, and that the equation $A = Ra_{\overline{n}|i}$, or $a_{\overline{n}|i} = W$ where $W = A/R$, is not true for *any* integer n. Suppose that

$$a_{\overline{k}|i} < W < a_{\overline{k+1}|i},$$

* The function of n represented by $a_{\overline{n}|i}$ is defined only when n is a *positive integer*.

where k is an integer. Assume that we apply linear interpolation in a column of values of $a_{\overline{n}i}$, as in Table VIII, to solve $W = a_{\overline{n}i}$ for n, and obtain $n = k + h$. The process is equivalent to defining $a_{\overline{k+h}i}$ by the following equation (3). It is obtained as usual from an interpolation table (we omit i temporarily):

$$(a_{\overline{k+1}} - a_{\overline{k}}) \left[(W - a_{\overline{k}}) \left[\begin{array}{c|c} a_{\overline{n}} & n \\ \hline a_{\overline{k}} & k \\ \hline W & k + h \\ \hline a_{\overline{k+1}} & k + 1 \end{array} \right] h \right] 1$$

$$\frac{W - a_{\overline{k}}}{a_{\overline{k+1}} - a_{\overline{k}}} = \frac{h}{1}, \quad \text{or} \quad W - a_{\overline{k}} = h(a_{\overline{k+1}} - a_{\overline{k}}). \tag{2}$$

Or, on using $W = a_{\overline{k+h}}$, we define $a_{\overline{k+h}}$ as follows:

$$W = a_{\overline{k+h}} = a_{\overline{k}} + h(a_{\overline{k+1}} - a_{\overline{k}}). \tag{3}$$

Recall that $W = A/R$ and use (1) in (3). Also multiply all of the equal expressions by R. Then

$$A = Ra_{\overline{k+h}i}, \quad \text{or} \quad A = Ra_{\overline{k}i} + hR(1 + i)^{-(k+1)}. \tag{4}$$

In (4) we have justified the following conclusion.

Let $\{R, A, i\}$ be given and assume that $A = Ra_{\overline{n}i}$ is not satisfied by any integer n. Suppose that the solution of $A = Ra_{\overline{n}i}$ by interpolation in Table VIII is $n = k + h$, where k is an integer and $0 < h < 1$. Then(4) is true, or A is the present value of an annuity of R per period for k periods plus the present value of a payment $H = hR$ at the end of $(k + 1)$ periods.

The statement above justifies the preceding Summary.

Exercise 26

In each problem, assume that the final payment occurs one payment interval after the last regular payment unless otherwise specified. In finding any final irregular payment, use an equation of value as in Example 2 on page 100, inless the instructor directs use of the interpolation method. In any case, it would be instructive to check by use of both methods in a few problems.

1. A debt of \$10,000, with interest at 5% payable annually, will be discharged, interest included, by payments of \$2000 at the end of each year as long as necessary. Construct the amortization schedule.
2. Without using the amortization schedule in Problem 1, (a) find the

outstanding principal just after the 3rd payment; (b) find the final payment and when it is due.

3. A debt of $20,000, with interest at 6% payable semiannually, will be discharged, interest included, by payments of $3000 at the end of each 6 months as long as necessary. (a) Find the outstanding principal at the beginning of the 3rd year. (b) Find the final payment.

4. A man receives a loan of $2000 from a bank to make possible his purchase of a new automobile. He agrees to pay $70 at the end of each month as long as necessary to discharge the debt, interest included at 12% payable monthly on any unpaid balance. (a) What is the remaining principal unpaid just after his 7th payment? (b) How much of his 8th payment is interest and how much is a repayment of principal? (c) Find his final payment and when it is due.

5. A bank has granted a $2000 home improvement loan to a man, who agrees to pay $80 at the end of each month as long as necessary to pay all principal and interest at the rate 15% payable monthly. (a) What is his remaining liability just after his 4th payment? (b) How much principal does he repay on the 5th payment date? (c) Find his final payment and when it is due.

6. A man buys a house worth $26,000 cash, with the agreement to pay $6000 cash and $200 at the end of each month as long as necessary to discharge all liability, with interest payable monthly at the rate 7.5%. (a) Find the remaining liability just after the 35th payment. (b) How much interest is paid at the end of 3 years? (c) Find the final payment and when it is due.

7. A debt, with interest at 4% payable annually, will be discharged, interest included, by payments of $750 at the end of each year for 14 years. How much interest is paid at the end of 10 years?

8. The bill for a purchase of draperies is $1400. The buyer will pay $100, including interest at 18% payable monthly on the unpaid balance, at the end of each month as long as necessary. (a) Find the final payment and when it is due. (b) Obtain the total interest paid by the buyer in retiring his debt.

9. A man has an automobile which is 2 years old, with a Blue Book listed value of $3000. With this age, a bank in 1974 is willing to lend up to 90% of the Blue Book value. The man obtains a loan of $2500. He will pay $125 at the end of each month as long as necessary to pay principal and interest payable monthly at the rate 12%. (a) Find the principal remaining unpaid just after the 10th monthly payment; (b) find the final payment and when it is due; (c) obtain the total interest paid in discharging the debt.

10. In purchasing a house worth $35,000 cash, a man pays $5000 cash and agrees to discharge the balance by payments of $3000 at the end of each year as long as necessary. These payments include interest at 8% payable annually. How much interest and how much principal does he pay at the end of 5 years?

11. The outstanding principal of a debt now is $9350.40, just after a payment by the debtor, and interest is payable annually at the rate 6%. The debtor is discharging his debt by payments of $1100 at the end of each year as long as necessary. (*a*) Make up the amortization schedule for the next two years to find how much interest is paid two years from today. (*b*) Find the final payment and when it is due without making up an amortization schedule.

★12. A farm is worth $14,000 cash. The buyer pays $3000 cash and agrees to pay $2000 at the end of 1 year, $2500 at the end of 2 years, and $1000 at the end of each year thereafter as long as necessary to discharge all liability, with interest at 5% payable annually. (*a*) Find the unpaid principal just after the 4th payment of $1000. (*b*) Find the final payment and when it is due.

38. Sinking Funds

If an individual or corporation foresees the necessity of making a large payment at some future date, business prudence leads to the formation of a *fund*, probably by periodic deposits, to insure the accumulation of money to provide for the payment. Such a fund will be called a **sinking fund**. Its purpose may be to repay the principal of a loan in one installment, or to provide for replacement or modernization of a manufacturing plant, or for expansion of a business, etc. Unless something is said to the contrary, we shall assume that any sinking fund considered is created by investing equal periodic payments. Then the amount in the fund at any time is *the amount of the annuity formed by the payments*. On any payment date, the increase which occurs in the fund is *the sum of the new payment and interest on the previous balance in the fund.*

Example 1. A fund is being created by annual deposits of $250 invested at 3%. (*a*) Find the amount in the fund just after the 4th deposit. (*b*) What increase occurs in the fund on the 5th payment date?

SOLUTION. 1. Amount just after the 4th deposit is $250s_{\overline{4}|.03} = \$1045.907$.

2. The increase on the day of the 5th deposit is the difference between the amounts in the fund just after the 5th and the 4th deposits:

Amount just after 5th *deposit is* $250s_{\overline{5}|.03} = \$1327.284$.

Increase on 5th *deposit date is* $1327.284 - 1045.907 = \$281.377$.

CHECK. Also, the increase is equal to the interest for one year on $1045.907, or $31.377, plus the 5th payment, or $(31.377 + 250.000) = \$281.377$. The following table shows how the fund accumulates.

Table Showing Growth of Sinking Fund

Payment Interval	In Fund at Beginning of Interval	Interest at 3% Received on Fund at End of Interval	Payment to Fund at End of Interval	In Fund at End of Interval
1	0.000	0.000	$250	$ 250.000
2	$ 250.000	$ 7.500	250	507.500
3	507.500	15.225	250	772.725
4	772.725	23.182	250	1045.907
5	1045.907	31.377	250	1327.284

Example 2. A fund is being created by annual deposits of $500 invested at 6%. (*a*) When will the fund first exceed $9000? (*b*) What additional payment would be needed to complete a fund of exactly $9000 on the day when the last full deposit of $500 is required?

SOLUTION. 1. If n is an integer and n annual deposits of $500 would create a fund of $9000, then $9000 = 500s_{\overline{n}|.06}$; hence $s_{\overline{n}|.06} = 18$.

2. From the 6% column in Table VII, $s_{\overline{12}|} < 18$ and $s_{\overline{13}|} > 18$. Hence, without interpolation, we see that the fund never will contain exactly $9000 on an interest date. The fund will contain more than $9000 just after the 13th regular deposit, if it is made.

3. From Table VII,

amount in fund just after 12th *deposit is* $500s_{\overline{12}|.06} = \$8434.97$.

Additional deposit to complete fund of $9000 *on* 12th *payment date is*

$$(9000 - 8434.97), \quad or \quad \$565.03.$$

Example 3. A man will accumulate a fund to provide for purchasing an automobile worth $5000 cash at the end of three years, instead of asking for a loan on the new car at the usual high rate of 12%. He deposits $1000 in his fund immediately, and will place equal deposits in it at the end of each 3 months for 3 years. If the fund is invested with a savings and loan association paying $\{5\%, m = 4\}$, find the quarterly deposit if the fund is to contain $5000 at the end of 3 years.

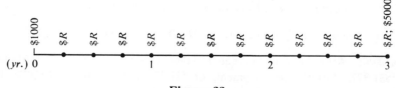

Figure 23

SOLUTION. Observe the time scale in Figure 23 where R is the periodic deposit. The following table of equivalent obligations, and Figure 23, are the basis for writing the associated equation of value with *the end of 3 years as the comparison date.*

Fund	Equivalent Deposits
$5000 *at end* 3 *years*	(*a*) $1000 *immediately*
	(*b*) $$R *at end of each* 3 *mo. for* 3 *yr.*

$$5000 = 1000(1.0125)^{12} + Rs_{\overline{12}|.0125}.$$

$$Rs_{\overline{12}|.0125} = 5000 - 1000(1.0125)^{12} = 3839.245.$$

$$R = 3839.245 \frac{1}{s_{\overline{12}|.0125}};$$

$$R = 3839.245(.09025831 - .0125) = \$298.54. \qquad \text{(Table IX)}$$

Exercise 27

1. A fund is being created by investing $500 at the end of each 6 months at 4.5% compounded semiannually. (*a*) How much is in the fund just after the 4th deposit? (*b*) Form a table showing the growth of the fund over $2\frac{1}{2}$ years.

2. A young man decides that he must have $8000 at the end of three years in order to make possible two years of college education. If he can invest at 5% compounded monthly, how much must he place in his fund at the end of each month?

3. In order to provide $20,000 for the replacement of a machine at the end of 3 years, a corporation will place equal deposits in a fund at the end of each 3 months. Find the periodic deposit if the money is invested at 5% compounded quarterly.

4. In order to modernize a factory at the end of 5 years at a cost of $500,000, a corporation will form a sinking fund by equal deposits at the end of each 6 months. Find the periodic deposit if the money is invested at 6.5% compounded semiannually.

5. In discharging a debt, a man foresees the necessity of paying $10,000 at the end of 6 years. To provide this money, he will create a sinking fund by investing equal deposits at the end of each month, at 7.5% compounded monthly. Find the monthly deposit.

6. A depreciation fund, to replace machinery, will be accumulated by investing $5000 at the end of each year for 9 years, at 4% effective. (*a*) How

much is in the fund just after the 6th deposit? (b) How much new interest is added to the fund at the end of 7 years? (c) Find the increase which occurs in the fund at the end of 7 years.

7. How much must be deposited in a fund at the end of each month for 15 years to accumulate $20,000 by the end of that time if money is worth $\{.06, m = 12\}$?

8. Deposits of $500 will be invested annually at 6%. How much new interest is added to the fund on the day of the 7th deposit?

9. Deposits of $1000 will be invested at 4% at the beginning of each year. How much is in the fund just after the 8th deposit? (The beginning of any year is the same instant as the end of the preceding year.)

10. In order to pay off the principal of a $5000 loan as soon as possible, a man will invest $100 at the end of each month at 5% compounded monthly. On what date will he first be able to pay the $5000 and what will he have to add to the fund on that day?

11. A man will invest $250 at the end of each 3 months at 5% compounded quarterly in order to provide $5000 for the purchase of an automobile for cash. On what date will he first be able to make the purchase, and what payment, if any, to his fund will be necessary to complete it on that date?

12. A fund is being created by investing $1000 at the end of each year at 6%. Find the date on which the fund first will exceed $26,500, and what payment, if any, will be needed to complete a fund of exactly $26,500 (a) on that date; (b) just after the preceding payment date.

13. A man has $2000 in his passbook account at a savings and loan association. He will make equal deposits in the fund at the end of each 3 months in order to have $6000 to his credit at the end of 4 years. Find his quarterly deposit if the association pays interest at the rate 5% compounded quarterly.

14. If money is worth $\{.06, m = 12\}$, what payment at the end of each year would be just as satisfactory as (a) $100 payable at the end of each month; (b) $100 payable at the beginning of each month for the year?

15. If money is worth $\{.07, m = 4\}$, what payment at the end of each year would be just as satisfactory as $200 payable (a) at the end of each 3 months; (b) at the beginning of each 3 months of the year?

16. At what nominal rate compounded monthly will investment of $100 at the beginning of each month for 5 years accumulate a fund of $6700 at the end of 5 years?

17. At what rate compounded quarterly will payments of $200 at the end of each 3 months accumulate a fund of $6000 by the end of 6 years?

18. Find the amount in a fund at the end of 15 years if the fund is invested at 5% compounded annually, and $500 is deposited in the fund at the end of each year for 10 years. (Insert fictitious deposits at the end of each of the last 5 years and write an equation of value at the end of 15 years.)

19. An investment of $20,000 in a mine will yield a 5% dividend at the end of each year, and the investor will reinvest all dividends at 3%. At the end of 12 years, after receiving a dividend, he sells his share of the mine for $20,000. How much does he have on hand as a result of his original investment?

★**20.** Suppose that a principal P is invested for n years (or, periods) with interest payable at the rate i at the end of each year, and that the investor can reinvest all interest at the rate r per year. (*a*) Find the resulting amount at the end of n years. (*b*) If $i = .035$ and $r = .055$, what principal must be invested in order to have $5000 at the end of 16 years?

COMMENT. The result for (*a*) in Problem 20 may be called the *generalized compound amount* when the reinvestment rate is not assumed to be the rate earned by the original principal.

39. Sinking Fund Method for Retiring a Debt

Some of the enormous long-term loans used in the financing of modern business are in the form of issues of bonds, which will be considered in the next chapter. Other long term loans may be payable in installments, just as is the case of loans of smaller size such as mortgages on homes, or loans for purchases by consumers.

Sometimes the principal of a loan may be payable all in one installment, with the interest payable periodically as due. If the principal of such a loan is large, the creditor probably is certain that the debtor corporation, or individual, has such a good credit rating that no precautions need be taken to be certain that the principal will be paid at maturity. Or, the debtor might merely ask to have the loan renewed for a given length of time when the principal falls due.

Suppose, now, that a corporation K borrows A from a bank B with interest payable at the rate i per period, and that the principal A is due in one install-ment at the end of n periods. Suppose that K generates surplus funds in profits. Then it is possible for K to withdraw money periodically from its working capital in order to accumulate a sinking fund, designed to contain A for payment of the debt when the principal falls due. Or, in extreme cases, if the creditor B feels it essential to have assurance of the payment of A, then B might require K to accumulate the sinking fund just mentioned. If either one of the preceding two cases occurs, then it is said that the corporation K is retiring its debt by the *sinking fund method*. This procedure is not common currently in the business world and hence will be emphasized only moderately in future problems.

A borrower K of a moderate sum, as a matter of financial prudence, might voluntarily accumulate a sinking fund to contain the principal when it is due, if it is to be paid in one installment. However, the typical loan of moderate size to an individual, and the typical mortgage, is discharged by the *amortization method*, as considered earlier in this chapter. The data for retirement of a debt by a sinking fund method is as follows.

I. *A creditor B loans $A to a debtor K who agrees to pay interest at the rate i per interest period on $A for n periods, and to pay $A in one installment at the end of n periods.*

II. *The debtor K will accumulate a sinking fund to contain $A at the end of n periods by investing equal deposits in the fund at the end of each period, with the fund earning interest at the rate r per period.*

In II, it is not assumed that $r = i$, the rate mentioned in I. When the preceding sinking fund method is used, we define the **book value** of the debtor's debt at any time as $A minus the sum in the sinking fund. That is, the debtor K owes $A but has $S in his fund, so that the net indebtedness in his bookkeeping is ($A − S), now being called the *book value* of the debt. The conditions of II will apply whenever we mention a sinking fund for retiring a debt.

Example 1. A debt of $10,000 is contracted with the agreement that interest shall be paid semiannually at the rate 6%, and that the principal shall be paid in one installment at the end of $2\frac{1}{2}$ years. (*a*) Under the sinking fund method, what is the semiannual expense of the debt if the debtor invests his fund at 4% compounded semiannually? (*b*) Find the book value of the debt just after the 4th deposit in the fund. (*c*) Find the semiannual expense of the debt if it were to be discharged, principal and interest included at 6% payable semiannually, by equal payments at the end of each 6 months for $2\frac{1}{2}$ years.

SOLUTION. 1. Let R be the semiannual deposit in the sinking fund. The amount in the fund at the end of $2\frac{1}{2}$ years should be $10,000. From $S = Rs_{\overline{n}|}$ with $S = \$10,000$,

$$10,000 = Rs_{\overline{5}|.02}; \qquad R = \frac{10,000}{s_{\overline{5}|.02}} = \$1921.584. \qquad \text{(Table IX)}$$

2. Interest payable semiannually to the creditor is (10,000)(.03) or $300. Hence, the semiannual expense of the debt is $1921.58 + 300 = \$2221.58$.

3. Just after the 4th deposit, the fund contains $1921.584 s_{\overline{4}|.02} = \$7920.02$; the book value of the debt is $10,000 − 7920.02 = \$2079.98$.

4. If H is the semiannual amortization payment, at 6% payable semiannually, then

$$10,000 = Ha_{\overline{5}|.03}; \qquad H = 10,000\,\frac{1}{a_{\overline{5}|.03}} = \$2183.55.$$

Observe that H is *less* than the expense $2221.58 in Step 2 above. We shall investigate this fact below.

If the sinking fund method is used for the data described in {I, II}, the periodic interest is Ai. The periodic deposit R for the sinking fund satisfies $A = Rs_{\overline{n}|r}$, or $R = A/s_{\overline{n}|r}$. Hence, the periodic expense E_1 is $(A + R)$, or

$$\left\{\begin{array}{c}\textbf{expense, sinking}\\ \textbf{fund method}\end{array}\right\} \qquad E_1 = Ai + \frac{A}{s_{\overline{n}|r}}. \qquad (1)$$

If a debt of $\$A$ is *amortized* at the interest rate i per period by equal payments at the end of each period for n periods, the periodic expense E_2 satisfies the equation $A = E_2 a_{\overline{n}|i}$, or

$$\textbf{(amortization expense)} \qquad E_2 = A\left(\frac{1}{a_{\overline{n}|i}}\right). \qquad (2)$$

Since $\dfrac{1}{a_{\overline{n}|i}} = i + \dfrac{1}{s_{\overline{n}|i}}$ $\qquad E_2 = Ai + \dfrac{A}{s_{\overline{n}|i}}. \qquad (3)$

Compare (1) and (3). If $r < i$ then $s_{\overline{n}|r} < s_{\overline{n}|i}$, because *amounts* at compound interest *increase* when the interest rate *increases*. Hence,

if $r < i$ *then* $\qquad \dfrac{1}{s_{\overline{n}|i}} < \dfrac{1}{s_{\overline{n}|r}} \qquad$ *and thus* $\qquad E_2 < E_1$.

Similarly, if $r > i$ then $E_1 < E_2$. Suppose that $r = i$; then E_1 in (1) and E_2 in (3) are the same. Thus we have established the following results.

Let i and r be the interest rates on the debt and the sinking fund, respectively. If the expense of discharging a debt by the sinking fund method is E_1, and by the amortization method is E_2, then the following facts are true.

$$E_1 = E_2 \text{ if } i = r; \quad E_1 > E_2 \text{ if } r < i; \quad E_1 < E_2 \text{ if } r > i. \qquad (4)$$

In case a corporation K is accumulating a sinking fund at a rate r to repay a debt which bears interest at a rate i, it might be possible for K to find means for investment where $r > i$. Then, by (4), the periodic expense of the debt for K would be *less* than the cost with amortization at the rate i. However, if business prudence is the main feature which leads K to accumulate a sinking fund, it is sensible to assume that K will seek such a safe form of investment for the sinking fund that its rate of investment r will be *less* than i. Hence, the natural expectation when method {I, II} is in use will be that $r < i$ and thus, by (4), the expense of the sinking fund method will be greater than the corresponding expense if the debt were to be amortized.

NOTE 1. We may refer to Table IX for $1/a_n$ as a table of *amortization charges* for a debt of $\$1$. A table for $1/s_{\overline{n}|}$ would give *sinking fund charges* for a debt of $\$1$.

Exercise 28

1. The principal of a debt of $10,000 will be paid at the end of 8 years by the accumulation of a sinking fund by quarterly deposits, and interest will be payable on the debt quarterly at the rate 6.5%. Find the quarterly expense of the debt to the debtor if his sinking fund is invested at (a) {3%, $m = 4$}; (b) {6.5%, $m = 4$}; (c) {8%, $m = 4$}. Notice which method is best for the debtor.

2. A loan of $5000 bears interest at 8% payable semiannually, and the debtor will create a sinking fund by semiannual payments to repay the principal in one installment at the end of 6 years. Find the debtor's semiannual expense if his fund is invested at {5%, $m = 2$}.

3. A loan of $80,000 is made with interest payable semiannually at the rate 7%. Find the semiannual expense of the debt to the debtor (a) if he discharges all liability as to principal and interest by paying his creditor equal sums at the end of each 6 months for 7 years; (b) if he pays interest as due and accumulates a sinking fund to pay the principal at the end of 7 years, with the fund invested at 4.5% compounded semiannually.

4. A loan of $15,000 bears interest at 7% payable semiannually. The debtor will accumulate a sinking fund by investing $1000 at the end of each six months at 5% compounded semiannually. He will pay the principal of the loan in one installment on the first interest date when his sinking fund contains at least $15,000. (a) When will he pay the principal? (b) Find the book value of his indebtedness at the end of 6 years. (c) Obtain the periodic expense of the debt.

5. A debt of $20,000 bears interest payable annually. The principal will be paid at the end of 10 years by the accumulation of a sinking fund by equal deposits at the end of each year invested at 5%. If the annual expense of the debt is $2900, find the rate at which interest is paid on the debt.

6. A corporation is offered a loan of $50,000 with interest at 7%, provided the debt is retired, principal and interest included, by equal payments at the end of each year for 5 years. Or, the loan can be obtained with 8% interest payable annually, if the corporation will pay all principal in one installment at the end of 5 years; in this case, the corporation would accumulate a sinking fund at 5% to pay the principal at the end of 5 years. How much does the corporation save annually by choosing the cheaper method?

7. A city issues $1,000,000 of tax exempt bonds paying 4.5% interest annually, and is required by law to create a sinking fund to retire the bonds at the end of 11 years. If the fund is invested at 6%, find the book value of the city's indebtedness at the beginning of the 6th year.

8. A debt of $10,000, with interest at $6\frac{1}{2}$% payable semiannually, will be discharged by the sinking fund method with the principal payable at the

end of 6 years. By interpolation find the rate at which the sinking fund accumulates if the semiannual expense of the debt is $1055.

9. A man borrows $6000, with interest payable semiannually at the rate 6%, and the principal must be paid in one installment on some interest date. He can invest a sinking fund at 5% compounded semiannually, and has $425 available at the end of each 6 months to provide for interest and a sinking fund. When will he first be able to pay the principal?

10. A debt of $100,000, with interest payable annually at the rate 7% will be retired at the end of 10 years through the accumulation of a sinking fund invested at 6%. At what rate of interest could the debtor just as well agree to pay off his debt by equal payments, including all interest and principal, at the end of each year for 10 years? (We call the result the *equivalent amortization rate.*)

HINT. The annual expense is found to be $14,586.80. If i is the equivalent amortization rate, then $100,000 = 14,586.80a_{\overline{10}|i}$.

(divide by $100,000a_{\overline{10}|i}$) $$\frac{1}{a_{\overline{10}|i}} = .1458680.$$

Solve for i by interpolation in Table IX.

11. A man can invest a sinking fund at 5%. He is offered a loan of $50,000, with interest at 6% payable annually, if he agrees to pay the principal in one installment at the end of 8 years. At what rate could he just as well afford to borrow if he were allowed to extinguish the debt, interest included, by equal payments at the end of each year for 8 years?

12. From one source a man can borrow $9000, with interest at 6.5% payable semiannually, and all principal due at the end of 6 years; he would accumulate a sinking fund at $\{.05, m = 2\}$ to pay the principal. He can borrow from another source, with an agreement to discharge the debt, interest included, by equal payments at the end of each 6 months for 6 years. Find the equivalent amortization rate.

40. Approximate Amortization Rate

Suppose that a debt of A is to be discharged, interest included, by an annuity of n payments of R each, as described in (2) on page 95. Then the interest rate i per payment interval satisfies the equation $A = Ra_{\overline{n}|i}$. Without the use of annuity tables, the method of the following Summary frequently gives a useful approximation to the value of i. The good sense of the method can be checked by reference to the amortization schedule on page 93. In that case, notice that the first payment is composed heavily of interest. The last payment consists largely of principal. Example 1 on page 92 is used below as a basis for the first illustration of the following method.

Summary

Approximation to an amortization rate:

I. *Compute the average interest paid per payment interval:*

$$(total\ interest) = nR - A; \qquad (average\ int.\ per\ payt.\ interval) = \frac{nR - A}{n}.$$

II. *Assume that the last payment R is wholly principal; then the outstanding principal during the 1st period is A and during the last period is R:*

$$(average\ outstanding\ principal) = \frac{A + R}{2}.$$

III. *An approximation to the interest rate i per payment interval is**

$$i = \frac{\text{average interest per payment interval}}{\text{average outstanding principal}}. \tag{1}$$

Example 1. A debt of $15,000 will be discharged, with interest payable annually, by payments of $3465 at the end of each year for 5 years. Find an approximate value for the interest rate.

SOLUTION. 1. Each payment involves both interest and principal:

$$(total\ payments) = 5(3465) = \$17{,}325;$$

$$(total\ principal\ repaid) = \$15{,}000;$$

$$(total\ interest\ paid\ in\ 5\ years) = 17{,}325 - 15{,}000 = \$2325;$$

$$(average\ annual\ interest) = \tfrac{1}{5}(2325) = \$465.$$

2. Let us assume (contrary to fact) that the *whole* of the last payment is principal. Then, the outstanding principal is $15,000 in the 1st year and $3465 in the 5th year. Hence, approximately,

$$(average\ outst.\ principal) = \frac{15{,}000 + 3465}{2} = \$9232.$$

3. An approximate value for the interest rate is

$$i = \frac{average\ annual\ interest}{average\ outstanding\ principal} = \frac{465}{9232} = 5.04\%. \tag{2}$$

We conclude that the rate i is close to 5.0%. We would not be justified in making a more exact statement. Compare with Example 1, page 92.

---

* By use of Taylor's Theorem from calculus, it can be proved that the error of (1) is approximately $(n - 4)i^2/6$, where i is the exact rate.

COMMENT.   See the footnote on page 114. In Example 1, $(n - 4)i^2/6$ becomes $(.05)^2/6 = .0025/6$, or .0004, approximately. This is exactly the error in (2) as compared to the correct interest rate.

41.   The True Interest Rate for a Consumer Debt

A large part of sales at retail involve installment contracts, of a type where the purchaser makes a cash payment, and agrees to discharge his remaining liability by a sequence of future payments. We shall assume that they are of equal size and occur at equal intervals of time. The typical contract thus involves an original liability $A of the purchaser after he makes his down payment, and a set of future payments of $R each, forming an *ordinary annuity* with a term of n payment intervals. Then, the *true interest rate i* per payment interval which is paid by the purchaser is that rate at which *the payments of $R each will pay all interest as due and also pay off the original liability $A in installments.* From (2) on page 95 we conclude that $A = Ra_{\overline{n}|i}$, or that *the payments amortize the original debt.* Thus, with R, n, and A given, i can be found very closely by interpolation if Table VIII applies. For the typical installment contract, where the payments extend over a relatively short period of time, the method of Section 40 gives an approximation to the true interest rate without use of an annuity table.

The preceding discussion also applies to the discharge of loans obtained from small loan agencies, banks, automobile financing companies, and so on.

When money is loaned for any purpose, including consumer loans of the variety just described, the federal Truth in Lending Act of 1968 now applies (abbreviated "T.L. Act" hereafter). This excellent law for protection of the borrower requires the lender to tell him in simple language the true interest rate i at which the periodic payments R satisfy the amortization equation $A = Ra_{\overline{n}|i}$. Naturally, the technical language of this text about annuities and the amortization process would not be used in the typical promissory note which would be the basis for any loan. The method would be described in the simple but equivalent language of "*interest payable periodically,*" as in (2) on page 95 . Or, the lender might present the borrower with an amortization schedule showing how the payments discharge all interest and principal as due.

A loan agreement may specify various charges, which are confusing to the uninformed borrower. He should be alert to focus on the following simple features:

I. *How much money, or its equivalent in the cost of goods, is received on the date of the loan?*

II. *What payments are to be made?*

III. *What is the true interest rate on any unpaid principal (this information now required of every lender)?*

With information {I, II, III} available, anybody who knows arithmetic and is acquainted with simple interest could make up an amortization table for himself, even though this name for the table would not be known to him.

Example 1. The buyer of a used automobile, listed at $900, makes a cash payment of $200 and signs a contract with the following terms: a "*carrying charge*" of $50 is added by the seller to cover incidentals; the resulting "*liability*" is $750; the buyer agrees to make payments of $50 at the end of each month for 15 months. Find the nominal rate at which the buyer pays interest monthly.

SOLUTION. 1. *By interpolation.* On the date of purchase, the buyer's remaining liability *actually* is $700, and he agrees to pay an annuity of $50 per month for 15 months. The true interest rate i per month satisfies $700 = 50a_{\overline{15}|i}$ or $a_{\overline{15}|i} = 14$. By interpolation in Table VIII, $i = \frac{7}{8}\%$, approximately; the nominal rate, $12i$, is $10\frac{1}{2}\%$.

2. By use of Section 40, we proceed as follows.

(*Total payments*) = 15(50) = 750.

(*Total principal repaid*) = 700.

(*Total interest paid*) = 50.

(*Average monthly interest*) = (50/15) = (10/3).

(*Outstanding principal in* 1*st mo.*) = 700.

(*Outstanding principal in last mo.*) $\doteq$ 50.

(*Average outstanding principal*) $\doteq \frac{1}{2}(700 + 50) = 375$.

$$(\textit{Approximate int. rate per mo.}) = \frac{10/3}{375} = \frac{10}{1125} = i.$$

$$(\textit{Annual interest rate}) \doteq 12i = \frac{120}{1125} = .10\frac{2}{3} = 10\frac{2}{3}\%.$$

Before the T.L. Act was passed by Congress, a deceptive form of statement, as in the next example, was common in the description of charges on small loans. The method was called the ADD-ON system. Our reason for considering this former method is met later.

Example 2. A bank B offers a $2000 loan on a new automobile, with equal payments required at the end of each month for 36 months. (*Old form of charges follows.*) B states that 6% interest ADD-ON will be charged. Find the true rate of interest payable monthly which is being charged.

SOLUTION. 1. *Computation of the monthly payment.* The creditor B computes 6% simple interest for 3 years on $2000, obtaining $360; B ADDS-ON this $360 to $2000 and obtains $2360; then B computes (2360/36) = $65.555. This is specified as the payment which must be made by the debtor at the end of each month for 36 months.

2. *To find the true amortization rate.* Let i be the interest rate per month. The nominal rate will be $12i$. Then,

$$2000 = 65.56a_{\overline{36}|i}; \qquad \frac{65.56}{2000} = \frac{1}{a_{\overline{36}|i}} = .03278. \qquad (1)$$

We prefer to divide as above to simplify the arithmetic. Division by 65.56 would lead to interpolation in Table VIII. By interpolation in Table IX, with .03278 bracketted by the values of $1/a_{\overline{36}|i}$ for $\frac{7}{8}\%$ and 1%, from (1) we obtain

$$i \doteq \tfrac{7}{8}\% + \frac{28}{71} \cdot \tfrac{1}{8}\%; \qquad j \doteq 12i = 10.5\% + .6\% = 11.1\% = \textit{nominal rate.}$$

Hence, the "6% rate" was purely fictitious and unrelated to the true interest rate, 11.1%. This fact, and other similar practices, were primary reasons for passage of the T.L. Act.

The description of payments as in Example 2 NO LONGER MAY BE USED. However, a lender B may continue to use the add-on device* in computing charges, because of its simplicity. Then, however, B merely should tell the borrower the periodic charge and the nominal rate of interest which is being included monthly on all principal remaining unpaid.

Exercise 29

When an approximate result is requested, use the method of Section 40. *When a solution by interpolation is required, sometimes it is more convenient numerically to interpolate in Table* IX *rather than in Table* VIII.

1. A buyer purchases a refrigerator and a garbage disposal unit with a total value of $1100. He signs a promissory note requiring the payment of $100 at the end of each month for one year. Find approximately the nominal rate at which interest is included, payable monthly on any unpaid balance.
2. In purchasing furniture worth $2000 cash, a buyer pays $500 cash, and contracts to pay $96 at the end of each month for 18 months. Find approximately the nominal rate at which the buyer pays interest at the end of each month on the outstanding principal of his debt in the preceding month.
3. A dealer in used cars tells a customer that the cash price of a certain car is $1025 and that the "time" price is $1200, payable without added interest by installments of $75 at the end of each month for 16 months. In spite of absence of mention of an interest rate, at what nominal rate does the buyer pay interest in taking the car at the "time" price? (*a*) Solve by the approximate method. (*b*) Solve by interpolation.

---

* In 1974, various prominent banks and other lending agencies used this method to compute charges for loans of various types. This accounts for the strangely uneven interest rates such as 11.08%, 11.93%, and so on, which were available on loans of various sorts in 1974.

4. A bank B grants a loan of 70% of the cost of a new automobile. The debtor agrees to make equal payments, including all interest payable monthly on unpaid principal, at the end of each month for 24 months. The bank will use the add-on method at 6% in computing the monthly payment. (*a*) Find the required payment for a $3000 loan. (*b*) Find approximately the nominal rate at which B must inform the debtor that he is paying interest each month (on account of the T.L. Act). (*c*) Also find the rate by interpolation in Table IX.

5. A bank B grants a $4000 home improvement loan to a man. The loan will be repaid by equal payments of R at the end of each month for 4 years. (*a*) If B computes R by using the add-on method at $7\frac{3}{4}$%, find R. (*b*) By the approximate method, find the nominal rate which B will state in the contract as the rate at which each installment R pays interest for the preceding month on all unpaid principal of the loan. (*c*) Solve for the rate by interpolation in Table IX.

6. A bank will use the add-on method at 7% to compute the monthly payment for a $1000 loan which the borrower will discharge by payments at the end of each month for (*a*) 12 months; (*b*) 24 months; (*c*) 36 months. For each case find the monthly payment and, approximately, the nominal rate at which the borrower pays interest monthly on all unpaid principal.

Exercise 30 | *Review of Chapter 4*

1. A debt is being discharged, interest included at 6% payable semiannually, by payments of $1000 at the end of each 6 months. At the beginning of the 3rd year, the outstanding principal is $22,050.75. Make up the amortization schedule for the next year. How much principal is paid at the end of that year?

2. A debt will be discharged, interest included at 8% payable quarterly, by payments of $1100 at the end of each 3 months for 10 years. (*a*) Find the outstanding principal at the beginning of the 4th year. (*b*) What part of the 13th payment is interest?

3. A man borrows $12,000 with interest at 7% payable annually. He agrees to discharge the debt, interest included, by paying $1000 at the end of each year as long as necessary. When is the last $1000 payment due, and what payment closes the transaction one year later?

4. In Problem 3, find the outstanding principal just after the 4th payment of $1000.

5. A house is worth $30,000 cash. A purchaser will pay $10,000 cash and will discharge the balance, interest included at the rate 8% payable quarterly, by equal payments at the end of each 3 months for 8 years. (*a*) Find the

quarterly payment. (*b*) What is the unpaid principal just after the 10th quarterly payment? (*c*) At the end of 5 years, the purchase contract is sold by the original creditor to a new investor, to whom money is worth 9% compounded quarterly. How much does he pay? Find results only to the nearest dollar.

6. A corporation can obtain a $50,000 loan with interest payable annually at the rate 7%. The creditor will require that a sinking fund be created by deposits of $5000 invested at the end of each year at 5%. The principal of the debt is to be repaid on the first date when the regular sinking fund deposit would cause the fund to exceed $50,000. (*a*) Find the annual expense of the debt. (*b*) Obtain the corporation's net indebtedness at the end of 3 years. (*c*) When will the corporation repay the principal?

7. A man obtains a $3000 loan from a bank which uses the add-on method at 7% in computing payments. He will discharge his debt by making equal payments, including interest on unpaid principal, at the end of each month for 18 months. (*a*) Find the monthly payment. Obtain the nominal rate at which he pays interest monthly (*b*) by the approximate method of Section 40; (*c*) by interpolation in Table IX.

8. At what interest rate payable quarterly will payments of $225 at the beginning of each 3 months for 6 years amortize a debt of $4680? Use interpolation.

9. A debt of $14,500, with interest at 7% payable monthly, will be amortized by equal payments at the beginning of each month for 9 years. Find the periodic payment.

10. A man buys a farm worth $25,000 cash. He pays $5000 cash and agrees to discharge the balance, with interest at 8% compounded semiannually, by a sequence of 12 equal semiannual payments, where the first one is due at the end of 3 years. Find the periodic payment.

11. To provide $200,000 for replacement of a machine at the end of 10 years, what equal deposits should a corporation invest at the end of each year in a depreciation fund which earns 5% compounded annually?

12. A man will accumulate a fund by deposits of $100 at the end of each month for three years in order to buy an automobile for cash at the end of that time. If the fund earns interest at the rate $\{5\%, m = 12\}$, how much will be in the fund (*a*) at the end of 15 months; (*b*) at the end of 3 years? (*c*) How much interest is added to the fund on the day of the 8th deposit?

13. In order to accumulate a fund of $100,000 needed for overhauling a factory, a corporation invests $10,000 at the end of each year at $5\frac{1}{2}\%$. On what date will the corporation first be able to begin the overhauling, and what smaller deposit completes the necessary fund on that date?

14. A sinking fund is being accumulated by the investment of $7000 at the end of each 6 months at 5% compounded semiannually. Just after the 6th deposit, how much larger is the fund than after the preceding deposit, and how much of this increase is due to new interest credited on the day of the 6th deposit?

15. A man obtains from a bank B a loan of $4000 which requires him to make equal payments at the end of each month for 3 years. The monthly payments are computed by the add-on method at $7\frac{3}{4}\%$, and include all interest payable monthly on unpaid principal. (a) Find the monthly payment. (b) By the approximate method of Section 40, and (c) by interpolation in Table IX, find the true interest rate payable monthly which is charged on the debt.

16. A debt of $10,000 will be paid, principal and interest payable annually included, by payments of $1000 at the end of each year for 16 years. Find the rate at which interest is charged by interpolation in Table VIII.

17. A man considers borrowing from a creditor who will demand that interest be paid annually at the rate 5%, and that the principal will be paid in one installment at the end of 12 years. In this case, the debtor would accumulate a sinking fund to pay the principal by investing equal annual deposits at 3%. Find the equivalent interest rate at which he could borrow with the agreement to amortize his debt by equal payments at the end of each year for 12 years. Use interpolation in Table IX.

★18. A man borrows $10,000 and agrees that interest shall be paid annually at the rate 7% for the first 5 years on all unpaid principal, and at the rate 6% for the next 10 years. What equal payments at the end of each year for 15 years will discharge his debt, interest included? (An equation of value with the end of 5 years as a comparison date would be useful.)

★19. A yacht is worth $20,000 cash. A buyer pays $4000 cash and agrees to pay $2000 at the end of 1 year, $3000 at the end of 2 years, and $1000 at the end of each year thereafter as long as necessary to discharge all liability, with interest at 5% payable annually. (a) Find the unpaid principal just after the 4th payment of $1000. (b) Find the final payment and when it is due. (Use an equation of value.)

5/ Bonds

42. Terminology for Bonds

A bond is a written contract by a debtor to pay a final **redemption value** $V on an indicated redemption date, or maturity date, and to pay a certain sum $K periodically. The typical bond mentions a borrowed principal $H, called the **face value** or **par value** of the bond, and describes the payments of $K as periodic payments of *interest* on $H at a specified nominal rate r, called the **bond rate**. In many cases, a small dated **coupon** is attached to the bond corresponding to each payment of $K. Any coupon thus is a contract to pay $K on a corresponding date. The owner of the bond cuts off each coupon when it becomes due, and presents it for payment through his bank. An abbreviated bond contract is shown on page 122. A bond is named after its face $H and bond rate r. For convenience, we shall talk as if the periodic payments of $K each on a bond always correspond to attached coupons. Then these payments will be referred to as the **coupon annuity**.

ILLUSTRATION 1.   For the bond on page 122, the face value is $H = \$1000$. The redemption value is $V = \$1000$, payable on the redemption date April 1, 1989. The bond rate is $r = .056$. Each coupon payment is 2.8% of $1000, or $K = \$28$, payable semiannually. This bond is a $1000, 5.6% bond. Since it is issued by a public agency of a state, the coupon payments of this bond would be exempt from Federal income tax. Also, as a rule, any state exempts from income tax the coupon payments of subdivisions or public agencies in the state. Thus this bond illustrates a tax-exempt bond. On account of the tax-exempt feature, the bond rates and (as discussed later) the yields to investors of tax-exempt bonds usually are less than those of bonds which are not tax-exempt. The tax-exempt bonds of one state are not exempt from income tax in other states.

Most bonds promise coupon payments semiannually and are redeemable at par, so that $V = H$. However, no inconvenience occurs in our future discussion if either of the preceding facts is not true.

School Building Bond of 1975

Independent School District Number 5

of Jackson County, Minnesota

Bond 136   *April 1, 1975*

The Independent School District Number 5 of Jackson County, Minnesota, acknowledges itself to owe and, for value received, promises to pay to bearer ONE THOUSAND DOLLARS on April 1, 1989, with interest on said sum after April 1, 1975, at the rate of 5.6% per annum, payable semiannually, until the principal is paid. Furthermore, all such sums are payable at the main office of the First National Bank of Minneapolis.

Signed by authority of the School Board of said school district.

James Forsythe
Chairman of the School Board

No. 28   *Bond 136*   *$28.00*

On April 1, 1989, Independent School District No. 5 of Jackson County, Minnesota, will pay to bearer at the First National Bank of Minneapolis, in Minneapolis, Minnesota, the sum of Twenty-Eight and no-100 Dollars for interest due then on its School Building Bond of 1975 dated April 1, 1975.

James Forsythe
Chairman of the School Board

---

etc.

No. 27   *Bond 136*   *$28.00*

On October 1, 1988, Independent School District No. 5 of Jackson County, Minnesota, will pay to bearer at the First National Bank of Minneapolis, in Minneapolis, Minnesota, the sum of Twenty-Eight and no-100 Dollars for interest due then on its School Building Bond of 1975, dated April 1, 1975.

James Forsythe
Chairman of the School Board

---

etc.

No. 2   *Bond 136*   *$28.00*

On April 1, 1976, Independent School District No. 5 of Jackson County, Minnesota, will pay to bearer at the First National Bank of Minneapolis, in Minneapolis, Minnesota, the sum of Twenty-Eight and no-100 Dollars for interest due then on its School Building Bond of 1975, dated April 1, 1975.

James Forsythe
Chairman of the School Board

No. 1   *Bond 136*   *$28.00*

On October 1, 1975, Independent School District No. 5 of Jackson County, Minnesota, will pay to bearer at the First National Bank of Minneapolis, in Minneapolis, Minnesota, the sum of Twenty-Eight and no-100 Dollars for interest due then on its School Building Bond of 1975, dated April 1, 1975.

James Forsythe
Chairman of the School Board

Suppose that a corporation or public agency W has need for a large loan. Then it is common practice for W to conduct an auction at which combinations of banks or brokers present sealed bids specifying what bonds, with what bond rates, should be issued to obtain the money desired by W. The combination of bond dealers which makes the lowest bid, in regard to the cost of the loan to W, is called the *underwriting group G* for the bond issue. G gives the desired principal of the loan to W. Then G has the responsibility for selling the bonds, and tries to dispose of them at such prices that G will make a profit. However, G may incur a loss, if its specifications of bond rates for bonds of various maturities are so low that the bonds, at specified prices, do not appeal to investors. In such a case, G would have to lower the prices at which it had hoped to sell the bonds. After a bond has been issued, it can be bought and sold subject to the law of supply and demand. We shall discuss the price at which an investor will be willing to buy a specified bond when the investor declares that he must obtain interest at a certain rate on any investment.

The essential features of a bond are its promises (*a*) *to pay a single sum $V at maturity*, and (*b*) *to pay an annuity, consisting of the periodic coupon payments of $K each*. Any financial contract with these features can be called a *bond*, and can be treated by the methods of this chapter.

43. Price on an Interest Date

Any date on which a coupon of a bond becomes due will be referred to as a **coupon date**, or **interest date**, for the bond. The owner of a bond is free to sell it on any date. If a bond is sold on a coupon date, *the seller takes the coupon payment which is due*. Problems arising when a bond is sold between two successive coupon dates will be considered later.

Consider a purchaser of a bond who demands that his money be invested at a specified rate, which we shall call *the investment rate*. Then, the price* P which he would be willing to pay for a bond on any date, or the VALUE of the bond at the investor's rate, can be found as follows:

$$P = \left\{ \begin{array}{l} \textbf{(pres. val. of final redemption payt.)} \\ + \textbf{ (pres. val. of the remaining coupon annuity payts.),} \end{array} \right\} \quad (1)$$

where present values are computed at the investor's rate. We shall refer to (1) as furnishing the *general method* for computing the value of a bond. When it is bought on a coupon date, the future coupon payments form an ordinary annuity whose term begins on the date of purchase.

Example 1. A \$1000, 6% bond pays coupons semiannually and will be redeemed on July 1, 1978. Find the price if the bond is bought on July 1, 1975

---

* Unless otherwise stated, any sales commission, tax, or other minor item payable at the time of purchase will be disregarded in this chapter.

to yield 4% compounded semiannually, (a) if the bond is redeemable at par; (b) if the bond is redeemable at 110%.

SOLUTION. (a) The redemption value is $1000, due in 3 years. The coupon payments are $30 payable semiannually for 3 years. Hence,

$$price = 1000(1.02)^{-6} + 30a_{\overline{6}|.02} = 887.97 + 168.04 = \$1056.01.$$

(b) "At 110%" means that the redemption payment is 110% of $1000, or $1100, due at the end of 3 years. The periodic payment is $30. Hence, from (1),

$$price = 1100(1.02)^{-6} + 30a_{\overline{6}|.02} = 976.77 + 168.04 = \$1144.81.$$

In dealing with any bond, unless contrary directions are met, it is customary to assume that (1) **the bond is redeemable at par,** and that (2) **the interest rate, stipulated by the investor, is compounded as often per year as coupons are payable on the bond.**

ILLUSTRATION 1. "To find the price of a $1000, 5% bond with *quarterly* coupons, which is bought to yield 6%," means to find the price under the assumptions that (1) the bond will be redeemed at par, and that (2) the investor wishes interest payable or compounded *quarterly* at the rate 6%.

Summary

To find the value $P of a bond on a coupon date to yield a specified investment rate, when the coupon period is equal to the investor's interest period:

$$\left\{ \begin{aligned} &H = (face\ value); \quad V = (redemp.\ payt.); \quad r = (bond\ rate\ per\ period); \\ &K = (coupon\ payt.) = Hr; \quad i = (investor's\ rate\ per\ period); \\ &n = (number\ of\ periods\ from\ purchase\ date\ to\ redemption\ date). \end{aligned} \right\} \quad (2)$$

$$P = V(1 + i)^{-n} + K(a_{\overline{n}|i}). \tag{3}$$

With the data in (2), the present value of the redemption payment is $V(1+i)^{-n}$; the future coupons form an ordinary annuity of $K payable at the end of each period for n periods, and the present value of this annuity is $K(a_{\overline{n}|i})$. Hence, from (1) we obtain (3). The student may prefer to remember (1) instead of memorizing (3) mechanically.

To say that a bond pays "*interest*" annually, semiannually, etc. means that *the coupons are paid annually, semiannually,* etc., respectively. However, it is essential for the student to avoid thinking of the *bond rate, r,* as an interest rate. A coupon payment is not necessarily identical with "*interest on the investment*" from the investor's standpoint, as will be emphasized later. The only "*interest rate*" is *i*, in connection with (3). The bond rate *r*, called an interest rate in the bond, is merely a convenient basis for computing the coupon payment $K.

If the price P of a bond is *greater* than the redemption value V, we say that the bond is purchased at a premium, where $P - V$ is defined as the **premium**. Similarly, if P is *less* than V we call $V - P$ the **discount** and say that the bond is purchased at a discount.

ILLUSTRATION 2.   In Example 1(*a*), the bond is purchased at a premium of $56.01. In Example 1(*b*) the premium is $44.81.

Exercise 31

1. A $1000, 5% bond with annual coupons will be redeemed at the end of 9 years. Find the price to yield (*a*) 4%; (*b*) 5%; (*c*) 6%.
2. A $100, 4.5% bond with semiannual coupons will be redeemed at the end of 15 years. Find the price to yield (*a*) 3%; (*b*) 4.5%; (*c*) 5.5%. State a general conclusion about the effect on the price if there is a change in the investment rate.

The par value of each bond in the table is $1000; *the* **life** *is the time to the redemption date. Find the price.*

Problem	Life	Redeemable at	Bond Rate	Coupon Payable	Investment Rate
3.	27 yr.	par	7%	annually	.05, $m = 1$
4.	5 yr.	115%	5%	quarterly	.08, $m = 4$
5.	16 yr.	par	6%	semiann.	.04, $m = 2$
6.	20 yr.	par	8%	annually	.05, $m = 1$
7.	10 yr.	105%	4%	quarterly	.06, $m = 4$
8.	16 yr.	par	5%	annually	.07, $m = 1$

9. A $10,000, 5% bond with semiannual coupons is priced to yield 7%. Find the price if the bond is redeemable at par at the end of (*a*) 10 years; (*b*) 15 years; (*c*) 20 years.
10. Repeat Problem 9 with the bond rate 8% and the investment rate 5%.
11. Nelson sells the following promissory note to a banker on June 1, 1976. What does Nelson receive if the banker discounts at 6% compounded semiannually?

Omaha, Nebraska, *June 1, 1974*
At the end of five years I *promise to pay* $2000 *to* Robert Nelson *and to pay interest semiannually on this sum at the rate* $6\frac{1}{2}$% *per annum.*
(Signed) James Costello

NOTE. A promissory note which requires *the periodic payment of interest* on an original principal during the whole life of the note, and the payment of the principal in *one installment*, is an illustration of a *bond* in the sense of the present chapter.

12. Loomis borrows $15,000 from Roberts and signs a note promising to pay interest semiannually at the rate 5%, and to pay the principal in one installment at the end of 6 years. Find the price Roberts would receive if he sold this note 4 years before it is due to yield an investor 8%.

13. On February 1, 1975, Harris borrows $1000 from Jones and signs a note promising to pay Jones, at the end of 4 years, the principal and accumulated interest at 5% compounded annually. On February 1, 1976 Jones sells this note to yield the investor 4% compounded annually. What price does Jones receive?

14. To retire a debt, principal and interest included, a man agrees to pay $100 at the end of each month for 15 months, and an additional final "*balloon*" payment of $500 at the end of 15 months. Find the original sum borrowed, if interest is at the rate 9% compounded monthly.

44. Premium or Discount Equation

It is possible to compute the premium or the discount involved in the purchase price of a bond without first computing the price.

Example 1. A $1000, 6% bond with semiannual coupons will be redeemed at the end of 20 years. Find the price to yield (*a*) 5%; (*b*) 7%.

SOLUTION. (*a*) *When the investor's rate is 5%.* **IF** he should pay $1000 for the bond, his demand for a return of principal would be exactly satisfied on the redemption date. In addition,

> *he would demand $25 interest semiannually;*
> *he would receive a $30 coupon semiannually; or,*
> *he would receive an* **excess** *of $5 semiannually for 20 years.*

Hence, a price of $1000 was *too small*; the investor should pay a *premium* equal to the present value of the excess income:

$$premium = 5a_{\overline{40}|.025} = \$125.51;$$

$$price = 1000 + 125.51 = \$1125.51.$$

(*b*) *When the investor's rate is 7%.* An investment of $1000 in the bond would require $35 interest semiannually but the coupon is only $30. Hence, there will be a semiannual **deficiency** of $5 in income whose present value should be subtracted from \$1000 in order to find the proper price; the bond should sell at a *discount:*

$$discount = (35 - 30)a_{\overline{40}|.035} = \$106.78;$$
$$price = 1000 - 106.78 = \$893.22.$$

Let \$$H$ be the face value of a bond whose bond rate per period is r; each coupon payment is \$$Hr$. If the investor's rate per period is i, then any investment of \$$H$ by him requires \$$Hi$ as interest at the end of each period. Suppose that this investor pays \$$H$ for the bond and $r > i$; then there is an *excess* of (\$$Hr - \$Hi$) in the payment at the end of each coupon period, and the investor should pay an *added premium* for the bond. If $i > r$, there is a *deficiency* (\$$Hi - \$Hr$) when a coupon payment is made; hence the investor should get the bond at a *discount.* Thus, with reasoning as in the special case of Example 1, we obtain the following general results.

Summary

Premium-discount method *for a bond redeemable at par at end of n periods, with face* \$$H$; *bond rate r and investment rate i per period:*

Bond rate greater than investment rate, $r > i$. *Investor pays*

$$\text{premium = (pr. val. of excess of coupons over int. on } \$H), \quad or \tag{1}$$

$$\textbf{premium} = (Hr - Hi)a_{\overline{n}|i}; \tag{2}$$

$$\textbf{price} = H + \textbf{premium}, \quad or \quad P = H + (Hr - Hi)a_{\overline{n}|i}. \tag{3}$$

Bond rate less than investment rate, $r < i$. *The investor obtains the bond at a discount, where*

$$\text{discount = (pr. val. of deficiency of coupons under int. on } \$H), \quad or \tag{4}$$

$$\textbf{discount} = (Hi - Hr)a_{\overline{n}|i}; \tag{5}$$

$$\textbf{price} = H - \textbf{discount}, \quad or \quad P = H - (Hi - Hr)a_{\overline{n}|i}. \tag{6}$$

NOTE 1. Of course, (6) is the same as (3) with the order of the terms Hi and Hr reversed. This similarity is to be expected, because a *discount* can be thought of as a *negative premium*. By the premium-discount method, we find the price by use of just one table, Table VIII, whereas the general method of (3) on page 124 uses Table VI as well as Table VIII. Hence, the numerical simplicity of the premium-discount method justifies the advice to employ it whenever a bond is redeemable at par. The student is advised to use the direct reasoning of Example 1 rather than to employ (3) and (6) as formulas.

NOTE 2. To facilitate work with bonds, extensive tables have been computed showing the purchase prices of bonds redeemable at par. The following table illustrates those found in bond tables.

Values to the Nearest Cent of a $100,000, 5% Bond with Semiannual Coupons

Investment Rate	Time to Redemption Date			
	10½ years	11 Years	11½ Years	12 Years
.0400	108 505.60	108 829.02	109 146.10	109 456.96
.0405	108 060.01	108 365.61	108 665.14	108 958.72
.0410	107 616.62	107 904.58	108 186.75	108 463.25
.0415	107 175.43	107 445.93	107 710.93	107 970.54
.0420	106 736.43	106 989.64	107 237.65	107 480.56
.0425	106 299.59	106 535.71	106 766.91	106 993.30
.0430	105 864.92	106 084.11	106 298.69	106 508.75
.0435	105 432.40	105 634.84	105 832.97	106 026.89
.0440	105 002.01	105 187.88	105 369.74	105 547.69
.0445	104 573.75	104 743.21	104 908.99	105 071.16
.0450	104 147.61	104 300.84	104 450.70	104 597.26

Exercise 32

1. A $1000, 6% bond with semiannual coupons will be redeemed at the end of 15 years. Find the price by use of the general method of (3) on page 124 and also by the premium-discount method, to yield (a) 4%; (b) 8%.

Use the premium-discount method in each problem

2. A $100, 7% bond with semiannual coupons will be redeemed at the end of 12 years. Find the value of the bond to an investor whose interest rate is (a) 4%; (b) 7%; (c) 9%.
3. Verify the entries in the preceding extract from a bond table for the investment rates 4% and 4.5%.
4. A $2000 bond pays a $75 coupon semiannually and will be redeemed at the end of 9 years. Find the price to yield 6%.
5. Dixon borrows $9000 from Burkhart and signs a note promising to pay interest at the rate 6.5% semiannually and to pay the principal in one installment at the end of 7 years. Burkhart sells the note 5 years before maturity to yield the investor 8%. Find the price paid.
6. The Baker Construction Company borrows $25,000 from the First National Bank and signs a note promising to pay interest quarterly at the rate 9% and to pay the principal in one installment at the end of 6 years. Two years later the bank sells this note to an investor to yield 7%. Find the price paid.
7. It is estimated that a mine will yield net income of $50,000 at the end of each year for 14 years, and that the property can be sold then for $125,000. Find the present worth of the mine to an investor whose interest rate is 8%.

45. Amortization of a Premium

Let $P be the price an investor pays for a bond when his interest rate is i per conversion period. Then, the coupons $K and the final redemption payment $V are just sufficient to pay interest at the rate i periodically on the investment and to return the invested principal P in installments. If $P > V$, then only V of the original principal is returned on the redemption date. Therefore, the remaining principal $(P - V)$, or the original premium, is returned in installments as a part of the coupon payments. We speak of the premium $(P - V)$ being *amortized by the coupon payments*. Each coupon, in addition to paying interest on the investment, provides a *partial return of the principal P*. These payments of principal reduce the *book value* of the bond, or its *value* in the investor's private *bookkeeping*, from the original price P to the value V on the maturity date.

Example 1. A $1000, 6% bond pays coupons on January 1 and July 1 and will be redeemed on July 1, 1978. The bond is bought on January 1, 1976 to yield 4%. Find the price and form an investment schedule.

SOLUTION. 1. To find the price P, use Section 44. Each coupon is $30; interest at 2% on $1000 is $20. Hence, the bond is bought at a premium:

$$premium = (30 - 20)a_{\overline{5}|.02} = \$47.135; \qquad P = \$1047.135.$$

We shall refer to a table such as we proceed to construct as an "*investment schedule*" because, on each interest date, the table will show how much interest is received, and how much principal remains invested in the bond.

2. *Construction of the schedule.* On July 1, 1976 the semiannual interest due is .02(1047.135) or $20.943. Hence, the $30 coupon pays $20.943 interest and leaves $30 - 20.943$ or $9.057 for repayment of principal. The principal which remains invested in the bond is $1047.135 - 9.057$ or $1038.078. Each other row of the table is computed similarly. A check is that the final book value should be $1000, paid on the redemption date. On any date, the value in the table is the principal which the investor may consider as remaining invested in the bond.

Investment Schedule for a Bond Bought at a Premium

Date	Interest at 4% Due on Book Value	Coupon Payment Received	For Amortization of Premium	Final Book Value
Jan. 1, 1976	$ 0.000	$ 0.000	$ 0.000	$1047.135
July 1, 1976	20.943	30.000	9.057	1038.078
Jan. 1, 1977	20.762	30.000	9.238	1028.840
July 1, 1977	20.577	30.000	9.423	1019.417
Jan. 1, 1978	20.388	30.000	9.612	1009.805
July 1, 1978	20.196	30.000	9.804	1000.001

Summary

For a bond bought at a **premium:** *Each coupon payment is* **greater than the interest due** *on the investor's principal. The difference between the coupon payment and the interest due is a partial repayment of principal which is available to amortize the premium:*

$$\textbf{(coupon payt.)} = \textbf{(int. on invest.)} + \textbf{(amortization payt.).} \tag{1}$$

46. Accumulation of a Discount

If a bond is bought at a discount, the price P is less than the redemption payment V and the discount is $(V - P)$. The redemption payment V exceeds the original invested principal P by $(V - P)$. On any coupon date, the coupon payment is *too small to pay all the interest* desired by the investor; he can consider the unpaid interest as a *new investment* which increases the *book value* of the bond, or its *value* in his private bookkeeping. The sum of these new investments during the bond's life is equal to the discount $(V - P)$ because the value of the bond increases from P to V, which is the final redemption payment. This bookkeeping performance of adding unpaid interest to the value of the bond is spoken of as the *accumulation of the discount*.

Example 1. A \$1000, 4% bond pays coupons on January 1 and July 1 and will be redeemed on January 1, 1979. Find the price on July 1, 1976 to yield 6%, and form an investment schedule.

SOLUTION. 1. To find the price P, use Section 44. Each coupon is \$20; 3% of \$1000 is \$30. Hence, the bond is bought at a discount:

$$discount = (30 - 20)a_{\overline{5}|.03} = \$45.797; \qquad P = \$954.203. \tag{1}$$

Investment Schedule Showing Accumulation of the Discount

Date	Interest at 6% Due on Book Value	Coupon Payment Received	For Accumulation of Discount	Final Book Value
July 1, 1976	\$ 0.000	\$ 0.000	\$ 0.000	\$ 954.203
Jan. 1, 1977	28.626	20.000	8.626	962.829
July 1, 1977	28.885	20.000	8.885	971.714
Jan. 1, 1978	29.151	20.000	9.151	980.865
July 1, 1978	29.426	20.000	9.426	990.291
Jan. 1, 1979	29.709	20.000	9.709	1000.000

2. *Construction of the schedule.* In forming the row for January 1, 1977, the interest due is .03(954.203) or $28.626. The coupon payment falls $8.626 short of paying all interest due. Hence, the investor arranges his accounts by saying that he *receives* $28.626 *interest, but immediately makes a new investment of* $8.626 *in the bond.* A check on the arithmetic is that $1000 should be the value on January 1, 1979, after the coupon is paid.

Summary

For a bond bought at a **discount**: *Each coupon payment is* **too small to pay all interest due** *on the investor's principal. The unpaid interest on each coupon date is thought of as a new investment in the bond:*

$$\text{(int. on princ.)} = \text{(coup. payt.)} + \text{(unpaid int.); } \textit{or,} \tag{2}$$

$$\text{(int. on princ.)} = \text{(coup. payt.)} + \text{(payt. for accum. of disct.)} \tag{3}$$

We may find any entry in the "*book value*" column of an investment schedule without computing any other items. Each book value is the price of the bond on the associated date at the investor's rate.

Example 2. For the bond in Example 1, find the book value on 7/1/1977.

SOLUTION. The remaining life of the bond is 3 interest periods.

$Discount = (30 - 20)a_{\overline{3}|.03} = \$28.286;$ $price = (book\ value) = \$971.714.$

NOTE 1. The following equation summarizes the method used in finding each book value in an investment schedule. $\$Q_0$ and $\$Q_1$ represent book values on two successive coupon dates; $\$I$ is simple interest on Q_0 for one coupon period at the investor's rate; $\$K$ is the coupon.

$$Q_1 = Q_0 + I - K. \tag{4}$$

The preceding statement is true for a bond bought at either a premium or a discount as compared to the redemption price.

NOTE 2. The theoretical book values in investment schedules, as constructed for bonds in preceding examples, are specified as the legal values of bonds in regulations governing the valuation of assets of trusts or insurance companies in some states. Also, these book values actually should guide the thinking of an investor, regardless of how he may choose, or be required by law, to handle the premium or discount on a bond in income tax accounting.

Exercise 33

1. A $1000, 7% bond pays coupons on February 1 and August 1 and will be redeemed on 8/1/1980. (*a*) Find the price of the bond on 2/1/1978 to

yield 5%, and form a schedule showing the amortization of the premium. (b) Without the schedule, find the book value on 2/1/1979 to yield 5%.

2. A $1000, 5% bond pays coupons annually on March 1 and will be redeemed on 3/1/1983. (a) Find the price of the bond on 3/1/1977 to yield 7%, and form a schedule showing the accumulation of the discount. (b) Without the schedule, find the book value on 3/1/1979 to yield 7%.

3. A $100, 6% bond pays coupons annually on March 1. The value of the bond is $115.75 on 3/1/1977 to yield an investor 4%. On 3/1/1978: (a) what part of the coupon payment is used for amortization of the premium; (b) what is the new book value of the bond after the coupon is paid? (Make up a row in an investment schedule.)

4. A $1000, 5% bond pays coupons semiannually and is bought to yield 6.5%. On a certain coupon date, the book value is $915. Find the book value just after the next coupon payment is made.

5. A $1000, 7% bond pays coupons semiannually and is bought to yield 5%. On a certain coupon date, the book value of the bond is $1125. Find (a) the book value just after the next coupon date; (b) the part of the coupon just paid which is a partial payment of the principal invested in the bond.*

6. A $1000, 5% bond pays coupons semiannually, and is bought to yield 7%. On a certain coupon date, the book value of the bond is $850. On the next coupon date, in the bookkeeping of the investor, (a) how much interest does he list as received on his investment; (b) how much does he list as a new investment in the bond; (c) what is the final new book value of the bond?

7. A $1000, 5% bond with annual coupons is bought on a coupon date 3 years before the redemption date, to yield 5%. Construct an investment schedule for the bond.

8. A $2000, 6.5% bond pays coupons semiannually, and is bought to yield 5.5%. On a certain coupon date, the book value is $2100. Find the book value just after payment of the next coupon.

9. A $1000, 6% bond, with coupons payable annually on August 1, will be redeemed on 8/1/1990. An investor buys the bond on 8/1/1978 to yield 4%. In the investor's bookkeeping on 8/1/1985, what interest does he list as received and what principal does he consider repaid on that date?

HINT. First find the book value, or price, on 8/1/1984.

10. Repeat Problem 9, properly altered, with the investment rate 8%.

★11. A $1000, 7% bond pays coupons annually on February 1 and is not redeemable at par. On 2/1/1978, the price of the bond to yield an investor 6% is $1075. Find the value of the bond for this investor on 2/1/1981

* In problems of this nature, the bond is not necessarily redeemable at par. The redemption value does not enter in the solution.

without making up an investment schedule. Use a retrospective method. (Write an equation of value on 2/1/1981.)

47. Professional Practices in Pricing Bonds for Sale

Bonds are sold on bond exchanges, or in the offices of brokers, at prices regulated by the law of supply and demand. Since a bond may be sold on any date, the typical situation as now considered will deal with a bond bought between two successive coupon dates.

In buying or selling bonds, it is customary to think of each coupon payment K of a bond as being earned or *accruing* continuously during the corresponding period, although K is not due until the end of the period. Since a bond describes its coupon payment as "*interest*" on the face value H for one period at the bond rate, it is common practice to speak of the "**accrued interest**" rather than the "**accrued coupon**," on any date. We shall employ the word "*interest*" frequently in this sense when it does not cause confusion with actual interest at the investment rate. Thus, on a day between two successive coupon dates which is w days after a coupon date,

$$\text{(accrued int.)} = \text{(simp. int. for } w \text{ days on } H \text{ at bond rate.)} \tag{1}$$

ILLUSTRATION 1.   A $100, 6% bond pays interest on January 1 and July 1. On August 16, approximately 45 days after July 1,

$$(\textit{accrued interest}) = 1000(.06)\frac{45}{360} = \$7.50.$$

NOTE 1.   In this text, when finding simple interest in bond problems, use the approximate time between dates and ordinary interest.

In the sale of a bond, the actual purchase price P on any day is called the **flat price**. When a man sells a bond between coupon dates, w days after the preceding coupon date, it is sensible for him to feel that he is entitled to the accrued interest (disregarding the minor feature that the next coupon is not yet payable). Any buyer likewise realizes the justification of such an attitude. Hence, it is customary to consider the flat price as consisting of two parts, *the accrued interest* k and a second part Q, a "**quoted price**," which is thought of as the price paid on account of the future accruals of interest on the bond, and the final redemption payment:

$$\text{(flat price)} = \text{(accrued interest)} + \text{(quoted price)}, \textit{ or} \tag{2}$$

$$P = k + Q. \tag{3}$$

When the flat price is described to a buyer as in (2), by telling him the quoted price, it is said that the bond is being sold **at a "price and accrued interest."** Then, the *quoted price* may be called the "**and-interest-price**," and is described as a percentage of the face value of the bond; the **market quotation** is the corresponding rate percent. On an interest date, the accrued interest is zero and then, from (2), the flat price and the and-interest-price are the same. Sometimes the flat price itself may be specified directly. Then we say that the bond is **sold flat**.

Hereafter, we may use the words *flat price* instead of simply *price*, or *purchase price*, even on a coupon date where the flat price and quoted "price" are the same.

ILLUSTRATION 2. If a $1000 bond is quoted at $104\frac{1}{2}$ *flat*, the flat price is $104\frac{1}{2}\%$ of $1000, or $1045.

Example 1. A $1000, 6% bond, which pays interest semiannually, is quoted at 103 and accrued interest 2 months after an interest date. Find the flat price.

SOLUTION. The and-interest-price is 103% of $1000, or $1030;

$$k = (accrued\ interest) = 1000(.06)(\tfrac{2}{12}) = \$10.$$

Hence, from (3), $\qquad\qquad (flat\ price) = 1030 + 10 = \$1040.$

Example 2. A $1000, 5% bond, which pays interest semiannually on February 1 and August 1, is sold at a flat price of $942.08 on October 1. Find the market quotation on that day on an "and interest" basis.

SOLUTION. October 1 is 2 months after August 1. Hence,

$$k = (accrued\ interest\ on\ \text{October 1}) = 1000(.05)(\tfrac{2}{12}) = \$8.33;$$

$$(and\text{-}interest\text{-}price) = 942.08 - 8.33 = \$933.75.$$

Since $933.75 is 93.375% of $1000, the market quotation is $93\frac{3}{8}$.

Exercise 34

1. Find the accrued interest on October 16 for a $1000, 8% bond which pays coupons on January 1 and July 1.
2. Find the accrued interest on August 16 for a $1000, 5% bond which pays interest on May 1 and November 1.
3. A $1000, 6% bond pays interest on February 1 and August 1. (*a*) Find the flat price on April 1 if the bond is quoted at $96\frac{3}{4}$ and accrued interest. (*b*) If the flat price on October 1 is $985, find the market quotation then on a price and accrued interest basis.
4. A $1000, 7% bond pays coupons on March 1 and September 1. (*a*) Find the flat price on May 16 if the bond is quoted at $103\frac{3}{8}$ and accrued interest. (*b*) If the flat price is $1043.75 on February 1, find the quotation then on a price and accrued interest basis.

5. A $100, 6% bond pays interest on April 1 and October 1, and is quoted at $103\frac{1}{4}$ and accrued interest on November 16. Find the flat price.

Find the flat price of a $1000 bond of the given variety on the specified day, corresponding to the given market quotation. The quotations are approximately those which existed on the given dates.

6. American Telephone and Telegraph Company,* $8\frac{3}{4}$'s; due 5/15/2000; interest dates 5/15 and 11/15; quoted at 104 on 3/15/74.
7. General Eelectric Company $3\frac{1}{2}$'s; due 5/1/76; interest dates 5/1 and 11/1; quoted at 91 on 4/1/74.
8. Commonwealth Edison Company 8's; due 4/1/75; interest dates 4/1 and 10/1; quoted at 99 on 5/1/74.
9. Dow Chemical Corporation 4.35's; due 3/15/88; interest dates 3/15 and 9/15; quoted at 68 on 4/15/74.
10. Dow Chemical Corporation 8.9's; due 5/1/2000; interest dates 5/1 and 11/1; quoted at 100 on 6/1/74.
11. General Motors Acceptance Corporation $6\frac{1}{4}$'s; due 2/1/88; interest dates 2/1 and 8/1; quoted at 81 on 5/1/74.
12. Sears Roebuck Company $4\frac{3}{4}$'s; due 2/1/83; interest dates 2/1 and 8/1; quoted at 80 on 5/1/74.

48. Flat Price at a Given Yield Between Interest Dates

In early sections of the chapter, it was shown how to compute the *price* (also called the *flat price*) of a bond on an interest date. Suppose now that A and C are successive interest dates of a bond, and that B is a day between A and C. Then, as yet, we have not defined the *flat price* P and the *and-interest* price Q of the bond at B to yield an investor a specified rate i. The following procedure provides definitions of P and Q.

Summary

To find the flat price P and the and-interest price Q of a bond on a day B between successive interest dates A and C to yield the investment rate i:

  I. *Compute the flat price P_1 of the bond to yield the rate i at A.*

  II. *Add to P_1 simple interest on P_1 at the rate i for the time from A to B in order to obtain the flat price P at B to yield the rate i.*

  III. *Subtract the accrued interest I on day B from P to find the and-interest price Q of the bond at B to yield the rate i.*

---

* This means that the bond rate is $8\frac{3}{4}\%$.

Example 1. A \$1000, 6% bond pays interest on March 1 and September 1, and will be redeemed on September 1, 1990. On October 16, 1985, find the flat price and the and-interest price to yield an investor 5%.

SOLUTION.   1. The immediately preceding interest date is 9/1/85. The flat price P_1 then to yield 5% is found by the premium method:

$$premium = (30 - 25)a_{\overline{10}|.025} = \$43.76; \qquad P_1 = \$1043.76.$$

2. Interest at 5% on P_1 from 9/1/85 to 10/16/85, for 45 days, is

$$1043.76(.05)\left(\frac{45}{360}\right) = \$6.52.$$

Flat price on 10/16/85 is $P = 1043.76 + 6.52 = \$1050.28.$

3. Accrued interest on bond on 10/16/85 for 45 days is

$$I = 1000(.06)\left(\frac{45}{360}\right) = \$7.50.$$

$$Q = (and\text{-}interest\ price\ on\ 10/16/85) = 1050.28 - 7.50,\ or$$

$Q = \$1042.78.$ The corresponding market quotation is 104.278 on 10/16/85. The details of the solution are illustrated in Figure 24.

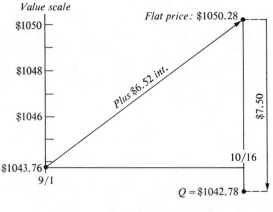

Figure 24

In view of the fact that, in a case like Example 1, $Q = P - k$, where k is the accrued interest, we think of Q as the *value* of the bond on account of its *future history*, for the investor whose interest rate is i. Or, we may call the *and-interest price Q* on any date the **book value** of the bond from the investor's standpoint. On an interest date, $P = Q$ because then $k = 0$.

★49. Graphical Study of the Book Value of a Bond

Consider a bond with face value H and bond rate r per interest period. Let i be the investor's interest rate per period. Suppose that A and C are successive interest dates and that B is A, or is a day between A and C. We introduce the following notations:

$u = $ (*length in days of one coupon period*).

$w = $ (*time in days from A to B*).

$t = \dfrac{w}{u}$; *hence* $\{0 \leq t < 1\}$.

$Q = $ (*and-interest price, or book value to yield rate i on any day*).

$P_1 = $ (*flat price to yield rate i at A*) $= (Q$ *at* $A)$.

$P = $ (*flat price to yield rate i on any day*).

If the method of Section 48 is applied to these data, we obtain the following results.

For t periods:

(*simple interest at rate i on* P_1) $= t P_1 i$.

(*accrued interest on bond at B*) $= t H r$.

Then, $\qquad\qquad P = P_1 + t P_1 i; \qquad Q = P - t H r,$ \hfill (1)

or $\qquad\qquad\qquad Q = P_1 + t(P_1 i - Hr).$ \hfill (2)

Let $m = P_1 i - Hr$. Then, from (2),

$$Q = P_1 + mt. \qquad (3)$$

Although we mentioned that $\{0 \leq t < 1\}$ in obtaining (3), it is true also when $t = 1$; then (2) states that we add interest, $P_1 i$, for one period to P_1 and subtract the coupon payment Hr, to obtain the flat price $Q = P$ on the next interest date C. Hence (3) is true when $\{0 \leq t \leq 1\}$. Since (3) is *linear* in t, the graph of (3) in a tQ-plane is a *line segment*, shown as RK in Figure 25 on page 138. (The scales are distorted to emphasize certain features.) From (1),

$$P = P_1 + P_1 it. \qquad (4)$$

Hence, P is a *linear function of t*, so that the graph of (4) also is a line segment, shown as RZ in Figure 25. However, P is not defined by (4) when $t = 1$, because this gives the interest date C, where the coupon payment Hr is subtracted from P in (4); then P drops down to the value Q. To emphasize this feature in Figure 25, a small circle is used to indicate that Z is not on the graph of (4).

In the next coupon period, from C to D, the graphical situation over the time-interval AC is repeated; and so on, throughout the life of the bond. Thus, the graph of the book value Q at a constant yield rate i is a sequence of *connected line segments*, like *RKT* in Figure 25. The graph of the flat price *P* is a sequence of *disconnected line segments*, like *RZ* and *KW* in Figure 25, which exhibit a drop equal to the coupon payment at each interest date. The main features of Figure 25 relative to increasing slopes of lines illustrate the situation for a bond where $i > r$.

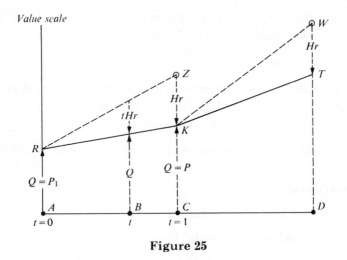

Figure 25

Exercise 35

Find the flat price and book value of the bond if it is purchased to yield the specified investment rate. Also, on the date of purchase, find the market quotation of the bond on an "and-interest" basis to obtain the specified yield.

Prob.	Par Value	Bond Rate	Interest Dates	Redemption Date	Purchase Date	Invest. Rate
1.	$1000	8%	6/1; 12/1	6/1/91	8/1/75	5%
2.	100	7%	2/1; 8/1	2/1/85	10/16/77	8%
3.	5000	8%	4/1; 10/1	4/1/88	7/1/80	6%
4.	1000	6%	3/1; 9/1	9/1/92	1/1/79	9%
5.	100	6%	1/1; 7/1	7/1/88	10/1/77	6%
6.	1000	5%	5/1; 11/1	11/1/89	10/1/81	4%

7. A $1000, $8\frac{7}{8}$%, General Foods Corporation bond, due January 1, 1990; coupon dates 1/1 and 7/1; bought on 3/1/77 to yield 6%.

8. A $1000, $8\frac{7}{8}$%, General Mills Company bond, due April 15, 1995; coupon dates 4/15 and 10/15; bought on 6/15/80 to yield 8%.

9. A $1000, $6\frac{3}{4}\%$, Standard Brands Company bond, due June 1, 1993; coupon dates 6/1 and 12/1; bought on 10/1/79 to yield 9%.
10. A $1000, 7.4%, Safeway Stores Company bond, due April 1, 1997; coupon dates 4/1 and 10/1; bought on 7/1/81 to yield 6%.
11. On 3/1/78, Freeman receives a loan of $3000 from King and signs a note promising to pay to him interest annually at the rate 5%, and the principal on 3/1/84. This note is sold by King on 6/1/81 to yield the new investor 6%. What price does he pay?

★NOTE 1.   Recall that (3) on page 137 is linear in t. In the discussion of linear interpolation on page 38, it was emphasized that the method assumes that the graph of the function f involved is a straight line. This means that f is a *linear function for the values of the independent variable which are met.* Thus, linear interpolation gives an *exact* result if the graph of the function involved is a line. Hence, the following method is available for obtaining the and-interest price, or book value, of a bond to yield a specified rate i on a day B between two successive interest dates A and C for the bond.

Find the flat prices, or book values to yield the rate i on the interest dates A and C. Then use linear interpolation to obtain the book value at the rate i on day B.

★12–15. Find the book values in Problems 1–4, respectively, by interpolation as described in Note 1. Thus, commence by obtaining the prices on the two interest dates A and C which bracket the purchase date.

50.   Approximation to a Bond Yield Without Tables

Up to this point, we have been concerned mainly with the book values of bonds to yield given investment rates. We now consider the converse problem: *given the book value of a bond on a specified date, we ask for the investment rate which the bond will yield to a purchaer.* In computing a yield, it is customary to neglect any accrued interest paid at the date of purchase. This part of the flat price essentially is canceled by part of the first interest payment after the purchase date. First we shall consider a method for obtaining the yield without use of interest or annuity tables.

From Sections 45 and 46 we recall the following facts. When a bond is bought at a premiun, the periodic coupon payments of the bond provide all interest required at the investment rate and, also, repay the premium in installments. Hence, during the life of the bond after the purchase date,

$$\begin{Bmatrix} \textbf{bond} \\ \textbf{at a} \\ \textbf{premium} \end{Bmatrix} : \qquad \begin{Bmatrix} investor's \\ total \\ interest \end{Bmatrix} = \begin{Bmatrix} sum\ of\ all \\ coupon \\ payments \end{Bmatrix} - \begin{Bmatrix} the \\ premium \end{Bmatrix}. \qquad (1)$$

When a bond is bought at a discount, the coupon payments are not sufficient to pay all interest at the investor's rate. He may act as if the interest which is not paid when due accumulates until the redemption date, when the total accumulation is equal to the original discount, and then is paid. Hence,

$$\begin{Bmatrix} \textbf{bond} \\ \textbf{at a} \\ \textbf{discount} \end{Bmatrix}: \qquad \begin{Bmatrix} investor's \\ total \\ interest \end{Bmatrix} = \begin{Bmatrix} sum\ of\ all \\ coupon \\ payments \end{Bmatrix} + \begin{Bmatrix} the \\ discount \end{Bmatrix}. \qquad (2)$$

Example 1. A $1000, 5% bond will be redeemed at the end of 11 years and 1 month. Estimate the yield obtained by an investor who buys the bond at a quotation of 112 and accrued interest.

SOLUTION. 1. The buyer's book value for the bond changes from $1120 on the purchase date to $1000 on the redemption date due to the amortization of the premium:

$$(average\ invested\ principal) = \tfrac{1}{2}(1120 + 1000) = \$1060. \qquad (3)$$

2. The premium is $120. The sum of the coupon payments in one year is $50. Hence, from (1), with the life of the bond taken as 11 years.

$$(total\ interest\ in\ 11\ years) = 11(50) - 120 = \$430;$$

$$(average\ annual\ interest) = \tfrac{1}{11}(430) = \$39. \qquad (4)$$

3. From (3) and (4), $\qquad (approximate\ yield) = \dfrac{39}{1060} = 3.7\%.$

Summary

To estimate the yield of a bond purchased with a book value $Q, n years before the bond is to be redeemed for $V:

  I. *Compute the average invested principal, $\tfrac{1}{2}(V + Q)$.*

 II. *Compute the total interest received by the investor in the n years, from (1) or (2), whichever applies, and divide by n to find the average interest per year.*

III. *An estimate j for the yield is*

$$j = \frac{\textbf{average annual interest}}{\textbf{average investment}}. \qquad (5)$$

Example 2. A $1000, 7% bond will be redeemed at the end of 12 years and 2 months. Estimate the yield obtained by an investor who buys the bond when it is quoted at 78 and accrued interest.

SOLUTION. 1. Statement (2) applies. We approximate the life as 12 years. The buyer's book value for the bond changes from $780 to $1000 due to the accumulation of the discount:

$$(average\ invested\ principal) = \tfrac{1}{2}(780 + 1000) = \$890. \qquad (6)$$

2. The discount on the purchase date is $220. The total of the coupon payments in 12 years is $840. Hence, by (2),

$$(\textit{total interest in } 12 \textit{ years}) = 840 + 220 = \$1060;$$

$$(\textit{average annual interest}) = \frac{1060}{12} = \frac{\$265}{3}. \tag{7}$$

3. From (6) and (7),

$$(\textit{approx. yield}) = \frac{265}{3(890)} = 9.9\%.$$

NOTE 1. Observe that, since averages were employed in the preceding method, it is not refined enough to allow the frequency of interest payments on a bond to affect the result. However, experience shows that the method gives a result within a few tenths of 1% of the true yield for the usual type of problem. In applying the method, express the remaining life of the bond to the *nearest* interest date. Round off the final estimated yield to tenths of 1% because greater refinement is not justified.

Exercise 36

All quotations are on an "and-interest" basis, so that the quoted price is the book value for the investor. Estimate the yield of each bond to tenths of 1% without using a table. The student will find it convenient to take either $100 or $1000 as par value.

Prob.	Redeemable at	Quotation	Bond Rate	Life
1.	par	120	6%	9 yr.
2.	par	60	5%	20 yr.
3.	par	93	$4\frac{3}{8}\%$	15 yr.
4.	par	109	8%	10 yr.
5.	par	90	$6\frac{1}{2}\%$	8 yr.
6.	105%	100	7%	6 yr.
7.	110%	104	8%	9 yr.

8. The Allied Chemical Corporation $7\frac{7}{8}\%$ bonds of 1996 were quoted at 95 on 3/27/74. Coupons are payable on 3/1 and 9/1. The bonds are to be redeemed on 3/1/1996.

9. The Consolidated Edison Company $4\frac{5}{8}\%$ bonds of 1993 were quoted at 55 on 3/27/74. Coupons are payable on 6/1 and 12/1. The bonds are to be redeemed on 6/1/93.

10. The B. F. Goodrich Company 7% bonds of 1997 were quoted at 80 on 5/27/74. Coupons are payable on 2/15 and 8/15. The bonds are to be redeemed on 2/15/97.

51. Yield Determined by Interpolation

In this section, we shall assume that any bond which we discuss is bought on an interest date, where the *book value* of a bond is the same as its flat price, or purchase price. Suppose that we are told the book value at which an investor purchases a certain bond. Then, if a bond table* is available, the yield received by the investor can be found easily by interpolation, with the accuracy of the result determined by the nature of the table. With somewhat more labor, the yield can be found with reasonable accuracy by interpolation with the aid of Table VIII, or Tables VI and VIII. The following procedure is designed for use without a bond table.

Summary

To find the yield i of a bond with a known book value $Q:$

I. *Decide on an estimate j for the yield, perhaps with the aid of Section* 50.
II. *Compute the book value at the rate i_1 nearest to j for which the tables can be used. Inspect the result to decide whether $i < i_1$ or $i > i_1$. Then, compute the book value for a second rate i_2 chosen so that i probably lies between i_1 and i_2.*
III. *After two rates i_1 and i_2 are found so that the corresponding book values* **bracket** *Q, determine i by interpolation.*

Example 1. A \$100, 6% bond with interest payable semiannually will be redeemed at the end of $10\frac{1}{2}$ years. Find the yield if the bond is bought at the flat price \$111.98.

SOLUTION. 1. By use of Section 50, we obtain 4.6% as an estimated yield. Hence, we compute the bond's book value, or flat price, $10\frac{1}{2}$ years before maturity to yield $4\frac{1}{2}\%$:

$$premium = (3.00 - 2.25)a_{\overline{21}|.0225} = \$12.44; \qquad value = \$112.44.$$

2. Since \$112.44 is *greater* than \$111.98, the yield is *greater* than $4\frac{1}{2}\%$, because an *increase* must occur in the rate in order to *decrease* any present value. Therefore, the yield probably is between $4\frac{1}{2}\%$ and 5%, and we compute the value of the bond to yield 5%:

$$premium = (3.00 - 2.50)a_{\overline{21}|.025} = \$8.09; \qquad value = \$108.09.$$

Thus, $108.09 < 111.98 < 112.44$, or we have found book values which **bracket** 111.98.

---

* The usual bond table applies only to bonds redeemable at par.

3. *The yield i is between* $4\frac{1}{2}\%$ *and* 5%. We obtain $i = .0455$ by interpolation below. As usual, we acted as if all interest rates were compounded semiannually because coupons are payable semiannually. Thus, we have found that the yield is approximately .0455, compounded semiannually.

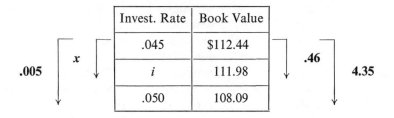

Invest. Rate	Book Value
.045	$112.44
i	111.98
.050	108.09

$$\frac{x}{.005} = \frac{.46}{4.35}; \qquad x = \frac{46}{435}(.005) = .0005; \qquad i = .045 + x = .0455.$$

★ COMMENT. A more exact solution of Example 1 can be obtained as follows. We compute the value of the bond at the investment rate .0455, just found, by use of (5), page 64, and logarithms, or a computing machine: the result is $111.998. Since this is greater than $111.98, we decide that the true yield probably is between .0455 and .0456; by use of computation again, the value to yield .0456 is found to be $111.910. Then, by interpolation between .0455 and .0456, we obtain $x = .04552$.*

If a bond is bought between two successive interest dates, a reasonable approximation to the yield is obtained if the known book value is assumed to be the value on the nearest interest date, and the yield then is determined by interpolation. If the yield is desired more accurately, the preceding Summary applies, where it is understood that the method of Section 48 would be used to obtain book values at the *exact* purchase date. The interested student may solve problems of this nature in the next exercise.

Exercise 37

Solve by use of the extract from a bond table on page 128.

1. A $1000, 5% bond pays interest semiannually and will be redeemed at the end of $11\frac{1}{2}$ years. Find the yield if the book value is $1064.25.
2. A 5% bond with semiannual coupons is quoted at $106\frac{3}{8}$ and accrued interest eleven years before maturity. Find the yield.

* Experience shows that a solution as in Example 1 gives a result which usually is in error by not more than 1/30 of the difference between the rates used in the interpolation. Essentially, such a solution is equivalent to interpolating in Table VIII.

Find the yield of each bond by interpolation. The quotation is on a price and accrued interest basis. Approximate the life to the nearest interest period.

Prob.	Redeemable at	Bond Rate	Life	Quotation
3.	par	4%, semiann.	10 yr.	80
4.	par	$4\frac{1}{2}$%, semiann.	15 yr.	65
5.	par	6%, semiann.	20 yr.	89
6.	par	9%, annually	12 yr., 3 mo.	121
7.	par	8%, semiann.	$10\frac{1}{2}$ yr.	109
8.	par	7%, semiann.	8 yr., 11 mo.	112
9.	110%	5%, annually	19 yr., 9 mo.	$84\frac{1}{2}$
10.	105%	5%, semiann.	14 yr., 2 mo.	92

11–13. By interpolation, find the yields for the bonds in Problems 8–10, respectively, in Exercise 36. Use the quotation on the nearest interest date.

★ *Find the yield in each case by interpolation, using book values on the dates of sales as determined by use of Note 1 on page 139.*

14. A \$100, 4% bond pays interest annually on 12/1 and will be redeemed on 12/1/83. Find the yield if the bond is quoted at $95\frac{5}{8}$ and accrued interest on 2/1/78.

HINT. By the approximate method of Section 50, the yield is near 4.8%. We prefer to find any book value Q on 2/1/78 by first finding book values on 12/1/77 and 12/1/78, and then interpolating, as in Note 1 on page 139. Thus, at 5%, the book values on 12/1/77 and 12/1/78 are 94.924 and 95.671;

$$Q = 94.924 + \tfrac{1}{6}(95.671 - 94.924) = 95.048.$$

An interpolation table for obtaining the yield could be arranged as follows. The process could be referred to as *double interpolation*, because each central entry in the 1st and 3rd rows is obtained by interpolation; the yield is found by interpolation in the 2nd column of entries.

Table of Book Values

Investment Rate	Dec. 1, 1977	Feb. 1, 1978	Dec. 1, 1978
5%	94.924	95.048	95.671
i		95.625	
$4\frac{1}{2}$%	97.421	97.485	97.805

15. A 5% bond pays interest on 3/1 and 9/1 and will be redeeeed on 9/1/88. If the bond is quoted at 106.72 and accrued interest on 11/1/77, find the yield by use of the bond table extract on page 128.

52. Valuation of Miscellaneous Contracts

When a corporation issues a set of bonds in securing a loan, it may be decided to redeem the bonds in installments instead of all on one date. In such a case, the bonds are referred to as a **serial issue**. Similarly, a *serial bond* is one whose face value is redeemable in installments, with interest payable periodically as due on outstanding principal. Serial bonds arise frequently in the sale of real estate. A serial bond is essentially several bonds combined in one contract, and can be thought of as a serial bond issue. On any date, the flat price of a serial bond issue is the sum of the corresponding prices of all bonds of the issue which remain unredeemed.

Example 1. A man borrows $10,000, contracting to pay $2000 of the principal at the end of each year for 5 years, and to pay interest semiannually at the rate 7%. His contract is sold 2 years later to yield the investor 6% compounded semiannually. Find the price he pays.

SOLUTION.   1. The contract is a serial bond involving *five distinct bonds* of $2000 each. At the end of 2 years, *three* bonds remain alive. The price of the contract is the sum of the prices of three $2000 bonds, to be redeemed at the ends of 1, 2, and 3 years, respectively.

2. We find the following prices by use of the premium method of page 127. Observe that $2000(.035 - .03) = \$10$.

(Bond due in 1 year) $Price = 2000 + 10a_{\overline{2}|.03} = \$2019.135$.

(Bond due in 2 years) $Price = 2000 + 10a_{\overline{4}|.03} = \$2037.171$.

(Bond due in 3 years) $Price = 2000 + 10a_{\overline{6}|.03} = \$2054.172$.

The price of the contract is the sum of these: $6110.48.

An **annuity bond**, with face value H, is a contract promising the payment of an annuity whose present value is H at the bond rate. When H and the bond rate are given, the periodic payment R of the bond can be computed. At any date, the price of the annuity bond is obtained by computing the present value of the future payments of the bond at the investor's interest rate. Problems of this nature have been solved already in this text, and will be met again in the next exercise.

Exercise 38

1. A $1,000,000 serial issue of 7% bonds pays coupons on 2/1 and 8/1 and will be redeemed in 5 equal annual installments. The bonds were issued on 2/1/76. An insurance company buys all bonds outstanding on 8/1/78, to yield 8%. Find the price paid.

2. On 3/1/77, a corporation sells a $2,000,000 issue of 8% bonds paying coupons on 3/1 and 9/1. The issue is redeemable in equal installments at the end of each 2 years for 10 years. On 9/1/79, find the value of all outstanding bonds to yield 7%.

3. Jackson borrows from Hansen and signs a contract to discharge the debt, interest included payable semiannually, by paying $1200 at the end of each 6 months for 8 years. At the end of 3 years, Hansen sells the contract to yield the new investor 6.5% payable semiannually. What does Hansen receive? (The contract could be called an annuity bond.)

4. Kelly borrows $5000 from Harlow, and promises to pay the principal plus accumulated interest at 4% compounded semiannually at the end of 6 years. At the end of 2 years, Harlow sells the contract to yield 5% compounded semiannually. What does the buyer pay?

5. On 5/1/78, Davis obtains a loan of $20,000 from Cameron and signs a contract to pay interest quarterly at the rate 4.5% and to pay the principal in one installment at the end of 7 years. On 11/1/81, Cameron sells the the contract to yield the investor 5% compounded quarterly. What does Cameron receive? Use the premium-discount method.

6. On 4/16/76, Sloan buys a house from Miller worth $38,000 cash. He pays $14,000 cash and signs a contract to pay interest annually at 5.5% and to pay the remaining principal in equal installments at the end of each 3 years for 12 years. What does Miller receive if he sells the contract to yield the new investor 6% (a) on 4/16/81; (b) on 12/16/81.

7. On 2/1/77, Lawrence buys a farm worth $40,000 cash from Watkins, paying $10,000 cash and signing a contract to pay interest semiannually at the rate 7% and to pay the remaining principal in 6 equal semiannual installments. What does an investor pay on buying this contract to yield 8% compounded semiannually (a) on 8/1/78; (b) 12/1/78.

8. On 3/1/78, Norris buys a house worth $30,000 cash from Griswold. Norris pays $6000 cash and signs a contract to discharge the balance, interest included at the rate 7% payable monthly, by equal payments at the end of each month for 12 years. On 8/1/83, how much does Griswold receive on selling this contract to yield the new investor 9% compounded monthly?

9. On 4/1/78, Ewing buys a hardware store from Thompson at a price of $50,000 cash. Ewing pays $10,000 cash and signs a contract to pay the principal in equal installments at the end of each year for 5 years, and to pay interest semiannually at the rate 5% on all principal outstanding. On 10/1/81, what does Thompson receive on selling the contract to yield the new investor 5.5% compounded semiannually?

★10. Consider a serial bond with the bond rate r per interest period, whose face value will be redeemed in equal installments of M at the end of each period for h periods. By use of Problem 16 on page 88, prove that the price $\$P$ to yield the investor the rate i per period is given by

$$P = Ma_{\overline{n}|i} + \frac{Mr}{i}(h - a_{\overline{n}|i}).$$

★11. A man buys a house worth \$40,000 cash, and pays \$10,000 cash. He signs a contract to pay \$200 of the remaining principal at the end of each month and to pay interest monthly at the rate 6% on outstanding principal. At the end of 15 months this contract is sold to yield an investor $7\frac{1}{2}\%$ compounded monthly. Find the price he pays.

Exercise 39 / Review of Chapter 5

1. A \$10,000, 6% bond pays interest quarterly and will be redeemed at the end of 7 years. Find the price to yield 4%, (a) by the general method; (b) by the premium or discount method.

2. Repeat Problem 1 to find the price to yield 7%.

3. A \$1000, 5% bond will pay interest semiannually and will be redeemed at 105% at the end of 6 years. (a) Find the book value of the bond to yield the investor 6%, and construct the first two rows of an investment schedule for the bond. (b) What is the book value two years before the bond is due?

4. A \$1000, 8% bond pays interest annually and will be redeemed at the end of two years. (a) Find the flat price of the bond to yield an investor 7%. (b) Construct an investment schedule for the bond.

5. A \$100, 7% bond pays interest semiannually and is not redeemable at par. If the book value of the bond to yield 9% is \$83.25 on a certain interest date, find the book value to yield 9% on the next interest date, without tables. (Make up a row of an investment schedule.)

6. Find the accrued interest on August 25 for a \$1000, 5% bond which pays interest on May 25 and November 25.

7. A \$1000, 4% bond pays interest on March 1 and September 1. (a) If the bond is quoted at 93 and accrued interest on June 1, find the flat price then. (b) If the flat price is \$1072.08 on November 1, find the market quotation then on a price and accrued interest basis.

8. A 5% bond pays interest semiannually and will be redeemed at the end of 14 years. Estimate the yield without interpolation if the bond is quoted (a) at 87; (b) at 107.

9. Find the yield in each case in Problem 8 by interpolation.

10. A $1000, 7% bond pays interest annually and will be redeemed on 4/1/81. If the bond is purchased on 4/1/79 to yield 6%, construct a schedule showing the retirement of the investment.

11. A $100, 5% bond pays interest on March 1 and September 1, and will be redeemed on 9/1/89. (*a*) Find the flat price and book value of the bond to yield an investor 6% on 11/1/80. (*b*) Find the market quotation then on a price and accrued interest basis to yield the purchaser 6%.

12. On 6/1/74, a man borrows $5000 and signs a note promising to pay interest semiannually at the rate 7% and to pay the principal at the end of 9 years. (*a*) Find the price of this note on 6/1/77, to yield the purchaser 6%. (*b*) Find the price to yield 6% on 10/1/77.

13. A man borrows $1000 and signs a note promising to pay the principal and accumulated interest at the rate 4% compounded quarterly at the end of 5 years. Three years before the note is due, find its price to yield a buyer 5.5% compounded quarterly.

14. Find the effective rate at which interest is earned if a man invests all of his money in 5% bonds which pay interest quarterly, with the bonds bought at par on interest dates.

15. A man borrows $15,000 with interest payable monthly at the rate 5%. He signs a contract to discharge the debt, interest included, by equal payments at the end of each month for 20 years. The contract was sold 4 years later to yield the purchaser 4% compounded monthly. Find the price.

16. A $1,000,000 issue of 5% bonds will pay interest annually and will be redeemed in annual installments of $100,000 each. Seven years after the date of issue, find the price of the outstanding bonds to yield 7%.

17. On 1/1/79, a man signs a note promising to pay $2000 at the end of 6 years, and interest annually on this sum at the rate 5%. If this note is purchased for $1850 on 1/1/81, estimate the yield to the buyer, without interpolation. This contract is equivalent to a bond.

18. A $1000, 4% bond pays interest annually. It is stipulated in the bond contract that the bond may be redeemed on any interest date after the end of 6 years, and certainly will be redeemed by the end of 20 years. At what price should the bond sell so that an investor will obtain a yield of at least 6%?

19. A $1000 bond pays interest annually and will be redeemed at a premium of 5% at the end of 12 years. If the price to yield 5% is $967, what would be the price if the redemption premium were increased to 10%?

20. A $100 bond pays interest annually and will be redeemed at the end of 10 years. If the book value is at a premium of $6.55 when the bond is purchased to yield 4%, find the book value if the dividend rate were increased by 2%.

★**21.** A $1000, 5% bond pays interest annually. It is stipulated that, at the option of the debtor corporation which issued the bond, it may be redeemed at par on any interest date after the end of 10 years and will certainly be redeemed on or before the end of 16 years. An investor buys the bond at such a price that he is certain to obtain a yield of 6% or more on his investment. Without interpolation, estimate the yield under the possibility as to redemption which is most favorable to him.

★**22.** A $1000, 4% bond pays interest semiannually and will be redeemed at par. If the book value of the bond is $1043.62 to yield 3.5%, find when the bond is to be redeemed.

★**23.** A $100, 6% bond pays interest annually on 6/1, and will be redeemed on 6/1/86. The bond is purchased by an investor on 6/1/76 to yield 8%. In the bookkeeping of this investor on 6/1/80 what new investment in the bond will be recorded?

6/ Depreciation, Capitalization, Perpetuities

53. Depreciation

Consider a business enterprise, referred to hereafter as a corporation. The financial items in its accounting may be labeled, for our purposes, as *capital expenditures, income*, and *expenses*. The corporation will have a certain accounting period or fiscal year. In any period, the excess, if any, of income over expense gives the *profit*. This is the basis for income taxes which the corporation will pay. Also, the profit and the amount of cash on hand determine the decision of the corporation in regard to the payment of dividends to its stockholders. The cost of any item which will be consumed in the conduct of the business during a single accounting period legitimately is labeled as an *expense*. Thus, the cost of paper used in publishing a newspaper clearly is an expense of the business, just as well as the wages and salaries. However, the cost of the purchase of a new press on which to print the newspaper would *not* be labeled as an expense. The cost of the machine would be a *capital investment*, and thus would increase the capital in use in the business.

Let us refer to any item representing a capital investment as a *capital asset*, or simply as an *asset*. The cost of routine upkeep of the asset, to maintain it in an efficient condition, would be an expense item in the accounting. However, regardless of current upkeep, or because of increasing repair costs as the asset grows older, or because of obsolescence as improved similar assets come on the market, the asset can be expected to have only a limited useful life, say *n* years. Then, income tax regulations and ordinary business prudence make it appropriate to charge off as an expense in each accounting period that part of the original cost of any asset which can be considered to have disappeared due to use. This expense on account of the aging of an asset is called a **depreciation charge** for it. Depreciation charges are deductible from income as part of business expense before income taxes are paid, and hence are subject to federal and state regulations.

Consider an asset with price $P. Suppose that the asset will be retired from use with a final scrap value or salvage value $L at the end of n years. The difference (P − L) is called the **wearing value** $W of the asset. By some systematic procedure, at the end of each year, the corporation will decide on a depreciation charge $D on account of the use of the asset in that year. At the end of any year in the life of the machine, the

$$(\text{accrued depreciation}) = (\text{sum of deprec. charges to date}). \qquad (1)$$

Each depreciation charge is considered as a reduction in the value of the asset. Hence, at the end of any year, after the depreciation charge is made, the **book value** $B of the asset is defined as follows:

$$B = P - (\text{accrued depreciation}). \qquad (2)$$

Then $B is the value listed for the asset in the summary of capital assets of the corporation. The book value $B at any date is the capital still considered as invested in the asset.

The depreciation charge $D at the end of any year is placed by the accountant of the corporation in a depreciation account, which is a part of the capital funds used in the operation of the corporation. All depreciation charges thus are expense items, to be removed from cash income before any of it is considered as available for consideration as profit.

No question of investment of depreciation charges is involved. Hence no interest rate is met in the description of depreciation. We shall consider three of the most common methods for computing depreciation charges.

54. Straight Line Method of Depreciation

Consider an asset which costs $P and will have a salvage value $L when the asset is retired from use at the end of n years. The wearing value is $W = P - L$. Let $d = 1/n$, which we shall call the *annual rate of depreciation*. Let the depreciation charge $D at the end of each year be

$$D = dW, \quad or \quad D = \frac{P - L}{n}. \qquad (1)$$

Then it is said that the *straight line method of depreciation* is used. At the end of t years, the accrued depreciation $E and book value $B are given by

$$E = tD \quad and \quad B = P - tD. \qquad (2)$$

The equation $E = tD$ is *linear* in E and t; hence, the graph of the equation in a tE-system of rectangular coordinates would be a *straight line*. Similarly, the graph of $B = P - tD$ in a tB-system would be a straight line. These facts justify the name "*straight line method*".

ILLUSTRATION 1. Consider a machine which costs $1000 and will wear out in 10 years with a final salvage value of $50; the wearing value is $W = \$950$.

The rate of depreciation is $d = \frac{1}{10}$, or $d = 10\%$. From (1) we have $D = .10(950) = \$95$. From (2), at the end of t years,

$$E = 95t \quad and \quad B = 1000 - 95t. \tag{3}$$

A depreciation schedule showing D, B, and E for each year is as follows:

Depreciation Schedule, Straight Line Method

At End of Year	Depreciation Charge, D	Accrued Depreciation, E	Book Value, E
0	$ 0	$ 0	$1000
1	95	95	905
2	95	190	810
⋮	⋮	⋮	⋮
10	95	950	50

55. Sum of the Years' Digits Method of Depreciation

Some capital assets, such as automobiles, lose their original market values very rapidly in early years. Also, due to the effects of inflation, the replacement cost of a machine is likely to be much higher than the original cost of the old machine. Hence, equal depreciation charges during its life, as in the case of the straight line method, may under-estimate the expense of the operation of the business during early years of the life of the asset. The obsolescence of machinery due to the continuous development of new improved models also is not taken into account suitably when there is slow reduction of book value with the straight line method. Another influence which bears on depreciation is the desire of national and state authorities to have businesses increase their speed in modernizing their plants. This objective is encouraged by permitting use of depreciation methods where relatively large depreciation charges occur in the early years of use of an asset. This so-called "*accelerated*" depreciation has the effect of reducing income taxes in early years and increasing retained cash, which encourages faster replacement of old assets. In this section we consider one of the methods for accelerated depreciation which income tax regulations permit.

Suppose that an asset costs P and will have the salvage value L at the end of n years, when the asset is retired from use. Then the wearing value $W = P - L$. Let

$$k = 1 + 2 + 3 + \cdots + (n - 1) + n, \tag{1}$$

where k will be referred to as the *sum of the years' digits*. By use of (6) on page 271 for the sum of an arithmetic progression,

$$k = \frac{n(n + 1)}{2}. \tag{2}$$

With k taken as a denominator, and the terms on the right of (1) **in reverse order** taken as *numerators*, we obtain the following fractions:

$$d_1 = \frac{n}{k}; \quad d_2 = \frac{n-1}{k}; \quad \cdots; \quad d_{n-1} = \frac{2}{k}; \quad d_n = \frac{1}{k}. \tag{3}$$

Then, d_h is the *rate of depreciation* to be applied to the wearing value $\$W$ to obtain the depreciation charge $\$D_h$ for the hth year:

$$D_h = d_h W. \tag{4}$$

Since the sum of the numerators in (3) is the right-hand side of (1),

$$d_1 + d_2 + \cdots + d_n = \frac{k}{k} = 1;$$

$$D_1 + D_2 + \cdots + D_n = W(d_1 + d_2 + \cdots + d_n) = W. \tag{5}$$

Hence, by (5), the *accrued depreciation* for the whole life, n years, will be exactly $\$W$. When the rates (3) are applied to $\$W$, it is said that the *sum of the years' digits* method of depreciation is being used. This system was legalized for tax returns by the Federal Revenue Act of 1954.

Example 1. A machine costs $5000 and will have a salvage value of $1250 when retired at the end of 5 years. By the sum of the years' digits method, find the depreciation charges for the successive years.

SOLUTION. 1. From (1), $k = 1 + 2 + 3 + 4 + 5 = 15$. From (3),

$$d_1 = \tfrac{5}{15}; d_2 = \tfrac{4}{15}; d_3 = \tfrac{3}{15}; d_4 = \tfrac{2}{15}; d_5 = \tfrac{1}{15}.$$

2. We have $W = 5000 - 1250 = \$3750$. Since $\tfrac{1}{15}(3750) = 250$, the successive depreciation charges are 5(250), 4(250), etc., or $1250, $1000, $750, $500, and $250.

NOTE 1. Sometimes a corporation obtains permission from the tax commissioner to assign a fairly arbitrary sequence of rates, $d_1, d_2, \ldots, d_n$ to be used as in (4). In the straight line method all $d_n = 1/n$, whereas in (3) the rates *decrease* during the life of the machine.

Exercise 40

Prepare a depreciation schedule for the asset (a) by the straight line method; (b) by the sum of the years' digits method.

1. A machine costs $4500 and will have a salvage value of $3000 when retired at the end of 6 years.
2. A machine costs $12,000 and will have a salvage value of $800 when retired at the end of 7 years.
3. A machine costs $6000 and will have a salvage value of $500 when retired at the end of 4 years.

4. A machine costs $7500 and will have a salvage value of $300 when retired at the end of 8 years.

5. A machine costs $10,000 and will have a salvage value of $1000 when retired at the end of 9 years.

56. Depreciation by a Constant Percentage of Declining Book Value

Let $P be the cost of an asset which will be retired at the end of n years. Let d, expressed as a decimal, be an assigned constant annual rate of depreciation which will be applied as follows:

(depr. charge for any yr.) = d × (book val. at beginning of yr.) (1)

When (1) is used, it is said that depreciation is being computed by a constant percentage of the declining book value. With the straight line method in use, the constant rate $d = 1/n$ is applied each year to the *original* book value. Suppose that we call $d = 1/n$ the **natural rate** of depreciation. Then, the Federal Revenue Act of 1954 legalized use of (1) with

$$d = \frac{2}{n}.$$ (2)

which is *twice* the natural rate. Since (2) is applied to the declining book value, the effect is to create large depreciation charges in early years as compared to later years. Hence, (2) provides another method of accelerated depreciation.

Example 1. By the method using a fixed percentage of declining book value, with the rate as twice the natural rate, find the depreciation charges and book values during the life of a $5000 machine with life 5 years.

SOLUTION. The natural rate of depreciation is $\frac{1}{5}$. Hence, in (2), $d = \frac{2}{5}$ or $d = 40\%$. Since $P = 5000$, the depreciation charge at the end of the 1st year is $D = .40(5000) = \$2000$, leaving a book value of $3000. At the end of the 2nd year, $D = .40(3000) = \$1200$, etc.

Depreciation Schedule, Fixed Percentage of Declining Book Value

At End of Year	Depreciation Charge, D	Accrued Depreciation, B	Book Value, B
0	$ 0	$ 0	$5000
1	2000	2000	3000
2	1200	3200	1800
3	720	3920	1080
4	432	4352	648
5	259	4611	389

COMMENT. With the preceding method, there is no point in estimating the salvage value in advance. In Example 1, if the machine is sold for scrap at the end of 5 years for *less than* $389, the difference is claimed by the accountant as *an added expense* of operation in the 5th year. If *more than* $389 is realized from the sale, the difference is a *profit* for the 5th year.

Consider a machine which costs $P and will be retired at the end of n years with a salvage value $L. Suppose that we desire to use (1) with d chosen so that, at the end of n years, *the remaining book value will be equal to* $L. Then, from (1), the decrease in book value for the 1st year is dP and the book value at the end of this year is $P - Pd$, or $P(1 - d)$. Similarly, the book value at the end of any year is $(1 - d)$ times the book value at the beginning of the year. Hence, by the end of n years, the original value $P has been multiplied n times by $(1 - d)$, or by $(1 - d)^n$, and the value at the end of n years is $P(1 - d)^n$. Therefore, we require d to satisfy

$$L = P(1 - d)^n. \tag{3}$$

If the (probably inconvenient) value of d from (3) is to be used, the book value, B_k, at the end of k years would be computed from

$$B_k = P(1 - d)^k, \quad or \quad B_k = (1 - d)B_{k-1}, \tag{4}$$

and the corresponding depreciation charge D_k by use of

$$D_k = B_k - B_{k-1}, \tag{5}$$

where logarithmic computation could be used in (4) and (5). Such exact computations would be met *very seldom* in practice. More frequently, after d is computed from (3), an approximation to d would be chosen for computation of depreciation charges by use of (1), as in Example 1.

Example 2. A machine costs $3000 and will have a salvage value of approximately $290 when retired at the end of 6 years. Find the annual rate of depreciation, d, if we use a constant percentage of declining book value with d chosen so that the final book value will be $290.

SOLUTION. From (3), $3000(1 - d)^6 = 290.$

$$(1 - d)^6 = \frac{290}{3000} = .096667, \quad 1 - d = \sqrt[6]{.096667} = .67745, \quad and \quad d = .32255,$$

where 5-place logarithms were used to compute the 6th root.

★ NOTE 1. Consider an asset with original cost $P, salvage value $L, wearing value $W = $P - $L, and life n years. Let an interest rate i be specified for invested funds. Suppose that $R is such that the investment of $R at the end of each year for n years will create a fund to contain $W at the end of n years. Then $W = Rs_{\overline{n}|i}$. Many years ago, the increase in such a fund at the end of any year sometimes was recommended as the depreciation charge for the asset for that year. This "*sinking fund method*" for depreciation no longer is used. The assumptions involved in it were unrealistic on the basis of accepted accounting principles.

Exercise 41

Prepare a depreciation schedule for the machine by the constant percentage of declining book value method, with the specified annual rate.

1. A machine costs $600 and has a life of 6 years. Use twice the natural rate, as permitted by Federal rules. If the machine is sold as scrap for $600 at the end of 6 years, what profit or loss at that date in addition to the final depreciation charge will the corporation report?
2. A machine costs $10,000 and has a life of 10 years. Use twice the natural rate of the straight line method. If the machine is sold as scrap for $500 at the end of 10 years, what profit or loss will the corporation list in its accounts in addition to the final depreciation charge at the end of 10 years?
★3. For the machine in Problem 1, suppose that the scrap value is estimated in advance to be $500. First compute the constant rate of depreciation on declining book value which will make the final book value exactly $500. Round off this rate to the nearest 5% and then, by use of this approximation, prepare a depreciation schedule by the constant percentage of declining book value method.

57. Perpetuities, Simple Case

A *perpetuity* is an annuity whose payments continue forever. Present values of perpetuities are useful in capitalization problems. Since there is no end to the term of a perpetuity, we have no possibility of defining a concept for a perpetuity similar to the amount of an annuity.

Consider a perpetuity of $R payable at the end of each interest period and let i be the interest rate per conversion period. Let $A be the present value of the perpetuity. Then it is evident intuitively that, if $A is invested at the rate i, the *interest alone* on this fund must provide $R at the end of each interest period, so that the capital of the fund may remain intact and permit the payments to continue unchanged forever. Thus $Ai = R$ or

$$A = \frac{R}{i}. \tag{1}$$

Example 1. If money is worth 10% compounded semiannually, find the present value (*a*) of a perpetuity of $50 payable semiannually; (*b*) of an annuity of $50 payable semiannually for 50 years.

SOLUTION.   1. Let A be the present value of the perpetuity, and let K be the present value of the annuity just described.

2. From (1), $\qquad A = \dfrac{50}{.05} = \$1000, \quad while \quad K = 50a_{\overline{100}|.05} = \$992.40.$

The value of $a_{\overline{100}|.05}$ was computed by use of Table VI and

$$a_{\overline{100}|.05} = \frac{1 - (1.05)^{-100}}{.05} = \frac{1 - [(1.05)^{-50}]^2}{.05}.$$

COMMENT.   We have illustrated the fact that the present value of an annuity whose term is *very long* is closely approximated by the present value of the corresponding perpetuity. Hence, if the term of an annuity is very long, especially if this term is not known *exactly*, it may be convenient to act as if the annuity is a *perpetuity* and to use (1) instead of $A = Ra_{\overline{n}|}$ in finding the present value.

Methods for finding present values of annuities due and deferred annuities extend to similar perpetuity problems.

Example 2. If money is worth 4%, find the present value of a perpetuity of \$100 payable at the *beginning* of each year.

SOLUTION.   The payments form a perpetuity *due* whose present value is the sum of the *first payment* and the present value of the *future payments*, which form an *ordinary* perpetuity to which (1) applies:

$$(present\ value\ of\ perpetuity\ due) = 100 + \frac{100}{.04} = \$2600.$$

★ NOTE 1.   For a rigorous derivation of (1), we write an equation of value. Observe that, one period after the beginning of the term of the perpetuity whose present value is A, the first payment R is due and the remaining payments form a perpetuity of R per period whose term commences on this new date. The original perpetuity is equivalent to the following payments:

I. *The single payment R due at the end of the first period;*
II. *A perpetuity of R per period whose term begins at the end of the first period.*

Therefore, if we accumulate the present value of the original perpetuity for one period, the result will equal the sum of the values of I and II at the end of the first period. The result of accumulating A is $A(1 + i)$. At the end of one period, the value of I is simply R; the value of II is A itself, because the term of the perpetuity II begins at the end of the first period. Hence, the equation of value at the end of one period is

$$A(1 + i) = R + A;$$

$$A + Ai = R + A; \quad Ai = R, \quad or \quad A = \frac{R}{i}.$$

★ NOTE 2.   Sometimes $a_{\overline{\infty}|i}$ is used to represent the present value of a perpetuity of \$1 per interest period, when i is the rate per period. From (1)

$$a_{\overline{\infty}|i} = \frac{1}{i} \quad and \quad A = Ra_{\overline{\infty}|i}. \tag{2}$$

Example 3.   If money is worth 8%, obtain the present value of a perpetuity of \$1000 payable annually, with the first payment due at the end of 5 years.

SOLUTION.   1. The payments form a deferred perpetuity. The payments are indicated by dots on the time scale in Figure 26. Insert fictitious payments of \$1000 at the end of each year for 4 years, as shown by small circles in Figure 26.

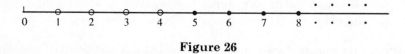

Figure 26

2. The fictitious payments have the present value $1000a_{\overline{4}|.08}$. The fictitious payments plus the actual payments form a perpetuity whose term begins immediately; its present value is 1000/.08. Hence, the present value, A, of the actual payments is given by

$$A = \left\{ \begin{array}{l} pr.\ val.\ actual\ and\ fictitious\ payments) \\ -\ (pr.\ val.\ of\ the\ fictitious\ payments) \end{array} \right\} \quad or$$

$$A = \frac{1000}{.08} - 1000a_{\overline{4}|.08} = 12{,}500 - 3312.13 = \$9187.87.$$

58.   Perpetuity at End of Each k Interest Periods

Consider a perpetuity of \$$W$ payable at the end of each k interest periods, where k is in integer. Let \$$A$ be the present value of this perpetuity. Before finding A, let us ask *what payment \$$R$ at the end of each period could equitably replace \$$W$ at the end of k periods?* The amount of the annuity of \$$R$ per period for k periods should equal \$$W$; hence $Rs_{\overline{k}|i} = W$ or

$$R = \frac{W}{s_{\overline{k}|i}}. \tag{1}$$

The present value of the perpetuity of \$$W$ payable at the end of each k periods is the same as the present value of the perpetuity of \$$R$ per period. Hence $A = R/i$ or, from (1),

$$P = \frac{W}{i(s_{\overline{k}|i})}. \tag{2}$$

Example 1. Find the present value of a perpetuity of $100 payable semi-annually if money is worth 4% compounded quarterly.

SOLUTION. From (2) with $k = 2$,

$$A = \frac{100}{.01} \frac{1}{(s_{\overline{2}|.01})} = \$4975.12. \qquad \text{(Table IX)}$$

Exercise 42

1. If money is worth 8% compounded quarterly, find the present value of a sequence of payments of $200 each, (*a*) at the end of each 3 months forever; (*b*) at the beginning of each 3 months forever; (*c*) at the end of each 3 months for 25 years, and compare with the result of (*a*).
2. If money is worth 6% compounded semiannually, find the present value (*a*) of an annuity of $100 payable semiannually for 50 years; (*b*) of a perpetuity of $100 payable semiannually.
3. What payment at the end of each year forever can be provided by an endowment of $100,000 invested at 8%?
4. If money is worth 5%, how much money is necessary for the permanent endowment of a hospital ward which will require $10,000 at the beginning of each year?
5. If money is worth 7%, find the present value of a perpetuity of $700 per year, if the first payment is due at the end of 5 years.
6. What payment at the end of each 3 months would be equivalent to $1000 paid at the end of each year, if money is worth (.08, $m = 4$)?
7. What payment at the end of each month would be equivalent to $500 paid at the end of each 6 months if money is worth (.06, $m = 12$)?
8. If money is worth 6%, find the present value of a perpetuity of $500 payable at the end of each 4 years.
9. To maintain a bridge, $3000 will be required at the end of 3 years and annually thereafter. Find the capitalized expense (present value) of all future maintenance, if money is worth 5%.

NOTE 1. The **capitalized value** of an enterprise is the present value of all future earnings. Similarly, to speak of *capitalizing* any sequence of equal periodic payments due in the future means to find their present value. In following problems, we shall assume that such payments continue forever and thus form a *perpetuity*, although actually the annuity term only would be *very long*, and *not accurately known*. Our basis for this use of perpetuities is in the *Comment* following Example 1 on page 157.

10. If it costs $2500 at the end of each year to maintain a section of an unpaved road, how much would it pay to spend immediately to reduce the annual cost to $500, if money is worth 6%?

11. It is estimated that maintenance of a certain section of a railroad will require \$2000 per mile at the end of each 4 years. If money is worth 8%, find the capitalized cost of this maintenance per mile.

12. A philanthropist desires to endow perpetual care, at a cost of \$5000 at the end of each 6 months, for a city playground. If money is worth 9% compounded quarterly, what endowment is necessary?

13. In building a town hall, it is estimated that, with a wooden exterior, a repainting cost of \$4500 would be involved at the end of each 3 years. How much could the town afford to pay, beyond the cost of the wooden exterior, to install an aluminum exterior needing no future upkeep, if money is worth 5%?

14. Find the capitalized value of an enterprise which will yield net profit of \$20,000 at the end of each 2 years, if money is worth 8%.

15. What income for a university at the end of each year will be provided by an endowment of \$200,000 invested at 6% compounded quarterly?

16. An enterprise will yield \$700 profit at the end of each month. At what nominal rate compounded monthly will the capitalized value of the enterprise be \$125,000?

17. A sequence of annual payments of \$2000 each will start with the 1st payment at the end of 5 years, and then will continue forever. Find the present value of the perpetuity when money is worth 5%.

★18. Prove that $\lim_{n \to \infty} a_{\overline{n}|i} = 1/i$, and thus obtain $a_{\overline{\infty}|i} = 1/i$. Also, prove that $a_{\overline{\infty}|i} = 1/i$ by calculating the sum of the infinite geometric progression whose terms are $(1 + i)^{-1}, (1 + i)^{-2}, \cdots$.

59. Annual Investment Cost

In this section, in any reference to an *asset*, it may be merely a single machine or capital asset of some sort used in a business. Or, perhaps the asset might be a whole corporation which some investor may buy. Also, we include the case where the asset may have no earning power. This possibility is illustrated by the investment that a state or governmental agency might make in roads, schools, and any other public works.

Suppose that money is worth the rate i. Let \$$P$ be the original cost of an asset T which will have a residual or scrap value \$$L$ at the end of n years, when the investor G who buys T will end his use of it. The *wearing value* of T is \$$W =$ \$$P -$ \$$L$, which will disappear in n years due to use of T. In our present discussion, we shall not consider the effects of depreciation charges or taxes on the earning power of T, if such earning power exists.

The investor G who buys T at the cost \$$P$ could get \$$Pi$ elsewhere as income at the end of each year. Also, if G buys T, then \$$W$ of G's capital will disappear due to use of T in n years. Hence, G should establish a sinking fund, invested at the rate i, to replace the disappearing capital \$$W$ at the end of n years. If

$R is invested in this fund at the end of each year, the amount of the annuity at the end of n years should be W, or

$$W = Rs_{\overline{n}|i}, \quad \text{or} \quad R = \frac{W}{s_{\overline{n}|i}}.$$

Hence, an investor G, who can invest P at the interest rate i elsewhere, would desire the asset T to produce *at least* the following income M at the end of each year:

$$M = \text{(int. at rate } i \text{ on } \$P) + \text{(replacement deposit } \$R);^* \tag{1}$$

$$M = Pi + \frac{W}{s_{\overline{n}|i}}. \tag{2}$$

We shall call M the **annual investment cost** of owning T when money is worth the rate i. This cost exists even if T produces no income.

Example 1. Suppose that a machine T costs \$11,000 and will have a salvage value of \$1000 when retired from use at the end of 15 years. If money is worth 8% to an investor G, find the annual investment cost, or the minimum income per year which G would desire T to produce.

SOLUTION. The wearing value of T is \$10,000. Hence, from (2), the annual investment cost of T is

$$M = 880 + 10,000 \frac{1}{s_{\overline{15}|.08}} = 880 + 10,000(.03682954); \quad \text{(Table IX)}$$

$$M = 880 + 368.30 = \$1248.30.$$

If the salvage value of the asset in (2) is $L = 0$, then the equation $W = P - L$ gives $W = P$. Thus, from (2),

$$M = P\left(i + \frac{1}{s_{\overline{n}|i}}\right).$$

Hence, by use of (1) on page 69.

(*when* $W = P$) $\qquad\qquad M = P\frac{1}{a_{\overline{n}|i}}, \quad \text{or} \quad P = Ma_{\overline{n}|i}. \tag{3}$

We could have foreseen (3) immediately. A cost P, none of which is salvaged, is equivalent to an annuity of M per year for n years in case $P = Ma_{\overline{n}|i}$.

If two different assets are considered by an investor for performing a certain service, we agree that the assets are equally economical, when money is worth the rate i, if their annual investment costs are the same. This statement applies even if the assets have no earning power.

---

* We could assume that the investor's interest rate for investment of his capital replacement fund is a rate r, possibly less than i. Then $s_{\overline{n}|i}$ in (2) would become $s_{\overline{n}|r}$. We shall not include this added complication in (2).

Example 2. A certain type of pavement costs $12 per unit area and must be renewed at the same cost at the end of each 10 years. If money is worth 4%, how much could a highway commission afford to pay for a different variety of pavement if it would require renewal at its original cost at the end of each 15 years?

SOLUTION. Let x be the new cost per unit area, with 15 years as the life. The new variety can be used if its annual investment cost M per unit is the same as for the old variety. We use (3) to obtain M for one unit of each type.

$$\text{Annual cost for original pavement} = \frac{12}{a_{\overline{10}|.04}}.$$

$$\text{Annual cost for new pavement} = \frac{x}{a_{\overline{15}|.04}}.$$

Hence, $\qquad \dfrac{x}{a_{\overline{15}|.04}} = \dfrac{12}{a_{\overline{10}|.04}}; \qquad x = \dfrac{12a_{\overline{15}|}}{a_{\overline{10}|}} = \$16.45.$ $\qquad$ (Table VIII)

NOTE 1. We have $W = P - L$ in (2), where L is the final salvage value. Without added demonstration, we may allow the case where L is negative and thus $W > P$. For instance, a machine might cost $5000 and it might be necessary to pay $500 to get rid of it at the end of its life. In such a case, we consider $L = -\$500$ and the replacement cost is $W = P - L = \$5500$. The same possibility of $W > P$ occurs in connection with (5) below.

Suppose that money is worth the rate i. Then, for the asset involved in (2), the **capitalized cost** is defined as the sum K such that annual interest on it at the rate i is equal to the annual investment cost of the asset. Thus, $M = Ki$. From (2),

$$\left\{ \begin{matrix} \text{interest on} \\ \text{capitalized cost } \$K \end{matrix} \right\} = \left\{ \begin{matrix} \text{interest on} \\ \text{investment, } \$P \end{matrix} \right\} + \left\{ \begin{matrix} \text{replace. deposit} \\ \text{to restore capital} \end{matrix} \right\}. \qquad (4)$$

From $Ki = M$, we obtain $K = M/i$. Then (2) gives

$$\left\{ \begin{matrix} \text{capitalized} \\ \text{cost} \end{matrix} \right\} \qquad\qquad K = P + \frac{W}{is_{\overline{n}|i}}. \qquad (5)$$

From (4), K is a convenient sum such that, if operation of the asset yields profit equal to interest at the rate i on K, then the sum on the right in (4) is provided. This feature sometimes causes use of K in estimating the desirable profit from operations of public utility companies.

ILLUSTRATION 1. If a machine costs $3000 with life 15 years and final salvage value $500, the capitalized cost at 5% is found by use of (5):

$$T = 3000 + \frac{2500}{.05} \cdot \frac{1}{s_{\overline{15}|.05}} = 3000 + 50,000(.04634229) = \$5317.11.$$

In connection with the machine involved in (5) let us make the unrealistic assumption that replacements will continue *forever*, with the *same cost* $P for the machine at the end of each n years. Then, the replacement costs form a perpetuity of $W at the end of each n years: from (2) on page 158 the present value of this perpetuity is the fraction in (5). Hence, the capitalized cost, $K could be defined as *the original cost*, $P, *plus the present value of infinitely many future replacements*. It may be more convenient to remember the preceding definition than to use (5) as a formula.

Two assets are equally desirable for a given purpose if *their capitalized costs are the same*. The preceding statement gives a basis for a second method, equivalent to that used in Example 2, for comparing assets, by use of (2).

Exercise 43

Find the annual investment cost $M and also the capitalized cost $K of the machine, by first finding K and then using $M = Ki$. Money is worth 4%.

1. Machine with cost $15,000; life 8 years; final salvage value $3000.
2. Machine with cost $20,000; life 12 years; final salvage value $2000.
3-4. What cash return would an investor demand annually from operation of the machines in Problems 1 and 2, respectively, if he desires interest annually at the rate 8% on his investment and accumulates a replacement fund by investing annual deposits at 5%?
5. At 5% find the capitalized cost of an asset whose cost is $100,000, life is 15 years, and final salvage value is $10,000.
6. At 6%, find the capitalized cost of a bridge whose cost is $250,000 and life is 20 years, if the bridge must be partially rebuilt at a cost of $100,000 at the end of each 20 years.
7. A black-top pavement on a street would cost $10,000 and would last for 5 years with negligible repairs. At the end of each 5 years, $1000 would be spent to remove the old surface before $10,000 is spent again to lay a new surface. Find the capitalized cost of the pavement, at 5%.
8. For the street of Problem 7, it would cost $35,000 to install a thick cement pavement, which would last indefinitely, with a cost of $3000 for minor repairs at the end of each 5 years. If money is worth 5%, find the capitalized cost of the pavement, and compare its desirability with the pavement of Problem 7.
9. For a hot water boiler in a factory, we could use either a galvanized iron tank costing $500, which would need replacement at the same cost at the end of each 4 years, or a stainless steel tank costing $900, which would require replacement at the same cost at the end of each 8 years. If money is worth 6%, how much is saved in the annual investment cost by the more economical choice?

10. A corporation uses a type of motor truck which costs $5000, with life 2 years and final salvage value $800. How much could the corporation afford to pay for another type of truck for the same purpose whose life is 3 years, with final salvage value $1000? Money is worth 4%.

11. A machine costs $20,000, lasts for 6 years, and has a final salvage value of $2000. If money is worth 3%, how much could we afford to pay for a new machine for the same purpose whose life would be 9 years, with no final salvage value?

12. A machine costs $8000, lasts for 9 years, and has no final salvage value. If money is worth 5%, how much could we afford to pay for an improvement which would double the output of the machine but would reduce its life to 6 years, with the salvage value zero as before?

★60. Valuation of a Wasting Resource

A natural resource such as a mine, an oil or gas well, or a piece of timber land, wastes away as the units comprising the resource are removed and sold. The corresponding reduction in the value of the resource is called **depletion**. We shall call the typical asset of this nature a *mine*.

Consider a mine which will yield a cash dividend M from operations at the end of each year for n years and will be without value at the end of that time. If an investor pays P for the mine, he must take account of the fact that, due to depletion, P of his capital wastes away during the life of the mine. Hence, part of each dividend should be used to accumulate a capital replacement fund to return P at the end of n years. Consider an investor who desires interest at the rate i on his invested capital P, and will accumulate a replacement fund by investing R annually at his reinvestment rate r. Then, (1) of page 161 applies in the form

$$\left\{\begin{array}{c}\textbf{annual}\\\textbf{dividend } M\end{array}\right\} = \left\{\begin{array}{c}\textbf{int. at rate}\\\textbf{i on price } P\end{array}\right\} + \left\{\begin{array}{c}\textbf{replace. deposit } R,\\\textbf{to return capital}\end{array}\right\}. \quad (1)$$

In our application, the final salvage value of the asset (the mine) is $0, so that the replacement cost is $W = P$. Thus, (2) on page 161, with r as the rate for the replacement fund, gives

$$\left\{\begin{array}{c}\textit{final}\\\textit{value }\$0\end{array}\right\} \qquad M = P\left(i + \frac{1}{s_{\overline{n}|r}}\right) \qquad \textit{or} \qquad P = \frac{M}{i + \dfrac{1}{s_{\overline{n}|r}}}. \quad (2)$$

The result for P in (2) is referred to as the **mine valuation formula**; it applies to valuation of any dividend-paying enterprise where the final value of the producing asset is zero. Sometimes, (1) by itself is useful.

Example 1. The revenue from a mine will be $30,000 at the end of each year until the mine becomes exhausted at the end of 25 years. Find the price of the mine for an investor with $i = .08$ and $r = .05$.

SOLUTION $\quad P = \dfrac{30,000}{.08 + \dfrac{1}{s_{\overline{25}|.05}}} = \dfrac{30,000}{.08 + .02095246} = \$297,170.$ (Table IX)

★Exercise 44

Find each result correct only to four significant figures.

1. The annual dividend from a mine will be $75,000 until the ore is exhausted at the end of 30 years, and the mine becomes valueless. Find the price of the mine to yield the investor 6.5%, if he accumulates a replacement fund to restore his capital by annual investments at (*a*) 5%; (*b*) 6.5%.

2. A piece of timber land will yield a dividend of $50,000 at the end of each year for 8 years, when the timber rights will become valueless. Find the price of the timber to yield an investor 7%, if he accumulates his capital replacement fund at 4%.

3. The privileges of a patent will last for 20 more years, and the royalty from it will be $60,000 at the end of each year during that time. Find the value of these patent rights to an investor who desires interest at 8% on his investment and will accumulate a capital replacement fund at 5%.

4. A purchaser pays $500,000 for a mine which will become exhausted and valueless at the end of 25 years. What dividend from the mine will be required at the end of each year for 25 years to pay interest at 7% on the investment, and to accumulate a capital replacement fund at 4%?

5. An investor pays $110,000 for a mine which will yield a dividend of $20,000 at the end of each year for 10 years and then will become valueless. If he plans to accumulate a capital replacement fund at 4.5%, at what rate does he receive interest on his investment at the end of each year?

6. A wasting asset will pay a dividend $\$M$ at the end of each year for n years, and then will be sold for $\$L$. By use of (1) on page 164, obtain a formula for the price $\$P$ which the investor would be willing to pay for the asset if he accumulates his capital replacement fund at the rate r.

7. An investor pays $250,000 for an oil well which then will pay a dividend of $30,000 at the end of each 6 months for 9 years, and will be sold for $40,000 at the end of 9 years. He will accumulate a capital replacement fund by semi-annual deposits invested at 5% compounded semiannually. At what nominal rate will he receive interest on his investment at the end of each 6 months?

8. It is estimated that a certain wooden ship can be used efficiently for 10 years, and then can be sold, essentially as scrap, for $50,000. Operation of the ship will produce a dividend of $50,000 at the end of each year for 10 years. Find

the price of the ship to yield an investor 7.5%, if he accumulates a capital replacement fund at 4%.

Exercise 45 / Cumulative Review of Chapters 1–6

1. If $2037 is invested at 5% simple interest from March 13 to October 9, find the ordinary and the exact interest for (a) the actual number of days; (b) the approximate time.

2. Without logarithms, compute (a) $(1.02)^{150}$ accurate to one decimal place; (b) $(1.02)^{-150}$ accurate to three decimal places. Use Tables V and VI and laws of exponents.

3. A debt of $100,000 will be discharged, interest at 5% payable semi-annually included, by equal payments at the end of each 6 months for 9 years. (a) Find the semiannual payment. (b) Compute the first two rows in an amortization schedule for the debt.

4. A debt of $50,000 bears interest at 6.5% payable semiannually. The debtor will accumulate a sinking fund by equal deposits, on interest dates, invested at 5% compounded semiannually, to pay the principal at the end of 10 years. Find the debtor's semiannual expense on account of the debt.

5. Find the effective rate if the nominal rate 5% is compounded monthly.

6. By interpolation, find the rate at which interest is compounded quarterly if payments of $1000 at the end of each 3 months accumulate to $200,000 in 22 years.

7. If money is worth 4% effective, what equal payments at the ends of 2 years and 4 years will discharge all liability of the following debts: (a) $1000 due without interest at the end of 3 years; (b) $2000 due with accumulated interest at the rate 5% compounded semiannually at the end of 5 years? Use an equation of value. Obtain the result only to the nearest dollar.

8. (a) By interpolation, find how long it will take $1000 to accumulate to $1750 if invested at 5% compounded quarterly. (b) Accumulate $1000 for the resulting time by the approximate method of page 36, to verify the property mentioned after Example 2 on page 42.

9. At what interest rate payable semiannually will payments of $500 at the end of each 6 months for 10 years discharge a loan of $8000, principal and interest included? Use interpolation.

10. The purchaser of a farm paid $8000 cash and agreed to pay $1000 at the end of each year for 8 years. (a) Find the equivalent all-cash price if money is worth 5.5% payable annually. (b) At the end of 5 years, what must the purchaser pay, in addition to his regular payment, to discharge the debt immediately? (c) How much interest and how much principal does the purchaser pay at the end of 4 years?

11. On 3/1/78, Harris obtains a loan of $1500 from Roberts, and signs a note promising to pay the principal and accumulated simple interest at the rate 5% at the end of 120 days. On May 15, Roberts discounts the note at a bank whose discount rate is 6%. What does he receive?

12. A capital replacement fund is being accumulated by quarterly deposits of $300 each, invested at 6% compounded quarterly. (a) How much is in the fund just after the 25th deposit? (b) By how much does the fund increase on the day of the 26th deposit?

13. Find the nominal rate which, if compounded quarterly, is equivalent to $6\frac{1}{2}\%$ compounded (a) annually; (b) semiannually.

14. A machine costs $9000 and will have a salvage value of $600 at the end of 6 years. Find the depreciation charge at the end of each year (a) by the straight line method; (b) by the sum of the years' digits method; (c) by a constant percentage of declining book value, with the percentage as twice the "natural" rate as used in (a), and no assigned salvage value. (d) In Part (b), find the accrued depreciation and the remaining book value at the end of 3 years.

15. A man will deposit $200 with a savings and loan association at the beginning of each 3 months for 9 years. If the association pays interest at the rate 5.5% quarterly, find the sum to his credit (a) just after the last deposit; (b) at the end of 9 years.

16. A bridge will need painting repair at a cost of $3000 at the end of each year for a very long time. If money is worth 4%, find an approximation to the present value of all future painting repair.

17. A machine costs $150,000, and will have a scrap value of $10,000 when retired at the end of 15 years. If money is worth 4%, (a) find the annual investment cost of the machine; (b) find the capitalized cost.

18. If money now is worth (4%, $m = 1$), what payment at the end of 4 years, in addition to $1500 at the end of 2 years, will discharge all liability as to the following debts: (a) $1000 due at the end of 3 years with accumulated interest from today at {3%, $m = 1$}; (b) $2000 due at the end of 5 years with accumulated simple interest from today at 4%? Find the result only to the nearest $1.

19. To discharge a loan, including all interest compounded quarterly at the rate 8%, Hansen will make a sequence of 10 quarterly payments of $1000 each, the first due at the end of $3\frac{1}{2}$ years. (a) Find the sum borrowed. (b) Find his remaining liability just after his 4th payment.

20. An annuity is payable daily for 15 years. Find its present value if the amount of the annuity is $60,000 when interest is at the rate $\{4\%, m = 12\}$. Give a very simple solution.

21. Compute the ordinary interest on $3175.83 for 198 days by the 6% method (a) at 6%; (b) at 5%.

22. Find the present value of $1250 due at the end of 9 months if money can be invested at 8% simple interest. What is the discount on the $1250 involved?

23. Accumulate $5000 for 10 months at 6% simple interest.

24. Find the simple interest rate at which $1000 is the present value of $1150 due at the end of 18 months.

25. Find the amount due at the end of 18 months whose present value is $2730 at 6% simple discount.

26. Find the simple interest rate equivalent to the specified discount rate in the transaction of Problem 25.

27. By use of geometrical progressions, find expressions for the present value and the amount of an annuity of $50 payable quarterly for 8 years, if money is worth 8% compounded quarterly.

28. Jacobs borrowed $1000 from Gallagher on 3/15/77, agreeing to pay the compound amount at 5% compounded semiannually when the debt is settled. Jacob pays off the debt on 12/15/79. What does he pay if simple interest is used for the fractional part of an interest period?

29. A U.S. Treasury Bill for $10,000 is due in 120 days. It is quoted for sale at the discount rate 9%. (a) Find the purchase price. (b) Find the simple interest rate yielded by the transaction.

30. How long will it take for money to double itself, if invested at (a) 4% simple interest; (b) 4% effective (interpolate)?

31. If a given principal doubles in 11 years, find the interest rate if we use (a) simple interest; (b) interest compounded annually (interpolate).

32. A man will deposit $500 in a fund at the end of each 6 months for 5 years. Find the size of the fund at the end of 9 years if it is invested at $\{.06, m = 2\}$.

33. At what interest rate payable quarterly will payments of $500 at the beginning of each 3 months for 7 years discharge a debt of $12,500 due immediately? Use interpolation.

34. Find the discount if $2000 is discounted for 3 years at 5% compounded monthly.

35. Accumulate $3000 for 4 years at 7% compounded quarterly.

36. By approximate methods using simple interest for times less than an interest period, with money worth $\{.06, m = 4\}$, (a) find the compound amount if $1000 is invested for 2 years and 5 months; (b) find the present value if $1000 is discounted for 3 years and 7 months.

37. At 5% compounded monthly, find the capitalized value approximately of an income of $50 at the beginning of each month for an indefinitely long time.

38. A $1000, 5% bond pays coupons semiannually and will be redeemed at par at the end of $9\frac{1}{2}$ years. By use of both the general method and the premium or discount method, find the price of the bond to yield an investor (a) 4%; (b) 6%. (c) In each case, make up an investment schedule for the bond for one year after the purchase date.

39. In buying a farm worth $30,000 cash, the purchaser pays $10,000 cash and agrees to pay the balance, including interest at 5.5% compounded semiannually, by a sequence of 8 equal semiannual payments, the first due at the end of 4 years. Find the semiannual payment.

40. Find the compound interest earned by the end of 3 years if $2000 is invested at $\{5\%, m = 4\}$.

41. By interpolation in Table V, find the nominal rate compounded quarterly at which $2000 is the present value of $2600 due at the end of $3\frac{1}{2}$ years.

42. A man will invest $1000 at 6% in a fund at the end of each year for 12 years, and then allow the fund to accumulate at 6% for 8 more years. (a) By how much does the fund increase on the day of the 10th deposit? (b) Find the amount in the fund at the end of 20 years by use of Table VII alone. (Insert eight fictitious deposits.)

43. A debt of $15,000 will be discharged, interest at 5% payable annually included, by payments of $1000 at the end of each year as long as necessary, with a final smaller payment one year after the last $1000 is paid. (a) Find the outstanding principal just after the 6th payment. (b) What part of the 7th payment is interest on unpaid principal? (c) Find the final payment and when it is due. Use interpolation if desired.

44. If the compound amount on $1000 for 30 years at 3% compounded monthly is $2456.84, find $s_{\overline{360}|.0025}$.

45. Robinson borrows $1000 from Kasper and signs a note promising to pay the principal and accumulated simple interest at 5% at the end of 180 days. What does Kasper receive on selling the note 120 days before it is due to a man who discounts it (*a*) at 6% simple interest; (*b*) at 6% simple discount?

46. A $1000, 4% tax-exempt bond pays interest on 2/1 and 8/1, and is quoted at 105 and accrued interest on 11/1. Find the flat price then.

47. A $100, 6.5% bond pays interest semiannually and will be redeemed at a premium of 5% at the end of 12 years. Find the value of the bond to yield an investor 8%.

48. A machine costs $9000 and will last for 5 years. (*a*) Find the depreciation charge at the end of each year by the method using a constant percentage of declining book value, with the annual rate as twice the rate under the straight line method. (*b*) If the machine is sold as scrap for $750 at the end of 5 years, what profit or added expense will the owner have to declare in his tax report just after the machine is sold? (The profit or loss is based on the book value at the end of 5 years.)

49. If an investor's funds are invested in 9% bonds, at par, paying interest quarterly, at what rate compounded semiannually is his money invested?

50. A $1000, 5.5% bond pays interest on 4/1 and 10/1 and will be redeemed at par on 10/1/88. (*a*) Find the price of the bond to yield an investor 7% on 4/1/77. (*b*) Find the flat price and quotation to yield 7% on 8/1/77.

51. To discharge a debt due now, a debtor agrees to make $1000 payments at the beginning of each 6 months for 8 years, with these payments to include all interest at 7% payable semiannually. (*a*) Find the outstanding principal just after the 5th payment. (*b*) What part of the 6th payment is interest?

52. Find the nominal rate which, if compounded annually, is equivalent to accumulated simple interest at the rate 6% in a 4-year transaction. Use logarithms or interpolation.

53. A man can borrow $20,000, with interest payable semiannually at the rate 7.5% and the principal payable in one installment at the end of 9 years. To pay the principal, he would accumulate a sinking fund by equal deposits at the end of each 6 months, invested at 5% compounded semiannually. Find his total semiannual expense on account of the debt.

54. In Problem 53, at what rate payable semiannually could the man just as well borrow if he were allowed to discharge the debt, interest included, by equal payments at the end of each 6 months for 9 years? Interpolate in Table IX.

55. A 5% bond pays interest on 2/1 and 8/1 and will be redeemed at par on 8/1/88. The bond is quoted at 109 and accrued interest on 4/1/76. With the specified price assumed as given on the nearest interest date, find the yield of the bond (*a*) by an approximate method not involving use of any table; (*b*) by interpolation.

56. A man signs a contract to discharge a debt of $25,000, with interest at 5% payable semiannually, by equal payments including all interest at the end of each 6 months for 10 years. At the end of $3\frac{1}{2}$ years, this contract is sold to yield the new owner 6% compounded semiannually. Find the price paid, to the nearest $10.

57. A $100, 4% bond pays interest semiannually and will be redeemed at the end of 7 years. If the book value of the bond is 92\frac{1}{4}$, find the yield to an investor (*a*) by a method not involving use of a table; (*b*) by interpolation.

58. A debtor is paying 8% interest semiannually on a debt of $50,000, and has the privilege of paying the principal in one installment on any interest date. In order to repay the principal, he is accumulating a sinking fund by depositing $2000 at the end of each 6 months in a fund invested at $\{7\%, m = 2\}$. When will he be able to pay the principal of his debt?

59. At the end of each 6 months, $100,000 is placed in a fund which accumulates at 4% compounded semiannually. (*a*) Find the last payment date on which the fund contains less than $1,000,000. (*b*) On the next payment date, what payment, if any, is needed to complete a fund of $1,000,000?

60. Given that $.0006631399$ is the present value of $1 due at the end of 150 years if money can be invested at 5%, find $a_{\overline{150}|.05}$.

61. A payment of $250,000 is to be made at the end of 15 years through the accumulation of a fund by equal semiannual deposits, starting with one at the end of 1 year. Find the deposit if the fund accumulates at 6% compounded semiannually.

62. One type of telephone pole costs a corporation $250 installed and lasts for 12 years. If money is worth 4%, how much could the corporation afford to pay for a different variety which would last for 18 years, if the poles have no salvage value when worn out? Find the result only to the nearest dollar.

63. If money is worth 4%, find the present value (*a*) of a perpetuity of $200 payable annually, with the first payment due at the end of 5 years; (*b*) of a perpetuity of $5000 payable at the end of each 3 years.

64. A debt of $10,000 will be discharged, with interest payable annually included, by payments of $625 at the end of each six months for 12 years. Find the rate at which interest is paid, by interpolation.

65. A bank B offers a loan of $3000 to Richards on a new automobile, with equal payments including interest payable at the end of each month for 24 months. The bank will compute the monthly payment by the add-on method at 7%. (*a*) Find the monthly payment. (*b*) By interpolation in Table IX, find the true interest rate which B (because of the Truth in Lending Act) will inform Richards he is paying.

66. In purchasing a color television set for $950, a buyer will pay $250 cash. Also, he will make equal payments including interest at the end of each month for 12 months. The seller will compute the monthly payment by the add-on method at 8%. (*a*) Find the monthly payment. (*b*) By interpolation in Table IX, find the true rate of interest which the seller will specify to the buyer.

67. A man borrows $30,000 and signs a note promising to pay interest semi-annually at the rate 8% on all unpaid principal and to pay the principal in equal installments at the ends of the next 6 years. At the end of $3\frac{1}{2}$ years, this note is sold to yield the new investor 7% compounded semiannually. Find the price paid, by the premium or discount method.

68. A $1000, 5% bond pays interest on 3/1 and 9/1 and is redeemable at par on 3/1/87. (*a*) Find the price on 3/1/76 to yield 4%. (*b*) Find the market quotation on a price and accrued interest basis on 5/1/76 to yield an investor 4%.

69. A sinking fund will be accumulated by investing $400 at the end of each 6 months at 7% compounded semiannually. At the end of $4\frac{1}{2}$ years, how much of the increase in the fund is interest credited then?

70. If it costs $3000 at the end of each year to maintain a certain unpaved road, how much would it pay to spend immediately to build a practically permanent paved road, if money is worth 5%?

71. An industrial commission awards $50,000 damages, plus attorney fees, to the wife of a workman killed in an accident. It is ordered that this sum shall be invested with an insurance company at 3% payable monthly, to provide $300 at the beginning of each month until the fund is exhausted. Find the concluding payment and when it is due. Use interpolation if desired.

72. A debt will be discharged by paying $500 at the end of each 3 months for 11 years. If the payments include all interest at 7% payable quarterly, (*a*) find the original principal of the debt; (*b*) what part of the 12th payment is a repayment of principal and what part is interest on unpaid principal?

73. Griffith buys a house worth $45,000 cash from Wilder. Griffith signs a contract to pay $10,000 cash, the remaining principal in equal installments at the end of each year for 7 years, and interest semiannually at 8% on all outstanding principal. Wilder sells this contract five years later to yield the buyer 9% compounded semiannually. How much does he pay for the contract? Use the premium or discount method.

74. Colson has promised to pay Fox $2000 plus accumulated interest at 5% compounded quarterly at the end of 6 years. Fox agrees to let Colson pay equivalent equal sums at the end of each 6 months for 6 years under the assumption that money now is worth 4% compounded semiannually. Find the semiannual payment to the nearest dollar.

75. It is estimated that a certain mine will yield net profit of $30,000 at the end of each year practically forever. Find the capitalized value of this mine approximately if money is worth 8%.

76. If money is worth 8%, find the annual investment cost to the nearest dollar of an asset whose original cost is $10,000, useful life is 6 years, and salvage value is $1000.

77. An investor pays $500,000 for an oil well which will pay a dividend of $75,000 at the end of each 6 months for 10 years. He will accumulate a capital replacement fund by semiannual deposits invested at $\{6\%, m = 2\}$. At what nominal rate will he receive interest on his investment at the end of each six months, if the well will have a market value of $100,000 at the end of 10 years?

78. A debt of $20,000 will bear interest at 4.5% compounded semiannually. To discharge the debt, interest included, the debtor will pay $2000 at the end of 3 years and semiannually thereafter until a final date when less than the usual installment completes payment of the debt. (*a*) Find the outstanding principal just after the 5th payment. (*b*) Find the final payment and when it is due.

79. On 3/15/75, Dolan borrows $5000 from Jacobson, and signs a note promising to pay interest semiannually at the rate $5\frac{1}{4}\%$, and to pay the principal at the end of 6 years. (*a*) On 9/15/78, Jacobson sells this note to yield a new investor 6%. What does he pay? (*b*) What would this investor pay on 11/15/78?

80. In place of a creditor requiring $250 at the end of each 3 months, how much would he be willing to receive instead at the end of each year, if money is worth $\{7\%, m = 4\}$?

81. In place of a creditor requiring payments of $150 at the end of each month, what would he be willing to accept at the beginning of each year if money is worth 9% compounded monthly?

82. In order to have $8000 available at the end of 7 years, a sinking fund will be accumulated by investing equal deposits at the beginning of each 6 months for the 7 years. Find the deposit if the fund is invested at 4.5% compounded semiannually.

★83. To provide $40,000 at the end of 12 years, $2000 will be deposited in a fund at the end of each year for 4 years, and then other equal deposits at the end of each year for the remaining 8 years. If the fund is invested at 3%, find the unknown annual deposit.

★84. A mine will yield a dividend of $25,000 at the end of each year for 20 years, when the mine will become valueless. Find the value of the mine, to the nearest $100, for an investor who desires interest at the rate 7% on his original investment and will accumulate a capital replacement fund by investing equal deposits at the end of each year at 4%.

★85. A $1000, 5% bond pays interest on 12/1. At the option of the debtor corporation, the bond may be redeemed at par on any 12/1 from 1980 to 1989, with redemption certain on or before 12/1/89. (a) Find the price to yield an investor at least 6% on 12/1/76. (b) If he buys at the preceding price, find his yield by the approximate method if the option most favorable to him is taken by the corporation.

★86. A $1000, 6% bond pays interest on 2/1 and will be redeemed on any interest date from 2/1/84 to 2/1/93. (a) Find the price on 2/1/76 to yield the investor at least 4%. (b) If the bond is purchased at this price, find the yield obtained if the bond actually is redeemed on the date most favorable to the purchaser (use an approximate method).

★87. A $1000, 7% bond pays interest on 5/1 and will be redeemed at par on 5/1/91. The bond is bought to yield 8% by an investor on 5/1/78. In his bookkeeping on 5/1/80, how much interest will he list as received, and how much of his original invested principal will he list as repaid by accumulation of the discount? (Notice that the price on 5/1/78 is not needed. What more convenient price should be computed?)

★88. A man will buy into a business when his savings amount to $15,000. He now has $5000 and can invest at 4% compounded semiannually. What equal sums should he invest at the beginning of each 6 months in order to have the desired amount at the end of 6 years?

★89. In order to accumulate a fund at the end of 9 years, $1000 will be placed in the fund at the end of each year for 9 years. Find the final amount in the fund to the nearest $10 if it is invested at 7% for the first 4 years and at 5% for the last 5 years.

★90. A $1000 bond with interest payable annually will be redeemed at par at the end of 11 years. Find the annual coupon payment if the bond yields 5.5% when bought for $1110.

★**91.** A debt of $150,000 will be discharged, interest included, by equal payments at the end of each 6 months for 15 years, with interest at 4% compound semiannually for the first 10 years, and at 5% compounded semiannually for the last 5 years. What single interest rate over the 15 years would result in the same periodic payment?

★**92.** A man borrows $15,000 and agrees to discharge all principal and accumulated interest by a sequence of 9 successive annual payments of $2200 each, with the 1st payment at the end of 4 years. At what rate compounded annually is the transaction executed?

★**93.** A $1000, 5% bond pays interest on 4/1. On 4/1/77, the flat price of the bond is $900 to yield the investor 6%. Find the flat price to yield the investor 6% on 4/1/81. The bond is not assumed to be redeemable at par.

7/ General Annuity Formulas

61. Annuity Problems Not Under Simple Case

Up to this point in the text, each annuity problem has come under the simple case, where the payment interval is the same as the interest period.* As a rule, any annuity problem which does not come under the simple case presents one or other of the following features, where Case I is more simple to deal with than Case II.

I. *The payment interval of the annuity may be an integral multiple of the interest period.*

II. *The interest period may be an integral multiple of the payment interval.*

In a later section we shall derive formulas which will cover not only possibilities I and II, but also any other conceivable case. In all formulas which we shall obtain, our procedure will involve a reduction of any complicated data to an equivalent problem under the simple case, where we may use the standard formulas $A = Ra_{\overline{m}|i}$ and $S = Rs_{\overline{m}|i}$.

62. Payment Interval is k Interest Periods, k an Integer

The method to be used later in deriving certain general formulas is illustrated in the solution of the following problem.

Example 1. If money is worth 4% compounded quarterly, find the present value of an annuity of $100 payable semiannually for 15 years.

SOLUTION. 1. **Auxiliary Problem.** *What payment $W at the end of each 3 months would be equivalent to $100 at the end of each 6 months?* Or, we may ask

---

* Except for perpetuities as met on page 158.

what payment W at the end of each interest period (that is, at the end of each 3 months) will create a sinking fund to provide $100 at the end of each 6 months? Then, $100 is the amount of an annuity of W payable quarterly for 6 months:

$$100 = Ws_{\overline{2}|.01}; \qquad W = \frac{100}{s_{\overline{2}|.01}} = \$49.7512. \qquad \text{(Table IX)}$$

2. The present value A of the annuity of $100 payable *semiannually* is the same as the present value of the annuity of $49.75 payable *quarterly*, for the 15 years. Hence, by use of $A = Ra_{\overline{n}|i}$ and Table VIII,

$$A = 49.7512a_{\overline{60}|.01} = \$2236.57.$$

In Example 1 we met a special case of the following results, where k is an integer. This Summary covers all problems under Case I of Section 61.

Summary

If an ordinary annuity pays $R at the end of each k interest periods for a term of n interest periods, and i is the interest rate per period, the present value A and amount S of the annuity are given by

$$A = \frac{R}{s_{\overline{k}|i}} a_{\overline{n}|i}; \qquad S = \frac{R}{s_{\overline{k}|i}} s_{\overline{n}|i}. \tag{1}$$

PROOF.   1. First, we ask for the solution of the following auxiliary problem: *What payment W, if made at the end of each interest period, is equivalent to a payment of $R at the end of each k interest periods?* To solve this problem, consider just one payment interval; R paid *at the end of k periods* is equivalent to k payments of W each, paid *at the end of each interest period*. Then, R is the amount of an annuity of W per interest period for k periods. Or,

$$R = Ws_{\overline{k}|i}, \qquad or \qquad W = \frac{R}{s_{\overline{k}|i}}. \tag{2}$$

2. The annuity of R at the end of each k periods for n interest periods is equivalent to an annuity of W at the end of each interest period for n periods, where the data now come under the simple case. Hence, with $R/s_{\overline{k}|i}$ as *the equivalent payment per interest period*,

$$A = Ws_{\overline{n}|i}, \qquad or \qquad A = \frac{R}{s_{\overline{k}|i}} a_{\overline{n}|i}.$$

Example 2.   To discharge a loan of $2000 with interest at the rate 6% compounded quarterly, a debtor agrees to make equal payments at the end of each year for 8 years. Find the annual payment.

SOLUTION.   1. The payment interval is *four times the interest period*.

> **Analysis:** $k = 4$; $i = .015$; $A = 2000$; $n = 32$.

2. Hence, from (1),
$$2000 = \frac{R}{s_{\overline{4}|.015}}\, a_{\overline{32}|.015};$$

$$R = \frac{2000 s_{\overline{4}|.015}}{a_{\overline{32}|.015}}\,;\qquad R = \frac{2000(4.09090)}{25.2671} = \$323.81.\qquad \text{(Tables VII, VIII, II)}$$

Example 3. To discharge a debt of \$10,000 with interest at the rate $4\frac{1}{2}\%$ compounded monthly, a debtor agrees to make equal payments at the beginning of each 6 months for 20 years. Find the semiannual payment.

SOLUTION. Let the periodic payment be R. The present value of the payments is \$10,000. The payments form an annuity *due*, with 40 payments. Just after the first payment, the remaining 39 payments form an ordinary annuity whose term is $19\frac{1}{2}$ years. From (1),

$$(pr.\ val.) = (1\text{st } payt.) + (pr.\ value\ of\ remaining\ payments);\qquad (3)$$

$$10{,}000 = R + \frac{R}{s_{\overline{6}|\frac{3}{8}\%}}\, a_{\overline{234}|\frac{3}{8}\%};\qquad\qquad [\text{In (1), } k = 6 \text{ and } n = 234]$$

$$10{,}000 s_{\overline{6}|} = R s_{\overline{6}|} + R a_{\overline{234}|};\qquad R = \frac{10{,}000 s_{\overline{6}|}}{s_{\overline{6}|} + a_{\overline{234}|}}\,;\qquad (\text{at } \tfrac{3}{8}\%)$$

$$R = (60{,}565.3/161.655) = \$374.66.$$

Exercise 46

1. If money is worth 4% compounded monthly, what payment at the end of each month could replace \$1000 paid at the end of each year?
2. If money is worth 6% compounded quarterly, what payment at the end of each 3 months could replace \$500 paid at the end of each 6 months?

*Find the present value A or the amount S of the annuity.**

Prob.	Payment	Payment Interval	Term	Interest Rate	Find
3.	\$ 200	1 yr.	9 yr.	$5\%,\ m = 4$	S
4.	500	3 mo.	$5\frac{1}{2}$ yr.	$3\%,\ m = 12$	A
5.	250	3 mo.	8 yr.	$4\frac{1}{2}\%,\ m = 12$	A
6.	200	3 mo.	14 yr.	$6\%,\ m = 4$	S
7.	1000	6 mo.	15 yr.	$4\%,\ m = 12$	S
8.	500	6 mo.	20 yr.	$5\frac{1}{2}\%,\ m = 4$	A
9.	100	2 yr.	28 yr.	$6\frac{1}{2}\%,\ m = 2$	A

* Problems in this chapter involve elaborate computation. Answers are given usually as obtained with a ten-place computer. However, the teacher may desire to accept results as computed by use of only five-place or six-place logarithms.

10. Find the amount of an annuity of $300 payable annually for 29 years if money is worth 3% compounded semiannually.

11. A purchaser of a house will pay $6000 cash and $1000 at the end of each 6 months for 8 years. If money is worth $5\frac{1}{2}$% compounded quarterly, find the cash valuation of the house.

12. A man will deposit $1000 at the end of each 6 months in a bank which credits interest quarterly at the rate 3%. Find the sum to the man's credit at the beginning of the 7th year.

13. The purchaser of a farm will pay $1200 at the end of each 6 months for 7 years. If money is worth 5% compounded monthly, find the equivalent cash price.

14. A debtor agreed to pay $200 at the beginning of each 6 months for 9 years. If money is worth 5% compounded quarterly, find the outstanding principal of the debt just after his third payment.

15. At the end of each 2 years, $2400 will be invested in an account at a savings and loan association at 4% compounded semiannually. Find the size of the fund at the beginning of the 19th year.

16. Find the periodic payment of an annuity payable semiannually for 15 years whose amount is $4000 if interest is at the rate 6% compounded quarterly.

17. A debt of $7000 will be discharged by equal payments at the end of each 6 months for 7 years. Find the semiannual payment if money is worth 5% compounded quarterly.

18. A $1000, 5% bond pays interest on February 1 and August 1 and will be redeemed at 110% on February 1, 1993. Find the price of the bond on February 1, 1979 to yield $4\frac{1}{2}$% compounded quarterly.

19. In order to create a sinking fund of $5000 at the end of 12 years, equal deposits will be invested at the end of each 6 months at 4% compounded quarterly. Find the semiannual deposit.

20. In order to have $8000 at the end of 3 years to use for a college education, what equal deposits must a war veteran invest at the end of each year at 5% compounded quarterly?

21. The buyer of a cannery promises to pay $5000 cash, and a sequence of 20 semiannual payments of $2000 each, the first due at the end of $2\frac{1}{2}$ years. If these payments discharge all liability as to interest and principal, find the equivalent cash price if money is worth 5% compounded monthly.

22. A debt of $7500 will be discharged, interest included, by a sequence of 14 equal semiannual payments, the first due at the end of 4 years. Find the payment if money is worth 4% compounded quarterly.

63. General Formulas for A and S

The data for any problem involving computation of the present value A and amount S of an annuity can be described by use of the following symbols.

$$R = (periodic\ payment\ of\ the\ annuity). \tag{1}$$

$$i = (interest\ rate\ per\ conversion\ period). \tag{2}$$

$$n = (length\ of\ term\ of\ the\ annuity\ in\ interest\ periods). \tag{3}$$

$$p = \frac{interest\ period}{payment\ interval} \quad or \quad k = \frac{payment\ interval}{interest\ period}\ ; \quad k = \frac{1}{p}. \tag{4}$$

The simple case occurs when $p = k = 1$. Case I of page 176 occurs when k is an integer, and Case II when p is an integer and thus k is a fraction $1/p$.

ILLUSTRATION 1. Consider an annuity of $60 payable quarterly for 5 years. If interest is at the rate 4% compounded semiannually,

$$R = 60; \quad i = .02; \quad n = 10; \quad p = 2; \quad k = \tfrac{1}{2}.$$

For any data (1)–(4), where $k \neq 1$, we shall propose finding equivalent new data under the simple case. Then, A and S for the *given data* will be obtained as the values of A and S corresponding to the *new data*, where formulas of the simple case can be used.

Example 1. Find the present value A of an annuity of $100 payable quarterly for $12\tfrac{1}{2}$ years, if money is worth $\{.05, m = 2\}$.

SOLUTION. 1. We first propose the following problem:

$$\left\{ \begin{array}{l} With\ 3\ mo.\ as\ a\ new\ interest\ period,\ what\ is\ the\ rate\ r\ per \\ new\ period\ if\ the\ new\ rate\ is\ equivalent\ to\ \{.05, m = 2\}? \end{array} \right\} \tag{5}$$

To solve (5), invest $1 at the rate r per 3 mo., for a term of 6 mo.; also invest $1 for 6 mo. at $\{.05, m = 2\}$. The results are equal when r satisfies (5). We use $F = P(1 + i)^n$ with $P = 1$:

At $\{.05, m = 2\}$, $\qquad\qquad\qquad\qquad F = 1.025.$

At rate r per 3 mo., $\qquad\qquad\qquad F = (1 + r)^2.$

$$(1 + r)^2 = 1.025; \quad 1 + r = (1.025)^{.5}; \quad r = (1.025)^{.5} - 1. \tag{6}$$

2. With interest at the rate r per 3 mo., we have data of the simple case. From $A = Ra_{\overline{n}|i}$ with $i = r$, $R = 100$, and $n = 50$, and from (8) on page 64,

$$A = 100a_{\overline{50}|r} = 100\frac{1 - (1 + r)^{-50}}{r}. \tag{7}$$

From (6), $\qquad\qquad (1 + r)^{-50} = [(1.025)^{.5}]^{-50} = (1.025)^{-25}. \tag{8}$

From (6), (7), and (8), $\qquad\qquad A = 100\frac{1 - (1.025)^{-25}}{(1.025)^{.5} - 1}.$

By use of Tables VI, XIV, and I, we compute $A = 3708.

To obtain A and S for data (1)–(4), we first propose the following problem:

$$\left\{\begin{array}{l}\textit{If the payment interval is taken as a new interest period,}\\ \textit{find the new interest rate } r \textit{ per new period which is}\\ \textit{equivalent to the given rate } i \textit{ per old interest period.}\end{array}\right\} \quad (9)$$

To solve (9), we invest \$1 at each of the rates r and i for one *old* interest period, and state that the amounts* F are the same. From (4), the old interest period is p payment intervals, or p new interest periods.

Comp. amt. F, on \$1 at rate r after one old conversion period, or p new periods:

$$F = (1 + r)^p.$$

Comp. amt. F at rate i after one old conversion period:

$$F = 1 + i.$$

Since the rates are equivalent,

$$(1 + r)^p = 1 + i; \quad 1 + r = (1 + i)^{1/p}; \quad r = (1 + i)^{1/p} - 1. \quad (10)$$

We obtained $1 + r = (1 + i)^{1/p}$ by taking the pth root of both sides of $(1 + r)^p = 1 + i$.

Now, we consider the following data which are equivalent to (1)–(4), because amounts and present values at the old rate i are the same as at the new rate r, whose interest period is the *payment interval*. From (3) and (4), since each interest period is p payment intervals, the term of the annuity is np *payment intervals*. The new data under the simple case are as follows:

$$R = (\textit{periodic payt.}); \quad r = (\textit{int. rate per new period}); \quad \textit{term} = (np \textit{ periods}).$$

Then, from (8) on page 64, the amount S of the annuity is

$$S = Rs_{\overline{np}|r} = R\frac{(1 + r)^{np} - 1}{r}. \quad (11)$$

From (10),

$$(1 + r)^{np} = [(1 + r)^p]^n = (1 + i)^n. \quad (12)$$

From (10), (11), and (12),

$$S = R\frac{(1 + i)^n - 1}{(1 + i)^{1/p} - 1}. \quad (13)$$

Similarly,

$$A = R\frac{1 - (1 + i)^{-n}}{(1 + i)^{1/p} - 1}. \quad (14)$$

From (13),

$$S = R\frac{i}{(1 + i)^{1/p} - 1} \cdot \frac{(1 + i)^n - 1}{i}. \quad (15)$$

Recall

$$s_{\overline{k}|i} = \frac{(1 + i)^k - 1}{i} \quad \textit{and} \quad \frac{1}{s_{\overline{k}|i}} = \frac{i}{(1 + i)^k - 1}. \quad (16)$$

---

* We imply use of the theoretical amount as obtained from $F = P(1 + i)^n$ when n is not an integer, if this case should arise. See Problems 11–17 on page 38.

In (15), the last fraction is $s_{\overline{n}|i}$. Previously, we have employed $s_{\overline{k}|i}$ only when k is a positive integer, and then $s_{\overline{k}|i}$ represents the amount (in dollars) of an annuity of \$1 per interest period for k periods. Now, however, think of $s_{\overline{k}|i}$ *merely as an algebraic symbol* defined by the first equation in (16), *even when k is not an integer*. Then, in (15), the 1st fraction is simply $1/s_{\overline{k}|i}$ with $k = 1/p$. Thus, (15) becomes

$$\left(\text{with } k = \frac{1}{p}\right) \qquad\qquad S = R\frac{1}{s_{\overline{k}|i}}\, s_{\overline{n}|i}. \qquad\qquad (17)$$

Similarly, from (14) we obtain A in the following Summary.

Summary

For an annuity whose periodic payment is R and term is n interest periods, with i as the interest rate per conversion period, and

$$k = \frac{\text{payment interval}}{\text{interest period}}: \qquad\qquad (18)$$

$$A = \frac{R}{s_{\overline{k}|i}}\, a_{\overline{n}|i}; \quad S = \frac{R}{s_{\overline{k}|i}}\, s_{\overline{n}|i}. \qquad\qquad (19)$$

Notice that (19) is the same as (1) on page 177 except that *now we have the right to use k as a fraction $1/p$ in* (19). Thus, the single set of formulas (19) applies in both of Cases I and II on page 176. When k is a fraction $1/p$, Table XI or Table XII is used with $s_{\overline{k}|i}$.

ILLUSTRATION 2. From Table XI, $s_{\overline{.5}|.02} = .49752469$. From Table XII.

$$\frac{1}{s_{\overline{.5}|.02}} = 2.00995049.$$

In (19), let $W = R/s_{\overline{k}|i}$. Then, (19) shows that $A = Wa_{\overline{n}|i}$, or A is the present value of an annuity of W paid at the end of each interest period. That is, in both of Cases I and II on page 176, $R/s_{\overline{k}|i}$ is the payment at the end of each interest period which is equivalent to R paid at the end of each payment interval.

Example 2. Find the amount of an annuity of \$50 payable monthly for 18 years, if money is worth 5% compounded quarterly.

SOLUTION. Interest period is 3 months; payment interval is 1 month.

> **Analysis:** $k = \dfrac{1\text{ mo.}}{3\text{ mo.}} = \dfrac{1}{3}$; $R = 50$; $n = 72$; $i = .0125$.

From (19), $$S = 50\frac{1}{s_{\overline{1/3}|.0125}}(s_{\overline{72}|.0125});$$

$$S = 50(3.01246549)(115.67362145) = \$17,423. \qquad \text{(Tables VII and XII)}$$

NOTE 1. Consider an annuity *due*, with data (R, n, i, k) as in (1)–(4), and with $\ddot{A}$ and $\ddot{S}$ as the present value and amount, respectively. This annuity *due*, paying R at the *beginning* of each k interest periods, is equivalent to an *ordinary* annuity paying $R(1 + i)^k$ at the *end* of each k periods. Hence, $\ddot{A}$ is obtained from A in (19) on replacing R by $R(1 + i)^k$:

$$\ddot{A} = \frac{R(1 + i)^k}{s_{\overline{k}|i}} a_{\overline{n}|i} = \frac{R}{(1 + i)^{-k}s_{\overline{k}|i}} a_{\overline{n}|i} = \frac{R}{a_{\overline{k}|i}} a_{\overline{n}|i}, \tag{20}$$

where we use $(1 + i)^{-k}s_{\overline{k}|i} = a_{\overline{k}|i}$, from (3) on page 64, and define $a_{\overline{k}|i}$ by the customary formula even when k is a fraction. Similarly, we obtain $\ddot{S}$ from (19), and thus have the following results, where we apply Table IX when k is an integer, and Table X or Table XII when $k = 1/p$, p an integer:

$$\left\{ \begin{array}{c} \text{annuity} \\ \text{due} \end{array} \right\} \qquad \ddot{A} = \frac{R}{a_{\overline{k}|i}} a_{\overline{n}|i}; \qquad \ddot{S} = \frac{R}{a_{\overline{k}|i}} s_{\overline{n}|i}. \tag{21}$$

Example 3. At the death of a man, his wife becomes the beneficiary of his life insurance policy, which has a cash value of $20,000. She is allowed the option of leaving this sum with the insurance company, which then promises to pay her or her heirs equal payments at the end of each month for 20 years, with payments computed under the assumption that money is worth $3\frac{1}{2}\%$ effective (a common rate in insurance practice). Find the monthly payment.

SOLUTION. The interest rate is $3\frac{1}{2}\%$ compounded annually. The term of the annuity is 20 interest periods. The payment interval is 1 month.

> **Analysis:** $i = .035$; $k = \frac{1}{12}$; $A = 20,000$; $n = 20$.

From (19), $\qquad\qquad 20,000 = R\dfrac{1}{s_{\overline{1/12}|.035}} a_{\overline{20}|.035};$

$$20,000s_{\overline{1/12}|} = Ra_{\overline{20}|}; \quad R = 20,000s_{\overline{1/12}|}\frac{1}{a_{\overline{20}|}}; \qquad\qquad (at\ .035)$$

$$R = 20,000(.08202568)(.07036108) = \$115.42. \qquad \text{(Tables IX, XI)}$$

Exercise 47

1. An annuity will pay $200 at the end of each 3 months for 8 years. Find the present value of the annuity if money is worth 4% compounded (*a*) semi-annually; (*b*) monthly; (*c*) quarterly.
2. An annuity will pay $100 at the end of each 6 months for 12 years. Find

the amount of the annuity if money is worth $4\frac{1}{2}\%$ compounded (a) quarterly; (b) semiannually; (c) annually.

Compute the present value A or amount S as specified.

Prob.	Payment	Payment Interval	Term of Annuity	Investment Rate	Find
3.	$1000	3 mo.	$5\frac{1}{2}$ yr.	.06, $m = 2$	S
4.	250	1 mo.	18 yr.	.05, $m = 4$	A
5.	125	6 mo.	21 yr.	.035, $m = 2$	A
6.	500	1 yr.	8 yr.	.08, $m = 4$	S
7.	300	6 mo.	7 yr.	.07, $m = 1$	A

8. A debtor agrees to pay $500 at the end of each 3 months for 10 years. If money is worth 5% compounded semiannually, what did he borrow?

9. In place of a payment of $250 at the end of each month for 4 years, what equivalent payment should be made at the end of 4 years, if money is worth $4\frac{1}{2}\%$ compounded quarterly?

10. The purchaser of a farm will pay $2000 cash and $500 at the end of each 3 months for 15 years. If money is worth 4% compounded semiannually, find the cash value of the farm.

11. Find the periodic payment of an annuity, payable quarterly for 11 years, whose present value is $10,000 if interest is at $\{.04, m = 2\}$.

12. What sum paid at the end of each 3 months for 2 years is equivalent to $3000 paid at the end of 2 years if money is worth $\{.05, m = 2\}$?

13. If $200 is invested in a fund at the end of each 3 months for 6 years, how much is in the fund just after the last deposit if interest is at the rate 4% compounded monthly?

14. The maturity value of an insurance policy is $15,000. The beneficiary, or his estate, is entitled to equal payments at the end of each month for 20 years, with money considered worth .035 compounded semiannually. Find the monthly payment.

15. In order to accumulate a fund of $15,000 to pay a debt at the end of 12 years, a man will invest equal deposits at the end of each 3 months for the 12 years, at $3\frac{1}{2}\%$ compounded quarterly. Find the deposit.

16. If money is worth 5% compounded semiannually, find the present value of a sequence of 12 quarterly payments of $500 each, the first of which is due at the end of $5\frac{1}{4}$ years.

17. If money is worth 4% effective, find the present value of a sequence of quarterly payments of $300 each, the first due at the end of $2\frac{1}{4}$ years and the last at the end of 7 years.

18. Find the periodic payment of an annuity, payable semiannually for 15 years, whose amount is $8000 when interest is at $\{.06, m = 4\}$.

19. If money is worth $\{.04, m = 4\}$, what equal payments at the end of each 6 months for 5 years would discharge a loan of $7500?

20. An insurance endowment policy on maturing gives the option of an immediate payment of $25,000 or an annuity payable quarterly for 10 years. If money is worth $3\frac{1}{2}\%$ effective in the policies of the insurance company, find the quarterly payment of the annuity.

21. To discharge a debt, a man will pay $400 at the beginning of each 3 months for 5 years. Find the sum borrowed, if the payments discharge all liability as to principal and interest at $4\frac{1}{2}\%$ compounded (a) quarterly; (b) monthly; (c) semiannually. See (21) on page 183.

22. A man will deposit $300 in a fund at the beginning of each 3 months for 6 years. How much will be in the fund at the end of 6 years if the money accumulates at $3\frac{1}{2}\%$ compounded (a) quarterly; (b) monthly?

23. In order to buy a $3500 automobile for cash at the end of 3 years, what equal payments must a man deposit in a bank at the end of each 6 months if the bank accumulates the money at 3% compounded quarterly?

24. At retirement, a worker finds that his accumulated reserve in a pension fund is $50,000. He or his estate will receive equivalent payments at the end of each month for 25 years. Find the monthly payment, if money is considered worth 4% compounded quarterly.

25. If money is worth $5\frac{1}{2}\%$ compounded semiannually, what equal quarterly payments for 12 years will amortize a debt of $15,000 if the payments occur at (a) the end of each 3 months; (b) the beginning of each 3 months?

26. A man creates a trust fund by placing $50,000 in the hands of an insurance company, to provide his wife or her estate with equal payments at the end of each month for 20 years. If the company computes the payments under the assumption that money is worth 4% compounded quarterly, find the monthly payment from the fund.

27. Take the following new definitions of R, p, and n. Let R be the annual rent* of an ordinary annuity payable p times per year for n years. Suppose that interest is at the nominal rate j compounded m times per year and, with w as the effective rate, obtain $(1 + w)$ from page 28. Then obtain the following formulas for A and S by substituting $(1 + w)$ for $(1 + i)$ in (13) and (14) on page 181.

$$A = R\frac{1 - \left(1 + \frac{j}{m}\right)^{-mn}}{p\left[\left(1 + \frac{j}{m}\right)^{m/p} - 1\right]}; \qquad S = R\frac{\left(1 + \frac{j}{m}\right)^{mn} - 1}{p\left[\left(1 + \frac{j}{m}\right)^{m/p} - 1\right]}.$$

These formulas once were fundamental, when the interest period was not recognized as the best time unit for theory.

* The *annual rent* is defined as the sum of the payments of the annuity made in one year.

★64. Other General Formulas for A and S

With data (1) to (4) on page 180, define $a_{\overline{n}|i}^{(p)}$ and $s_{\overline{n}|i}^{(p)}$ by

$$a_{\overline{n}|i}^{(p)} = \frac{1 - (1 + i)^{-n}}{p[(1 + i)^{1/p} - 1]} \; ; \qquad s_{\overline{n}|i}^{(p)} = \frac{(1 + i)^n - 1}{p[(1 + i)^{1/p} - 1]} \cdot \tag{1}$$

Let $W = pR$. Then, in (13) and (14) on page 181, we find that $A = Wa_{\overline{n}|i}^{(p)}$ and $S = Ws_{\overline{n}|i}^{(p)}$. From (1) with $n = 1$,

$$s_{\overline{1}|i}^{(p)} = \frac{i}{j_p}, \qquad \text{where} \qquad j_p = p[(1 + i)^{1/p} - 1]. \tag{2}$$

Then, from (1) and (2), on multiplying each numerator and denominator in (1) by i, we obtain

$$A = Wa_{\overline{n}|i}^{(p)} = Ws_{\overline{1}|i}^{(p)} a_{\overline{n}|i}; \qquad S = Ws_{\overline{n}|i}^{(p)} = Ws_{\overline{1}|i}^{(p)} s_{\overline{n}|i}; \tag{3}$$

or, from (2),
$$A = W\frac{i}{j_p} a_{\overline{n}|i}; \qquad S = W\frac{i}{j_p} a_{\overline{n}|i}. \tag{4}$$

With p either an integer or a fraction, (3) covers general annuity problems as thoroughly as (19) on page 182. However, the only extensive tables of values of $s_{\overline{1}|i}^{(p)}$ and j_p are restricted to *integral* values of p. Notice the common features of (19) on page 182, (21) on page 183, and (1) on page 177. This feature, and the fact that the most extensive available tables for the mathematics of investment now give $s_{\overline{k}|i}$ with $k = 1/p$, p an integer, rather than $s_{\overline{1}|i}^{(p)}$, cause us to emphasize (19) on page 182.

NOTE 1.   The symbols j_p, $a_{\overline{n}|i}^{(p)}$, and $s_{\overline{n}|i}^{(p)}$, are classical in actuarial science. The teacher may desire to direct use of (4) in some problems of Exercise 48; Table XIII is available for j_p with p an integer or $p = 1/k$, k an integer. Formulas (4) will not be used in any illustrative examples in this text.

★65. Cases where the Tables Do Not Apply

Formulas (19) of page 182 remain desirable even if one of the necessary tables fails to apply. This may occur due to an unusual value of i or k, or a non-integral value of n. In such a case the data should be substituted in the proper explicit algebraic formula.

Example 1.   Find the present value of an annuity paying $600 at the end of each 6 months for $8\frac{1}{2}$ years, if interest is at 5% effective.

PARTIAL SOLUTION.   The interest period is 1 year.

> **Analysis:** $i = .05$; $n = 8\frac{1}{2}$; $k = \frac{6}{12} = \frac{1}{2}$; $R = 600$.

From (19) on page 182, $\qquad\qquad A = \dfrac{600}{s_{\overline{.5}|.05}} a_{\overline{8.5}|.05}.$

We obtain $1/s_{\overline{5}|}$ from Table XII, but (8) of page 64 must be used for $a_{\overline{8.5}|}$. Thus, we must compute

$$A = 600(2.02469508)\frac{1 - (1.05)^{-8.5}}{.05}. \tag{1}$$

From Tables VI and XIV,

$$(1.05)^{-8.5} = (1.05)^{-9}(1.05)^{.5} = (.64460892)(1.02469508).$$

To find A, we would compute $(1.05)^{-8.5}$, insert the result in (1), and then compute by use of logarithms or an electronic computer.

★66. Unknown Interest Rate or Term in General Case

If the rate is unknown in an annuity problem not under the simple case, the solution can be found by first solving a new problem which does come under the simple case.

Example 1. At what rate converted semiannually is $7150 the present value of an annuity of $220 payable quarterly for $12\frac{1}{2}$ years?

SOLUTION. 1. *First solve the following new problem:* At what rate converted *quarterly* is $7150 the present value of the annuity? This problem comes under the simple case: if i is the unknown rate per 3 months, $7150 = 220a_{\overline{50}|i}$, and $4i$ is the corresponding nominal rate. This problem was solved in Example 1, page 72 ; the result is $i = .01843$, and $4i = .0737$.

2. Now let j be the unknown nominal rate, compounded *semiannually*, at which $7150 is the present value of the annuity. Then, the rate $\{j, m = 2\}$ is equivalent to $\{.0737, m = 4\}$. To find j, write an equation where the left-hand member is the compound amount at the end of 1 year if $1 is invested at $\{j, m = 2\}$ and the right-hand member is the amount at $\{.0737, m = 4\}$:

$$\left(1 + \frac{j}{2}\right)^2 = \left(1 + \frac{.0737}{4}\right)^4;$$

$$1 + \frac{j}{2} = (1.0184)^2 = 1.03714; \qquad j = .07428. \qquad \text{(Using logarithms)}$$

The solution is approximately .0743, with doubt as to the last digit because the preliminary result, .0737, was equally doubtful.

Example 2. A man borrows $36,000 and agrees to pay $2400 at the end of each 6 months as long as necessary. How long will his payments continue if interest is at the rate $\{.06, m = 12\}$?

SOLUTION. If a certain whole number of $2400 payments were to satisfy the creditor exactly, the analysis of the problem would be as follows:

Analysis: $i = .005$; n *is unknown*; $k = \frac{6}{1} = 6$; $R = 2400$; $A = 36,000$.

$$36,000 = \frac{2400}{s_{\overline{6}|.5\%}} \, a_{\overline{n}|.5\%}; \qquad a_{\overline{n}|.5\%} = 15 s_{\overline{6}|.5\%}; \qquad a_{\overline{n}|.5\%} = 91.13.$$

By inspection of Table VIII, we see that $n = 121$ is too small and $n = 122$ is too large. Therefore the man must pay $2400 semiannually for 10 years and a smaller payment 6 months later.

★Exercise 48

1. At what rate compounded semiannually is $5500 the amount of an annuity of $100 payable quarterly for 9 years?
2. A man has deposited $50 with a savings and loan association at the end of each 3 months for the last 10 years. If he now has $2750 to his credit, at what rate compounded monthly does the association credit interest?
3. If money is worth $\{.04, m = 2\}$, for how long must payments of $1000 be made at the end of each 3 months to discharge a $16,000 loan?
4. At the end of each 6 months a man deposits $400 in a bank which credits interest quarterly at the rate 3%. On what payment date will the fund first amount to more than $6000?
5. A fund of $6000 is deposited with a trust company to provide an income of $400 at the end of each 6 months for 10 years. At what rate compounded quarterly is interest earned by the fund?
6. If money is worth $\{6\%, m = 2\}$, for how long must $1000 be paid at the end of each 3 months to discharge a loan of $17,000?
7. A man borrows $10,000, agreeing that money is worth 6% compounded quarterly. He will discharge all principal and interest obligations by paying $500 at the end of each 6 months as long as necessary. (*a*) Find the principal outstanding just after his 7th payment. (*b*) Find the final payment and when it is due.
8. Find the present value of an annuity of $50 payable at the end of each 3 months for $7\frac{1}{4}$ years if money is worth 5% compounded semiannually.
9. Find the amount of an annuity of $50 per week for 3 years if money is worth 4% effective.

8/ Life Annuities

67. Orientation for Life Annuities and Life Insurance

A **life annuity** for a certain person is a sequence of payments which stops when he dies. A **life insurance** on the life of a person is a single payment or a set of payments which will be made only after he dies. Any payment that becomes due only after the occurrence of some uncertain event, such as the continued existence or the death of a particular person, is called a **contingent payment**. Hence, the theory of life insurance* deals with contingent payments, each of which has a certain probability of being made. In contrast, the mathematics of investment that has been studied up to this point in the text deals with payments *certain* to be made. Thus, to commence the study of life insurance, it is desirable to start with associated remarks about probability. The discussion which follows is given on an intuitional basis. A complete theoretical foundation for the mathematical statistics involved would be far above the level of this text.

68. Background Relating to Probability

The language of probability is in use colloquially as a means for expressing varying degrees of confidence in the occurrence of an *uncertain event E*, whenever it has an opportunity to occur or fail to occur. In the fields of mathematics and statistics, formal definitions of probability are given corresponding to various possible situations about the data. We proceed to discuss briefly the most simple setting for a definition of probability.

Consider an *experiment T* which makes it possible for an uncertain *event E* to occur or fail to occur. Any performance of *T* will be called a *trial* of *T*. At any trial, suppose that there are *N* possible *outcomes* for *T*. We shall call a particular trial, or its outcome, *a success if E occurs*, and *a failure if E does not*

---

* Life insurance and life annuities have similar theoretical bases. Any reference to a foundation for life insurance will be understood to apply also to life annuities.

occur. We assume that the N outcomes of T are **equally likely**,* with S successes and F failures, where $S + F = N$. Then, the **probability** p that E *will occur* at any trial, and the probability q that E *will not occur*, are defined by

$$p = \frac{S}{N} \quad and \quad q = \frac{F}{N}. \tag{1}$$

Since $S + F = N$, we verify that

$$p + q = 1. \tag{2}$$

ILLUSTRATION 1. Consider a die (a cube) with its faces numbered $\{1, 2, 3, 4, 5, 6\}$ respectively. Let the experiment T consist of tossing the die and observing the number on the face which is up when the die comes to rest. Let E be the event that $\{2 \text{ } or \text{ } 4\}$ appears, or is *tossed* at a trial of T. Then, in (1), we have $N = 6$ and $S = 2$. Hence the probability of $\{2 \text{ } or \text{ } 4\}$ being tossed is $p = \frac{2}{6}$, or $p = \frac{1}{3}$; $q = \frac{2}{3}$.

In (1) and (2), we observe certain results which are true for the *probability* of an event E, regardless of the corresponding definition of probability. That is, in any setting, $0 \le p \le 1$; $0 \le q \le 1$; $p + q = 1$; $\{p = 1 \text{ } and \text{ } q = 0\}$ means that the event E is *certain to occur* at each trial of the experiment involved; $\{p = 0 \text{ } and \text{ } q = 1\}$ means that E is *certain not to occur* at any trial.

In arriving at (1), we dealt with an experiment T where the number (finite) and nature of the possible outcomes of T at any trial remain constant and are known *in advance of the trial*. Hence, the corresponding concept of probability is called an "*a priori*" probability because it is based on advance knowledge of the outcomes of T. The mathematical foundation of life insurance does not bring in *a priori* probability. However, the theory involves methods whose validity is a consequence of advanced results about such a type of probability. This fact is suggested by the remainder of the section.

Consider an experiment T which is *not* of a type where all possible outcomes of T at any trial are known in advance. However, let us assume that an unknown probability p exists for the occurrence of some specified event E at any trial of T. Suppose that N trials of T have been made, and that just S of them were successes for E. Often it is desirable then to take the *relative frequency* S/N of successes for E in the *past N trials* as the probability that E will occur *at any future trial*. Let

$$p = \frac{S}{N}. \tag{3}$$

We refer to p in (3) as an *experimental* or *empirical probability* for E. Sometimes S/N of (3) is called an "*a posteriori*" probability because it is obtained from past experience.

---

* We take *equally likely* as an undefined phrase. In a more elaborate introduction, a meaning is defined for the phrase. See Chapter 13 on *Probability* in *Basic College Algebra*, by William L. Hart; D. C. Heath and Company, publishers, 1972; Lexington, Massachusetts.

ILLUSTRATION 2. Recall the die of Illustration 1, where the *a priori* probability of tossing {2 *or* 4} at any trial was $p = \frac{1}{3}$. Now consider obtaining a probability for tossing {2 *or* 4} by experimentation. It is possible that the results of many trials would be as follows, where S is the number of successes in the specified N tosses. It would be very satisfying if we could say that S/N will approach $\frac{1}{3}$ as

$N =$	12	25	36	48	60	120	140
$S =$	3	5	13	15	23	45	78
$S/N =$	.25	.20	.39	.31	.36	.375	.325

a *limit* if N grows large without bound. However, the preceding statement is *not* true. The correct conclusion, stated in a colloquial fashion, is as follows, and is known as the **law of large numbers**.

$$\left\{\begin{array}{l}\textit{Suppose that N trials of an experiment T are made, where the}\\\textit{probability, at any trial, of success for an event E is p. Then, it is}\\\textit{likely that the relative frequency of successes, S/N, for E in the N}\\\textit{trials will be as close to p as we desire if N is sufficiently large.}\end{array}\right\} \quad (4)$$

Later, we shall have occasion to mention the importance of (4) in the operation of a life insurance company.

69. A Mortality Table

An insurance company makes charges, called *premiums*, whenever it issues a contract (called a *policy*) requiring the company to pay a life annuity or life insurance. In order to compute the premiums for its policies, the company must know the probability that an individual of any specified age will live for the next year. At various times in the past, the prominent insurance companies in the United States have pooled their records about deaths among policy holders in order to obtain the desired probabilities. Let p_x represent the probability that a man of age x years will live to age $(x + 1)$. Then, the data just referred to are used to obtain all of the statistical or empirical probabilities

$$p_0, p_1, p_2, \ldots, p_{99}. \tag{1}$$

The assumption is made here that the upper limit of ages involved will be 99 years, with all individuals assumed to die on or before age 100 years. Each of (1), say p_x, would be obtained (with many complications unmentioned here) by considering the N people of age x in the past experience of the insurance companies, and learning the number S of these people who lived to age $(x + 1)$.

Then $p_x = S/N$. It might be thought that the most convenient form for the final record would be merely a list of the values of p_x from (1). However, it proves more desirable to proceed as follows.

First, the empirical probabilities in (1) are found. Then, an arbitrary large number is specified as the number of infants, all assumed to be born on the same day, whose deaths in subsequent years will be tabulated. This number is called the **radix** of the table to be formed, and is 10,000,000 in the corresponding Table XV of this text. Then, a Mortality Table is calculated showing how the radix group reduces in size due to deaths, year by year, under the assumption that the yearly statistical probabilities of living at least one year are those in (1). Table XV is called the *Commissioners' Standard Ordinary Mortality Table*, abbreviated hereafter as the CSO table. We think of it as giving the reduced size, due to deaths, of an original group of 10,000,000 people, all born on the same day.*

With the CSO table, we introduce standard notations as follows.†

$$[\, x\,] \text{ means a person from the radix group who is alive at age } x. \ddagger \tag{2}$$

$$l_x = \{\text{the number of the radix group remaining alive at age } x\}. \tag{3}$$

$$d_x = \left\{ \begin{array}{l} \text{the number of the } l_x \text{ people in the radix group alive at} \\ \text{age } x \text{ who die before age } (x + 1). \end{array} \right\} \tag{4}$$

$$p_x = \{\text{the probability of } [\, x\,] \text{ living to age } (x + 1)\}. \tag{5}$$

$$q_x = \{\text{the probability of } [\, x\,] \text{ dying before age } (x + 1)\}. \tag{6}$$

From (2)–(6), the following results are obtained.

$$p_x = \frac{l_{x+1}}{l_x}. \qquad or \qquad l_{x+1} = p_x l_x. \tag{7}$$

$$d_x = l_x - l_{x+1}, \qquad or \qquad l_{x+1} = l_x - d_x. \tag{8}$$

$$q_x = \frac{d_x}{l_x}, \qquad or \qquad d_x = q_x l_x. \tag{9}$$

---

* Table XV applies for males. A different table with the radix 10,014,660 and age limit 102 applies to females. This table, at age 15, dovetails with Table XV for age 12. Thereafter, each entry in Table XV at age x is the entry of the table for females at age $(x + 3)$.

† In a life insurance company, the division involved with the mathematical theory of insurance and its applications in company affairs is referred to as the *actuarial department*. In the United States and Canada, there is an organization named the *Society of Actuaries* (208 South La Salle Street, Chicago, Illinois, 60604). In cooperation with major life insurance companies, the Society of Actuaries prepares numerous standard tables of values of the functions which are basic in the mathematical work of insurance companies. These tables are referred to as *actuarial tables*. In this text, Table XVI is an actuarial table of the Society of Actuaries, published with its permission.

‡ The standard actuarial symbol is "(x)," with parentheses. However, in an elementary introduction to insurance as in this text, use of parentheses would lead to confusion with other similar expressions where parentheses are advisable for the elementary student. Hence, brackets will be used as in (2).

From (7), (8), and (9), we derive

$$p_x + q_x = \frac{l_{x+1}}{l_x} + \frac{d_x}{l_x} = \frac{l_{x+1} + (l_x - l_{x+1})}{l_x} = \frac{l_x}{l_x}. \quad or$$

$$p_x + q_x = 1, \tag{10}$$

which agrees with (2) on page 190.

In the next example, we illustrate how a mortality table can be formed after the probabilities (1) are found and the radix is chosen.

Example 1. If we have $\{p_0 = .9918, p_1 = .9941, p_2 = .9959\}$, and the radix $= 1,000,000$, obtain $\{l_1, l_2, l_3\}$.

SOLUTION.   1. We are given $l_0 = 1,000,000$;

$$q_0 = 1 - p_0 = .0082; \qquad q_1 = .0059; \qquad q_2 = .0041.$$

2. From (9), $d_0 = q_0 l_0 = .0082(1,000,000) = 8200$.

Hence, from (8), $l_1 = l_0 - d_0 = 991,800$.

3. From (9), $d_1 = q_1 l_1 = .0059(991,800) = 5852$.

Hence, from (8), $l_2 = l_1 - d_1 = 985,948$.

Similarly, $d_2 = 4042$; $l_3 = l_2 - d_2 = 981,906$.

In the management of any insurance company, different mortality tables are used for various types of contracts. Also, the mortality table used for computations about life annuities might not be the same as the table used for life insurance. In this text, the CSO table will be used in all cases where a probability about living or dying is to be found. In such a case, we use statistical probability based on the records in the CSO table about the times of death for 10,000,000 people all born on the same day.

ILLUSTRATION 1.   In a group of people of age 24, the probability of dying before age 25, or the probability of [**24**] dying in the next year is*

$$q_{24} = \frac{d_{24}}{l_{24}} = \frac{18,324}{9,593,960} = .00191.$$

* Entries in Tables XV and XVI are given to numerous significant figures. The objective of Chapters 8 and 9 is presentation of general principles, and not computation of results to the high degree of accuracy required in the actuarial work of an insurance company. Hence, in Chapters 8 and 9, the student is advised to round off data in problems so that computation will be minimized. This attitude is shown in Illustration 1. In certain places, results given as fractions may be considered satisfactory. As a rule, answers will be obtained by use of five-place logarithms. Each final result is rounded off to a stage which appears sensible for the objective in view.

The probability that [**24**] will live to age 38 is

$$\frac{l_{38}}{l_{24}} = \frac{9,299,482}{9,593,960} \doteq \frac{9299}{9594} = .969.$$

Symbols are summarized below for various probabilities frequently obtained from the CSO table. The variable n always will represent a positive integer.

> *Probability that [x] will live 1 year*: p_x.
>
> *Probability that [x] will live n years*: $_np_x$.
>
> *Probability that [x] will die within 1 year*: q_x.
>
> *Probability that [x] will die within n years*: $_nq_x$.

Thus, when $n = 1$ on $_np_x$ (or $_nq_x$), we omit 1 and write simply p_x (or q_x). Out of l_x people alive at age x, there are l_{x+1} alive one year later, and $d_x = l_x - l_{x+1}$, who died in the preceding year. Also, l_{x+n} are alive n years later, so that $(l_x - l_{x+n})$ died before reaching age $(x + n)$. Hence we obtain the following results.

$$p_x = \frac{l_{x+1}}{l_x} ; \qquad _np_x = \frac{l_{x+n}}{l_x} . \tag{11}$$

$$q_x = \frac{d_x}{l_x} = \frac{l_x - l_{x+1}}{l_x} ; \qquad _nq_x = \frac{l_x - l_{x+n}}{l_x} . \tag{12}$$

70. Expectation of Life

A question of general interest is as follows, in colloquial language: on the average, among the standard group of l_x people, how long may an individual [x] be expected to live? Of the l_x people, l_{x+1} will live for 1 year, l_{x+2} for 2 years, and so on. The number of *full* years to be lived by the l_x people is

$$l_{x+1} + l_{x+2} + \cdots + l_{99}. \tag{1}$$

The *average number* of full years to be lived by each of the l_x people then is obtained on dividing the sum in (1) by l_x. The result is called the **curtate expectation** of life at age x, and is denoted by e_x. If we assume that the deaths in any year are spread uniformly over the year, on the average a person will live $\frac{1}{2}$ year in the year of his death. Then, $(e_x + \frac{1}{2})$ finally is called the **expectation of life** at age x and is denoted by $\overset{\circ}{e}_x$, given by

$$\overset{\circ}{e}_x = \frac{l_{x+1} + l_{x+2} + \cdots + l_{99}}{l_x} + \frac{1}{2} . \tag{2}$$

Actuaries sometimes make use of $\overset{\circ}{e}_x$ in approximate analyses of problems met in the field of insurance and life annuities. We shall not employ $\overset{\circ}{e}_x$, but the student may be interested to compute it for various values of x in the next exercise. The values of $\mathring{e}_x$ are given in Table XV. The student should be interested to examine the column for $\mathring{e}_x$.

Exercise 49

Find the requested probability if the specified experiment is performed. The outcomes are assumed to be equally likely for each experiment.

1. A bag contains 20 balls alike except as to color, with five white, twelve black, and three green. The experiment consists of drawing one ball from the bag at random. Find the probability that, at any trial, the ball drawn will be (*a*) black; (*b*) white or black; (*c*) white or green.
2. What is the probability that you were born in a Monday or a Wednesday?
3. Each one of two true dice has its faces numbered {1, 2, 3, 4, 5, 6}, as usual. The experiment consists of tossing the two dice together, and adding the numbers on the faces which will fall up, as in the game of shooting craps. We speak of "*tossing a number*," say 7, if the sum of the face numbers which fall up is the specified number. (*a*) Find the number of outcomes in which each of the totals {2, 3,..., 12} will be tossed. (*b*) What is the total number of possible outcomes of the experiment? (*c*) Find the probability of tossing each of the possible totals at any trial.
4. Bag I contains 5 white and 10 black balls. Bag II contains 4 green and 6 white balls. The experiment consists of drawing a ball from each bag and observing the colors. (Thus, there are $15 \cdot 10$ or 150 possible outcomes.) Find the probability that, at any trial, (*a*) a black ball and a green ball will be obtained; (*b*) a black ball and a white ball will be obtained; (*c*) both balls will be white.
5. The experiment consists of drawing a ball from bag I in Problem 4, replacing the ball, and then drawing a ball again. (*a*) How many outcomes are there for the experiment? At any trial, find the probability that (*b*) both balls drawn will be white; (*c*) both will be black; (*d*) one will be black and one will be white.
6. Suppose that a mortality table has the radix 1,000,000 and that we have

$$\{p_0 = .990; p_1 = .992; p_2 = .996\}. \text{ Calculate } \{l_0, l_1, l_2, l_3\}.$$

Any requested probability for [x] is understood to be a relative frequency based upon the mortality among the l_x men involved at age x in the CSO table. Find the specified probability correct to three significant figures. Use the standard symbols $_np_x$ and $_nq_x$ in specifying results where these symbols apply. If the instructor permits, any quotient may be computed by use of a slide rule, or possibly each result may be obtained merely as a quotient.

7. That a man aged 26 will live at least (*a*) 30 years; (*b*) 50 years.
8. That a man aged 30 will die in his 41st year.

9. That a man aged 22 will die within 1 year.
10. That a man aged 39 will be alive at age 41.
11. That a man aged 32 will die in the year after reaching age 50.
12. That a man aged 22 will die sometime after reaching age 48.
13. That a man aged 27 will not live to age 39.
14. That a man aged 20 will (*a*) not live to age 40; (*b*) live at least 12 years.
15. That a man aged 40 will (*a*) not live to age 60; (*b*) live at least to age 60.
16. That a man aged 22 will (*a*) not live to age 50; (*b*) live at least 20 years; (*c*) live at most 20 years.

Check the results in the following problems by use of Table XV.

17. Compute $\overset{\circ}{e}_{95}$.   18. Compute $\overset{\circ}{e}_{97}$.
19. If a computing device is available, compute $\overset{\circ}{e}_{70}$; $\overset{\circ}{e}_{55}$; $\overset{\circ}{e}_{25}$. Round off each result to one decimal place.

71. Present Value of a Pure Endowment

Recall that any payment promised to [*x*] at a certain future date is *contingent* on his survival to that date.

In all future details in Chapters 8 and 9, if money is to be accumulated or discounted, we shall assume that interest is compounded annually. If the nominal rate is i, the discount factor for one year is $v = (1 + i)^{-1}$. Then, the present value of $1 due at the end of n years is $(1 + i)^{-n}$, or v^n.

If a payment of $1 is promised to [*x*] at the end of n years, or when he reaches age $(x + n)$, we shall say that he is promised an **n-year pure endowment** of $1. We wish to develop a sensible definition for the present value of such a contingent payment. For this purpose, visualize the possibility that all l_x *men of age x of the* CSO *table agree to create a* **mutual benefit fund** *by immediate contributions of a sum* $\$_n E_x$ *per person to insure payment of $1 to each survivor at age* $(x + n)$. Since l_{x+n} men will survive, the total payments will be $\$l_{x+n}$, whose present value is $l_{x+n}(1 + i)^{-n}$. To provide this present value, the share which each man should contribute immediately is $l_{x+n}(1 + i)^{-n}/l_x$. Or,

$$_n E_x = \frac{v^n l_{x+n}}{l_x}.$$ (1)

We shall call $_n E_x$ the **present value** of the n-year pure endowment of $1 to a man aged x. The present value $\$H$ of an n-year pure endowment of $\$R$ to [*x*] is $R(_n E_x)$, or

$$\begin{Bmatrix} pr.\ val.,\ n\text{-}yr. \\ endow.\ of\ \$R \end{Bmatrix} \qquad H = R(_n E_x) = \frac{R v^n l_{x+n}}{l_x}.$$ (2)

In (2), $\$H$ is the sum which each of l_x men would have to contribute today in order to provide $\$R$ as a payment for each of the l_{x+n} survivors at the end of n years.

Example 1. A man aged 35 is promised $3000 at age 39, if he is alive then. Find the present value H of this promise at 5%.

SOLUTION. By use of (2) and Tables VI and XV,

$$H = \frac{3000(1.05)^{-4}l_{39}}{l_{35}} = \frac{3000(.82270)(9,271,491)}{9,373,807} = \$2441.$$

In order to simplify computation of $_nE_x$ by use of tables, multiply the numerator and denominator by v^x on the right in (1), to obtain

$$_nE_x = \frac{v^{x+n}l_{x+n}}{v^x l_x}.$$

Now define

$$D_k = v^k l_k. \tag{3}$$

Then

$$_nE_x = \frac{D_{x+n}}{D_x}, \tag{4}$$

and (2) becomes

$$H = R\frac{D_{x+n}}{D_x}. \tag{5}$$

If y represents the age $(x + n)$ when the endowment is due in (5), then

$$\begin{Bmatrix} age\ x;\ pr.\ val.,\ \$R \\ payable\ at\ age\ y \end{Bmatrix} \qquad H = R\frac{D_y}{D_x}. \tag{6}$$

The values of D_k depend on the mortality table and the interest rate i being used. Table XVI* gives the values of D_k and other later symbols based on the CSO table with the interest rate 3%, which is standard in the operation and public regulation of many phases of the business of insurance companies. If $i = 3\%$ in a problem, use (6) and Table XVI to find H. If $i \neq 3\%$, then (2) must be used as in Example 1. Hereafter, **unless something is said to the contrary, we shall assume that $i = 3\%$.**

ILLUSTRATION 1. At 3%, the present value of a 10-year pure endowment of $1000 to a man aged 34 is as follows, with the D's rounded off:

$$H = \frac{1000D_{44}}{D_{34}} = \frac{1000(24,769)}{34,395} = \$720. \qquad \text{(Table XVI)}$$

The results in (1) and (2) also can be obtained by use of a probability concept which we proceed to introduce. As an aid to intuition, consider a player A who enters a game against a professional gambler, where the prize is $\$K$ if A wins and p is his probability of winning. Then the *mathematical expectation* $\$E$ of A is defined by $E = pK$:

$$\begin{Bmatrix} \textbf{math. expectation } of\ \$K,\ with \\ probability\ p\ of\ winning \end{Bmatrix} = \$pK. \tag{7}$$

* The symbols whose values are listed in Table XVI are called **commutation symbols.**

ILLUSTRATION 2. Suppose that a game is operated as a business G, where each player has the probability $p = \frac{3}{4}$ of winning a prize of $200 = \$E$. His mathematical expectation is $\frac{3}{4}(200)$ or $150. Assume that G charges each player $\$H$ for the privilege of playing the game, and that N players participate, with exactly S players winning. Then G receives $\$NH$ and must pay $200S$ in prizes. G will have no profit or loss if

$$NH = 200S \qquad or \qquad H = 200\,\frac{S}{N}. \tag{8}$$

By the law of large numbers from (4) on page 191, it is likely that S/N in (8) will be a close approximation to $p = \frac{3}{4}$ if N is large. If $S/N = \frac{3}{4}$, from (8) we obtain

$$H = 200(\tfrac{3}{4}) = \$150,$$

which also is the mathematical expectation of each player. However, even if N is very large, there is no assurance that only $\frac{3}{4}$ of the players will win. If G charges *only* $150, then G would experience loss if more than $\frac{3}{4}$ of the players should win. Thus, the mathematical expectation of a player certainly is the *least* entrance fee for the game which business prudence would permit G to charge. The preceding discussion leads to the following conclusions about entrance fees, if it is to be likely that G will obtain a profit by operating the game.

I. *The number of players should be so large that, by the law of large numbers, it will be likely that the relative frequency of wins will closely approximate the probability of winning.*
II. *The entrance fee of each player should be greater than his mathematical expectation.*

Now let us return to the consideration of an n-year pure endowment of $1 for $[\,x\,]$. The probability of $[\,x\,]$ receiving $1 at the end of n years is his probability of living until then, or $_np_x$. Hence, his mathematical expectation at the end of n years is $1 \cdot {}_np_x$, and its present value is

$$1 \cdot {}_np_x \cdot v^n = \frac{l_{x+n}v^n}{l_x}, \tag{9}$$

which is $_nE_x$ as in (1). Thus, instead of deriving (1) by the mutual benefit fund method of reasoning, the same result can be obtained by the following definition:

$$\left\{ \begin{array}{l} _nE_x \text{ is the present value of the mathematical expectation} \\ of\ [\,x\,]\ receiving\ an\ endowment\ of\ \$1\ at\ the\ end\ of\ n\ years. \end{array} \right\} \tag{10}$$

NOTE 1. In (5), D_{x+n}/D_x is the *discount factor* which must be applied to a contingent payment of $\$R$ due at age $(x + n)$ for a man now of age x. In this language, D_{x+n}/D_x plays a role in (5) with contingent payments similar to the role of $(1 + i)^{-n}$ in the present value, $K(1 + i)^{-n}$, of $\$K$ *certainly* due at the end of n years.

72. Net Single Premium for Contingent Benefits

A life insurance company issues contracts called *policies* to individuals called *policyholders*. In a policy contract, the company promises to pay certain sums of money, called **benefits**, if certain events occur. If a benefit is contingent on the *survival* of the policyholder, the present value of the benefit will be found by use of $R(_nE_x)$. A policy also may specify an *insurance benefit*, payable at the death of the policyholder, which will be considered in the next chapter. In return for the benefits of a policy, the policyholder agrees to pay various sums to the company on certain dates if he remains alive. Thus, these sums also are contingent payments, and are called the **gross premiums** by the company, but merely the *premiums* by the general public. The **policy date** is the day on which the contract is entered into by the company and the policyholder.

ILLUSTRATION 1.   Suppose that an insurance company promises to pay $2000 to a man now aged 25 when he reaches age 45. The policy benefit in this case is a $2000, 20-year pure endowment for a man aged 25. If the man agrees to pay equal premiums at the beginning of each year for 10 years, his payments are referred to as a *temporary life annuity due*.

The fundamental problem of an insurance company is to determine the premiums which should be charged in return for the *specified contingent benefits*. For a given type of policy, the company adopts a corresponding mortality table and an assumed rate of interest on invested funds as a basis. We shall always use the CSO table and 3% interest, except on rare occasions where a different interest rate may be specified. Let us think of the insurance company as similar to the business G of Illustration 2 of the preceding section. When a man takes out a policy with the company, he plays a game with it where the policy benefits are the prize of the game. The premiums paid by the policyholder are the fees he pays for playing the game. Then the company makes the assumption that the specified type of policy will be sold to a *safely large number of people*, as described in Item I on page 198. That is, the company assumes that the *observed relative frequency of deaths* in each year among the policyholders will be closely approximated by the corresponding probability as given by the CSO table. A set of premiums for a policy then is called a set of **net premiums** if their present value is equal to the *present value of the policy benefits* under the following assumption:

$$\left\{ \begin{array}{l} \textbf{deaths among the policyholders will occur at} \\ \textbf{exactly the rates shown by the mortality table.} \end{array} \right\} \tag{1}$$

With (1) as a basis, net premiums are defined by the statement

$$\textbf{(pr. val. of the net premiums)} = \textbf{(pr. val. of the benefits).} \tag{2}$$

If just a *single* premium is specified, payable on the policy date, this premium is called the **net single premium** for the policy:

$$\textbf{(the net single premium)} = \textbf{(pr. val. of the benefits).} \tag{3}$$

In view of Section 71, the left-hand side of (2) can be described as the present value for the insurance company of the *mathematical expectations of the contingent premiums* to be paid by the policy holder. The right-hand side of (2) is the present value of the *mathematical expectations for the policy holder of all contingent benefit payments*. Thus, as implied by the discussion in Illustration 2 of Section 71, the net premiums are the *least* premiums which the company could charge under the following conditions:

I. *The mortality experience among policyholders will be exactly as given by the CSO table.*

II. *All money will be invested at the assumed rate i.*

III. *There are no expenses, profits, or losses in investments.*

The discussion in Section 71 shows that the net premiums would not yield a single cent to the insurance company to cover possible investment losses; investments at less than the assumed interest rate; losses caused by greater or less mortality among the policy holders than specified by the CSO table; and profits. Hence, for any policy, the insurance company charges premiums called **gross premiums**, which are greater than the net premiums of (2). A gross premium is equal to the corresponding net premium plus a certain amount called **loading**, which provides for necessary profit, added expenses due to violations of items I–III, and to other features of insurance practice. In computing gross premiums, each insurance company uses its own methods. Our discussion of premiums will deal entirely with *net premiums*. In any reference to a *premium*, it will be assumed that the company is charging only *net premiums*. The net single premium for a policy is defined in (3). Thus, $_nE_x$ now may be called the net single premium for an *n*-year pure endowment of $1 promised to [*x*] by an insurance policy; $R(_nE_x)$ is the net single premium when the endowment is $R.

Example 1. What pure endowment payable at age 40 can be purchased now by a man aged 25, for a net single premium of $1000?

SOLUTION. In (6) on page 197, $H = 1000$, $y = 40$, $x = 25$, and R is the unknown payment. By use of Table XVI, with values of D_x rounded off to five significant figures,

$$1000 = R\frac{D_{40}}{D_{25}}; \qquad R = \frac{1000 D_{25}}{D_{40}} = \frac{1000(4,573,400)}{2,833,000} = \$1614.$$

Exercise 50

1. A bag contains fifteen balls of which three are white and twelve are black. The balls are alike except as to color. A game consists of drawing a ball at random from the bag. If a white ball is drawn, the player will receive a prize of $30. Find his mathematical expectation.

2. As an inducement to increase business, a theater announces that a jackpot of $50 will be given to a member of the audience selected at random from those who come on a certain night. If 600 people come, find the mathematical expectation of each person on account of the jackpot prize.

3. Compute D_{35} at 3% by use of Tables VI, XV, and logarithms, correct to four significant digits.

4. Find the net single premium for a 10-year pure endowment of $1000 for a man aged (*a*) 25; (*b*) 55.

5. A man aged 30 is promised a gift of $10,000 at age 40, if he is alive. Find the present value of this promise.*

6. A man aged 29 is promised $1000 at the end of 1 year and $2000 at the end of 2 years, if he remains alive. Find the sum of the present values of these payments. It will be useful to add fractions before computing any quotient by use of logarithms or other means.

7. What endowment payable at the end of 15 years can a man aged 30 purchase for a net single premium of $5000?

8. What endowment payable at age 50 can a man aged 40 purchase for $4000?

9. A will states that the estate shall be turned over to the heir, now aged 20, when he reaches age 30. If the estate then will be worth $200,000, find the present value of the expectation of the heir, at 3% interest.

10. A man aged 40 pays $5000 to an insurance company as the net single premium for a payment to be made to him at age 60, with no payment to be made to his estate at any time if he should die before age 60. (*a*) What will he receive at age 60 if he lives? (*b*) Find the compound amount at the end of 20 years if $5000 were invested at 3% effective.

11. Find the present value of a 15-year pure endowment of $3000 for a man now aged 32, if money is worth 4%.

12. A corporation promises a payment of $3000 as a gift to each employee when he retires at age 65. Find the present value of this promise to an employee of age 50 who is certain that he will continue to work for the corporation as long as he lives. Money is worth 5%.

73. Life Annuities

A *life annuity* is one which provides periodic payments on certain dates in case a certain individual (or individuals) remains alive. We shall consider only problems of the type where just *one* individual now of age x is involved. We may deal with *ordinary life annuities*, also called *life annuities immediate*, where the payments occur at the *ends* of payment intervals after the present date, either for the whole of the life of [x] or for a limited number of years (*temporary life*

---

* In cases like Problem 5 where no insurance company is involved, we agree to compute present values as if an insurance company were designated to make the payments.

annuities). Also, we may consider *deferred life annuities* and *life annuities due*, where the payments occur at the *beginnings* of the successive payment intervals. In any life annuity which we shall introduce, the periodic payments will be equal and will be made annually, unless something to the contrary is stated.

The *present value* or *net single premium* for a life annuity for [*x*] may be found by considering the annuity as a set of successive pure endowments, and obtaining their present values by use of Section 71.

Example 1. If money is worth 3%, find the net single premium for a life annuity of $1000 payable at the end of each year for 3 years to a man aged 30.

SOLUTION. He is promised pure endowments of $1000 payable at ages 31, 32, and 33. From (6) of page 197, the present value H of the annuity is

$$H = 1000({}_1E_{30}) + 1000({}_2E_{30}) + 1000({}_3E_{30}) = 1000\left(\frac{D_{31}}{D_{30}} + \frac{D_{32}}{D_{30}} + \frac{D_{33}}{D_{30}}\right);$$

$$H = 1000\frac{D_{31} + D_{32} + D_{33}}{D_{30}} = 1000\frac{11,000,543}{3,905,800} = \$2816. \qquad \text{(Table XVI)}$$

NOTE 1. If the interest rare were not 3% in Example 1, we would have used (1) on page 196.

Consider a life annuity which will pay $1 to a man now aged x when he reaches age y, and annually thereafter for the rest of his life. Let L be the net single premium for this annuity; it consists of pure endowments of $1 each due at ages $y, y + 1, \ldots, 99$. Then L is equal to the sum of the present values of these endowments, as obtained from (6) on page 197 with $R = 1$:

$$L = \frac{D_y}{D_x} + \frac{D_{y+1}}{D_x} + \frac{D_{y+2}}{D_x} + \cdots + \frac{D_{99}}{D_x}; \qquad (1)$$

$$L = \frac{D_y + D_{y+1} + D_{y+2} + \cdots + D_{99}}{D_x}. \qquad (2)$$

Define N_k as follows:

$$N_k = D_k + D_{k+1} + \cdots + D_{99}. \qquad (3)$$

Then, from (2), $$L = \frac{N_y}{D_x}. \qquad (4)$$

Let H represent the net single premium for the preceding life annuity if each payment is R instead of $1. Then $H = RL$ and (4) gives

$$\left\{\begin{array}{l} \$R \text{ annually to } [\,x\,], \\ \text{1st payt. at age } y \end{array}\right\} \qquad\qquad H = R\frac{N_y}{D_x}. \qquad (5)$$

Values of N_k for the CSO table at 3% are given in Table XVI.

ILLUSTRATION 1.   A whole life annuity due for a man now aged 30 promises $500 at the beginning of each year of his life. To find the net single premium H for this annuity due, apply (5) with $x = 30$ and $y = 30$:*

$$H = 500 \frac{N_{30}}{D_{30}} = 500 \frac{91,698,000}{3,905,800} = \$11,740. \qquad \text{(Table XVI)}$$

74.   Life Annuities Due and Deferred Life Annuities

The symbol $\ddot{a}_x$ represents the present value of a **whole life annuity due** of $1 paid annually to $[\,x\,]$. The first payment of $1 occurs at age x, and hence $\ddot{a}_x$ is obtained from (5) of Section 73 with $R = 1$ and $y = x$. The present value H of a whole life annuity due of R paid annually to $[\,x\,]$ is equal to $R\ddot{a}_x$. The results follow in (1) and (2).

$$\left\{ \begin{array}{l} \textit{Life ann. due;} \\ \$1 \textit{ annually to } [\,x\,] \end{array} \right\} \qquad\qquad \ddot{a}_x = \frac{N_x}{D_x}. \qquad\qquad (1)$$

$$\left\{ \begin{array}{l} \textit{Life ann. due;} \\ \$R \textit{ annually to } [\,x\,] \end{array} \right\} \qquad\qquad H = R\ddot{a}_x = R\frac{N_x}{D_x}. \qquad\qquad (2)$$

Consider a **deferred whole life annuity** of $1 paid annually to $[\,x\,]$ where the first payment occurs at the end of n years. These payments can be thought of as an annuity *due* deferred n years, and the symbol $_n|\ddot{a}_x$ is used to represent the present value of the payments. The first payment occurs at age $(x + n)$; hence $_n|\ddot{a}_x$ is obtained from (5) of Section 73 with $y = x + n$ and $R = \$1$. Let H represent the present value when the periodic payment is R. The results are given in (3) and (4).

$$\left\{ \begin{array}{l} \textit{Life ann., } \$1 \textit{ annually;} \\ \textrm{1st } \textit{payt. at age } (x + n) \end{array} \right\} \qquad\qquad _x|\ddot{a}_x = \frac{N_{x+n}}{D_x}. \qquad\qquad (3)$$

$$\left\{ \begin{array}{l} \textit{Life ann., } \$R \textit{ annually;} \\ \textrm{1st } \textit{payt. at age } (x + n) \end{array} \right\} \qquad\qquad H = R(_n|\ddot{a}_x) = R\frac{N_{x+n}}{D_x}. \qquad\qquad (4)$$

In (1)–(4), it should be noticed that (5) of Section 73 is the basic result that yields the later formulas.

NOTE 1.   The symbol a_x represents the present value of a **whole life annuity immediate** of $1 annually to (x); the first payment is at age $(x + 1)$. Let H be the present value if each payment is R. Then, from (5) on page 202,

$$a_x = \frac{N_{x+1}}{D_x}; \qquad H = Ra_x = R\frac{N_{x+1}}{D_x}. \qquad\qquad (5)$$

Our applications will not emphasize a_x.

* Any result in Chapters 8 and 9 will be given rounded off to four significant digits as a rule, or to the nearest dollar if the value is less than $1000.

Example 1. Find the annual payment of a whole life annuity due for a man aged 55 which can be purchased from an insurance company for a net single premium of $10,000.

SOLUTION. From (2), as below, we find $R = \$682$ by use of Table XVI, with entries rounded off.

$$10,000 = R\frac{N_{55}}{D_{55}}; \qquad R = \frac{10,000\,D_{55}}{N_{55}} = \frac{10,000(1,639,300)}{24,032,000}.$$

Exercise 51

Write the net single premium of the life annuity in terms of $\ddot{a}_x$ and $_n|\ddot{a}_x$; finally express the result as a quotient by use of Table XVI, *and compute.*

1. A whole life annuity due of $2000 payable annually to a man aged 45.
2. A whole life annuity due of $5000 payable annually to a man aged 35.
3. A pension of $4000 payable at the beginning of each year to a man aged 65.
4. A pension of $5000 payable annually for life with the first payment due at age 65, for a man now aged 40.
5. A deferred whole life annuity of $8000 payable annually to a man aged 30 with the first payment at age 60.
6. A man aged 29 takes out a life insurance policy on which he agrees to pay premiums of $200 at the beginning of each year for life. Find the present value of these premiums.
7. A man aged 38 takes out a life insurance policy on which he agrees to pay premiums of $400 at the beginning of each year for life. Find the present value of the premiums.
8. An insurance policy pays $10,000 at the death of the insured. The beneficiary is 36 years old, and has the option of receiving a whole life annuity due with annual payments instead of $10,000 cash. Find the equivalent annual payment.
9. A man aged 45 pays $20,000 to an insurance company as the net single premium in return for a contract to pay him a deferred whole life annuity whose first annual payment will occur when he is 65 years old. Find the annual payment.
10. The net single premium for a life insurance policy for a man aged 50 is $5000. He arranges to pay the insurance company a fixed premium at the beginning of each year of his life, instead of the single premium. Find the annual premium.
11. Solve Problem 10 if the net single premium is $10,000, at age 40.
12. Find the present value of a contract to pay $1000 at the end of each year for life to a man aged 53.

75. Temporary Life Annuity

An *n*-year **temporary life annuity due** of $1 paid annually to a man aged *x* consists of payments of $1 at the beginning of each year for *n* years to [*x*] while he remains alive. Let $\ddot{a}_{x:\overline{n}|}$ represent the present value of these payments. The last payment is due at age [*x* + (*n* − 1)], if the man is still alive. Now consider a whole life annuity due of $1 per year for *x*. From these payments, let us omit the *n* payments of the *n*-year temporary annuity due. There remain the payments of a deferred whole life annuity of $1 per year whose first payment is due at the end of *n* years, when the man is of age (*x* + *n*), one year after the last payment of the temporary annuity. Thus, the present value of the whole life annuity due is equal to *the present value of the temporary annuity due* plus *the present value of the deferred annuity*, or

$$\ddot{a}_x = \ddot{a}_{x:\overline{n}|} + {}_n|\ddot{a}_x; \quad \ddot{a}_{x:\overline{n}|} = \ddot{a}_x - {}_n|\ddot{a}_x. \tag{1}$$

By use of (1) and (3) of Section 74, we obtain

$$\ddot{a}_{x:\overline{n}|} = \frac{N_x}{D_x} - \frac{N_{x+n}}{D_x} ;$$

$$\begin{cases} \textit{n-yr. life ann. due;} \\ \$1 \textit{ annually to } [x] \end{cases} \qquad \ddot{a}_{x:\overline{n}|} = \frac{N_x - N_{x+n}}{D_x} . \tag{2}$$

Let $H represent the present value of an *n*-year temporary life annuity due of $R payable annually to [*x*]. Then,

$$\begin{cases} \textit{n-yr. life ann. due;} \\ \$R \textit{ annually to } [x] \end{cases} \qquad H = R\ddot{a}_{x:\overline{n}|} = R\frac{N_x - N_{x+n}}{D_x} . \tag{3}$$

ILLUSTRATION 1. To find the net single premium for a pension of $2500 payable at the beginning of each year for 20 years to a man now aged 50, use (3). Table XVI and five-place logarithms were employed to compute *H*.

$$H = 2500\ddot{a}_{50:\overline{20}|} = 2500\frac{N_{50} - N_{70}}{D_{50}} = \$33,870.$$

Example 1. A widow, at the death of her husband, has the option of receiving $25,000 cash as the proceeds of a life insurance policy, or an equivalent 20-year temporary life annuity due, with annual payments. Find the equivalent annual payment if she is 60 years old*

SOLUTION. From (3) with *H* = 25,000, where *R* is the unknown annual payment,

$$25,000 = R\frac{N_{60} - N_{80}}{D_{60}} ; \qquad R = \frac{25,000D_{60}}{N_{60} - N_{80}} = \$2161.$$

* We use Tables XV–XVI for females as well as males in this text. With more extensive tables, there would be separate tables for females.

Exercise 52

1. (a) Find the present value of a temporary life annuity due paying $1000 at the beginning of each year for 25 years to a man now aged 40. (b) For contrast, find the present value of an annuity due, certain, paying $1000 at the beginning of each year for 25 years, with money worth 3%.
2. Repeat (a) and (b) of Problem 1, for payments of $2000 at the beginning of each year for 20 years, with the man now of age 65.

Find the present value of the premiums specified for a policy. All premiums are payable at the beginnings of the years.

3. A man aged 25 will pay $1000 as a premium for 20 years.
4. A man aged 30 will pay $200 as a premium for 15 years.
5. A man aged 23 will pay $500 as a premium for 25 years.

6. A man aged 40 estimates his future earnings as the equivalent of $10,000 at the beginning of each year for 25 years, as long as he lives. Find the capitalized value of his future earning power.
7. A man aged 55 pays an insurance company $20,000 in return for a contract to pay him equal sums at the beginning of each year for 25 years, as long as he lives. Find the annual payment.
8. A $20,000 endowment insurance policy matures when a man is 60 years old. Instead of taking cash, he has the option of receiving equal sums at the beginning of each year for 20 years, if he lives. Find the equivalent annual payment. If he should die just before age 75, what would his estate receive from the insurance company?
9. (a) In Problem 8, what payment at the beginning of each year for 20 years, certain, would be provided by investment of $20,000 at 3%. (b) If the man dies at age 75, how much would his estate receive?
10. In a lawsuit over the death of a man aged 40 in an automobile accident, the court awards the widow, as damages, the present value of her deceased husband's earnings, estimated as $20,000 at the beginning of each year of life for 25 years. How much does she receive, if the value is computed by use of the CSO table at 3%?

The net single premium or present value of the benefits for an insurance policy is given. Find the net annual premium $P which the man should pay at the beginning of each year as specified. Use (2) on page 199 and (3) on page 205.

11. Net single premium is $10,000 at age 35; $P is payable for 10 years.

   HINT. The premiums form a 10-year life annuity due of $P per year with the present value $P\ddot{a}_{35:\overline{10}|}$. Hence,

$$10,000 = P\ddot{a}_{35:\overline{10}|}.$$

   Solve for P in terms of commutation symbols and then compute.
12. Net single premium is $5000 at age 26; $P is payable for 20 years.

13. The symbol $a_{x:\overline{n}|}$ represents the net single premium for an n-year life annuity *immediate*, paying \$1 at the end of each year for n years. By the method used in proving (2) on page 205 show that

$$a_{x:\overline{n}|} = \frac{N_{x+1} - N_{x+n+1}}{D_x}.$$

14. Find the present value of a 15-year life annuity immediate paying \$7500 per year to a man now aged 50.

15. A man aged 20 inherits an estate of \$100,000 invested at 5% payable annually. If he lives, he will receive the income annually for the next 10 years and the principal when he reaches age 30. If money is worth 3%, find the present worth of his expectation from the estate, as based on the CSO table.

76. Pension or Annuity Policy

Our later applications will emphasize the following present values.

Summary of Net Single Premiums at Age x

$\left\{\begin{array}{c} \$R \text{ pure endow.} \\ \text{in } n \text{ yr.} \end{array}\right\}$
    $\qquad H = R(_nE_x) = R\dfrac{D_{x+n}}{D_x}.$ (1)

$\left\{\begin{array}{c} \text{Whole life ann.} \\ \text{due, } \$R \text{ annually} \end{array}\right\}$
    $\qquad H = R\ddot{a}_x = R\dfrac{N_x}{D_x}.$ (2)

$\left\{\begin{array}{c} n\text{-yr. life ann.} \\ \text{due, } \$R \text{ annually} \end{array}\right\}$
    $\qquad H = R\ddot{a}_{x:\overline{n}|} = R\dfrac{N_x - N_{x+n}}{D_x}.$ (3)

$\left\{\begin{array}{c} \text{Whole life ann. due,} \\ \$R \text{ annually, defd. } n \text{ yr.} \end{array}\right\}$
    $\qquad H = R(_n|\ddot{a}_x) = R\dfrac{N_{x+n}}{D_x}.$ (4)

A familiar type of policy sold by insurance companies is one having the following benefit and premiums, and is called an **annuity policy**; it promises a self-created pension to the policyholder. The *annual* feature in the following description is nonessential and is designed to permit easy computation.

Benefit.   *A pension, or deferred whole life annuity, of \$R payable annually, with the first payment at the end of n years.*

Premiums.   *Equal sums payable at the beginning of each year for n years, thus forming an n-year temporary life annuity due.*

We emphasize again the fact that, for any policy,

$$\text{(pr. val. of premiums)} = \text{(net single prem. for benefits).} \qquad (5)$$

Example 1. An annuity policy for a man aged 45 will pay him $3000 annually for life, starting at age 65. Find the net annual premium P which he should pay at the beginning of each year for 20 years.

SOLUTION. Refer to (5). From (3) and (4),

$$(pres.\ value\ of\ premiums) = P\ddot{a}_{45:\overline{20}|} = P\frac{N_{45} - N_{65}}{D_{45}}, \tag{6}$$

$$(pres.\ value\ of\ benefit) = 3000(_{20|}\ddot{a}_{45}) = 3000\frac{N_{65}}{D_{45}}. \tag{7}$$

Hence,

$$P\frac{N_{45} - N_{65}}{D_{45}} = 3000\frac{N_{65}}{D_{45}}.$$

$$P = 3000\frac{N_{65}}{N_{45} - N_{65}} = \frac{3000(10,607,000)}{33,848,000} = \$940.$$

If the general annuity policy as described above is issued to a man aged x, and if the annual premium is P, the method employed in Example 1 would lead to the formula

$$P = R\frac{N_{x+n}}{N_x - N_{x+n}} \tag{8}$$

which the student will prove later. At present, it is advisable not to use (8) in problems, but to follow the method of Example 1.

Exercise 53

All annuities are assumed to consist of equal annual payments.

1. In return for a net single premium of $15,000, what annual income can a man aged 60 obtain from an insurance company if he buys (*a*) a whole life annuity due; (*b*) a 20-year life annuity due; (*c*) a deferred whole life annuity with the first payment to occur at the end of 5 years.

Find the net annual premium, P, if it is payable at the beginning of each year as specified, for a life annuity policy with the benefit which is described, for the given age.

2. Man aged 25; the insurance company will pay $2000 at age 65 and annually thereafter; premiums payable for 40 years.
3. Man aged 30; the annuity will pay $4000 at age 55 and annually thereafter for life; premiums payable for 25 years.
4. Man aged 35; the annuity will pay $5000 at age 65 and annually thereafter for life; premiums payable for 30 years.
5. The annuity will pay $1000 at age 65 and annually thereafter for life; premiums payable at the beginning of each year, with the last payment at

age 64; find the annual premium if the policy is taken out at age (*a*) 25 years; (*b*) 50 years.

6. Prove formula (8) in Section 76.

7. In terms of l_x and $v = (1 + i)^{-1}$, prove that (1) on page 202 leads to

$$\ddot{a}_x = \frac{l_x + l_{x+1}v + \cdots + l_{99}v^{99-x}}{l_x}.$$

The preceding formula makes it clear that $\ddot{a}_x$ is the sum which each of the l_x men of the CSO table, at age x, should contribute to a mutual benefit fund to provide each survivor with \$1 at the beginning of each year of life. This fact also follows from the similar property of the present value of a pure endowment as used in proving (1) on page 196.

8. A man aged 45 will pay \$1000 as a premium at the beginning of each year, with the last premium due when he is of age 64, on a policy which will pay him a deferred whole life annuity with the first payment due at age 65. Find the annual payment of the annuity.

9. A father wishes to take out a policy with an insurance company for his son aged 10 to provide annual payments of \$2500 to him for 6 years starting at age 17, to guarantee his education. Find the net single premium which the father would pay.

10. In Problem 9, if the father desires to pay premiums, in the name of his son, at the beginning of each year for five years in buying the policy, find the premium.

9/ Life Insurance

77. Background for Insurance

Insurance is an indemnity or protection against loss. The business of insuring people against any variety of disaster is on a scientific basis only when a large number of individuals are insured under one organization, so that individual losses may be distributed over the whole group according to some principle of mutuality. In this chapter we shall discuss the principles and the most simple aspects of the type of life insurance furnished by *old line* or *legal reserve* companies. A company of this nature usually engages in the sale of life annuities and pure endowments as well as of life insurance, and various combinations of the resulting types of benefits may appear in a policy contract. When an *insurance* benefit is involved, the policyholder may be referred to as the *insured*. A person to whom a benefit of a policy is to be payable is called a *beneficiary*.

We recall that any specified premiums for a policy are called *net* premiums when *their present value is equal to the present value of the policy benefits*. In the case of all policies considered in this chapter, we shall be concerned entirely with *net* premiums.

78. Whole Life and Term Insurance

If a policyholder agrees to pay all premiums in one installment, it is payable on the policy date and is called the **single premium**. The **net single premium** for an insurance benefit in a policy is computed under assumptions I, II, and III on page 200 and, in addition, the following assumption:

$$\left\{ \begin{array}{l} \textbf{any death benefit will be paid at the end of} \\ \textbf{the policy year in which the death occurs.} \end{array} \right\} \tag{1}$$

A whole life insurance of \$1 on the life of [x] is a contract by the insurance company to pay \$1 to a specified beneficiary B at the end of the year in which

210

[x] dies. Let A_x represent the present value of this benefit on the policy date, when the insured is of age x. We shall derive the value of A_x by use of a mutual benefit fund type of reasoning.

Conceive of a policy with the preceding insurance benefit of \$1 at death being issued by the insurance company to each of the l_x men of age x in the CSO table. The number dying between ages x and $(x + 1)$ is $d_x = l_x - l_{x+1}$; hence the company must provide \$$d_x$ at the end of the 1st policy year; the present value of this payment is $d_x(1 + i)^{-1}$ or vd_x. The number who will die in the next year is d_{x+1} which will require payments of \$$d_{x+1}$ at the end of the 2nd policy year; etc., as seen in the following table. The last survivors will die in the year after they are 99 years old, so that \$$d_{99}$ will be paid in insurance benefits when the men

Policy Year	Deaths During Year	Benefits Due at End of Year	Present Value of Benefits
1	d_x	\$$d_x$	vd_x
2	d_{x+1}	\$$d_{x+1}$	v^2d_{x+1}
3	d_{x+2}	\$$d_{x+2}$	v^2d_{x+2}
.	.	.	.
.	.	.	.
.	.	.	.
$100 - x$	d_{99}	\$$d_{99}$	$v^{100-x}d_{99}$

would have been 100 years old, or at the end of the $(100 - x)$th year. To provide these insurance payments, the company must collect from the l_x men, on the policy date, the sum of the present values of all payments, which is the numerator at the right below. The share of this mutual benefit fund which each of the l_x men should pay on the policy date is the fraction at the right below. This quotient is defined as the *present value* or *net single premium* of the insurance benefit for a man aged x.

$$A_x = \frac{vd_x + v^2d_{x+1} + v^3d_{x+2} + \cdots + v^{100-x}d_{99}}{l_x}. \tag{2}$$

On multiplying numerator and denominator in (2) by v^x we obtain

$$A_x = \frac{v^{x+1}d_x + v^{x+2}d_{x+1} + \cdots + v^{100}d_{99}}{v^xl_x}. \tag{3}$$

Let us define new commutation symbols C_k and M_k as follows:

$$C_k = v^{k+1}d_k; \qquad M_k = C_k + C_{k+1} + \cdots + C_{99}. \tag{4}$$

Then, the numerator in (3) is seen to be

$$C_x + C_{x+1} + \cdots + C_{99} = M_x. \tag{5}$$

Thus, from (3) and (5) for [x],

$$\begin{Bmatrix} \text{net single prem.,} \\ \$1 \text{ whole life ins.} \end{Bmatrix} \qquad A_x = \frac{M_x}{D_x}. \tag{6}$$

Let $\$K$ represent the net single premium for a whole life insurance of $\$R$ for [x]. Then,

$$\begin{Bmatrix} \text{net single prem.,} \\ \$R \text{ whole life ins.} \end{Bmatrix} \qquad K = RA_x = R\frac{M_x}{D_x}. \tag{7}$$

ILLUSTRATION 1.　From (7) with $\$R = 1000$ and $x = 45$, by use of Table XVI we obtain

$$K = 1000A_{45} = 1000\frac{M_{45}}{D_{45}} = 1000\frac{1,098,094}{2,392,900} = \$459.$$

Example 1.　How much whole life insurance for a man aged 60 can be purchased for a net single premium of $\$5000$?

SOLUTION.　In (7) we have $K = \$5000$. Hence, by use of Table XVI,

$$5000 = R\frac{M_{60}}{D_{60}}; \qquad R = 5000\frac{D_{60}}{M_{60}} = \$7911. \tag{8}$$

An ***n-year term insurance*** of $\$1$ on the life of [x] promises the payment of $\$1$ at the end of the year in which [x] dies, only on condition that his death occurs before the end of n years. Let $A^1_{x:\overline{n}|}$ be the net single premium for this insurance benefit in a policy. If all l_x men of age x considered in the CSO table take out policies promising the preceding insurance, the last insurance payments will occur at the end of n years, due to the death of d_{x+n-1} men in the nth year. Thus, for the present insurance, the last term in the numerator, corresponding to that in (2), will be $v^n d_{x+n-1}$. Hence,

$$A^1_{x:\overline{n}|} = \frac{vd_x + v^2 d_{x+1} + \cdots + v^n d_{x+n-1}}{l_x}. \tag{9}$$

From (9), on multiplying numerator and denominator by v^x and on using the symbol $C_k = v^{k+1} d_k$, we obtain

$$A^1_{x:\overline{n}|} = \frac{C_x + C_{x+1} + \cdots + C_{x+n-1}}{D_x}. \tag{10}$$

Since $\qquad M_x = C_x + C_{x+1} + \cdots + C_{x+n-1} + C_{x+n} + \cdots + C_{99},$

and $\qquad M_{x+n} = \qquad\qquad\qquad\qquad\qquad\qquad C_{x+n} + \cdots + C_{99},$

it is seen that the numerator in (10) is $M_x - M_{x+n}$; hence,

$$\begin{Bmatrix} \text{net single prem.;} \\ \$1 \text{ } n\text{-yr. term ins.} \end{Bmatrix} \qquad A^1_{x:\overline{n}|} = \frac{M_x - M_{x+n}}{D_x}. \tag{11}$$

The net single premium, K, for n-year term insurance of R on the life of $[x]$ is

$$\left\{ \begin{array}{l} \text{net single prem.;} \\ \$R \text{ n-yr. term ins.} \end{array} \right\} \qquad K = RA^1_{x:\overline{n}|} = R\,\frac{M_x - M_{x+n}}{D_x}. \tag{12}$$

Example 2. How much 10-year term insurance can be purchased for a net single premium of $1000 by a man of age 40?

SOLUTION. From (12) with $K = 1000$, and R as the unknown amount of term insurance, by use of Table XVI we obtain

$$1000 = R\,\frac{M_{40} - M_{50}}{D_{40}}\,; \qquad R = \frac{1000\,D_{40}}{M_{40} - M_{50}} = \$23{,}060.$$

It is instructive to derive (2) as the present value on the policy date of the mathematical expectation of the beneficiary B of the policy, which promises $1 to B at the end of the year in which $[x]$ dies. Thus, the probability of $[x]$ dying in policy year 1 is d_x/l_x; then B would receive $1 at the end of 1 year; the mathematical expectation of B at the end of 1 year is $1 \cdot (d_x/l_x)$, as in the following table; the discounted value of this expectation on the policy date is $(d_x/l_x)\cdot v$. The similar present values for all policy years in the table should be verified by the student. The sum of these present values is seen to be the right-hand side of (2).

Policy Year	Probability [x] Dies in the Year	Math. Expect of B at End of Year	Pres. Value of the Expect.
1	d_x/l_x	$1 \cdot (d_x/l_x)$	$v(d_x/l_x)$
2	d_{x+1}/l_x	$1 \cdot (d_{x+1}/l_x)$	$v^2(d_{x+1}/l_x)$
3	d_{x+2}/l_x	$1 \cdot (d_{x+2}/l_x)$	$v^3(d_{x+2}/l_x)$
.	.	.	.
.	.	.	.
.	.	.	.
$100 - x$	d_{99}/l_x	$1 \cdot (d_{99}/l_x)$	$v^{100-x}(d_{99}/l_x)$

That is, the net single premium, or A_x, is equal to the present value of the future mathematical expectations of the beneficiary B who will receive $1 at the end of the year when $[x]$ dies. Or, A_x is the sum of the entries in the fourth column of the table, as in (2).

Exercise 54

Find the net single premium for a whole life insurance of $1000 on the life of a person of the specified age.

1. 20 years.　　**2.** 25 years.　　**3.** 40 years.　　**4.** 60 years.　　**5.** 90 years.

How much whole life insurance can a person of the specified age purchase for $3000 *cash?*

6. 25 years.   **7.** 35 years.   **8.** 65 years.

Find the net single premium for the specified insurance.

9. A 10-year term insurance for $1000 on the life of a man aged (*a*) 20 years; (*b*) 30 years; (*c*) 60 years.

10. A 5-year term insurance of $5000 for a man aged 25.

11. A 20-year term insurance of $1000 for a man aged 30.

12. How much 10-year term insurance can be purchased for a net single premium of $400 by a man who is (*a*) 40 years old; (*b*) 60 years old?

13. Find the net single premium for a 5-year term insurance of $10,000 at age 65.

14. (*a*) For a net single premium of $1000, how much 10-year term insurance can be purchased by a man aged 50? (*b*) How much whole life insurance can be purchased for this premium?

79. Endowment Insurance

An **n-year endowment insurance** of $R on the life of a man aged x promises the following benefits.

I. **An n-year term insurance for $R**; *that is, $R at the end of the year in which the man dies, if his death occurs before the end of n years.*

II. **A pure endowment of $R payable to the man at the end of n years** *if he is alive then.*

ILLUSTRATION 1. A $1000, 20-year endowment insurance will pay $1000 at the end of the year of death if death occurs within 20 years, and $1000 at the end of 20 years if the insured person remains alive.

Let $A_{x:\overline{n}|}$ represent the net single premium or present value of an *n*-year endowment insurance of $1 on the life of [x]. $A_{x:\overline{n}|}$ is the sum of the present values of *n*-year term insurance for $1 on the life of [x] and an *n*-year pure endowment of $1 to [x]. From the preceding definition, on using Sections 71 and 78 we obtain

$$A_{x:\overline{n}|} = A^1_{x:\overline{n}|} + {}_nE_x = \frac{M_x - M_{x+n}}{D_x} + \frac{D_{x+n}}{D_x} ;$$

$$\left\{ \begin{array}{l} \textit{net single pr.; } \$1 \\ \textit{n-yr. endow. ins.} \end{array} \right\} \qquad A_{x:\overline{n}|} = \frac{M_x - M_{x+n} + D_{x+n}}{D_x} . \qquad (1)$$

If the endowment insurance is for $R, the net single premium $K is given by

$$\left\{ \begin{array}{l} \textit{net single pr.; } \$R \\ \textit{n-yr. endow. ins.} \end{array} \right\} \qquad K = RA_{x:\overline{n}|} = \frac{R(M_x - M_{x+n} + D_{x+n})}{D_x} . \qquad (2)$$

ILLUSTRATION 2.   The net single premium for a $1000, 10-year endowment insurance for a man aged 30 is given by

$$K = 1000 \frac{M_{30} - M_{40} + D_{40}}{D_{30}}.$$

Exercise 55

1. Separately compute the net single premiums for a pure endowment of $1000 due at the end of 20 years, and for a $1000, 20-year term insurance for a man aged 25. Add the results to get the net single premium for a 20-year endowment insurance for a man aged 25.
2. Repeat Problem 1 for a person of your age.
3. Find the net single premium for a $1000, 20-year endowment insurance for a person aged (*a*) 20 years; (*b*) 40 years; (*c*) 60 years.
4. How much 20-year endowment insurance can be purchased for $2500 cash by a man aged (*a*) 25 years; (*b*) 40 years?
5. In taking out a policy for a 20-year endowment insurance, a man aged 25 agrees to pay premiums of $150 at the beginning of each year for 20 years. How much 20-year endowment insurance does he obtain?
6. Repeat Problem 5 if the man is 40 years old and the annual premium is $300.

80.   Annual Premiums

Suppose that the net premiums for a policy are payable annually, instead of in one installment on the date the policy is written. Then these annual premiums satisfy the following equation:

$$\textbf{(pres. value of annual premiums) = (net single premium).} \qquad (1)$$

When premiums are payable annually, they are always payable at the beginnings of the policy years and cease when the insured person dies. Let an annual premium be represented by P. The annual premiums may be payable during the whole of the life of the policyholder, and thus form a *whole life annuity due*. Or, the premiums may be payable only for n years, and thus form an *n-year life annuity due*. For future convenience, we give the expression for the present value H of the annual premiums under each of these possibilities. The formulas are obtained by replacing R by P in (2) and (3) on page 207, for a man of age x.

$$\left\{ \begin{matrix} \$P \ annually \ for \\ whole \ life \end{matrix} \right\} \qquad H = P\ddot{a}_x = P\frac{N_x}{D_x}. \qquad (2)$$

$$\left\{ \begin{matrix} \$P \ annually \\ for \ n \ yrs. \end{matrix} \right\} \qquad H = P\ddot{a}_{x:\overline{n}|} = P\frac{N_x - N_{x+n}}{D_x}. \qquad (3)$$

The following rephrasing of (1) will be called the *fundamental equation for finding a premium*, annual or otherwise:

$$\text{(pres. value of premiums)} = \text{(pres. value of benefits).} \qquad (4)$$

The most common types of insurance policies are as follows:

Name of Policy	Policy Benefits	Premiums Paid
Ordinary life	Whole life insurance	Annually for life
n-payment life	Whole life insurance	Annually for n years
n-year term	n-year term insurance	Annually for n years
n-year endowment insurance	(a) n-year pure endowment (b) n-year term insurance	Annually for n years

In using (4) to find the annual premium for a particular policy, or for a general type of policy, the outline below is useful.

Summary

To find an annual premium P:

Write an expression in commutation symbols for the sum of the net single premiums of the policy benefits.

Write an expression in commutation symbols for the present value of the premiums.

Equate the preceding results as in (4) and solve for P.

Example 1. Find the net annual premium for a 20-payment life policy for $1000 for a man aged 26.

SOLUTION. 1. *Benefit*: $1000 whole life insurance. From page 212,

$$(\text{pres. value of benefit}) = 1000A_{26} = 1000\,\frac{M_{26}}{D_{26}}\,.$$

2. *Premiums:* payable for 20 years. From (3),

$$(\text{pres. value of premiums}) = P\ddot{a}_{26:\overline{20|}} = P\,\frac{N_{26} - N_{46}}{D_{26}}\,.$$

3. *Premium equation:*

$$P\,\frac{N_{26} - N_{46}}{D_{26}} = 1000\,\frac{M_{26}}{D_{26}}\,;$$

$$P = \frac{1000M_{26}}{N_{26} - N_{46}} = \$19.05. \qquad \text{(Table XVI)}$$

Example 2. Find the net annual premium for a 20-year endowment insurance policy for $1000 for a man aged 24.

PARTIAL SOLUTION. 1. *Benefits*: 20-year term insurance for $1000 and a 20-year pure endowment of $1000:

$$(\text{pres. val. of benefits}) = 1000A_{24:\overline{20}|} = 1000\,\frac{M_{24} - M_{44} + D_{44}}{D_{24}}.$$

2. *Premiums*: payable for 20 years. Therefore,

$$(\text{pres. val. of premiums}) = P\ddot{a}_{24:\overline{20}|} = P\,\frac{N_{24} - N_{44}}{D_{24}}.$$

Hence,

$$P\,\frac{N_{24} - N_{44}}{D_{24}} = 1000\,\frac{M_{24} - M_{44} + D_{44}}{D_{24}};$$

$$P(N_{24} - N_{44}) = 1000(M_{24} - M_{44} + D_{44});$$

$$P = 1000\,\frac{M_{24} - M_{44} + D_{44}}{N_{24} - N_{44}}.$$

The following formulas for annual premiums, with each benefit payment as $1, can be proved by the method of Examples 1 and 2. The annual premium for a corresponding benefit of R would be R times the premium as given in (5)–(8). The student may prove (5)–(7) in the next exercise.

ANNUAL PREMIUM AT AGE x

$\begin{cases} \text{Ordinary life} \\ \text{policy for \$1} \end{cases}$
$$P_x = \frac{M_x}{N_x}. \tag{5}$$

$\begin{cases} \text{n-payment life} \\ \text{policy for \$1} \end{cases}$
$$_nP_x = \frac{M_x}{N_x - N_{n+n}}. \tag{6}$$

$\begin{cases} \text{n-year term} \\ \text{policy for \$1} \end{cases}$
$$P^1_{x:\overline{n}|} = \frac{M_x - M_{x+n}}{N_x - N_{x+n}}. \tag{7}$$

$\begin{cases} \text{n-yr. endowment} \\ \text{insurance for \$1} \end{cases}$
$$P_{x:\overline{n}|} = \frac{M_x - M_{x+n} + D_{x+n}}{N_x - N_{x+n}}. \tag{8}$$

PROOF OF (8). The benefit is an n-year endowment insurance of $1 for $[x]$ with the net single premium $A_{x:\overline{n}|}$, in (1) on page 214. The premiums consist of P payable at the beginning of each year for n years, with present value $P\ddot{a}_{x:\overline{n}|}$. Hence,

$$P\ddot{a}_{x:\overline{n}|} = A_{x:\overline{n}|}, \quad \text{or} \quad P\,\frac{N_x - N_{x+n}}{D_x} = \frac{M_x - M_{x+n} + D_{x+n}}{D_x}.$$

Hence,

$$P = \frac{M_x - M_{x+n} + D_{x+n}}{N_x - N_{x+n}}.$$

denoted by the customary actuarial symbol $P_{x:\overline{n}|}$ in (8).

Example 3. What amount of 20-year term insurance can be bought by a man aged 35 for a net annual premium of $100?

SOLUTION. Let $\$W$ be the death benefit of the policy. The annual premium is $WP^1_{35:\overline{20}|}$. From (7), with the result given to the nearest $10,

$$100 = WP^1_{35:\overline{20}|} = W\frac{M_{35} - M_{55}}{N_{35} - N_{55}}; \quad W = \frac{100(N_{35} - N_{55})}{M_{35} - M_{55}} = \$19,310. \quad (9)$$

NOTE. The student should inquire from some insurance agent about the actual gross premiums for the policies of the illustrative examples and some of the problems in the next exercise. Such data will show approximately what percentage of a gross premium is loading.

Exercise 56

1. The net single premium is $4000 for a policy written for a man aged 25. Find the net annual premium if he agrees to pay premiums (a) for the whole of his life; (b) for 15 years.

The student is advised to do some of the next nine problems by the direct method of Examples 1 and 2 of Section 80, without using (5)–(8) on page 217. In later problems, use (5)–(8) if they apply.

Find the net annual premium for a person of the given age.

2. Man aged 25; a $10,000, ordinary life policy.
3. Man aged 30; a $10,000, 20-payment life policy.
4. Man aged 50; a $5000, ordinary life policy.
5. Man aged 50; a $10,000, 20-payment life policy.
6. A ten-year term policy for $5000 for a man aged (a) 32 years; (b) 52 years.
7. Man aged 25; a $5000, 20-year endowment insurance policy.
8. For yourself; a $5000, 20-year endowment insurance policy.
9. Man aged 40; a 5-year term policy for $10,000.
10. Man aged 60; a 5-year term policy for $10,000.

11. Prove formulas (5)–(7) on page 217.
12. How much whole life insurance on the ordinary life plan can a man aged 35 purchase for a net annual premium of $100?
13. How much 15-year term insurance on the 15-year term plan can a man aged 30 purchase for a net annual premium of $200?
14. How much insurance on the 20-payment life plan can a man aged 32 purchase for a net annual premium of $75?
15. How large a 20-year endowment insurance policy can a man aged 23 purchase for a net annual premium of $100?
16. (a) For a man aged 20, find the net annual premium for a $1000 endowment insurance policy which matures at age 85. (b) Find the net annual premium

for an ordinary life policy for $1000 taken at age 20. (c) Explain the small difference between the results.

17. A policy, which will mature at age 55, offers the option of a pure endowment of $5000, or an equivalent amount of *paid-up whole life insurance*, that is, as much insurance as the $5000, considered as a net single premium, will buy. Find the amount of paid-up insurance.

81. Policies of Irregular Type

The premium equation (4) on page 216 enables us to find the premiums for any policy for which the present value of the benefits is known.

Example 1. A policy written for a man aged 32 promises the following benefits: (a) term insurance of $5000 for 28 years; (b) a life annuity of $10,000 payable annually with the first payment due at age 60. Premiums are to be paid annually for 28 years. Find the net annual premium P.

INCOMPLETE SOLUTION. Let P be the annual premium. The student may verify that the premium equation is

$$P\ddot{a}_{32:\overline{28|}} = 5000A^1_{32:\overline{28|}} + 10,000(_{28|}\ddot{a}_{32}),$$

from which
$$P = \frac{10,000N_{60} + 5000(M_{32} - M_{60})}{N_{32} - N_{60}}.$$

Exercise 57

Find the net annual premium for each policy described for a man of the given age.

1. Age 47; 10 annual premiums; benefits are a 10-year term insurance of $5000 and a pure endowment of $10,000 at the end of 10 years.
2. Age 45; 20 annual premiums; benefits are a 20-year term insurance for $10,000 and a life annuity of $4000 paid annually with the first payment at age 65.
3. Age 30; 35 annual premiums; benefits are a life annuity of $5000 paid annually with the first payment at age 65, and 35-year term insurance for $10,000.
4. Age 45; 20 annual premiums; benefits are a life annuity of $2000 paid annually with the first payment at age 65, and a whole life insurance of $10,000.
5. Age 50; 20 annual premiums; benefits are a 20-year term insurance for $10,000 and a life annuity of $4000 paid annually with the first payment at age 70.

82. Level Premiums, Cost of Insurance, and Reserve Fund

The net single premium for a 1-year term insurance of R for $[x]$ is called the **natural premium** for R insurance at age x. Hence,

$$\left\{ \begin{array}{l} \text{natural premium,} \\ \$R \text{ insurance, age } x \end{array} \right\} = RA^1_{x:\overline{1}|} = R\,\frac{M_x - M_{x+1}}{D_x}. \tag{1}$$

Let c_x represent the natural premium for $1 insurance for $[x]$. Then, from (1), and (4) on page 211,

$$c_x = \frac{M_x - M_{x+1}}{D_x} = \frac{C_x}{D_x}. \tag{2}$$

ILLUSTRATION 1. The natural premium for $1000 insurance for a man of age 30 is

$$1000c_{30} = 1000\,\frac{C_{30}}{D_{30}} = \$2.07.$$

We refer to c_x as the **cost of $1 insurance** for 1 year at age x. This cost increases continually during life after an early age. However, for each type of life insurance which we have mentioned, the insurance company charges a fixed annual premium, or a **level premium** (considered by us to be payable annually) although c_x increases.

ILLUSTRATION 2. At 3%, the natural premium for $1000 insurance

$$\left. \begin{array}{l} \textit{at age } 30 \textit{ is } \$\ \ 2.07; \\ \textit{at age } 55 \textit{ is } \$\ 12.62; \\ \textit{at age } 80 \textit{ is } \$106.78; \end{array} \right\} = \textit{cost of 1-year term insurance.}$$

Suppose that either an R, n-year term, or an R, ordinary life policy for $[x]$ is issued by an insurance company T. Assume that a particular person $[x]$ is involved who, in the case of the n-year term policy, will live to age $(x + n - 1)$; in the case of the ordinary life policy, assume that he will live to age 99. During the early years after the policy date, the *cost* of insurance, or the *expense* of T per survivor with the policy, will be *less* than *the annual level premium*. In these years, the *surplus* of each premium over T's cost of insurance for each man is considered to be placed in a reserve fund which accumulates with interest at 3%. This fund is held in trust by T for all surviving policyholders with identical policies. During later years, the *level premium* is *less* than the *annual cost* of T for insurance per policyholder. This requires T to withdraw money annually from the reserve fund which grew in earlier years. Then, the method by which the level premiums are computed makes it certain that, for the n-year term policy, the corresponding reserve fund is exactly exhausted by expenses of death benefits n years after the policy date. For the ordinary life policy, the reserve is exactly exhausted at the date when each policyholder would have reached* 100. The amount in the reserve fund for a policy at the end of any year is called the *terminal reserve* for that year.

The nature of an insurance reserve is best appreciated if we recall the notion of a mutual benefit fund formed by the premiums paid by a great many people of the same age x who take out the same sort of policy. The net level premiums of these people are just sufficient to pay all benefits for the policies. The reserve at any date credited to the policy of a survivor of the group is his pro rata share of the total amount remaining in the joint benefit fund for all policyholders. The fund grows during early policy years and provides an increasing part of the cost of the insurance for the group in later years.

ILLUSTRATION 3. Consider a $1000, 10-year term insurance policy written for each of the large group G of men aged 50 who, we assume, obtain this type of policy at the same time from an insurance company T. The level annual premium P for the policy is found from (7) on page 217:

$$P = 1000P^1_{50:\overline{10|}} = \$12.10.$$

The following table shows the costs of $1000 insurance per person, or the natural premium $1000c_x$ for $1000 insurance in each of the 10 years, as obtained from (2). At the beginning of year 1, T receives $12.10 from each policyholder; T removes from it the cost, $8.08, to provide for $1000 death benefits on account of deaths which will occur in the group of policyholders in the first year. The balance, $(12.10 - 8.08)$ or $4.02, is placed in a reserve fund for the group, to provide some of the expense of future death benefits. At the beginning of year 2, each survivor in the group pays $12.10; the cost of insurance in year 2 for T is

Contributions (+ or −) of Level Premiums to Reserve for $1000, 10-Year Term Insurance Policy for [50]

Year	Level Premium	Cost of Death Benefits for Year	Contribution to Reserve Fund
1	$12.10	$8.08	(+) $4.02
2	$12.10	$8.84	(+) $3.26
3	$12.10	$9.67	(+) $2.43
4	$12.10	$10.57	(+) $1.53
5	$12.10	$11.55	(+) $ .55
6	$12.10	$12.62	(−) $ .52
7	$12.10	$13.80	(−) $1.70
8	$12.10	$15.09	(−) $2.99
9	$12.10	$16.50	(−) $4.40
10	$12.10	$18.05	(−) $5.95

* If he should live to age 100, the reserve fund would contain $1000, for a $1000 policy, credited to him. Then it is sometimes customary for T to pay [100] $1000 as if he were the beneficiary.

$8.84; the surplus (12.10 − 8.84), or $3.26 per surviving policyholder, is placed in the reserve fund. Etc., as shown in the table. At the beginning of year 6, *T* needs $12.62 for the cost of insurance per survivor but receives only the level premium $12.10. The deficit (12.62 − 12.10), or $.52 per survivor, is taken from the reserve fund for the group. In each of the remaining years, the cost of insurance is greater than the level premium, and the balance comes from the reserve. The manner in which the net level premium is computed assures us that the surplus contributions from the premiums in the first 5 years, plus interest accumulation at 3%, and the future premiums are sufficient to pay all death benefits for the given type of policyholder. The reserve will be exactly exhausted at the end of the tenth year. Figure 27 represents the level premiums by black dots, connected by a horizontal line to emphasize that the premiums remain constant. The costs of insurance for the 10 years are the ordinates on the light curve at the integral values {0, 1, 2, 3, 4, 5, 6, 7, 8, 9} of the years.

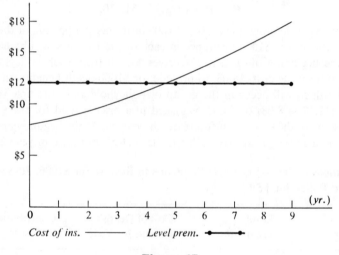

Figure 27

A complete discussion of the reserve per policyholder, and related considerations in the conduct of an insurance company *T* are above the level of this text.* Only an illustration of the most simple manner of computation of a reserve will be presented.

Example 1. Find the terminal reserve at the end of 5 years for a $1000, 20-payment whole life insurance policy for a man who took out the policy when he was 25 years old.

* See the subject of reserves in *The Mathematicians of Life Insurance*, by Walter O. Menge and Carl H. Fischer, 1965; distributed by Ulrich's Books, Inc., Ann Arbor, Michigan.

SOLUTION.   1. The net annual premium P is obtained from (6) on page 217, with the aid of Table XVI:

$$P = 1000 \, \frac{M_{25}}{N_{25} - N_{45}} = \$18.573.$$

2. At the end of any policy year, a given policy promises certain remaining benefits; it has a certain terminal reserve V; the policyholder is required to pay remaining premiums. We can write an equation of value, with the basic investment rate $i = .03$, involving the features just mentioned about the policy. The comparison date is the end of the specified policy year.

$$\left\{\begin{array}{c}\textbf{net single premium}\\ \textbf{or present value,}\\ \textbf{of remaining benefits}\end{array}\right\} = \left\{\begin{array}{c}\textbf{pr. value of}\\ \textbf{remaining}\\ \textbf{premiums}\end{array}\right\} + \left\{\begin{array}{c}\textbf{terminal}\\ \textbf{reserve}\\ V\end{array}\right\}. \qquad (3)$$

3. In our problem, the remaining benefits are a $1000 whole life insurance for a man now aged 30. The remaining premiums form a 15-year life annuity due of $18.573 payable annually. Hence, from (3) we obtain

$$1000A_{30} = 18.573\ddot{a}_{30:\overline{15|}} + V; \qquad (4)$$

$$V = \frac{1000M_{30} - 185.73(N_{30} - N_{45})}{D_{30}} = \$91.53. \qquad (5)$$

Statement (3) is available for the computation of the reserve for any policy of the types we have considered.

Exercise 58

1. A $1000, 10-year term insurance policy is written for each man in a large group of men aged 55 by an insurance company T. (*a*) Find the level annual premium for the policy. (*b*) Find the cost for T of the insurance per survivor for each of the 10 years. (*c*) Make up a table as in Section 82 showing the surplus or deficit of the premium for each year as compared to the cost of the insurance per survivor.

2. At an attained age of 50, the net single premium for the remaining benefits of a policy is $750. There are ten annual premiums of $50 remaining to be paid, the first due immediately. Find the policy reserve.

3. At the attained age of 44, the reserve on a certain policy is $500. Annual premiums of $75, the first due immediately, must be paid for the remainder of life. Find the present value of the remaining policy benefits.

4. Find the terminal reserve at the end of 5 years for a $1000 ordinary life policy written for a man of age 25.

5. A $1000, 10-payment life policy is written for a man of age 30. What is the terminal reserve at the end of 10 years?

6. A man aged 30 pays the net single premium for a whole life insurance for $10,000. Twenty years later, what is the terminal reserve?

7. Find the terminal reserve at the end of 5 years for a $1000, 20-year endowment insurance policy written for a man aged 25.

8. For the policy in Example 1 of Section 80, find the terminal reserve at the end of 10 years. Use the premium as found in Section 80.

9. Find the terminal reserve at the end of 5 years for a $1000, 10-year term policy written for a man aged 35.

Auxiliary Topics

10/ Certain Basic Topics

83. Real Numbers

Algebra uses numbers of the following two varieties: *real numbers*, with which we deal in this section, and *imaginary numbers*, which we shall not need in this text. The system R of real numbers consists of the positive numbers, the negative numbers, and zero, which is not called either positive or negative. A **rational number** is a real number that can be expressed as a fraction p/q where p and q are integers and $q \neq 0$. An **irrational number** is a real number that is not rational. Unless implied otherwise, any single letter introduced in a discussion will represent a real number.

ILLUSTRATION 1.   The numbers $\{7, -2, \frac{2}{3}, 0\}$ are rational numbers. The endless nonrepeating decimals $\pi = 3.14159\ldots$ and $\sqrt{2} = 1.414\ldots$ are irrational numbers. The terminating decimal 15.709, or 15.709000..., is a rational number which can be written 15709/1000. The endless repeating decimal .1666... is the rational number $\frac{1}{6}$.

DEFINITION I.   *To **divide** a by $b \neq 0$ means to find a number c such that $a = bc$.*

In Definition I, we call a the *dividend*, b the *divisor*, and c the *quotient* of a divided by b. This quotient is represented by $a \div b$, $\dfrac{a}{b}$, or a/b, where we read the fraction as "*a divided by b*," or simply "*a over b*." If a and b are real numbers with $b \neq 0$, there exists a single number c such that $c = a/b$. Also, the fraction a/b is referred to as the **ratio** of a to b.

ILLUSTRATION 2.   Notice that, by Definition I, division by 0 is *not defined* in algebra. However, addition of 0, multiplication by 0, and division of 0 by any number not 0, present no peculiarities. Thus, for any number b, we have $(b + 0) = b$; $b \cdot 0 = 0$. If $b \neq 0$, then $0 = 0/b$. Also, a product $bc = 0$ *if and only if $b = 0$ or $c = 0$.*

227

A *minus sign* before a symbol for a number indicates multiplication of it by -1. A *plus sign* before a symbol for a number indicates multiplication of it by $+1$, or 1, which does not alter the number. A sign, $+$ or $-$, preceding a number symbol will be called *its sign*. If no sign is used, this is equivalent to the presence of a *plus sign* which has no effect on the value of the symbol. Thus, every symbol will be said to have a preceding sign, $+$ or $-$. We recall that

$$(-1)(-1) = +1 = 1; \qquad (-1)(+1) = -1. \tag{1}$$

The **negative** of any number b is defined as $(-1)(b)$, or simply $-b$. As a consequence of (1), the negative of a positive number is a negative number. The negative of a negative number is a positive number.

ILLUSTRATION 3.   The negative of -4 is $-(-4) = (-1)(-1)(4) = 4$.
The negative of 6, or $+6$, is $(-1)(+1)(6) = -6$.
The negative of 0 is $(-1)(0) = 0$.

The **difference** of a first number A and a second number B is defined as $[A + (-B)]$, or simply $(A - B)$.

ILLUSTRATION 4.   The difference of 7 and -12 is $7 - (-12) = 7 + 12 = 19$.

Parentheses, ( ), brackets, [ ], braces, { }, and the vinculum, —— are used to enclose terms whose sum is to act as a single number. In general remarks, the word *parentheses* will refer to any symbols of grouping.

To remove parentheses preceded by a minus sign, the implied multiplication by -1 should be performed on each included term, which thus will have its sign changed. Suppose that a symbol of grouping encloses other symbols of grouping. Then, to remove the symbols, we commence by removing the innermost symbol first, then the next innermost; and so forth. Usually we enclose parentheses within brackets; brackets within braces.

ILLUSTRATION 5. $-[3y - (2x - 5 + z)]$
$$= -[3y - 2x + 5 - z] = -3y + 2x - 5 + z.$$

Suppose that any number to be used as a divisor is not zero. Then the following properties of fractions are recalled.

$$\frac{a}{b} \cdot \frac{c}{d} = \frac{ac}{bd}; \qquad \left(\frac{a}{b} \div \frac{c}{d}\right) = \frac{a}{b} \cdot \frac{d}{c} = \frac{ad}{bc}. \tag{2}$$

Let h be any number not zero. Then,

$$a \cdot \frac{1}{h} = \frac{a}{1} \cdot \frac{1}{h} = \frac{a}{h} = (a \div h).$$

In other words, *division* by h is equivalent to *multiplication* by $1/h$. We verify that, if $k \neq 0$,

$$\frac{a}{b} = \frac{a}{b} \cdot \frac{k}{k} = \frac{ak}{bk}, \qquad because \qquad \frac{k}{k} = 1. \tag{3}$$

Hence, the value of a fraction is unaltered if its numerator and denominator are multiplied by the same number, not zero. Since *division* by a number $h \neq 0$ is equivalent to *multiplication* by $1/h$, the value of a fraction is unaltered if its numerator and denominator are *divided* by the same number $h \neq 0$.

ILLUSTRATION 6.
$$\frac{3}{4}\cdot\frac{5}{7} = \frac{15}{28}. \qquad \frac{2}{3} \div \frac{5}{11} = \frac{2}{3}\cdot\frac{11}{5} = \frac{22}{15}.$$

$$\frac{5}{7} = \frac{5}{7}\cdot\frac{2}{2} = \frac{10}{14}; \qquad \frac{12}{15} = \frac{12 \div 3}{15 \div 3} = \frac{4}{5}.$$

DEFINITION II.   *The* **reciprocal** *of a number $b \neq 0$ is $1/b$.*

ILLUSTRATION 7.   The reciprocal of 6 is $\frac{1}{6}$.

The reciprocal of $\dfrac{3}{7}$ is $\left(1 \div \dfrac{3}{7}\right) = \dfrac{1}{1}\cdot\dfrac{7}{3} = \dfrac{7}{3}.$

The reciprocal of $\dfrac{a}{b}$ is $\left(1 \div \dfrac{a}{b}\right) = \dfrac{1}{1}\cdot\dfrac{b}{a} = \dfrac{b}{a}.$

Thus, *the reciprocal of a fraction a/b is the fraction* **inverted**.

To *multiply* a fraction by a number k, multiply the *numerator* by k. To *divide* a fraction by $k \neq 0$, multiply the *denominator* by k. These results are a consequence of (2).

ILLUSTRATION 8.
$$\frac{a}{b}\cdot k = \frac{a}{b}\cdot\frac{k}{1} = \frac{ak}{b}; \qquad \frac{3}{5}(7) = \frac{21}{5}.$$

$$\left(\frac{a}{b} \div k\right) = \left(\frac{a}{b} \div \frac{k}{1}\right) = \frac{a}{b}\cdot\frac{1}{k} = \frac{a}{bk}; \qquad \left(\frac{2}{7} \div 5\right) = \frac{2}{35}.$$

A fraction is said to be in **lowest terms** if its numerator and denominator have no common factor* except ± 1 (read "*plus or minus* 1"). To change a fraction to lowest terms, we divide both numerator and denominator by the product of all of their common factors.

ILLUSTRATION 9.   To change the following fraction to lowest terms, divide out the factor $8kw$ from the numerator and denominator:

$$\frac{16hkw}{24ukw} = \frac{2h(8kw)}{3u(8kw)} = \frac{2h}{3u}.$$

DEFINITION III.   *The* **absolute value** *of a positive number or of zero is the given number. The absolute value of a negative number is its negative.*

"*The absolute value of b*" is represented by "$|\,b\,|$." Hence,

$$|\,b\,| = b \qquad \text{if } b \text{ is } \textbf{zero } \textit{or } \textbf{positive};$$
$$|\,b\,| = -b \qquad \text{if } b \text{ is } \textbf{negative.}$$

---

* The word *factor* is assumed to have a meaning fitting the circumstances involved.

ILLUSTRATION 10. $|0| = 0$; $|-6| = 6$; $\left|\frac{7}{2}\right| = \frac{7}{2}$.

Observe that bc and $|b| \cdot |c|$ are equal if bc is positive of zero. Otherwise $bc = -|b| \cdot |c|$. In either case,

$$|bc| = |b| \cdot |c|.$$

With $b \neq 0$ and $c = a/b$, or $a = bc$, we have

$$|a| = |b| \cdot |c|, \quad \text{and then} \quad |c| = \frac{|a|}{|b|}. \quad \text{or}$$

$$\left|\frac{a}{b}\right| = \frac{|a|}{|b|}.$$

To compute a/b when $a \neq 0$ and $b \neq 0$, first we obtain $|a/b|$, and then multiply by -1 if necessary.

ILLUSTRATION 11. $\quad \dfrac{-120}{45} = -\dfrac{120}{45} = -\dfrac{8}{3}. \quad \dfrac{-36}{-32} = +\dfrac{9 \cdot 4}{8 \cdot 4} = \dfrac{9}{8}.$

84. Sets, Variables, and Constants

The concept of a "*set*" of "*elements*" is very useful in many places in mathematics. For instance, the negative integers form a set of numbers. The members of the Armed Forces of the United States form a set of people. Each object or element of a set is called a *member* of it. For simplicity in some statements, it is convenient to introduce the concept of the **empty set**, or **null set**, represented by $\varnothing$, which has no members. If a set T has exactly n members, where n is a nonnegative integer, then T is called a *finite set*. If T is *not* a finite set, then T is called an *infinite set*. In such a case, corresponding to every positive integer n, there exists more than n elements in T. Thus, for example, the set of real numbers is an infinite set.

A **subset** S of a set M is a set consisting of some, and possibly all, of the elements of M. If S is a subset of M, it is said that S is *included* in M, and we write "$S \subset M$," which is read "S *is included in* M." It is seen that $M \subset M$. Also, it is agreed that the empty set is a subset of every set, or $\varnothing \subset M$ for every M. If all elements of a set T are in a set M, and all elements of M are in T, then T and M are the same set, and we say that $T = M$. If $T \neq M$ and $T \subset M$, then T is called a **proper subset** of T. In such a case there is at least one element of M that is *not* in T.

ILLUSTRATION 1. The set P of positive numbers is an infinite proper subset of the set R of all real numbers, or $P \subset R$ and $P \neq R$.

To describe a set, sometimes symbols for its elements are written within braces. This notation is referred to as the **roster description** of a set.

ILLUSTRATION 2.   If $K = \{2, 4, 6, 8, 10, 12\}$ and $H = \{4, 6, 8\}$, then $H \subset K$ and H is a proper subset of K.

A **variable** is a symbol, such as x, that may represent any element of some specified nonempty set T, called the **domain** of the variable. Each element of T is called a *value* of the variable, where value does not necessarily mean a number. However, in this text, the domain of any variable will be a set of numbers unless otherwise indicated.

ILLUSTRATION 3.   If y represents any member of the Congress of the United States, then all the members form the domain for y.

ILLUSTRATION 4.   Let S be the set of all numbers $u \neq 6$. The set S also could be described as the set of all numbers $v \neq 6$. The letter u, or v, that is used for the arbitrary member of S is immaterial.

In a given mathematical discussion, a **constant** is a fixed number. A constant k also can be thought of as a variable whose domain consists of a single element, k. Whenever we refer to a variable, it will *not* be a constant unless otherwise specified.

ILLUSTRATION 5.   In the formula $V = \pi r^2 h$ for the volume of a cylinder with radius r and altitude h, if all cylinders are being considered, then V, r, and h are variables and π is a constant.

Exercise 59

State the absolute value of the expression.

1. $|-7|$.   **2.** $|0|$.   **3.** $|6(-7)(-3)|$.   **4.** $|9(0)(-4)|$.

Find the sum, difference, and product of the numbers. Also find the quotient of the first number divided by the second number, if possible.

5. 10 and 4.   **6.** -3 and -9.   **7.** -20 and 5.   **8.** 36 and 0.
9. Find the ratio of 68 to 12; of -72 to 48.

Rewrite by removing any parentheses and collecting similar terms.

10. $5(x - 3y + 5) - 2(x + 2y - 4) - 3(-4x - y + 6)$.
11. $-[4a - (2a + 3)]$.   **12.** $-[2t - (3 - 4t)]$.

13. If M represents the set $\{3, 4, 5, 6, 7, 8\}$, use the roster notation to describe six proper subsets of M consisting of five elements each.
14. If R is the set of all real numbers, describe two infinite proper subsets of R.

Perform any indicated operation, and express the result as a fraction in lowest terms without any minus sign in the numerator or denominator.

15. $\dfrac{-5}{3}$.   **16.** $\dfrac{4}{-7}$.   **17.** $\dfrac{-15}{-12}$.   **18.** $\dfrac{-78}{-26}$.

19. $\frac{3}{5} \cdot \frac{4}{7}$.　　**20.** $\frac{4}{5} \cdot \frac{3}{8}$.　　**21.** $(2\frac{1}{7})(5\frac{1}{4})$.　　**22.** $\frac{4}{5} \div \frac{2}{3}$.

23. $\frac{22}{7} \div \frac{11}{5}$.　　**24.** $5 \div \frac{15}{4}$.　　**25.** $\frac{16}{21} \div \frac{4}{7}$.　　**26.** $16(\frac{3}{40})$.

27. $\frac{b}{2} \cdot \frac{8}{d}$.　　**28.** $\frac{4cd}{16c}$.　　**29.** $\frac{3}{5cd} \cdot (4c)$.　　**30.** $\frac{8a}{15} \div \frac{2a}{5}$.

31. $\frac{21x}{28xy}$.　　**32.** $\frac{27a}{6ad}$.　　**33.** $\frac{-bc}{3c}$.　　**34.** $\frac{4a}{-3ad}$.

35. $-\frac{-3}{12b}$.　　　　**36.** $-\frac{5ad}{3a}$.　　　　**37.** $(4\frac{5}{9}) \div \frac{x}{3}$.

38. $\frac{3}{4} \cdot \frac{5x}{7} \cdot \frac{2}{9x}$.　　　**39.** $15x \div \frac{10x}{7}$.　　　**40.** $\frac{5d}{c} \div 10d$.

Find the reciprocal of the number.

41. 12.　　　**42.** $\frac{3}{5}$.　　　**43.** $\frac{1}{2}cd$.　　　**44.** $-\frac{2}{3}$.

85.　A Number Line and Inequality Relations

In this text, the word *length* or the unqualified word *distance* will refer to a non-negative number that is the measure of some distance or straight line segment between two points. On a given line L, select a point O, to be called the **origin**, and let it represent the number 0. For convenience in referring to directions, we shall assume that L is horizontal, as in Figure 28. Choose a unit for measuring distance on L. If p is any positive number, let it be represented by the point on L that is p units of distance from O to the right. Let $-p$ be represented by the point on L that is p units of distance from O to the left. Thus, each real number is represented by a point on L, and each point on L represents just one number. Hereafter, if r is any number, we may refer to *the point r*, meaning the point representing r on L. We call L a **number line**.

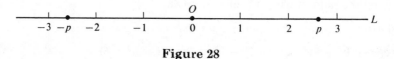

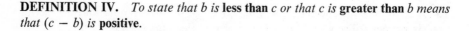

Figure 28

DEFINITION IV.　*To state that b is* **less than** *c or that c is* **greater than** *b means that $(c - b)$ is* **positive.**

The sign "$<$" is used for "*is less than*" and "$>$" for "*is greater than*":

$$b < c \qquad \text{means that} \qquad (c - b) \text{ is \textbf{positive}.} \tag{1}$$

We refer to "$b < c$" as an *inequality*. By definition, $b < c$ and $c > b$ have the same meaning. The statement "$b \leq c$" is read "b *is less than or equal to c,*" and "$c \geq b$" is read "c *is greater than or equal to b.*" Each of $b \leq c$ and $c \geq b$ also is called an *inequality.*

ILLUSTRATION 1.   We have $4 < 6$ because $(6 - 4) = 2$, which is positive.

$-7 < -3$ because $-3 - (-7) = -3 + 7 = 4$, which is positive.

$-10 < 0$ because $0 - (-10) = 10$, which is positive.

To say that $p > 0$ means that $(p - 0)$, or p, is *positive;* to say that $h < 0$ means that $(0 - h)$, or $-h$, is *positive,* and hence that h is *negative:*

$$p > 0 \qquad \textit{means that} \qquad p \textit{ is \textbf{positive.}} \qquad\qquad (2)$$

$$h < 0 \qquad \textit{means that} \qquad h \textit{ is \textbf{negative.}} \qquad\qquad (3)$$

To state that b and c are *numerically equal* means that $|b| = |c|$. To state that b is *numerically less than* c means that $|b| < |c|$.

ILLUSTRATION 2. $-7 < 2$ but -7 is numerically greater than 2 because we have $|-7| > |2|$, or $7 > 2$.

If x is any number, and P is the point representing x on a number line, as in Figure 29, we shall call x the **coordinate** of P. We shall write "$P:(x)$" to be read simply "P, x" or, if desired, "P *with the coordinate x.*"

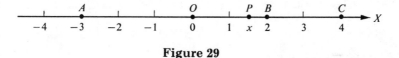

Figure 29

ILLUSTRATION 3.   In Figure 29, observe $A:(-3)$, $B:(2)$, $C:(4)$, and $P:(x)$, where points are labeled above the line.

If $P_1:(x_1)$ and $P_2:(x_2)$ are distinct points on a number line L, as in Figure 30, then P_1P_2 will represent, or be the *name,* of the line segment with P_1 as the initial point and P_2 as the terminal point. P_1P_2 is thought of as *directed* from P_1 to P_2, and P_1P_2 is referred to as a *directed line segment.* P_1P_2 is said to have *positive* direction if P_1P_2 is directed to the right, and then will be assigned a positive value. P_1P_2 is said to have negative direction if P_1P_2 is directed to the *left,* and then will be assigned a negative value. If P_1 and P_2 are the same point, then P_1P_2 is referred to as having no direction; it consists of a single point, and later will be assigned the value 0.

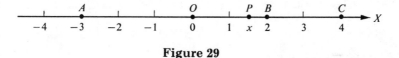

Figure 30

If $P_1:(x_1)$ and $P_2:(x_2)$ are any points on a number line L, as in Figure 30, let $\overline{P_1P_2}$ represent the *directed distance* from P_1 to P_2, defined by

$$\overline{P_1P_2} = x_2 - x_1. \tag{4}$$

We read "$\overline{P_1P_2}$" as "P_1, P_2, *bar*," and call it the *value* of P_1P_2. From (4), $\overline{P_1P_2}$ is either plus or minus the number of units of distance between P_1 and P_2. Then,

$$\textbf{(length of } P_1P_2\textbf{)} = |\ \overline{P_1P_2}\ | = |\ x_2 - x_1\ |. \tag{5}$$

We shall call $|\ x_2 - x_1\ |$ the *scale distance* between P_1 and P_2 on L. With the preceding agreements, we refer to L as a *directed line*. If $P:(x)$ is any point on L, as in Figure 29, by use of (4) we obtain $\overline{OP} = x - 0$, or $\overline{OP} = x$. Hence, the *coordinate* of P is the directed distance from the origin to P, with $\overline{OP}$ positive when P is to the right of O, and $\overline{OP}$ negative when P is to the left of O. We indicate the positive direction on L by an arrowhead.

ILLUSTRATION 4.   With A, B, and C as in Figure 29.

$$\overline{AB} = 2 - (-3) = 5; \qquad \textit{(length of AB)} = |\ \overline{AB}\ | = 5. \tag{6}$$

$$\overline{BA} = -3 - 2 = -5; \qquad \textit{(length of BA)} = |\ \overline{BA}\ | = 5. \tag{7}$$

$$\overline{OC} = 4 - 0 = 4; \qquad \textit{(length of OC)} = |\ \overline{OC}\ | = 4. \tag{8}$$

$$\overline{OA} = -3 - 0 = -3; \qquad \textit{(length of OA)} = |\ \overline{OA}\ | = 3. \tag{9}$$

In (6) and (7), notice that

$$\overline{AB} = -\overline{BA}. \tag{10}$$

For any points A and B on L, it is seen that (10) is true, because *reversal* of the direction of a line segment multiplies its value by -1.

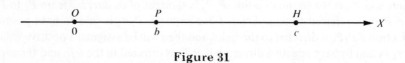

Figure 31

Suppose that $P:(b)$ and $H:(c)$ are points on a number line, as in Figure 31. By (4), we have $\overline{PH} = c - b$. Hence, to state that b is to the *left* of c on a number line means that PH is directed to the *right*, or that $(c - b)$ is positive, which is equivalent to $b < c$. Thus, we have the following geometrical meaning for "*less than*":

$$b < c \text{ means that } b \text{ is to the \textbf{left} of } c \text{ on a number line.} \tag{11}$$

ILLUSTRATION 5. Since -4 is to the left of 7 on a number line, we have $-4 < 7$.

A statement such as "$a < x < b$" is read "*a is less than x and x is less than b.*" Hence, by (11), x is to the *right* of a and to the *left* of b. Or, $a < x < b$ means that the number x is *between* a and b on a number line.

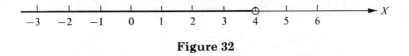

Figure 32

ILLUSTRATION 6. The values of x for which $x < 4$ are called the *solutions* of the inequality, and they form its *solution set*, or set of solutions. On a number line, the solutions of $x < 4$ are the points to the left of 4, as shown in Figure 32 by the thick part of the line. The point 4 is not included; this is emphasized by the open circle at 4. A representation of the solutions of an inequality as in Figure 32 is called the **graph** of the inequality on the number line.

86. Nonnegative Integral Exponents

We write a^2 to abbreviate $a \cdot a$, and a^3 to abbreviate $a \cdot a \cdot a$. We call a^2 the *square* of a, and a^3 the *cube* of a. If n is any positive integer, then a^n is read "*a nth,*" and is defined by

$$a^n = a \cdot a \cdot a \cdots a \qquad (n \text{ factors } a). \qquad (1)$$

We call a^n the *n*th **power** of the **base** a; n is referred to as the **exponent** of this power. When the exponent is 1, usually we omit it. Thus, y means y^1.

ILLUSTRATION 1. $\qquad 5^3 = 5 \cdot 5 \cdot 5 = 125$.

$$(-4)^3 = (-4)(-4)(-4) = -4 \cdot 4 \cdot 4 = -4^3 = -64.$$

Until specified otherwise, any exponent to which we refer will be a positive integer, as in (1). The following familiar theorems, called **index laws**, are recalled. We assume that no base for a power in a denominator is zero.

I. *Law of exponents for multiplication:* $\qquad a^m a^n = a^{m+n}$.

II. *Law for finding a power of a power:* $\qquad (a^m)^n = a^{mn}$.

III. *Law of exponents for division (with $a \neq 0$):*

$$\frac{a^n}{a^n} = 1; \qquad \frac{a^m}{a^n} = a^{m-n} \quad (\text{if } m > n); \qquad \frac{a^m}{a^n} = \frac{1}{a^{n-m}} \quad (\text{if } n > m).$$

IV. *Law for finding a power of a product:* $\qquad (ab)^n = a^n b^n$.

V. *Law for finding a power of a fraction:* $\qquad \left(\dfrac{a}{b}\right)^n = \dfrac{a^n}{b^n}$.

ILLUSTRATION 2. $a^2 a^3 = a^5$; $(a^2)^3 = a^6$.

$$\frac{a^6}{a^2} = a^{6-2} = a^4; \qquad \frac{a^2}{a^6} = \frac{1}{a^{6-2}} = \frac{1}{a^4}.$$

$$(3a^2 b^4)^3 = 3^3 (a^2)^3 (b^4)^3 = 27 a^6 b^{12}.$$

$$\left(\frac{3}{2}\right)^4 = \frac{3^4}{2^4} = \frac{81}{16}. \qquad \left(\frac{4cd^2}{3x}\right)^2 = \frac{(4cd^2)^2}{(3x)^2} = \frac{16c^2 d^4}{9x^2}.$$

$$\frac{-15 a^3 x^5}{10 a x^9} = -\frac{3}{2} \cdot \frac{a^3}{a} \cdot \frac{x^5}{x^9} = -\frac{3a^{3-1}}{2x^{9-5}} = -\frac{3a^2}{2x^4}.$$

Suppose that we wish to use zero as an exponent, and that a^0 is to obey the law of exponents for multiplication. Then, if n is any positive integer and $a \neq 0$,

$$a^0 a^n = a^{0+n} = a^n, \qquad or \qquad a^0 a^n = a^n, \qquad so\ that \qquad a^0 = \frac{a^n}{a^n} = 1.$$

Hence, if $a \neq 0$, we decide to *define* a^0 as follows:

$$a^0 = 1. \tag{2}$$

Hereafter, until otherwise specified, any exponent that occurs will be a non-negative integer. Observe that all of the index laws remain true if each exponent is 0 or a positive integer. For a reason that is discussed in calculus, a^0 is *not defined* if $a = 0$. However, by (1), $0^n = 0$ for every positive integer n.

A **monomial**, not 0, in a set of variables is defined as a product of nonnegative integral powers of the variables, multiplied by a constant, not zero, called the *coefficient* of the monomial. The **degree** of the monomial is defined as the sum of the exponents of the powers of the variables that are factors of the monomial. In addition to monomials as just described, 0 is called the monomial with *no degree*.

ILLUSTRATION 3.   If $\{b, x, y\}$ are variables, then $9bx^3 y^2$, or $9b^1 x^3 y^2$ is a monomial with the coefficient 9 and degree 6, because $1 + 3 + 2 = 6$.

ILLUSTRATION 4.   If $x \neq 0$, any constant $b \neq 0$ can be thought of as bx^0, which is of degree 0 in x.

A sum of monomials in specified variables is called a **polynomial** in them. A polynomial is called a *binomial* if it is a sum of two monomials, and a *trinomial* if it is a sum of three monomials. Each monomial in a polynomial is called a *term* of it. The **degree of a polynomial** is the degree of its term of *highest degree*. A polynomial in any variables is said to be a *linear, quadratic, cubic,* or *quartic* polynomial according as its degree is 1, 2, 3, or 4, respectively.

ILLUSTRATION 5.   If x and y are variables, with each of $\{a, b, c\}$ as a constant, not zero, then $(5ax^2 - 2bxy^4 + cy^3)$ is of degree 5, because $2bx^1 y^4$ is of degree 5. The terms in this polynomial are $5ax^2$, $-2bxy^4$, and cy^3.

A *linear polynomial* in x is of the form $(a + bx)$ where a and b are constants with $b \neq 0$. A *quadratic polynomial* in x is of the form $(ax^2 + bx + c)$ where $\{a, b, c\}$ are constants with $a \neq 0$. A linear polynomial in two variables x and y is of the form $(ax + by + c)$, where $\{a, b\}$ are not both zero. A constant, not zero, such as 6, is a polynomial of degree 0. The constant 0 by itself may be referred to as the polynomial with *no degree*. Unless specified otherwise, in any polynomial it will be assumed that any literal number symbol represents a variable.

Exercise 60

Insert the proper symbol, $<$ or $>$ between the numbers.,

1. 6 and 12.   **2.** 3 and 9.   **3.** 6 and 0.   **4.** 0 and -7.
5. -2 and -5.   **6.** -5 and 2.   **7.** -2 and 9.   **8.** -4 and -14.

Apply the laws of exponents and simplify any fraction to lowest terms. Wherever no literal symbol is involved, compute to a form not involving an exponent. Collect similar terms in multiplying polynomials.

9. 4^3.   **10.** 10^2.   **11.** $(-1)^6$.   **12.** $(-7)^0$.
13. $(-10)^5$.   **14.** $(.1)^3$.   **15.** $(\frac{1}{3})^4$.   **16.** $(\frac{2}{5})^3$.
17. $(3^2)^3$.   **18.** $2(4^3)$.   **19.** $(2^2)^3$.   **20.** $(10^2)^4$.
21. $a^5 a^4 a^0$.   **22.** $x x^3$.   **23.** $a^h a^{2h}$.   **24.** $y y^7$.

25. $\dfrac{y^3}{y}$.   **26.** $\dfrac{a^2}{a^8}$.   **27.** $\dfrac{x^3}{x^5}$.   **28.** $\dfrac{a^7}{a^2}$.

29. $-3ax^4(-2a^2x)$.   **30.** $5x^2y(-2xy^3)$.   **31.** $2a^3b^2(-49a^2b^4)$.
32. $(u + y)^2$.   **33.** $(a - 2y)^2$.   **34.** $(2y^3 - 4y + 5y^2 - 3)(y + 3)$.
35. $(24a^3b^5 - 36a^4b^2) \div 16a^3b^6$.   **36.** $(21x^3y^2 - 28y^4) \div 14x^2y$.

87. Radicals and Rational Exponents

If $R^2 = A$, then R is called a **square root** of A. If $A > 0$, then A is found to have two square roots, one positive and one negative, with equal absolute values. The positive square root is represented by $+\sqrt{A}$, or simply $\sqrt{A}$, and the negative square root by $-\sqrt{A}$. We read "$\sqrt{A}$" as "*the square root of A*," meaning the *positive* square root of A. We refer to $\sqrt{A}$ as a **radical** whose **radicand** is A. The only number R such that $R^2 = 0$ is $R = 0$. That is, 0 has just one square root, and we use $\sqrt{0} = 0$. By the definition of $\sqrt{A}$ it is seen that

$$(\sqrt{A})^2 = A. \tag{1}$$

ILLUSTRATION 1.   The square roots of 25 are $\pm\sqrt{25}$, or 5 and -5.

If $A < 0$ and R is a square root of A, then $R \neq 0$ and $R^2 = A$. If R is real and $R \neq 0$, then $R^2 > 0$. Hence, *no real number satisfies* $R^2 = A$ *when* $A < 0$, or *a negative number has no real number as a square root*.

If $x \neq 0$, the two square roots of x^2 are $\pm x$ (read "*plus and minus* x"), because $(x)^2 = x^2$ and $(-x)^2 = x^2$. Thus, if $x > 0$ then the *positive* square root of x^2 is x; if $x < 0$ then the *positive* square root of x^2 is $-x$. Since $\sqrt{x^2}$ in each case represents the *positive* square root, we have

$$\sqrt{x^2} = x \text{ if } x > 0; \qquad \sqrt{x^2} = -x \text{ if } x < 0. \tag{2}$$

In all of our applications of (2), we shall have $x > 0$, so that

$$\sqrt{x^2} = x \tag{3}$$

in all cases in this text.

To state that a rational number is a **perfect square** will mean that the number is the square of some rational number. Suppose that the coefficient of any monomial to be mentioned is a rational number. Such a monomial, or a quotient of such monomials, will be called a *perfect square* if it is the square of an expression of the same type. To obtain the square root of a perfect square, we use (3).

ILLUSTRATION 2. Notice that $25a^2b^4 = (5ab^2)^2$ and $16x^6 = (4x^3)^2$. Hence, by use of (3), with $\{a > 0, b > 0, x > 0\}$,

$$\sqrt{\frac{25a^2b^4}{16x^6}} = \sqrt{\left(\frac{5ab^2}{4x^3}\right)^2} = \frac{5ab^2}{4x^3}.$$

To state that R is an **nth root** of a number A means that n is a positive integer and

$$R^n = A. \tag{4}$$

An *n*th root is called a *square root* if $n = 2$, a *cube root* if $n = 3$, and simply an *n*th root if $n > 3$. As in the case of square roots, we find that, if $A < 0$ and n is even, then A has no real *n*th root. If $A = 0$ then the only *n*th root of A is 0. In advanced college algebra, it is proved that, if $A \neq 0$, then A has n distinct *n*th roots, some or all of which may be imaginary numbers. In this text, *we shall restrict consideration of* (4) *to the case where* $A > 0$. Then, (4) is satisfied by just one positive number R, which is referred to as the **principal nth root** of A, and is represented by $\sqrt[n]{A}$, called a **radical** whose **index** is n and **radicand** is A. We shall refer to $\sqrt[n]{A}$ simply as *the nth root of* A. If $n = 2$, the index of $\sqrt[n]{A}$ usually is omitted, so that $\sqrt{A}$ means $\sqrt[2]{A}$, as earlier in this section.

ILLUSTRATION 3. $\sqrt[4]{81} = 3$ because $3^4 = 81$. $\sqrt[3]{125} = 5$ because $5^3 = 125$.

By the definition of $\sqrt[n]{A}$, we have

$$(\sqrt[n]{A})^n = A. \tag{5}$$

ILLUSTRATION 4. $(\sqrt[5]{7})^5 = 7.$ $(\sqrt[3]{x})^3 = x.$

With $A > 0$ and $B > 0$, the student should recall that

$$\sqrt[n]{AB} = \sqrt[n]{A}\, \sqrt[n]{B}; \qquad \sqrt[n]{\frac{A}{B}} = \frac{\sqrt[n]{A}}{\sqrt[n]{B}} \,. \tag{6}$$

Suppose that $x > 0$. Then, by the definition of an nth root,

$$\sqrt[n]{x^n} = x, \tag{7}$$

because $(x)^n = x^n$. A monomial, or a quotient of monomials, is said to be a **perfect nth power** in case it is the nth power of some expression of the same type. In this text, we shall assume that all variables involved in any monomial in a radical have positive values. Then, the nth root of a perfect nth power with a positive coefficient is obtained by use of (7).

ILLUSTRATION 5. $8b^6$ is a perfect cube because $8b^6 = (2b^2)^3$. Hence, by (7),

$$\sqrt[3]{8b^6} = \sqrt[3]{(2b^2)^3} = 2b^2.$$

$$\sqrt[4]{\frac{16y^{12}}{x^4}} = \sqrt[4]{\left(\frac{2y^3}{x}\right)^4} = \frac{2y^3}{x} \,.$$

If m, n, and m/n are positive integers, then

$$\sqrt[n]{x^m} = \sqrt[n]{(x^{m/n})^n} = x^{m/n}, \tag{8}$$

because $(x^{m/n})^n = x^{(m/n)\cdot n} = x^m$. We use (8) in obtaining the result in Illustration 6 below.

ILLUSTRATION 6. $\sqrt[4]{16y^{12}} = \sqrt[4]{2^4 y^{12}} = 2^{4/4} y^{12/4} = 2y^3.$

Up to this point in the text, all exponents employed have been 0 or positive integers. We proceed to define powers of numbers where the exponents are any rational numbers. If such exponents are to obey the laws of exponents on page 235 then, for instance, it should be true that

$$(a^{5/3})^3 = a^{3 \cdot (5/3)} = a^5.$$

Hence $a^{5/3}$ would be a cube root of a^5. These remarks motivate the following definition of an optional form to substitute for a radical.

DEFINITION V.   *If m and n are positive integers, then $A^{m/n}$ represents the principal nth root of A^m, or*

$$A^{m/n} = \sqrt[n]{A^m}. \tag{9}$$

when $m = 1$ in (9), $A^{1/n} = \sqrt[n]{A}.$ $\qquad(10)$

Notice that, when m/n is an integer, (9) is consistent with (8). In this text, we shall use $A^{m/n}$ only when $A > 0$, if m/n is not an integer.

ILLUSTRATION 7. $8^{1/3} = \sqrt[3]{8} = 2.$ $8^{2/3} = \sqrt[3]{8^2} = \sqrt[3]{64} = 4.$

THEOREM I. $$A^{m/n} = (\sqrt[n]{A})^m. \tag{11}$$

PROOF.   By use of the product form $\sqrt[n]{A}\ \sqrt[n]{B}$ in (6).

$$(\sqrt[n]{A})^m = \sqrt[n]{A}\ \sqrt[n]{A}\cdots\sqrt[n]{A} \qquad (m\ factors\ \sqrt[n]{A})$$

$$= \sqrt[n]{A\cdot A\cdots A} \qquad (m\ factors\ A)$$

$$= \sqrt[n]{A^m} = A^{m/n}.$$

Notice that we have *two forms* for $A^{m/n}$ in (9) and (11).

ILLUSTRATION 8.   By (11): $64^{5/6} = (\sqrt[6]{2^6})^5 = 2^5 = 32.$

By (9): $64^{5/6} = \sqrt[6]{(2^6)^5} = \sqrt[6]{2^{30}} = 2^{30/6} = 2^5 = 32.$

It is seen that (11) is more convenient than (9) above.

If a negative exponent is to obey the laws of exponents, and if p is any positive rational number, we should have $a^p a^{-p} = a^{p-p} = a^0 = 1$. Then $a^{-p} = 1/a^p$. Hence, if $a \neq 0$ we decide to define

$$a^{-p} = \frac{1}{a^p}. \tag{12}$$

By use of (12), we have $a^p a^{-p} = 1$, and hence also

$$a^p = \frac{1}{a^{-p}}.$$

Hereafter, until much later in the text, we shall restrict exponents to be positive or negative rational numbers, or zero. If m/n is any negative rational exponent, we agree to choose $m < 0$ and $n > 0$. Thus, an exponent $-\frac{2}{3}$ is taken as $(-2)/3$. Then, the definition of $A^{m/n}$ in (9) or (11) applies when m/n is positive or negative. To calculate any power with a negative exponent we employ (12).

ILLUSTRATION 9. $a^{-3} = 1/a^3.$ $a^3 = 1/a^{-3}.$

$$5^{-3} = \frac{1}{5^3} = \frac{1}{125}. \qquad 8^{-1/3} = \frac{1}{8^{1/3}} = \frac{1}{2}.$$

We accept the fact that the index laws, as stated for positive integral exponents on page 235, remain true if the exponents are any rational numbers.

ILLUSTRATION 10. $(x^6)^{2/3} = x^4;$ $x^{1/4}x^{2/3} = x^{(1/4)+(2/3)} = x^{11/12}.$

$$\left(\frac{1}{125}\right)^{-2/3} = \left[\left(\frac{1}{5}\right)^3\right]^{-2/3} = \left(\frac{1}{5}\right)^{-2} = \frac{1}{(5)^{-2}} = (5)^2 = 25.$$

$$(1.04)^{3/2} = \sqrt{(1.04)^3}; \qquad (1.02)^{1/12} = \sqrt[12]{1.02}.$$

Exercise 61

Find the two square roots of the number or the specified root.

1. 25.   **2.** 49.   **3.** $\frac{4}{9}$.   **4.** $\sqrt{\frac{36}{121}}$.

5. $\sqrt{9x^8}$.   **6.** $\sqrt{16y^4}$.   **7.** $\sqrt{49z^8}$.   **8.** $\sqrt{64z^4}$.

9. $\sqrt{\frac{144}{81}}$.   **10.** $\sqrt{\frac{x^4}{64}}$.   **11.** $\sqrt{\frac{y^6}{16}}$.

12. $\sqrt{\frac{4x^4}{25y^2}}$.   **13.** $\sqrt{\frac{9a^4b^6}{121z^4}}$.   **14.** $\sqrt{\frac{36u^8w^4}{81x^6}}$.

Find the indicated root or power.

15. $\sqrt[3]{y^3}$.   **16.** $\sqrt[4]{x^8}$.   **17.** $(\sqrt[3]{29})^3$.   **18.** $(\sqrt[5]{31})^5$.

19. $\sqrt[3]{.008}$.   **20.** $\sqrt[4]{\frac{1}{16}}$.   **21.** $\sqrt{900}$.   **22.** $\sqrt[3]{\frac{27}{64}}$.

23. $\sqrt[3]{8u^3w^6}$.   **24.** $\sqrt[4]{256v^8}$.   **25.** $\sqrt[5]{u^5v^{10}}$.   **26.** $\sqrt[5]{243}$.

27. $\sqrt[4]{\frac{625a^8}{b^{12}x^{16}}}$.   **28.** $\sqrt[3]{\frac{216}{b^3x^6}}$.   **29.** $\sqrt[5]{\frac{32}{a^5v^{10}}}$.   **30.** $\sqrt[4]{\frac{16u^8}{81x^4}}$.

Obtain the value of the symbol in a form without any exponent or radical.

31. 6^{-3}.   **32.** $16^{1/4}$.   **33.** $(32)^{1/5}$.   **34.** $36^{3/2}$.

35. $(\frac{2}{3})^{-1}$.   **36.** $(\frac{25}{9})^{3/2}$.   **37.** $(8)^{5/3}$.   **38.** $(64)^{2/3}$.

39. $(125)^{4/3}$.   **40.** $(27)^{-1/3}$.   **41.** $(\frac{4}{49})^{-1/2}$.   **42.** $(\frac{1}{16})^{3/4}$.

Change to a form involving no radical.

43. $\sqrt[12]{1.05}$.   **44.** $\sqrt[6]{(1.03)^5}$.   **45.** $\sqrt[3]{(1.02)^2}$.   **46.** $\sqrt[12]{(1.04)^5}$.

Change to forms involving negative exponents and no denominators.

47. $\frac{5}{x^4}$.   **48.** $\frac{30}{x^2y^2}$.   **49.** $\frac{6}{(1.02)^3}$.   **50.** $\frac{5}{(1.04)^n}$.

88. Coordinates on a Plane

If the order in which we refer to a pair of numbers is important, then it is called an **ordered pair**. That is, one number is called the first number and, in writing, will be listed at the left. The other number is called the second number of the pair, and in writing will be listed at the right. Thus, the ordered pairs $(2, 7)$ and $(7, 2)$ are different although they involve the same two numbers. Each number in an ordered pair is called a *component* of it. To state that two ordered pairs (h, k) and (u, v) are the same means that $h = u$ and $k = v$. In the familiar introduction of coordinates in a plane, as discussed in this section, we associate an ordered pair of numbers with each point in the plane.

In a given plane, draw two perpendicular lines OX and OY, each of which will be called a *coordinate axis*. In Figure 33, we refer to OX as horizontal; then OY is vertical. On OX and also on OY, choose arbitrarily a scale unit for distance as the basis for establishing number lines on OX and on OY, where O represents zero on both lines. The units for distance on OX and OY need *not* be equal. The positive direction is chosen to the *right* on OX and *upward* on OY. Any horizontal line segment in the plane will be a *directed segment*, with the positive direction as on OX, and will be measured in terms of the scale unit on OX. Any vertical line segment will be a *directed segment*, with the positive direction as on OY, and will be measured in terms of the scale unit on OY. Let P be any point in the plane of OX and OY. Then, an ordered pair of coordinates (x, y) for P is defined as follows.

The **horizontal coordinate**, *or the x-coordinate, of P is the directed distance x, measured parallel to OX from the vertical axis OY to P. The* **vertical coordinate**, *or the y-coordinate, of P is the directed distance y, measured parallel to OY from the horizontal axis OX to P.*

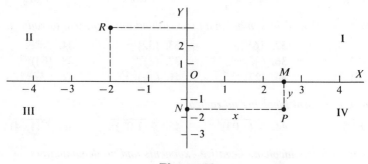

Figure 33

Sometimes the horizontal coordinate of a point P is called its **abscissa**, and the vertical coordinate is called the **ordinate** of P.

Coordinates as just described are called **rectangular coordinates**, because the coordinate axes are perpendicular. The intersection, O of the axis is called the **origin** of the coordinates. The plane in which OX and OY lie is referred to as the *xy*-plane, when x and y are used for the coordinates. We shall use "$P:(x, y)$" to mean "P *with coordinates* (x, y)." We may read "$P:(x, y)$" as just described or simply "P, x, y." For each point P in the *xy*-plane there is just one pair of coordinates; for each ordered pair of numbers (x, y) there is just one point P having the pair as coordinates. The coordinate axes divide the plane into four **quadrants**, numbered I, II, III, and IV counterclockwise, as in Figure 33. A point on a coordinate axis is not said to lie in any quadrant.

ILLUSTRATION 1. The point $R:(-2, 3)$ is shown in Figure 33. We refer to R as "*the point* $(-2, 3)$."

89. Terminology for Equations

An *equation* is a statement that two numbers are equal. A **solution** of an equation in just one variable x is a value $x = r$ such that the equation becomes a true statement, or is satisfied, when r is substituted for x. The set of all solutions of an equation is called its **solution set**. *To solve* an equation means to find all of its solutions.

ILLUSTRATION 1. The equation $3x + 5 = 11$, or $3x = 6$, has just one solution, $x = 2$. The equation

$$x^2 - x - 6 = 0, \quad or \quad (x - 3)(x + 2) = 0, \tag{1}$$

is satisfied if $x - 3 = 0$ and if $x + 2 = 0$. Hence, the solutions of (1) are $x = 3$ and $x = -2$, and the solution set is the set $\{3, -2\}$.

An equation is said to be *inconsistent* if it has *no solution*, and otherwise is called *consistent*. If an equation is satisfied by *all* values of any variable or variables involved, then the equation is called an *identical equation*, or for short, an *identity*. Two equations are said to be **equivalent** if they have *the same solutions*.

ILLUSTRATION 2. With the number system consisting only of real numbers, the equation $x^2 = -8$ is inconsistent, because the square of any real number x is not negative. The equations $x + 3 = 2$ and $x(x + 3) = 2x$ are *not* equivalent, because $x = 0$ satisfies the second equation but not the first equation.

Suppose that U and V are polynomials in a variable x. Then, the equation $U = V$ is said to be a *linear equation* in case it is equivalent to a form $ax = b$ where a and b are constants and $a \neq 0$. The single solution of $ax = b$ is $x = b/a$.

ILLUSTRATION 3. To solve $3x + 5 = 0$, we write $3x = -5$ and then obtain $x = -\frac{5}{3}$ as the single solution.

A solution of an equation in two variables, say x and y, is an ordered pair of numbers (a, b) such that, if we substitute $x = a$ and $y = b$ in the equation, it becomes a true statement. With the word *solution* thus defined, the definitions for the *solution set, consistency, inconsistency,* and *equivalence,* as given for an equation in one variable, are seen to apply unchanged for an equation in two variables. Similar terminology can be given for an equation in any number of variables.

ILLUSTRATION 4. Let $x = 2$ in $3y + 4x = 17$.

$$3y + 8 = 17, \quad or \quad 3y = 9, \quad or \quad y = 3.$$

Hence $(x = 2, y = 3)$ is a solution of $3y + 4x = 17$. Similarly, we may obtain as many solutions of the equation as we desire, by substituting a value for one variable, and solving for the corresponding value of the other variable.

Suppose that U and V are polynomials in the variables x and y. Then the equation $U = V$ is said to be a *linear equation* in x and y if $U = V$ is equivalent to an equation of the form $Ax + By = C$ where $\{A, B, C\}$ are constants, with A and B not both zero.

ILLUSTRATION 5.   The equation $3y + 4x = 17$ is a linear equation in x and y.

90.   Graph of an Equation in Two Variables

Consider any equation in two variables x and y. If a value, say a, is assigned to x in the equation, as a rule we can expect to obtain one or more values, say b, for y so that the ordered pair $(x = a, y = b)$ forms a solution of the equation. We have called the *set of all solutions of an equation* its *solution set*. It is said that x and y are *related* by the equation, or that it defines a *relation between x and y*. Each solution $(x = a, y = b)$ of the equation may be taken as the coordinates of a point in a plane provided with an xy-system of coordinates, as in Figure 33. This leads to the following familiar terminology.

DEFINITION VI.   *The* **graph** *of an equation in two variables x and y in an xy-plane is the set of points whose coordinates are solutions of the equation.*

That is, the graph of an equation $U = V$ in x and y is the *graph of its solution set* in an xy-plane. If an equation is inconsistent, or has no solution, then the equation has no graph. We accept the fact that the graph of any linear equation $Ax + By = C$ is a *line*.

The values of x where a graph in an xy-plane meets the x-axis are called the **x-intercepts** of the graph. The value of y where the graph meets the y-axis are called the **y-intercepts** of the graph. To find the x-intercepts of the graph of an equation $U = V$ in x and y, let $y = 0$ in the equation and find the corresponding values of x to form solutions of the equation. To obtain the y-intercepts, let $x = 0$ in the equation and find the corresponding values of y.

Example 1.   Graph the equation: $\qquad\qquad 3x - 5y = 15.$ $\qquad\qquad$ (1)

SOLUTION.   1. Place $x = 0$; then $-5y = 15$, or $y = -3$. Thus $(x = 0, y = -3)$ is a solution of (1), and -3 is the y-intercept of the graph. Place $y = 0$ and obtain $x = 5$. Thus $(x = 5, y = 0)$ is a solution of (1), and 5 is the x-intercept of the graph. Similarly, by substituting other values for x, or y, in (1) and solving for the second variable, we obtain solutions as shown in the following table.

2. The points with coordinates (x, y) as given in the table were plotted in Figure 34. The line L through these points is the graph of (1).

$y =$	-6	$-4\frac{1}{5}$	-3	0	$\frac{3}{5}$
$x =$	-5	-2	0	5	6

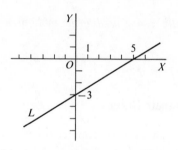

Figure 34

ILLUSTRATION 1. To graph $\qquad y - x^2 + 2x + 1 = 0,$
first solve for y: $\qquad\qquad y = x^2 - 2x - 1.$ $\qquad$ (2)

On substituting values for x and computing y, solutions of (2) are obtained as in the following table. The graph in Figure 35 was drawn through the corresponding points and is called a **parabola**.

$y =$	7	-1	-2	-1	7
$x =$	-2	0	1	2	4

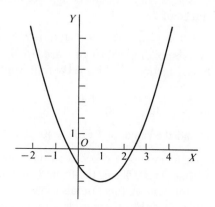

Figure 35

Exercise 62

Graph the equation in an xy-plane by use of the x-intercept and y-intercept (whichever exists), and at most two other points.

1. $3x - 2y = 6.$ $\qquad$ **2.** $3y + 4x = 12.$ $\qquad$ **3.** $2x + 5y = 0.$
4. $x + 5 = 0.$ $\qquad\qquad$ **5.** $y = -3.$ $\qquad\qquad$ **6.** $y - 2x = 0.$
7. $3y - 4 = 0.$ $\qquad\quad$ **8.** $5x + 4y = -20.$ $\qquad$ **9.** $4y = -3x.$

Graph the equation with $x = 2$ *used in the table of solutions. The graph is a parabola.*

10. $y = x^2 - 4x + 3$.   **11.** $y = 5 + 4x - x^2$.

91.   Functions and their Graphs

Very frequently in mathematics, we encounter situations involving two variables x and y where, for each value of one variable, say x, a *single* value of y is given by some rule. Then, it is said that "*y as a function of x*," where the meaning of this phrase is made precise as follows.

DEFINITION VII.   *Let D be a given set of numbers. Suppose that, for each number x in D, some rule specifies just one corresponding value for y, and let K be the set of all of these values of y. Then, the resulting set of ordered pairs of numbers* (x, y) *is called a* **function** *F, whose* **domain** *is D and* **range** *is K.*

In Definition VII, each value of y in K is called a *value* of the function F. We refer to x as the **independent variable**, and to y as the **dependent variable**. We call F "*a function of x*," to indicate that x has been adopted as a symbol for the independent variable. Also, F is said to be a function of a single variable, because the domain of F consists of single numbers. The domain of the dependent variable is called the **range** of F.

ILLUSTRATION 1.   Let $D = \{-4, -3, -2, -1, 0, 1, 2, 3\}$. For each number x in D, let $y = x^2$; the corresponding values of y are $\{16, 9, 4, 1, 0, 1, 4, 9\}$. The preceding rule describes a function F, which is the following set of ordered pairs of numbers:

$$F = \{(-4, 16), (-3, 9), (-2, 4), (-1, 1), (0, 0), (1, 1), (2, 4), (3, 9)\}$$

The domain of F is D and the range of F is $K = \{0, 1, 4, 9, 16\}$.

Suppose that a formula in a variable x specifies a single number corresponding to each value of x in some set D. Then, the formula defines a function whose values are given by the formula. A function also may be defined merely by its tabulated ordered pairs (x, y), or by other means without a formula. If a function is defined by a formula, the function frequently is given a name corresponding to the nature of the formula. Elementary levels in mathematics deal with *algebraic, exponential, logarithmic,* and *trigonometric functions.*

ILLUSTRATION 2.   In Definition VII, if $y = k$, a constant, for all x in D, then F is called a *constant function.*

DEFINTION VIII.   *In an xy-plane, the* **graph** *of a function of x is the set of points whose coordinates* (x, y) *form pairs of corresponding values of x and the function.*

On the basis of Definition VIII, we have the following procedure for obtaining the graph of a function whose values are defined by a formula in the independent variable x: *place y equal to the formula and graph the resulting equation.*

ILLUSTRATION 3.   To graph the function $(x^2 - 2x - 1)$, we let

$$y = x^2 - 2x - 1,$$

and graph this equation. The graph is the parabola in Figure 35 on page 245.

If F is a function of x, we may represent the value of F corresponding to any value of x by $F(x)$, to be read "F of x", or "F at x." Hence,

$F(x)$ *is the* **value** *of F corresponding to any number x.*   (1)

We refer to $F(x)$ as a symbol in **functional notation**, with x as the **argument**. Symbols like F, G, H, f, g, h, etc., are used for functions.

ILLUSTRATION 4.   If we write $F(x) = 3x^2 + x - 5$, this assigns F as a symbol for the function, and gives a formula, $3x^2 + x - 5$, for the values of F. Thus, the value of F at $x = -1$ is $F(-1) = 3 - 1 - 5 = -3$.

ILLUSTRATION 5.   If $f(x) = 5x^2 + 2$ and $g(y) = 4/y$, then

$$[f(3)]^2 = [5(9) + 2]^2 = 47^2 = 2209;$$

$$f(x)g(x) = (5x^2 + 2)\left(\frac{4}{x}\right) = 20x + \frac{8}{x};$$

In functional notation, Definition VIII yields the following conclusion.

$\left.\begin{array}{l}\textit{The } \textbf{graph of a function } F\textit{, with the independent variable } x\textit{, in an}\\ \textit{xy-plane, is the graph of the equation } y = F(x).\end{array}\right\}$ (2)

Frequently, hereafter, we shall use the terminology "*y is a function of x*," to mean that there exists some function F where we shall let $y = F(x)$.

ILLUSTRATION 6.   If $y = 5x + 7x^2$, then y is a function of x.

Let n be a nonnegative integer and suppose that $F(x)$ is a polynomial,

$$F(x) = a_0 + a_1 x + a_2 x^2 + \cdots + a_n x^n,$$

where $\{a_0, a_1, a_2, \ldots, a_n\}$ are constants and $a_n \neq 0$. Then F is called a *polynomial function* of degree n. Polynomial functions of degrees 1, 2, 3, and 4 are called *linear, quadratic, cubic,* and *quartic functions*, respectively. Thus, a linear function of x is of the form $f(x) = mx + b$ where $\{m, b\}$ are constants and $m \neq 0$. A quadratic function is of the form $f(x) = ax^2 + bx + c$ where $\{a, b, c\}$ are constants and $a \neq 0$. If $F(x) = P(x)/Q(x)$ where $P(x)$ and $Q(x)$ are polynomials in x and $Q(x) \neq 0$, then F is called a *rational function* of x. Since $P(x) = P(x)/1$, where 1 is a simple polynomial (of degree 0), any polynomial function $P(x)$ also may be called a rational function. If $F(x)$ is defined by a formula involving only the operations of algebra applied to x, then F is called an *algebraic* function* of

---

* There is a more general definition for an algebraic function. It does not have to be defined by an algebraic formula.

x. An algebraic function which is not a rational function is referred to as an *irrational function* of *x*.

ILLUSTRATION 7.   The graph of a linear function ($mx + b$) is the graph of the equation $y = mx + b$, which is a line. The graph of a quadratic function ($ax^2 + bx + c$) is the graph of the equation $y = ax^2 + bx + c$, and is a parabola, illustrated by Figure 35 on page 245.

92.   Functions of More than One Variable

Let D be a set of ordered pairs of numbers (x, y). We may interpret D as a set of points in an *xy*-plane. For each point (x, y) in D, suppose that some rule specifies a single number z, and let K be the set of all values of z. Then, this correspondence between ordered pairs in D and numbers z in K, or the resulting *ordered triples* of numbers (x, y, z), is called a function F of the two independent variables x and y. We refer to D as the *domain* and to K as the *range* of F, and call z the dependent variable. We write $z = F(x, y)$, meaning that both z and $F(x, y)$ may represent the value of F corresponding to an assigned pair (x, y) in D.

Similarly, functions of three or more variables may be considered. For instance, $f(x, y, z)$ would represent the value of a function f of the three independent variables x, y, and z. Hereafter, unless otherwise indicated, in any reference to a *function* we shall mean a function of a *single variable*. In the mathematics of investment, we deal with functions of several variables.

ILLUSTRATION 1.   If $g(x, y) = 3x^2 + xy$, then $g(-2, 3) = 3(4) - 6 = 6$.

Exercise 63

Describe the range K of the function F, and tabulate the whole set of ordered pairs of numbers that forms F. Then graph F in an xy-plane.

1. The domain of F is the set $D = \{-2, -1, 0, 1, 2, 4\}$. The value of F corresponding to any number x in D is $3x$.
2. The domain of F is the set $D = \{-5, -3, 1, 2, 4\}$. The value of F corresponding to any number x in D is $(x^2 - 4)$.

Graph the function of x.

3. $2x - 5$.   4. $x + 4$.   5. 6.
6. $(x^2 - 6x - 4)$, with $x = 3$ used in the table of ordered pairs (x, y).

If $f(x) = 3x - 2$, find the value of the symbol.

7. $f(3)$.   8. $f(-2)$.   9. $f(\tfrac{1}{4})$.   10. $[f(2)]^2$.

If $F(x, y) = x^2 + xy$, find the value of the symbol.

11. $F(2, 3)$.   12. $F(-1, 2)$.   13. $F(-2, -4)$.

11/ Computation and Logarithms

93. Approximate Values

In this chapter, we shall assume that each number is written in decimal form. In any number N, let us read its digits from left to right. Then, by definition, the **significant digits** or **figures** of N are its digits, in sequence, starting with the first one not zero and ending with the last one definitely specified. Notice that this definition does not involve any reference to the position of the decimal point in N. Usually we do not mention *final zeros* at the right in referring to the significant digits of N, except when it is the approximate value of some item of data.

ILLUSTRATION 1.   The significant digits of .0041058 are {4, 1, 0, 5, 8}.

If T is the *true value*, and A is an *approximate value* of a quantity, we agree to call $|A - T|$ the **error** of A.

ILLUSTRATION 2.   If $T = 35.62$, and if $A = 35.60$ is an approximation to T, then the error of A is $|35.60 - 35.62|$ or .02.

The significant digits in an approximate value A should indicate the maximum possible error of A. This error is understood to be *at most one half of a unit in the last significant place in A* or, which is the same, *not more than 5 units in the next place to the right.*

ILLUSTRATION 3.   If a surveyor measures a distance as 256.8 yards, he should mean that the true result lies between 256.75 and 256.85, inclusive.

In referring to the significant digits of an *approximate* value A, *it is essential to mention all final zeros designated in A.*

ILLUSTRATION 4.   To state that a measured weight is 35.60 pounds should mean that the true weight differs from 35.60 pounds by at most .005 pound; "35.6 pounds" would indicate a possible error of .05 pound.

For abbreviation, or to indicate how many digits in a large number are significant, we may write a number N in the following form, called the **scientific notation** for a number:

Express the number N as the product of an integral power of 10 and a number equal to or greater than 1 but less than 10, with as many significant digits as are justified by the data.

ILLUSTRATION 5. $385{,}720 = 3.8572(100{,}000) = 3.8572(10^5)$.

$.000'000'368 = 3.68(.000'000'1) = 3.68(10^{-7})$.

ILLUSTRATION 6.   If 5,630,000 is an approximate value, its appearance fails to show how many zeros are significant. If five digits are significant, we write $5.6300(10^6)$, and if just three are significant, $5.63(10^6)$.

Observe that the following facts are true concerning the scientific notation.

$$\left\{ \begin{array}{l} \textit{If } N \geq 1 \textit{ and } N \textit{ has } k \textit{ digits to the left of the decimal point, then} \\ N = W(10^{k-1}), \textit{ where } 1 \leq W < 10. \end{array} \right\} \quad (1)$$

$$\left\{ \begin{array}{l} \textit{If } 0 < N < 1 \textit{ and the first significant digit of } N \textit{ appears in the} \\ h\textit{th decimal place, then } N = W(10^{-h}), \textit{ where } 1 \leq W < 10. \end{array} \right\} \quad (2)$$

In referring to a *place* in a number, we shall mean any place where a significant digit stands. In referring to a *decimal place*, the word *decimal* will be used explicitly. *To round off N to k places* means to write an approximate value for N with k significant digits.

Summary

To round off a number N to k places, drop off the part of N beyond the kth place* and then proceed as follows:

  I. *If the omitted part of N is less than 5 units in the $(k + 1)$th place, leave the digit in the kth place unchanged.*

 II. *If the omitted part of N is more than 5 units in the $(k + 1)$th place, increase the digit in the kth place by 1.*

III. †*If the omitted part of N is exactly equal to 5 units in the $(k + 1)$th place, increase the digit in the kth place by 1 or leave it unchanged, with the object of making the final choice an even digit.*

ILLUSTRATION 7.   The seven-place approximation to π is 3.141593. On rounding off to five places, we obtain 3.1416. In rounding off 315.475 to five figures, in accordance with III of the Summary, we choose 315.48.

* Filling in zeros if necessary to the left of the decimal point.
† Item III could be replaced by other equally justified agreements.

By illustrations, we can verify that the following rules do not *underestimate* the accuracy of computation with approximate values. On the other hand, we must admit that the rules sometimes *overestimate* the accuracy.

In adding approximate values, round off the result in the first place where the last significant digit of any given value is found.

In multiplying or dividing approximate values, round off the result to the smallest number of significant figures in any given value.

Exercise 64

Round off, first to five and then to three significant digits.

1. 15.32573.   **2.** .00132146.   **3.** .3148638.   **4.** 5.62653.
5. 195.635.   **6.** .00128558.   **7.** .0345645.   **8.** 392.462.

Tell the range of values on which the exact length of a line lies if its measured length in feet is as follows.

9. 567.   **10.** 567.0.   **11.** 567.4.   **12.** 35.18.

Assume that the numbers represent approximate data. Find their sum and product and state the results without false accuracy.

13. 31.52 and .0186.   **14.** .023424 and 1.14.   **15.** .0047 (11.3987126).

Write the number in ordinary decimal form.

16. 100(3.856).   **17.** 27.38(10^2).   **18.** 1.935(10^{-4}).   **19.** 2.056(10^6).

Write as the product of a power of 10 and a number between 1 and 10.

20. 38.075.   **21.** 675.38.   **22.** 153,720,000.   **23.** 45,726.
24. .0000578.   **25.** .00000036.   **26.** .00138.   **27.** .000242.

94. The Exponential Function

Suppose that $a > 0$. From page 239, if m and n are integers and $n > 0$,

$$a^{m/n} = \sqrt[n]{a^m}, \quad \text{and also} \quad a^{m/n} = (\sqrt[n]{a})^m. \tag{1}$$

Let x be any number. When x is *rational*, then a^x is defined by (1). It is essential to have meaning for a^x also when x is *irrational*.

ILLUSTRATION 1.   Recall the irrational number $\sqrt{3} = 1.732\ldots$, where the decimal is endless and nonrepeating. If $a > 0$, consider the sequence

$$a^1, \quad a^{1.7}, \quad a^{1.73}, \quad a^{1.732}, \ldots. \tag{2}$$

Each exponent in (2) is rational. For instance, $1.73 = 173/100$. Hence, each power in (2) has a meaning as described in (1). A discussion above the level of this text would prove that, when we proceed to the right in (2), the powers approach some number as a *limit*. This limit is defined as $a^{\sqrt{3}}$. Each power in

(2) is an approximation to $a^{\sqrt{3}}$, with the accuracy of the approximation improving as we move to the right. Thus, $a^{1.732}$ is a better approximation than $a^{1.73}$ to $a^{\sqrt{3}}$. The preceding remarks are an introduction to the following general discussion.

It is known that any irrational number x can be expressed as an *endless non-repeating decimal*. Suppose that $a > 0$. Then, if x is *rational*, a^x is defined in (1). If x is *irrational*, we define a^x as the *limit* of the sequence of rational powers obtained by using as exponents the successive decimal approximations to x, as was done in (2). For any real number x, let $E(x) = a^x$. Then E is called the **exponential function** with **base** a. At a more advanced level, it is proved that E is a *continuous function*, which means that the graph of $y = a^x$ is a *continuous curve (has no breaks)*. Hence, in obtaining a graph of $y = a^x$ for a particular value of a, we may use rational values of x in obtaining coordinates for points, and join these to obtain the curve. For reasons discussed in much more advanced mathematics, the exponential function a^x is not defined in case $a \le 0$.

ILLUSTRATION 2. To graph the function 3^x, first let $y = 3^x$. Values of x were substituted to compute the solutions (x, y) in the following table as a basis for the graph in Figure 36. Similarly, we obtain the graph of $y = (\frac{1}{3})^x$, or $y = 3^{-x}$,

$y = 3^x$	$0\leftarrow$	$\frac{1}{9}$	$\frac{1}{3}$	1	1.7	9	27
$x =$	$-\infty\leftarrow$	-2	-1	0	.5	2	3

in Figure 37. These graphs illustrate the nature of a^x for $a > 1$ and for $a < 1$, respectively. In the table, the arrows indicate that, if x is negative and $|x|$ grows large without bound or if "*x approaches minus infinity,*" then y *approaches zero through positive values*.

We accept the fact that the familiar laws of exponents apply with powers of the type a^x where $a > 0$, for all real values of x.

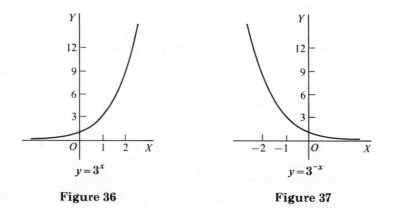

$y = 3^x$

Figure 36

$y = 3^{-x}$

Figure 37

95.   The Logarithm Function

Let $E(y) = a^y$ with $a > 1$. A graph, W, of $x = a^y$ is given in Figure 38 with $a = 10$. For later convenience, we are using y as the independent variable. The *domain* of the function E is the set D of *all real numbers*, y. The *range* of E, or the set of all values of x given by $x = a^y$ is the set H of *all positive values of x*, or $H = \{$*all x such that* $0 < x\}$. Notice that, for each positive value of x, the vertical line through the point x on the x-axis meets W in *just one point, $P:(x, y)$*. That is, for each value of $x > 0$, there is *just one value of y* so that $x = a^y$. If $x > 0$, let $L(x)$ represent the corresponding value of y such that $x = a^y$. Then,

$$x = a^y \qquad \textit{is equivalent to} \qquad y = L(x). \tag{1}$$

Instead of using $L(x)$, we shall let $L(y) = \log_a x$, which is read "*logarithm of x to the base a*." Then, from (1),

$$x = a^y \qquad \textit{is equivalent to} \qquad y = \log_a x. \tag{2}$$

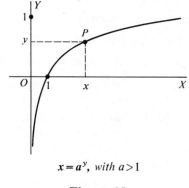

$x = a^y$, *with $a > 1$*

Figure 38

In (2), we have introduced a *new function*, called the *logarithm function to the base a*. On account of the equivalence in (2), the exponential function a^y, to the base a, and the logarithm function $\log_a x$, are referred to as *inverse functions*. The following statement is equivalent to (2), and from this place on will be taken as the definition of $\log_a x$.

$$\left\{ \begin{array}{l} \textit{The } \textbf{logarithm } \textit{of a number } x \textit{ to a base } a > 0 \textit{ is the exponent} \\ \textit{of the power of } a \textit{ which is equal to } x, \textit{ or} \end{array} \right\} \tag{3}$$

$$y = \log_a x \qquad \textit{is equivalent to} \quad x = a^y. \tag{4}$$

NOTE 1.   In arriving at (4) from Figure 38, we took $a > 1$, which we shall assume to be the case hereafter. The case $0 < a < 1$ is unimportant for our purposes.

In (4), we refer to $x = a^y$ as the *exponential form*, and to $y = \log_a x$ as the *logarithmic form* of the relation between x and y. If one form is given, then the other form can be written immediately.

ILLUSTRATION 1.   If $N = 4^5$, then 5 is the logarithm of N to the base 4.

"$\log_2 64$" is read "*the logarithm of 64 to the base 2*":

$$\text{since} \quad 64 = 2^6, \quad \log_2 64 = 6.$$

Since $$\sqrt[3]{5} = 5^{1/3}, \quad \log_5 \sqrt[3]{5} = \tfrac{1}{3} = .333\ldots.$$

Since $$\frac{1}{8} = \frac{1}{2^3} = 2^{-3}, \quad \log_2 \frac{1}{8} = -3.$$

If $\log_b 16 = 4$, then $b^4 = 16$; $b = \sqrt[4]{16} = 2$.

If $\log_{10} N = -4$, then $N = 10^{-4} = .0001$.

For any base a,

$$\log_a a = 1 \quad because \quad a^1 = a;$$
$$\log_a 1 = 0 \quad because \quad a^0 = 1.$$

To graph the function $\log_{10} x$, use (4) with $a = 10$:

$$y = \log_{10} x \quad is\ equivalent\ to \quad x = 10^y. \tag{5}$$

We assign values to y and use $x = 10^y$ to obtain solutions (x, y) of the equation $y = \log_{10} x$. In (5), if $y = -1$ then $x = 10^{-1} = .1$; if $y = 2$ then $x = 10^2 = 100$; if $y = -3$ then $x = 10^{-3} = .001$. If y is negative and $|y|$ grows large without bound, we say that "y *approaches minus infinity*," which is abbreviated by writing "$y \to -\infty$," where "$\to$" is read "*approaches*." Then "x *approaches* 0 *through positive values*," which is abbreviated by "$x \to 0+$." The following table of solutions (x, y) of $y = \log_{10} x$ was used to obtain the graph of $y = \log_{10} x$ in Figure 39.

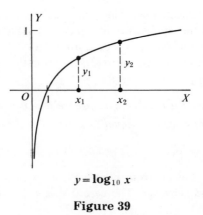

$$y = \log_{10} x$$

Figure 39

$x =$	$0 + \leftarrow$	.001	.01	.1	1	.3	10	100
$y = \log_{10} x$	$-\infty \leftarrow$	-3	-2	-1	0	.5	1	2

Since $x \to 0+$ as $y \to -\infty$, the graph approaches the y-axis as $x \to 0+$. For this reason we refer to the y-axis as an *asymptote* of the graph of $y = \log_{10} x$. This graph is typical of the graph of $y = \log_a x$ for any $a > 1$. Hereafter we shall deal mainly with $a = 10$. Hence we shall phrase the following facts only for $a = 10$, as observed from Figure 39.

  I. *The domain of the function* $\log_{10} x$ *consists of all positive values of x. Thus, negative numbers and 0 do not have logarithms.*

 II. *The function* $\log_{10} x$ *is an increasing function. That is, as in Figure 39,*

$$x_1 < x_2 \quad \text{is equivalent to} \quad \log_{10} x_1 < \log_{10} x_2. \tag{6}$$

 III. $\log_{10} x \to -\infty$ *as $x \to 0+$, or the y-axis is an asymptote of the graph of* $y = \log_{10} x$.

 IV. *If $x < 1$ then* $\log_{10} x < 0$; *if $x > 1$ then* $\log_{10} x > 0$.

Exercise 65

1. Obtain a graph of $y = \log_{10} x$. First make up an extensive table of solutions (x, y), and use a very large distance for one unit on the y-axis.

Write a logarithmic equation equivalent to the exponential equation.

2. $N = 2^6$.   **3.** $N = 5^3$.   **4.** $N = 10^4$.   **5.** $N = 10^{-2}$.
6. $H = 4^{1/4}$.   **7.** $H = 5^{2/5}$.   **8.** $K = 10^{5/3}$.   **9.** $N = 10^{.35}$.
10. $N = 10^{-4}$.   **11.** $36 = 6^2$.   **12.** $16 = 2^4$.   **13.** $32 = 2^5$.
14. $81 = 3^4$.   **15.** $625 = 25^2$.   **16.** $625 = 5^4$.   **17.** $\frac{1}{49} = 7^{-2}$.
18. $\frac{1}{64} = 2^{-6}$.   **19.** $\frac{1}{27} = 3^{-3}$.   **20.** $\frac{1}{216} = 6^{-3}$.   **21.** $.0001 = 10^{-4}$.

Find the number whose logarithm is given, by writing an exponential equation.

22. $\log_6 N = 2$.   **23.** $\log_2 N = 3$.   **24.** $\log_{10} N = 4$.
25. $\log_7 M = 2$.   **26.** $\log_5 M = 3$.   **27.** $\log_{10} K = 0$.
28. $\log_{15} K = 1$.   **29.** $\log_{10} N = 1$.   **30.** $\log_5 N = -1$.
31. $\log_{10} M = -2$.   **32.** $\log_b M = 1$.   **33.** $\log_{11} N = -2$.
34. $\log_9 N = \frac{1}{2}$.   **35.** $\log_{64} N = \frac{1}{3}$.   **36.** $\log_{216} N = -\frac{1}{3}$.
37. $\log_4 N = \frac{3}{2}$.   **38.** $\log_{27} N = \frac{2}{3}$.   **39.** $\log_8 N = \frac{5}{3}$.

Find the logarithm by expressing the number as a power of the base.

40. $\log_9 81$.   **41.** $\log_5 25$.   **42.** $\log_3 81$.   **43.** $\log_9 3$.
44. $\log_{10} 100$.   **45.** $\log_{10} 1000$.   **46.** $\log_3 243$.   **47.** $\log_{11} 121$.
48. $\log_{16} 4$.   **49.** $\log_{100} 10$.   **50.** $\log_7 \frac{1}{7}$.   **51.** $\log_4 \frac{1}{4}$.
52. $\log_3 \frac{1}{27}$.   **53.** $\log_2 \frac{1}{16}$.   **54.** $\log_{10} .001$.   **55.** $\log_{10} .0001$.

96. Basic Properties of Logarithms

Logarithms to the base 10 are called **common logarithms**, and are the most useful variety as aids in computation. Hereafter we shall write simply "log N" instead of "$\log_{10} N$" for the *common logarithm* of a number N. We remember that log N is defined just when $0 < N$, but log N may be *any* real number, that is, positive, negative, or zero. From previous discussion, and Figure 39 on page 254, we have the following facts.

$$\log 1 = 0; \quad \log N < 0 \quad \text{if} \quad 0 < N < 1; \tag{1}$$

$$\log N > 0 \quad \text{if} \quad 1 < N. \tag{2}$$

When $N_1 < N_2$ *then* $\log N_1 < \log N_2$. $\tag{3}$

Hereafter in this chapter, the unqualified word *logarithm* will refer to a *common logarithm*. The following properties of logarithms are true for any base, but we shall prove the results just for the base 10. Whenever the logarithm of a *number* is mentioned, it is assumed that the number is *positive*.

I. *The logarithm of a product is equal to the sum of the logarithms of the factors. For instance,*

$$\log MN = \log M + \log N. \tag{4}$$

II. *The logarithm of a fraction is equal to the logarithm of the numerator minus the logarithm of the denominator. Thus,*

$$\log \frac{M}{N} = \log M - \log N. \tag{5}$$

III. *The logarithm of the kth power of a number M is equal to k times the logarithm of M:*

$$\log M^k = k \log M. \tag{6}$$

ILLUSTRATION 1. $\log 17^3 = 3 \log 17$.

Since $\sqrt[3]{M} = M^{1/3}$, then $\log \sqrt[3]{M} = \frac{1}{3} \log M$

$\log (25)(54) = \log 25 + \log 54$.

$\log \dfrac{37}{189} = \log 37 - \log 189$.

PROOF OF PROPERTIES I–III. 1. Let $x = \log M$ and $y = \log N$. By the definition of a logarithm in (3) on page 253, $M = 10^x$ and $N = 10^y$. Then

$$MN = 10^x 10^y, \quad \text{or} \quad MN = 10^{x+y}.$$

Hence, by the definition of a logarithm in (3) on page 253, we obtain Property I:

$$\log MN = x + y = \log M + \log N.$$

2. From preceding details and a law of exponents,

$$\frac{M}{N} = \frac{10^x}{10^y}. \qquad or \qquad \frac{M}{N} = 10^{x-y}.$$

Hence, by (3) on page 253, we obtain Property II:

$$\log \frac{M}{N} = x - y = \log M - \log N.$$

3. For any number k, by use of preceding details and a law of exponents,

$$M^k = (10^x)^k = 10^{kx}.$$

Hence, by (3) on page 253, we obtain Property III:

$$\log M^k = kx = k \log M.$$

Recall the following logarithms of integral powers of 10.

$N =$	.0001	.001	.01	.1	1	10	100	1000	10,000	100,000
$\log N =$	-4	-3	-2	-1	0	1	2	3	4	5

ILLUSTRATION 2. If we are given $\log 3 = .4771$ and $\log 2 = .3010$, then we obtain the following results by use of Properties I–III and logarithms of powers of 10.

$$\log 300 = \log 3(100) = \log 3 + \log 100 = .4771 + 2 = 2.4771.$$

$$\log .003 = \log \frac{3}{1000} = \log 3 - \log 1000 = .4771 - 3 = -2.5229.$$

$$\log 8 = \log 2^3 = 3 \log 2 = .9030.$$

$$\log 60 = \log 2(3)(10) = \log 2 + \log 3 + 1$$

$$= .3010 + .4771 + 1 = 1.7781.$$

ILLUSTRATION 3. By use of Property I applied twice.

$$\log MNP = \log (MN)P = \log MN + \log P$$

$$= \log M + \log N + \log P.$$

Similarly, the logarithm of a product of any number of positive factors is the sum of the logarithms of the factors.

Suppose that h is a positive integer, and recall that $\sqrt[h]{N} = N^{1/h}$. Hence, by use of Property III,

IV. $$\log \sqrt[h]{N} = \frac{1}{h} \log N. \qquad (7)$$

ILLUSTRATION 4. $\log \sqrt{N} = \frac{1}{2} \log N.$ $\log \sqrt[3]{25} = \frac{1}{3} \log 25.$

Exercise 66

Find the common logarithm of the number by use of the following common logarithms, logarithms of powers of 10, *and Properties* I–IV *of logarithms.*

log 2 = .3010;   log 3 = .4771;   log 7 = .8451;   log 17 = 1.2304.

1. 14.	**2.** 51.	**3.** 30.	**4.** 170.	**5.** 21.
6. 42.	**7.** $\frac{7}{2}$.	**8.** $\frac{17}{3}$.	**9.** $\frac{3}{7}$.	**10.** $\frac{10}{3}$.
11. $\frac{17}{14}$.	**12.** .7.	**13.** 200.	**14.** $\frac{34}{3}$.	**15.** $\frac{2}{21}$.
16. $\frac{100}{17}$.	**17.** $\frac{100}{21}$.	**18.** 49.	**19.** 32.	**20.** 81.

21. $\sqrt{3}$.   **22.** $\sqrt{14}$.   **23.** $\sqrt{\frac{7}{3}}$.   **24.** $\sqrt{\frac{2}{17}}$.

97. Characteristic and Mantissa

Every number, and hence *every logarithm*, can be written as the sum of *an integer and a decimal fraction* which is *positive or zero* and *less than* 1. When log N is written in this way, we call the integer the *characteristic* and the fraction the *mantissa* of log N.

$$\log N = \text{(an integer)} + \text{(a fraction, } \geq 0, < 1\text{)};$$

$$\log N = \text{characteristic} + \text{mantissa.} \tag{1}$$

ILLUSTRATION 1.   If log N = 4.6832 = 4 + .6832, then .6832 is the mantissa and 4 is the characteristic of log N.

We notice that the **characteristic of log N is negative if and only if log N itself is negative.**

ILLUSTRATION 2.   If log N = −3.75, then log N lies between −4 and −3. Hence, log N = −4 + (*a fraction*). To find the fraction, subtract: 4 − 3.75 = .25. Hence, log N = −3.75 = −4 + .25; the characteristic is −4.

ILLUSTRATION 3.   The following logarithms were obtained by later methods. The student should verify the three columns at the right.

	Logarithm		Characteristic	Mantissa
log 300 = 2.4771	=	2+.4771	2	.4771
log 50 = 1.6990	=	1+.6990	1	.6990
log .0001 = −3	=	−3+.0000	−3	.0000
log 6.5 = 0.8129	=	0+.8129	0	.8129
log .0385 = −1.4145	=	−2+.5855	−2	.5855

ILLUSTRATION 4. All numbers whose logarithms are given below have the same significant digits, {3, 8, 0, 4}. To obtain the logarithms, log 3.804 was found from a table to be discussed later; the other logarithms were obtained then by the use of Properties I and II of logarithms.

$$\log 380.4 \;=\; \log 100(3.804) = \log 100 + \log 3.804 \;=\; \quad 2 + .5802;$$

$$\log 38.04 \;=\; \log 10(3.804) \;\; = \log 10 + \log 3.804 \;\; = \quad 1 + .5802;$$

$$\log 3.804 \;=\; .5802 \qquad\qquad\qquad\qquad = \quad 0 + .5802;$$

$$\log .3804 \;=\; \log \frac{3.804}{10} \quad = \log 3.804 - \log 10 \;\; = \;\; -1 + .5802;$$

$$\log .03804 = \log \frac{3.804}{100} \quad = \log 3.804 - \log 100 = -2 + .5802.$$

Similarly, if N is *any* number whose significant digits are (3, 8, 0, 4), then N is equal to 3.804 multiplied, or else divided, by a positive integral power of 10; hence, as before, .5802 is the mantissa of log N. A general discussion of the same nature would lead us to the following theorems.

THEOREM I. *The mantissa of* log N *depends only on the sequence of significant digits in* N. Or, **if two numbers differ only in the positions of the decimal points, their logarithms have the same mantissa.**

THEOREM II. **When** $N > 1$, *the characteristic of* log N *is an integer, positive or zero,* **which is one less than the number of digits in** N **to the left of the decimal point.**

THEOREM III. **If** $N < 1$, *the characteristic of* log N *is a negative integer*: **if the first significant digit of** N **is in the** k**th decimal place, then** $-k$ **is the characteristic of log** N.

ILLUSTRATION 5. By Theorem III, the characteristic of log .00039 is -4 because "3" is in the 4th decimal place. By Theorem II, the characteristic of log 1578.6 is 3.

Hereafter, for convenience in computation, **if the characteristic of log** N **is negative,** $-k$, **change it to the equivalent value**

$$[(10 - k) - 10], \quad or \quad [(20 - k) - 20], \text{ and so on.}$$

ILLUSTRATION 6. Given that log .000843 $= -4 + .9258$, we write

$$\log .000843 = -4 + .9258 = (6 - 10) + .9258 = 6.9258 - 10.$$

The characteristics of the following logarithms are obtained by use of Theorem III; the mantissas are identical, by Theorem I.

1st Signif. Digit in	Illustration	Log N Standard Form
1st *decimal place*	$N = .843$	$-1 + .9258 = 9.9258 - 10$
2nd *decimal place*	$N = .0843$	$-2 + .9258 = 8.9258 - 10$
6th *decimal place*	$N = .00000843$	$-6 + .9258 = 4.9258 - 10$

98. A Table of Logarithms

Mantissas can be computed by advanced methods and, except in special cases, are endless decimal fractions. Computed mantissas are found in tables of logarithms, also called *tables of mantissas.*

Table I gives the mantissa of log N correct to five decimal places if N is any number with at most four significant digits. If N lies between 1 and 10, the characteristic of log N is *zero* so that log N is the *same as its mantissa*. Hence, a five-place table of mantissas is also a table of the *actual logarithms* of all numbers with at most four significant digits, from $N = 1.000$ to $N = 9.999$. In case N is less than 1 or greater than 10, we must supply the characteristic of log N by use of Theorems II and III of Section 97. A decimal point is understood in front of each mantissa in Table I.

Example 1. Find log .03162 from Table I.

SOLUTION. 1. *To find the mantissa.* In Table I, we find the first three digits, 316, in the column headed "N." In the *row* of 316, in the *column* headed by 2 (the *fourth* digit of 3162) we find 996, the last three digits of the mantissa; its *first two* digits are 49, which appear in the column headed by 0. The complete mantissa is .49996.

2. By Theorem III, the characteristic is -2. Hence,

$$\log .03162 = -2 + .49996 = 8.49996 - 10.$$

Example 2. Find log 31,680 from Table I.

SOLUTION. 1. In the row of 316, in the column headed by 8, in Table I, we find *079; the asterik (*) means that the first two digits are 50, instead of 49 as at the beginning of the row. The mantissa is .50079.

2. The characteristic is 4. Hence, log 31,680 = 4.50079.

Example 3. Find N from Table I if log $N = 2.88468$.

SOLUTION. 1. The mantissa is .88468. We find the first two digits 88 in the column headed by 0. Among the table entries belonging to 88, we find 468 in the row with 766 at the left-hand margin and in the column headed by 8. Hence, the significant digits of N are 7668.

2. The characteristic of log N is 2; by Theorem II, N has *one more than two* digits, or *three* digits, to the left of the decimal point: $N = 766.8$.

DEFINITION I. *A number N is called the* **antilogarithm** *of L in case* log $N = L$. *We write $N = $* **antilog L.**

ILLUSTRATION 1.   In Example 3, antilog 2.88468 = 766.8.

Example 4.   Find N from Table I if log $N = 6.40209 - 10$.

SOLUTION.   1. The mantissa is .40209. We find the first two digits 40 in the column headed by 0. Among the entries belonging to 40 we find 209 in the row with 252 at the left-hand margin, and in the column headed by 4. Hence the significant part of N is 2524.

2. The characteristic is -4. Therefore, by Theorem III, the first significant digit of N is in the fourth decimal place: $N = .0002524$.

Exercise 67

Find the five-place logarithm of each number.

1. 198.7.	**2.** 18.56.	**3.** 1.389.	**4.** 2.633.	**5.** .2866.
6. .1118.	**7.** .2563.	**8.** .0356.	**9.** .0078.	**10.** 3100.
11. 99,500.	**12.** .00146.	**13.** .00583.	**14.** 59,600.	**15.** 69,990.

Find the antilogarithms of the following logarithms.

16. 1.25115.	**17.** 2.47305.	**18.** 4.68538.	**19.** 3.77663.
20. 0.11361.	**21.** 0.30081.	**22.** 9.42716 − 10.	**23.** 8.58726 − 10.
24. 7.49094 − 10.	**25.** 9.09237 − 10.	**26.** 8.57043 − 10.	**27.** −3.16941.

99.   Interpolation in a Five-place Table of Logarithms

Recall *linear interpolation* as met on page 38. When used in Table I, the interpolation method yields the following statement:

$$\left\{ \begin{array}{l} \textit{for small changes in the number N, it is assumed that the changes} \\ \textit{in log N are proportional to the changes in N.} \end{array} \right\} \quad (1)$$

We refer to (1) as the *principle of proportional parts* for use with logarithms. The principle is only an approximation to the truth, but yields results which are accurate to a very useful stage, as will be described later. This accuracy is due to the fact that, as can be seen from Figure 39 on page 254, any small arc of the graph of $y = \log x$ can be well approximated by a segment of a straight line.

Example 1. Find $\log 25.637$ by use of Table I.

SOLUTION. By the principle of proportional parts, since 25.637 is $\frac{7}{10}$ of the way from 25.630 to 25.640, we assume that

$\log 25.637$ *is* $\frac{7}{10}$ *of the way from* $\log 25.630$ *to* $\log 25.640$.

From table: $\log 25.630 = 1.40875$ **Tabular difference** *is*
          $\log 25.637 = \quad ?$ 17 $.40892 - .40875 = .00017$.
From table: $\log 25.640 = 1.40892$ $.7(17) = 11.9$ or 12.
      $\log 25.637 = 1.40875 + .7(.00017) = 1.40875 + .00012$;
                 $\log 25.637 = 1.40887$.

We obtained .7(17) from the column of proportional parts.

Example 2. Find $\log .0012397$.

SOLUTION. 1. Since 12397 is $\frac{7}{10}$ of the way from 12390 to 12400, the mantissa for 12397 is $\frac{7}{10}$ of the way from the mantissa for 12390 to the mantissa for 12400. We read these last two mantissas from Table I. In the following table we assume that

$$\frac{x}{35} = \frac{7}{10}, \quad or \quad x = .7(35),$$

   10   7   12390: *mantissa is* .09307 x 35   **Tabular difference** *is*
             12397: *mantissa is*   ? $.09342 - .09307 = .00035$.
             12400: *mantissa is* .09342 $x = .7(35) = 24.5$.
       Mantissa for $\log 12397$ *is* $.09307 + .00025 = .09332$.

We chose $x = 25$ to make the final result of the interpolation end in an **even digit; we agree to act similarly in all interpolation** in this book whenever ambiguity arises in rounding off.

2. The characteristic is -3, or $7 - 10$; $\log .0012397 = 7.09332 - 10$.

In finding N when the *five*-place $\log N$ is given, specify just *five* significant digits in N. No greater refinement is justified by the interpolation.

Example 3. Find N from Table I if $\log N = 8.33094 - 10$.

SOLUTION. 1. The mantissa is .33094. In Table I, .33094 is not an entry, but this number lies between the table entries .33082 and .33102, the mantissas for 2142 and 2143.

2. Since .33094 is $\frac{12}{20}$ of the way from .33082 to .33102, we assume that the significant part of N is $\frac{12}{20}$ of the way from 21420 to 21430.

$$20 \begin{bmatrix} 12 \begin{bmatrix} .33082, \textit{mantissa for } 21420 \\ .33094, \textit{mantissa for } N \\ .33102, \textit{mantissa for } 21430 \end{bmatrix} x \end{bmatrix} 10 \qquad \begin{matrix} \frac{12}{20} = .6. \textit{ Hence,} \\ x = .6(10) = 6. \\ 21420 + 6 = 21426. \end{matrix}$$

Hence, .33094 *is the mantissa for* 21426.

3. Since the characteristic of log N is $8 - 10$, or -2, $N = .021426$.

Example 4. Find N from Table I if log $N = 2.40971$.

SOLUTION. 1. In Table I, the mantissa .40971 is between the entries .40960 and .40976, which correspond to 2568 and 2569.

2. Since .40971 is $\frac{11}{16}$ of the way from .40960 to .40976, we assume that the significant part of N is $\frac{11}{16}$ of the way from 25680 to 25690.

$$16 \begin{bmatrix} 11 \begin{bmatrix} .40960, \textit{mantissa for } 25680 \\ .40971, \textit{mantissa for } ? \\ .40976, \textit{mantissa for } 25690 \end{bmatrix} x \end{bmatrix} 10 \qquad \begin{matrix} \frac{11}{16} = .7, \textit{ to nearest tenth}; \\ x = .7(10) = 7. \\ 25680 + 7 = 25687. \end{matrix}$$

3. Since the characteristic of log N is 2, we obtain $N = 256.87$.

COMMENT. We obtained $\frac{11}{16} = .7$ by inspection of the tenths of 16 in the column of proportional parts.

Exercise 68

Find the five-place logarithm of each number.

1. 18,563.	**2.** 25,632.	**3.** 5.3217.	**4.** 21.285.	**5.** .30129.
6. .042087.	**7.** 4.7178.	**8.** 31.648.	**9.** .073563.	**10.** .89316.
11. .75362.	**12.** 53.193.	**13.** 61.597.	**14.** .071384.	**15.** 896,910.
16. .0040063.	**17.** .0062873.	**18.** .00078651	**19.** 1,300,600.	
20. 966,910.	**21.** .00041569.	**22.** .000000000061.	**23.** 5,000,600,000.	

Find the antilogarithm of each five-place logarithm.

24. 2.21388.	**25.** 3.21631.	**26.** 1.33740.	**27.** 2.05297.
28. 9.65328 − 10.	**29.** 8.12277 − 10.	**30.** 7.94014 − 10.	**31.** 9.77817 − 10.
32. 6.03271.	**33.** 5.45698.	**34.** 0.97035.	**35.** 0.28779.
36. 9.00858 − 10.	**37.** 3.33412 − 10.	**38.** 6.24049 − 20.	**39.** 8.73168 − 20.

100. Computation of Products and Quotients

Unless otherwise specified, we shall assume that the data of any given problem are exact. Then, the accuracy of a product, quotient, or power computed by use of logarithms depends on the number of places in the table being used. The result frequently is subject to an unavoidable error, which usually is at most a few units in the last significant place given by interpolation. Hence, usually we must compute with at least *five*-place logarithms to obtain *four*-place accuracy. However, as a general custom, in any result we shall give *all digits obtainable by interpolation*.

Example 1. Compute: $P = 787.97(.0033238)(14.431)$.

SOLUTION. By Property I of logarithms, $\log P$ is the sum of the logarithms of the factors. The computing form, given below in bold face type, was made up as the first step in the solution.

$$
\left\{
\begin{array}{lll}
\textbf{log 787.97} = & 2.89651 & \text{(Table I)} \\
\textbf{log .0033238} = & 7.52163 - 10 & \text{(Table I)} \\
\textbf{log 14.431} = & 1.15930 & \text{(Table I)}
\end{array}
\right.
$$

(**Add**) $\log P = 11.57744 - 10 = 1.57744$

Hence, $P = 37.795.$ ($=$ antilog 1.57744, from Table I)

Example 2. Compute: $q = \dfrac{432.9132}{15.68278}$.

SOLUTION. 1. By Property II of logarithms, $\log q$ is equal to the logarithm of the numerator minus the logarithm of the denominator.

2. First, we round off each number to *five* significant digits because we shall use a *five*-place table. Thus, $432.9132 \rightarrow 432.91$.

$$
\begin{array}{lll}
\textbf{log 432.91} = 2.63640 & & \text{(Table I)} \\
(-)\,\textbf{log 15.683} = 1.19543 & & \text{(Table I)} \\
\hline
\textbf{log } q = 1.44097. & \textbf{Hence, } q = \textbf{27.604.} & \text{(Table I)}
\end{array}
$$

Whenever it is necessary to subtract a *larger* logarithm from a *smaller* one in computing a quotient, add 10 to the smaller logarithm and then subtract 10 to compensate for the change.

Example 3. Compute: $q = 257/8956$.

SOLUTION. $\qquad\textbf{log 257} = 2.40993 = 12.40993 - 10$

$\qquad\qquad (-)\,\textbf{log 8956} = 3.95211 = \quad 3.95211$

$\qquad\qquad\qquad\qquad \textbf{log } q = \quad ? \quad = 8.45782 - 10; \quad q = .028696.$

COMMENT. In order that $\log q$ should appear in the *standard form for a negative logarithm*, we changed log 257 by adding 10 and then subtracting 10 to compensate for the first change. Actually,

$$\log q = 2.40993 - 3.95211 = -1.54218 = 8.45782 - 10.$$

Example 4. Compute: $\quad q = \dfrac{(4.803)(269.9)(1.636)}{(7880)(253.6)}$.

INCOMPLETE SOLUTION. The computing form is as follows.

$$(+) \begin{cases} \log 4.803 = \\ \log 269.9 = \\ \log 1.636 = \end{cases}$$
$$\overline{}$$
$$\log \text{ numer.} =$$
$$(-) \quad \log \text{ denom.} =$$
$$\overline{}$$
$$\log q =$$

$$(+) \begin{cases} \log 7880 = \\ \log 253.6 = \end{cases}$$
$$\overline{}$$
$$\log \text{ denom.} =$$

Hence, $\quad q =$

Example 5. Compute the reciprocal of 189 by use of Table I.

SOLUTION. Let $R = \dfrac{1}{189}$.

$$\begin{aligned} \log 1 &= 0.00000 = 10.00000 - 10 \\ (-)\ \log 189 &= 2.27646 = 2.27646 \\ \hline \text{loh } R &= ? = 7.72354 - 10. \end{aligned}$$

Hence, $\quad R = .0052910.$

Exercise 69

Compute by use of five-place logarithms.

1. $31.57 \times .789.$
2. $925.6 \times .137.$
3. $.8475 \times .0937.$
4. $.0179 \times .35641.$
5. $925.618 \times .000217.$
6. $3.41379 \times .0142.$
7. $168 \times .213143.$
8. $56.1214 \times .00326.$
9. $.03195 \times .003149.$
10. $563.7 \times 8.2156 \times .00565.$
11. $4.321 \times 21.98 \times .99315.$

12. $\dfrac{675}{13.21}$.
13. $\dfrac{568.5}{23.14}$.
14. $\dfrac{728.72}{895}$.
15. $\dfrac{753.17}{9273.8}$.

16. $\dfrac{.0894}{.6358}$.
17. $\dfrac{.0421}{.53908}$.
18. $\dfrac{1}{325.93}$.
19. $\dfrac{1}{100,940}$.

20. $\dfrac{.42173(.217)}{.3852(.956)}$.
21. $\dfrac{16.083(256)}{(47.0158)}$.
22. $\dfrac{9.32(531)}{.8319(.5685)}$.

Compute the reciprocal of the number by use of Table I.

23. 853.
24. 958.3.
25. .00356278.
26. .0000139902.

Compute the product by use of Table I.

27. $(-84.75)(.00368)(.02458).$
28. $(-16.8)(-136.94)(.00038).$

HINT. Recall that only positive numbers have logarithms. Compute as if all factors were positive, and then determine the proper sign for the result by inspecting the signs of the factors.

101. Computation of Powers and Roots

Recall that

$$\log M^k = k \log M. \tag{1}$$

From (1) with $k = 1/h$,

$$\log \sqrt[h]{M} = \frac{1}{h} \log M. \tag{2}$$

Thus, $\qquad \log \sqrt{N} = \tfrac{1}{2} \log N; \qquad \log \sqrt[3]{N} = \tfrac{1}{3} \log N. \tag{3}$

Example 1. Compute $(.3156)^4$.

SOLUTION.   From (1) with $k = 4$, $\qquad \log (.3156)^4 = 4 \log .3156.$

$\log .3156 = \;\; 9.49914 - 10 \qquad\qquad\qquad\qquad$ (Table I)

$4 \log .3156 = 37.99656 - 40 = 7.99656 - 10$

Hence, $(.3156)^4 = .0099210.$ $\qquad\qquad$ [$=$ antilog $(7.99656 - 10)$, Table I]

Example 2. Compute $\sqrt[3]{856.31}$.

SOLUTION.   From (3), $\qquad \log \sqrt[3]{856.31} = \tfrac{1}{3} \log 856.31.$

$\log 856.31 = 2.93264 \qquad\qquad\qquad\qquad\qquad$ (Table I)

$\tfrac{1}{3} \log 856.31 = 0.97755 = \log \sqrt[3]{856.31}$

Hence, $\sqrt[3]{856.31} = 9.4962.$ $\qquad\qquad\qquad$ ($=$antilog 0.97755, Table I)

Before dividing a *negative* logarithm by a positive integer, we write the logarithm so that *the negative part, when divided by the integer, will give* -10 *as the quotient*.

Example 3. Find $\sqrt[6]{.08351}$.

SOLUTION.   From (2), $\qquad\qquad \log \sqrt[6]{.08351} = \tfrac{1}{6} \log .08351.$

$\log .08351 = \;\; 8.92174 - 10 \qquad\qquad\qquad\qquad$ (Table I)

$\log .08351 = 58.92174 - 60 \qquad\quad$ (Add 50 and subtract 50 above)

$\tfrac{1}{6} \log .08351 = \;\; 9.82029 - 10 = \log \sqrt[6]{.08351}$

Hence, $\sqrt[6]{.08351} = \;\; .66113.$

Exercise 70

Compute by use of five-place logarithms.

1. $(175)^2$.
2. $(56.73)^3$.
3. $(.013821)^4$.
4. $\sqrt{531.2}$.
5. $\sqrt[3]{.079677}$.
6. $(.38956)^{1/4}$.

7. $(353.3 \times 1.6888)^2$.   **8.** $\sqrt[5]{199.62}$.   **9.** $(1.05)^7$.

10. $(1.06)^{1/4}$.   **11.** $(1.03)^{14}$.   **12.** $(1.06)^{29}$.

13. $\dfrac{1}{85.75}$.   **14.** $\dfrac{1}{(45.6)^2}$.

15. $(1.03)^{-6} = \dfrac{1}{(1.03)^6}$.   **16.** $\sqrt{\dfrac{56.35 \times 4.3157}{21.36 \times \sqrt{521.9}}}$.

HINT for Problem 16. First find the logarithm of the fraction.

17. $\dfrac{535 \times 831.5 \times (1.03)^5}{475 \times 938}$.   **18.** $(189.5)^4$.   **19.** $\sqrt[4]{.00356}$.

20. $\sqrt{896.33}$.   **21.** $\dfrac{(153.2)^2 \times 257.3}{1893.2 \times 35830}$.   **22.** $\dfrac{.03156 \times 75.31}{221.38 \times (.3561)^2}$.

23. $(1.04)^{25}$.   **24.** $(1.035)^{-6}$.   **25.** $(1.0225)^{100}$.

HINT for Problems 23–25. To increase accuracy, start by using a logarithm from Table III. Thus, from Table III, $\log 1.04 = 0.0170333$; $25 \log 1.04 = 0.42583$; then use Table I.

★ *Solve for x in the exponential equation.*

26. $12^x = 31$.   **27.** $5^{2x} = 64$.   **28.** $(1.02)^x = 2.15$.

HINT for Problem 26. Take the logarithm of each side. Then

$$x \log 12 = \log 31; \qquad x = \frac{\log 31}{\log 12}.$$

29. $(1.03)^{-x} = .475$.   **30.** $(1.02)^{-x} = .642$.   **31.** $(1.0125)^x = 1.485$.

★**32.** Find the logarithm of 25 to the base $e = 2.71828\ldots$. That is, solve the exponential equation $e^x = 25$.

NOTE 1. Logarithms to the base e are called **natural logarithms**, and are of fundamental importance in advanced mathematics and in the advanced theory of life insurance.

102. Use of a Six-place Table of Logarithms

Table II gives the mantissa of $\log N$ correct to six decimal places if N is any number with at most four significant digits.

ILLUSTRATION 1. From Table II, $\log 219{,}500 = 5.341435$. If we are given $\log N = 7.420781 - 10$, then $N = .002635$.

If N is expressed with five or with six significant figures, we can obtain the mantissa of $\log N$ with reasonable accuracy by interpolation in Table II. In obtaining a number N by interpolation in Table II when the six-place log N is given, we shall specify *just six significant digits* in N. As a rule, the result will be subject to an error of at most 1 unit in the sixth significant place. If N is given to more than six significant places, round off N to *just six significant figures* before finding log N from Table II. Use of more figures as a rule could not increase the accuracy of the interpolation for log N. In using Table II for log N, *act as if every number N has just six significant figures*.

Example 1. Find log 18.6237 from Table II.

SOLUTION. In Table II, we find the mantissas for 186200 and for 186300. We assume that the mantissa for 186237 is $\frac{37}{100}$ of the way from the mantissa for 1862 to the mantissa for 1863.

$$100 \begin{bmatrix} 37 \begin{bmatrix} 186200: \textit{mantissa is } .269980 \\ 186237: \textit{mantissa is } \quad ? \\ 186300: \textit{mantissa is } .270213 \end{bmatrix} x \end{bmatrix} \qquad \begin{array}{c} \textit{Tabular difference is} \\ 233 \ .270213 - .269980 = .000233 \\ x = .37(233) = 86. \end{array}$$

$$\textit{Mantissa for } \log 18.6237 \textit{ is } .269980 + .000086 = .270066.$$

$$\text{Hence, } \log 18.6236 = 1.270066.$$

Example 2. Find N if log N = 6.134279 − 10.

SOLUTION. 1. The mantissa is .134279, which lies between the mantissas .134177 and .134496 in Table II, corresponding to the significant figures 1362 and 1363.

2. From below, since .134279 is $\frac{102}{319}$ of the way from .134177 to .134496, we assume that the significant part of N is $\frac{102}{319}$ of the way from 136200 to 136300, where we have prepared for interpolation to six figures.

$$319 \begin{bmatrix} 102 \begin{bmatrix} .134177, \textit{mantissa for } 136200 \\ .134279, \textit{mantissa for } \quad N \\ .134496, \textit{mantissa for } 136300 \end{bmatrix} x \end{bmatrix} \quad 100 \ \begin{array}{c} \dfrac{102}{319} = .32. \quad \textit{Hence,} \\ x = .32(100) = 32. \end{array}$$

$$136200 + 32 = 136232.$$

$$\text{Hence, } .134279 \textit{ is the mantissa for } 136232.$$

3. Since the characteristic of log N is −4, N = .000136232.

NOTE 1. The arithmetic of interpolation in Table II cannot be done safely without carrying out the necessary division, such as 102/319 in Example 2, on scratch paper. In order to have interpolation as convenient for six-place logarithms as for five-place logarithms in Table I, we would need a six-place table *expanded to* **180** *pages.* Excellent tables of this type are available.

Exercise 71

Find the six-place logarithm of the number.

1. 215,600.   **2.** 314,576.   **3.** .0815469.   **4.** .00345163.
5. 13.5946.   **6.** 24.1459.   **7.** 470.342.   **8.** .0196195.

Find the antilogarithm of each six-place logarithm.

9. 2.724639.   **10.** 4.343305.   **11.** $8.224199 - 10$.   **12.** $7.070195 - 10$.
13. 4.889996.   **14.** 6.454037.   **15.** $6.679857 - 10$.   **16.** $8.377831 - 10$.

Compute by use of six-place logarithms.

17. 925.6183(.000217).   **18.** 56.12139(.00326).   **19.** $\sqrt[4]{.3895627}$.

20-22. Problems 23-25, respectively, on page 267 starting in Table III.
23-24. Problems 21-22, respectively, on page 267.

12/Sequences and Series

103. Arithmetic Progressions

A *sequence*, *S*, is a *function* whose domain, *D*, is a set of positive integers. Unless otherwise mentioned, let us infer that *D* consists of either (*a*) all positive integers $n \leq k$, where *k* is a certain fixed integer, or (*b*) all positive integers. In (*a*), it is said that *S* is a *finite sequence*, $\{S(1), S(2), \ldots, S(k)\}$. In (*b*), it is said that *S* is an *infinite sequence*, and its range consists of the endless set of numbers

$$S(1), S(2), \ldots, S(n), \ldots. \tag{1}$$

In (1), we list $S(n)$ to establish the general notation, and the final dots..., to be read "*and so forth*," indicate that the values of *S* extend endlessly to the right. Instead of (1), we usually write the range of *S* as follows:

$$S_1, S_2, S_3, \ldots, S_n, \ldots, \tag{2}$$

where subscripts are employed, instead of functional notation, to indicate that the domain of the independent variable, *n*, consists of all integers.

An **arithmetic progression** (abbreviated **A.P.**) is a sequence of numbers, called *terms*, each of which, after the first, is obtained from the preceding one by adding to it a fixed number, called the **common difference**. Unless otherwise stated, any A.P. will be assumed to have just a finite number of terms.

ILLUSTRATION 1. In the arithmetic progression 9, 6, 3, 0, $-3, \ldots$, the common difference is -3. The 6th term would be -6.

Let *b* be the 1st term and *d* be the common difference in an A.P. Then, the 2nd term is $b + d$; the 3rd term is $b + 2d$; the 4th term is $b + 3d$. In each of these terms, the coefficient of *d* is 1 less than the number of the term. The *n*th term is the $(n - 1)$th after the 1st term and is obtained after *d* has been added $(n - 1)$ times. Hence, if *l* represents the *n*th term,

$$l = b + (n - 1)d. \tag{3}$$

Let S be the sum of the A.P. involved in (3). The first term is b; the common difference is d; the last term is l; the next to the last term is $l - d$, etc. On writing the sum of the n terms, forward and backward, we obtain

$$S = b + (b + d) + (b + 2d) + \cdots + (l - 2d) + (l - d) + l; \qquad (4)$$

$$S = l + (l - d) + (l - 2d) + \cdots + (b + 2d) + (b + d) + b. \qquad (5)$$

In (4), the three dots "$\cdots$" may be read "*and so forth up to.*" On adding corresponding sides of (4) and (5), we obtain

$$2S = (b + l) + (b + l) + (b + l) + \cdots + (b + l) + (b + l) + (b + l),$$

where there are n terms $(b + l)$. Hence, $2S = n(b + l)$ or

$$S = \frac{n}{2}(b + l). \qquad (6)$$

Example 1. Find the sum of the A.P. $8 + 5 + 2 + \cdots$ *to twelve terms.*

SOLUTION. First obtain l from (3) with $b = 8$, $d = -3$, and $n = 12$:

$$l = 8 + 11(-3) = -25; \quad \textit{from (6),} \quad S = 6(8 - 25) = -102.$$

On substituting $l = b + (n - 1)d$ in (6) we obtain

$$S = \frac{n}{2}[2b + (n - 1)d]. \qquad (7)$$

We call b, d, l, n, and S the **elements** of the general A.P.

Example 2. Find d and S in an A.P. where $b = 2$, $l = 402$, and $n = 26$.

SOLUTION. 1. From (6), $\qquad\qquad S = 13(404) = 5252.$

2. From (3), $\qquad\qquad 402 = 2 + 25d; \quad \textit{hence,} \quad d = 16.$

Exercise 72

Does the sequence form an arithmetic progression?

1. 3, 7, 11, 15.   **2.** 15, 17, 20, 22.   **3.** 23, 20, 17.   **4.** 35. 32. 30, 28.

Find the value of k for which the sequence forms an A.P.

5. 3; 8; k.   **6.** 25; 21; k.   **7.** 15; k; 13.   **8.** k; 17; 23.

HINT. If b, h, and w form an A.P., then $h - b = w - h$.

Find the specified term of the A.P. *by use of a formula.*

9. Given terms: 4, 7, 10; find the 50th term.
10. Given terms: -5, -8, -11; find the 29th term.
11. Given terms: 3, $3\frac{1}{4}$, $3\frac{1}{2}$; find the 83rd term.

Find the last term and the sum of the A.P. *by use of formulas.*

12. 8, 13, 18,... *to 15 terms.*   **13.** 13, 8, 3,... *to 17 terms.*

14. 3, 5, 7,... *to 41 terms.*   **15.** 2.06, 2.02, 1.98,... *to 33 terms.*

16. 9, 6, 3,... *to 28 terms.*   **17.** 5, $4\frac{1}{2}$, 4,... *to 81 terms.*

Certain of b, d, l, n, and S are given. Find the other elements.

18. $b = 10, l = 410, n = 26.$ **19.** $b = 27, l = 11, d = -\frac{1}{4}.$

20. $b = 4, l = 72, n = 18.$ **21.** $b = 50, l = 0, d = -\frac{5}{2}.$

104. Geometric Progressions

A **geometric progression**, abbreviated **G.P.**, is a sequence of numbers called terms, each of which, after the first, is obtained by multiplying the preceding term by a fixed number called the **common ratio.** The common ratio is equal to *the ratio of any term, after the first, to the one preceding it.*

ILLUSTRATION 1. In the geometric progression 16, -8, $+4$, -2,..., the common ratio is $-\frac{1}{2}$; the 5th term would be $(-\frac{1}{2})(-2) = +1$.

ILLUSTRATION 2. If 3, 8, and x form a G.P., then $\dfrac{8}{3} = \dfrac{x}{8}$, or $x = \dfrac{64}{3}$.

If the terms of a G.P. are *reversed*, the terms will form a G.P. whose common ratio is the *reciprocal* of the ratio for the given G.P.

ILLUSTRATION 3. The common ratio of the G.P. (16, 8, 4, 2) is $\frac{1}{2}$. On reversing terms, we obtain (2, 4, 8, 16), a G.P. whose ratio is 2.

Let b represent the 1st term, and u the common ratio. Then the 2nd term is bu; the 3rd term in bu^2. In each of these terms the exponent of u is 1 *less* than the number of the term. Similarly, the 8th term is bu^7. The nth term is the $(n-1)$th after the 1st term, and hence is found by multiplying b by $(n-1)$ factors u or by u^{n-1}. Thus, if l represents the nth term,

$$l = bu^{n-1}. \tag{1}$$

ILLUSTRATION 4. If $b = 3$ and $u = 2$, the 7th term is $3(2^6) = 192$.

Let S be the sum of the G.P. involved in (1). The terms are

$$b, \quad bu, \quad bu^2, \ldots, bu^{n-2}, \quad bu^{n-1}, \tag{2}$$

and $\qquad\qquad S = b + bu + bu^2 + \cdots + bu^{n-2} + bu^{n-1}. \tag{3}$

Hence, $\qquad\qquad uS = \quad bu + bu^2 + bu^3 + \cdots + bu^{n-1} + bu^n. \tag{4}$

On subtracting each side of (3) from the corresponding side of (4), all terms on the right in (4) are canceled except bu^n, and $-b$ remains from (3). Thus,

$$uS - S = bu^n - b; \qquad S(u - 1) = bu^n - b. \tag{5}$$

On dividing by $(u - 1)$ in (5) we obtain

$$S = \frac{bu^n - b}{u - 1}.$$ (6)

Since $l = bu^{n-1}$, we have $ul = bu^{n-1}u = bu^n$. Therefore we may replace bu^n by ul in (6) and obtain

$$S = \frac{ul - b}{u - 1}.$$ (7)

ILLUSTRATION 5.   In the G.P. (3, 6, 12, 24, 48, 96), we have $b = 3$, $u = 2$, and $l = 96$. By use of (7), $S = 2(96) - 3 = 189$.

ILLUSTRATION 6.   In $S = 1 + (1.05) + (1.05)^2 + \cdots + (1.05)^{10}$,

notice that $b = 1$, $u = 1.05$, and $l = (1.05)^{10}$. Hence,

$$ul = (1.05)(1.05)^{10} = (1.05)^{11}; \qquad u - 1 = 1.05 - 1 = .05;$$

$$S = \frac{(1.05)^{11} - 1}{.05}.$$ [Using (7)]

ILLUSTRATION 7.   To find a compact expression for the sum

$$S = (1.04)^{-10} + (1.04)^{-9} + (1.04)^{-8} + \cdots + (1.04)^{-2} + (1.04)^{-1},$$

observe that, by use of a law of exponents,

$$u = \frac{(1.04)^{-9}}{(1.04)^{-10}} = (1.04)^{-9+10} = (1.04)^1; \quad b = (1.04)^{-10}; \quad l = (1.04)^{-1}.$$

Hence, $ul = (1.04)^1(1.04)^{-1} = (1.04)^0 = 1; \quad u - 1 = .04;$

$$S = \frac{1 - (1.04)^{-10}}{.04}.$$ [Using (7)]

Exercise 73

State the common ratio and write the next two terms of the progression.

1. 2, 4, 8, 16, ...   **2.** 8, 4, 2, 1, ...   **3.** 36, -12, 4, ...

4. $-\frac{3}{2}$, 3, -6, ...   **5.** 10, -5, $\frac{5}{2}$, ...   **6.** 1, h, h^2, h^3, ...

7. $r, r^3, r^5, r^7, \ldots$ **8.** 1, (1.04), $(1.04)^2$, $(1.04)^3$, $(1.04)^4$, . . .

9. 1, (1.06), $(1.06)^2$, ...   **10.** 1, (1.03), $(1.03)^2$, ...

11. 1, $(1.02)^2$, $(1.02)^4$, ...   **12.** $(1.01)^2$, $(1.01)^5$, $(1.01)^8$, ...

13. $(1.01)^{-9}$, $(1.01)^{-8}$, $(1.01)^{-7}$, ...   **14.** $(1.03)^{-11}$, $(1.03)^{-10}$, $(1.03)^{-9}$, ...

Find an expression for the sum by use of (7) on this page.

15. 3, 6, 12, 24, 48, 96, 192.   **16.** -8, 4, -2, 1, $-\frac{1}{2}$.

17. $1 + 1.06 + (1.06)^2 + (1.06)^3 + (1.06)^4 + (1.06)^5 + (1.06)^6$.

18. $1 + 1.03 + (1.03)^2 + (1.03)^3 + (1.03)^4 + (1.03)^5$.
19. $1 + (1.02)^2 + (1.02)^4 + (1.02)^6 + (1.02)^8 + (1.02)^{10}$.
20. $1 + (1.03)^3 + (1.03)^6 + \cdots + (1.03)^{27}$.
21. $(1.03)^{-5} + (1.03)^{-4} + (1.03)^{-3} + (1.03)^{-2} + (1.03)^{-1}$.
22. $(1.04)^{-8} + (1.04)^{-7} + (1.04)^{-6} + \cdots + (1.04)^{-1}$.

105. Geometric Progressions with Infinitely Many Terms

Let S_n represent the sum of the progression $b, bu, bu^2, \ldots, bu^{n-1}$. Then, from (6) on page 273,

$$b + bu + bu^2 + \cdots + bu^{n-1} = S_n = \frac{b}{1-u} - \frac{bu^n}{1-u}. \tag{1}$$

Now consider ($b, bu, bu^2, \ldots$ *to infinitely many terms*), under the condition that u is a number between -1 and $+1$. Then, as n grows large without bound (abbreviated $n \to \infty$; read n *becomes infinite*), the absolute value of bu^n in (1) grows smaller, and is as near zero as we please for all values of n sufficiently large. Hence, from (1) we see that, as n grows large without bound, S_n approaches the limit

$$\frac{b}{1-u} - \frac{0}{1-u} \quad or \quad \frac{b}{1-u}.$$

That is,
$$\operatorname*{limit}_{n \to \infty} S_n = \frac{b}{1-u}, \tag{2}$$

which we read "*the limit of S_n as $n \to \infty$ is $b/(1-u)$.*" The limit in (2) is called *the sum of the geometric progression $b, bu, bu^2, \ldots, bu^{n-1}, \ldots$, to infinitely many terms.* If S represents this sum, then

$$S = \frac{b}{1-u}. \tag{3}$$

Hence we write, if $|u| < 1$,

$$(b + bu + bu^2 + \cdots \textit{ to infinitely many terms}) = \frac{b}{1-u}. \tag{4}$$

The indicated sum of a finite number of terms sometimes is called a *series*. An expression $a_1 + a_2 + a_3 + \ldots$ *to infinitely many terms* is called an **infinite series.** Thus, the expression at the left in (4) is referred to as the **infinite geometric series.** It has a "*sum,*" as defined in (2), when $|u| < 1$ and hence is called a **convergent infinite series.** The infinite geometric series does *not* have a sum when $|u| \geq 1$ because, in this case, S_n in (1) does not approach a limit as $n \to \infty$. Thus, for the G.P. $(1, 2, 4, \ldots)$ where $u = 2$, we find that S_n increases beyond all bounds as $n \to \infty$.

ILLUSTRATION 1. From (4) with $b = 5$ and $u = \frac{1}{2}$,

$$\left(5 + \frac{5}{2} + \frac{5}{4} + \cdots \textit{ to infinitely many terms}\right) = \frac{5}{1 - \frac{1}{2}} = 10. \qquad (5)$$

That is, by adding enough terms on the left in (5) we could obtain a result as close as we please to 10. Thus, $S_{11} = 9\frac{1019}{1024}$.

ILLUSTRATION 2. Any endless repeating decimal may be shown to represent a rational number, as in the following case.

$$.58181\cdots = .5 + .081 + .00081 + \cdots \textit{ to infinitely many terms.} \qquad (6)$$

On the right in (6), aside from .5, we have an infinite geometric series with $b = .081$ and $u = .01$. Hence, by (4),

$$.58181\cdots = .5 + \frac{.081}{1 - .01} = \frac{5}{10} + \frac{.081}{.99} = \frac{5}{10} + \frac{9}{110} = \frac{32}{55}.$$

Example 1. Find the sum of the progression

$$(1.04)^{-2} + (1.04)^{-4} + (1.04)^{-6} + \cdots \textit{ to infinitely many terms.}$$

SOLUTION. The ratio is $u = (1.04)^{-2}$; $b = (1.04)^{-2}$. From (4),

$$S = \frac{(1.04)^{-2}}{1 - (1.04)^{-2}}.$$

Exercise 74

Find the sum of the geometric progression.

1. $2 + 1 + \frac{1}{2} + \cdots$ *to infinitely many terms.*
2. $5 + 1 + \frac{1}{5} + \frac{1}{25} + \cdots$ *to infinitely many terms.*
3. $(1.04)^{-1} + (1.04)^{-2} + (1.04)^{-3} + \cdots$ *to infinitely many terms.*
4. $(1.03)^{-2} + (1.03)^{-4} + (1.03)^{-6} + \cdots$ *to infinitely many terms.*
5. $(1.01)^{-1} + (1.01)^{-2} + (1.01)^{-3} + \cdots$ *to infinitely many terms.*

Express the endless repeating decimal as a rational number.

6. $.333333\ldots$ 7. $.666666\ldots.$ 8. $.111111\ldots.$ 9. $.41111\ldots.$

106. Expansion of a Positive Integral Power of a Binomial

By multiplication, we obtain the following results:

$$(x + y)^1 = x + y;$$
$$(x + y)^2 = x^2 + 2xy + y^2;$$
$$(x + y)^3 = x^3 + 3x^2y + 3xy^2 + y^3;$$
$$(x + y)^4 = x^4 + 4x^3y + 6x^2y^2 + 4xy^3 + y^4.$$

Observe that, if $n = 1$, 2, 3, or 4, the expansion of $(x + y)^n$ *in descending powers of* x consists of $(n + 1)$ terms with the following properties.

I. *In any term, the sum of the exponents of* x *and* y *is* n.

II. *The first term is* x^n, *and in each other term the exponent of* x *is 1 less than in the preceding term.*

III. *The second term is* $nx^{n-1}y$, *and in each succeeding term the exponent of* y *is 1 more than in the preceding term.*

IV. *If the coefficient of any term is multiplied by the exponent of* x *in that term, and if the product then is divided by the number of that term, the quotient obtained is the coefficient of the next term.*

V. *The coefficients of terms equidistant from the ends are the same.*

ILLUSTRATION 1. In the expansion of $(x + y)^3$, the 2nd term is $3x^2y$. By Property IV, we obtain $(3 \cdot 2) \div 2$, or 3, as the coefficient of the 3rd term.

We shall assume that Properties I to V are true if n is any positive integer, although we merely have verified their truth when $n = 1$, 2, 3, and 4. The theorem that justifies this assumption is called the **binomial theorem**.

Example 1. Expand $(c + w)^7$.

SOLUTION. 1. By use of Properties I, II, and III, we obtain

$$(c + w)^7 = c^7 + 7c^6w + \quad c^5w^2 + \quad c^4w^3 + \quad c^3w^4 + \quad c^2w^5 + \quad cw^6 + w^7,$$

where spaces are left for the unknown coefficients.

2. By Property IV, the coefficient of the third term is $(7 \cdot 6) \div 2$, or 21; that of the fourth term is $(21 \cdot 5) \div 3$, or 35.

3. By Property V, we obtain the other coefficients; hence,

$$(c + w)^7 = c^7 + 7c^6w + 21c^5w^2 + 35c^4w^3 + 35c^3w^4$$
$$+ 21c^2w^5 + 7cw^6 + w^7.$$

The following array is called **Pascal's triangle**. The rows give the coefficients of the successive positive integral powers of $(x + y)$. To form any row after the second, first place 1 at the left; the 2nd number is the sum of the 1st and 2nd numbers in the preceding row; the 3rd number in the new row is the sum of the 2nd and 3rd numbers in the preceding row; etc. This triangle was known to Chinese mathematicians in the early fourteenth century. The triangle is named after BLAISE PASCAL (1623–1662), a French scientist.

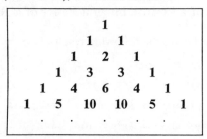

ILLUSTRATION 2. From above, the coefficients in $(x + y)^6$ are $\{1, 6, 15, 20, 15, 6, 1\}$, so that

$$(x + y)^6 = x^6 + 6x^5y + 15x^4y^2 + 20x^3y^3 + 15x^2y^4 + 6xy^5 + y^6.$$

It is recommended that Pascal's triangle should be used, rather than Properties I–V in obtaining the expansion of $(x + y)^n$ in particular cases, except when *only the first few terms are desired.*

Example 2. Expand $\left(2a - \dfrac{w}{3}\right)^6$.

SOLUTION. 1. $\left(2a - \dfrac{w}{3}\right)^6 = \left[(2a) + \left(-\dfrac{w}{3}\right)\right]^6.$

2. By use of Pascal's triangle, the coefficients are found to be $\{1, 6, 15, 20, 15, 6, 1\}$, as below.

$$\left(2a - \frac{w}{3}\right)^6 = (2a)^6 + 6(2a)^5 \left(-\frac{w}{3}\right) + 15(2a)^4 \left(-\frac{w}{3}\right)^2 + 20(2a)^3 \left(-\frac{w}{3}\right)^3$$

$$+ 15(2a)^2 \left(-\frac{w}{3}\right)^4 + 6(2a)\left(-\frac{w}{3}\right)^5 + \left(-\frac{w}{3}\right)^6$$

$$= 64a^6 - 64a^5w + \frac{80}{3} a^4w^2 - \frac{160}{27} a^3w^3 + \frac{20}{27} a^2w^4 - \frac{4}{81} aw^5 + \frac{w^6}{729}.$$

Exercise 75

Expand each power by use of Pascal's triangle.

1. $(a + b)^5$.   **2.** $(c - d)^6$.   **3.** $(x - y)^8$.   **4.** $(c + 3)^5$.
5. $(2 + a)^4$.   **6.** $(x - 2a)^7$.   **7.** $(3b - y)^6$.   **8.** $(2c + 3d)^3$.
9. $(a + b^2)^3$.   **10.** $(c^3 - 3d)^4$.   **11.** $(a^2 - b^2)^6$.   **12.** $(c - x^3)^5$.
13. $(x - \frac{1}{2})^5$.   **14.** $(1 - a)^9$.   **15.** $(\sqrt{x} - \sqrt{y})^6$.   **16.** $(x^{1/4} + a)^5$.
17. $(-a + y^{-2})^4$.   **18.** $(z^{-3} - x)^5$.   **19.** $(x^{1/2} - 2a^{-1})^4$.

Find only the first three terms of the expansion by use of Properties I–V on page 276.

20. $(a + 12)^{15}$.   **21.** $(c - 3)^{25}$.   **22.** $(a^2 + b^3)^{20}$.   **23.** $(1 + 2a)^{10}$.
24. $(1 - .1)^{22}$.   **25.** $(1 + .2)^{12}$.   **26.** $(1 - \sqrt{2})^{12}$.   **27.** $(1 - 3x^3)^{18}$.
28. $(2x - a^2)^{30}$.   **29.** $(x^{1/2} + b)^{14}$.   **30.** $(a^{-1} + 3)^{26}$.   **31.** $(x - a^{-2})^{11}$.
32. $(x - y)^n$.   **33.** $(a + x)^k$.   **34.** $(x^2 - y)^m$.   **35.** $(w^2 + z)^h$.

Compute the power correct to three decimal places by using only as many terms as necessary in a binomial expansion.

36. $(1.01)^8$.   **37.** $(1.02)^9$.   **38.** $(1.03)^{11}$.   **39.** $(1.01)^{20}$.

HINT. $(1.01)^8 = (1 + .01)^8 = 1 + 8(.01) + 28(.01)^2 + \cdots.$

Answers to Exercises

Sometimes, in a problem, a special method of computation to a stipulated degree of accuracy is requested. Otherwise, each answer which is a numeral is given to a number of significant digits which will appear reasonable in view of the nature of the data and the main feature illustrated by the problem. There is no merit to the assumption that each answer which is an amount of money must be given correct to the nearest cent. This may be true in many business affairs. However, a standard of accuracy of this nature in a college textbook would create the need for an unreasonable amount of computation by the student who, it is safe to assume, does not as a rule have access to a modern sophisticated computer. If such assistance is available, the teacher may request answers with many more significant digits than are found in the listed results.

Exercise 1

1. $180; $5180.
3. $93; $8093.
5. $48; $3048.
7. $10.17; $2510.17.
9. Actual, 182; approx., 179.
11. $971.83; $21,371.83.
13. $5337.50.
15. $18.40.
17. $25.50.
19. $310.05.

Exercise 2

1. $1210.
3. $1597.50.
5. $1000.
7. $1617.65; disct. = $32.35.
9. $174.42.
11. $r = .12; I = $150.
13. $P = $1309.01; I = $215.99.
15. (a) $2083.33; (b) $1923.08. For Hansen, 4%.
17. Gain $40 at end of 2 years, by use of 9%.
19. $1233.55.
21. 21.4%.
23. 19.1%.

Exercise 3

1. $I = \$157.50; P = \$2842.50.$ **3.** $I = \$50; P = \$2950.$
5. $1179.$ **7.** (a) $8510.64; (b) $8480.
9. (a) $d = .064;$ (b) $r = .067.$ **11.** (a) $2000.00; (b) $1996.80.
13. $r = .08\frac{1}{3}.$ **15.** .049.   **17.** .0783.

Exercise 4

1. $4970.16.
3. (a) Date, Dec. 12; mat. val. = $2058.33; (b) proceeds = $1996.58.
5. $1183.00.   **7.** $2017.05.   **9.** $3050.85.

Exercise 5

1. $61.36.   **3.** Int. = $3174.14; amt. = $5174.14.
5. Int. = $500.33; amt. = $2000.33.
7. Int. = $566.99; amt. = $1566.99.
9. Int. = $666.00; amt. = $1416.00.   **11.** $1572.96.
13. $6413.14.   **15.** (a) $1842.02; (b) $400.   **17.** See table.

19. (a) $\left(1 + \dfrac{j}{m}\right)^m$; (b) $\left(1 + \dfrac{j}{m}\right)^{km}$.   **23.** $2665.84.

Exercise 6

3. $638.22.   **5.** $6839.97.   **7.** $175.50.   **9.** $1761.11.
11. $8167.45.   **13.** $5250.30.   **15.** (a) $376.89; (b) $258.42.
17. (a) $2000.00; (b) $1428.57; (c) $1600.00.
19. (a) $481.02; (b) $571.43.

Exercise 7

1. (a) .05; (b) .050625; (c) .05094534; (d) .05116190.
3. (a) .03033919; (b) .06136355; (c) .08243216; (d) .09308332.
5. .05912602.   **7.** (a) .0296683; (b) .0394136; (c) .0682341.
9. The better investment yields .136355% greater effective rate.
11. Yes; bonds yield .049375% better effective rate.

Exercise 8

1. .0604500.   **3.** .0298883.   **5.** .0808000.
7. .0401335.   **9.** .11762776.   **11.** (a) .0700; (b) .0749.

Exercise 9

1. $1166.34.   **3.** $4701.85.   **5.** $1394.88.
7. $1874.43.   **9.** $1797.17.   **11.** $1000(1.04)^{16/3}$
13. $1000(1.015)^{31/3}.$ **15.** $3000(1.08)^{35/6}.$ **17.** $2000(1.07)^{-16/3}.$

Exercise 10

1. 2.98%.   **3.** In 4.57 years.   **5.** 31.19 years.
7. 5.97%.   **9.** 6.66%.   **11.** 3.23%.
13. At end of 6.288 years.
15. In years: 11.72; 17.41; 14.21; 9.99; 9.01.

Exercise 11

NOTE. The answer as obtained by use of Table I is given first.

1. 3.0420; 3.04204. Without preliminary use of Table III, two places of accuracy are lost in multiplying the logarithm, so that the results are as follows: 3.04; 3.042.
3. $1304.6; $1304.59.   **5.** .0489.   **7.** 22.182; 22.1827, in years.

Exercise 12

1. $9235.   **3.** (a) $1641;   (b) $2319.   **5.** $2075.
7. In present values, $16 in favor of the most valuable obligation.
9. As compared at end of 3 years, (a) is $249 more valuable.

Exercise 13

1. (a) $500(1.045)^{-3} + 2000(1.045)^{-7} = x(1.045)^{-5}$.

$500(1.045) + 2000(1.045)^{-3} = x(1.045)^{-1}$.

$500(1.045)^4 + 2000 = x(1.045)^2$.

(b) $2377.

3. $\dfrac{7530}{2.94938705}$.

5. (a) $800(1.03)^{-3} + 600(1.03)^{-6} = x(1.03)^{-4} + x(1.03)^{-8}$.

$800 + 600(1.03)^{-3} = x(1.03)^{-1} + x(1.03)^{-5}$.

$800(1.03)^2 + 600(1.03)^{-1} = x(1.03) + x(1.03)^{-3}$.

(b) Each is $736.
7. (a) $500(1.03)^8 + 1500(1.05)^7(1.03)^{-2} = x(1.03)^4$.   (b) $2330.
9. (a) $1000 + 2000(1.04)^6(1.05)^{-2} = 1500(1.05) + x(1.05)^{-1}$.   (b) $1806.
11. $972.

Exercise 14

1. Ord. = $70.75; exact = $69.78.
3. (a) $76.92;   (b) $80.00;   (c) $77.66.
5. (a) $8264.46;   (b) $8162.98;   (c) $7900.00.
7. (a) .07;   (b) .071225;   (c) .07229008;   (d) .07185903.

9. $6122.45.   **11.** .0710288.   **13.** $3019.35.   **15.** 6.49%.
17. (a) 10.24; (b) 10.25.   **19.** At end of 7.132 years.
21. $1000(1.05)^{15}(1.07)^{10}$.   **23.** 5.59%.

Exercise 15

1. $A = \$550.813$; $S = \$638.774$.

Exercise 16

1. $A = 200\,\dfrac{1 - (1.06)^{-4}}{.06} = \$693.02$; $S = 200\,\dfrac{(1.06)^4 - 1}{.06} = \$874.92$.

3. $A = 100\,\dfrac{1 - (1.015)^{-32}}{.015} = \$2526.71$; $S = 100\,\dfrac{(1.015)^{32} - 1}{.015} = \$4068.83$.

5. $A = 25\,\dfrac{1 - (1.005)^{-186}}{.005} = \$3022.65$; $S = 25\,\dfrac{(1.005)^{186} - 1}{.005} = \$7643.21$.

Exercise 17

1. $A = \$15,622$; $S = \$41,646$.   **3.** $A = \$11,364$; $S = \$30,828$.
5. $A = \$10,953$; $S = \$27,550$.   **7.** $A = \$10,349$; $S = \$24,767$.
9. $A = \$22,561$; $S = \$33,623$.   **11.** (a) $132,958; (b) $73,333.
13. $98,040.   **15.** $9020.   **17.** $3926.05.

Exercise 18

1. (a) $36,670; (b) $25,363; (c) $26,363.
3. (a) $7256; (b) $4990; (c) $4269.   **5.** $8920.
7. $10,819.   **9.** $16,181.   **11.** $911.45.

Exercise 19

1. $336.08.   **3.** $65.28.   **5.** $55.08.
7. $1942.14.   **9.** $415.17.   **11.** $652.04.
13. $98.10.   **15.** $515.72.   **17.** $248.13.

Exercise 20

1. 6.34%.   **3.** 4.93%.   **5.** 7.42%.
7. At end of 8 years.   **9.** At end of $6\frac{1}{2}$ years.

Exercise 21

1. $A = \$3291$; $S = \$6668$.   **3.** $A = \$4265$; $S = \$5520$.
5. $12,385.   **7.** (a) $3905; (b) $3954.
9. (a) $11,799; (b) $11,065; (c) $10,580.
11. (a) $10,032; (b) $4655; (c) $4155.   **13.** $1700.
15. $1197.   **17.** $641.   **19.** 6.73%.   **21.** 5.16%.

Exercise 22

1. $833. **3.** $1192. **5.** $3689. **7.** $29,560.
9. $7500 cash is better by $675 in present value.
11. $1,337,438. **13.** $3835. **15.** $1,472,963. **17.** $45,918.

Exercise 23

1. (a) $100a_{\overline{8}|.05}$; $(100s_{\overline{8}|.05})(1.05)^{-8}$.

(b) $(100a_{\overline{8}|.05})(1.05)^{8}$; $100s_{\overline{8}|.05}$.

(c) $(100a_{\overline{8}|.05})(1.05)^{14}$; $(100s_{\overline{8}|.05})(1.05)^{6}$.

(d) $(100a_{\overline{8}|.05})(1.05)^{-4}$; $(100s_{\overline{8}|.05})(1.05)^{-12}$.

3. $36,336. **5.** $19,938. **7.** 67.58816. **9.** $2965.
11. $6620. **13.** $16,430. **19.** $17,736.

Exercise 24

1. (a) $38,695; (b) $32,072. **3.** $773.98. **5.** $45,647.
7. $22,492. **9.** $a_{\overline{140}|.03} = 32.801633$; $s_{\overline{140}|.03} = 2056.3968$.
11. $1359.21. **13.** At end $4\frac{1}{4}$ years. **15.** 5.23%.
17. $3650. **19.** $1270.

Exercise 25

1. $922.9875. **3.** (a) $14,720.174; (c) $11,164.76.
5. (a) $1018.06; (b) int. = $9.41; princ. = $65.59.
7. (a) $1970.1747. **9.** $13,006.54.
11. Int. = $324.44; princ. = $675.56. **13.** $501.30.
15. 2.73%. **17.** $9398.

Exercise 26

3. (a) $9959.30; (b) $1658.39.
5. (a) $1775.94; (b) $57.80; (c) $13.06 at end of 2 years and 7 months.
7. $133.55.
9. (a) $1453.78; (b) $53.37 at end of 23 months; (c) $303.37.
11. (a) $528.69; (b) $273.37 at end of 13 years.

Exercise 27

1. $2068.52. **3.** $1555.17. **5.** $110.40. **7.** $68.77.
9. $9214.23. **11.** $238.45 at end of 18 months. **13.** $202.39.
15. (a) $821.25; (b) $835.62. **17.** 7.54%. **19.** $34,192.

Exercise 28

1. (a) $440.16; (b) $403.24; (c) $388.61.
3. (a) $7325.66; (b) $7724.98. **5.** 6.55%.
7. $623,482. **9.** At end of 10 years. **11.** 6.57%.

Exercise 29

1. $16\frac{2}{3}\%$.   **3.** (a) 23.9%;   (b) 23.02%.
5. (a) \$109.167;   (b) 15.1%;   (c) 13.93%.

Exercise 30

1. \$348.63.   **3.** Last \$1000 at end 27 years; last, \$88.37.
5. (a) \$852.212;   (b) \$15,048;   (c) \$8875.
7. (a) \$184.17;   (b) 13.2%;   (c) 12.88%.   **9.** \$180.29.   **11.** \$15.901.
13. At the end of 9 years; no deposit is needed because, without it, the fund contains \$2563 more than needed.
15. (a) \$136.94;   (b) 15.0%;   (c) 14.12%.   **17.** 6.18%.
19. (a) \$10,932;   (b) \$217 at end of 23 years.

Exercise 31

1. (a) \$1074.35;   (b) \$1000;   (c) \$931.98.   **3.** \$760.27.
5. \$1234.68.   **7.** \$877.98.
9. (a) \$8578.76;   (b) \$8160.80;   (c) \$7864.49.
11. \$2027.09.   **13.** \$1080.58.

Exercise 32

1. (a) \$1223.96;   (b) \$827.08.   **5.** \$8452.51.   **7.** \$454,769.

Exercise 33

1. (a) \$1046.458;   (b) \$1028.560.   **3.** (a) \$1.37;   (b) \$114.38.
5. (a) \$1118.125;   (b) \$6.875.   **7.** Price = \$1000.
9. (a) \$44.19;   (b) \$15.81.   **11.** \$1057.49.

Exercise 34

1. \$23.33.   **3.** (a) \$977.50;   (b) 97.5.   **5.** \$104.
7. \$924.58.   **9.** \$683.63.   **11.** \$825.62.

Exercise 35

1. Price = \$1338.80;   B.V. = \$1325.57;   quot. = 132.56.
3. Price = \$5712.48;   B.V. = \$5612.48;   quot. = 112.25.
5. Price = \$101.50;   B.V. = \$100.00;   quot. = 100.
7. Price = \$1269.55;   B.V. = \$1254.76;   quot. = 125.48.
9. Price = \$847.58;   B.V. = \$825.08;   quot. = 82.508.
11. \$2963.61.

Exercise 36

1. 3.4%.   **3.** 5.0%.   **5.** 8.2%.   **7.** 8.1%.
9. 9.0%; the deep discount and long term cause this result to be a relatively poor approximation to the true yield.

Exercise 37

1. .04287.   **3.** 6.79%.   **5.** 7.04%.   **7.** 6.79%.
9. 6.68%.   **11.** 8.39%.   **13.** 9.11%.   **15.** 4.22%.

Exercise 38

1. $591,812.   **3.** $10,107.   **5.** $19.681.
7. (*a*) $14,859;   (*b*) $15,256.   **9.** $15,924.   **11.** $25,240.

Exercise 39

1. $11,215.82.   **3.** (*a*) $985.30;   (*b*) $1025.84.   **5.** $83.50.
7. (*a*) $940;   (*b*) 106.54.   **9.** (*a*) 6.42%;   (*b*) 4.33%.
11. (*a*) Flat = $94.054;   B.V. = $93.221;   (*b*) quot. = 93.221.
13. $1035.76.   **15.** $14,022.   **17.** 7.1%.
19. $994.84.   **21.** 6.2%.   **23.** $1.17.

Exercise 40

1. (*a*) Each annual charge is $700.   (*b*) The annual charges are $1200, $1000, $800, etc.
3. (*a*) Each annual charge is $1375.   (*b*) The annual charges are $2200, $1650, etc.
5. (*a*) Each annual charge is $1000.   (*b*) The annual charges are $1800, $1600, etc.

Exercise 41

1. Rate is $\frac{1}{3}$; final B.V. is $527. Profit is $73.
3. $d = .3391$; use $d = .35$.

Exercise 42

1. (*a*) $10,000;   (*b*) $10,200;   (*c*) $8620.   **3.** $8000.   **5.** $7628.95.
7. $82.30.   **9.** $54.421.77.   **11.** $5548.02.   **13.** $28,549.
15. $12,272.71 (which is the compound interest earned in one year by the endowment). The result also can be obtained by use of (2) in Section 58.
17. $32,908.10.

Exercise 43

1. $K = $47,558$; $M = 1902.33.   **3.** $2456.66.   **5.** $183,416.
7. $49,814.   **9.** $.64 saved.   **11.** $26,338.

Exercise 44

1. (*a*) $936,900;   (*b*) $979,400.   **3.** $544,300.
5. 10.044%.   **7.** 16.495%.

Exercise 45

1. (a) Actual time: Ord. = \$59.41; exact = \$58.60.
   (b) Approximate time: Ord. = \$58.28; exact = \$57.48.
3. (a) \$6967.008.   5. .05116190.   7. \$1682.   9. 4.45%.
11. \$1513.56.   13. (a) .0634731;   (b) .0644803.
15. (a) \$9236; (b) \$9363.   17. (a) \$12,992; (b) \$324,794.
19. (a) \$6943.83. (b) \$5601.43.   21. (a) \$104.80; (b) \$87.33.
23. \$5250.   25. \$3000.   27. Check with (8) on page 64.
29. (a) \$9700; (b) .0928.   31. (a) $9\frac{1}{11}\%$; (b) 6.50%.
33. .0344.   35. \$3959.79.   37. \$12,050.
39. \$3408.73.   41. .0756.
43. (a) \$13,299.52; (b) \$664.98; (c) \$419.32 at end of 29 years.
45. (a) \$1004.90; (b) \$1004.50.   47. \$90.52.   49. .09101250.
51. (a) \$9001.55; (b) \$315.05.   53. \$1643.40
55. (a) .041; (b) .0408.   57. (a) .053; (b) .0534.
59. (a) 9th; (b) \$5027.90.   61. \$5528.67.   63. \$241,400.
65. (a) \$142.50; (b) 12.91%.   67. \$15,207.07.   69. \$126.72.
71. At the end of 17 years and 11 months, \$46.62.
73. \$9863.50.   75. \$375,000.   77. .1202.
79. (a) \$4914.13; (b) \$4963.27.   81. \$1751.24.   83. \$3306.29.
85. (a) \$911.473; (b) 7.5%.
87. Int. = \$73.97; accum. of disct. = \$3.97.
89. \$11,192.   91. 4.10%.   93. \$917.50.

Exercise 46

1. \$81.82.   3. \$2214.   5. \$6683.   7. \$40,675.
9. \$610.52.   11. \$18,786.   13. \$14,004.   15. \$30,276.
17. \$599.40.   19. \$164.16.   21. \$33,148.

Exercise 47

1. (a) \$5458; (b) \$5451; (c) \$5454.   3. \$25,806.
5. \$3696.   7. \$3289.   9. \$13,117.   11. \$281.76.
13. \$5397.   15. \$252.80.   17. \$5013.   19. \$835.39.
21. (a) \$7208; (b) \$6806; (c) \$7212.   23. \$561.76.
25. (a) \$428.09; (b) \$422.32.

Exercise 48

1. 9.3%.
3. \$1000 for $4\frac{1}{4}$ years and a smaller payment at the end of $4\frac{1}{2}$ years.
5. 5.8%.   7. (a) \$8484; (b) \$76.70.   9. \$8274.30.

Exercise 49

1. (a) $\frac{3}{5}$; (b) $\frac{17}{20}$; (c) $\frac{2}{5}$.

3. (a) $\{1, 2, 3, 4, 5, 6, 5, 4, 3, 2, 1\}$ for totals at any throw
$\{2, 3, 4, 5, 6, 7, 8, 9, 10, 11, 12\}$, respectively. (b) 36.
(c) $\frac{1}{36}, \frac{1}{18}$, etc. Largest probability is $\frac{1}{6}$ for tossing 7.

5. (a) 225; (b) $\frac{1}{9}$; (c) $\frac{4}{9}$; (d) $\frac{4}{9}$.

7. (a) $_{30}p_{26} = .860$; (b) $_{50}p_{26} = .400$. **9.** $q_{22} = .00186$.

11. .00772. **13.** $_{12}q_{27} = .0280$.

15. (a) $_{20}q_{40} = .167$; (b) $_{20}p_{40} = .833$.

Exercise 50

1. $6. **3.** See Table XVI. **5.** $7253.

7. $8161. **9.** $145,976. **11.** $1579.

Exercise 51

1. $37,156. **3.** $42,611. **5.** $33,817.

7. $8421. **9.** $4512. **11.** $490.82.

Exercise 52

1. (a) $16,630; (b) $17,936. **3.** $15,029. **5.** $8753.

7. $1448. **9.** (a) $1305; (b) $6157. **11.** $1152.80.

15. $115,220.

Exercise 53

1. (a) $1187; (b) $1297; (c) $1848. **3.** $1421.

5. (a) $103.40; (b) $467.51. **9.** $11,190.

Exercise 54

1. $247.02. **3.** $406.58. **5.** $902.15. **7.** $8364.

9. (a) $16.24; (b) $21.28; (c) $230.08. **11.** $52.73. **13.** $1623.

Exercise 55

1. $562. **3.** (a) $561; (b) $576; (c) $663. **5.** $4010.

Exercise 56

1. (a) $161.62; (b) $329.79. **3.** $211.45. **5.** $380.00.

7. $187.05. **9.** $40.53. **13.** $69,039. **15.** $2679.

17. $8726.

Exercise 57

1. $841. **3.** $722. **5.** $1104.

Exercise 58

1. (*a*) $18.82.
   (*b*) {$12.62, $13.80, $15.09, $16.50, $18.05, $19.75, $21.59, $23.60, $25.80, $28.19}.
3. $1921.   5. $406.58.
7. Annual premium = $37.411; reserve = $195.19.
9. Annual premium = $3.347; reserve = $3.31.

Exercise 59

1. 7.   3. 126.   5. 14; 6; 40; $\frac{5}{2}$.
7. -15; -25; -100; -4.   9. $\frac{17}{3}$; $-\frac{3}{2}$.   11. $3 - 2a$.
13. {4, 5, 6, 7, 8}; {3, 5, 6, 7, 8}; {3, 4, 6, 7, 8};
    {3, 4, 5, 7, 8}; {3, 4, 5, 6, 8}; {3, 4, 5, 6, 7}.

15. $-\dfrac{5}{3}$.   17. $\dfrac{5}{4}$.   19. $\dfrac{12}{35}$.   21. $\dfrac{45}{4}$.   23. $\dfrac{10}{7}$.

25. $\dfrac{4}{3}$.   27. $\dfrac{4b}{d}$.   29. $\dfrac{12}{5d}$.   31. $\dfrac{3}{4y}$ 33. $-\dfrac{b}{3}$.

35. $\dfrac{1}{4b}$.   37. $\dfrac{41}{3x}$.   39. $\dfrac{21}{2}$.   41. $\dfrac{1}{12}$.   43. $\dfrac{2}{cd}$.

Exercise 60

1. $<$ 3. $>$ 5. $>$ 7. $<$
9. 64.   11. 1.   13. $-100,000$.   15. $\frac{1}{81}$.
17. 729.   19. 64.   21. a^9.   23. a^{3h}.

25. y^2.   27. $\dfrac{1}{x^2}$.   29. $6a^3x^5$.   31. $-98a^5b^6$.

33. $a^2 - 4ay + 4y^2$.   35. $\dfrac{3}{2b} - \dfrac{9a}{4b^4}$.

Exercise 61

1. ± 5.   3. $\pm\frac{2}{3}$.   5. $3x^4$.   7. $7z^4$.   9. $\frac{12}{9}$.

11. $\dfrac{y^3}{4}$.   13. $\dfrac{3a^2b^3}{11z^2}$.   15. y.   17. 29.   19. .2.

21. 30.   23. $2uw^2$.   25. uv^2.   27. $\dfrac{5a^2}{b^3x^4}$.   29. $\dfrac{2}{av^2}$.

31. $\dfrac{1}{216}$.   33. 2.   35. $\dfrac{3}{2}$.   37. 32.   39. 625.

41. $\frac{7}{2}$.   43. $1.05^{1/12}$.   45. $1.02^{2/3}$.   47. $5x^{-4}$.   49. $6(1.02^{-3})$.

Exercise 62

11. A parabola concave downward.

Exercise 63

1. $K = \{-6, -3, 0, 3, 6, 12\}$. F is the set of ordered pairs:

$$\{(-2, -6), (-1, -3), (0, 0), (1, 3), (2, 6), (4, 12)\}.$$

7. 7.   **9.** $-\frac{5}{4}$.   **11.** 10.   **13.** 12.

Exercise 64

1. 15.326; 15.3.   **3.** .31486; .315.   **5.** 195.64; 196.
7. .034564; .0346.   **9.** 566.5 to 567.5.   **11.** 567.35 to 567.45.
13. 31.54; .586.   **15.** 11.4034; .054.   **17.** 2738.
19. 2,056,000.   **21.** $6.7538(10^2)$.   **23.** $4.5726(10^4)$.
25. $3.6(10^{-7})$.   **27.** $2.42(10^{-4})$.

Exercise 65

3. $\log_5 N = 3$.   **5.** $\log_{10} N = -2$.   **7.** $\log_5 H = \frac{2}{5}$.
9. $\log_{10} N = .35$.   **11.** $\log_6 36 = 2$.   **13.** $\log_2 32 = 5$.

15. $\log_{25} 625 = 2$.   **17.** $\log_7 \dfrac{1}{49} = -2$.   **19.** $\log_3 \dfrac{1}{27} = -3$.

21. $\log_{10} .0001 = -4$.   **23.** $N = 9$.   **25.** $M = 49$.

27. $K = 1$.   **29.** $N = 10$.   **31.** $M = .01$.   **33.** $N = \dfrac{1}{121}$.

35. $N = 4$.   **37.** $N = 8$.   **39.** $N = 32$.   **41.** 2.
43. $\frac{1}{2}$.   **45.** 3.   **47.** 2.   **49.** $\frac{1}{2}$.
51. -1.   **53.** -4.   **55.** -4.

Exercise 66

1. 1.1461.   **3.** 1.4771.   **5.** 1.3222.   **7.** .5441.
9. $-.3680$.   **11.** .0843.   **13.** 2.3010.   **15.** -1.0212.
17. .6778.   **19.** 1.5050.   **21.** .2386.   **23.** .1840.

Exercise 67

1. 2.29820.   **3.** 0.14270.   **5.** $9.45728 - 10$.
7. $9.40875 - 10$.   **9.** $7.89209 - 10$.   **11.** 4.99782.
13. $7.76567 - 10$.   **15.** 4.84504.   **17.** 297.2.
19. 5979.   **21.** 1.999.   **23.** .03866.
25. .1237.   **27.** .0006770.

Exercise 68

1. 4.26865.
3. 0.72605.
5. 9.47898 − 10.
7. 0.67374.
9. 8.86666 − 10.
11. 9.87715 − 10.
13. 1.78956.
15. 5.95274.
17. 7.79846 − 10.
19. 6.11414.
21. 6.61877 − 10.
23. 9.69902.
25. 1645.5.
27. 112.97.
29. .013267.
31. .60003.
33. $2.8641(10^5)$.
35. 1.9400.
37. .00000021584.
39. $5.3911(10^{-12})$.

Exercise 69

1. 24.909.
3. .079410.
5. .20086.
7. 35.808.
9. .00010061.
11. 94.326.
13. 24.568.
15. .081214.
17. .078096.
19. $9.9070(10^{-6})$.
21. 87.572.
23. .0011723.
25. 280.68.
27. −.0076660.

Exercise 70

1. 30,625.
3. $3.6489(10^{-8})$.
5. .43031.
7. $3.5599(10^5)$.
9. 1.4071.
11. 1.5127.
13. .011662.
15. .83746.
17. 1.1575.
19. .24426.
21. .089024.
23. 2.6658.
25. 9.2540.
27. 1.2921.
29. 25.18.
31. (Table III was used) 31.831.

Exercise 71

1. 5.333649.
3. 8.911408 − 10.
5. 1.133366.
7. 2.672414.
9. 530.443.
11. .0167571.
13. 77,623.9.
15. .000478473.
17. .200859.
19. .790031.
21. .813500.
23. .0890254.

Exercise 72

5. 13.
7. 14.
9. 151.
11. $23\frac{1}{2}$.
13. $l = -67$; $S = -459$.
15. $l = .78$; $S = 46.86$.
17. $l = -35$; $S = -1215$.
19. $n = 65$; $S = 1235$.
21. $n = 21$; $S = 525$.

Exercise 73

1. Ratio 2.
3. Ratio $-\frac{1}{3}$.
5. Ratio $-\frac{1}{2}$.
7. Ratio r^2.
9. Ratio 1.06.
11. Ratio $(1.02)^2$.
13. Ratio 1.01.
15. $3(2^7) - 3$.

17. $\dfrac{(1.06)^7 - 1}{.06}$.

19. $\dfrac{(1.02)^{12} - 1}{(1.02)^2 - 1}$.

21. $\dfrac{1 - (1.03)^{-5}}{.03}$.

Exercise 74

1. 4.
3. 25.
5. 100.
7. $\frac{2}{3}$.
9. $\frac{37}{90}$.

Exercise 75

1. $a^5 + 5a^4b + 10a^3b^2 + 10a^2b^3 + 5ab^4 + b^5$.

3. $x^8 - 8x^7y + 28x^6y^2 - 56x^5y^3 + 70x^4y^4 + $ etc.

5. $16 + 32a + 24a^2 + 8a^3 + a^4$.

7. $729b^6 - 1458b^5y + 1215b^4y^2 - 540b^3y^3 + 135b^2y^4 - 18by^5 + y^6$.

9. $a^3 + 3a^2b^2 + 3ab^4 + b^6$.

11. $a^{12} - 6a^{10}b^2 + 15a^8b^4 - 20a^6b^6 + 15a^4b^8 - 6a^2b^{10} + b^{12}$.

13. $x^5 - \frac{5}{2}x^4 + \frac{5}{2}x^3 - \frac{5}{4}x^2 + \frac{5}{16}x - \frac{1}{32}$.

15. $x^3 - 6x^{5/2}y^{1/2} + 15x^2y - 20x^{3/2}y^{3/2} + 15xy^2 - 6x^{1/2}y^{5/2} + y^3$.

17. $a^4 - 4a^3y^{-2} + 6a^2y^{-4} - 4ay^{-6} + y^{-8}$.

19. $x^2 - 8x^{3/2}a^{-1} + 24xa^{-2} - 32x^{1/2}a^{-3} + 16a^{-4}$.

21. $c^{25} - 75c^{24} + 2700c^3$.   **23.** $1 + 20a + 180a^2$.

25. $1 + 2.4 + 2.64$.   **27.** $1 - 54x^3 + 1377x^6$.

29. $x^7 + 14x^{13/2}b + 91x^6b^2$.   **31.** $x^{11} - 11x^{10}a^{-2} + 55x^9a^{-4}$.

33. $a^k + ka^{k-1}x + \frac{1}{2}k(k - 1)a^{k-2}y^2$.

35. $w^{2h} + hw^{2h-2}z + \frac{1}{2}h(h - 1)w^{2h-4}z^2$.   **37.** 1.195.   **39.** 1.220.

Index

Tables for
Mathematics of
Investment

Introduction

These tables were compiled for use with the author's Mathematics of Investment, Fifth Edition. However, the tables are so extensive that they provide a reasonable basis for the solution of the typical problems relating to investment theory and accounting as involved in all parts of the curriculum in a college of business administration. In addition to tables for the fundamental functions relating to compound interest and annuities certain, the following tables are included: Both five-place and six-place tables of logarithms, for use on those numerous occasions when some modern type of computer is not available; a few minor tables; certain currently standard actuarial tables of 1958 at 3% interest relating to life annuities and life insurance, for use in the brief introduction to that subject in the text.

In the interest tables, emphasis is placed on small rates to permit convenient solution of problems involving nominal rates payable on a monthly basis. The interest and annuity Tables V–XIV (for the same rates) involve entries for thirty-two interest rates.* In particular, they include eight common monthly rates with the tabulated values extending to 250 periods, to facilitate work with data involving monthly payments. However, no table for student use can be expected to provide entries for all interest rates arising in business practice, particularly in a period of history when interest rates are subject to rapid oscillation. For much more extensive interest tables, the author recommends the *Financial Compound Interest and Annuity Tables*, in its current edition, published by the Financial Publishing Company, Boston, Massachusetts. Also, in business practice, a modern computer must be used when a nonstandard interest rate is met, so that no existing tables apply.

Sources. Tables XVI compiled from current tables of the Society of Actuaries, with its permission. The interest tables for $\frac{3}{8}\%$ and $\frac{5}{8}\%$ were taken (in the fourth edition of these tables), with a moderate reduction in the number of decimal places, from entries in the *Financial Compound Interest and Annuity Tables*, with the permission of its publishers (loc. cit. above). The entries for $3\frac{1}{4}\%$ were obtained in an earlier edition by use of *Die Zusammengesetzte Zinsen and Zeitrenten oder Annuitatenrechnung*, by W. M. J. Werker, published by Bejerf, Utrecht. For all interest rates other than those just mentioned, the original source was *Kent and Kent's Compound Interest and Annuity Tables*, McGraw-Hill Book Company, Publishers, who permitted reproduction (with fewer decimal places) in the third edition of the present tables. Tables X, XI, and XII were computed by the author and checked against various printed tables where similar entries appear.

*The interest and annuity tables are the same as in the Fourth Edition of these tables.

List of Tables

**Compound Interest And
Annuity Tables For The Interest Rates**

$\frac{1}{4}\%$, $\frac{7}{24}\%$, $\frac{1}{3}\%$, $\frac{3}{8}\%$, $\frac{5}{12}\%$, $\frac{1}{2}\%$, $\frac{7}{12}\%$, $\frac{5}{8}\%$, $\frac{3}{4}\%$, $\frac{7}{8}\%$, 1%,
$1\frac{1}{8}\%$, $1\frac{1}{4}\%$, $1\frac{3}{8}\%$, $1\frac{1}{2}\%$, $1\frac{5}{8}\%$, $1\frac{3}{4}\%$, 2%, $2\frac{1}{4}\%$, $2\frac{1}{2}\%$, $2\frac{3}{4}\%$,
3%, $3\frac{1}{4}\%$, $3\frac{1}{2}\%$, 4%, $4\frac{1}{2}\%$, 5%, $5\frac{1}{2}\%$, 6%, $6\frac{1}{2}\%$, 7%, 8%

Selected Actuarial Tables

[1]

N	0	1	2	3	4	5	6	7	8	9
100	00 000	043	087	130	173	217	260	303	346	389
01	432	475	518	561	604	647	689	732	775	817
02	00 860	903	945	988	*030	*072	*115	*157	*199	*242
03	01 284	326	368	410	452	494	536	578	620	662
04	01 703	745	787	828	870	912	953	995	*036	*078
05	02 119	160	202	243	284	325	366	407	449	490
06	531	572	612	653	694	735	776	816	857	898
07	02 938	979	*019	*060	*100	*141	*181	*222	*262	*302
08	03 342	383	423	463	503	543	583	623	663	703
09	03 743	782	822	862	902	941	981	*021	*060	*100
110	04 139	179	218	258	297	336	376	415	454	493
11	532	571	610	650	689	727	766	805	844	883
12	04 922	961	999	*038	*077	*115	*154	*192	*231	*269
13	05 308	346	385	423	461	500	538	576	614	652
14	05 690	729	767	805	843	881	918	956	994	*032
15	06 070	108	145	183	221	258	296	333	371	408
16	446	483	521	558	595	633	670	707	744	781
17	06 819	856	893	930	967	*004	*041	*078	*115	*151
18	07 188	225	262	298	335	372	408	445	482	518
19	555	591	628	664	700	737	773	809	846	882
120	07 918	954	990	*027	*063	*099	*135	*171	*207	*243
21	08 279	314	350	386	422	458	493	529	565	600
22	636	672	707	743	778	814	849	884	920	955
23	08 991	*026	*061	*096	*132	*167	*202	*237	*272	*307
24	09 342	377	412	447	482	517	552	587	621	656
25	09 691	726	760	795	830	864	899	934	968	*003
26	10 037	072	106	140	175	209	243	278	312	346
27	380	415	449	483	517	551	585	619	653	687
28	10 721	755	789	823	857	890	924	958	992	*025
29	11 059	093	126	160	193	227	261	294	327	361
130	394	428	461	494	528	561	594	628	661	694
31	11 727	760	793	826	860	893	926	959	992	*024
32	12 057	090	123	156	189	222	254	287	320	352
33	385	418	450	483	516	548	581	613	646	678
34	12 710	743	775	808	840	872	905	937	969	*001
35	13 033	066	098	130	162	194	226	258	290	322
36	354	386	418	450	481	513	545	577	609	640
37	672	704	735	767	799	830	862	893	925	956
38	13 988	*019	*051	*082	*114	*145	*176	*208	*239	*270
39	14 301	333	364	395	426	457	489	520	551	582
140	613	644	675	706	737	768	799	829	860	891
41	14 922	953	983	*014	*045	*076	*106	*137	*168	*198
42	15 229	259	290	320	351	381	412	442	473	503
43	534	564	594	625	655	685	715	746	776	806
44	15 836	866	897	927	957	987	*017	*047	*077	*107
45	16 137	167	197	227	256	286	316	346	376	406
46	435	465	495	524	554	584	613	643	673	702
47	16 732	761	791	820	850	879	909	938	967	997
48	17 026	056	085	114	143	173	202	231	260	289
49	319	348	377	406	435	464	493	522	551	580
150	17 609	638	667	696	725	754	782	811	840	869
N	0	1	2	3	4	5	6	7	8	9

Prop. Parts

	44	43	42
1	4.4	4.3	4.2
2	8.8	8.6	8.4
3	13.2	12.9	12.6
4	17.6	17.2	16.8
5	22.0	21.5	21.0
6	26.4	25.8	25.2
7	30.8	30.1	29.4
8	35.2	34.4	33.6
9	39.6	38.7	37.8

	41	40	39
1	4.1	4	3.9
2	8.2	8	7.8
3	12.3	12	11.7
4	16.4	16	15.6
5	20.5	20	19.5
6	24.6	24	23.4
7	28.7	28	27.3
8	32.8	32	31.2
9	36.9	36	35.1

	38	37	36
1	3.8	3.7	3.6
2	7.6	7.4	7.2
3	11.4	11.1	10.8
4	15.2	14.8	14.4
5	19.0	18.5	18.0
6	22.8	22.2	21.6
7	26.6	25.9	25.2
8	30.4	29.6	28.8
9	34.2	33.3	32.4

	35	34	33
1	3.5	3.4	3.3
2	7.0	6.8	6.6
3	10.5	10.2	9.9
4	14.0	13.6	13.2
5	17.5	17.0	16.5
6	21.0	20.4	19.8
7	24.5	23.8	23.1
8	28.0	27.2	26.4
9	31.5	30.6	29.7

	32	31	30
1	3.2	3.1	3
2	6.4	6.2	6
3	9.6	9.3	9
4	12.8	12.4	12
5	16.0	15.5	15
6	19.2	18.6	18
7	22.4	21.7	21
8	25.6	24.8	24
9	28.8	27.9	27

Prop. Parts

I. FIVE-PLACE LOGARITHMS: 150—200

Prop. Parts

	29	28
1	2.9	2.8
2	5.8	5.6
3	8.7	8.4
4	11.6	11.2
5	14.5	14.0
6	17.4	16.8
7	20.3	19.6
8	23.2	22.4
9	26.1	25.2

	27	26
1	2.7	2.6
2	5.4	5.2
3	8.1	7.8
4	10.8	10.4
5	13.5	13.0
6	16.2	15.6
7	18.9	18.2
8	21.6	20.8
9	24.3	23.4

	25
1	2.5
2	5.0
3	7.5
4	10.0
5	12.5
6	15.0
7	17.5
8	20.0
9	22.5

	24	23
1	2.4	2.3
2	4.8	4.6
3	7.2	6.9
4	9.6	9.2
5	12.0	11.5
6	14.4	13.8
7	16.8	16.1
8	19.2	18.4
9	21.6	20.7

	22	21
1	2.2	2.1
2	4.4	4.2
3	6.6	6.3
4	8.8	8.4
5	11.0	10.5
6	13.2	12.6
7	15.4	14.7
8	17.6	16.8
9	19.8	18.9

N	0	1	2	3	4	5	6	7	8	9
150	17 609	638	667	696	725	754	782	811	840	869
51	17 898	926	955	984	*013	*041	*070	*099	*127	*156
52	18 184	213	241	270	298	327	355	384	412	441
53	469	498	526	554	583	611	639	667	696	724
54	18 752	780	808	837	865	893	921	949	977	*005
55	19 033	061	089	117	145	173	201	229	257	285
56	312	340	368	396	424	451	479	507	535	562
57	590	618	645	673	700	728	756	783	811	838
58	19 866	893	921	948	976	*003	*030	*058	*085	*112
59	20 140	167	194	222	249	276	303	330	358	385
160	412	439	466	493	520	548	575	602	629	656
61	683	710	737	763	790	817	844	871	898	925
62	20 952	978	*005	*032	*059	*085	*112	*139	*165	*192
63	21 219	245	272	299	325	352	378	405	431	458
64	484	511	537	564	590	617	643	669	696	722
65	21 748	775	801	827	854	880	906	932	958	985
66	22 011	037	063	089	115	141	167	194	220	246
67	272	298	324	350	376	401	427	453	479	505
68	531	557	583	608	634	660	686	712	737	763
69	22 789	814	840	866	891	917	943	968	994	*019
170	23 045	070	096	121	147	172	198	223	249	274
71	300	325	350	376	401	426	452	477	502	528
72	553	578	603	629	654	679	704	729	754	779
73	23 805	830	855	880	905	930	955	980	*005	*030
74	24 055	080	105	130	155	180	204	229	254	279
75	304	329	353	378	403	428	452	477	502	527
76	551	576	601	625	650	674	699	724	748	773
77	24 797	822	846	871	895	920	944	969	993	*018
78	25 042	066	091	115	139	164	188	212	237	261
79	285	310	334	358	382	406	431	455	479	503
180	527	551	575	600	624	648	672	696	720	744
81	25 768	792	816	840	864	888	912	935	959	983
82	26 007	031	055	079	102	126	150	174	198	221
83	245	269	293	316	340	364	387	411	435	458
84	482	505	529	553	576	600	623	647	670	694
85	717	741	764	788	811	834	858	881	905	928
86	26 951	975	998	*021	*045	*068	*091	*114	*138	*161
87	27 184	207	231	254	277	300	323	346	370	393
88	416	439	462	485	508	531	554	577	600	623
89	646	669	692	715	738	761	784	807	830	852
190	27 875	898	921	944	967	989	*012	*035	*058	*081
91	28 103	126	149	171	194	217	240	262	285	307
92	330	353	375	398	421	443	466	488	511	533
93	556	578	601	623	646	668	691	713	735	758
94	28 780	803	825	847	870	892	914	937	959	981
95	29 003	026	048	070	092	115	137	159	181	203
96	226	248	270	292	314	336	358	380	403	425
97	447	469	491	513	535	557	579	601	623	645
98	667	688	710	732	754	776	798	820	842	863
99	29 885	907	929	951	973	994	*016	*038	*060	*081
200	30 103	125	146	168	190	211	233	255	276	298

Prop. Parts

| N | 0 | 1 | 2 | 3 | 4 | 5 | 6 | 7 | 8 | 9 |

N	0	1	2	3	4	5	6	7	8	9
200	30 103	125	146	168	190	211	233	255	276	298
01	320	341	363	384	406	428	449	471	492	514
02	535	557	578	600	621	643	664	685	707	728
03	750	771	792	814	835	856	878	899	920	942
04	30 963	984	*006	*027	*048	*069	*091	*112	*133	*154
05	31 175	197	218	239	260	281	302	323	345	366
06	387	408	429	450	471	492	513	534	555	576
07	597	618	639	660	681	702	723	744	765	785
08	31 806	827	848	869	890	911	931	952	973	994
09	32 015	035	056	077	098	118	139	160	181	201
210	222	243	263	284	305	325	346	366	387	408
11	428	449	469	490	510	531	552	572	593	613
12	634	654	675	695	715	736	756	777	797	818
13	32 838	858	879	899	919	940	960	980	*001	*021
14	33 041	062	082	102	122	143	163	183	203	224
15	244	264	284	304	325	345	365	385	405	425
16	445	465	486	506	526	546	566	586	606	626
17	646	666	686	706	726	746	766	786	806	826
18	33 846	866	885	905	925	945	965	985	*005	*025
19	34 044	064	084	104	124	143	163	183	203	223
220	242	262	282	301	321	341	361	380	400	420
21	439	459	479	498	518	537	557	577	596	616
22	635	655	674	694	713	733	753	772	792	811
23	34 830	850	869	889	908	928	947	967	986	*005
24	35 025	044	064	083	102	122	141	160	180	199
25	218	238	257	276	295	315	334	353	372	392
26	411	430	449	468	488	507	526	545	564	583
27	603	622	641	660	679	698	717	736	755	774
28	793	813	832	851	870	889	908	927	946	965
29	35 984	*003	*021	*040	*059	*078	*097	*116	*135	*154
230	36 173	192	211	229	248	267	286	305	324	342
31	361	380	399	418	436	455	474	493	511	530
32	549	568	586	605	624	642	661	680	698	717
33	736	754	773	791	810	829	847	866	884	903
34	36 922	940	959	977	996	*014	*033	*051	*070	*088
35	37 107	125	144	162	181	199	218	236	254	273
36	291	310	328	346	365	383	401	420	438	457
37	475	493	511	530	548	566	585	603	621	639
38	658	676	694	712	731	749	767	785	803	822
39	37 840	858	876	894	912	931	949	967	985	*003
240	38 021	039	057	075	093	112	130	148	166	184
41	202	220	238	256	274	292	310	328	346	364
42	382	399	417	435	453	471	489	507	525	543
43	561	578	596	614	632	650	668	686	703	721
44	739	757	775	792	810	828	846	863	881	899
45	38 917	934	952	970	987	*005	*023	*041	*058	*076
46	39 094	111	129	146	164	182	199	217	235	252
47	270	287	305	322	340	358	375	393	410	428
48	445	463	480	498	515	533	550	568	585	602
49	620	637	655	672	690	707	724	742	759	777
250	39 794	811	829	846	863	881	898	915	933	950
N	0	1	2	3	4	5	6	7	8	9

Prop. Parts

	22	21
1	2.2	2.1
2	4.4	4.2
3	6.6	6.3
4	8.8	8.4
5	11.0	10.5
6	13.2	12.6
7	15.4	14.7
8	17.6	16.8
9	19.8	18.9

	20
1	2
2	4
3	6
4	8
5	10
6	12
7	14
8	16
9	18

	19
1	1.9
2	3.8
3	5.7
4	7.6
5	9.5
6	11.4
7	13.3
8	15.2
9	17.1

	18
1	1.8
2	3.6
3	5.4
4	7.2
5	9.0
6	10.8
7	12.6
8	14.4
9	16.2

	17
1	1.7
2	3.4
3	5.1
4	6.8
5	8.5
6	10.2
7	11.9
8	13.6
9	15.3

Prop. Parts

N	0	1	2	3	4	5	6	7	8	9
250	39 794	811	829	846	863	881	898	915	933	950
51	39 967	985	*002	*019	*037	*054	*071	*088	*106	*123
52	40 140	157	175	192	209	226	243	261	278	295
53	312	329	346	364	381	398	415	432	449	466
54	483	500	518	535	552	569	586	603	620	637
55	654	671	688	705	722	739	756	773	790	807
56	824	841	858	875	892	909	926	943	960	976
57	40 993	*010	*027	*044	*061	*078	*095	*111	*128	*145
58	41 162	179	196	212	229	246	263	280	296	313
59	330	347	363	380	397	414	430	447	464	481
260	497	514	531	547	564	581	597	614	631	647
61	664	681	697	714	731	747	764	780	797	814
62	830	847	863	880	896	913	929	946	963	979
63	41 996	*012	*029	*045	*062	*078	*095	*111	*127	*144
64	42 160	177	193	210	226	243	259	275	292	308
65	325	341	357	374	390	406	423	439	455	472
66	488	504	521	537	553	570	586	602	619	635
67	651	667	684	700	716	732	749	765	781	797
68	813	830	846	862	878	894	911	927	943	959
69	42 975	991	*008	*024	*040	*056	*072	*088	*104	*120
270	43 136	152	169	185	201	217	233	249	265	281
71	297	313	329	345	361	377	393	409	425	441
72	457	473	489	505	521	537	553	569	584	600
73	616	632	648	664	680	696	712	727	743	759
74	775	791	807	823	838	854	870	886	902	917
75	43 933	949	965	981	996	*012	*028	*044	*059	*075
76	44 091	107	122	138	154	170	185	201	217	232
77	248	264	279	295	311	326	342	358	373	389
78	404	420	436	451	467	483	498	514	529	545
79	560	576	592	607	623	638	654	669	685	700
280	716	731	747	762	778	793	809	824	840	855
81	44 871	886	902	917	932	948	963	979	994	*010
82	45 025	040	056	071	086	102	117	133	148	163
83	179	194	209	225	240	255	271	286	301	317
84	332	347	362	378	393	408	423	439	454	469
85	484	500	515	530	545	561	576	591	606	621
86	637	652	667	682	697	712	728	743	758	773
87	788	803	818	834	849	864	879	894	909	924
88	45 939	954	969	984	*000	*015	*030	*045	*060	*075
89	46 090	105	120	135	150	165	180	195	210	225
290	240	255	270	285	300	315	330	345	359	374
91	389	404	419	434	449	464	479	494	509	523
92	538	553	568	583	598	613	627	642	657	672
93	687	702	716	731	746	761	776	790	805	820
94	835	850	864	879	894	909	923	938	953	967
95	46 982	997	*012	*026	*041	*056	*070	*085	*100	*114
96	47 129	144	159	173	188	202	217	232	246	261
97	276	290	305	319	334	349	363	378	392	407
98	422	436	451	465	480	494	509	524	538	553
99	567	582	596	611	625	640	654	669	683	698
300	47 712	727	741	756	770	784	799	813	828	842

Prop. Parts

18	
1	1.8
2	3.6
3	5.4
4	7.2
5	9.0
6	10.8
7	12.6
8	14.4
9	16.2

17	
1	1.7
2	3.4
3	5.1
4	6.8
5	8.5
6	10.2
7	11.9
8	13.6
9	15.3

16	
1	1.6
2	3.2
3	4.8
4	6.4
5	8.0
6	9.6
7	11.2
8	12.8
9	14.4

15	
1	1.5
2	3.0
3	4.5
4	6.0
5	7.5
6	9.0
7	10.5
8	12.0
9	13.5

14	
1	1.4
2	2.8
3	4.2
4	5.6
5	7.0
6	8.4
7	9.8
8	11.2
9	12.6

N	0	1	2	3	4	5	6	7	8	9
300	47 712	727	741	756	770	784	799	813	828	842
01	47 857	871	885	900	914	929	943	958	972	986
02	48 001	015	029	044	058	073	087	101	116	130
03	144	159	173	187	202	216	230	244	259	273
04	287	302	316	330	344	359	373	387	401	416
05	430	444	458	473	487	501	515	530	544	558
06	572	586	601	615	629	643	657	671	686	700
07	714	728	742	756	770	785	799	813	827	841
08	855	869	883	897	911	926	940	954	968	982
09	48 996	*010	*024	*038	*052	*066	*080	*094	*108	*122
310	49 136	150	164	178	192	206	220	234	248	262
11	276	290	304	318	332	346	360	374	388	402
12	415	429	443	457	471	485	499	513	527	541
13	554	568	582	596	610	624	638	651	665	679
14	693	707	721	734	748	762	776	790	803	817
15	831	845	859	872	886	900	914	927	941	955
16	49 969	982	996	*010	*024	*037	*051	*065	*079	*092
17	50 106	120	133	147	161	174	188	202	215	229
18	243	256	270	284	297	311	325	338	352	365
19	379	393	406	420	433	447	461	474	488	501
320	515	529	542	556	569	583	596	610	623	637
21	651	664	678	691	705	718	732	745	759	772
22	786	799	813	826	840	853	866	880	893	907
23	50 920	934	947	961	974	987	*001	*014	*028	*041
24	51 055	068	081	095	108	121	135	148	162	175
25	188	202	215	228	242	255	268	282	295	308
26	322	335	348	362	375	388	402	415	428	441
27	455	468	481	495	508	521	534	548	561	574
28	587	601	614	627	640	654	667	680	693	706
29	720	733	746	759	772	786	799	812	825	838
330	851	865	878	891	904	917	930	943	957	970
31	51 983	996	*009	*022	*035	*048	*061	*075	*088	*101
32	52 114	127	140	153	166	179	192	205	218	231
33	244	257	270	284	297	310	323	336	349	362
34	375	388	401	414	427	440	453	466	479	492
35	504	517	530	543	556	569	582	595	608	621
36	634	647	660	673	686	699	711	724	737	750
37	763	776	789	802	815	827	840	853	866	879
38	52 892	905	917	930	943	956	969	982	994	*007
39	53 020	033	046	058	071	084	097	110	122	135
340	148	161	173	186	199	212	224	237	250	263
41	275	288	301	314	326	339	352	364	377	390
42	403	415	428	441	453	466	479	491	504	517
43	529	542	555	567	580	593	605	618	631	643
44	656	668	681	694	706	719	732	744	757	769
45	782	794	807	820	832	845	857	870	882	895
46	53 908	920	933	945	958	970	983	995	*008	*020
47	54 033	045	058	070	083	095	108	120	133	145
48	158	170	183	195	208	220	233	245	258	270
49	283	295	307	320	332	345	357	370	382	394
350	54 407	419	432	444	456	469	481	494	506	518
N	0	1	2	3	4	5	6	7	8	9

Prop. Parts

	15		14		13		12
1	1.5	1	1.4	1	1.3	1	1.2
2	3.0	2	2.8	2	2.6	2	2.4
3	4.5	3	4.2	3	3.9	3	3.6
4	6.0	4	5.6	4	5.2	4	4.8
5	7.5	5	7.0	5	6.5	5	6.0
6	9.0	6	8.4	6	7.8	6	7.2
7	10.5	7	9.8	7	9.1	7	8.4
8	12.0	8	11.2	8	10.4	8	9.6
9	13.5	9	12.6	9	11.7	9	10.8

N	0	1	2	3	4	5	6	7	8	9
350	54 407	419	432	444	456	469	481	494	506	518
51	531	543	555	568	580	593	605	617	630	642
52	654	667	679	691	704	716	728	741	753	765
53	777	790	802	814	827	839	851	864	876	888
54	54 900	913	925	937	949	962	974	986	998	*011
55	55 023	035	047	060	072	084	096	108	121	133
56	145	157	169	182	194	206	218	230	242	255
57	267	279	291	303	315	328	340	352	364	376
58	388	400	413	425	437	449	461	473	485	497
59	509	522	534	546	558	570	582	594	606	618
360	630	642	654	666	678	691	703	715	727	739
61	751	763	775	787	799	811	823	835	847	859
62	871	883	895	907	919	931	943	955	967	979
63	55 991	*003	*015	*027	*038	*050	*062	*074	*086	*098
64	56 110	122	134	146	158	170	182	194	205	217
65	229	241	253	265	277	289	301	312	324	336
66	348	360	372	384	396	407	419	431	443	455
67	467	478	490	502	514	526	538	549	561	573
68	585	597	608	620	632	644	656	667	679	691
69	703	714	726	738	750	761	773	785	797	808
370	820	832	844	855	867	879	891	902	914	926
71	56 937	949	961	972	984	996	*008	*019	*031	*043
72	57 054	066	078	089	101	113	124	136	148	159
73	171	183	194	206	217	229	241	252	264	276
74	287	299	310	322	334	345	357	368	380	392
75	403	415	426	438	449	461	473	484	496	507
76	519	530	542	553	565	576	588	600	611	623
77	634	646	657	669	680	692	703	715	726	738
78	749	761	772	784	795	807	818	830	841	852
79	864	875	887	898	910	921	933	944	955	967
380	57 978	990	*001	*013	*024	*035	*047	*058	*070	*081
81	58 092	104	115	127	138	149	161	172	184	195
82	206	218	229	240	252	263	274	286	297	309
83	320	331	343	354	365	377	388	399	410	422
84	433	444	456	467	478	490	501	512	524	535
85	546	557	569	580	591	602	614	625	636	647
86	659	670	681	692	704	715	726	737	749	760
87	771	782	794	805	816	827	838	850	861	872
88	883	894	906	917	928	939	950	961	973	984
89	58 995	*006	*017	*028	*040	*051	*062	*073	*084	*095
390	59 106	118	129	140	151	162	173	184	195	207
91	218	229	240	251	262	273	284	295	306	318
92	329	340	351	362	373	384	395	406	417	428
93	439	450	461	472	483	494	506	517	528	539
94	550	561	572	583	594	605	616	627	638	649
95	660	671	682	693	704	715	726	737	748	759
96	770	780	791	802	813	824	835	846	857	868
97	879	890	901	912	923	934	945	956	966	977
98	59 988	999	*010	*021	*032	*043	*054	*065	*076	*086
99	60 097	108	119	130	141	152	163	173	184	195
400	60 206	217	228	239	249	260	271	282	293	304

Prop. Parts

	13		12		11		10
1	1.3	1	1.2	1	1.1	1	1.0
2	2.6	2	2.4	2	2.2	2	2.0
3	3.9	3	3.6	3	3.3	3	3.0
4	5.2	4	4.8	4	4.4	4	4.0
5	6.5	5	6.0	5	5.5	5	5.0
6	7.8	6	7.2	6	6.6	6	6.0
7	9.1	7	8.4	7	7.7	7	7.0
8	10.4	8	9.6	8	8.8	8	8.0
9	11.7	9	10.8	9	9.9	9	9.0

N	0	1	2	3	4	5	6	7	8	9	Prop. Parts	
400	60 206	217	228	239	249	260	271	282	293	304		
01	314	325	336	347	358	369	379	390	401	412		
02	423	433	444	455	466	477	487	498	509	520		
03	531	541	552	563	574	584	595	606	617	627		
04	638	649	660	670	681	692	703	713	724	735		
05	746	756	767	778	788	799	810	821	831	842		
06	853	863	874	885	895	906	917	927	938	949		**11**
07	60 959	970	981	991	*002	*013	*023	*034	*045	*055	1	1.1
08	61 066	077	087	098	109	119	130	140	151	162	2	2.2
09	172	183	194	204	215	225	236	247	257	268	3	3.3
410	278	289	300	310	321	331	342	352	363	374	4	4.4
11	384	395	405	416	426	437	448	458	469	479	5	5.5
12	490	500	511	521	532	542	553	563	574	584	6	6.6
13	595	606	616	627	637	648	658	669	679	690	7	7.7
14	700	711	721	731	742	752	763	773	784	794	8	8.8
15	805	815	826	836	847	857	868	878	888	899	9	9.9
16	61 909	920	930	941	951	962	972	982	993	*003		
17	62 014	024	034	045	055	066	076	086	097	107		
18	118	128	138	149	159	170	180	190	201	211		
19	221	232	242	252	263	273	284	294	304	315		
420	325	335	346	356	366	377	387	397	408	418		
21	428	439	449	459	469	480	490	500	511	521		**10**
22	531	542	552	562	572	583	593	603	613	624	1	1.0
23	634	644	655	665	675	685	696	706	716	726	2	2.0
24	737	747	757	767	778	788	798	808	818	829	3	3.0
25	839	849	859	870	880	890	900	910	921	931	4	4.0
26	62 941	951	961	972	982	992	*002	*012	*022	*033	5	5.0
27	63 043	053	063	073	083	094	104	114	124	134	6	6.0
28	144	155	165	175	185	195	205	215	225	236	7	7.0
29	246	256	266	276	286	296	306	317	327	337	8	8.0
430	347·	357	367	377	387	397	407	417	428	438	9	9.0
31	448	458	468	478	488	498	508	518	528	538		
32	548	558	568	579	589	599	609	619	629	639		
33	649	659	669	679	689	699	709	719	729	739		
34	749	759	769	779	789	799	809	819	829	839		
35	849	859	869	879	889	899	909	919	929	939		
36	63 949	959	969	979	988	998	*008	*018	*028	*038		**9**
37	64 048	058	068	078	088	098	108	118	128	137	1	0.9
38	147	157	167	177	187	197	207	217	227	237	2	1.8
39	246	256	266	276	286	296	306	316	326	335	3	2.7
440	345	355	365	375	385	395	404	414	424	434	4	3.6
41	444	454	464	473	483	493	503	513	523	532	5	4.5
42	542	552	562	572	582	591	601	611	621	631	6	5.4
43	640	650	660	670	680	689	699	709	719	729	7	6.3
44	738	748	758	768	777	787	797	807	816	826	8	7.2
45	836	846	856	865	875	885	895	904	914	924	9	8.1
46	64 933	943	953	963	972	982	992	*002	*011	*021		
47	65 031	040	050	060	070	079	089	099	108	118		
48	128	137	147	157	167	176	186	196	205	215		
49	225	234	244	254	263	273	283	292	302	312		
450	65 321	331	341	350	360	369	379	389	398	408		
N	0	1	2	3	4	5	6	7	8	9	Prop. Parts	

Prop. Parts	N	0	1	2	3	4	5	6	7	8	9
	450	65 321	331	341	350	360	369	379	389	398	408
	51	418	427	437	447	456	466	475	485	495	504
	52	514	523	533	543	552	562	571	581	591	600
	53	610	619	629	639	648	658	667	677	686	696
	54	706	715	725	734	744	753	763	772	782	792
	55	801	811	820	830	839	849	858	868	877	887
	56	896	906	916	925	935	944	954	963	973	982
	57	65 992	*001	*011	*020	*030	*039	*049	*058	*068	*077
	58	66 087	096	106	115	124	134	143	153	162	172
	59	181	191	200	210	219	229	238	247	257	266
	460	276	285	295	304	314	323	332	342	351	361
	61	370	380	389	398	408	417	427	436	445	455
	62	464	474	483	492	502	511	521	530	539	549
	63	558	567	577	586	596	605	614	624	633	642
	64	652	661	671	680	689	699	708	717	727	736
	65	745	755	764	773	783	792	801	811	820	829
	66	839	848	857	867	876	885	894	904	913	922
	67	66 932	941	950	960	969	978	987	997	*006	*015
	68	67 025	034	043	052	062	071	080	089	099	108
	69	117	127	136	145	154	164	173	182	191	201
	470	210	219	228	237	247	256	265	274	284	293
	71	302	311	321	330	339	348	357	367	376	385
	72	394	403	413	422	431	440	449	459	468	477
	73	486	495	504	514	523	532	541	550	560	569
	74	578	587	596	605	614	624	633	642	651	660
	75	669	679	688	697	706	715	724	733	742	752
	76	761	770	779	788	797	806	815	825	834	843
	77	852	861	870	879	888	897	906	916	925	934
	78	67 943	952	961	970	979	988	997	*006	*015	*024
	79	68 034	043	052	061	070	079	088	097	106	115
	480	124	133	142	151	160	169	178	187	196	205
	81	215	224	233	242	251	260	269	278	287	296
	82	305	314	323	332	341	350	359	368	377	386
	83	395	404	413	422	431	440	449	458	467	476
	84	485	494	502	511	520	529	538	547	556	565
	85	574	583	592	601	610	619	628	637	646	655
	86	664	673	681	690	699	708	717	726	735	744
	87	753	762	771	780	789	797	806	815	824	833
	88	842	851	860	869	878	886	895	904	913	922
	89	68 931	940	949	958	966	975	984	993	*002	*011
	490	69 020	028	037	046	055	064	073	082	090	099
	91	108	117	126	135	144	152	161	170	179	188
	92	197	205	214	223	232	241	249	258	267	276
	93	285	294	302	311	320	329	338	346	355	364
	94	373	381	390	399	408	417	425	434	443	452
	95	461	469	478	487	496	504	513	522	531	539
	96	548	557	566	574	583	592	601	609	618	627
	97	636	644	653	662	671	679	688	697	705	714
	98	723	732	740	749	758	767	775	784	793	801
	99	810	819	827	836	845	854	862	871	880	888
	500	69 897	906	914	923	932	940	949	958	966	975
Prop. Parts	N	0	1	2	3	4	5	6	7	8	9

Prop. Parts

	10
1	1.0
2	2.0
3	3.0
4	4.0
5	5.0
6	6.0
7	7.0
8	8.0
9	9.0

	9
1	0.9
2	1.8
3	2.7
4	3.6
5	4.5
6	5.4
7	6.3
8	7.2
9	8.1

	8
1	0.8
2	1.6
3	2.4
4	3.2
5	4.0
6	4.8
7	5.6
8	6.4
9	7.2

N	0	1	2	3	4	5	6	7	8	9
500	69 897	906	914	923	932	940	949	958	966	975
01	69 984	992	*001	*010	*018	*027	*036	*044	*053	*062
02	70 070	079	088	096	105	114	122	131	140	148
03	157	165	174	183	191	200	209	217	226	234
04	243	252	260	269	278	286	295	303	312	321
05	329	338	346	355	364	372	381	389	398	406
06	415	424	432	441	449	458	467	475	484	492
07	501	509	518	526	535	544	552	561	569	578
08	586	595	603	612	621	629	638	646	655	663
09	672	680	689	697	706	714	723	731	740	749
510	757	766	774	783	791	800	808	817	825	834
11	842	851	859	868	876	885	893	902	910	919
12	70 927	935	944	952	961	969	978	986	995	*003
13	71 012	020	029	037	046	054	063	071	079	088
14	096	105	113	122	130	139	147	155	164	172
15	181	189	198	206	214	223	231	240	248	257
16	265	273	282	290	299	307	315	324	332	341
17	349	357	366	374	383	391	399	408	416	425
18	433	441	450	458	466	475	483	492	500	508
19	517	525	533	542	550	559	567	575	584	592
520	600	609	617	625	634	642	650	659	667	675
21	684	692	700	709	717	725	734	742	750	759
22	767	775	784	792	800	809	817	825	834	842
23	850	858	867	875	883	892	900	908	917	925
24	71 933	941	950	958	966	975	983	991	999	*008
25	72 016	024	032	041	049	057	066	074	082	090
26	099	107	115	123	132	140	148	156	165	173
27	181	189	198	206	214	222	230	239	247	255
28	263	272	280	288	296	304	313	321	329	337
29	346	354	362	370	378	387	395	403	411	419
530	428	436	444	452	460	469	477	485	493	501
31	509	518	526	534	542	550	558	567	575	583
32	591	599	607	616	624	632	640	648	656	665
33	673	681	689	697	705	713	722	730	738	746
34	754	762	770	779	787	795	803	811	819	827
35	835	843	852	860	868	876	884	892	900	908
36	916	925	933	941	949	957	965	973	981	989
37	72 997	*006	*014	*022	*030	*038	*046	*054	*062	*070
38	73 078	086	094	102	111	119	127	135	143	151
39	159	167	175	183	191	199	207	215	223	231
540	239	247	255	263	272	280	288	296	304	312
41	320	328	336	344	352	360	368	376	384	392
42	400	408	416	424	432	440	448	456	464	472
43	480	488	496	504	512	520	528	536	544	552
44	560	568	576	584	592	600	608	616	624	632
45	640	648	656	664	672	679	687	695	703	711
46	719	727	735	743	751	759	767	775	783	791
47	799	807	815	823	830	838	846	854	862	870
48	878	886	894	902	910	918	926	933	941	949
49	73 957	965	973	981	989	997	*005	*013	*020	*028
550	74 036	044	052	060	068	076	084	092	099	107
N	0	1	2	3	4	5	6	7	8	9

Prop. Parts

	9
1	0.9
2	1.8
3	2.7
4	3.6
5	4.5
6	5.4
7	6.3
8	7.2
9	8.1

	8
1	0.8
2	1.6
3	2.4
4	3.2
5	4.0
6	4.8
7	5.6
8	6.4
9	7.2

	7
1	0.7
2	1.4
3	2.1
4	2.8
5	3.5
6	4.2
7	4.9
8	5.6
9	6.3

I. FIVE-PLACE LOGARITHMS: 550—600

N	0	1	2	3	4	5	6	7	8	9
550	74 036	044	052	060	068	076	084	092	099	107
51	115	123	131	139	147	155	162	170	178	186
52	194	202	210	218	225	233	241	249	257	265
53	273	280	288	296	304	312	320	327	335	343
54	351	359	367	374	382	390	398	406	414	421
55	429	437	445	453	461	468	476	484	492	500
56	507	515	523	531	539	547	554	562	570	578
57	586	593	601	609	617	624	632	640	648	656
58	663	671	679	687	695	702	710	718	726	733
59	741	749	757	764	772	780	788	796	803	811
560	819	827	834	842	850	858	865	873	881	889
61	896	904	912	920	927	935	943	950	958	966
62	74 974	981	989	997	*005	*012	*020	*028	*035	*043
63	75 051	059	066	074	082	089	097	105	113	120
64	128	136	143	151	159	166	174	182	189	197
65	205	213	220	228	236	243	251	259	266	274
66	282	289	297	305	312	320	328	335	343	351
67	358	366	374	381	389	397	404	412	420	427
68	435	442	450	458	465	473	481	488	496	504
69	511	519	526	534	542	549	557	565	572	580
570	587	595	603	610	618	626	633	641	648	656
71	664	671	679	686	694	702	709	717	724	732
72	740	747	755	762	770	778	785	793	800	808
73	815	823	831	838	846	853	861	868	876	884
74	891	899	906	914	921	929	937	944	952	959
75	75 967	974	982	989	997	*005	*012	*020	*027	*035
76	76 042	050	057	065	072	080	087	095	103	110
77	118	125	133	140	148	155	163	170	178	185
78	193	200	208	215	223	230	238	245	253	260
79	268	275	283	290	298	305	313	320	328	335
580	343	350	358	365	373	380	388	395	403	410
81	418	425	433	440	448	455	462	470	477	485
82	492	500	507	515	522	530	537	545	552	559
83	567	574	582	589	597	604	612	619	626	634
84	641	649	656	664	671	678	686	693	701	708
85	716	723	730	738	745	753	760	768	775	782
86	790	797	805	812	819	827	834	842	849	856
87	864	871	879	886	893	901	908	916	923	930
88	76 938	945	953	960	967	975	982	989	997	*004
89	77 012	019	026	034	041	048	056	063	070	078
590	085	093	100	107	115	122	129	137	144	151
91	159	166	173	181	188	195	203	210	217	225
92	232	240	247	254	262	269	276	283	291	298
93	305	313	320	327	335	342	349	357	364	371
94	379	386	393	401	408	415	422	430	437	444
95	452	459	466	474	481	488	495	503	510	517
96	525	532	539	546	554	561	568	576	583	590
97	597	605	612	619	627	634	641	648	656	663
98	670	677	685	692	699	706	714	721	728	735
99	743	750	757	764	772	779	786	793	801	808
600	77 815	822	830	837	844	851	859	866	873	880

Prop. Parts

8	
1	0.8
2	1.6
3	2.4
4	3.2
5	4.0
6	4.8
7	5.6
8	6.4
9	7.2

7	
1	0.7
2	1.4
3	2.1
4	2.8
5	3.5
6	4.2
7	4.9
8	5.6
9	6.3

N	0	1	2	3	4	5	6	7	8	9
600	77 815	822	830	837	844	851	859	866	873	880
01	887	895	902	909	916	924	931	938	945	952
02	77 960	967	974	981	988	996	*003	*010	*017	*025
03	78 032	039	046	053	061	068	075	082	089	097
04	104	111	118	125	132	140	147	154	161	168
05	176	183	190	197	204	211	219	226	233	240
06	247	254	262	269	276	283	290	297	305	312
07	319	326	333	340	347	355	362	369	376	383
08	390	398	405	412	419	426	433	440	447	455
09	462	469	476	483	490	497	504	512	519	526
610	533	540	547	554	561	569	576	583	590	597
11	604	611	618	625	633	640	647	654	661	668
12	675	682	689	696	704	711	718	725	732	739
13	746	753	760	767	774	781	789	796	803	810
14	817	824	831	838	845	852	859	866	873	880
15	888	895	902	909	916	923	930	937	944	951
16	78 958	965	972	979	986	993	*000	*007	*014	*021
17	79 029	036	043	050	057	064	071	078	085	092
18	099	106	113	120	127	134	141	148	155	162
19	169	176	183	190	197	204	211	218	225	232
620	239	246	253	260	267	274	281	288	295	302
21	309	316	323	330	337	344	351	358	365	372
22	379	386	393	400	407	414	421	428	435	442
23	449	456	463	470	477	484	491	498	505	511
24	518	525	532	539	546	553	560	567	574	581
25	588	595	602	609	616	623	630	637	644	650
26	657	664	671	678	685	692	699	706	713	720
27	727	734	741	748	754	761	768	775	782	789
28	796	803	810	817	824	831	837	844	851	858
29	865	872	879	886	893	900	906	913	920	927
630	79 934	941	948	955	962	969	975	982	989	996
31	80 003	010	017	024	030	037	044	051	058	065
32	072	079	085	092	099	106	113	120	127	134
33	140	147	154	161	168	175	182	188	195	202
34	209	216	223	229	236	243	250	257	264	271
35	277	284	291	298	305	312	318	325	332	339
36	346	353	359	366	373	380	387	393	400	407
37	414	421	428	434	441	448	455	462	468	475
38	482	489	496	502	509	516	523	530	536	543
39	550	557	564	570	577	584	591	598	604	611
640	618	625	632	638	645	652	659	665	672	679
41	686	693	699	706	713	720	726	733	740	747
42	754	760	767	774	781	787	794	801	808	814
43	821	828	835	841	848	855	862	868	875	882
44	889	895	902	909	916	922	929	936	943	949
45	80 956	963	969	976	983	990	996	*003	*010	*017
46	81 023	030	037	043	050	057	064	070	077	084
47	090	097	104	111	117	124	131	137	144	151
48	158	164	171	178	184	191	198	204	211	218
49	224	231	238	245	251	258	265	271	278	285
650	81 291	298	305	311	318	325	331	338	345	351
N	0	1	2	3	4	5	6	7	8	9

Prop. Parts

	8
1	0.8
2	1.6
3	2.4
4	3.2
5	4.0
6	4.8
7	5 6
8	6.4
9	7.2

	7
1	0.7
2	1.4
3	2.1
4	2.8
5	3.5
6	4.2
7	4.9
8	5.6
9	6.3

	6
1	0.6
2	1.2
3	1.8
4	2.4
5	3.0
6	3.6
7	4.2
8	4.8
9	5.4

Prop. Parts

7

1	0.7
2	1.4
3	2.1
4	2.8
5	3.5
6	4.2
7	4.9
8	5.6
9	6.3

6

1	0.6
2	1.2
3	1.8
4	2.4
5	3.0
6	3.6
7	4.2
8	4.8
9	5.4

N	0	1	2	3	4	5	6	7	8	9
650	81 291	298	305	311	318	325	331	338	345	351
51	358	365	371	378	385	391	398	405	411	418
52	425	431	438	445	451	458	465	471	478	485
53	491	498	505	511	518	525	531	538	544	551
54	558	564	571	578	584	591	598	604	611	617
55	624	631	637	644	651	657	664	671	677	684
56	690	697	704	710	717	723	730	737	743	750
57	757	763	770	776	783	790	796	803	809	816
58	823	829	836	842	849	856	862	869	875	882
59	889	895	.902	908	915	921	928	935	941	948
660	81 954	961	968	974	981	987	994	*000	*007	*014
61	82 020	027	033	040	046	053	060	066	073	079
62	086	092	099	105	112	119	125	132	138	145
63	151	158	164	171	178	184	191	197	204	210
64	217	223	230	236	243	249	256	263	269	276
65	282	289	295	302	308	315	321	328	334	341
66	347	354	360	367	373	380	387	393	400	406
67	413	419	426	432	439	445	452	458	465	471
68	478	484	491	497	504	510	517	523	530	536
69	543	549	556	562	569	575	582	588	595	601
670	607	614	620	627	633	640	646	653	659	666
71	672	679	685	692	698	705	711	718	724	730
72	737	743	750	756	763	769	776	782	789	795
73	802	808	814	821	827	834	840	847	853	860
74	866	872	879	885	892	898	905	911	918	924
75	930	937	943	950	956	963	969	975	982	988
76	82 995	*001	*008	*014	*020	*027	*033	*040	*046	*052
77	83 059	065	072	078	085	091	097	104	110	117
78	123	129	136	142	149	155	161	168	174	181
79	187	193	200	206	213	219	225	232	238	245
680	251	257	264	270	276	283	289	296	302	308
81	315	321	327	334	340	347	353	359	366	372
82	378	385	391	398	404	410	417	423	429	436
83	442	448	455	461	467	474	480	487	493	499
84	506	512	518	525	531	537	544	550	556	563
85	569	575	582	588	594	601	607	613	620	626
86	632	639	645	651	658	664	670	677	683	689
87	696	702	708	715	721	727	734	740	746	753
88	759	765	771	778	784	790	797	803	809	816
89	822	828	835	841	847	853	860	866	872	879
690	885	891	897	904	910	916	923	929	935	942
91	83 948	954	960	967	973	979	985	992	998	*004
92	84 011	017	023	029	036	042	048	055	061	067
93	073	080	086	092	098	105	111	117	123	130
94	136	142	148	155	161	167	173	180	186	192
95	198	205	211	217	223	230	236	242	248	255
96	261	267	273	280	286	292	298	305	311	317
97	323	330	336	342	348	354	361	367	373	379
98	386	392	398	404	410	417	423	429	435	442
99	448	454	460	466	473	479	485	491	497	504
700	84 510	516	522	528	535	541	547	553	559	566

Prop. Parts	N	0	1	2	3	4	5	6	7	8	9

N	0	1	2	3	4	5	6	7	8	9
700	84 510	516	522	528	535	541	547	553	559	566
01	572	578	584	590	597	603	609	615	621	628
02	634	640	646	652	658	665	671	677	683	689
03	696	702	708	714	720	726	733	739	745	751
04	757	763	770	776	782	788	794	800	807	813
05	819	825	831	837	844	850	856	862	868	874
06	880	887	893	899	905	911	917	924	930	936
07	84 942	948	954	960	967	973	979	985	991	997
08	85 003	009	016	022	028	034	040	046	052	058
09	065	071	077	083	089	095	101	107	114	120
710	126	132	138	144	150	156	163	169	175	181
11	187	193	199	205	211	217	224	230	236	242
12	248	254	260	266	272	278	285	291	297	303
13	309	315	321	327	333	339	345	352	358	364
14	370	376	382	388	394	400	406	412	418	425
15	431	437	443	449	455	461	467	473	479	485
16	491	497	503	509	516	522	528	534	540	546
17	552	558	564	570	576	582	588	594	600	606
18	612	618	625	631	637	643	649	655	661	667
19	673	679	685	691	697	703	709	715	721	727
720	733	739	745	751	757	763	769	775	781	788
21	794	800	806	812	818	824	830	836	842	848
22	854	860	866	872	878	884	890	896	902	908
23	914	920	926	932	938	944	950	956	962	968
24	85 974	980	986	992	998	*004	*010	*016	*022	*028
25	86 034	040	046	052	058	064	070	076	082	088
26	094	100	106	112	118	124	130	136	141	147
27	153	159	165	171	177	183	189	195	201	207
28	213	219	225	231	237	243	249	255	261	267
29	273	279	285	291	297	303	308	314	320	326
730	332	338	344	350	356	362	368	374	380	386
31	392	398	404	410	415	421	427	433	439	445
32	451	457	463	469	475	481	487	493	499	504
33	510	516	522	528	534	540	546	552	558	564
34	570	576	581	587	593	599	605	611	617	623
35	629	635	641	646	652	658	664	670	676	682
36	688	694	700	705	711	717	723	729	735	741
37	747	753	759	764	770	776	782	788	794	800
38	806	812	817	823	829	835	841	847	853	859
39	864	870	876	882	888	894	900	906	911	917
740	923	929	935	941	947	953	958	964	970	976
41	86 982	988	994	999	*005	*011	*017	*023	*029	*035
42	87 040	046	052	058	064	070	075	081	087	093
43	099	105	111	116	122	128	134	140	146	151
44	157	163	169	175	181	186	192	198	204	210
45	216	221	227	233	239	245	251	256	262	268
46	274	280	286	291	297	303	309	315	320	326
47	332	338	344	349	355	361	367	373	379	384
48	390	396	402	408	413	419	425	431	437	442
49	448	454	460	466	471	477	483	489	495	500
750	87 506	512	518	523	529	535	541	547	552	558
N	0	1	2	3	4	5	6	7	8	9

Prop. Parts

	7
1	0.7
2	1.4
3	2.1
4	2.8
5	3.5
6	4.2
7	4.9
8	5.6
9	6.3

	6
1	0.6
2	1.2
3	1.8
4	2.4
5	3.0
6	3.6
7	4.2
8	4.8
9	5.4

	5
1	0.5
2	1.0
3	1.5
4	2.0
5	2.5
6	3.0
7	3.5
8	4.0
9	4.5

Prop. Parts	N	0	1	2	3	4	5	6	7	8	9
	750	87 506	512	518	523	529	535	541	547	552	558
	51	564	570	576	581	587	593	599	604	610	616
	52	622	628	633	639	645	651	656	662	668	674
	53	679	685	691	697	703	708	714	720	726	731
	54	737	743	749	754	760	766	772	777	783	789
	55	795	800	806	812	818	823	829	835	841	846
	56	852	858	864	869	875	881	887	892	898	904
	57	910	915	921	927	933	938	944	950	955	961
	58	87 967	973	978	984	990	996	*001	*007	*013	*018
	59	88 024	030	036	041	047	053	058	064	070	076
	760	081	087	093	098	104	110	116	121	127	133
	61	138	144	150	156	161	167	173	178	184	190
6	62	195	201	207	213	218	224	230	235	241	247
1 0.6	63	252	258	264	270	275	281	287	292	298	304
2 1.2	64	309	315	321	326	332	338	343	349	355	360
3 1.8	**65**	366	372	377	383	389	395	400	406	412	417
4 2.4	66	423	429	434	440	446	451	457	463	468	474
5 3.0	67	480	485	491	497	502	508	513	519	525	530
6 3.6	68	536	542	547	553	559	564	570	576	581	587
7 4.2	69	593	598	604	610	615	621	627	632	638	643
8 4.8	**770**	649	655	660	666	672	677	683	689	694	700
9 5.4	71	705	711	717	722	728	734	739	745	750	756
	72	762	767	773	779	784	790	795	801	807	812
	73	818	824	829	835	840	846	852	857	863	868
	74	874	880	885	891	897	902	908	913	919	925
	75	930	936	941	947	953	958	964	969	975	981
	76	88 986	992	997	*003	*009	*014	*020	*025	*031	*037
	77	89 042	048	053	059	064	070	076	081	087	092
	78	098	104	109	115	120	126	131	137	143	148
	79	154	159	165	170	176	182	187	193	198	204
	780	209	215	221	226	232	237	243	248	254	260
	81	265	271	276	282	287	293	298	304	310	315
5	82	321	326	332	337	343	348	354	360	365	371
1 0.5	83	376	382	387	393	398	404	409	415	421	426
2 1.0	84	432	437	443	448	454	459	465	470	476	481
3 1.5	**85**	487	492	498	504	509	515	520	526	531	537
4 2.0	86	542	548	553	559	564	570	575	581	586	592
5 2.5	87	597	603	609	614	620	625	631	636	642	647
6 3.0	88	653	658	664	669	675	680	686	691	697	702
7 3.5	89	708	713	719	724	730	735	741	746	752	757
8 4.0	**790**	763	768	774	779	785	790	796	801	807	812
9 4.5	91	818	823	829	834	840	845	851	856	862	867
	92	873	878	883	889	894	900	905	911	916	922
	93	927	933	938	944	949	955	960	966	971	977
	94	89 982	988	993	998	*004	*009	*015	*020	*026	*031
	95	90 037	042	048	053	059	064	069	075	080	086
	96	091	097	102	108	113	119	124	129	135	140
	97	146	151	157	162	168	173	179	184	189	195
	98	200	206	211	217	222	227	233	238	244	249
	99	255	260	266	271	276	282	287	293	298	304
	800	90 309	314	320	325	331	336	342	347	352	358
Prop. Parts	N	0	1	2	3	4	5	6	7	8	9

N	0	1	2	3	4	5	6	7	8	9	Prop. Parts
800	90 309	314	320	325	331	336	342	347	352	358	
01	363	369	374	380	385	390	396	401	407	412	
02	417	423	428	434	439	445	450	455	461	466	
03	472	477	482	488	493	499	504	509	515	520	
04	526	531	536	542	547	553	558	563	569	574	
05	580	585	590	596	601	607	612	617	623	628	
06	634	639	644	650	655	660	666	671	677	682	
07	687	693	698	703	709	714	720	725	730	736	
08	741	747	752	757	763	768	773	779	784	789	
09	795	800	806	811	816	822	827	832	838	843	
810	849	854	859	865	870	875	881	886	891	897	
11	902	907	913	918	924	929	934	940	945	950	
12	90 956	961	966	972	977	982	988	993	998	*004	
13	91 009	014	020	025	030	036	041	046	052	057	
14	062	068	073	078	084	089	094	100	105	110	
15	116	121	126	132	137	142	148	153	158	164	
16	169	174	180	185	190	196	201	206	212	217	
17	222	228	233	238	243	249	254	259	265	270	
18	275	281	286	291	297	302	307	312	318	323	
19	328	334	339	344	350	355	360	365	371	376	
820	381	387	392	397	403	408	413	418	424	429	
21	434	440	445	450	455	461	466	471	477	482	
22	487	492	498	503	508	514	519	524	529	535	
23	540	545	551	556	561	566	572	577	582	587	
24	593	598	603	609	614	619	624	630	635	640	
25	645	651	656	661	666	672	677	682	687	693	
26	698	703	709	714	719	724	730	735	740	745	
27	751	756	761	766	772	777	782	787	793	798	
28	803	808	814	819	824	829	834	840	845	850	
29	855	861	866	871	876	882	887	892	897	903	
830	908	913	918	924	929	934	939	944	950	955	
31	91 960	965	971	976	981	986	991	997	*002	*007	
32	92 012	018	023	028	033	038	044	049	054	059	
33	065	070	075	080	085	091	096	101	106	111	
34	117	122	127	132	137	143	148	153	158	163	
35	169	174	179	184	189	195	200	205	210	215	
36	221	226	231	236	241	247	252	257	262	267	
37	273	278	283	288	293	298	304	309	314	319	
38	324	330	335	340	345	350	355	361	366	371	
39	376	381	387	392	397	402	407	412	418	423	
840	428	433	438	443	449	454	459	464	469	474	
41	480	485	490	495	500	505	511	516	521	526	
42	531	536	542	547	552	557	562	567	572	578	
43	583	588	593	598	603	609	614	619	624	629	
44	634	639	645	650	655	660	665	670	675	681	
45	686	691	696	701	706	711	716	722	727	732	
46	737	742	747	752	758	763	768	773	778	783	
47	788	793	799	804	809	814	819	824	829	834	
48	840	845	850	855	860	865	870	875	881	886	
49	891	896	901	906	911	916	921	927	932	937	
850	92 942	947	952	957	962	967	973	978	983	988	
N	0	1	2	3	4	5	6	7	8	9	Prop. Parts

Prop. Parts:

	6
1	0.6
2	1.2
3	1.8
4	2.4
5	3.0
6	3.6
7	4.2
8	4.8
9	5.4

	5
1	0.5
2	1.0
3	1.5
4	2.0
5	2.5
6	3.0
7	3.5
8	4.0
9	4.5

Prop. Parts		N	0	1	2	3	4	5	6	7	8	9
		850	92 942	947	952	957	962	967	973	978	983	988
		51	92 993	998	*003	*008	*013	*018	*024	*029	*034	*039
		52	93 044	049	054	059	064	069	075	080	085	090
		53	095	100	105	110	115	120	125	131	136	141
		54	146	151	156	161	166	171	176	181	186	192
		55	197	202	207	212	217	222	227	232	237	242
		56	247	252	258	263	268	273	278	283	288	293
	6	57	298	303	308	313	318	323	328	334	339	344
1	0.6	58	349	354	359	364	369	374	379	384	389	394
2	1.2	59	399	404	409	414	420	425	430	435	440	445
3	1.8	**860**	450	455	460	465	470	475	480	485	490	495
4	2.4											
5	3.0	61	500	505	510	515	520	526	531	536	541	546
6	3.6	62	551	556	561	566	571	576	581	586	591	596
7	4.2	63	601	606	611	616	621	626	631	636	641	646
8	4.8	64	651	656	661	666	671	676	682	687	692	697
9	5.4	**65**	702	707	712	717	722	727	732	737	742	747
		66	752	757	762	767	772	777	782	787	792	797
		67	802	807	812	817	822	827	832	837	842	847
		68	852	857	862	867	872	877	882	887	892	897
		69	902	907	912	917	922	927	932	937	942	947
		870	93 952	957	962	967	972	977	982	987	992	997
		71	94 002	007	012	017	022	027	032	037	042	047
	5	72	052	057	062	067	072	077	082	086	091	096
1	0.5	73	101	106	111	116	121	126	131	136	141	146
2	1.0											
3	1.5	74	151	156	161	166	171	176	181	186	191	196
4	2.0	**75**	201	206	211	216	221	226	231	236	240	245
5	2.5	76	250	255	260	265	270	275	280	285	290	295
6	3.0	77	300	305	310	315	320	325	330	335	340	345
7	3.5	78	349	354	359	364	369	374	379	384	389	394
8	4.0	79	399	404	409	414	419	424	429	433	438	443
9	4.5	**880**	448	453	458	463	468	473	478	483	488	493
		81	498	503	507	512	517	522	527	532	537	542
		82	547	552	557	562	567	571	576	581	586	591
		83	596	601	606	611	616	621	626	630	635	640
		84	645	650	655	660	665	670	675	680	685	689
		85	694	699	704	709	714	719	724	729	734	738
		86	743	748	753	758	763	768	773	778	783	787
	4	87	792	797	802	807	812	817	822	827	832	836
1	0.4	88	841	846	851	856	861	866	871	876	880	885
2	0.8	89	890	895	900	905	910	915	919	924	929	934
3	1.2	**890**	939	944	949	954	959	963	968	973	978	983
4	1.6											
5	2.0	91	94 988	993	998	*002	*007	*012	*017	*022	*027	*032
6	2.4	92	95 036	041	046	051	056	061	066	071	075	080
7	2.8	93	085	090	095	100	105	109	114	119	124	129
8	3.2	94	134	139	143	148	153	158	163	168	173	177
9	3.6	**95**	182	187	192	197	202	207	211	216	221	226
		96	231	236	240	245	250	255	260	265	270	274
		97	279	284	289	294	299	303	308	313	318	323
		98	328	332	337	342	347	352	357	361	366	371
		99	376	381	386	390	395	400	405	410	415	419
		900	95 424	429	434	439	444	448	453	458	463	468
Prop. Parts		N	0	1	2	3	4	5	6	7	8	9

N	0	1	2	3	4	5	6	7	8	9	Prop. Parts
900	95 424	429	434	439	444	448	453	458	463	468	
01	472	477	482	487	492	497	501	506	511	516	
02	521	525	530	535	540	545	550	554	559	564	
03	569	574	578	583	588	593	598	602	607	612	
04	617	622	626	631	636	641	646	650	655	660	
05	665	670	674	679	684	689	694	698	703	708	
06	713	718	722	727	732	737	742	746	751	756	
07	761	766	770	775	780	785	789	794	799	804	
08	809	813	818	823	828	832	837	842	847	852	
09	856	861	866	871	875	880	885	890	895	899	
910	904	909	914	918	923	928	933	938	942	947	
11	952	957	961	966	971	976	980	985	990	995	
12	95 999	*004	*009	*014	*019	*023	*028	*033	*038	*042	
13	96 047	052	057	061	066	071	076	080	085	090	
14	095	099	104	109	114	118	123	128	133	137	
15	142	147	152	156	161	166	171	175	180	185	
16	190	194	199	204	209	213	218	223	227	232	
17	237	242	246	251	256	261	265	270	275	280	
18	284	289	294	298	303	308	313	317	322	327	
19	332	336	341	346	350	355	360	365	369	374	
920	379	384	388	393	398	402	407	412	417	421	
21	426	431	435	440	445	450	454	459	464	468	
22	473	478	483	487	492	497	501	506	511	515	
23	520	525	530	534	539	544	548	553	558	562	
24	567	572	577	581	586	591	595	600	605	609	
25	614	619	624	628	633	638	642	647	652	656	
26	661	666	670	675	680	685	689	694	699	703	
27	708	713	717	722	727	731	736	741	745	750	
28	755	759	764	769	774	778	783	788	792	797	
29	802	806	811	816	820	825	830	834	839	844	
930	848	853	858	862	867	872	876	881	886	890	
31	895	900	904	909	914	918	923	928	932	937	
32	942	946	951	956	960	965	970	974	979	984	
33	96 988	993	997	*002	*007	*011	*016	*021	*025	*030	
34	97 035	039	044	049	053	058	063	067	072	077	
35	081	086	090	095	100	104	109	114	118	123	
36	128	132	137	142	146	151	155	160	165	169	
37	174	179	183	188	192	197	202	206	211	216	
38	220	225	230	234	239	243	248	253	257	262	
39	267	271	276	280	285	290	294	299	304	308	
940	313	317	322	327	331	336	340	345	350	354	
41	359	364	368	373	377	382	387	391	396	400	
42	405	410	414	419	424	428	433	437	442	447	
43	451	456	460	465	470	474	479	483	488	493	
44	497	502	506	511	516	520	525	529	534	539	
45	543	548	552	557	562	566	571	575	580	585	
46	589	594	598	603	607	612	617	621	626	630	
47	635	640	644	649	653	658	663	667	672	676	
48	681	685	690	695	699	704	708	713	717	722	
49	727	731	736	740	745	749	754	759	763	768	
950	97 772	777	782	786	791	795	800	804	809	813	
N	0	1	2	3	4	5	6	7	8	9	Prop. Parts

Prop. Parts:

	5
1	0.5
2	1.0
3	1.5
4	2.0
5	2.5
6	3.0
7	3.5
8	4.0
9	4.5

	4
1	0.4
2	0.8
3	1.2
4	1.6
5	2.0
6	2.4
7	2.8
8	3.2
9	3.6

Prop. Parts	N	0	1	2	3	4	5	6	7	8	9
	950	97 772	777	782	786	791	795	800	804	809	813
	51	818	823	827	832	836	841	845	850	855	859
	52	864	868	873	877	882	886	891	896	900	905
	53	909	914	918	923	928	932	937	941	946	950
	54	97 955	959	964	968	973	978	982	987	991	996
	55	98 000	005	009	014	019	023	028	032	037	041
	56	046	050	055	059	064	068	073	078	082	087
	57	091	096	100	105	109	114	118	123	127	132
	58	137	141	146	150	155	159	164	168	173	177
	59	182	186	191	195	200	204	209	214	218	223
	960	227	232	236	241	245	250	254	259	263	268
5	61	272	277	281	286	290	295	299	304	308	313
	62	318	322	327	331	336	340	345	349	354	358
1 0.5	63	363	367	372	376	381	385	390	394	399	403
2 1.0	64	408	412	417	421	426	430	435	439	444	448
3 1.5	65	453	457	462	466	471	475	480	484	489	493
4 2.0	66	498	502	507	511	516	520	525	529	534	538
5 2.5	67	543	547	552	556	561	565	570	574	579	583
6 3.0	68	588	592	597	601	605	610	614	619	623	628
7 3.5	69	632	637	641	646	650	655	659	664	668	673
8 4.0	970	677	682	686	691	695	700	704	709	713	717
9 4.5	71	722	726	731	735	740	744	749	753	758	762
	72	767	771	776	780	784	789	793	798	802	807
	73	811	816	820	825	829	834	838	843	847	851
	74	856	860	865	869	874	878	883	887	892	896
	75	900	905	909	914	918	923	927	932	936	941
	76	945	949	954	958	963	967	972	976	981	985
	77	98 989	994	998	*003	*007	*012	*016	*021	*025	*029
	78	99 034	038	043	047	052	056	061	065	069	074
	79	078	083	087	092	096	100	105	109	114	118
	980	123	127	131	136	140	145	149	154	158	162
	81	167	171	176	180	185	189	193	198	202	207
	82	211	216	220	224	229	233	238	242	247	251
4	83	255	260	264	269	273	277	282	286	291	295
1 0.4	84	300	304	308	313	317	322	326	330	335	339
2 0.8	85	344	348	352	357	361	366	370	374	379	383
3 1.2	86	388	392	396	401	405	410	414	419	423	427
4 1.6	87	432	436	441	445	449	454	458	463	467	471
5 2.0	88	476	480	484	489	493	498	502	506	511	515
6 2.4	89	520	524	528	533	537	542	546	550	555	559
7 2.8	990	564	568	572	577	581	585	590	594	599	603
8 3.2	91	607	612	616	621	625	629	634	638	642	647
9 3.6	92	651	656	660	664	669	673	677	682	686	691
	93	695	699	704	708	712	717	721	726	730	734
	94	739	743	747	752	756	760	765	769	774	778
	95	782	787	791	795	800	804	808	813	817	822
	96	826	830	835	839	843	848	852	856	861	865
	97	870	874	878	883	887	891	896	900	904	909
	98	913	917	922	926	930	935	939	944	948	952
	99	99 957	961	965	970	974	978	983	987	991	996
	1000	00 000	004	009	013	017	022	026	030	035	039
Prop. Parts	N	0	1	2	3	4	5	6	7	8	9

[19]

N	0	1	2	3	4	5	6	7	8	9
100	00 0000	0434	0868	1301	1734	2166	2598	3029	3461	3891
01	4321	4751	5181	5609	6038	6466	6894	7321	7748	8174
02	00 8600	9026	9451	9876	*0300	*0724	*1147	*1570	*1993	*2415
03	01 2837	3259	3680	4100	4521	4940	5360	5779	6197	6616
04	01 7033	7451	7868	8284	8700	9116	9532	9947	*0361	*0775
05	02 1189	1603	2016	2428	2841	3252	3664	4075	4486	4896
06	5306	5715	6125	6533	6942	7350	7757	8164	8571	8978
07	02 9384	9789	*0195	*0600	*1004	*1408	*1812	*2216	*2619	*3021
08	03 3424	3826	4227	4628	5029	5430	5830	6230	6629	7028
09	03 7426	7825	8223	8620	9017	9414	9811	*0207	*0602	*0998
110	04 1393	1787	2182	2576	2969	3362	3755	4148	4540	4932
11	5323	5714	6105	6495	6885	7275	7664	8053	8442	8830
12	04 9218	9606	9993	*0380	*0766	*1153	*1538	*1924	*2309	*2694
13	05 3078	3463	3846	4230	4613	4996	5378	5760	6142	6524
14	05 6905	7286	7666	8046	8426	8805	9185	9563	9942	*0320
15	06 0698	1075	1452	1829	2206	2582	2958	3333	3709	4083
16	4458	4832	5206	5580	5953	6326	6699	7071	7443	7815
17	06 8186	8557	8928	9298	9668	*0038	*0407	*0776	*1145	*1514
18	07 1882	2250	2617	2985	3352	3718	4085	4451	4816	5182
19	5547	5912	6276	6640	7004	7368	7731	8094	8457	8819
120	07 9181	9543	9904	*0266	*0626	*0987	*1347	*1707	*2067	*2426
21	08 2785	3144	3503	3861	4219	4576	4934	5291	5647	6004
22	6360	6716	7071	7426	7781	8136	8490	8845	9198	9552
23	08 9905	*0258	*0611	*0963	*1315	*1667	*2018	*2370	*2721	*3071
24	09 3422	3772	4122	4471	4820	5169	5518	5866	6215	6562
25	09 6910	7257	7604	7951	8298	8644	8990	9335	9681	*0026
26	10 0371	0715	1059	1403	1747	2091	2434	2777	3119	3462
27	3804	4146	4487	4828	5169	5510	5851	6191	6531	6871
28	10 7210	7549	7888	8227	8565	8903	9241	9579	9916	*0253
29	11 0590	0926	1263	1599	1934	2270	2605	2940	3275	3609
130	3943	4277	4611	4944	5278	5611	5943	6276	6608	6940
31	11 7271	7603	7934	8265	8595	8926	9256	9586	9915	*0245
32	12 0574	0903	1231	1560	1888	2216	2544	2871	3198	3525
33	3852	4178	4504	4830	5156	5481	5806	6131	6456	6781
34	12 7105	7429	7753	8076	8399	8722	9045	9368	9690	*0012
35	13 0334	0655	0977	1298	1619	1939	2260	2580	2900	3219
36	3539	3858	4177	4496	4814	5133	5451	5769	6086	6403
37	6721	7037	7354	7671	7989	8303	8618	8934	9249	9564
38	13 9879	*0194	*0508	*0822	*1136	*1450	*1763	*2076	*2389	*2702
39	14 3015	3327	3639	3851	4263	4574	4885	5196	5507	5818
140	6128	6438	6748	7058	7367	7676	7985	8294	8603	8911
41	14 9219	9527	9835	*0142	*0449	*0756	*1063	*1370	*1676	*1982
42	15 2288	2594	2900	3205	3510	3815	4120	4424	4728	5032
43	5336	5640	5943	6246	6549	6852	7154	7457	7759	8061
44	15 8362	8664	8965	9266	9567	9868	*0168	*0469	*0769	*1068
45	16 1368	1667	1967	2266	2564	2863	3161	3460	3758	4055
46	4353	4650	4947	5244	5541	5838	6134	6430	6726	7022
47	16 7317	7613	7908	8203	8497	8792	9086	9380	9674	9968
48	17 0262	0555	0848	1141	1434	1726	2019	2311	2603	2895
49	3186	3478	3769	4060	4351	4641	4932	5222	5512	5802
150	17 6091	6381	6670	6959	7248	7536	7825	8113	8401	8689
N	**0**	**1**	**2**	**3**	**4**	**5**	**6**	**7**	**8**	**9**

N	0	1	2	3	4	5	6	7	8	9
150	17 6091	6381	6670	6959	7248	7536	7825	8113	8401	8689
51	17 8977	9264	9552	9839	*0126	*0413	*0699	*0986	*1272	*1558
52	18 1844	2129	2415	2700	2985	3270	3555	3839	4123	4407
53	4691	4975	5259	5542	5825	6108	6391	6674	6956	7239
54	18 7521	7803	8084	8366	8647	8928	9209	9490	9771	*0051
55	19 0332	0612	0892	1171	1451	1730	2010	2289	2567	2846
56	3125	3403	3681	3959	4237	4514	4792	5069	5346	5623
57	5900	6176	6453	6729	7005	7281	7556	7832	8107	8382
58	19 8657	8932	9206	9481	9755	*0029	*0303	*0577	*0850	*1124
59	20 1397	1670	1943	2216	2488	2761	3033	3305	3577	3848
160	4120	4391	4663	4934	5204	5475	5746	6016	6286	6556
61	6826	7096	7365	7634	7904	8173	8441	8710	8979	9247
62	20 9515	9783	*0051	*0319	*0586	*0853	*1121	*1388	*1654	*1921
63	21 2188	2454	2720	2986	3252	3518	3783	4049	4314	4579
64	4844	5109	5373	5638	5902	6166	6430	6694	6957	7221
65	21 7484	7747	8010	8273	8536	8798	9060	9323	9585	9846
66	22 0108	0370	0631	0892	1153	1414	1675	1936	2196	2456
67	2716	2976	3236	3496	3755	4015	4274	4533	4792	5051
68	5309	5568	5826	6084	6342	6600	6858	7115	7372	7630
69	22 7887	8144	8400	8657	8913	9170	9426	9682	9938	*0193
170	23 0449	0704	0960	1215	1470	1724	1979	2234	2488	2742
71	2996	3250	3504	3757	4011	4264	4517	4770	5023	5276
72	5528	5781	6033	6285	6537	6789	7041	7292	7544	7795
73	23 8046	8297	8548	8799	9049	9299	9550	9800	*0050	*0300
74	24 0549	0799	1048	1297	1546	1795	2044	2293	2541	2790
75	3038	3286	3534	3782	4030	4277	4525	4772	5019	5266
76	5513	5759	6006	6252	6499	6745	6991	7237	7482	7728
77	24 7973	8219	8464	8709	8954	9198	9443	9687	9932	*0176
78	25 0420	0664	0908	1151	1395	1638	1881	2125	2368	2610
79	2853	3096	3338	3580	3822	4064	4306	4548	4790	5031
180	5273	5514	5755	5996	6237	6477	6718	6958	7198	7439
81	25 7679	7918	8158	8398	8637	8877	9116	9355	9594	9833
82	26 0071	0310	0548	0787	1025	1263	1501	1739	1976	2214
83	2451	2688	2925	3162	3399	3636	3873	4109	4346	4582
84	4818	5054	5290	5525	5761	5996	6232	6467	6702	6937
85	7172	7406	7641	7875	8110	8344	8578	8812	9046	9279
86	26 9513	9746	9980	*0213	*0446	*0679	*0912	*1144	*1377	*1609
87	27 1842	2074	2306	2538	2770	3001	3233	3464	3696	3927
88	4158	4389	4620	4850	5081	5311	5542	5772	6002	6232
89	6462	6692	6921	7151	7380	7609	7838	8067	8296	8525
190	27 8754	8982	9211	9439	9667	9895	*0123	*0351	*0578	*0806
91	28 1033	1261	1488	1715	1942	2169	2396	2622	2849	3075
92	3301	3527	3753	3979	4205	4431	4656	4882	5107	5332
93	5557	5782	6007	6232	6456	6681	6905	7130	7354	7578
94	28 7802	8026	8249	8473	8696	8920	9143	9366	9589	9812
95	29 0035	0257	0480	0702	0925	1147	1369	1591	1813	2034
96	2256	2478	2699	2920	3141	3363	3584	3804	4025	4246
97	4466	4687	4907	5127	5347	5567	5787	6007	6226	6446
98	6665	6884	7104	7323	7542	7761	7979	8198	8416	8635
99	29 8853	9071	9289	9507	9725	9943	*0161	*0378	*0595	*0813
200	30 1030	1247	1464	1681	1898	2114	2331	2547	2764	2980
N	0	1	2	3	4	5	6	7	8	9

N	0	1	2	3	4	5	6	7	8	9
200	30 1030	1247	1464	1681	1898	2114	2331	2547	2764	2980
01	3196	3412	3628	3844	4059	4275	4491	4706	4921	5136
02	5351	5566	5781	5996	6211	6425	6639	6854	7068	7282
03	7496	7710	7924	8137	8351	8564	8778	8991	9204	9417
04	30 9630	9843	*0056	*0268	*0481	*0693	*0906	*1118	*1330	*1542
05	31 1754	1966	2177	2389	2600	2812	3023	3234	3445	3656
06	3867	4078	4289	4499	4710	4920	5130	5340	5551	5760
07	5970	6180	6390	6599	6809	7018	7227	7436	7646	7854
08	31 8063	8272	8481	8689	8898	9106	9314	9522	9730	9938
09	32 0146	0354	0562	0769	0977	1184	1391	1598	1805	2012
210	2219	2426	2633	2839	3046	3252	3458	3665	3871	4077
11	4282	4488	4694	4899	5105	5310	5516	5721	5926	6131
12	6336	6541	6745	6950	7155	7359	7563	7767	7972	8176
13	32 8380	8583	8787	8991	9194	9398	9601	9805	*0008	*0211
14	33 0414	0617	0819	1022	1225	1427	1630	1832	2034	2236
15	2438	2640	2842	3044	3246	3447	3649	3850	4051	4253
16	4454	4655	4856	5057	5257	5458	5658	5859	6059	6260
17	6460	6660	6860	7060	7260	7459	7659	7858	8058	8257
18	33 8456	8656	8855	9054	9253	9451	9650	9849	*0047	*0246
19	34 0444	0642	0841	1039	1237	1435	1632	1830	2028	2225
220	2423	2620	2817	3014	3212	3409	3606	3802	3999	4196
21	4392	4589	4785	4981	5178	5374	5570	5766	5962	6157
22	6353	6549	6744	6939	7135	7330	7525	7720	7915	8110
23	34 8305	8500	8694	8889	9083	9278	9472	9666	9860	*0054
24	35 0248	0442	0636	0829	1023	1216	1410	1603	1796	1989
25	2183	2375	2568	2761	2954	3147	3339	3532	3724	3916
26	4108	4301	4493	4685	4876	5068	5260	5452	5643	5834
27	6026	6217	6408	6599	6790	6981	7172	7363	7554	7744
28	7935	8125	8316	8506	8696	8886	9076	9266	9456	9646
29	35 9835	*0025	*0215	*0404	*0593	*0783	*0972	*1161	*1350	*1539
230	36 1728	1917	2105	2294	2482	2671	2859	3048	3236	3424
31	3612	3800	3988	4176	4363	4551	4739	4926	5113	5301
32	5488	5675	5862	6049	6236	6423	6610	6796	6983	7169
33	7356	7542	7729	7915	8101	8287	8473	8659	8845	9030
34	36 9216	9401	9587	9772	9958	*0143	*0328	*0513	*0698	*0883
35	37 1068	1253	1437	1622	1806	1991	2175	2360	2544	2728
36	2912	3096	3280	3464	3647	3831	4015	4198	4382	4565
37	4748	4932	5115	5298	5481	5664	5846	6029	6212	6394
38	6577	6759	6942	7124	7306	7488	7670	7852	8034	8216
39	37 8398	8580	8761	8943	9124	9306	9487	9668	9849	*0030
240	38 0211	0392	0573	0754	0934	1115	1296	1476	1656	1837
41	2017	2197	2377	2557	2737	2917	3097	3277	3456	3636
42	3815	3995	4174	4353	4533	4712	4891	5070	5249	5428
43	5606	5785	5964	6142	6321	6499	6677	6856	7034	7212
44	7390	7568	7746	7924	8101	8279	8456	8634	8811	8989
45	38 9166	9343	9520	9698	9875	*0051	*0228	*0405	*0582	*0759
46	39 0935	1112	1288	1464	1641	1817	1993	2169	2345	2521
47	2697	2873	3048	3224	3400	3575	3751	3926	4101	4277
48	4452	4627	4802	4977	5152	5326	5501	5676	5850	6025
49	6199	6374	6548	6722	6896	7071	7245	7419	7592	7766
250	39 7940	8114	8287	8461	8634	8808	8981	9154	9328	9501
N	0	1	2	3	4	5	6	7	8	9

N	0	1	2	3	4	5	6	7	8	9
250	39 7940	8114	8287	8461	8634	8808	8981	9154	9328	9501
51	39 9674	9847	*0020	*0192	*0365	*0538	*0711	*0883	*1056	*1228
52	40 1401	1573	1745	1917	2089	2261	2433	2605	2777	2949
53	3121	3292	3464	3635	3807	3978	4149	4320	4492	4663
54	4834	5005	5176	5346	5517	5688	5858	6029	6199	6370
55	6540	6710	6881	7051	7221	7391	7561	7731	7901	8070
56	8240	8410	8579	8749	8918	9087	9257	9426	9595	9764
57	40 9933	*0102	*0271	*0440	*0609	*0777	*0946	*1114	*1283	*1451
58	41 1620	1788	1956	2124	2293	2461	2629	2796	2964	3132
59	3300	3467	3635	3803	3970	4137	4305	4472	4639	4806
260	4973	5140	5307	5474	5641	5808	5974	6141	6308	6474
61	6641	6807	6973	7139	7306	7472	7638	7804	7970	8135
62	8301	8467	8633	8798	8964	9129	9295	9460	9625	9791
63	41 9956	*0121	*0286	*0451	*0616	*0781	*0945	*1110	*1275	*1439
64	42 1604	1768	1933	2097	2261	2426	2590	2754	2918	3082
65	3246	3410	3574	3737	3901	4065	4228	4392	4555	4718
66	4882	5045	5208	5371	5534	5697	5860	6023	6186	6349
67	6511	6674	6836	6999	7161	7324	7486	7648	7811	7973
68	8135	8297	8459	8621	8783	8944	9106	9268	9429	9591
69	42 9752	9914	*0075	*0236	*0398	*0559	*0720	*0881	*1042	*1203
270	43 1364	1525	1685	1846	2007	2167	2328	2488	2649	2809
71	2969	3130	3290	3450	3610	3770	3930	4090	4249	4409
72	4569	4729	4888	5048	5207	5367	5526	5685	5844	6004
73	6163	6322	6481	6640	6799	6957	7116	7275	7433	7592
74	7751	7909	8067	8226	8384	8542	8701	8859	9017	9175
75	43 9333	9491	9648	9806	9964	*0122	*0279	*0437	*0594	*0752
76	44 0909	1066	1224	1381	1538	1695	1852	2009	2166	2323
77	2480	2637	2793	2950	3106	3263	3419	3576	3732	3889
78	4045	4201	4357	4513	4669	4825	4981	5137	5293	5449
79	5604	5760	5915	6071	6226	6382	6537	6692	6848	7003
280	7158	7313	7468	7623	7778	7933	8088	8242	8397	8552
81	44 8706	8861	9015	9170	9324	9478	9633	9787	9941	*0095
82	45 0249	0403	0557	0711	0865	1018	1172	1326	1479	1633
83	1786	1940	2093	2247	2400	2553	2706	2859	3012	3165
84	3318	3471	3624	3777	3930	4082	4235	4387	4540	4692
85	4845	4997	5150	5302	5454	5606	5758	5910	6062	6214
86	6366	6518	6670	6821	6973	7125	7276	7428	7579	7731
87	7882	8033	8184	8336	8487	8638	8789	8940	9091	9242
88	45 9392	9543	9694	9845	9995	*0146	*0296	*0447	*0597	*0748
89	46 0898	1048	1198	1348	1499	1649	1799	1948	2098	2248
290	2398	2548	2697	2847	2997	3146	3296	3445	3594	3744
91	3893	4042	4191	4340	4490	4639	4788	4936	5085	5234
92	5383	5532	5680	5829	5977	6126	6274	6423	6571	6719
93	6868	7016	7164	7312	7460	7608	7756	7904	8052	8200
94	8347	8495	8643	8790	8938	9085	9233	9380	9527	9675
95	46 9822	9969	*0116	*0263	*0410	*0557	*0704	*0851	*0998	*1145
96	47 1292	1438	1585	1732	1878	2025	2171	2318	2464	2610
97	2756	2903	3049	3195	3341	3487	3633	3779	3925	4071
98	4216	4362	4508	4653	4799	4944	5090	5235	5381	5526
99	5671	5816	5962	6107	6252	6397	6542	6687	6832	6976
300	47 7121	7266	7411	7555	7700	7844	7989	8133	8278	8422
N	0	1	2	3	4	5	6	7	8	9

N	0	1	2	3	4	5	6	7	8	9
300	47 7121	7266	7411	7555	7700	7844	7989	8133	8278	8422
01	47 8566	8711	8855	8999	9143	9287	9431	9575	9719	9863
02	48 0007	0151	0294	0438	0582	0725	0869	1012	1156	1299
03	1443	1586	1729	1872	2016	2159	2302	2445	2588	2731
04	2874	3016	3159	3302	3445	3587	3730	3872	4015	4157
05	4300	4442	4585	4727	4869	5011	5153	5295	5437	5579
06	5721	5863	6005	6147	6289	6430	6572	6714	6855	6997
07	7138	7280	7421	7563	7704	7845	7986	8127	8269	8410
08	8551	8692	8833	8974	9114	9255	9396	9537	9677	9818
09	48 9958	*0099	*0239	*0380	*0520	*0661	*0801	*0941	*1081	*1222
310	49 1362	1502	1642	1782	1922	2062	2201	2341	2481	2621
11	2760	2900	3040	3179	3319	3458	3597	3737	3876	4015
12	4155	4294	4433	4572	4711	4850	4989	5128	5267	5406
13	5544	5683	5822	5960	6099	6238	6376	6515	6653	6791
14	6930	7068	7206	7344	7483	7621	7759	7897	8035	8173
15	8311	8448	8586	8724	8862	8999	9137	9275	9412	9550
16	49 9687	9824	9962	*0099	*0236	*0374	*0511	*0648	*0785	*0922
17	50 1059	1196	1333	1470	1607	1744	1880	2017	2154	2291
18	2427	2564	2700	2837	2973	3109	3246	3382	3518	3655
19	3791	3927	4063	4199	4335	4471	4607	4743	4878	5014
320	5150	5286	5421	5557	5693	5828	5964	6099	6234	6370
21	6505	6640	6776	6911	7046	7181	7316	7451	7586	7721
22	7856	7991	8126	8260	8395	8530	8664	8799	8934	9068
23	50 9203	9337	9471	9606	9740	9874	*0009	*0143	*0277	*0411
24	51 0545	0679	0813	0947	1081	1215	1349	1482	1616	1750
25	1883	2017	2151	2284	2418	2551	2684	2818	2951	3084
26	3218	3351	3484	3617	3750	3883	4016	4149	4282	4415
27	4548	4681	4813	4946	5079	5211	5344	5476	5609	5741
28	5874	6006	6139	6271	6403	6535	6668	6800	6932	7064
29	7196	7328	7460	7592	7724	7855	7987	8119	8251	8382
330	8514	8646	8777	8909	9040	9171	9303	9434	9566	9697
31	51 9828	9959	*0090	*0221	*0353	*0484	*0615	*0745	*0876	*1007
32	52 1138	1269	1400	1530	1661	1792	1922	2053	2183	2314
33	2444	2575	2705	2835	2966	3096	3226	3356	3486	3616
34	3746	3876	4006	4136	4266	4396	4526	4656	4785	4915
35	5045	5174	5304	5434	5563	5693	5822	5951	6081	6210
36	6339	6469	6598	6727	6856	6985	7114	7243	7372	7501
37	7630	7759	7888	8016	8145	8274	8402	8531	8660	8788
38	52 8917	9045	9174	9312	9430	9559	9687	9815	9943	*0072
39	53 0200	0328	0456	0584	0712	0840	0968	1096	1223	1351
340	1479	1607	1734	1862	1990	2117	2245	2372	2500	2627
41	2754	2882	3009	3136	3264	3391	3518	3645	3772	3899
42	4026	4153	4280	4407	4534	4661	4787	4914	5041	5167
43	5294	5421	5547	5674	5800	5927	6053	6180	6306	6432
44	6558	6685	6811	6937	7063	7189	7315	7441	7567	7693
45	7819	7945	8071	8197	8322	8448	8574	8699	8825	8951
46	53 9076	9202	9327	9452	9578	9703	9829	9954	*0079	*0204
47	54 0329	0455	0580	0705	0830	0955	1080	1205	1330	1454
48	1579	1704	1829	1953	2078	2203	2327	2452	2576	2701
49	2825	2950	3074	3199	3323	3447	3571	3696	3820	3944
350	54 4068	4192	4316	4440	4564	4688	4812	4936	5060	5183
N	0	1	2	3	4	5	6	7	8	9

N	0	1	2	3	4	5	6	7	8	9
350	54 4068	4192	4316	4440	4564	4688	4812	4936	5060	5183
51	5307	5431	5555	5678	5802	5925	6049	6172	6296	6419
52	6543	6666	6789	6913	7036	7159	7282	7405	7529	7652
53	7775	7898	8021	8144	8267	8389	8512	8635	8758	8881
54	54 9003	9126	9249	9371	9494	9616	9739	9861	9984	*0106
55	55 0228	0351	0473	0595	0717	0840	0962	1084	1206	1328
56	1450	1572	1694	1816	1938	2060	2181	2303	2425	2547
57	2668	2790	2911	3033	3155	3276	3398	3519	3640	3762
58	3883	4004	4126	4247	4368	4489	4610	4731	4852	4973
59	5094	5215	5336	5457	5578	5699	5820	5940	6061	6182
360	6303	6423	6544	6664	6785	6905	7026	7146	7267	7387
61	7507	7627	7748	7868	7988	8108	8228	8349	8469	8589
62	8709	8829	8948	9068	9188	9308	9428	9548	9667	9787
63	55 9907	*0026	*0146	*0265	*0385	*0504	*0624	*0743	*0863	*0982
64	56 1101	1221	1340	1459	1578	1698	1817	1936	2055	2174
65	2293	2412	2531	2650	2769	2887	3006	3125	3244	3362
66	3481	3600	3718	3837	3955	4074	4192	4311	4429	4548
67	4666	4784	4903	5021	5139	5257	5376	5494	5612	5730
68	5848	5966	6084	6202	6320	6437	6555	6673	6791	6909
69	7026	7144	7262	7379	7497	7614	7732	7849	7967	8084
370	8202	8319	8436	8554	8671	8788	8905	9023	9140	9257
71	56 9374	9491	9608	9725	9842	9959	*0076	*0193	*0309	*0426
72	57 0543	0660	0776	0893	1010	1126	1243	1359	1476	1592
73	1709	1825	1942	2058	2174	2291	2407	2523	2639	2755
74	2872	2988	3104	3220	3336	3452	3568	3684	3800	3915
75	4031	4147	4263	4379	4494	4610	4726	4841	4957	5072
76	5188	5303	5419	5534	5650	5765	5880	5996	6111	6226
77	6341	6457	6572	6687	6802	6917	7032	7147	7262	7377
78	7492	7607	7722	7836	7951	8066	8181	8295	8410	8525
79	8639	8754	8868	8983	9097	9212	9326	9441	9555	9669
380	57 9784	9898	*0012	*0126	*0241	*0355	*0469	*0583	*0697	*0811
81	58 0925	1039	1153	1267	1381	1495	1608	1722	1836	1950
82	2063	2177	2291	2404	2518	2631	2745	2858	2972	3085
83	3199	3312	3426	3539	3652	3765	3879	3992	4105	4218
84	4331	4444	4557	4670	4783	4896	5009	5122	5235	5348
85	5461	5574	5686	5799	5912	6024	6137	6250	6362	6475
86	6587	6700	6812	6925	7037	7149	7262	7374	7486	7599
87	7711	7823	7935	8047	8160	8272	8384	8496	8608	8720
88	8832	8944	9056	9167	9279	9391	9503	9615	9726	9838
89	58 9950	*0061	*0173	*0284	*0396	*0507	*0619	*0730	*0842	*0953
390	59 1065	1176	1287	1399	1510	1621	1732	1843	1955	2066
91	2177	2288	2399	2510	2621	2732	2843	2954	3064	3175
92	3286	3397	3508	3618	3729	3840	3950	4061	4171	4282
93	4393	4503	4614	4724	4834	4945	5055	5165	5276	5386
94	5496	5606	5717	5827	5937	6047	6157	6267	6377	6487
95	6597	6707	6817	6927	7037	7146	7256	7366	7476	7586
96	7695	7805	7914	8024	8134	8243	8353	8462	8572	8681
97	8791	8900	9009	9119	9228	9337	9446	9556	9665	9774
98	9883	9992	*0101	*0210	*0319	*0428	*0537	*0646	*0755	*0864
99	60 0973	1082	1191	1299	1408	1517	1625	1734	1843	1951
400	60 2060	2169	2277	2386	2494	2603	2711	2819	2928	3036
N	0	1	2	3	4	5	6	7	8	9

N	0	1	2	3	4	5	6	7	8	9
400	60 2060	2169	2277	2386	2494	2603	2711	2819	2928	3036
01	3144	3253	3361	3469	3577	3686	3794	3902	4010	4118
02	4226	4334	4442	4550	5658	4766	4874	4982	5089	5197
03	5305	5413	5521	5628	5736	5844	5951	6059	6166	6274
04	6381	6489	6596	6704	6811	˙6919	7026	7133	7241	7348
05	7455	7562	7669	7777	7884	7991	8098	8205	8312	8419
06	8526	8633	8740	8847	8954	9061	9167	9274	9381	9488
07	60 9594	9701	9808	9914	*0021	*0128	*0234	*0341	*0447	*0554
08	61 0660	0767	0873	0979	1086	1192	1298	1405	1511	1617
09	1723	1829	1936	2042	2148	2254	2360	2466	2572	2678
410	2784	2890	2996	3102	3207	3313	3419	3525	3630	3736
11	3842	3947	4053	4159	4264	4370	4475	4581	4686	4792
12	4897	5003	5108	5213	5319	5424	5529	5634	5740	5845
13	5950	6055	6160	6265	6370	6476	6581	6686	6790	6895
14	7000	7105	7210	7315	7420	7525	7629	7734	7839	7943
15	8048	8153	8257	8362	8466	8571	8676	8780	8884	8989
16	61 9093	9198	9302	9406	9511	9615	9719	9824	9928	*0032
17	62 0136	0240	0344	0448	0552	0656	0760	0864	0968	1072
18	1176	1280	1384	1488	1592	1695	1799	1903	2007	2110
19	2214	2318	2421	2525	2628	2732	2835	2939	3042	3146
420	3249	3353	3456	3559	3663	3766	3869	3973	4076	4179
21	4282	4385	4488	4591	4695	4798	4901	5004	5107	5210
22	5312	5415	5518	5621	5724	5827	5929	6032	6135	6238
23	6340	6443	6546	6648	6751	6853	6956	7058	7161	7263
24	7366	7468	7571	7673	7775	7878	7980	8082	8185	8287
25	8389	8491	8593	8695	8797	8900	9002	9104	9206	9308
26	62 9410	9512	9613	9715	9817	9919	*0021	*0123	*0224	*0326
27	63 0428	0530	0631	0733	0835	0936	1038	1139	1241	1342
28	1444	1545	1647	1748	1849	1951	2052	2153	2255	2356
29	2457	2559	2660	2761	2862	2963	3064	3165	3266	3367
430	3468	3569	3670	3771	3872	3973	4074	4175	4276	4376
31	4477	4578	4679	4779	4880	4981	5081	5182	5283	5383
32	5484	5584	5685	5785	5886	5986	6087	6187	6287	6388
33	6488	6588	6688	6789	6889	6989	7089	7189	7290	7390
34	7490	7590	7690	7790	7890	7990	8090	8190	8290	8389
35	8489	8589	8689	8789	8888	8988	9088	9188	9287	9387
36	63 9486	9586	9686	9785	9885	9984	*0084	*0183	*0283	*0382
37	64 0481	0581	0680	0779	0879	0978	1077	1177	1276	1375
38	1474	1573	1672	1771	1871	1970	2069	2168	2267	2366
39	2465	2563	2662	2761	2860	2959	3058	3156	3255	3354
440	3453	3551	3650	3749	3847	3946	4044	4143	4242	4340
41	4439	4537	4636	4734	4832	4931	5029	5127	5226	5324
42	5422	5521	5619	5717	5815	5913	6011	6110	6208	6306
43	6404	6502	6600	6698	6796	6894	6992	7089	7187	7285
44	7383	7481	7579	7676	7774	7872	7969	8067	8165	8262
45	8360	8458	8555	8653	8750	8848	8945	9043	9140	9237
46	64 9335	9432	9530	9627	9724	9821	9919	*0016	*0113	*0210
47	65 0308	0405	0502	0599	0696	0793	0890	0987	1084	1181
48	1278	1375	1472	1569	1666	1762	1859	1956	2053	2150
49	2246	2343	2440	2536	2633	2730	2826	2923	3019	3116
450	65 3213	3309	3405	3502	3598	3695	3791	3888	3984	4080
N	0	1	2	3	4	5	6	7	8	9

N	0	1	2	3	4	5	6	7	8	9
450	65 3213	3309	3405	3502	3598	3695	3791	3888	3984	4080
51	4177	4273	4369	4465	4562	4658	4754	4850	4946	5042
52	5138	5235	5331	5427	5523	5619	5715	5810	5906	6002
53	6098	6194	6290	6386	6482	6577	6673	6769	6864	6960
54	7056	7152	7247	7343	7438	7534	7629	7725	7820	7916
55	8011	8017	8202	8298	8393	8488	8584	8679	8774	8870
56	8965	9060	9155	9250	9346	9441	9536	9631	9726	9821
57	65 9916	*0011	*0106	*0201	*0296	*0391	*0486	*0581	*0676	*0771
58	66 0865	0960	1055	1150	1245	1339	1434	1529	1623	1718
59	1813	1907	2002	2096	2191	2286	2380	2475	2569	2663
460	2758	2852	2947	3041	3135	3230	3324	3418	3512	3607
61	3701	3795	3889	3983	4078	4172	4266	4360	4454	4548
62	4642	4736	4830	4924	5018	5112	5206	5200	5393	5487
63	5581	5675	5769	5862	5956	6050	6143	6237	6331	6424
64	6518	6612	6705	6799	6892	6986	7079	7173	7266	7360
65	7453	7546	7640	7733	7826	7920	8013	8106	8199	8293
66	8386	8479	8572	8665	8759	8852	8945	9038	9131	9224
67	66 9317	9410	9503	9506	9689	9782	9875	9967	*0060	*0153
68	67 0246	0339	0431	0524	0617	0710	0802	0895	0988	1080
69	1173	1265	1358	1451	1543	1636	1728	1821	1913	2005
470	2098	2190	2283	2375	2467	2560	2652	2744	2836	2929
71	3021	3113	3205	3207	3390	3482	3574	3666	3758	3850
72	3942	4034	4126	4218	4310	4402	4494	4586	4677	4769
73	4861	4953	5045	5137	5228	5320	5412	5503	5595	5687
74	5778	5870	5962	6053	6145	6236	6328	6419	6511	6602
75	6694	6785	6876	6968	7059	7151	7242	7333	7424	7516
76	7607	7698	7789	7881	7972	8063	8154	8245	8336	8427
77	8518	8609	8700	8791	8882	8973	9064	9155	9246	9337
78	67 9428	9519	9610	9700	9791	9882	9973	*0063	*0154	*0245
79	68 0336	0426	0517	0607	0698	0789	0879	0970	1060	1151
480	1241	1332	1422	1513	1603	1693	1784	1874	1964	2055
81	2145	2235	2326	2416	2506	2596	2686	2777	2867	2957
82	3047	3137	3227	3317	3407	3497	3587	3677	3767	3857
83	3947	4037	4127	4217	4307	4396	4486	4576	4666	4756
84	4845	4935	5025	5114	5204	5294	5383	5473	5563	5652
85	5742	5831	5921	6010	6100	6189	6279	6368	6458	6547
86	6636	6726	6815	6904	6994	7083	7172	7261	7351	7440
87	7529	7618	7707	7796	7886	7975	8064	8153	8242	8331
88	8420	8509	8598	8687	8776	8865	8953	9042	9131	9220
89	68 9309	9398	9486	9575	9664	9753	9841	9930	*0019	*0107
490	69 0196	0285	0373	0462	0550	0639	0728	0816	0905	0993
91	1081	1170	1258	1347	1435	1524	1612	1700	1789	1877
92	1965	2053	2142	2230	2318	2406	2494	2583	2671	2759
93	2847	2935	3023	3111	3199	3287	3375	3463	3551	3639
94	3727	3815	3903	3991	4078	4166	4254	4342	4430	4517
95	4605	4693	4781	4868	4956	5044	5131	5219	5307	5394
96	5482	5569	5657	5744	5832	5919	6007	6094	6182	6269
97	6356	6444	6531	6618	6706	6793	6880	6968	7055	7142
98	7229	7317	7404	7491	7578	7665	7752	7839	7926	8014
99	8101	8188	8275	8362	8449	8535	8622	8709	8796	8883
500	69 8970	9051	9144	9231	9317	9404	9491	9578	9664	9751
N	0	1	2	3	4	5	6	7	8	9

N	0	1	2	3	4	5	6	7	8	9
500	69 8970	9057	9144	9231	9317	9404	9491	9578	9664	9751
01	69 9838	9924	*0011	*0098	*0184	*0271	*0358	*0444	*0531	*0617
02	70 0704	0790	0877	0963	1050	1136	1222	1309	1395	1482
03	1568	1654	1741	1827	1913	1999	2086	2172	2258	3244
04	2431	2517	2603	2689	2775	2861	2947	3033	3119	3205
05	3291	3377	3463	3549	3635	3721	3807	3893	3979	4065
06	4151	4236	4322	4408	4494	4579	4665	4751	4837	4922
07	5008	5094	5179	5265	5350	5436	5522	5607	5693	5778
08	5864	5949	6035	6120	6206	6291	6376	6462	6547	6632
09	6718	6803	6888	6974	7059	7144	7229	7315	7400	7485
510	7570	7655	7740	7826	7911	7996	8081	8166	8251	8336
11	8421	8506	8591	8676	8761	8846	8931	9015	9100	9185
12	70 9270	9355	9440	9524	9609	9694	9779	9863	9948	*0033
13	71 0117	0202	0287	0371	0456	0540	0625	0710	0794	0879
14	0963	1048	1132	1217	1301	1385	1470	1554	1639	1723
15	1807	1892	1976	2060	2144	2229	2313	2397	2481	2566
16	2650	2734	2818	2902	2986	3070	3154	3238	3323	3407
17	3491	3575	3659	3742	3826	3910	3994	4078	4162	4246
18	4330	4414	4497	4581	4665	4749	4833	4916	5000	5084
19	5167	5251	5335	5418	5502	5586	5669	5753	5836	5920
520	6003	6087	6170	6254	6337	6421	6504	6588	6671	6754
21	6838	6921	7004	7088	7171	7254	7338	7421	7504	7587
22	7671	7754	7837	7920	8003	8086	8169	8253	8336	8419
23	8502	8585	8668	8751	8834	8917	9000	9083	9165	9248
24	71 9331	9414	9497	9580	9663	9745	9828	9911	9994	*0077
25	72 0159	0242	0325	0407	0490	0573	0655	0738	0821	0903
26	0986	1068	1151	1233	1316	1398	1481	1563	1646	1728
27	1811	1893	1975	2058	2140	2222	2305	2387	2469	2552
28	2634	2716	2798	2881	2963	3045	3127	3209	3291	3374
29	3456	3538	3620	3702	3784	3866	3948	4030	4112	4194
530	4276	4358	4440	4522	4604	4685	4767	4849	4931	5013
31	5095	5176	5258	5340	5422	5503	5585	5667	5748	5830
32	5912	5993	6075	6156	6238	6320	6401	6483	6564	6646
33	6727	6809	6890	6972	7053	7134	7216	7297	7379	7460
34	7541	7623	7704	7785	7866	7948	8029	8110	8191	8273
35	8354	8435	8516	8597	8678	8759	8841	8922	9003	9084
36	9165	9246	9327	9408	9489	9570	9651	9732	9813	9893
37	72 9974	*0055	*0136	*0217	*0298	*0378	*0459	*0540	*0621	*0702
38	73 0782	0863	0944	1024	1105	1186	1266	1347	1428	1508
39	1589	1669	1750	1830	1911	1991	2072	2152	2233	2313
540	2394	2474	2555	2635	2715	2796	2876	2956	3037	3117
41	3197	3278	3358	3438	3518	3598	3679	3759	3839	3919
42	3999	4079	4160	4240	4320	4400	4480	4560	4640	4720
43	4800	4880	4960	5040	5120	5200	5279	5359	5439	5519
44	5599	5679	5759	5838	5918	5998	6078	6157	6237	6317
45	6397	6476	6556	6635	6715	6795	6874	6954	7034	7113
46	7193	7272	7352	7431	7511	7590	7670	7749	7829	7908
47	7987	8067	8146	8225	8305	8384	8463	8543	8622	8701
48	8781	8860	8939	9018	9097	9177	9256	9335	9414	9493
49	73 9572	9651	9731	9810	9889	9968	*0047	*0126	*0205	*0284
550	74 0363	0442	0521	0600	0678	0757	0836	0915	0994	1073
N	0	1	2	3	4	5	6	7	8	9

N	0	1	2	3	4	5	6	7	8	9
550	74 0363	0442	0521	0600	0678	0757	0836	0915	0994	1073
51	1152	1230	1309	1388	1467	1546	1624	1703	1782	1800
52	1939	2018	2096	2175	2254	2332	2411	2489	2568	2647
53	2725	2804	2882	2961	3039	3118	3196	3275	3353	3431
54	3510	3588	3667	3745	3823	3902	3980	4058	4136	4215
55	4293	4371	4449	4528	4606	4684	4762	4840	4919	4997
56	5075	5153	5231	5309	5387	5465	5543	5621	5699	5777
57	5855	5933	6011	6089	6167	6245	6323	6401	6479	6556
58	6634	6712	6790	6868	6945	7023	7101	7179	7256	7334
59	7412	7489	7567	7645	7722	7800	7878	7955	8033	8110
560	8188	8266	8343	8421	8498	8576	8653	8731	8808	8885
61	8963	9040	9118	9195	9272	9350	9427	9504	9582	9659
62	74 9736	9814	9891	9968	*0045	*0123	*0200	*0277	*0354	*0431
63	75 0508	0586	0663	0740	0817	0894	0971	1048	1125	1202
64	1279	1356	1433	1510	1587	1664	1741	1818	1895	1972
65	2048	2125	2202	2279	2356	2433	2509	2586	2663	2740
66	2816	2893	2970	3047	3123	3200	3277	3353	3430	3506
67	3583	3660	3736	3813	3889	3966	4042	4119	4195	4272
68	4348	4425	4501	4578	4654	4730	4807	4883	4960	5036
69	5112	5189	5265	5341	5417	5494	5570	5646	5722	5799
570	5875	5951	6027	6103	6180	6256	6332	6408	6484	6560
71	6636	6712	6788	6864	6940	7016	7092	7168	7244	7320
72	7396	7472	7548	7624	7700	7775	7851	7927	8003	8079
73	8155	8230	8306	8382	8458	8533	8609	8685	8761	8836
74	8912	8988	9063	9139	9214	9290	9366	9441	9517	9592
75	75 9668	9743	9819	9894	9970	*0045	*0121	*0196	*0272	*0347
76	76 0422	0498	0573	0649	0724	0799	0875	0950	1025	1101
77	1176	1251	1326	1402	1477	1552	1627	1702	1778	1853
78	1928	2003	2078	2153	2228	2303	2378	2453	2529	2604
79	2679	2754	2829	2904	2978	3053	3128	3203	3278	3353
580	3428	3503	3578	3653	3727	3802	3877	3952	4027	4101
81	4176	4251	4326	4400	4475	4550	4624	4699	4774	4848
82	4923	4998	5072	5147	5221	5296	5370	5445	5520	5594
83	5669	5743	5818	5892	5966	6041	6115	6190	6264	6338
84	6413	6487	6562	6636	6710	6785	6859	6933	7007	7082
85	7156	7230	7304	7379	7453	7527	7601	7675	7749	7823
86	7898	7972	8046	8120	8194	8268	8342	8416	8490	8564
87	8638	8712	8786	8860	8934	9008	9082	9156	9230	9303
88	76 9377	9451	9525	9599	9673	9746	9820	9894	9968	*0042
89	77 0115	0189	0263	0336	0410	0484	0557	0631	0705	0778
590	0852	0926	0999	1073	1146	1220	1293	1367	1440	1514
91	1587	1661	1734	1808	1881	1955	2028	2102	2175	2248
92	2322	2395	2468	2542	2615	2688	2762	2835	2908	2981
93	3055	3128	3201	3274	3348	3421	3494	3567	3640	3713
94	3786	3860	3933	4006	4079	4152	4225	4298	4371	4444
95	4517	4590	4663	4736	4809	4882	4955	5028	5100	5173
96	5246	5319	5392	5465	5538	5610	5683	5756	5829	5902
97	5974	6047	6120	6193	6265	6338	6411	6483	6556	6629
98	6701	6774	6846	6919	6992	7064	7137	7209	7282	7354
99	7427	7499	7572	7644	7717	7789	7862	7934	8006	8079
600	77 8151	8224	8296	8368	8441	8513	8585	8658	8730	8802
N	0	1	2	3	4	5	6	7	8	9

N	0	1	2	3	4	5	6	7	8	9
600	77 8151	8224	8296	8368	8441	8513	8585	8658	8730	8802
01	8874	8947	9019	9091	9163	9236	9308	9380	9452	9524
02	77 9596	9669	9741	9813	9885	9957	*0029	*0101	*0173	*0245
03	78 0317	0389	0461	0533	0605	0677	0749	0821	0893	0965
04	1037	1109	1181	1253	1324	1396	1468	1540	1612	1684
05	1755	1827	1899	1971	2042	2114	2186	2258	2329	2401
06	2473	2544	2616	2688	2759	2831	2902	2974	3046	3117
07	3189	3260	3332	3403	3475	3546	3618	3689	3761	3832
08	3904	3975	4046	4118	4189	4261	4332	4403	4475	4546
09	4617	4689	4760	4831	4902	4974	5045	5116	5187	5259
610	5330	5401	5472	5543	5615	5686	5757	5828	5899	5970
11	6041	6112	6183	6254	6325	6396	6467	6538	6609	6680
12	6751	6822	6893	6964	7035	7106	7177	7248	7319	7390
13	7460	7531	7602	7673	7744	7815	7885	7956	8027	8098
14	8168	8239	8310	8381	8451	8522	8593	8663	8734	8804
15	8875	8946	9016	9087	9157	9228	9299	9369	9440	9510
16	78 9581	9651	9722	9792	9863	9933	*0004	*0074	*0144	*0215
17	79 0285	0356	0426	0496	0567	0637	0707	0778	0848	0918
18	0988	1059	1129	1199	1269	1340	1410	1480	1550	1620
19	1691	1761	1831	1901	1971	2041	2111	2181	2252	2322
620	2392	2462	2532	2602	2672	2742	2812	2882	2952	3022
21	3092	3162	3231	3301	3371	3441	3511	3581	3651	3721
22	3790	3860	3930	4000	4070	4139	4209	4279	4349	4418
23	4488	4558	4627	4697	4767	4836	4906	4976	5045	5115
24	5185	5254	5324	5393	5463	5532	5602	5672	5741	5811
25	5880	5949	6019	6088	6158	6227	6297	6366	6436	6505
26	6574	6644	6713	6782	6852	6921	6990	7060	7129	7198
27	7268	7337	7406	7475	7545	7614	7683	7752	7821	7890
28	7960	8029	8098	8167	8236	8305	8374	8443	8513	8582
29	8651	8720	8789	8858	8927	8996	9065	9134	9203	9272
630	79 9341	9409	9478	9547	9616	9685	9754	9823	9892	9961
31	80 0029	0098	0167	0236	0305	0373	0442	0511	0580	0648
32	0717	0786	0854	0923	0992	1061	1129	1198	1266	1335
33	1404	1472	1541	1609	1678	1747	1815	1884	1952	2021
34	2089	2158	2226	2295	2363	2432	2500	2568	2637	2705
35	2774	2842	2910	2979	3047	3116	3184	3252	3321	3389
36	3457	3525	3594	3662	3730	3798	3867	3935	4003	4071
37	4139	4208	4276	4344	4412	4480	4548	4616	4685	4753
38	4821	4889	4957	5025	5093	5161	5229	5297	5365	5433
39	5501	5569	5637	5705	5773	5841	5908	5976	6044	6112
640	6180	6248	6316	6384	6451	6519	6587	6655	6723	6790
41	6858	6926	6994	7061	7129	7197	7264	7332	7400	7467
42	7535	7603	7670	7738	7806	7873	7941	8008	8076	8143
43	8211	8279	8346	8414	8481	8549	8616	8684	8751	8818
44	8886	8953	9021	9088	9156	9223	9290	9358	9425	9492
45	80 9560	9627	9694	9762	9829	9896	9964	*0031	*0098	*0165
46	81 0233	0300	0367	0434	0501	0569	0636	0703	0770	0837
47	0904	0971	1039	1106	1173	1240	1307	1374	1441	1508
48	1575	1642	1709	1776	1843	1910	1977	2044	2111	2178
49	2245	2312	2379	2445	2512	2579	2646	2713	2780	2847
650	81 2913	2980	3047	3114	3181	3247	3314	3381	3448	3514
N	0	1	2	3	4	5	6	7	8	9

N	0	1	2	3	4	5	6	7	8	9
650	81 2913	2980	3047	3114	3181	3247	3314	3381	3448	3514
51	3581	3648	3714	3781	3848	3914	3981	4048	4114	4181
52	4248	4314	4381	4447	4514	4581	4647	4714	4780	4847
53	4913	4980	5046	5113	5179	5246	5312	5378	5445	5511
54	5578	5644	5711	5777	5843	5910	5976	6042	6109	6175
55	6241	6308	6374	6440	6506	6573	6639	6705	6771	6838
56	6904	6970	7036	7102	7169	7235	7301	7367	7433	7499
57	7565	7631	7698	7764	7830	7896	7962	8028	8094	8160
58	8226	8292	8358	8424	8490	8556	8622	8688	8754	8820
59	8885	8951	9017	9083	9149	9215	9281	9346	9412	9478
660	81 9544	9610	9676	9741	9807	9873	9939	*0004	*0070	*0136
61	82 0201	0267	0333	0399	0464	0530	0595	0661	0727	0792
62	0858	0924	0989	1055	1120	1186	1251	1317	1382	1448
63	1514	1579	1645	1710	1775	1841	1906	1972	2037	2103
64	2168	2233	2299	2364	2430	2495	2560	2626	2691	2756
65	2822	2887	2952	3018	3083	3148	3213	3279	3344	3409
66	3474	3539	3605	3670	3735	3800	3865	3930	3996	4061
67	4126	4191	4256	4321	4386	4451	4516	4581	4646	4711
68	4776	4841	4906	4971	5036	5101	5166	5231	5296	5361
69	5426	5491	5556	5621	5686	5751	5815	5880	5945	6010
670	6075	6140	6204	6269	6334	6399	6464	6528	6593	6658
71	6723	6787	6852	6917	6981	7046	7111	7175	7240	7305
72	7369	7434	7499	7563	7628	7692	7757	7821	7886	7951
73	8015	8080	8144	8209	8273	8338	8402	8467	8531	8595
74	8660	8724	8789	8853	8918	8982	9046	9111	9175	9239
75	9304	9368	9432	9497	9561	9625	9690	9754	9818	9882
76	82 9947	*0011	*0075	*0139	*0204	*0268	*0332	*0396	*0460	*0525
77	83 0589	0653	0717	0781	0845	0909	0973	1037	1102	1166
78	1230	1294	1358	1422	1486	1550	1614	1678	1742	1806
79	1870	1934	1998	2062	2126	2189	2253	2317	2381	2445
680	2509	2573	2637	2700	2764	2828	2892	2956	3020	3083
81	3147	3211	3275	3338	3402	3466	3530	3593	3657	3721
82	3784	3848	3912	3975	4039	4103	4166	4230	4294	4357
83	4421	4484	4548	4611	4675	4739	4802	4866	4929	4993
84	5056	5120	5183	5247	5310	5373	5437	5500	5564	5627
85	5691	5754	5817	5881	5944	6007	6071	6134	6197	6261
86	6324	6387	6451	6514	6577	6641	6704	6767	6830	6894
87	6957	7020	7083	7146	7210	7273	7336	7399	7462	7525
88	7588	7652	7715	7778	7841	7904	7967	8030	8093	8156
89	8219	8282	8345	8408	8471	8534	8597	8660	8723	8786
690	8849	8912	8975	9038	9101	9164	9227	9289	9352	9415
91	83 9478	9541	9604	9667	9729	9792	9855	9918	9981	*0043
92	84 0106	0169	0232	0294	0357	0420	0482	0545	0608	0671
93	0733	0796	0859	0921	0984	1046	1109	1172	1234	1297
94	1359	1422	1485	1547	1610	1672	1735	1797	1860	1922
95	1985	2047	2110	2172	2235	2297	2360	2422	2484	2547
96	2609	2672	2734	2796	2859	2921	2983	3046	3108	3170
97	3233	3295	3357	3420	3482	3544	3606	3669	3731	3793
98	3855	3918	3980	4042	4104	4166	4229	4291	4353	4415
99	4477	4539	4601	4664	4726	4788	4850	4912	4974	5036
700	84 5098	5160	5222	5284	5346	5408	5470	5532	5594	5656
N	0	1	2	3	4	5	6	7	8	9

N	0	1	2	3	4	5	6	7	8	9
700	84 5098	5160	5222	5284	5346	5408	5470	5532	5594	5656
01	5718	5780	5842	5904	5966	6028	6090	6151	6213	6275
02	6337	6399	6461	6523	6585	6646	6708	6770	6832	6894
03	6955	7017	7079	7141	7202	7264	7326	7388	7449	7511
04	7573	7634	7696	7758	7819	7881	7943	8004	8066	8128
05	8189	8251	8312	8374	8435	8497	8559	8620	8682	8743
06	8805	8866	8928	8989	9051	9112	9174	9235	9297	9358
07	84 9419	9481	9542	9604	9665	9726	9788	9849	9911	9972
08	85 0033	0095	0156	0217	0279	0340	0401	0462	0524	0585
09	0646	0707	0769	0830	0891	0952	1014	1075	1136	1197
710	1258	1320	1381	1442	1503	1564	1625	1686	1747	1809
11	1870	1931	1992	2053	2114	2175	2236	2297	2358	2419
12	2480	2541	2602	2663	2724	2785	2846	2907	2968	3029
13	3090	3150	3211	3272	3333	3394	3455	3516	3577	3637
14	3698	3759	3820	3881	3941	4002	4063	4124	4185	4245
15	4306	4367	4428	4488	4549	4610	4670	4731	4792	4852
16	4913	4974	5034	5095	5156	5216	5277	5337	5398	5459
17	5519	5580	5640	5701	5761	5822	5882	5943	6003	6064
18	6124	6185	6245	6306	6366	6427	6487	6548	6608	6668
19	6729	6789	6850	6910	6970	7031	7091	7152	7212	7272
720	7332	7393	7453	7513	7574	7634	7694	7755	7815	7875
21	7935	7995	8056	8116	8176	8236	8297	8357	8417	8477
22	8537	8597	8657	8718	8778	8838	8898	8958	9018	9078
23	9138	9198	9258	9318	9379	9439	9499	9559	9619	9679
24	85 9739	9799	9859	9918	9978	*0038	*0098	*0158	*0218	*0278
25	86 0338	0398	0458	0518	0578	0637	0697	0757	0817	0877
26	0937	0996	1056	1116	1176	1236	1295	1355	1415	1475
27	1534	1594	1654	1714	1773	1833	1893	1952	2012	2072
28	2131	2191	2251	2310	2370	2430	2489	2549	2608	2668
29	2728	2787	2847	2906	2966	3025	3085	3144	3204	3263
730	3323	3382	3442	3501	3561	3620	3680	3739	3799	3858
31	3917	3977	4036	4096	4155	4214	4274	4333	4392	4452
32	4511	4570	4630	4689	4748	4808	4867	4926	4985	5045
33	5104	5163	5222	5282	5341	5400	5459	5519	5578	5637
34	5696	5755	5814	5874	5933	5992	6051	6110	6169	6228
35	6287	6346	6405	6465	6524	6583	6642	6701	6760	6819
36	6878	6937	6996	7055	7114	7173	7232	7291	7350	7409
37	7467	7526	7585	7644	7703	7762	7821	7880	7939	7998
38	8056	8115	8174	8233	8292	8350	8409	8468	8527	8586
39	8644	8703	8762	8821	8879	8938	8997	9056	9114	9173
740	9232	9290	9349	9408	9466	9525	9584	9642	9701	9760
41	86 9818	9877	9935	9994	*0053	*0111	*0170	*0228	*0287	*0345
42	87 0404	0462	0521	0579	0638	0696	0755	0813	0872	0930
43	0989	1047	1106	1164	1223	1281	1339	1398	1456	1515
44	1573	1631	1690	1748	1806	1865	1923	1981	2040	2098
45	2156	2215	2273	2331	2389	2448	2506	2564	2622	2681
46	2739	2797	2855	2913	2972	3030	3088	3146	3204	3262
47	3321	3379	3437	3495	3553	3611	3669	3727	3785	3844
48	3902	3960	4018	4076	4134	4192	4250	4308	4366	4424
49	4482	4540	4598	4656	4714	4772	4830	4888	4945	5003
750	87 5061	5119	5177	5235	5293	5351	5409	5466	5524	5582
N	0	1	2	3	4	5	6	7	8	9

N	0	1	2	3	4	5	6	7	8	9
750	87 5061	5119	5177	5235	5293	5351	5409	5466	5524	5582
51	5640	5698	5756	5813	5871	5929	5987	6045	6102	6160
52	6218	6276	6333	6391	6449	6507	6564	6622	6680	6737
53	6795	6853	6910	6968	7026	7083	7141	7199	7256	7314
54	7371	7429	7487	7544	7602	7659	7717	7774	7832	7889
55	7947	8004	8062	8119	8177	8234	8292	8349	8407	8464
56	8522	8579	8637	8694	8752	8809	8866	8924	8981	9039
57	9096	9153	9211	9268	9325	9383	9440	9497	9555	9612
58	87 9669	9726	9784	9841	9898	9956	*0013	*0070	*0127	*0185
59	88 0242	0299	0356	0413	0471	0528	0585	0642	0699	0756
760	0814	0871	0928	0985	1042	1099	1156	1213	1271	1328
61	1385	1442	1499	1556	1613	1670	1727	1784	1841	1898
62	1955	2012	2069	2126	2183	2240	2297	2354	2411	2468
63	2525	2581	2638	2695	2752	2809	2866	2923	2980	3037
64	3093	3150	3207	3264	3321	3377	3434	3491	3548	3605
65	3661	3718	3775	3832	3888	3945	4002	4059	4115	4172
66	4229	4285	4342	4399	4455	4512	4569	4625	4682	4739
67	4795	4852	4909	4965	5022	5078	5135	5192	5248	5305
68	5361	5418	5474	5531	5587	5644	5700	5757	5813	5870
69	5926	5983	6039	6096	6152	6209	6265	6321	6378	6434
770	6491	6547	6604	6660	6716	6773	6829	6885	6942	6998
71	7054	7111	7167	7223	7280	7336	7392	7449	7505	7561
72	7617	7674	7730	7786	7842	7898	7955	8011	8067	8123
73	8179	8236	8292	8348	8404	8460	8516	8573	8629	8685
74	8741	8797	8853	8909	8965	9021	9077	9134	9190	9246
75	9302	9358	9414	9470	9526	9582	9638	9694	9750	9806
76	88 9862	9918	9974	*0030	*0086	*0141	*0197	*0253	*0309	*0365
77	89 0421	0477	0533	0589	0645	0700	0756	0812	0868	0924
78	0980	1035	1091	1147	1203	1259	1314	1370	1426	1482
79	1537	1593	1649	1705	1760	1816	1872	1928	1983	2039
780	2095	2150	2206	2262	2317	2373	2429	2484	2540	2595
81	2651	2707	2762	2818	2873	2929	2985	3040	3096	3151
82	3207	3262	3318	3373	3429	3484	3540	3595	3651	3706
83	3762	3817	3873	3928	3984	4039	4094	4150	4205	4261
84	4316	4371	4427	4482	4538	4593	4648	4704	4759	4814
85	4870	4925	4980	5036	5091	5146	5201	5257	5312	5367
86	5423	5478	5533	5588	5644	5699	5754	5809	5864	5920
87	5975	6030	6085	6140	6195	6251	6306	6361	6416	6471
88	6526	6581	6636	6692	6747	6802	6857	6912	6967	7022
89	7077	7132	7187	7242	7297	7352	7407	7462	7517	7572
790	7627	7682	7737	7792	7847	7902	7957	8012	8067	8122
91	8176	8231	8286	8341	8396	8451	8506	8561	8615	8670
92	8725	8780	8835	8890	8944	8999.	9054	9109	9164	9218
93	9273	9328	9383	9437	9492	9547	9602	9656	9711	9766
94	89 9821	9875	9930	9985	*0039	*0094	*0149	*0203	*0258	*0312
95	90 0367	0422	0476	0531	0586	0640	0695	0749	0804	0859
96	0913	0968	1022	1077	1131	1186	1240	1295	1349	1404
97	1458	1513	1567	1622	1676	1731	1785	1840	1894	1948
98	2003	2057	2112	2166	2221	2275	2329	2384	2438	2492
99	2547	2601	2655	2710	2764	2818	2873	2927	2981	3036
800	90 3090	3144	3199	3253	3307	3361	3416	3470	3524	3578
N	0	1	2	3	4	5	6	7	8	9

N	0	1	2	3	4	5	6	7	8	9
800	90 3090	3144	3199	3253	3307	3361	3416	3470	3524	3578
01	3633	3687	3741	3795	3849	3904	3958	4012	4066	4120
02	4174	4229	4283	4337	4391	4445	4499	4553	4607	4661
03	4716	4770	4824	4878	4932	4986	5040	5094	5148	5202
04	5256	5310	5364	5418	5472	5526	5580	5634	5688	5742
05	5796	5850	5904	5958	6012	6066	6119	6173	6227	6281
06	6335	6389	6443	6497	6551	6604	6658	6712	6766	6820
07	6874	6927	6981	7035	7089	7143	7196	7250	7304	7358
08	7411	7465	7519	7573	7626	7680	7734	7787	7841	7895
09	7949	8002	8056	8110	8163	8217	8270	8324	8378	8431
810	8485	8539	8592	8646	8699	8753	8807	8860	8914	8967
11	9021	9074	9128	9181	9235	9289	9342	9396	9449	9503
12	90 9556	9610	9663	9716	9770	9823	9877	9930	9984	*0037
13	91 0091	0144	0197	0251	0304	0358	0411	0464	0518	0571
14	0624	0678	0731	0784	0838	0891	0944	0998	1051	1104
15	1158	1211	1264	1317	1371	1424	1477	1530	1584	1637
16	1690	1743	1797	1850	1903	1956	2009	2063	2116	2169
17	2222	2275	2328	2381	2435	2488	2541	2594	2647	2700
18	2753	2806	2859	2913	2966	3019	3072	3125	3178	3231
19	3284	3337	3390	3443	3496	3549	3602	3655	3708	3761
820	3814	3867	3920	3973	4026	4079	4132	4184	4237	4290
21	4343	4396	4449	4502	4555	4608	4660	4713	4766	4819
22	4872	4925	4977	5030	5083	5136	5189	5241	5294	5347
23	5400	5453	5505	5558	5611	5664	5716	5769	5822	5875
24	5927	5980	6033	6085	6138	6191	6243	6296	6349	6401
25	6454	6507	6559	6612	6664	6717	6770	6822	6875	6927
26	6980	7033	7085	7138	7190	7243	7295	7348	7400	7453
27	7506	7558	7611	7663	7716	7768	7820	7873	7925	7978
28	8030	8083	8135	8188	8240	8293	8345	8397	8450	8502
29	8555	8607	8659	8712	8764	8816	8869	8921	8973	9026
830	9078	9130	9183	9235	9287	9340	9392	9444	9496	9549
31	91 9601	9653	9706	9758	9810	9862	9914	9967	*0019	*0071
32	92 0123	0176	0228	0280	0332	0384	0436	0489	0541	0593
33	0645	0697	0749	0801	0853	0906	0958	1010	1062	1114
34	1166	1218	1270	1322	1374	1426	1478	1530	1582	1634
35	1686	1738	1790	1842	1894	1946	1998	2050	2102	2154
36	2206	2258	2310	2362	2414	2466	2518	2570	2622	2674
37	2725	2777	2829	2881	2933	2985	3037	3089	3140	3192
38	3244	3296	3348	3399	3451	3503	3555	3607	3658	3710
39	3762	3814	3865	3917	3969	4021	4072	4124	4176	4228
840	4279	4331	4383	4434	4486	4538	4589	4641	4693	4744
41	4796	4848	4899	4951	5003	5054	5106	5157	5209	5261
42	5312	5364	5415	5467	5518	5570	5621	5673	5725	5776
43	5828	5879	5931	5982	6034	6085	6137	6188	6240	6291
44	6342	6394	6445	6497	6548	6600	6651	6702	6754	6805
45	6857	6908	6959	7011	7062	7114	7165	7216	7268	7319
46	7370	7422	7473	7524	7576	7627	7678	7730	7781	7832
47	7883	7935	7986	8037	8088	8140	8191	8242	8293	8345
48	8396	8447	8498	8549	8601	8652	8703	8754	8805	8857
49	8908	8959	9010	9061	9112	9163	9215	9266	9317	9368
850	92 9419	9470	9521	9572	9623	9674	9725	9776	9827	9879
N	0	1	2	3	4	5	6	7	8	9

N	0	1	2	3	4	5	6	7	8	9
850	92 9419	9470	9521	9572	9623	9674	9725	9776	9827	9879
51	92 9930	9981	*0032	*0083	*0134	*0185	*0236	*0287	*0338	*0389
52	93 0440	0491	0542	0592	0643	0694	0745	0796	0847	0898
53	0949	1000	1051	1102	1153	1204	1254	1305	1356	1407
54	1458	1509	1560	1610	1661	1712	1763	1814	1865	1915
55	1966	2017	2068	2118	2169	2220	2271	2322	2372	2423
56	2474	2524	2575	2626	2677	2727	2778	2829	2879	2930
57	2981	3031	·3082	3133	3183	3234	3285	3335	3386	3437
58	3487	3538	3589	3639	3690	3740	3791	3841	3892	3943
59	3993	4044	4094	4145	4195	4246	4296	4347	4397	4448
860	4498	4549	4599	4650	4700	4751	4801	4852	4902	4953
61	5003	5054	5104	5154	5205	5255	5306	5356	5406	5457
62	5507	5558	5608	5658	5709	5759	5809	5860	5910	5960
63	6011	6061	6111	6162	6212	6262	6313	6363	6413	6463
64	6514	6564	6614	6665	6715	6765	6815	6865	6916	6966
65	7016	7066	7117	7167	7217	7267	7317	7367	7418	7468
66	7518	7568	7618	7668	7718	7769	7819	7869	7919	7969
67	8019	8069	8119	8169	8219	8269	8320	8370	8420	8470
68	8520	8570	8620	8670	8720	8770	8820	8870	8920	8970
69	9020	9070	9120	9170	9220	9270	9320	9369	9419	9469
870	93 9519	9569	9619	9669	9719	9769	9819	9869	9918	9968
71	94 0018	0068	0118	0168	0218	0267	0317	0367	0417	0467
72	0516	0566	0616	0666	0716	0765	0815	0865	0915	0964
73	1014	1064	1114	1163	1213	1263	1313	1362	1412	1462
74	1511	1561	1611	1660	1710	1760	1809	1859	1909	1958
75	2008	2058	2107	2157	2207	2256	2306	2355	2405	2455
76	2504	2554	2603	2653	2702	2752	2801	2851	2901	2950
77	3000	3049	3099	3148	3198	3247	3297	3346	3396	3445
78	3495	3544	3593	3643	3692	3742	3791	3841	3890	3939
79	3989	4038	4088	4137	4186	4236	4285	4335	4384	4433
880	4483	4532	4581	4631	4680	4729	4779	4828	4877	4927
81	4976	5025	5074	5124	5173	5222	5272	5321	5370	5419
82	5469	5518	5567	5616	5665	5715	5764	5813	5862	5912
83	5961	6010	6059	6108	6157	6207	6256	6305	6354	6403
84	6452	6501	6551	6600	6649	6698	6747	6796	6845	6894
85	6943	6992	7041	7090	7140	7189	7238	7287	7336	7385
86	7434	7483	7532	7581	7630	7679	7728	7777	7826	7875
87	7924	7973	8022	8070	8119	8168	8217	8266	8315	8364
88	8413	8462	8511	8560	8609	8657	8706	8755	8804	8853
89	8902	8951	8999	9048	9097	9146	9195	9244	9292	9341
890	9390	9439	9488	9536	9585	9634	9683	9731	9780	9829
91	94 9878	9926	9975	*0024	*0073	*0121	*0170	*0219	*0267	*0316
92	95 0365	0414	0462	0511	0560	0608	0657	0706	0754	0803
93	0851	0900	0949	0997	1046	1095	1143	1192	1240	1289
94	1338	1386	1435	1483	1532	1580	1629	1677	1726	1775
95	1823	1872	1920	1969	2017	2066	2114	2163	2211	2260
96	2308	2356	2405	2453	2502	2550	2599	2647	2696	2744
97	2792	2841	2889	2938	2986	3034	3083	3131	3180	3228
98	3276	3325	3373	3421	3470	3518	3566	3615	3663	3711
99	3760	3808	3856	3905	3953	4001	4049	4098	4146	4194
900	95 4243	4291	4339	4387	4435	4484	4532	4580	4628	4677
N	0	1	2	3	4	5	6	7	8	9

N	0	1	2	3	4	5	6	7	8	9
900	95 4243	4291	4339	4387	4435	4484	4532	4580	4628	4677
01	4725	4773	4821	4869	4918	4966	5014	5062	5110	5158
02	5207	5255	5303	5351	5399	5447	5495	5543	5592	5640
03	5688	5736	5784	5832	5880	5928	5976	6024	6072	6120
04	6168	6216	6265	6313	6361	6409	6457	6505	6553	6601
05	6649	6697	6745	6793	6840	6888	6936	6984	7032	7080
06	7128	7176	7224	7272	7320	7368	7416	7464	7512	7559
07	7607	7655	7703	7751	7799	7847	7894	7942	7990	8038
08	8086	8134	8181	8229	8277	8325	8373	8421	8468	8516
09	8564	8612	8659	8707	8755	8803	8850	8898	8946	8994
910	9041	9089	9137	9185	9232	9280	9328	9375	9423	9471
11	9518	9566	9614	9661	9709	9757	9804	9852	9900	9947
12	95 9995	*0042	*0090	*0138	*0185	*0233	*0280	*0328	*0376	*0423
13	96 0471	0518	0566	0613	0661	0709	0756	0804	0851	0899
14	0946	0994	1041	1089	1136	1184	1231	1279	1326	1374
15	1421	1469	1516	1563	1611	1658	1706	1753	1801	1848
16	1895	1943	1990	2038	2085	2132	2180	2227	2275	2322
17	2369	2417	2464	2511	2559	2606	2653	2701	2748	2795
18	2843	2890	2937	2985	3032	3079	3126	3174	3221	3268
19	3316	3363	3410	3457	3504	3552	3599	3646	3693	3741
920	3788	3835	3882	3929	3977	4024	4071	4118	4165	4212
21	4260	4307	4354	4401	4448	4495	4542	4590	4637	4684
22	4731	4778	4825	4872	4919	4966	5013	5061	5108	5155
23	5202	5249	5296	5343	5390	5437	5484	5531	5578	5625
24	5672	5719	5766	5813	5860	5907	5954	6001	6048	6095
25	6142	6189	6236	6283	6329	6376	6423	6470	6517	6564
26	6611	6658	6705	6752	6799	6845	6892	6939	6986	7033
27	7080	7127	7173	7220	7267	7314	7361	7408	7454	7501
28	7548	7595	7642	7688	7735	7782	7829	7875	7922	7969
29	8016	8062	8109	8156	8203	8249	8296	8343	8390	8436
930	8483	8530	8576	8623	8670	8716	8763	8810	8856	8903
31	8950	8996	9043	9090	9136	9183	9229	9276	9323	9369
32	9416	9463	9509	9556	9602	9649	9695	9742	9789	9835
33	96 9882	9928	9975	*0021	*0068	*0114	*0161	*0207	*0254	*0300
34	97 0347	0393	0440	0486	0533	0579	0626	0672	0719	0765
35	0812	0858	0904	0951	0997	1044	1090	1137	1183	1229
36	1276	1322	1369	1415	1461	1508	1554	1601	1647	1693
37	1740	1786	1832	1879	1925	1971	2018	2064	2110	2157
38	2203	2249	2295	2342	2388	2434	2481	2527	2573	2619
39	2666	2712	2758	2804	2851	2897	2943	2989	3035	3082
940	3128	3174	3220	3266	3313	3359	3405	3451	3497	3543
41	3590	3636	3682	3728	3774	3820	3866	3913	3959	4005
42	4051	4097	4143	4189	4235	4281	4327	4374	4420	4466
43	4512	4558	4604	4650	4696	4742	4788	4834	4880	4926
44	4972	5018	5064	5110	5156	5202	5248	5294	5340	5386
45	5432	5478	5524	5570	5616	5662	5707	5753	5799	5845
46	5891	5937	5983	6029	6075	6121	6167	6212	6258	6304
47	6350	6396	6442	6488	6533	6579	6625	6671	6717	6763
48	6808	6854	6900	6946	6992	7037	7083	7129	7175	7220
49	7266	7312	7358	7403	7449	7495	7541	7586	7632	7678
950	97 7724	7769	7815	7861	7906	7952	7998	8043	8089	8135
N	0	1	2	3	4	5	6	7	8	9

II. SIX-PLACE LOGARITHMS: 950—1000

N	0	1	2	3	4	5	6	7	8	9
950	97 7724	7769	7815	7861	7906	7952	7998	8043	8089	8135
51	8181	8226	8272	8317	8363	8409	8454	8500	8546	8591
52	8637	8683	8728	8774	8819	8865	8911	8956	9002	9047
53	9093	9138	9184	9230	9275	9321	9366	9412	9457	9503
54	97 9548	9594	9639	9685	9730	9776	9821	9867	9912	9958
55	98 0003	0049	0094	0140	0185	0231	0276	0322	0367	0412
56	0458	0503	0549	0594	0640	0685	0730	0776	0821	0867
57	0912	0957	1003	1048	1093	1139	1184	1229	1275	1320
58	1366	1411	1456	1501	1547	1592	1637	1683	1728	1773
59	1819	1864	1909	1954	2000	2045	2090	2135	2181	2226
960	2271	2316	2362	2407	2452	2497	2543	2588	2633	2678
61	2723	2769	2814	2859	2904	2949	2994	3040	3085	3130
62	3175	3220	3265	3310	3356	3401	3446	3491	3536	3581
63	3626	3671	3716	3762	3807	3852	3897	3942	3987	4032
64	4077	4122	4167	4212	4257	4302	4347	4392	4437	4482
65	4527	4572	4617	4662	4707	4752	4797	4842	4887	4932
66	4977	5022	5067	5112	5157	5202	5247	5292	5337	5382
67	5426	5471	5516	5561	5606	5651	5696	5741	5786	5830
68	5875	5920	5965	6010	6055	6100	6144	6189	6234	6279
69	6324	6369	6413	6458	6503	6548	6593	6637	6682	6727
970	6772	6817	6861	6906	6951	6996	7040	7085	7130	7175
71	7219	7264	7309	7353	7398	7443	7488	7532	7577	7622
72	7666	7711	7756	7800	7845	7890	7934	7979	8024	8068
73	8113	8157	8202	8247	8291	8336	8381	8425	8470	8514
74	8559	8604	8648	8693	8737	8782	8826	8871	8916	8960
75	9005	9049	9094	9138	9183	9227	9272	9316	9361	9405
76	9450	9494	9539	9583	9628	9672	9717	9761	9806	9850
77	98 9895	9939	9983	*0028	*0072	*0117	*0161	*0206	*0250	*0294
78	99 0339	0383	0428	0472	0516	0561	0605	0650	0694	0738
79	0783	0827	0871	0916	0960	1004	1049	1093	1137	1182
980	1226	1270	1315	1359	1403	1448	1492	1536	1580	1625
81	1669	1713	1758	1802	1846	1890	1935	1979	2023	2067
82	2111	2156	2200	2244	2288	2333	2377	2421	2465	2509
83	2554	2598	2642	2686	2730	2774	2819	2863	2907	2951
84	2995	3039	3083	3127	3172	3216	3260	3304	3348	3392
85	3436	3480	3524	3568	3613	3657	3701	3745	3789	3833
86	3877	3921	3965	4009	4053	4097	4141	4185	4229	4273
87	4317	4361	4405	4449	4493	4537	4581	4625	4669	4713
88	4757	4801	4845	4889	4933	4977	5021	5065	5108	5152
89	5196	5240	5284	5328	5372	5416	5460	5504	5547	5591
990	5635	5679	5723	5767	5811	5854	5898	5942	5986	6030
91	6074	6117	6161	6205	6249	6293	6337	6380	6424	6468
92	6512	6555	6599	6643	6687	6731	6774	6818	6862	6906
93	6949	6993	7037	7080	7124	7168	7212	7255	7299	7343
94	7386	7430	7474	7517	7561	7605	7648	7692	7736	7779
95	7823	7867	7910	7954	7998	8041	8085	8129	8172	8216
96	8259	8303	8347	8390	8434	8477	8521	8564	8608	8652
97	8695	8739	8782	8826	8869	8913	8956	9000	9043	9087
98	9131	9174	9218	9261	9305	9348	9392	9435	9479	9522
99	99 9565	9609	9652	9696	9739	9783	9826	9870	9913	9957
1000	00 0000	0043	0087	0130	0174	0217	0260	0304	0347	0391
N	0	1	2	3	4	5	6	7	8	9

III. SEVEN-PLACE LOGARITHMS

N	0	1	2	3	4	5	6	7	8	9
1000	000 0000	0434	0869	1303	1737	2171	2605	3039	3473	3907
1001	4341	4775	5208	5642	6076	6510	6943	7377	7810	8244
1002	8677	9111	9544	9977	*0411	*0844	*1277	*1710	*2143	*2576
1003	001 3009	3442	3875	4308	4741	5174	5607	6039	6472	6905
1004	7337	7770	8202	8635	9067	9499	9932	*0364	*0796	*1228
1005	002 1661	2093	2525	2957	3389	3821	4253	4685	5116	5548
1006	5980	6411	6843	7275	7706	8138	8569	9001	9432	9863
1007	003 0295	0726	1157	1588	2019	2451	2882	3313	3744	4174
1008	4605	5036	5467	5898	6328	6759	7190	7620	8051	8481
1009	8912	9342	9772	*0203	*0633	*1063	*1493	*1924	*2354	*2784
1010	004 3214	3644	4074	4504	4933	5363	5793	6223	6652	7082
1011	7512	7941	8371	8800	9229	9659	*0088	*0517	*0947	*1376
1012	005 1805	2234	2663	3092	3521	3950	4379	4808	5237	5666
1013	6094	6523	6952	7380	7809	8238	8666	9094	9523	9951
1014	006 0380	0808	1236	1664	2092	2521	2949	3377	3805	4233
1015	4660	5088	5516	5944	6372	6799	7227	7655	8082	8510
1016	8937	9365	9792	*0219	*0647	*1074	*1501	*1928	*2355	*2782
1017	007 3210	3637	4064	4490	4917	5344	5771	6198	6624	7051
1018	7478	7904	8331	8757	9184	9610	*0037	*0463	*0889	*1316
1019	008 1742	2168	2594	3020	3446	3872	4298	4724	5150	5576
1020	6002	6427	6853	7279	7704	8130	8556	8981	9407	9832
1021	009 0257	0683	1108	1533	1959	2384	2809	3234	3659	4084
1022	4509	4934	5359	5784	6208	6633	7058	7483	7907	8332
1023	8756	9181	9605	*0030	*0454	*0878	*1303	*1727	*2151	*2575
1024	010 3000	3424	3848	4272	4696	5120	5544	5967	6391	6815
1025	7239	7662	8086	8510	8933	9357	9780	*0204	*0627	*1050
1026	011 1474	1897	2320	2743	3166	3590	4013	4436	4859	5282
1027	5704	6127	6550	6973	7396	7818	8241	8664	9086	9509
1028	9931	*0354	*0776	*1198	*1621	*2043	*2465	*2887	*3310	*3732
1029	012 4154	4576	4998	5420	5842	6264	6685	7107	7529	7951
1030	8372	8794	9215	9637	*0059	*0480	*0901	*1323	*1744	*2165
1031	013 2587	3008	3429	3850	4271	4692	5113	5534	5955	6376
1032	6797	7218	7639	8059	8480	8901	9321	9742	*0162	*0583
1033	014 1003	1424	1844	2264	2685	3105	3525	3945	4365	4785
1034	5205	5625	6045	6465	6885	7305	7725	8144	8564	8984
1035	9403	9823	*0243	*0662	*1082	*1501	*1920	*2340	*2759	*3178
1036	015 3598	4017	4436	4855	5274	5693	6112	6531	6950	7369
1037	7788	8206	8625	9044	9462	9881	*0300	*0718	*1137	*1555
1038	016 1974	2392	2810	3229	3647	4065	4483	4901	5319	5737
1039	6155	6573	6991	7409	7827	8245	8663	9080	9498	9916
1040	017 0333	0751	1168	1586	2003	2421	2838	3256	3673	4090
1041	4507	4924	5342	5759	6176	6593	7010	7427	7844	8260
1042	8677	9094	9511	9927	*0344	*0761	*1177	*1594	*2010	*2427
1043	018 2843	3259	3676	4092	4508	4925	5341	5757	6173	6589
1044	7005	7421	7837	8253	8669	9084	9500	9916	*0332	*0747
1045	019 1163	1578	1994	2410	2825	3240	3656	4071	4486	4902
1046	5317	5732	6147	6562	6977	7392	7807	8222	8637	9052
1047	9467	9882	*0296	*0711	*1126	*1540	*1955	*2369	*2784	*3198
1048	020 3613	4027	4442	4856	5270	5684	6099	6513	6927	7341
1049	7755	8169	8583	8997	9411	9824	*0238	*0652	*1066	*1479
1050	021 1893	2307	2720	3134	3547	3961	4374	4787	5201	5614
N	0	1	2	3	4	5	6	7	8	9

N	0	1	2	3	4	5	6	7	8	9
1050	021 1893	2307	2720	3134	3547	3961	4374	4787	5201	5614
1051	6027	6440	6854	7267	7680	8093	8506	8919	9332	9745
1052	022 0157	0570	0983	1396	1808	2221	2634	3046	3459	3871
1053	4284	4696	5109	5521	5933	6345	6758	7170	7582	7994
1054	8406	8818	9230	9642	*0054	*0466	*0878	*1289	*1701	*2113
1055	023 2525	2936	3348	3759	4171	4582	4994	5405	5817	6228
1056	6639	7050	7462	7873	8284	8695	9106	9517	9928	*0339
1057	024 0750	1161	1572	1982	2393	2804	3214	3625	4036	4446
1058	4857	5267	5678	6088	6498	6909	7319	7729	8139	8549
1059	8960	9370	9780	*0190	*0600	*1010	*1419	*1829	*2239	*2649
1060	025 3059	3468	3878	4288	4697	5107	5516	5926	6335	6744
1061	7154	7563	7972	8382	8791	9200	9609	*0018	*0427	*0836
1062	026 1245	1654	2063	2472	2881	3289	3698	4107	4515	4924
1063	5333	5741	6150	6558	6967	7375	7783	8192	8600	9008
1064	9416	9824	*0233	*0641	*1049	*1457	*1865	*2273	*2680	*3088
1065	027 3496	3904	4312	4719	5127	5535	5942	6350	6757	7165
1066	7572	7979	8387	8794	9201	9609	*0016	*0423	*0830	*1237
1067	028 1644	2051	2458	2865	3272	3679	4086	4492	4899	5306
1068	5713	6119	6526	6932	7339	7745	8152	8558	8964	9371
1069	9777	*0183	*0590	*0996	*1402	*1808	*2214	*2620	*3026	*3432
1070	029 3838	4244	4649	5055	5461	5867	6272	6678	7084	7489
1071	7895	8300	8706	9111	9516	9922	*0327	*0732	*1138	*1543
1072	030 1948	2353	2758	3163	3568	3973	4378	4783	5188	5592
1073	5997	6402	6807	7211	7616	8020	8425	8830	9234	9638
1074	031 0043	0447	0851	1256	1660	2064	2468	2872	3277	3681
1075	4085	4489	4893	5296	5700	6104	6508	6912	7315	7719
1076	8123	8526	8930	9333	9737	*0140	*0544	*0947	*1350	*1754
1077	032 2157	2560	2963	3367	3770	4173	4576	4979	5382	5785
1078	6188	6590	6993	7396	7799	8201	8604	9007	9409	9812
1079	033 0214	0617	1019	1422	1824	2226	2629	3031	3433	3835
1080	4238	4640	5042	5444	5846	6248	6650	7052	7453	7855
1081	8257	8659	9060	9462	9864	*0265	*0667	*1068	*1470	*1871
1082	034 2273	2674	3075	3477	3878	4279	4680	5081	5482	5884
1083	6285	6686	7087	7487	7888	8289	8690	9091	9491	9892
1084	035 0293	0693	1094	1495	1895	2296	2696	3096	3497	3897
1085	4297	4698	5098	5498	5898	6298	6698	7098	7498	7898
1086	8298	8698	9098	9498	9898	*0297	*0697	*1097	*1496	*1896
1087	036 2295	2695	3094	3494	3893	4293	4692	5091	5491	5890
1088	6289	6688	7087	7486	7885	8284	8683	9082	9481	9880
1089	037 0279	0678	1076	1475	1874	2272	2671	3070	3468	3867
1090	4265	4663	5062	5460	5858	6257	6655	7053	7451	7849
1091	8248	8646	9044	9442	9839	*0237	*0635	*1033	*1431	*1829
1092	038 2226	2624	3022	3419	3817	4214	4612	5009	5407	5804
1093	6202	6599	6996	7393	7791	8188	8585	8982	9379	9776
1094	039 0173	0570	0967	1364	1761	2158	2554	2951	3348	3745
1095	4141	4538	4934	5331	5727	6124	6520	6917	7313	7709
1096	8106	8502	8898	9294	9690	*0086	*0482	*0878	*1274	*1670
1097	040 2066	2462	2858	3254	3650	4045	4441	4837	5232	5628
1098	6023	6419	6814	7210	7605	8001	8396	8791	9187	9582
1099	9977	*0372	*0767	*1162	*1557	*1952	*2347	*2742	*3137	*3532
1100	041 3927	4322	4716	5111	5506	5900	6295	6690	7084	7479
N	0	1	2	3	4	5	6	7	8	9

IV. THE NUMBER OF EACH DAY OF THE YEAR

Day of Month	Jan.	Feb.	Mar.	April	May	June	July	Aug.	Sept.	Oct.	Nov.	Dec.	Day of Month
1	1	32	60	91	121	152	182	213	244	274	305	335	1
2	2	33	61	92	122	153	183	214	245	275	306	336	2
3	3	34	62	93	123	154	184	215	246	276	307	337	3
4	4	35	63	94	124	155	185	216	247	277	308	338	4
5	5	36	64	95	125	156	186	217	248	278	309	339	5
6	6	37	65	96	126	157	187	218	249	279	310	340	6
7	7	38	66	97	127	158	188	219	250	280	311	341	7
8	8	39	67	98	128	159	189	220	251	281	312	342	8
9	9	40	68	99	129	160	190	221	252	282	313	343	9
10	10	41	69	100	130	161	191	222	253	283	314	344	10
11	11	42	70	101	131	162	192	223	254	284	315	345	11
12	12	43	71	102	132	163	193	224	255	285	316	346	12
13	13	44	72	103	133	164	194	225	256	286	317	347	13
14	14	45	73	104	134	165	195	226	257	287	318	348	14
15	15	46	74	105	135	166	196	227	258	288	319	349	15
16	16	47	75	106	136	167	197	228	259	289	320	350	16
17	17	48	76	107	137	168	198	229	260	290	321	351	17
18	18	49	77	108	138	169	199	230	261	291	322	352	18
19	19	50	78	109	139	170	200	231	262	292	323	353	19
20	20	51	79	110	140	171	201	232	263	293	324	354	20
21	21	52	80	111	141	172	202	233	264	294	325	355	21
22	22	53	81	112	142	173	203	234	265	295	326	356	22
23	23	54	82	113	143	174	204	235	266	296	327	357	23
24	24	55	83	114	144	175	205	236	267	297	328	358	24
25	25	56	84	115	145	176	206	237	268	298	329	359	25
26	26	57	85	116	146	177	207	238	269	299	330	360	26
27	27	58	86	117	147	178	208	239	270	300	331	361	27
28	28	59	87	118	148	179	209	240	271	301	332	362	28
29	29		88	119	149	180	210	241	272	302	333	363	29
30	30		89	120	150	181	211	242	273	303	334	364	30
31	31		90		151		212	243		304		365	31

NOTE. In leap years, after February 28, add 1 to the tabulated number.

V. COMPOUND AMOUNT OF 1

$$(1 + i)^n$$

n	$\frac{1}{4}\%$	$\frac{7}{24}\%$	$\frac{1}{3}\%$	$\frac{3}{8}\%$	n
1	1.0025 0000	1.0029 1667	1.0033 3333	1.0037 5000	1
2	1.0050 0625	1.0058 4184	1.0066 7778	1.0075 1406	2
3	1.0075 1877	1.0087 7555	1.0100 3337	1.0112 9224	3
4	1.0100 3756	1.0117 1781	1.0134 0015	1.0150 8459	4
5	1.0125 6266	1.0146 6865	1.0167 7815	1.0188 9115	5
6	1.0150 9406	1.0176 2810	1.0201 6741	1.0227 1200	6
7	1.0176 3180	1.0205 9618	1.0235 6797	1.0265 4717	7
8	1.0201 7588	1.0235 7292	1.0269 7986	1.0303 9672	8
9	1.0227 2632	1.0265 5834	1.0304 0313	1.0342 6070	9
10	1.0252 8313	1.0295 5247	1.0338 3780	1.0381 3918	10
11	1.0278 4634	1.0325 5533	1.0372 8393	1.0420 3220	11
12	1.0304 1596	1.0355 6695	1.0407 4154	1.0459 3983	12
13	1.0329 9200	1.0385 8736	1.0442 1068	1.0498 6210	13
14	1.0355 7448	1.0416 1657	1.0476 9138	1.0537 9908	14
15	1.0381 6341	1.0446 5462	1.0511 8369	1.0577 5083	15
16	1.0407 5882	1.0477 0153	1.0546 8763	1.0617 1739	16
17	1.0433 6072	1.0507 5732	1.0582 0326	1.0656 9883	17
18	1.0459 6912	1.0538 2203	1.0617 3060	1.0696 9521	18
19	1.0485 8404	1.0568 9568	1.0652 6971	1.0737 0656	19
20	1.0512 0550	1.0599 7829	1.0688 2060	1.0777 3296	20
21	1.0538 3352	1.0630 6990	1.0723 8334	1.0817 7446	21
22	1.0564 6810	1.0661 7052	1.0759 5795	1.0858 3111	22
23	1.0591 0927	1.0692 8018	1.0795 4448	1.0899 0298	23
24	1.0617 5704	1.0723 9891	1.0831 4296	1.0939 9012	24
25	1.0644 1144	1.0755 2674	1.0867 5344	1.0980 9258	25
26	1.0670 7247	1.0786 6370	1.0903 7595	1.1022 1043	26
27	1.0697 4015	1.0818 0980	1.0940 1053	1.1063 4372	27
28	1.0724 1450	1.0849 6508	1.0976 5724	1.1104 9251	28
29	1.0750 9553	1.0881 2956	1.1013 1609	1.1146 5685	29
30	1.0777 8327	1.0913 0327	1.1049 8715	1.1188 3682	30
31	1.0804 7773	1.0944 8624	1.1086 7044	1.1230 3245	31
32	1.0831 7892	1.0976 7849	1.1123 6601	1.1272 4383	32
33	1.0858 8687	1.1008 8005	1.1160 7389	1.1314 7099	33
34	1.0886 0159	1.1040 9095	1.1197 9414	1.1357 1401	34
35	1.0913 2309	1.1073 1122	1.1235 2679	1.1399 7293	35
36	1.0940 5140	1.1105 4088	1.1272 7187	1.1442 4783	36
37	1.0967 8653	1.1137 7995	1.1310 2945	1.1485 3876	37
38	1.0995 2850	1.1170 2848	1.1347 9955	1.1528 4578	38
39	1.1022 7732	1.1202 8648	1.1385 8221	1.1571 6895	39
40	1.1050 3301	1.1235 5398	1.1423 7748	1.1615 0834	40
41	1.1077 9559	1.1268 3101	1.1461 8541	1.1658 6399	41
42	1.1105 6508	1.1301 1760	1.1500 0603	1.1702 3598	42
43	1.1133 4149	1.1334 1378	1.1538 3938	1.1746 2437	43
44	1.1161 2485	1.1367 1957	1.1576 8551	1.1790 2921	44
45	1.1189 1516	1.1400 3500	1.1615 4446	1.1834 5057	45
46	1.1217 1245	1.1433 6010	1.1654 1628	1.1878 8851	46
47	1.1245 1673	1.1466 9490	1.1693 0100	1.1923 4309	47
48	1.1273 2802	1.1500 3943	1.1731 9867	1.1968 1438	48
49	1.1301 4634	1.1533 9371	1.1771 0933	1.2013 0243	49
50	1.1329 7171	1.1567 5778	1.1810 3303	1.2058 0732	50

$$(1 + i)^n$$

n	$\frac{1}{4}\%$	$\frac{7}{24}\%$	$\frac{1}{3}\%$	$\frac{3}{8}\%$	n
51	1.1358 0414	1.1601 3165	1.1849 6981	1.2103 2909	51
52	1.1386 4365	1.1635 1537	1.1889 1971	1.2148 6783	52
53	1.1414 9026	1.1669 0896	1.1928 8277	1.2194 2358	53
54	1.1443 4398	1.1703 1244	1.1968 5905	1.2239 9642	54
55	1.1472 0484	1.1737 2585	1.2008 4858	1.2285 8641	55
56	1.1500 7285	1.1771 4922	1.2048 5141	1.2331 9361	56
57	1.1529 4804	1.1805 8257	1.2088 6758	1.2378 1808	57
58	1.1558 3041	1.1840 2594	1.2128 9714	1.2424 5990	58
59	1.1587 1998	1.1874 7935	1.2169 4013	1.2471 1912	59
60	1.1616 1678	1.1909 4283	1.2209 9659	1.2517 9582	60
61	1.1645 2082	1.1944 1641	1.2250 6658	1.2564 9005	61
62	1.1674 3213	1.1979 0013	1.2291 5014	1.2612 0189	62
63	1.1703 5071	1.2013 9400	1.2332 4730	1.2659 3140	63
64	1.1732 7658	1.2048 9807	1.2373 5813	1.2706 7864	64
65	1.1762 0977	1.2084 1235	1.2414 8266	1.2754 4369	65
66	1.1791 5030	1.2119 3689	1.2456 2093	1.2802 2660	66
67	1.1820 9817	1.2154 7171	1.2497 7300	1.2850 2745	67
68	1.1850 5342	1.2190 1683	1.2539 3891	1.2898 4630	68
69	1.1880 1605	1.2225 7230	1.2581 1871	1.2946 8323	69
70	1.1909 8609	1.2261 3813	1.2623 1244	1.2995 3829	70
71	1.1939 6356	1.2297 1437	1.2665 2015	1.3044 1156	71
72	1.1969 4847	1.2333 0104	1.2707 4188	1.3093 0310	72
73	1.1999 4084	1.2368 9816	1.2749 7769	1.3142 1299	73
74	1.2029 4069	1.2405 0578	1.2792 2761	1.3191 4129	74
75	1.2059 4804	1.2441 2393	1.2834 9170	1.3240 8807	75
76	1.2089 6291	1.2477 5262	1.2877 7001	1.3290 5340	76
77	1.2119 8532	1.2513 9190	1.2920 6258	1.3340 3735	77
78	1.2150 1528	1.2550 4179	1.2963 6945	1.3390 3999	78
79	1.2180 5282	1.2587 0233	1.3006 9068	1.3440 6139	79
80	1.2210 9795	1.2623 7355	1.3050 2632	1.3491 0162	80
81	1.2241 5070	1.2660 5547	1.3093 7641	1.3541 6075	81
82	1.2272 1108	1.2697 4813	1.3137 4099	1.3592 3885	82
83	1.2302 7910	1.2734 5156	1.3181 2013	1.3643 3600	83
84	1.2333 5480	1.2771 6580	1.3225 1386	1.3694 5226	84
85	1.2364 3819	1.2808 9086	1.3269 2224	1.3745 8770	85
86	1.2395 2928	1.2846 2680	1.3313 4532	1.3797 4241	86
87	1.2426 2811	1.2883 7362	1.3357 8314	1.3849 1644	87
88	1.2457 3468	1.2921 3138	1.3402 3575	1.3901 0988	88
89	1.2488 4901	1.2959 0010	1.3447 0320	1.3953 2279	89
90	1.2519 7114	1.2996 7980	1.3491 8554	1.4005 5525	90
91	1.2551 0106	1.3034 7054	1.3536 8283	1.4058 0733	91
92	1.2582 3882	1.3072 7233	1.3581 9510	1.4110 7911	92
93	1.2613 8441	1.3110 8520	1.3627 2242	1.4163 7066	93
94	1.2645 3787	1.3149 0920	1.3672 6483	1.4216 8205	94
95	1.2676 9922	1.3187 4435	1.3718 2238	1.4270 1335	95
96	1.2708 6847	1.3225 9069	1.3763 9512	1.4323 6465	96
97	1.2740 4564	1.3264 4825	1.3809 8310	1.4377 3602	97
98	1.2772 3075	1.3303 1706	1.3855 8638	1.4431 2753	98
99	1.2804 2383	1.3341 9715	1.3902 0500	1.4485 3926	99
100	1.2836 2489	1.3380 8856	1.3948 3902	1.4539 7128	100

$$(1 + i)^n$$

n	$\frac{1}{4}\%$	$\frac{7}{24}\%$	$\frac{1}{3}\%$	$\frac{3}{8}\%$	n
101	1.2868 3395	1.3419 9131	1.3994 8848	1.4594 2367	101
102	1.2900 5104	1.3459 0546	1.4041 5344	1.4648 9651	102
103	1.2932 7616	1.3498 3101	1.4088 3395	1.4703 8988	103
104	1.2965 0935	1.3537 6802	1.4135 3007	1.4759 0384	104
105	1.2997 5063	1.3577 1651	1.4182 4183	1.4814 3848	105
106	1.3030 0000	1.3616 7652	1.4229 6931	1.4869 9387	106
107	1.3062 5750	1.3656 4807	1.4277 1254	1.4925 7010	107
108	1.3095 2315	1.3696 3121	1.4324 7158	1.4981 6724	108
109	1.3127 9696	1.3736 2597	1.4372 4649	1.5037 8536	109
110	1.3160 7895	1.3776 3238	1.4420 3731	1.5094 2456	110
111	1.3193 6915	1.3816 5047	1.4468 4410	1.5150 8490	111
112	1.3226 6757	1.3856 8029	1.4516 6691	1.5207 6647	112
113	1.3259 7424	1.3897 2186	1.4565 0580	1.5264 6934	113
114	1.3292 8917	1.3937 7521	1.4613 6082	1.5321 9360	114
115	1.3326 1240	1.3978 4039	1.4662 3202	1.5379 3933	115
116	1.3359 4393	1.4019 1742	1.4711 1946	1.5437 0660	116
117	1.3392 8379	1.4060 0635	1.4760 2320	1.5494 9550	117
118	1.3426 3200	1.4101 0720	1.4809 4327	1.5553 0611	118
119	1.3459 8858	1.4142 2001	1.4858 7975	1.5611 3851	119
120	1.3493 5355	1.4183 4482	1.4908 3268	1.5669 9278	120
121	1.3527 2693	1.4224 8166	1.4958 0212	1.5728 6900	121
122	1.3561 0875	1.4266 3057	1.5007 8813	1.5787 6726	122
123	1.3594 9902	1.4307 9157	1.5057 9076	1.5846 8764	123
124	1.3628 9777	1.4349 6471	1.5108 1006	1.5906 3021	124
125	1.3663 0501	1.4391 5003	1.5158 4609	1.5965 9508	125
126	1.3697 2077	1.4433 4755	1.5208 9892	1.6025 8231	126
127	1.3731 4508	1.4475 5731	1.5259 6858	1.6085 9199	127
128	1.3765 7794	1.4517 7935	1.5310 5514	1.6146 2421	128
129	1.3800 1938	1.4560 1371	1.5361 5866	1.6206 7905	129
130	1.3834 6943	1.4602 6042	1.5412 7919	1.6267 5660	130
131	1.3869 2811	1.4645 1951	1.5464 1678	1.6328 5694	131
132	1.3903 9543	1.4687 9103	1.5515 7151	1.6389 8015	132
133	1.3938 7142	1.4730 7500	1.5567 4341	1.6451 2633	133
134	1.3973 5609	1.4773 7147	1.5619 3256	1.6512 9555	134
135	1.4008 4948	1.4816 8047	1.5671 3900	1.6574 8791	135
136	1.4043 5161	1.4860 0204	1.5723 6279	1.6637 0349	136
137	1.4078 6249	1.4903 3621	1.5776 0400	1.6699 4238	137
138	1.4113 8214	1.4946 8302	1.5828 6268	1.6762 0466	138
139	1.4149 1060	1 4990 4252	1.5881 3889	1.6824 9043	139
140	1.4184 4787	1.5034 1472	1.5934 3269	1.6887 9977	140
141	1.4219 9399	1.5077 9968	1.5987 4413	1.6951 3277	141
142	1.4255 4898	1.5121 9743	1.6040 7328	1.7014 8951	142
143	1.4291 1285	1.5166 0801	1.6094 2019	1.7078 7010	143
144	1.4326 8563	1.5210 3145	1.6147 8492	1.7142 7461	144
145	1.4362 6735	1.5254 6779	1.6201 6754	1.7207 0314	145
146	1.4398 5802	1.5299 1707	1.6255 6810	1.7271 5578	146
147	1.4434 5766	1.5343 7933	1.6309 8666	1.7336 3261	147
148	1.4470 6631	1.5388 5460	1.6364 2328	1.7401 3373	148
149	1.4506 8397	1.5433 4293	1.6418 7802	1.7466 5924	149
150	1.4543 1068	1.5478 4434	1.6473 5095	1.7532 0921	150

$$(1 + i)^n$$

n	$\frac{1}{4}\%$	$\frac{7}{24}\%$	$\frac{1}{3}\%$	$\frac{3}{8}\%$	n
151	1.4579 4646	1.5523 5889	1.6528 4212	1.7597 8374	151
152	1.4615 9132	1.5568 8660	1.6583 5160	1.7663 8293	152
153	1.4652 4530	1.5614 2752	1.6638 7943	1.7730 0687	153
154	1.4689 0842	1.5659 8169	1.6694 2570	1.7796 5564	154
155	1.4725 8069	1.5705 4913	1.6749 9045	1.7863 2935	155
156	1.4762 6214	1.5751 2990	1.6805 7375	1.7930 2809	156
157	1.4799 5279	1.5797 2403	1.6861 7566	1.7997 5194	157
158	1.4836 5268	1.5843 3156	1.6917 9625	1.8065 0101	158
159	1.4873 6181	1.5889 5253	1.6974 3557	1.8132 7539	159
160	1.4910 8021	1.5935 8697	1.7030 9369	1.8200 7517	160
161	1.4948 0791	1.5982 3493	1.7087 7067	1.8269 0046	161
162	1.4985 4493	1.6028 9645	1.7144 6657	1.8337 5133	162
163	1.5022 9129	1.6075 7157	1.7201 8146	1.8406 2790	163
164	1.5060 4702	1.6122 6032	1.7259 1540	1.8475 3025	164
165	1.5098 1214	1.6169 6274	1.7316 6845	1.8544 5849	165
166	1.5135 8667	1.6216 7888	1.7374 4068	1.8614 1271	166
167	1.5173 7064	1.6264 0878	1.7432 3215	1.8683 9301	167
168	1.5211 6406	1.6311 5247	1.7490 4292	1.8753 9948	168
169	1.5249 6697	1.6359 1000	1.7548 7306	1.8824 3223	169
170	1.5287 7939	1.6406 8140	1.7607 2264	1.8894 9135	170
171	1.5326 0134	1.6454 6673	1.7665 9172	1.8965 7695	171
172	1.5364 3284	1.6502 6600	1.7724 8035	1.9036 8911	172
173	1.5402 7393	1.6550 7928	1.7783 8862	1.9108 2794	173
174	1.5441 2461	1.6599 0659	1.7843 1658	1.9179 9355	174
175	1.5479 8492	1.6647 4799	1.7902 6431	1.9251 8602	175
176	1.5518 5488	1.6696 0350	1.7962 3185	1.9324 0547	176
177	1.5557 3452	1.6744 7318	1.8022 1929	1.9396 5199	177
178	1.5596 2386	1.6793 5706	1.8082 2669	1.9469 2569	178
179	1.5635 2292	1.6842 5518	1.8142 5411	1.9542 2666	179
180	1.5674 3172	1.6891 6760	1.8203 0163	1.9615 5501	180
181	1.5713 5030	1.6940 9433	1.8263 6930	1.9689 1084	181
182	1.5752 7868	1.6990 3544	1.8324 5720	1.9762 9426	182
183	1.5792 1688	1.7039 9096	1.8385 6539	1.9837 0536	183
184	1.5831 6492	1.7089 6094	1.8446 9394	1.9911 4425	184
185	1.5871 2283	1.7139 4541	1.8508 4292	1.9986 1104	185
186	1.5910 9064	1.7189 4441	1.8570 1240	2.0061 0584	186
187	1.5950 6836	1.7239 5800	1.8632 0244	2.0136 2873	187
188	1.5990 5604	1.7289 8621	1.8694 1311	2.0211 7984	188
189	1.6030 5368	1.7340 2909	1.8756 4449	2.0287 5927	189
190	1.6070 6131	1.7390 8667	1.8818 9664	2.0363 6711	190
191	1.6110 7896	1.7441 5901	1.8881 6963	2.0440 0349	191
192	1.6151 0666	1.7492 4614	1.8944 6352	2.0516 6850	192
193	1.6191 4443	1.7543 4811	1.9007 7840	2.0593 6226	193
194	1.6231 9229	1.7594 6496	1.9071 1433	2.0670 8487	194
195	1.6272 5027	1.7645 9673	1.9134 7138	2.0748 3644	195
196	1.6313 1839	1.7697 4347	1.9198 4962	2.0826 1707	196
197	1.6353 9669	1.7749 0522	1.9262 4912	2.0904 2689	197
198	1.6394 8518	1.7800 8203	1.9326 6995	2.0982 6599	198
199	1.6435 8390	1.7852 7393	1.9391 1218	2.1061 3448	199
200	1.6476 9285	1.7904 8098	1.9455 7589	2.1140 3249	200

$$(1 + i)^n$$

n	$\frac{1}{4}\%$	$\frac{7}{24}\%$	$\frac{1}{3}\%$	$\frac{3}{8}\%$	n
201	1.6518 1209	1.7957 0322	1.9520 6114	2.1219 6011	201
202	1.6559 4162	1.8009 4069	1.9585 6801	2.1299 1746	202
203	1.6600 8147	1.8061 9343	1.9650 9657	2.1379 0465	203
204	1.6642 3168	1.8114 6149	1.9716 4689	2.1459 2179	204
205	1.6683 9225	1.8167 4492	1.9782 1905	2.1539 6900	205
206	1.6725 6323	1.8220 4376	1.9848 1311	2.1620 4638	206
207	1.6767 4464	1.8273 5806	1.9914 2915	2.1701 5406	207
208	1.6809 3650	1.8326 8785	1.9980 6725	2.1782 9214	208
209	1.6851 3885	1.8380 3319	2.0047 2748	2.1864 6073	209
210	1.6893 5169	1.8433 9412	2.0114 0990	2.1946 5996	210
211	1.6935 7507	1.8487 7069	2.0181 1460	2.2028 8993	211
212	1.6978 0901	1.8541 6294	2.0248 4165	2.2111 5077	212
213	1.7020 5353	1.8595 7091	2.0315 9112	2.2194 4259	213
214	1.7063 0867	1.8649 9466	2.0383 6309	2.2277 6550	214
215	1.7105 7444	1.8704 3423	2.0451 5764	2.2361 1962	215
216	1.7148 5087	1.8758 8966	2.0519 7483	2.2445 0507	216
217	1.7191 3800	1.8813 6101	2.0588 1474	2.2529 2196	217
218	1.7234 3585	1.8868 4831	2.0656 7746	2.2613 7042	218
219	1.7277 4444	1.8923 5162	2.0725 6305	2.2698 5056	219
220	1.7320 6380	1.8978 7097	2.0794 7159	2.2783 6250	220
221	1.7363 9396	1.9034 0643	2.0864 0317	2.2869 0636	221
222	1.7407 3494	1.9089 5803	2.0933 5784	2.2954 8225	222
223	1.7450 8678	1.9145 2583	2.1003 3570	2.3040 9031	223
224	1.7494 4950	1.9201 0986	2.1073 3682	2.3127 3065	224
225	1.7538 2312	1.9257 1018	2.1143 6128	2.3214 0339	225
226	1.7582 0768	1.9313 2684	2.1214 0915	2.3301 0865	226
227	1.7626 0320	1.9369 5987	2.1284 8051	2.3388 4656	227
228	1.7670 0970	1.9426 0934	2.1355 7545	2.3476 1724	228
229	1.7714 2723	1.9482 7528	2.1426 9403	2.3564 2080	229
230	1.7758 5580	1.9539 5775	2.1498 3635	2.3652 5738	230
231	1.7802 9544	1.9596 5680	2.1570 0247	2.3741 2709	231
232	1.7847 4617	1.9653 7246	2.1641 9248	2.3830 3007	232
233	1.7892 0804	1.9711 0480	2.1714 0645	2.3919 6643	233
234	1.7936 8106	1.9768 5385	2.1786 4447	2.4009 3631	234
235	1.7981 6526	1.9826 1968	2.1859 0662	2.4099 3982	235
236	1.8026 6068	1.9884 0232	2.1931 9298	2.4189 7709	236
237	1.8071 6733	1.9942 0183	2.2005 0362	2.4280 4826	237
238	1.8116 8525	2.0000 1825	2.2078 3863	2.4371 5344	238
239	1.8162 1446	2.0058 5163	2.2151 9809	2.4462 9276	239
240	1.8207 5500	2.0117 0203	2.2225 8209	2.4554 6636	240
241	1.8253 0688	2.0175 6950	2.2299 9069	2.4646 7436	241
242	1.8298 7015	2.0234 5408	2.2374 2400	2.4739 1689	242
243	1.8344 4483	2.0293 5582	2.2448 8208	2.4831 9408	243
244	1.8390 3094	2.0352 7477	2.2523 6502	2.4925 0605	244
245	1.8436 2851	2.0412 1099	2.2598 7290	2.5018 5295	245
246	1.8482 3759	2.0471 6452	2.2674 0581	2.5112 3490	246
247	1.8528 5818	2.0531 3542	2.2749 6383	2.5206 5203	247
248	1.8574 9033	2.0591 2373	2.2825 4704	2.5301 0448	248
249	1.8621 3405	2.0651 2951	2.2901 5553	2.5395 9237	249
250	1.8667 8939	2.0711 5280	2.2977 8938	2.5491 1584	250

V. COMPOUND AMOUNT OF 1

$$(1 + i)^n$$

n	$\frac{5}{12}\%$	$\frac{1}{2}\%$	$\frac{7}{12}\%$	$\frac{5}{8}\%$	n
1	1.0041 6667	1.0050 0000	1.0058 3333	1.0062 5000	1
2	1.0083 5069	1.0100 2500	1.0117 0069	1.0125 3906	2
3	1.0125 5216	1.0150 7513	1.0176 0228	1.0188 6743	3
4	1.0167 7112	1.0201 5050	1.0235 3830	1.0252 3535	4
5	1.0210 0767	1.0252 5125	1.0295 0894	1.0316 4307	5
6	1.0252 6187	1.0303 7751	1.0355 1440	1.0380 9084	6
7	1.0295 3379	1.0355 2940	1.0415 5490	1.0445 7891	7
8	1.0338 2352	1.0407 0704	1.0476 3064	1.0511 0753	8
9	1.0381 3111	1.0459 1058	1.0537 4182	1.0576 7695	9
10	1.0424 5666	1.0511 4013	1.0598 8865	1.0642 8743	10
11	1.0468 0023	1.0563 9583	1.0660 7133	1.0709 3923	11
12	1.0511 6190	1.0616 7781	1.0722 9008	1.0776 3260	12
13	1.0555 4174	1.0669 8620	1.0785 4511	1.0843 6780	13
14	1.0599 3983	1.0723 2113	1.0848 3662	1.0911 4510	14
15	1.0643 5625	1.0776 8274	1.0911 6483	1.0979 6476	15
16	1.0687 9106	1.0830 7115	1.0975 2996	1.1048 2704	16
17	1.0732 4436	1.0884 8651	1.1039 3222	1.1117 3221	17
18	1.0777 1621	1.0939 2894	1.1103 7182	1.1186 8053	18
19	1.0822 0670	1.0993 9858	1.1168 4899	1.1256 7229	19
20	1.0867 1589	1.1048 9558	1.1233 6395	1.1327 0774	20
21	1.0912 4387	1.1104 2006	1.1299 1690	1.1397 8716	21
22	1.0957 9072	1.1159 7216	1.1365 0808	1.1469 1083	22
23	1.1003 5652	1.1215 5202	1.1431 3771	1.1540 7902	23
24	1.1049 4134	1.1271 5978	1.1498 0602	1.1612 9202	24
25	1.1095 4526	1.1327 9558	1.1565 1322	1.1685 5009	25
26	1.1141 6836	1.1384 5955	1.1632 5955	1.1758 5353	26
27	1.1188 1073	1.1441 5185	1.1700 4523	1.1832 0262	27
28	1.1234 7244	1.1498 7261	1.1768 7049	1.1905 9763	28
29	1.1281 5358	1.1556 2197	1.1837 3557	1.1980 3887	29
30	1.1328 5422	1.1614 0008	1.1906 4069	1.2055 2661	30
31	1.1375 7444	1.1672 0708	1.1975 8610	1.2130 6115	31
32	1.1423 1434	1.1730 4312	1.2045 7202	1.2206 4278	32
33	1.1470 7398	1.1789 0833	1.2115 9869	1.2282 7180	33
34	1.1518 5346	1.1848 0288	1.2186 6634	1.2359 4850	34
35	1.1566 5284	1.1907 2689	1.2257 7523	1.2436 7318	35
36	1.1614 7223	1.1966 8052	1.2329 2559	1.2514 4614	36
37	1.1663 1170	1.2026 6393	1.2401 1765	1.2592 6767	37
38	1.1711 7133	1.2086 7725	1.2473 5167	1.2671 3810	38
39	1.1760 5121	1.2147 2063	1.2546 2789	1.2750 5771	39
40	1.1809 5142	1.2207 9424	1.2619 4655	1.2830 2682	40
41	1.1858 7206	1.2268 9821	1.2693 0791	1.2910 4574	41
42	1.1908 1319	1.2330 3270	1.2767 1220	1.2991 1477	42
43	1.1957 7491	1.2391 9786	1.2841 5969	1.3072 3424	43
44	1.2007 5731	1.2453 9385	1.2916 5062	1.3154 0446	44
45	1.2057 6046	1.2516 2082	1.2991 8525	1.3236 2573	45
46	1.2107 8446	1.2578 7892	1.3067 6383	1.3318 9839	46
47	1.2158 2940	1.2641 6832	1.3143 8662	1.3402 2276	47
48	1.2208 9536	1.2704 8916	1.3220 5388	1.3485 9915	48
49	1.2259 8242	1.2768 4161	1.3297 6586	1.3570 2790	49
50	1.2310 9068	1.2832 2581	1.3375 2283	1.3655 0932	50

V. COMPOUND AMOUNT OF 1

$$(1 + i)^n$$

n	$\frac{5}{12}\%$	$\frac{1}{2}\%$	$\frac{7}{12}\%$	$\frac{5}{8}\%$	n
51	1.2362 2022	1.2896 4194	1.3453 2504	1.3740 4375	51
52	1.2413 7114	1.2960 9015	1.3531 7277	1.3826 3153	52
53	1.2465 4352	1.3025 7060	1.3610 6628	1.3912 7297	53
54	1.2517 3745	1.3090 8346	1.3690 0583	1.3999 6843	54
55	1.2569 5302	1.3156 2887	1.3769 9170	1.4087 1823	55
56	1.2621 9033	1.3222 0702	1.3850 2415	1.4175 2272	56
57	1.2674 4946	1.3288 1805	1.3931 0346	1.4263 8224	57
58	1.2727 3050	1.3354 6214	1.4012 2990	1.4352 9713	58
59	1.2780 3354	1.3421 3946	1.4094 0374	1.4442 6773	59
60	1.2833 5868	1.3488 5015	1.4176 2526	1.4532 9441	60
61	1.2887 0601	1.3555 9440	1.4258 9474	1.4623 7750	61
62	1.2940 7561	1.3623 7238	1.4342 1246	1.4715 1736	62
63	1.2994 6760	1.3691 8424	1.4425 7870	1.4807 1434	63
64	1.3048 8204	1.3760 3016	1.4509 9374	1.4899 6881	64
65	1.3103 1905	1.3829 1031	1.4594 5787	1.4992 8111	65
66	1.3157 7872	1.3898 2486	1.4679 7138	1.5086 5162	66
67	1.3212 6113	1.3967 7399	1.4765 3454	1.5180 8069	67
68	1.3267 6638	1.4037 5785	1.4851 4766	1.5275 6869	68
69	1.3322 9458	1.4107 7664	1.4938 1102	1.5371 1600	69
70	1.3378 4580	1.4178 3053	1.5025 2492	1.5467 2297	70
71	1.3434 2016	1.4249 1968	1.5112 8965	1.5563 8999	71
72	1.3490 1774	1.4320 4428	1.5201 0550	1.5661 1743	72
73	1.3546 3865	1.4392 0450	1.5289 7279	1.5759 0566	73
74	1.3602 8298	1.4464 0052	1.5378 9179	1.5857 5507	74
75	1.3659 5082	1.4536 3252	1.5468 6283	1.5956 6604	75
76	1.3716 4229	1.4609 0069	1.5558 8620	1.6056 3896	76
77	1.3773 5746	1.4682 0519	1.5649 6220	1.6156 7420	77
78	1.3830 9645	1.4755 4622	1.5740 9115	1.6257 7216	78
79	1.3888 5935	1.4829 2395	1.5832 7334	1.6359 3324	79
80	1.3946 4627	1.4903 3857	1.5925 0910	1.6461 5782	80
81	1.4004 5729	1.4977 9026	1.6017 9874	1.6564 4631	81
82	1.4062 9253	1.5052 7921	1.6111 4257	1.6667 9910	82
83	1.4121 5209	1.5128 0561	1.6205 4090	1.6772 1659	83
84	1.4180 3605	1.5203 6964	1.6299 9405	1.6876 9920	84
85	1.4239 4454	1.5279 7148	1.6395 0235	1.6982 4732	85
86	1.4298 7764	1.5356 1134	1.6490 6612	1.7088 6136	86
87	1.4358 3546	1.5432 8940	1.6586 8567	1.7195 4175	87
88	1.4418 1811	1.5510 0585	1.6683 6134	1.7302 8888	88
89	1.4478 2568	1.5587 6087	1.6780 9344	1.7411 0319	89
90	1.4538 5829	1.5665 5468	1.6878 8232	1.7519 8508	90
91	1.4599 1603	1.5743 8745	1.6977 2830	1.7629 3499	91
92	1.4659 9902	1.5822 5939	1.7076 3172	1.7739 5333	92
93	1.4721 0735	1.5901 7069	1.7175 9290	1.7850 4054	93
94	1.4782 4113	1.5981 2154	1.7276 1219	1.7961 9704	94
95	1.4844 0047	1.6061 1215	1.7376 8993	1.8074 2328	95
96	1.4905 8547	1.6141 4271	1.7478 2646	1.8187 1967	96
97	1.4967 9624	1.6222 1342	1.7580 2211	1.8300 8667	97
98	1.5030 3289	1.6303 2449	1.7682 7724	1.8415 2471	98
99	1.5092 9553	1.6384 7611	1.7785 9219	1.8530 3424	99
100	1.5155 8426	1.6466 6849	1.7889 6731	1.8646 1570	100

V. COMPOUND AMOUNT OF 1

$$(1 + i)^n$$

n	$\frac{5}{12}\%$	$\frac{1}{2}\%$	$\frac{7}{12}\%$	$\frac{5}{8}\%$	n
101	1.5218 9919	1.6549 0183	1.7994 0295	1.8762 6955	101
102	1.5282 4044	1.6631 7634	1.8098 9947	1.8879 9624	102
103	1.5346 0811	1.6714 9223	1.8204 5722	1.8997 9621	103
104	1.5410 0231	1.6798 4969	1.8310 7655	1.9116 6994	104
105	1.5474 2315	1.6882 4894	1.8417 5783	1.9236 1788	105
106	1.5538 7075	1.6966 9018	1.8525 0142	1.9356 4049	106
107	1.5603 4521	1.7051 7363	1.8633 0768	1.9477 3824	107
108	1.5668 4665	1.7136 9950	1.8741 7697	1.9599 1161	108
109	1.5733 7518	1.7222 6800	1.8851 0967	1.9721 6105	109
110	1.5799 3091	1.7308 7934	1.8961 0614	1.9844 8706	110
111	1.5865 1395	1.7395 3373	1.9071 6676	1.9968 9010	111
112	1.5931 2443	1.7482 3140	1.9182 9190	2.0093 7067	112
113	1.5997 6245	1.7569 7256	1.9294 8194	2.0219 2923	113
114	1.6064 2812	1.7657 5742	1.9407 3725	2.0345 6629	114
115	1.6131 2157	1.7745 8621	1.9520 5822	2.0472 8233	115
116	1.6198 4291	1.7834 5914	1.9634 4522	2.0600 7785	116
117	1.6265 9226	1.7923 7644	1.9748 9865	2.0729 5333	117
118	1.6333 6973	1.8013 3832	1.9864 1890	2.0859 0929	118
119	1.6401 7543	1.8103 4501	1.9980 0634	2.0989 4622	119
120	1.6470 0950	1.8193 9673	2.0096 6138	2.1120 6464	120
121	1.6538 7204	1.8284 9372	2.0213 8440	2.1252 6504	121
122	1.6607 6317	1.8376 3619	2.0331 7581	2.1385 4795	122
123	1.6676 8302	1.8468 2437	2.0450 3600	2.1519 1387	123
124	1.6746 3170	1.8560 5849	2.0569 6538	2.1653 6333	124
125	1.6816 0933	1.8653 3878	2.0689 6434	2.1788 9685	125
126	1.6886 1603	1.8746 6548	2.0810 3330	2.1925 1496	126
127	1.6956 5193	1.8840 3880	2.0931 7266	2.2062 1818	127
128	1.7027 1715	1.8934 5900	2.1053 8284	2.2200 0704	128
129	1.7098 1181	1.9029 2629	2.1176 6424	2.2338 8209	129
130	1.7169 3602	1.9124 4092	2.1300 1728	2.2478 4385	130
131	1.7240 8992	1.9220 0313	2.1424 4238	2.2618 9287	131
132	1.7312 7363	1.9316 1314	2.1549 3996	2.2760 2970	132
133	1.7384 8727	1.9412 7121	2.1675 1044	2.2902 5489	133
134	1.7457 3097	1.9509 7757	2.1801 5425	2.3045 6898	134
135	1.7530 0485	1.9607 3245	2.1928 7182	2.3189 7254	135
136	1.7603 0903	1.9705 3612	2.2056 6357	2.3334 6612	136
137	1.7676 4365	1.9803 8880	2.2185 2994	2.3480 5028	137
138	1.7750 0884	1.9902 9074	2.2314 7137	2.3627 2559	138
139	1.7824 0471	2.0002 4219	2.2444 8828	2.3774 9263	139
140	1.7898 3139	2.0102 4340	2.2575 8113	2.3923 5196	140
141	1.7972 8902	2.0202 9462	2.2707 5036	2.4073 0416	141
142	1.8047 7773	2.0303 9609	2.2839 9640	2.4223 4981	142
143	1.8122 9763	2.0405 4808	2.2973 1971	2.4374 8950	143
144	1.8198 4887	2.0507 5082	2.3107 2074	2.4527 2380	144
145	1.8274 3158	2.0610 0457	2.3241 9995	2.4680 5333	145
146	1.8350 4588	2.0713 0959	2.3377 5778	2.4834 7866	146
147	1.8426 9190	2.0816 6614	2.3513 9470	2.4990 0040	147
148	1.8503 6978	2.0920 7447	2.3651 1117	2.5146 1916	148
149	1.8580 7966	2.1025 3484	2.3789 0765	2.5303 3553	149
150	1.8658 2166	2.1130 4752	2.3927 8461	2.5461 5012	150

$$(1 + i)^n$$

n	$\frac{5}{12}\%$	$\frac{1}{2}\%$	$\frac{7}{12}\%$	$\frac{5}{8}\%$	n
151	1.8735 9591	2.1236 1276	2.4067 4252	2.5620 6356	151
152	1.8814 0256	2.1342 3082	2.4207 8186	2.5780 7646	152
153	1.8892 4174	2.1449 0197	2.4349 0308	2.5941 8944	153
154	1.8971 1358	2.1556 2648	2.4491 0668	2.6104 0312	154
155	1.9050 1822	2.1664 0462	2.4633 9314	2.6267 1814	155
156	1.9129 5580	2.1772 3664	2.4777 6293	2.6431 3513	156
157	1.9209 2645	2.1881 2282	2.4922 1655	2.6596 5472	157
158	1.9289 3031	2.1990 6344	2.5067 5448	2.6762 7756	158
159	1.9369 6752	2.2100 5875	2.5213 7722	2.6930 0430	159
160	1.9450 3821	2.2211 0905	2.5360 8525	2.7098 3558	160
161	1.9531 4254	2.2322 1459	2.5508 7908	2.7267 7205	161
162	1.9612 8063	2.2433 7566	2.5657 5921	2.7438 1437	162
163	1.9694 5264	2.2545 9254	2.5807 2614	2.7609 6321	163
164	1.9776 5869	2.2658 6551	2.5957 8037	2.7782 1923	164
165	1.9858 9893	2.2771 9483	2.6109 2242	2.7955 8310	165
166	1.9941 7351	2.2885 8081	2.6261 5280	2.8130 5550	166
167	2.0024 8257	2.3000 2371	2.6414 720?	2.8306 3710	167
168	2.0108 2625	2.3115 2383	2.6568 8062	2.8483 2858	168
169	2.0192 0469	2.3230 8145	2.6723 7909	2.8661 3063	169
170	2.0276 1804	2.3346 9686	2.6879 6796	2 8840 4395	170
171	2.0360 6645	2.3463 7034	2.7036 4778	2.9020 6922	171
172	2.0445 5006	2.3581 0219	2.7194 1906	2.9202 0715	172
173	2.0530 6902	2.3698 9270	2.7352 8233	2.9384 5845	173
174	2.0616 2347	2.3817 4217	2.7512 3815	2.9568 2381	174
175	2.0702 1357	2.3936 5088	2.7672 8704	2.9753 0396	175
176	2.0788 3946	2.4056 1913	2.7834 2954	2.9938 9961	176
177	2.0875 0129	2.4176 4723	2.7996 6622	3.0126 1149	177
178	2.0961 9921	2.4297 3546	2.8159 9760	3.0314 4031	178
179	2.1049 3338	2.4418 8414	2.8324 2426	3.0503 8681	179
180	2.1137 0393	2.4540 9356	2.8489 4673	3.0694 5173	180
181	2.1225 1103	2.4663 6403	2.8655 6559	3.0886 3580	181
182	2.1313 5483	2.4786 9585	2.8822 8139	3.1079 3977	182
183	2.1402 3547	2.4910 8933	2.8990 9469	3.1272 6440	183
184	2.1491 5312	2.5035 4478	2.9160 0608	3.1469 1043	184
185	2.1581 0793	2.5160 6250	2.9330 1612	3.1665 7862	185
186	2.1671 0004	2.5286 4281	2.9501 2538	3.1863 6973	186
187	2.1761 2963	2.5412 8603	2.9673 3444	3.2062 8454	187
188	2.1851 9683	2.5539 9246	2.9846 4389	3.2263 2382	188
189	2.1943 0182	2.5667 6242	3.0020 5431	3.2464 8834	189
190	2.2034 4474	2.5795 9623	3.0195 6630	3.2667 7890	190
191	2.2126 2576	2.5924 9421	3.0371 8043	3.2871 9627	191
192	2.2218 4504	2.6054 5668	3.0548 9732	3.3077 4124	192
193	2.2311 0272	2.6184 8397	3.0727 1755	3.3284 1462	193
194	2.2403 9899	2.6315 7639	3.0906 4174	3.3492 1722	194
195	2.2497 3398	2.6447 3427	3.1086 7048	3.3701 4982	195
196	2.2591 0787	2.6579 5794	3.1268 0440	3.3912 1326	196
197	2.2685 2082	2.6712 4773	3.1450 4409	3.4124 0834	197
198	2.2779 7299	2.6846 0397	3.1633 9018	3.4337 3589	198
199	2.2874 6455	2.6980 2699	3.1818 4329	3.4551 9674	199
200	2.2969 9565	2.7115 1712	3.2004 0404	3.4767 9172	200

V. COMPOUND AMOUNT OF 1

$$(1 + i)^n$$

n	$\frac{5}{12}\%$	$\frac{1}{2}\%$	$\frac{7}{12}\%$	$\frac{5}{8}\%$	n
201	2.3065 6646	2.7250 7471	3.2190 7306	3.4985 2167	201
202	2.3161 7716	2.7387 0008	3.2378 5099	3.5203 8743	202
203	2.3258 2790	2.7523 9358	3.2567 3845	3.5423 8985	203
204	2.3355 1885	2.7661 5555	3.2757 3609	3.5645 2979	204
205	2.3452 5017	2.7799 8633	3.2948 4456	3.5868 0810	205
206	2.3550 2205	2.7938 8626	3.3140 6448	3.6092 2565	206
207	2.3648 3464	2.8078 5569	3.3333 9652	3.6317 8331	207
208	2.3746 8812	2.8218 9497	3.3528 4134	3.6544 8196	208
209	2.3845 8265	2.8360 0444	3.3723 9958	3.6773 2247	209
210	2.3945 1841	2.8501 8447	3.3920 7191	3.7003 0574	210
211	2.4044 9557	2.8644 3539	3.4118 5900	3.7234 3265	211
212	2.4145 1431	2.8787 5757	3.4317 6151	3.7467 0410	212
213	2.4245 7478	2.8931 5135	3.4517 8012	3.7701 2100	213
214	2.4346 7718	2.9076 1711	3.4719 1550	3.7936 8426	214
215	2.4448 2167	2.9221 5520	3.4921 6834	3.8173 9478	215
216	2.4550 0842	2.9367 6597	3.5125 3932	3.8412 5350	216
217	2.4652 3762	2.9514 4980	3.5330 2913	3.8652 6134	217
218	2.4755 0945	2.9662 0705	3.5536 3847	3.8894 1922	218
219	2.4858 2407	2.9810 3809	3.5743 6803	3.9137 2809	219
220	2.4961 8167	2.9959 4328	3.5952 1851	3.9381 8889	220
221	2.5065 8243	3.0109 2299	3.6161 9062	3.9628 0257	221
222	2.5170 2652	3.0259 7761	3.6372 8506	3.9875 7009	222
223	2.5275 1413	3.0411 0750	3.6585 0256	4.0124 9240	223
224	2.5380 4544	3.0563 1303	3.6798 4382	4.0375 7048	224
225	2.5486 2063	3.0715 9460	3.7013 0958	4.0628 0529	225
226	2.5592 3988	3.0869 5257	3.7229 0055	4.0881 9783	226
227	2.5699 0338	3.1023 8733	3.7446 1747	4.1137 4906	227
228	2.5806 1131	3.1178 9927	3.7664 6107	4.1394 5999	228
229	2.5913 6386	3.1334 8877	3.7884 3210	4.1653 3162	229
230	2.6021 6121	3.1491 5621	3.8105 3128	4.1913 6494	230
231	2.6130 0355	3.1649 0199	3.8327 5938	4.2175 6097	231
232	2.6238 9106	3.1807 2650	3.8551 1715	4.2439 2073	232
233	2.6348 2394	3.1966 3013	3.8776 0533	4.2704 4523	233
234	2.6458 0238	3.2126 1329	3.9002 2469	4.2971 3552	234
235	2.6568 2655	3.2286 7635	3.9229 7600	4.3239 9261	235
236	2.6678 9666	3.2448 1973	3.9458 6003	4.3510 1757	236
237	2.6790 1290	3.2610 4383	3.9688 7755	4.3782 1143	237
238	2.6901 7545	3.2773 4905	3.9920 2933	4.4055 7525	238
239	2.7013 8452	3.2937 3580	4.0153 1617	4.4331 1009	239
240	2.7126 4029	3.3102 0448	4.0387 3885	4.4608 1703	240
241	2.7239 4295	3.3267 5550	4.0622 9816	4.4886 9714	241
242	2.7352 9272	3.3433 8928	4.0859 9490	4.5167 5150	242
243	2.7466 8977	3.3601 0622	4.1098 2987	4.5449 8119	243
244	2.7581 3431	3.3769 0675	4.1338 0388	4.5733 8732	244
245	2.7696 2654	3.3937 9129	4.1579 1773	4.6019 7100	245
246	2.7811 6665	3.4107 6024	4.1821 7225	4.6307 3331	246
247	2.7927 5484	3.4278 1404	4.2065 6826	4.6596 7540	247
248	2.8043 9132	3.4449 5311	4.2311 0657	4.6887 9837	248
249	2.8160 7628	3.4621 7788	4.2557 8803	4.7181 0336	249
250	2.8278 0993	3.4794 8877	4.2806 1346	4.7475 9150	250

V. COMPOUND AMOUNT OF 1

$$(1 + i)^n$$

n	$\frac{3}{4}\%$	$\frac{7}{8}\%$	1%	$1\frac{1}{8}\%$	n
1	1.0075 0000	1.0087 5000	1.0100 0000	1.0112 5000	1
2	1.0150 5625	1.0175 7656	1.0201 0000	1.0226 2656	2
3	1.0226 6917	1.0264 8036	1.0303 0100	1.0341 3111	3
4	1.0303 3919	1.0354 6206	1.0406 0401	1.0457 6509	4
5	1.0380 6673	1.0445 2235	1.0510 1005	1.0575 2994	5
6	1.0458 5224	1.0536 6192	1.0615 2015	1.0694 2716	6
7	1.0536 9613	1.0628 8147	1.0721 3535	1.0814 5821	7
8	1.0615 9885	1.0721 8168	1.0828 5671	1.0936 2462	8
9	1.0695 6084	1.0815 6327	1.0936 8527	1.1059 2789	9
10	1.0775 8255	1.0910 2695	1.1046 2213	1.1183 6958	10
11	1.0856 6441	1.1005 7343	1.1156 6835	1.1309 5124	11
12	1.0938 0690	1.1102 0345	1.1268 2503	1.1436 7444	12
13	1.1020 1045	1.1199 1773	1.1380 9328	1.1565 4078	13
14	1.1102 7553	1.1297 1701	1.1494 7421	1.1695 5186	14
15	1.1186 0259	1.1396 0203	1.1609 6896	1.1827 0932	15
16	1.1269 9211	1.1495 7355	1.1725 7864	1.1960 1480	16
17	1.1354 4455	1.1596 3232	1.1843 0443	1.2094 6997	17
18	1.1439 6039	1.1697 7910	1.1961 4748	1.2230 7650	18
19	1.1525 4009	1.1800 1467	1.2081 0895	1.2368 3611	19
20	1.1611 8414	1.1903 3980	1.2201 9004	1.2507 5052	20
21	1.1698 9302	1.2007 5527	1.2323 9194	1.2648 2146	21
22	1.1786 6722	1.2112 6188	1.2447 1586	1.2790 5071	22
23	1.1875 0723	1.2218 6042	1.2571 6302	1.2934 4003	23
24	1.1964 1353	1.2325 5170	1.2697 3465	1.3079 9123	24
25	1.2053 8663	1.2433 3653	1.2824 3200	1.3227 0613	25
26	1.2144 2703	1.2542 1572	1.2952 5631	1.3375 8657	26
27	1.2235 3523	1.2651 9011	1.3082 0888	1.3526 3442	27
28	1.2327 1175	1.2762 6052	1.3212 9097	1.3678 5156	28
29	1.2419 5709	1.2874 2780	1.3345 0388	1.3832 3989	29
30	1.2512 7176	1.2986 9280	1.3478 4892	1.3988 0134	30
31	1.2606 5630	1.3100 5636	1.3613 2740	1.4145 3785	31
32	1.2701 1122	1.3215 1935	1.3749 4068	1.4304 5140	32
33	1.2796 3706	1.3330 8265	1.3886 9009	1.4465 4398	33
34	1.2892 3434	1.3447 4712	1.4025 7699	1.4628 1760	34
35	1.2989 0359	1.3565 1366	1.4166 0276	1.4792 7430	35
36	1.3086 4537	1.3683 8315	1.4307 6878	1.4959 1613	36
37	1.3184 6021	1.3803 5650	1.4450 7647	1.5127 4519	37
38	1.3283 4866	1.3924 3462	1.4595 2724	1.5297 6357	38
39	1.3383 1128	1.4046 1843	1.4741 2251	1.5469 7341	39
40	1.3483 4861	1.4169 0884	1.4888 6373	1.5643 7687	40
41	1.3584 6123	1.4293 0679	1.5037 5237	1.5819 7611	41
42	1.3686 4969	1.4418 1322	1.5187 8989	1.5997 7334	42
43	1.3789 1456	1.4544 2909	1.5339 7779	1.6177 7079	43
44	1.3892 5642	1.4671 5534	1.5493 1757	1.6359 7071	44
45	1.3996 7584	1.4799 9295	1.5648 1075	1.6543 7538	45
46	1.4101 7341	1.4929 4289	1.5804 5885	1.6729 8710	46
47	1.4207 4971	1.5060 0614	1.5962 6344	1.6918 0821	47
48	1.4314 0533	1.5191 8370	1.6122 2608	1.7108 4105	48
49	1.4421 4087	1.5324 7655	1.6283 4834	1.7300 8801	49
50	1.4529 5693	1.5458 8572	1.6446 3182	1.7495 5150	50

V. COMPOUND AMOUNT OF 1

$$(1 + i)^n$$

n	$\frac{3}{4}\%$	$\frac{7}{8}\%$	1%	$1\frac{1}{8}\%$	n
51	1.4638 5411	1.5594 1222	1.6610 7814	1.7692 3395	51
52	1.4748 3301	1.5730 5708	1.6776 8892	1.7891 3784	52
53	1.4858 9426	1.5868 2133	1.6944 6581	1.8092 6564	53
54	1.4970 3847	1.6007 0602	1.7114 1047	1.8296 1988	54
55	1.5082 6626	1.6147 1219	1.7285 2457	1.8502 0310	55
56	1.5195 7825	1.6288 4093	1.7458 0982	1.8710 1788	56
57	1.5309 7509	1.6430 9328	1.7632 6792	1.8920 6684	57
58	1.5424 5740	1.6574 7035	1.7809 0060	1.9133 5259	58
59	1.5540 2583	1.6719 7322	1.7987 0960	1.9348 7780	59
60	1.5656 8103	1.6866 0298	1.8166 9670	1.9566 4518	60
61	1.5774 2363	1.7013 6076	1.8348 6367	1.9786 5744	61
62	1.5892 5431	1.7162 4766	1.8532 1230	2.0009 1733	62
63	1.6011 7372	1.7312 6483	1.8717 4443	2.0234 2765	63
64	1.6131 8252	1.7464 1340	1.8904 6187	2.0461 9121	64
65	1.6252 8139	1.7616 9452	1.9093 6649	2.0692 1087	65
66	1.6374 7100	1.7771 0934	1.9284 6015	2.0924 8949	66
67	1.6497 5203	1.7926 5905	1.9477 4475	2.1160 2999	67
68	1.6621 2517	1.8083 4482	1.9672 2220	2.1398 3533	68
69	1.6745 9111	1.8241 6783	1.9868 9442	2.1639 0848	69
70	1.6871 5055	1.8401 2930	2.0067 6337	2.1882 5245	70
71	1.6998 0418	1.8562 3043	2.0268 3100	2.2128 7029	71
72	1.7125 5271	1.8724 7245	2.0470 9931	2.2377 6508	72
73	1.7253 9685	1.8888 5658	2.0675 7031	2.2629 3994	73
74	1.7383 3733	1.9053 8408	2.0882 4601	2.2883 9801	74
75	1.7513 7486	1.9220 5619	2.1091 2847	2.3141 4249	75
76	1.7645 1017	1.9388 7418	2.1302 1975	2.3401 7659	76
77	1.7777 4400	1.9558 3933	2.1515 2195	2.3665 0358	77
78	1.7910 7708	1.9729 5292	2.1730 3717	2.3931 2675	78
79	1.8045 1015	1.9902 1626	2.1947 6754	2.4200 4942	79
80	1.8180 4398	2.0076 3066	2.2167 1522	2.4472 7498	80
81	1.8316 7931	2.0251 9742	2.2388 8237	2.4748 0682	81
82	1.8454 1691	2.0429 1790	2.2612 7119	2.5026 4840	82
83	1.8592 5753	2.0607 9343	2.2838 8390	2.5308 0319	83
84	1.8732 0196	2.0788 2537	2 3067 2274	2.5592 7473	84
85	1.8872 5098	2.0970 1510	2.3297 8997	2.5880 6657	85
86	1.9014 0536	2.1153 6398	2.3530 8787	2.6171 8232	86
87	1.9156 6590	2.1338 7341	2.3766 1875	2.6466 2562	87
88	1.9300 3339	2.1525 4481	2.4003 8494	2.6764 0016	88
89	1.9445 0865	2.1713 7957	2.4243 8879	2.7065 0966	89
90	1.9590 9246	2.1903 7914	2.4486 3267	2.7369 5789	90
91	1.9737 8565	2.2095 4496	2.4731 1900	2.7677 4867	91
92	1.9885 8905	2.2288 7848	2.4978 5019	2.7988 8584	92
93	2.0035 0346	2.2483 8117	2.5228 2869	2.8303 7331	93
94	2.0185 2974	2.2680 5450	2.5480 5698	2.8622 1501	94
95	2.0336 6871	2.2878 9998	2.5735 3755	2.8944 1492	95
96	2.0489 2123	2.3079 1910	2.5992 7293	2.9269 7709	96
97	2.0642 8814	2.3281 1340	2.6252 6565	2.9599 0559	97
98	2.0797 7030	2.3484 8439	2.6515 1831	2.9932 0452	98
99	2.0953 6858	2.3690 3363	2.6780 3349	3.0268 7807	99
100	2.1110 8384	2.3897 6267	2.7048 1383	3.0609 3045	100

V. COMPOUND AMOUNT OF 1

$$(1 + i)^n$$

n	$1\frac{1}{4}\%$	$1\frac{3}{8}\%$	$1\frac{1}{2}\%$	$1\frac{5}{8}\%$	n
1	1.0125 0000	1.0137 5000	1.0150 0000	1.0162 5000	1
2	1.0251 5625	1.0276 8906	1.0302 2500	1.0327 6406	2
3	1.0379 7070	1.0418 1979	1.0456 7838	1.0495 4648	3
4	1.0509 4534	1.0561 4481	1.0613 6355	1.0666 0161	4
5	1.0640 8215	1.0706 6680	1.0772 8400	1.0839 3388	5
6	1.0773 8318	1.0853 8847	1.0934 4326	1.1015 4781	6
7	1.0908 5047	1.1003 1256	1.1098 4491	1.1194 4796	7
8	1.1044 8610	1.1154 4186	1.1264 9259	1.1376 3899	8
9	1.1182 9218	1.1307 7918	1.1433 8998	1.1561 2563	9
10	1.1322 7083	1.1463 2740	1.1605 4083	1.1749 1267	10
11	1.1464 2422	1.1620 8940	1.1779 4894	1.1940 0500	11
12	1.1607 5452	1.1780 6813	1.1956 1817	1.2134 0758	12
13	1.1752 6395	1.1942 6656	1.2135 5244	1.2331 2545	13
14	1.1899 5475	1.2106 8773	1.2317 5573	1.2531 6374	14
15	1.2048 2918	1.2273 3469	1.2502 3207	1.2735 2765	15
16	1.2198 8955	1.2442 1054	1.2689 8555	1.2942 2248	16
17	1.2351 3817	1.2613 1843	1.2880 2033	1.3152 5359	17
18	1.2505 7739	1.2786 6156	1.3073 4064	1.3366 2646	18
19	1.2662 0961	1.2962 4316	1.3269 5075	1.3583 4664	19
20	1.2820 3723	1.3140 6650	1.3468 5501	1.3804 1977	20
21	1.2980 6270	1.3321 3492	1.3670 5783	1.4028 5160	21
22	1.3142 8848	1.3504 5177	1.3875 6370	1.4256 4793	22
23	1.3307 1709	1.3690 2048	1.4083 7715	1.4488 1471	23
24	1.3473 5105	1.3878 4451	1.4295 0281	1.4723 5795	24
25	1.3641 9294	1.4069 2738	1.4509 4535	1.4962 8377	25
26	1.3812 4535	1.4262 7263	1.4727 0953	1.5205 9838	26
27	1.3985 1092	1.4458 8388	1.4948 0018	1.5453 0810	27
28	1.4159 9230	1.4657 6478	1.5172 2218	1.5704 1936	28
29	1.4336 9221	1.4859 1905	1.5399 8051	1.5959 3868	29
30	1.4516 1336	1.5063 5043	1.5630 8022	1.6218 7268	30
31	1.4697 5853	1.5270 6275	1.5865 2642	1.6482 2811	31
32	1.4881 3051	1.5480 5986	1.6103 2432	1.6750 1182	32
33	1.5067 3214	1.5693 4569	1.6344 7918	1.7022 3076	33
34	1.5255 6629	1.5909 2419	1.6589 9637	1.7298 9201	34
35	1.5446 3587	1.6127 9940	1.6838 8132	1.7580 0275	35
36	1.5639 4382	1.6349 7539	1.7091 3954	1.7865 7030	36
37	1.5834 9312	1.6574 5630	1.7347 7663	1.8156 0207	37
38	1.6032 8678	1.6802 4633	1.7607 9828	1.8451 0560	38
39	1.6233 2787	1.7033 4971	1.7872 1025	1.8750 8857	39
40	1.6436 1946	1.7267 7077	1.8140 1841	1.9055 5875	40
41	1.6641 6471	1.7505 1387	1.8412 2868	1.9365 2408	41
42	1.6849 6677	1.7745 8343	1.8688 4712	1.9679 9260	42
43	1.7060 2885	1.7989 8396	1.8968 7982	1.9999 7248	43
44	1.7273 5421	1.8237 1999	1.9253 3302	2.0324 7203	44
45	1.7489 4614	1.8487 9614	1.9542 1301	2.0654 9970	45
46	1.7708 0797	1.8742 1708	1.9835 2621	2.0990 6407	46
47	1.7929 4306	1.8999 8757	2.0132 7910	2.1331 7387	47
48	1.8153 5485	1.9261 1240	2.0434 7829	2.1678 3794	48
49	1.8380 4679	1.9525 9644	2.0741 3046	2.2030 6531	49
50	1.8610 2237	1.9794 4464	2.1052 4242	2.2388 6512	50

n	$1\frac{1}{4}\%$	$1\frac{3}{8}\%$	$1\frac{1}{2}\%$	$1\frac{5}{8}\%$	n
51	1.8842 8515	2.0066 6201	2.1368 2106	2.2752 4668	51
52	1.9078 3872	2.0342 5361	2.1688 7337	2.3122 1944	52
53	1.9316 8670	2.0622 2460	2.2014 0647	2.3497 9300	53
54	1.9558 3279	2.0905 8019	2.2344 2757	2.3879 7714	54
55	1.9802 8070	2.1193 2566	2.2679 4398	2.4267 8177	55
56	2.0050 3420	2.1484 6639	2.3019 6314	2.4662 1697	56
57	2.0300 9713	2.1780 0780	2.3364 9259	2.5062 9300	57
58	2.0554 7335	2.2079 5541	2.3715 3998	2.5470 2026	58
59	2.0811 6676	2.2383 1480	2.4071 1308	2.5884 0934	59
60	2.1071 8135	2.2690 9163	2.4432 1978	2.6304 7099	60
61	2.1335 2111	2.3002 9164	2.4798 6807	2.6732 1614	61
62	2.1601 9013	2.3319 2065	2.5170 6609	2.7166 5590	62
63	2.1871 9250	2.3639 8456	2.5548 2208	2.7608 0156	63
64	2.2145 3241	2.3964 8934	2.5931 4442	2.8056 6459	64
65	2.2422 1407	2.4294 4107	2.6320 4158	2.8512 5664	65
66	2.2702 4174	2.4628 4589	2.6715 2221	2.8975 8956	66
67	2.2986 1976	2.4967 1002	2.7115 9504	2.9446 7539	67
68	2.3273 5251	2.5310 3978	2.7522 6896	2.9925 2636	68
69	2.3564 4442	2.5658 4158	2.7935 5300	3.0411 5492	69
70	2.3858 9997	2.6011 2190	2.8354 5629	3.0905 7368	70
71	2.4157 2372	2.6368 8732	2.8779 8814	3.1407 9551	71
72	2.4459 2027	2.6731 4453	2.9211 5796	3.1918 3343	72
73	2.4764 9427	2.7099 0026	2.9649 7533	3.2437 0073	73
74	2.5074 5045	2.7471 6139	3.0094 4996	3.2964 1086	74
75	2.5387 9358	2.7849 3486	3.0545 9171	3.3499 7754	75
76	2.5705 2850	2.8232 2771	3.1004 1059	3.4044 1467	76
77	2.6026 6011	2.8620 4710	3.1469 1674	3.4597 3641	77
78	2.6351 9336	2.9014 0024	3.1941 2050	3.5159 5713	78
79	2.6681 3327	2.9412 9450	3.2420 3230	3.5730 9143	79
80	2.7014 8494	2.9817 3730	3.2906 6279	3.6311 5417	80
81	2.7352 5350	3.0227 3618	3.3400 2273	3.6901 6042	81
82	2.7694 4417	3.0642 9881	3.3901 2307	3.7501 2553	82
83	2.8040 6222	3.1064 3291	3.4409 7492	3.8110 6507	83
84	2.8391 1300	3.1491 4637	3.4925 8954	3.8729 9488	84
85	2.8746 0191	3.1924 4713	3.5449 7838	3.9359 3104	85
86	2.9105 3444	3.2363 4328	3.5981 5306	3.9998 8992	86
87	2.9469 1612	3.2808 4300	3.6521 2535	4.0648 8813	87
88	2.9837 5257	3.3259 5459	3.7069 0723	4.1309 4257	88
89	3.0210 4948	3.3716 8646	3.7625 1084	4.1980 7038	89
90	3.0588 1260	3.4180 4715	3.8189 4851	4.2662 8903	90
91	3.0970 4775	3.4650 4530	3.8762 3273	4.3356 1622	91
92	3.1357 6085	3.5126 8967	3.9343 7622	4.4060 6999	92
93	3.1749 5786	3.5609 8916	3.9933 9187	4.4776 6863	93
94	3.2146 4483	3.6099 5276	4.0532 9275	4.5504 3074	94
95	3.2548 2789	3.6595 8961	4.1140 9214	4.6243 7524	95
96	3.2955 1324	3.7099 0897	4.1758 0352	4.6995 2134	96
97	3.3367 0716	3.7609 2021	4.2384 4057	4.7758 8856	97
98	3.3784 1600	3.8126 3287	4.3020 1718	4.8534 9675	98
99	3.4206 4620	3.8650 5657	4.3665 4744	4.9323 6607	99
100	3.4634 0427	3.9182 0110	4.4320 4565	5.0125 1702	100

V. COMPOUND AMOUNT OF 1

$$(1 + i)^n$$

n	$1\frac{3}{4}\%$	2%	$2\frac{1}{4}\%$	$2\frac{1}{2}\%$	n
1	1.0175 0000	1.0200 0000	1.0225 0000	1.0250 0000	1
2	1.0353 0625	1.0404 0000	1.0455 0625	1.0506 2500	2
3	1.0534 2411	1.0612 0800	1.0690 3014	1.0768 9063	3
4	1.0718 5903	1.0824 3216	1.0930 8332	1.1038 1289	4
5	1.0906 1656	1.1040 8080	1.1176 7769	1.1314 0821	5
6	1.1097 0235	1.1261 6242	1.1428 2544	1.1596 9342	6
7	1.1291 2215	1.1486 8567	1.1685 3901	1.1886 8575	7
8	1.1488 8178	1.1716 5938	1.1948 3114	1.2184 0290	8
9	1.1689 8721	1.1950 9257	1.2217 1484	1.2488 6297	9
10	1.1894 4449	1.2189 9442	1.2492 0343	1.2800 8454	10
11	1.2102 5977	1.2433 7431	1.2773 1050	1.3120 8666	11
12	1.2314 3931	1.2682 4179	1.3060 4999	1.3448 8882	12
13	1.2529 8950	1.2936 0663	1.3354 3611	1.3785 1104	13
14	1.2749 1682	1.3194 7876	1.3654 8343	1.4129 7382	14
15	1.2972 2786	1.3458 6834	1.3962 0680	1.4482 9817	15
16	1.3199 2935	1.3727 8571	1.4276 2146	1.4845 0562	16
17	1.3430 2811	1.4002 4142	1.4597 4294	1.5216 1826	17
18	1.3665 3111	1.4282 4625	1.4925 8716	1.5596 5872	18
19	1.3904 4540	1.4568 1117	1.5261 7037	1.5986 5019	19
20	1.4147 7820	1.4859 4740	1.5605 0920	1.6386 1644	20
21	1.4395 3681	1.5156 6634	1.5956 2066	1.6795 8185	21
22	1.4647 2871	1.5459 7967	1.6315 2212	1.7215 7140	22
23	1.4903 6146	1.5768 9926	1.6682 3137	1.7646 1068	23
24	1.5164 4279	1.6084 3725	1.7057 6658	1.8087 2595	24
25	1.5429 8054	1.6406 0599	1.7441 4632	1.8539 4410	25
26	1.5699 8269	1.6734 1811	1.7833 8962	1.9002 9270	26
27	1.5974 5739	1.7068 8648	1.8235 1588	1.9478 0002	27
28	1.6254 1290	1.7410 2421	1.8645 4499	1.9964 9502	28
29	1.6538 5762	1.7758 4469	1.9064 9725	2.0464 0739	29
30	1.6828 0013	1.8113 6158	1.9493 9344	2.0975 6758	30
31	1.7122 4913	1.8475 8882	1.9932 5479	2.1500 0677	31
32	1.7422 1349	1.8845 4059	2.0381 0303	2.2037 5694	32
33	1.7727 0223	1.9222 3140	2.0839 6034	2.2588 5086	33
34	1.8037 2452	1.9606 7603	2.1308 4945	2.3153 2213	34
35	1.8352 8970	1.9998 8955	2.1787 9356	2.3732 0519	35
36	1.8674 0727	2.0398 8734	2.2278 1642	2.4325 3532	36
37	1.9000 8689	2.0806 8509	2.2779 4229	2.4933 4870	37
38	1.9333 3841	2.1222 9879	2.3291 9599	2.5556 8242	38
39	1.9671 7184	2.1647 4477	2.3816 0290	2.6195 7448	39
40	2.0015 9734	2.2080 3966	2.4351 8897	2.6850 6384	40
41	2.0366 2530	2.2522 0046	2.4899 8072	2.7521 9043	41
42	2.0722 6624	2.2972 4447	2.5460 0528	2.8209 9520	42
43	2.1085 3090	2.3431 8936	2.6032 9040	2.8915 2008	43
44	2.1454 3019	2.3900 5314	2.6618 6444	2.9638 0808	44
45	2.1829 7522	2.4378 5421	2.7217 5639	3.0379 0328	45
46	2.2211 7728	2.4866 1129	2.7829 9590	3.1138 5086	46
47	2.2600 4789	2.5363 4352	2.8456 1331	3.1916 9713	47
48	2.2995 9872	2.5870 7039	2.9096 3961	3.2714 8956	48
49	2.3398 4170	2.6388 1179	2.9751 0650	3.3532 7680	49
50	2.3807 8893	2.6915 8803	3.0420 4640	3.4371 0872	50

V. COMPOUND AMOUNT OF 1

$$(1 + i)^n$$

n	1¾%	2%	2¼%	2½%	n
51	2.4224 5274	2.7454 1979	3.1104 9244	3.5230 3644	51
52	2.4648 4566	2.8003 2819	3.1804 7852	3.6111 1235	52
53	2.5079 8046	2.8563 3475	3.2520 3929	3.7013 9016	53
54	2.5518 7012	2.9134 6144	3.3252 1017	3.7939 2491	54
55	2.5965 2785	2.9717 3067	3.4000 2740	3.8887 7303	55
56	2.6419 6708	3.0311 6529	3.4765 2802	3.9859 9236	56
57	2.6882 0151	3.0917 8859	3.5547 4990	4.0856 4217	57
58	2.7352 4503	3.1536 2436	3.6347 3177	4.1877 8322	58
59	2.7831 1182	3.2166 9685	3.7165 1324	4.2924 7780	59
60	2.8318 1628	3.2810 3079	3.8001 3479	4.3997 8975	60
61	2.8813 7306	3.3466 5140	3.8856 3782	4.5097 8449	61
62	2.9317 9709	3.4135 8443	3.9730 6467	4.6225 2910	62
63	2.9831 0354	3.4818 5612	4.0624 5862	4.7380 9233	63
64	3.0353 0785	3.5514 9324	4.1538 6394	4.8565 4464	64
65	3.0884 2574	3.6225 2311	4.2473 2588	4.9779 5826	65
66	3.1424 7319	3.6949 7357	4.3428 9071	5.1024 0721	66
67	3.1974 6647	3.7688 7304	4.4406 0576	5.2299 6739	67
68	3.2534 2213	3.8442 5050	4.5405 1939	5.3607 1658	68
69	3.3103 5702	3.9211 3551	4.6426 8107	5.4947 3449	69
70	3.3682 8827	3.9995 5822	4.7471 4140	5.6321 0286	70
71	3.4272 3331	4.0795 4939	4.8539 5208	5.7729 0543	71
72	3.4872 0990	4.1611 4038	4.9631 6600	5.9172 2806	72
73	3.5482 3607	4.2443 6318	5.0748 3723	6.0651 5876	73
74	3.6103 3020	4.3292 5045	5.1890 2107	6.2167 8773	74
75	3.6735 1098	4.4158 3546	5.3057 7405	6.3722 0743	75
76	3.7377 9742	4.5041 5216	5.4251 5396	6.5315 1261	76
77	3.8032 0888	4.5942 3521	5.5472 1993	6.6948 0043	77
78	3.8697 6503	4.6861 1991	5.6720 3237	6.8621 7044	78
79	3.9374 8592	4.7798 4231	5.7996 5310	7.0337 2470	79
80	4.0063 9192	4.8754 3916	5.9301 4530	7.2095 6782	80
81	4.0765 0378	4.9729 4794	6.0635 7357	7.3898 0701	81
82	4.1478 4260	5.0724 0690	6.2000 0397	7.5745 5219	82
83	4.2204 2984	5.1738 5504	6.3395 0406	7.7639 1599	83
84	4.2942 8737	5.2773 3214	6.4821 4290	7.9580 1389	84
85	4.3694 3740	5.3828 7878	6.6279 9112	8.1569 6424	85
86	4.4459 0255	5.4905 3636	6.7771 2092	8.3608 8834	86
87	4.5237 0584	5.6003 4708	6.9296 0614	8.5699 1055	87
88	4.6028 7070	5.7123 5402	7.0855 2228	8.7841 5832	88
89	4.6834 2093	5.8266 0110	7.2449 4653	9.0037 6228	89
90	4.7653 8080	5.9431 3313	7.4079 5782	9.2288 5633	90
91	4.8487 7496	6.0619 9579	7.5746 3688	9.4595 7774	91
92	4.9336 2853	6.1832 3570	7.7450 6621	9.6960 6718	92
93	5.0199 6703	6.3069 0042	7.9193 3020	9.9384 6886	93
94	5.1078 1645	6.4330 3843	8.0975 1512	10.1869 3058	94
95	5.1972 0324	6.5616 9920	8.2797 0921	10.4416 0385	95
96	5.2881 5429	6.6929 3318	8.4660 0267	10.7026 4395	96
97	5.3806 9699	6.8267 9184	8.6564 8773	10.9702 1004	97
98	5.4748 5919	6.9633 2768	8.8512 5871	11.2444 6530	98
99	5.5706 6923	7.1025 9423	9.0504 1203	11.5255 7693	99
100	5.6681 5594	7.2446 4612	9.2540 4630	11.8137 1635	100

$$(1 + i)^n$$

n	$2\frac{3}{4}\%$	3%	$3\frac{1}{4}\%$	$3\frac{1}{2}\%$	n
1	1.0275 0000	1.0300 0000	1.0325 0000	1.0350 0000	1
2	1.0557 5625	1.0609 0000	1.0660 5625	1.0712 2500	2
3	1.0847 8955	1.0927 2700	1.1007 0308	1.1087 1788	3
4	1.1146 2126	1.1255 0881	1.1364 7593	1.1475 2300	4
5	1.1452 7334	1.1592 7407	1.1734 1140	1.1876 8631	5
6	1.1767 6836	1.1940 5230	1.2115 4727	1.2292 5533	6
7	1.2091 2949	1.2298 7387	1.2509 2255	1.2722 7926	7
8	1.2423 8055	1.2667 7008	1.2915 7754	1.3168 0904	8
9	1.2765 4602	1.3047 7318	1.3335 5381	1.3628 9735	9
10	1.3116 5103	1.3439 1638	1.3768 9430	1.4105 9876	10
11	1.3477 2144	1.3842 3387	1.4216 4337	1.4599 6972	11
12	1.3847 8378	1.4257 6089	1.4678 4678	1.5110 6866	12
13	1.4228 6533	1.4685 3371	1.5155 5180	1.5639 5606	13
14	1.4619 9413	1.5125 8972	1.5648 0723	1.6186 9452	14
15	1.5021 9896	1.5579 6742	1.6156 6347	1.6753 4883	15
16	1.5435 0944	1.6047 0644	1.6681 7253	1.7339 8604	16
17	1.5859 5595	1.6528 4763	1.7223 8814	1.7946 7555	17
18	1.6295 6973	1.7024 3306	1.7783 6575	1.8574 8920	18
19	1.6743 8290	1.7535 0605	1.8361 6264	1.9225 0132	19
20	1.7204 2843	1.8061 1123	1.8958 3792	1.9897 8886	20
21	1.7677 4021	1.8602 9457	1.9574 5266	2.0594 3147	21
22	1.8163 5307	1.9161 0341	2.0210 6987	2.1315 1158	22
23	1.8663 0278	1.9735 8651	2.0867 5464	2.2061 1448	23
24	1.9176 2610	2.0327 9411	2.1545 7416	2.2833 2849	24
25	1.9703 6082	2.0937 7793	2.2245 9782	2.3632 4498	25
26	2.0245 4575	2.1565 9127	2.2968 9725	2.4459 5856	26
27	2.0802 2075	2.2212 8901	2.3715 4641	2.5315 6711	27
28	2.1374 2682	2.2879 2768	2.4486 2167	2.6201 7196	28
29	2.1962 0606	2.3565 6551	2.5282 0188	2.7118 7798	29
30	2.2566 0173	2.4272 6247	2.6103 6844	2.8067 9370	30
31	2.3186 5828	2.5000 8035	2.6952 0541	2.9050 3148	31
32	2.3824 2138	2.5750 8276	2.7827 9959	3.0067 0759	32
33	2.4479 3797	2.6523 3524	2.8732 4058	3.1119 4235	33
34	2.5152 5626	2.7319 0530	2.9666 2089	3.2208 6033	34
35	2.5844 2581	2.8138 6245	3.0630 3607	3.3335 9045	35
36	2.6554 9752	2.8982 7833	3.1625 8475	3.4502 6611	36
37	2.7285 2370	2.9852 2668	3.2653 6875	3.5710 2543	37
38	2.8035 5810	3.0747 8348	3.3714 9323	3.6960 1132	38
39	2.8806 5595	3.1670 2698	3.4810 6676	3.8253 7171	39
40	2.9598 7399	3.2620 3779	3.5942 0143	3.9592 5972	40
41	3.0412 7052	3.3598 9893	3.7110 1298	4.0978 3381	41
42	3.1249 0546	3.4606 9589	3.8316 2090	4.2412 5799	42
43	3.2108 4036	3.5645 1677	3.9561 4858	4.3897 0202	43
44	3.2991 3847	3.6714 5227	4.0847 2341	4.5433 4160	44
45	3.3898 6478	3.7815 9584	4.2174 7692	4.7023 5855	45
46	3.4830 8606	3.8950 4372	4.3545 4492	4.8669 4110	46
47	3.5788 7093	4.0118 9503	4.4960 6763	5.0372 8404	47
48	3.6772 8988	4.1322 5188	4.6421 8983	5.2135 8898	48
49	3.7784 1535	4.2562 1944	4.7930 6100	5.3960 6459	49
50	3.8823 2177	4.3839 0602	4.9488 3548	5.5849 2686	50

V. COMPOUND AMOUNT OF 1

$$(1 + i)^n$$

n	$2\frac{3}{4}\%$	3%	$3\frac{1}{4}\%$	$3\frac{1}{2}\%$	n
51	3.9890 8562	4.5154 2320	5.1096 7263	5.7803 9930	51
52	4.0987 8547	4.6508 8590	5.2757 3700	5.9827 1327	52
53	4.2115 0208	4.7904 1247	5.4471 9845	6.1921 0824	53
54	4.3273 1838	4.9341 2485	5.6242 3240	6.4088 3202	54
55	4.4463 1964	5.0821 4859	5.8070 1995	6.6331 4114	55
56	4.5685 9343	5.2346 1305	5.9957 4810	6.8653 0108	56
57	4.6942 2975	5.3916 5144	6.1906 0991	7.1055 8662	57
58	4.8233 2107	5.5534 0098	6.3918 0473	7.3542 8215	58
59	4.9559 6239	5.7200 0301	6.5995 3839	7.6116 8203	59
60	5.0922 5136	5.8916 0310	6.8140 2339	7.8780 9090	60
61	5.2322 8827	6.0683 5120	7.0354 7915	8.1538 2408	61
62	5.3761 7620	6.2504 0173	7.2641 3222	8.4392 0793	62
63	5.5240 2105	6.4379 1379	7.5002 1651	8.7345 8020	63
64	5.6759 3162	6.6310 5120	7.7439 7355	9.0402 9051	64
65	5.8320 1974	6.8299 8273	7.9956 5269	9.3567 0068	65
66	5.9924 0029	7.0348 8222	8.2555 1140	9.6841 8520	66
67	6.1571 9130	7.2459 2868	8.5238 1552	10.0231 3168	67
68	6.3265 1406	7.4633 0654	8.8008 3953	10.3739 4129	68
69	6.5004 9319	7.6872 0574	9.0868 6681	10.7370 2924	69
70	6.6792 5676	7.9178 2191	9.3821 8999	11.1128 2526	70
71	6.8629 3632	8.1553 5657	9.6871 1116	11.5017 7414	71
72	7.0516 6706	8.4000 1727	10.0019 4227	11.9043 3624	72
73	7.2455 8791	8.6520 1778	10.3270 0540	12.3209 8801	73
74	7.4448 4158	8.9115 7832	10.6626 3307	12.7522 2259	74
75	7.6495 7472	9.1789 2567	11.0091 6865	13.1985 5038	75
76	7.8599 3802	9.4542 9344	11.3669 6663	13.6604 9964	76
77	8.0760 8632	9.7379 2224	11.7363 9304	14.1386 1713	77
78	8.2981 7869	10.0300 5991	12.1178 2582	14.6334 6873	78
79	8.5263 7861	10.3309 6171	12.5116 5516	15.1456 4013	79
80	8.7608 5402	10.6408 9056	12.9182 8395	15.6757 3754	80
81	9.0017 7751	10.9601 1727	13.3381 2818	16.2243 8835	81
82	9.2493 2639	11.2889 2079	13.7716 1734	16.7922 4195	82
83	9.5036 8286	11.6275 8842	14.2191 9491	17.3799 7041	83
84	9.7650 3414	11.9764 1607	14.6813 1874	17.9882 6938	84
85	10.0335 7258	12.3357 0855	15.1584 6160	18.6178 5881	85
86	10.3094 9583	12.7057 7981	15.6511 1160	19.2694 8387	86
87	10.5930 0696	13.0869 5320	16.1597 7273	19.9439 1580	87
88	10.8843 1465	13.4795 6180	16.6849 6534	20.6419 5285	88
89	11.1836 3331	13.8839 4865	17.2272 2672	21.3644 2120	89
90	11.4911 8322	14.3004 6711	17.7871 1158	22.1121 7595	90
91	11.8071 9076	14.7294 8112	18.3651 9271	22.8861 0210	91
92	12.1318 8851	15.1713 6556	18.9620 6147	23.6871 1568	92
93	12.4655 1544	15.6265 0652	19.5783 2847	24.5161 6473	93
94	12.8083 1711	16.0953 0172	20.2146 2415	25.3742 3049	94
95	13.1605 4584	16.5781 6077	20.8715 9943	26.2623 2856	95
96	13.5224 6085	17.0755 0559	21.5499 2641	27.1815 1006	96
97	13.8943 2852	17.5877 7076	22.2502 9902	28.1328 6291	97
98	14.2764 2255	18.1154 0388	22.9734 3374	29.1175 1311	98
99	14.6690 2417	18.6588 6600	23.7200 7034	30.1366 2607	99
100	15.0724 2234	19.2186 3198	24.4909 7262	31.1914 0798	100

V. COMPOUND AMOUNT OF 1

$$(1 + i)^n$$

n	4%	$4\frac{1}{2}$%	5%	$5\frac{1}{2}$%	n
1	1.0400 0000	1.0450 0000	1.0500 0000	1.0550 0000	1
2	1.0816 0000	1.0920 2500	1.1025 0000	1.1130 2500	2
3	1.1248 6400	1.1411 6613	1.1576 2500	1.1742 4138	3
4	1.1698 5856	1.1925 1860	1.2155 0625	1.2388 2465	4
5	1.2166 5290	1.2461 8194	1.2762 8156	1.3069 6001	5
6	1.2653 1902	1.3022 6012	1.3400 9564	1.3788 4281	6
7	1.3159 3178	1.3608 6183	1.4071 0042	1.4546 7916	7
8	1.3685 6905	1.4221 0061	1.4774 5544	1.5346 8651	8
9	1.4233 1181	1.4860 9514	1.5513 2822	1.6190 9427	9
10	1.4802 4428	1.5529 6942	1.6288 9463	1.7081 4446	10
11	1.5394 5406	1.6228 5305	1.7103 3936	1.8020 9240	11
12	1.6010 3222	1.6958 8143	1.7958 5633	1.9012 0749	12
13	1.6650 7351	1.7721 9610	1.8856 4914	2.0057 7390	13
14	1.7316 7645	1.8519 4492	1.9799 3160	2.1160 9146	14
15	1.8009 4351	1.9352 8244	2.0789 2818	2.2324 7649	15
16	1.8729 8125	2.0223 7015	2.1828 7459	2.3552 6270	16
17	1.9479 0050	2.1133 7681	2.2920 1832	2.4848 0215	17
18	2.0258 1652	2.2084 7877	2.4066 1923	2.6214 6627	18
19	2.1068 4918	2.3078 6031	2.5269 5020	2.7656 4691	19
20	2.1911 2314	2.4117 1402	2.6532 9771	2.9177 5749	20
21	2.2787 6807	2.5202 4116	2.7859 6259	3.0782 3415	21
22	2.3699 1879	2.6336 5201	2.9252 6072	3.2475 3703	22
23	2.4647 1554	2.7521 6635	3.0715 2376	3.4261 5157	23
24	2.5633 0416	2.8760 1383	3.2250 9994	3.6145 8990	24
25	2.6658 3633	3.0054 3446	3.3863 5494	3.8133 9235	25
26	2.7724 6978	3.1406 7901	3.5556 7269	4.0231 2893	26
27	2.8833 6858	3.2820 0956	3.7334 5632	4.2444 0102	27
28	2.9987 0332	3.4296 9999	3.9201 2914	4.4778 4307	28
29	3.1186 5145	3.5840 3649	4.1161 3560	4.7241 2444	29
30	3.2433 9751	3.7453 1813	4.3219 4238	4.9839 5129	30
31	3.3731 3341	3.9138 5745	4.5380 3949	5.2580 6861	31
32	3.5080 5875	4.0899 8104	4.7649 4147	5.5472 6238	32
33	3.6483 8110	4.2740 3018	5.0031 8854	5.8523 6181	33
34	3.7943 1634	4.4663 6154	5.2533 4797	6.1742 4171	34
35	3.9460 8899	4.6673 4781	5.5160 1537	6.5138 2501	35
36	4.1039 3255	4.8773 7846	5.7918 1614	6.8720 8538	36
37	4.2680 8986	5.0968 6049	6.0814 0694	7.2500 5008	37
38	4.4388 1345	5.3262 1921	6.3854 7729	7.6488 0283	38
39	4.6163 6599	5.5658 9908	6.7047 5115	8.0694 8699	39
40	4.8010 2063	5.8163 6454	7.0399 8871	8.5133 0877	40
41	4.9930 6145	6.0781 0094	7.3919 8815	8.9815 4076	41
42	5.1927 8391	6.3516 1548	7.7615 8756	9.4755 2550	42
43	5.4004 9527	6.6374 3818	8.1496 6693	9.9966 7940	43
44	5.6165 1508	6.9361 2290	8.5571 5028	10.5464 9677	44
45	5.8411 7568	7.2482 4843	8.9850 0779	11.1265 5409	45
46	6.0748 2271	7.5744 1961	9.4342 5818	11.7385 1456	46
47	6.3178 1562	7.9152 6849	9.9059 7109	12.3841 3287	47
48	6.5705 2824	8.2714 5557	10.4012 6965	13.0652 6017	48
49	6.8333 4937	8.6436 7107	10.9213 3313	13.7838 4948	49
50	7.1066 8335	9.0326 3627	11.4673 9979	14.5419 6120	50

V. COMPOUND AMOUNT OF 1

$$(1 + i)^n$$

n	6%	6½%	7%	8%	n
1	1.0600 0000	1.0650 0000	1.0700 0000	1.0800 0000	1
2	1.1236 0000	1.1342 2500	1.1449 0000	1.1664 0000	2
3	1.1910 1600	1.2079 4963	1.2250 4300	1.2597 1200	3
4	1.2624 7696	1.2864 6635	1.3107 9601	1.3604 8896	4
5	1.3382 2558	1.3700 8666	1.4025 5173	1.4693 2808	5
6	1.4185 1911	1.4591 4230	1.5007 3035	1.5868 7432	6
7	1.5036 3026	1.5539 8655	1.6057 8148	1.7138 2427	7
8	1.5938 4807	1.6549 9567	1.7181 8618	1.8509 3021	8
9	1.6894 7896	1.7625 7039	1.8384 5921	1.9990 0463	9
10	1.7908 4770	1.8771 3747	1.9671 5136	2.1589 2500	10
11	1.8982 9856	1.9991 5140	2.1048 5195	2.3316 3900	11
12	2.0121 9647	2.1290 9624	2.2521 9159	2.5181 7012	12
13	2.1329 2826	2.2674 8750	2.4098 4500	2.7196 2373	13
14	2.2609 0396	2.4148 7418	2.5785 3415	2.9371 9362	14
15	2.3965 5819	2.5718 4101	2.7590 3154	3.1721 6911	15
16	2.5403 5168	2.7390 1067	2.9521 6375	3.4259 4264	16
17	2.6927 7279	2.9170 4637	3.1588 1521	3.7000 1805	17
18	2.8543 3915	3.1066 5438	3.3799 3228	3.9960 1950	18
19	3.0255 9950	3.3085 8691	3.6165 2754	4.3157 0106	19
20	3.2071 3547	3.5236 4506	3.8696 8446	4.6609 5714	20
21	3.3995 6360	3.7526 8199	4.1405 6237	5.0338 3372	21
22	3.6035 3742	3.9966 0632	4.4304 0174	5.4365 4041	22
23	3.8197 4966	4.2563 8573	4.7405 2986	5.8714 6365	23
24	4.0489 3464	4.5330 5081	5.0723 6695	6.3411 8074	24
25	4.2918 7072	4.8276 9911	5.4274 3264	6.8484 7520	25
26	4.5493 8296	5.1414 9955	5.8073 5292	7.3963 5321	26
27	4.8223 4594	5.4756 9702	6.2138 6763	7.9880 6147	27
28	5.1116 8670	5.8316 1733	6.6488 3836	8.6271 0639	28
29	5.4183 8790	6.2106 7245	7.1142 5705	9.3172 7490	29
30	5.7434 9117	6.6143 6616	7.6122 5504	10.0626 5689	30
31	6.0881 0064	7.0442 9996	8.1451 1290	10.8676 6944	31
32	6.4533 8668	7.5021 7946	8.7152 7080	11.7370 8300	32
33	6.8405 8988	7.9898 2113	9.3253 3975	12.6760 4964	33
34	7.2510 2528	8.5091 5950	9.9781 1354	13.6901 3361	34
35	7.6860 8679	9.0622 5487	10.6765 8148	14.7853 4429	35
36	8.1472 5200	9.6513 0143	11.4239 4219	15.9681 7184	36
37	8.6360 8712	10.2786 3603	12.2236 1814	17.2456 2558	37
38	9.1542 5235	10.9467 4737	13.0792 7141	18.6252 7563	38
39	9.7035 0749	11.6582 8595	13.9948 2041	20.1152 9768	39
40	10.2857 1794	12.4160 7453	14.9744 5784	21.7245 2150	40
41	10.9028 6101	13.2231 1938	16.0226 6989	23.4624 8322	41
42	11.5570 3267	14.0826 2214	17.1442 5678	25.3394 8187	42
43	12.2504 5463	14.9979 9258	18.3443 5475	27.3666 4042	43
44	12.9854 8191	15.9728 6209	19.6284 5959	29.5559 7166	44
45	13.7646 1083	17.0110 9813	21.0024 5176	31.9204 4939	45
46	14.5904 8748	18.1168 1951	22.4726 2338	34.4740 8534	46
47	15.4659 1673	19.2944 1278	24.0457 0702	37.2320 1217	47
48	16.3938 7173	20.5485 4961	25.7289 0651	40.2105 7314	48
49	17.3775 0403	21.8842 0533	27.5299 2997	43.4274 1899	49
50	18.4201 5427	23.3066 7868	29.4570 2506	46.9016 1251	50

VI. PRESENT VALUE OF 1

$$v^n = (1 + i)^{-n}$$

n	$\frac{1}{4}\%$	$\frac{7}{24}\%$	$\frac{1}{3}\%$	$\frac{3}{8}\%$	n
1	0.9975 0623	0.9970 9182	0.9966 7774	0.9962 6401	1
2	0.9950 1869	0.9941 9209	0.9933 6652	0.9925 4198	2
3	0.9925 3734	0.9913 0079	0.9900 6630	0.9888 3385	3
4	0.9900 6219	0.9884 1791	0.9867 7704	0.9851 3958	4
5	0.9875 9321	0.9855 4341	0.9834 9871	0.9814 5911	5
6	0.9851 3038	0.9826 7727	0.9802 3127	0.9777 9238	6
7	0.9826 7370	0.9798 1946	0.9769 7469	0.9741 3936	7
8	0.9802 2314	0.9769 6996	0.9737 2893	0.9704 9999	8
9	0.9777 7869	0.9741 2875	0 9704 9395	0.9668 7421	9
10	0.9753 4034	0.9712 9581	0.9672 6972	0.9632 6198	10
11	0.9729 0807	0.9684 7110	0.9640 5620	0.9596 6324	11
12	0.9704 8187	0.9656 5461	0.9608 5335	0.9560 7795	12
13	0.9680 6171	0.9628 4631	0.9576 6115	0.9525 0605	13
14	0.9656 4759	0.9600 4617	0.9544 7955	0.9489 4750	14
15	0.9632 3949	0.9572 5418	0.9513 0852	0.9454 0224	15
16	0.9608 3740	0.9544 7031	0.9481 4803	0.9418 7022	16
17	0.9584 4130	0.9516 9453	0.9449 9803	0.9383 5141	17
18	0.9560 5117	0.9489 2683	0.9418 5851	0.9348 4573	18
19	0.9536 6700	0.9461 6718	0.9387 2941	0.9313 5316	19
20	0.9512 8878	0.9434 1555	0.9356 1071	0.9278 7363	20
21	0.9489 1649	6.9406 7192	0.9325 0236	0.9244 0711	21
22	0.9465 5011	0.9379 3627	0.9294 0435	0.9209 5353	22
23	0.9441 8964	0.9352 0858	0.9263 1663	0.9175 1286	23
24	0.9418 3505	0.9324 8882	0.9232 3916	0.9140 8504	24
25	0.9394 8634	0.9297 7697	0.9201 7192	0.9106 7003	25
26	0.9371 4348	0.9270 7301	0.9171 1487	0.9072 6777	26
27	0.9348 0646	0.9243 7691	0.9140 6798	0.9038 7823	27
28	0.9324 7527	0.9216 8865	0.9110 3121	0.9005 0135	28
29	0.9301 4990	0.9190 0821	0.9080 0453	0.8971 3709	29
30	0.9278 3032	0.9163 3557	0.9049 8790	0.8937 8539	30
31	0.9255 1653	0.9136 7069	0.9019 8130	0.8904 4622	31
32	0.9232 0851	0.9110 1357	0.8989 8468	0.8871 1952	32
33	0.9209 0624	0.9083 6417	0.8959 9802	0.8838 0525	33
34	0.9186 0972	0.9057 2248	0.8930 2128	0.8805 0336	34
35	0.9163 1892	0.9030 8848	0.8900 5444	0.8772 1381	35
36	0.9140 3384	0.9004 6213	0.8870 9745	0.8739 3655	36
37	0.9117 5445	0.8978 4342	0.8841 5028	0.8706 7153	37
38	0.9094 8075	0.8952 3232	0.8812 1290	0.8674 1871	38
39	0.9072 1272	0.8926 2882	0.8782 8528	0.8641 7804	39
40	0.9049 5034	0.8900 3289	0.8753 6739	0.8609 4948	40
41	0.9026 9361	0.8874 4451	0.8724 5920	0.8577 3298	41
42	0.9004 4250	0.8848 6366	0.8695 6066	0.8545 2850	42
43	0.8981 9701	0.8822 9031	0.8666 7175	0.8513 3899	43
44	0.8959 5712	0.8797 2445	0.8637 9245	0.8481 5541	44
45	0.8937 2281	0.8771 6605	0.8609 2270	0.8449 8671	45
46	0.8914 9407	0.8746 1509	0.8580 6249	0.8418 2985	46
47	0.8892 7090	0.8720 7155	0.8552 1179	0.8386 8478	47
48	0.8870 5326	0.8695 3540	0.8523 7055	0.8355 5146	48
49	0.8848 4116	0.8670 0663	0.8495 3876	0.8324 2985	49
50	0.8826 3457	0.8644 8522	0.8467 1637	0.8293 1990	50

VI. PRESENT VALUE OF 1

$$v^n = (1 + i)^{-n}$$

n	$\frac{1}{4}\%$	$\frac{7}{24}\%$	$\frac{1}{3}\%$	$\frac{3}{8}\%$	n
51	0.8804 3349	0.8619 7114	0.8439 0336	0.8262 2157	51
52	0.8782 3790	0.8594 6436	0.8410 9969	0.8231 3481	52
53	0.8760 4778	0.8569 6488	0.8383 0534	0.8200 5959	53
54	0.8738 6312	0.8544 7267	0.8355 2027	0.8169 9585	54
55	0.8716 8391	0.8519 8771	0.8327 4446	0.8139 4357	55
56	0.8695 1013	0.8495 0997	0.8299 7787	0.8109 0268	56
57	0.8673 4178	0.8470 3944	0.8272 2047	0.8078 7316	57
58	0.8651 7883	0.8445 7609	0.8244 7222	0.8048 5495	58
59	0.8630 2128	0.8421 1991	0.8217 3311	0.8018 4802	59
60	0.8608 6911	0.8396 7087	0.8190 0310	0.7988 5232	60
61	0.8587 2230	0.8372 2895	0.8162 8216	0.7958 6782	61
62	0.8565 8085	0.8347 9413	0.8135 7026	0.7928 9447	62
63	0.8544 4474	0.8323 6640	0.8108 6737	0.7899 3222	63
64	0.8523 1395	0.8299 4572	0.8081 7346	0.7869 8104	64
65	0.8501 8848	0.8275 3209	0.8054 8850	0.7840 4089	65
66	0.8480 6831	0.8251 2547	0.8028 1246	0.7811 1172	66
67	0.8459 5343	0.8227 2586	0.8001 4531	0.7781 9349	67
68	0.8438 4382	0.8203 3322	0.7974 8702	0.7752 8617	68
69	0.8417 3947	0.8179 4754	0.7948 3756	0.7723 8971	69
70	0.8396 4037	0.8155 6879	0.7921 9690	0.7695 0407	70
71	0.8375 4650	0.8131 9697	0.7895 6502	0.7666 2921	71
72	0.8354 5786	0.8108 3204	0.7869 4188	0.7637 6509	72
73	0.8333 7442	0.8084 7399	0.7843 2745	0.7609 1167	73
74	0.8312 9618	0.8061 2280	0.7817 2171	0.7580 6891	74
75	0.8292 2312	0.8037 7845	0.7791 2463	0.7552 3677	75
76	0.8271 5523	0.8014 4091	0.7765 3618	0.7524 1522	76
77	0.8250 9250	0.7991 1018	0.7739 5632	0.7496 0420	77
78	0.8230 3491	0.7967 8622	0.7713 8504	0.7468 0369	78
79	0.8209 8246	0.7944 6901	0.7688 2230	0.7440 1364	79
80	0.8189 3512	0.7921 5855	0.7662 6807	0.7412 3401	80
81	0.8168 9289	0.7898 5481	0.7637 2233	0.7384 6477	81
82	0.8148 5575	0.7875 5776	0.7611 8505	0.7357 0587	82
83	0.8128 2369	0.7852 6740	0.7586 5619	0.7329 5728	83
84	0.8107 9670	0.7829 8370	0.7561 3574	0.7302 1896	84
85	0.8087 7476	0.7807 0664	0.7536 2366	0.7274 9087	85
86	0.8067 5787	0.7784 3620	0.7511 1993	0.7247 7297	86
87	0.8047 4600	0.7761 7236	0.7486 2451	0.7220 6522	87
88	0.8027 3915	0.7739 1511	0.7461 3739	0.7193 6760	88
89	0.8007 3731	0.7716 6442	0.7436 5853	0.7166 8005	89
90	0.7987 4046	0.7694 2028	0.7411 8790	0.7140 0254	90
91	0.7967 4859	0.7671 8266	0.7387 2548	0.7113 3503	91
92	0.7947 6168	0.7649 5156	0.7362 7125	0.7086 7749	92
93	0.7927 7973	0.7627 2694	0.7338 2516	0.7060 2988	93
94	0.7908 0273	0.7605 0878	0.7313 8720	0.7033 9216	94
95	0.7888 3065	0.7582 9708	0.7289 5735	0.7007 6429	95
96	0.7868 6349	0.7560 9182	0.7265 3556	0.6981 4624	96
97	0.7849 0124	0.7538 9296	0.7241 2182	0.6955 3797	97
98	0.7829 4388	0.7517 0050	0.7217 1610	0.6929 3945	98
99	0.7809 9140	0.7495 1442	0.7193 1837	0.6903 5064	99
100	0.7790 4379	0.7473 3469	0.7169 2861	0.6877 7149	100

$$v^n = (1 + i)^{-n}$$

n	$\frac{1}{4}\%$	$\frac{7}{24}\%$	$\frac{1}{3}\%$	$\frac{3}{8}\%$	n
101	0.7771 0104	0.7451 6131	0.7145 4679	0.6852 0199	101
102	0.7751 6313	0.7429 9424	0.7121 7288	0.6826 4208	102
103	0.7732 3006	0.7408 3348	0.7098 0686	0.6800 9173	103
104	0.7713 0180	0.7386 7899	0.7074 4869	0.6775 5092	104
105	0.7693 7836	0.7365 3078	0.7050 9837	0.6750 1959	105
106	0.7674 5971	0.7343 8881	0.7027 5585	0.6724 9773	106
107	0.7655 4584	0.7322 5307	0.7004 2111	0.6699 8528	107
108	0.7636 3675	0.7301 2355	0.6980 9413	0.6674 8223	108
109	0.7617 3242	0.7280 0021	0.6957 7488	0.6649 8852	109
110	0.7598 3284	0.7258 8305	0.6934 6334	0.6625 0413	110
111	0.7579 3799	0.7237 7205	0.6911 5947	0.6600 2902	111
112	0.7560 4787	0.7216 6719	0.6888 6326	0.6575 6316	112
113	0.7541 6247	0.7195 6845	0.6865 7468	0.6551 0651	113
114	0.7522 8176	0.7174 7581	0.6842 9370	0.6526 5904	114
115	0.7504 0575	0.7153 8926	0.6820 2030	0.6502 2071	115
116	0.7485 3441	0.7133 0878	0.6797 5445	0.6477 9149	116
117	0.7466 6774	0.7112 3434	0.6774 9613	0.6453 7135	117
118	0.7448 0573	0.7091 6594	0.6752 4531	0 6429 6025	118
119	0.7429 4836	0.7071 0356	0.6730 0197	0.6405 5815	119
120	0.7410 9562	0.7050 4717	0.6707 6608	0.6381 6504	120
121	0.7392 4750	0.7029 9676	0.6685 3763	0.6357 8086	121
122	0.7374 0399	0.7009 5232	0.6663 1657	0.6334 0559	122
123	0.7355 6508	0.6989 1382	0.6641 0289	0.6310 3919	123
124	0.7337 3075	0.6968 8125	0.6618 9657	0.6286 8163	124
125	0.7319 0100	0.6948 5459	0.6596 9758	0.6263 3288	125
126	0.7300 7581	0.6928 3382	0.6575 0589	0.6239 9291	126
127	0.7282 5517	0.6908 1893	0.6553 2149	0.6216 6168	127
128	0.7264 3907	0.6888 0991	0.6531 4434	0.6193 3916	128
129	0.7246 2750	0.6868 0672	0.6509 7443	0.6170 2531	129
130	0.7228 2045	0.6848 0936	0.6488 1172	0.6147 2011	130
131	0.7210 1791	0.6828 1781	0.6466 5620	0.6124 2352	131
132	0.7192 1986	0.6808 3205	0.6445 0784	0.6101 3552	132
133	0.7174 2629	0.6788 5206	0.6423 6662	0.6078 5606	133
134	0.7156 3720	0.6768 7783	0.6402 3251	0.6055 8511	134
135	0.7138 5257	0.6749 0935	0.6381 0549	0.6033 2265	135
136	0.7120 7239	0.6729 4659	0.6359 8554	0.6010 6864	136
137	0.7102 9664	0.6709 8954	0.6338 7263	0.5988 2306	137
138	0.7085 2533	0.6690 3817	0.6317 6674	0.5965 8586	138
139	0.7067 5843	0.6670 9249	0.6296 6785	0.5943 5702	139
140	0.7049 9595	0.6651 5246	0.6275 7593	0.5921 3651	140
141	0.7032 3785	0.6632 1807	0.6254 9096	0.5899 2429	141
142	0.7014 8414	0.6612 8931	0.6234 1292	0.5877 2034	142
143	0.6997 3480	0.6593 6616	0.6213 4178	0.5855 2463	143
144	0.6979 8983	0.6574 4860	0.6192 7752	0.5833 3711	144
145	0.6962 4921	0.6555 3662	0.6172 2012	0.5811 5777	145
146	0.6945 1292	0.6536 3020	0.6151 6955	0.5789 8657	146
147	0.6927 8097	0.6517 2932	0.6131 2580	0.5768 2348	147
148	0.6910 5334	0.6498 3397	0.6110 8884	0.5746 6848	148
149	0.6893 3001	0.6479 4414	0.6090 5864	0.5725 2152	149
150	0.6876 1098	0.6460 5980	0.6070 3519	0.5703 8258	150

VI. PRESENT VALUE OF 1

$$v^n = (1 + i)^{-n}$$

n	$\frac{1}{4}\%$	$\frac{7}{24}\%$	$\frac{1}{3}\%$	$\frac{3}{8}\%$	n
151	0.6858 9624	0.6441 8093	0.6050 1846	0.5682 5164	151
152	0.6841 8578	0.6423 0754	0.6030 0843	0.5661 2866	152
153	0.6824 7958	0.6404 3959	0.6010 0508	0.5640 1361	153
154	0.6807 7764	0.6385 7707	0.5990 0839	0.5619 0646	154
155	0.6790 7994	0.6367 1997	0.5970 1833	0.5598 0718	155
156	0.6773 8647	0.6348 6827	0.5950 3488	0.5577 1575	156
157	0.6756 9723	0.6330 2196	0.5930 5802	0.5556 3213	157
158	0.6740 1220	0.6311 8101	0.5910 8773	0.5535 5629	158
159	0.6723 3137	0.6293 4542	0.5891 2398	0.5514 8821	159
160	0.6706 5473	0.6275 1517	0.5871 6676	0.5494 2786	160
161	0.6689 8228	0.6256 9024	0.5852 1604	0.5473 7520	161
162	0.6673 1399	0.6238 7062	0.5832 7180	0.5453 3021	162
163	0.6656 4987	0.6220 5629	0.5813 3402	0.5432 9286	163
164	0.6639 8989	0.6202 4723	0.5794 0268	0.5412 6313	164
165	0.6623 3406	0.6184 4344	0.5774 7775	0.5392 4097	165
166	0.6606 8235	0.6166 4489	0.5755 5922	0.5372 2637	166
167	0.6590 3476	0.6148 5158	0.5736 4706	0.5352 1930	167
168	0.6573 9129	0.6130 6347	0.5717 4126	0.5332 1973	168
169	0.6557 5191	0.6112 8057	0.5698 4179	0.5312 2762	169
170	0.6541 1661	0.6095 0285	0.5679 4862	0.5292 4296	170
171	0.6524 8540	0.6077 3031	0.5660 6175	0.5272 6572	171
172	0.6508 5826	0.6059 6292	0.5641 8115	0.5252 9586	172
173	0.6492 3517	0.6042 0066	0.5623 0679	0.5233 3336	173
174	0.6476 1613	0.6024 4354	0.5604 3866	0.5213 7819	174
175	0.6460 0112	0.6006 9152	0.5585 7674	0.5194 3032	175
176	0.6443 9015	0.5989 4460	0.5567 2100	0.5174 8974	176
177	0.6427 8319	0.5972 0276	0.5548 7143	0.5155 5640	177
178	0.6411 8024	0.5954 6598	0.5530 2801	0.5136 3029	178
179	0.6395 8129	0.5937 3426	0.5511 9070	0.5117 1137	179
180	0.6379 8632	0.5920 0757	0.5493 5950	0.5097 9962	180
181	0.6363 9533	0.5902 8590	0.5475 3439	0.5078 9501	181
182	0.6348 0831	0.5885 6924	0.5457 1534	0.5059 9752	182
183	0.6332 2525	0.5868 5757	0.5439 0233	0.5041 0712	183
184	0.6316 4613	0.5851 5088	0.5420 9535	0.5022 2378	184
185	0.6300 7096	0.5834 4916	0.5402 9437	0.5003 4748	185
186	0.6284 9971	0.5817 5238	0.5384 9937	0.4984 7819	186
187	0.6269 3238	0.5800 6053	0.5367 1033	0.4966 1588	187
188	0.6253 6895	0.5783 7361	0.5349 2724	0.4947 6053	188
189	0.6238 0943	0.5766 9159	0.5331 5008	0.4929 1211	189
190	0.6222 5380	0.5750 1447	0.5313 7881	0.4910 7059	190
191	0.6207 0204	0.5733 4222	0.5296 1343	0.4892 3596	191
192	0.6191 5416	0.5716 7484	0.5278 5392	0.4874 0817	192
193	0.6176 1013	0.5700 1230	0.5261 0025	0.4855 8722	193
194	0.6160 6996	0.5683 5460	0.5243 5241	0.4837 7307	194
195	0.6145 3362	0.5667 0172	0.5226 1038	0.4819 6570	195
196	0.6130 0112	0.5650 5365	0.5208 7413	0.4801 6508	196
197	0.6114 7244	0.5634 1037	0.5191 4365	0.4783 7119	197
198	0.6099 4757	0.5617 7186	0.5174 1892	0.4765 8400	198
199	0.6084 2650	0.5601 3813	0.5156 9992	0.4748 0349	199
200	0.6069 0923	0.5585 0914	0.5139 8663	0.4730 2963	200

VI. PRESENT VALUE OF 1

$$v^n = (1 + i)^{-n}$$

n	$\frac{1}{4}\%$	$\frac{7}{24}\%$	$\frac{1}{3}\%$	$\frac{3}{8}\%$	n
201	0.6053 9574	0.5568 8490	0.5122 7904	0.4712 6239	201
202	0.6038 8602	0.5552 6537	0.5105 7711	0.4695 0176	202
203	0.6023 8007	0.5536 5056	0.5088 8084	0.4677 4771	203
204	0.6008 7788	0.5520 4044	0.5071 9021	0.4660 0021	204
205	0.5993 7943	0.5504 3500	0.5055 0519	0.4642 5923	205
206	0.5978 8472	0.5488 3424	0.5038 2577	0.4625 2477	206
207	0.5963 9373	0.5472 3813	0.5021 5193	0.4607 9678	207
208	0.5949 0647	0.5456 4666	0.5004 8365	0.4590 7525	208
209	0.5934 2291	0.5440 5982	0.4988 2092	0.4573 6015	209
210	0.5919 4305	0.5424 7759	0.4971 6371	0.4556 5145	210
211	0.5904 6689	0.5408 9996	0.4955 1200	0.4539 4914	211
212	0.5889 9440	0.5393 2693	0.4938 6578	0.4522 5319	212
213	0.5875 2559	0.5377 5847	0.4922 2503	0.4505 6358	213
214	0.5860 6044	0.5361 9456	0.4905 8973	0.4488 8028	214
215	0.5845 9894	0.5346 3521	0.4889 5986	0.4472 0327	215
216	0.5831 4109	0.5330 8039	0.4873 3541	0.4455 3252	216
217	0.5816 8687	0.5315 3010	0.4857 1636	0.4438 6802	217
218	0.5802 3628	0.5299 8431	0.4841 0268	0.4422 0973	218
219	0.5787 8930	0.5284 4302	0.4824 9437	0.4405 5764	219
220	0.5773 4594	0.5269 0621	0.4808 9140	0.4389 1172	220
221	0.5759 0617	0.5253 7387	0.4792 9375	0.4372 7195	221
222	0.5744 7000	0.5238 4598	0.4777 0141	0.4356 3831	222
223	0.5730 3741	0.5223 2254	0.4761 1437	0.4340 1077	223
224	0.5716 0838	0.5208 0353	0.4745 3259	0.4323 8931	224
225	0.5701 8293	0.5192 8894	0.4729 5607	0.4307 7390	225
226	0.5687 6102	0.5177 7875	0.4713 8479	0.4291 6454	226
227	0.5673 4267	0.5162 7296	0.4698 1872	0.4275 6118	227
228	0.5659 2785	0.5147 7154	0.4682 5786	0.4259 6382	228
229	0.5645 1656	0.5132 7449	0.4667 0219	0.4243 7242	229
230	0.5631 0879	0.5117 8179	0.4651 5169	0.4227 8697	230
231	0.5617 0452	0.5102 9344	0.4636 0633	0.4212 0744	231
232	0.5603 0376	0.5088 0941	0.4620 6611	0.4196 3382	232
233	0.5589 0650	0.5073 2970	0.4605 3101	0.4180 6607	233
234	0.5575 1272	0.5058 5429	0.4590 0100	0.4165 0418	234
235	0.5561 2241	0.5043 8317	0.4574 7608	0.4149 4812	235
236	0.5547 3557	0.5029 1633	0.4559 5623	0.4133 9788	236
237	0.5533 5219	0.5014 5376	0.4544 4142	0.4118 5343	237
238	0.5519 7226	0.4999 9544	0.4529 3165	0.4103 1475	238
239	0.5505 9577	0.4985 4136	0.4514 2690	0.4087 8182	239
240	0.5492 2271	0.4970 9151	0.4499 2714	0.4072 5461	240
241	0.5478 5308	0.4956 4588	0.4484 3236	0.4057 3311	241
242	0.5464 8686	0.4942 0445	0.4469 4256	0.4042 1730	242
243	0.5451 2405	0.4927 6721	0.4454 5770	0.4027 0715	243
244	0.5437 6464	0.4913 3415	0.4439 7777	0.4012 0264	244
245	0.5424 0862	0.4899 0526	0.4425 0276	0.3997 0375	245
246	0.5410 5598	0.4884 8052	0.4410 3265	0.3982 1046	246
247	0.5397 0671	0.4870 5993	0.4395 6743	0.3967 2275	247
248	0.5383 6081	0.4856 4347	0.4381 0707	0.3952 4060	248
249	0.5370 1827	0.4842 3113	0.4366 5157	0.3937 6398	249
250	0.5356 7907	0.4828 2290	0.4352 0090	0.3922 9288	250

VI. PRESENT VALUE OF 1

$$v^n = (1 + i)^{-n}$$

n	$\frac{5}{12}\%$	$\frac{1}{2}\%$	$\frac{7}{12}\%$	$\frac{5}{8}\%$	n
1	0.9958 5062	0.9950 2488	0.9942 0050	0.9937 8882	1
2	0.9917 1846	0.9900 7450	0.9884 3463	0.9876 1622	2
3	0.9876 0345	0.9851 4876	0.9827 0220	0.9814 8196	3
4	0.9835 0551	0.9802 4752	0.9770 0301	0.9753 8580	4
5	0.9794 2457	0.9753 7067	0.9713 3688	0.9693 2750	5
6	0.9753 6057	0.9705 1808	0.9657 0361	0.9633 0683	6
7	0.9713 1343	0.9656 8963	0.9601 0301	0.9573 2356	7
8	0.9672 8308	0.9608 8520	0.9545 3489	0.9513 7745	8
9	0.9632 6946	0.9561 0468	0.9489 9906	0.9454 6827	9
10	0.9592 7249	0.9513 4794	0.9434 9534	0.9395 9580	10
11	0.9552 9211	0.9466 1487	0.9380 2354	0.9337 5980	11
12	0.9513 2824	0.9419 0534	0.9325 8347	0.9279 6005	12
13	0.9473 8082	0.9372 1924	0.9271 7495	0.9221 9632	13
14	0.9434 4978	0.9325 5646	0.9217 9779	0.9164 6840	14
15	0.9395 3505	0.9279 1688	0.9164 5182	0.9107 7604	15
16	0.9356 3657	0.9233 0037	0.9111 3686	0.9051 1905	16
17	0.9317 5426	0.9187 0684	0.9058 5272	0.8994 9719	17
18	0.9278 8806	0.9141 3616	0.9005 9922	0.8939 1025	18
19	0.9240 3790	0.9095 8822	0.8953 7619	0.8883 5802	19
20	0.9202 0372	0.9050 6290	0.8901 8346	0.8828 4027	20
21	0.9163 8544	0.9005 6010	0.8850 2084	0.8773 5679	21
22	0.9125 8301	0.8960 7971	0.8798 8815	0.8719 0736	22
23	0.9087 9636	0.8916 2160	0.8747 8524	0.8664 9179	23
24	0.9050 2542	0.8871 8567	0.8697 1192	0.8611 0985	24
25	0.9012 7013	0.8827 7181	0.8646 6802	0.8557 6135	25
26	0.8975 3042	0.8783 7991	0.8596 5338	0.8504 4606	26
27	0.8938 0623	0.8740 0986	0.8546 6782	0.8451 6378	27
28	0.8900 9749	0.8696 6155	0.8497 1117	0.8399 1432	28
29	0.8864 0414	0.8653 3488	0.8447 8327	0.8346 9746	29
30	0.8827 2611	0.8610 2973	0.8398 8394	0.8295 1300	30
31	0.8790 6335	0.8567 4600	0.8350 1303	0.8243 6075	31
32	0.8754 1578	0.8524 8358	0.8301 7037	0.8192 4050	32
33	0.8717 8335	0.8482 4237	0.8253 5580	0.8141 5205	33
34	0.8681 6599	0.8440 2226	0.8205 6914	0.8090 9520	34
35	0.8645 6365	0.8398 2314	0.8158 1025	0.8040 6976	35
36	0.8609 7624	0.8356 4492	0.8110 7896	0.7990 7554	36
37	0.8574 0373	0.8314 8748	0.8063 7510	0.7941 1234	37
38	0.8538 4604	0.8273 5073	0.8016 9853	0.7891 7997	38
39	0.8503 0311	0.8232 3455	0.7970 4907	0.7842 7823	39
40	0.8467 7488	0.8191 3886	0.7924 2659	0.7794 0693	40
41	0.8432 6129	0.8150 6354	0.7878 3091	0.7745 6590	41
42	0.8397 6228	0.8110 0850	0.7832 6188	0.7697 5493	42
43	0.8362 7779	0.8069 7363	0.7787 1935	0.7649 7384	43
44	0.8328 0776	0.8029 5884	0.7742 0316	0.7602 2245	44
45	0.8293 5212	0.7989 6402	0.7697 1317	0.7555 0057	45
46	0.8259 1083	0.7949 8907	0.7652 4922	0.7508 0802	46
47	0.8224 8381	0.7910 3390	0.7608 1115	0.7461 4462	47
48	0.8190 7102	0.7870 9841	0.7563 9883	0.7415 1018	48
49	0.8156 7238	0.7831 8250	0.7520 1209	0.7369 0453	49
50	0.8122 8785	0.7792 8607	0.7476 5079	0.7323 2748	50

VI. PRESENT VALUE OF 1

$$v^n = (1 + i)^{-n}$$

n	$\frac{5}{12}\%$	$\frac{1}{2}\%$	$\frac{7}{12}\%$	$\frac{5}{8}\%$	n
51	0.8089 1736	0.7754 0902	0.7433 1479	0.7277 7886	51
52	0.8055 6086	0.7715 5127	0.7390 0393	0.7222 5849	52
53	0.8022 1828	0.7677 1270	0.7347 1808	0.7187 6620	53
54	0.7988 8957	0.7638 9324	0.7304 5708	0.7143 0182	54
55	0.7955 7468	0.7600 9277	0.7262 2079	0.7098 6516	55
56	0.7922 7354	0.7563 1122	0.7220 0907	0.7054 5606	56
57	0.7889 8610	0.7525 4847	0.7178 2178	0.7010 7434	57
58	0.7857 1230	0.7488 0445	0.7136 5877	0.6967 1985	58
59	0.7824 5208	0.7450 7906	0.7095 1990	0.6923 9239	59
60	0.7792 0539	0.7413 7220	0.7054 0504	0.6880 9182	60
61	0.7759 7217	0.7376 8378	0.7013 1404	0.6838 1796	61
62	0.7727 5237	0.7340 1371	0.6972 4677	0.6795 7064	62
63	0.7695 4593	0.7303 6190	0.6932 0308	0.6753 4970	63
64	0.7663 5279	0.7267 2826	0.6891 8285	0.6711 5499	64
65	0.7631 7291	0.7231 1269	0.6851 8593	0.6669 8632	65
66	0.7600 0621	0.7195 1512	0.6812 1219	0.6628 4355	66
67	0.7568 5266	0.7159 3544	0.6772 6150	0.6587 2651	67
68	0.7537 1219	0.7123 7357	0.6733 3372	0.6546 3504	68
69	0.7505 8476	0.7088 2943	0.6694 2872	0.6505 6898	69
70	0.7474 7030	0.7053 0291	0.6655 4637	0.6465 2818	70
71	0.7443 6876	0.7017 9394	0.6616 8653	0.6425 1248	71
72	0.7412 8009	0.6983 0243	0.6578 4908	0.6385 2172	72
73	0.7382 0424	0.6948 2829	0.6540 3388	0.6345 5574	73
74	0.7351 4115	0.6913 7143	0.6502 4081	0.6306 1440	74
75	0.7320 9078	0.6879 3177	0.6464 6973	0.6266 9754	75
76	0.7290 5306	0.6845 0923	0.6427 2053	0.6228 0501	76
77	0.7260 2794	0.6811 0371	0.6389 9307	0.6189 3666	77
78	0.7230 1537	0.6777 1513	0.6352 8723	0.6150 9233	78
79	0.7200 1531	0.6743 4342	0.6316 0288	0.6112 7188	79
80	0.7170 2770	0.6709 8847	0.6279 3990	0.6074 7516	80
81	0.7140 5248	0.6676 5022	0.6242 9816	0.6037 0203	81
82	0.7110 8960	0.6643 2858	0.6206 7754	0.5999 5232	82
83	0.7081 3902	0.6610 2346	0.6170 7792	0.5962 2591	83
84	0.7052 0069	0.6577 3479	0.6134 9917	0.5925 2264	84
85	0.7022 7454	0.6544 6248	0.6099 4118	0.5888 4238	85
86	0.6993 6054	0.6512 0644	0.6064 0382	0.5851 8497	86
87	0.6964 5863	0.6479 6661	0.6028 8698	0.5815 5028	87
88	0.6935 6876	0.6447 4290	0.5993 9054	0.5779 3817	88
89	0.6906 9088	0.6415 3522	0.5959 1437	0.5743 4849	89
90	0.6878 2495	0.6383 4350	0.5924 5836	0.5707 8111	90
91	0.6849 7090	0.6351 6766	0.5890 2240	0.5672 3589	91
92	0.6821 2870	0.6320 0763	0.5856 0636	0.5637 1268	92
93	0.6792 9829	0.6288 6331	0.5822 1014	0.5602 1136	93
94	0.6764 7962	0.6257 3464	0.5788 3361	0.5567 3179	94
95	0.6736 7265	0.6226 2153	0.5754 7666	0.5532 7383	95
96	0.6708 7733	0.6195 2391	0.5721 3918	0.5498 3734	96
97	0.6680 9361	0.6164 4170	0.5688 2106	0.5464 2220	97
98	0.6653 2143	0.6133 7483	0.5655 2218	0.5430 2828	98
99	0.6625 6076	0.6103 2321	0.5622 4243	0.5396 5543	99
100	0.6598 1155	0.6072 8678	0.5589 8171	0.5363 0353	100

VI. PRESENT VALUE OF 1

$$v^n = (1 + i)^{-n}$$

n	$\frac{5}{12}\%$	$\frac{1}{2}\%$	$\frac{7}{12}\%$	$\frac{5}{8}\%$	n
101	0.6570 7374	0.6042 6545	0.5557 3989	0.5329 7246	101
102	0.6543 4730	0.6012 5915	0.5525 1688	0.5296 6207	102
103	0.6516 3216	0.5982 6781	0.5493 1255	0.5263 7225	103
104	0.6489 2829	0.5952 9136	0.5461 2681	0.5231 0285	104
105	0.6462 3565	0.5923 2971	0.5429 5955	0.5198 5377	105
106	0.6435 5417	0.5893 8279	0.5398 1065	0.5166 2486	106
107	0.6408 8382	0.5864 5054	0.5366 8002	0.5134 1601	107
108	0.6382 2455	0.5835 3288	0.5335 6754	0.5102 2709	108
109	0.6355 7632	0.5806 2973	0.5304 7312	0.5070 5798	109
110	0.6329 3907	0.5777 4102	0.5273 9664	0.5039 0855	110
111	0.6303 1277	0.5748 6669	0.5243 3800	0.5007 7868	111
112	0.6276 9736	0.5720 0666	0.5212 9710	0.4976 6826	112
113	0.6250 9281	0.5691 6085	0.5182 7383	0.4945 7715	113
114	0.6224 9906	0.5663 2921	0.5152 6810	0.4915 0524	114
115	0.6199 1608	0.5635 1165	0.5122 7980	0.4884 5242	115
116	0.6173 4381	0.5607 0811	0.5093 0884	0.4854 1855	116
117	0.6147 8222	0.5579 1852	0.5063 5510	0.4824 0353	117
118	0.6122 3126	0.5551 4280	0.5034 1849	0.4794 0723	118
119	0.6096 9088	0.5523 8090	0.5004 9891	0.4764 2955	119
120	0.6071 6104	0.5496 3273	0.4975 9627	0.4734 7036	120
121	0.6046 4170	0.5468 9824	0.4947 1046	0.4705 2955	121
122	0.6021 3281	0.5441 7736	0.4918 4138	0.4676 0700	122
123	0.5996 3434	0.5414 7001	0.4889 8895	0.4647 0261	123
124	0.5971 4623	0.5387 7612	0.4861 5305	0.4618 1626	124
125	0.5946 6844	0.5360 9565	0.4833 3361	0.4589 4784	125
126	0.5922 0094	0.5334 2850	0.4805 3051	0.4560 9723	126
127	0.5897 4367	0.5307 7463	0.4777 4367	0.4532 6433	127
128	0.5872 9660	0.5281 3396	0.4749 7300	0.4504 4902	128
129	0.5848 5969	0.5255 0643	0.4722 1839	0.4476 5120	129
130	0.5824 3288	0.5228 9197	0.4694 7976	0.4448 7076	130
131	0.5800 1615	0.5202 9052	0.4667 5701	0.4421 0759	131
132	0.5776 0944	0.5177 0201	0.4640 5005	0.4393 6158	132
133	0.5752 1273	0.5151 2637	0.4613 5879	0.4366 3262	133
134	0.5728 2595	0.5125 6356	0.4586 8314	0.4339 2062	134
135	0.5704 4908	0.5100 1349	0.4560 2301	0.4312 2546	135
136	0.5680 8207	0.5074 7611	0.4533 7830	0.4285 4704	136
137	0.5657 2488	0.5049 5135	0.4507 4893	0.4258 8526	137
138	0.5633 7748	0.5024 3916	0.4481 3481	0.4232 4001	138
139	0.5610 3981	0.4999 3946	0.4455 3585	0.4206 1119	139
140	0.5587 1185	0.4974 5220	0.4429 5197	0.4179 9870	140
141	0.5563 9354	0.4949 7731	0.4403 8306	0.4154 0243	141
142	0.5540 8485	0.4925 1474	0.4378 2906	0.4128 2229	142
143	0.5517 8574	0.4900 6442	0.4352 8987	0.4102 5818	143
144	0.5494 9618	0.4876 2628	0.4327 6541	0.4077 0999	144
145	0.5472 1611	0.4852 0028	0.4302 5558	0.4051 7763	145
146	0.5449 4550	0.4827 8635	0.4277 6031	0.4026 6100	146
147	0.5426 8432	0.4803 8443	0.4252 7952	0.4001 6000	147
148	0.5404 3252	0.4779 9446	0.4228 1311	0.3976 7453	148
149	0.5381 9006	0.4756 1637	0.4203 6100	0.3952 0451	149
150	0.5359 5690	0.4732 5012	0.4179 2312	0.3927 4982	150

VI. PRESENT VALUE OF 1

$$v^n = (1 + i)^{-n}$$

n	$\frac{5}{12}\%$	$\frac{1}{2}\%$	$\frac{7}{12}\%$	$\frac{5}{8}\%$	n
151	0.5337 3302	0.4708 9565	0.4154 9937	0.3903 1038	151
152	0.5315 1836	0.4685 5288	0.4130 8968	0.3878 8609	152
153	0.5293 1289	0.4662 2177	0.4106 9396	0.3854 7686	153
154	0.5271 1657	0.4639 0226	0.4083 1214	0.3830 8259	154
155	0.5249 2936	0.4615 9429	0.4059 4414	0.3807 0320	155
156	0.5227 5123	0.4592 9780	0.4035 8986	0.3783 3858	156
157	0.5205 8214	0.4570 1274	0.4012 4924	0.3759 8865	157
158	0.5184 2205	0.4547 3904	0.3989 2220	0.3736 5332	158
159	0.5162 7092	0.4524 7666	0.3966 0864	0.3713 3249	159
160	0.5141 2872	0.4502 2553	0.3943 0851	0.3690 2608	160
161	0.5119 9540	0.4479 8560	0.3920 2172	0.3667 3399	161
162	0.5098 7094	0.4457 5682	0.3897 4819	0.3644 5614	162
163	0.5077 5529	0.4435 3912	0.3874 8784	0.3621 9244	163
164	0.5056 4842	0.4413 3246	0.3852 4060	0.3599 4280	164
165	0.5035 5030	0.4391 3678	0.3830 0640	0.3577 0713	165
166	0.5014 6088	0.4369 5202	0.3807 8515	0.3554 8534	166
167	0.4993 8013	0.4347 7813	0.3785 7679	0.3532 7736	167
168	0.4973 0801	0.4326 1505	0.3763 8123	0.3510 8309	168
169	0.4952 4449	0.4304 6274	0.3741 9841	0.3489 0245	169
170	0.4931 8954	0.4283 2113	0.3720 2824	0.3467 3535	170
171	0.4911 4311	0.4261 9018	0.3698 7066	0.3445 8172	171
172	0.4891 0517	0.4240 6983	0.3677 2560	0.3424 4146	172
173	0.4870 7569	0.4219 6003	0.3655 9297	0.3403 1449	173
174	0.4850 5462	0.4198 6073	0.3634 7272	0.3382 0074	174
175	0.4830 4195	0.4177 7187	0.3613 6475	0.3361 0011	175
176	0.4810 3763	0.4156 9340	0.3592 6902	0.3340 1254	176
177	0.4790 4162	0.4136 2528	0.3571 8544	0.3319 3792	177
178	0.4770 5390	0.4115 6744	0.3551 1394	0.3298 7620	178
179	0.4750 7442	0.4095 1984	0.3530 5445	0.3278 2728	179
180	0.4731 0316	0.4074 8243	0.3510 0691	0.3257 9108	180
181	0.4711 4007	0.4054 5515	0.3489 7125	0.3237 6754	181
182	0.4691 8513	0.4034 3796	0.3469 4739	0.3217 5656	182
183	0.4672 3831	0.4014 3081	0.3449 3527	0.3197 5807	183
184	0.4652 9956	0.3994 3364	0.3429 3481	0.3177 7199	184
185	0.4633 6886	0.3974 4641	0.3409 4596	0.3157 9825	185
186	0.4614 4616	0.3954 6906	0.3389 6864	0.3138 3677	186
187	0.4595 3145	0.3935 0155	0.3370 0279	0.3118 8748	187
188	0.4576 2468	0.3915 4383	0.3350 4835	0.3099 5029	188
189	0.4557 2582	0.3895 9586	0.3331 0523	0.3080 2513	189
190	0.4538 3484	0.3876 5757	0.3311 7339	0.3061 1193	190
191	0.4519 5171	0.3857 2892	0.3292 5275	0.3042 1062	191
192	0.4500 7639	0.3838 0987	0.3273 4324	0.3023 2111	192
193	0.4482 0886	0.3819 0037	0.3254 4482	0.3004 4334	193
194	0.4463 4907	0.3800 0037	0.3235 5740	0.2985 7723	194
195	0.4444 9700	0.3781 0982	0.3216 8093	0.2967 2271	195
196	0.4426 5261	0.3762 2868	0.3198 1534	0.2948 7972	196
197	0.4408 1588	0.3743 5689	0.3179 6057	0.2930 4816	197
198	0.4389 8677	0.3724 9442	0.3161 1655	0.2912 2799	198
199	0.4371 6525	0.3706 4121	0.3142 8323	0.2894 1912	199
200	0.4353 5128	0.3687 9723	0.3124 6055	0.2876 2149	200

VI. PRESENT VALUE OF 1

$$v^n = (1 + i)^{-n}$$

n	$\frac{5}{12}\%$	$\frac{1}{2}\%$	$\frac{7}{12}\%$	$\frac{5}{8}\%$	n
201	0.4335 4484	0.3669 6242	0.3106 4843	0.2858 3502	201
202	0.4317 4590	0.3651 3673	0.3088 4683	0.2840 5964	202
203	0.4299 5443	0.3633 2013	0.3070 5567	0.2822 9530	203
204	0.4281 7038	0.3615 1257	0.3052 7490	0.2805 4191	204
205	0.4263 9374	0.3597 1400	0.3035 0445	0.2787 9941	205
206	0.4246 2447	0.3579 2438	0.3017 4428	0.2770 6774	206
207	0.4228 6255	0.3561 4366	0.2999 9431	0.2753 4682	207
208	0.4211 0793	0.3543 7180	0.2982 5450	0.2736 3660	208
209	0.4193 6059	0.3526 0876	0.2965 2477	0.2719 3699	209
210	0.4176 2051	0.3508 5448	0.2948 0507	0.2702 4794	210
211	0.4158 8764	0.3491 0894	0.2930 9535	0.2685 6938	211
212	0.4141 6197	0.3473 7208	0.2913 9554	0.2669 0125	212
213	0.4124 4345	0.3456 4386	0.2897 0559	0.2652 4348	213
214	0.4107 3207	0.3439 2424	0.2880 2544	0.2635 9600	214
215	0.4090 2779	0.3422 1317	0.2863 5504	0.2619 5876	215
216	0.4073 3058	0.3405 1062	0.2846 9432	0.2603 3169	216
217	0.4056 4041	0.3388 1654	0.2830 4324	0.2587 1472	217
218	0.4039 5725	0.3371 3088	0.2814 0173	0.2571 0780	218
219	0.4022 8108	0.3354 5361	0.2797 6974	0.2555 1085	219
220	0.4006 1187	0.3337 8469	0.2781 4721	0.2539 2383	220
221	0.3989 4958	0.3321 2407	0.2765 3410	0.2523 4666	221
222	0.3972 9418	0.3304 7171	0.2749 3033	0.2507 7929	222
223	0.3956 4566	0.3288 2757	0.2733 3588	0.2492 2166	223
224	0.3940 0398	0.3271 9162	0.2717 5066	0.2476 7370	224
225	0.3923 6911	0.3255 6380	0.2701 7464	0.2461 3535	225
226	0.3907 4102	0.3239 4408	0.2686 0777	0.2446 0656	226
227	0.3891 1969	0.3223 3241	0.2670 4997	0.2430 8726	227
228	0.3875 0508	0.3207 2877	0.2655 0122	0.2415 7740	228
229	0.3858 9718	0.3191 3310	0.2639 6144	0.2400 7692	229
230	0.3842 9594	0.3175 4538	0.2624 3060	0.2385 8576	230
231	0.3827 0136	0.3159 6555	0.2609 0863	0.2371 0386	231
232	0.3811 1338	0.3143 9358	0.2593 9549	0.2356 3117	232
233	0.3795 3200	0.3128 2944	0.2578 9112	0.2341 6762	233
234	0.3779 5718	0.3112 7307	0.2563 9548	0.2327 1316	234
235	0.3763 8889	0.3097 2445	0.2549 0852	0.2312 6774	235
236	0.3748 2711	0.3081 8353	0.2534 3018	0.2298 3129	236
237	0.3732 7181	0.3066 5028	0.2519 6041	0.2284 0377	237
238	0.3717 2297	0.3051 2466	0.2504 9916	0.2269 8511	238
239	0.3701 8055	0.3036 0662	0.2490 4639	0.2255 7527	239
240	0.3686 4453	0.3020 9614	0.2476 0205	0.2241 7418	240
241	0.3671 1488	0.3005 9318	0.2461 6608	0.2227 8179	241
242	0.3655 9159	0.2990 9769	0.2447 3844	0.2213 9806	242
243	0.3640 7461	0.2976 0964	0.2433 1907	0.2200 2291	243
244	0.3625 6392	0.2961 2899	0.2419 0794	0.2186 5631	244
245	0.3610 5951	0.2946 5572	0.2405 0500	0.2172 9820	245
246	0.3595 6134	0.2931 8977	0.2391 1019	0.2159 4852	246
247	0.3580 6938	0.2917 3111	0.2377 2347	0.2146 0722	247
248	0.3565 8362	0.2902 7971	0.2363 4479	0.2132 7426	248
249	0.3551 0402	0.2888 3553	0.2349 7411	0.2119 4957	249
250	0.3536 3056	0.2873 9854	0.2336 1138	0.2106 3312	250

VI. PRESENT VALUE OF 1

$$v^n = (1 + i)^{-n}$$

n	$\frac{3}{4}\%$	$\frac{7}{8}\%$	1%	$1\frac{1}{8}\%$	n
1	0.9925 5583	0.9913 2590	0.9900 9901	0.9888 7515	1
2	0.9851 6708	0.9827 2704	0.9802 9605	0.9778 7407	2
3	0.9778 3333	0.9742 0276	0.9705 9015	0.9669 9537	3
4	0.9705 5417	0.9657 5243	0.9609 8034	0.9562 3770	4
5	0.9633 2920	0.9573 7539	0.9514 6569	0.9455 9970	5
6	0.9561 5802	0.9490 7102	0.9420 4524	0.9350 8005	6
7	0.9490 4022	0.9408 3868	0.9327 1805	0.9246 7743	7
8	0.9419 7540	0.9326 7775	0.9234 8322	0.9143 9054	8
9	0.9349 6318	0.9245 8761	0.9143 3982	0.9042 1808	9
10	0.9280 0315	0.9165 6765	0.9052 8695	0.8941 5880	10
11	0.9210 9494	0.9086 1724	0.8963 2372	0.8842 1142	11
12	0.9142 3815	0.9007 3581	0.8874 4923	0.8743 7470	12
13	0.9074 3241	0.8929 2273	0.8786 6260	0.8646 4742	13
14	0.9006 7733	0.8851 7743	0.8699 6297	0.8550 2835	14
15	0.8939 7254	0.8774 9931	0.8613 4947	0.8455 1629	15
16	0.8873 1766	0.8698 8779	0.8528 2126	0.8361 1005	16
17	0.8807 1231	0.8623 4230	0.8443 7749	0.8268 0846	17
18	0.8741 5614	0.8548 6225	0.8360 1731	0.8176 1034	18
19	0.8676 4878	0.8474 4709	0.8277 3992	0.8085 1455	19
20	0.8611 8985	0.8400 9624	0.8195 4447	0.7995 1995	20
21	0.8547 7901	0.8328 0917	0.8114 3017	0.7906 2542	21
22	0.8484 1589	0.8255 8530	0.8033 9621	0.7818 2983	22
23	0.8421 0014	0.8184 2409	0.7954 4179	0.7731 3210	23
24	0.8358 3140	0.8113 2499	0.7875 6613	0.7645 3112	24
25	0.8296 0933	0.8042 8748	0.7797 6844	0.7560 2583	25
26	0.8234 3358	0.7973 1101	0.7720 4796	0.7476 1516	26
27	0.8173 0380	0.7903 9505	0.7644 0392	0.7392 9806	27
28	0.8112 1966	0.7835 3908	0.7568 3557	0.7310 7348	28
29	0.8051 8080	0.7767 4258	0.7493 4215	0.7229 4040	29
30	0.7991 8690	0.7700 0504	0.7419 2292	0.7148 9780	30
31	0.7932 3762	0.7633 2594	0.7345 7715	0.7069 4467	31
32	0.7873 3262	0.7567 0477	0.7273 0411	0.6990 8002	32
33	0.7814 7158	0.7501 4104	0.7201 0307	0.6913 0287	33
34	0.7756 5418	0.7436 3424	0.7129 7334	0.6836 1223	34
35	0.7698 8008	0.7371 8388	0.7059 1420	0.6760 0715	35
36	0.7641 4896	0.7307 8947	0.6989 2495	0.6684 8667	36
37	0.7584 6051	0.7244 5053	0.6920 0490	0.6610 4986	37
38	0.7528 1440	0.7181 6657	0.6851 5337	0.6536 9578	38
39	0.7472 1032	0.7119 3712	0.6783 6967	0.6464 2352	39
40	0.7416 4796	0.7057 6171	0.6716 5314	0.6392 3216	40
41	0.7361 2701	0.6996 3986	0.6650 0311	0.6321 2080	41
42	0.7306 4716	0.6935 7111	0.6584 1892	0.6250 8855	42
43	0.7252 0809	0.6875 5500	0.6518 9992	0.6181 3454	43
44	0.7198 0952	0.6815 9108	0.6454 4546	0.6112 5789	44
45	0.7144 5114	0.6756 7889	0.6390 5492	0.6044 5774	45
46	0.7091 3264	0.6698 1798	0.6327 2764	0.5977 3324	46
47	0.7038 5374	0.6640 0792	0.6264 6301	0.5910 8355	47
48	0.6986 1414	0.6582 4824	0.6202 6041	0.5845 0784	48
49	0.6934 1353	0.6525 3853	0.6141 1921	0.5780 0528	49
50	0.6882 5165	0 6468 7835	0.6080 3882	0.5715 7506	50

VI. PRESENT VALUE OF 1

$$v^n = (1 + i)^{-n}$$

n	$\frac{3}{4}\%$	$\frac{7}{8}\%$	1%	$1\frac{1}{8}\%$	n
51	0.6831 2819	0.6412 6726	0.6020 1864	0.5652 1637	51
52	0.6780 4286	0.6357 0484	0.5960 5806	0.5589 2843	52
53	0.6729 9540	0.6301 9067	0.5901 5649	0.5527 1044	53
54	0.6679 8551	0.6247 2433	0.5843 1336	0.5465 6162	54
55	0.6630 1291	0.6193 0541	0.5785 2808	0.5404 8120	55
56	0.6580 7733	0.6139 3349	0.5728 0008	0.5344 6843	56
57	0.6531 7849	0.6086 0817	0.5671 2879	0.5285 2256	57
58	0.6483 1612	0.6033 2904	0.5615 1365	0.5226 4282	58
59	0.6434 8995	0.5980 9571	0.5559 5411	0.5168 2850	59
60	0.6386 9970	0.5929 0776	0.5504 4962	0.5110 7887	60
61	0.6339 4511	0.5877 6482	0.5449 9962	0.5053 9319	61
62	0.6292 2592	0.5826 6649	0.5396 0358	0.4997 7077	62
63	0.6245 4185	0.5776 1238	0.5342 6097	0.4942 1090	63
64	0.6198 9266	0.5726 0211	0.5289 7126	0.4887 1288	64
65	0.6152 7807	0.5676 3530	0.5237 3392	0.4832 7602	65
66	0.6106 9784	0.5627 1158	0.5185 4844	0.4778 9965	66
67	0.6061 5170	0.5578 3056	0.5134 1429	0.4725 8309	67
68	0.6016 3940	0.5529 9188	0.5083 3099	0.4673 2568	68
69	0.5971 6070	0.5481 9517	0.5032 9801	0.4621 2675	69
70	0.5927 1533	0.5434 4007	0.4983 1486	0.4569 8566	70
71	0.5883 0306	0.5387 2622	0.4933 8105	0.4519 0177	71
72	0.5839 2363	0.5340 5325	0.4884 9609	0.4468 7443	72
73	0.5795 7681	0.5294 2082	0.4836 5949	0.4419 0302	73
74	0.5752 6234	0.5248 2857	0.4788 7078	0.4369 8692	74
75	0.5709 7999	0.5202 7615	0.4741 2949	0.4321 2551	75
76	0.5667 2952	0.5157 6322	0.4694 3514	0.4273 1818	76
77	0.5625 1069	0.5112 8944	0.4647 8726	0.4225 6433	77
78	0.5583 2326	0.5068 5447	0.4601 8541	0.4178 6337	78
79	0.5541 6701	0.5024 5796	0.4556 2912	0.4132 1470	79
80	0.5500 4170	0.4980 9959	0.4511 1794	0.4086 1775	80
81	0.5459 4710	0.4937 7902	0.4466 5142	0.4040 7194	81
82	0.5418 8297	0.4894 9593	0.4422 2913	0.3995 7670	82
83	0.5378 4911	0.4852 4999	0.4378 5063	0.3951 3148	83
84	0.5338 4527	0.4810 4089	0.4335 1547	0.3907 3570	84
85	0.5298 7123	0.4768 6829	0.4292 2324	0.3863 8882	85
86	0.5259 2678	0.4727 3188	0.4249 7350	0.3820 9031	86
87	0.5220 1169	0.4686 3136	0.4207 6585	0.3778 3961	87
88	0.5181 2575	0.4645 6640	0.4165 9985	0.3736 3621	88
89	0.5142 6873	0.4605 3671	0.4124 7510	0.3694 7956	89
90	0.5104 4043	0.4565 4197	0.4083 9119	0.3653 6916	90
91	0.5066 4063	0.4525 8187	0.4043 4771	0.3613 0448	91
92	0.5028 6911	0.4486 5613	0.4003 4427	0.3572 8503	92
93	0.4991 2567	0.4447 6444	0.3963 8046	0.3533 1029	93
94	0.4954 1009	0.4409 0651	0.3924 5590	0.3493 7976	94
95	0.4917 2217	0.4370 8204	0.3885 7020	0.3454 9297	95
96	0.4880 6171	0.4332 9075	0.3847 2297	0.3416 4941	96
97	0.4844 2850	0.4295 3234	0.3809 1383	0.3378 4861	97
98	0.4808 2233	0.4258 0654	0.3771 4241	0.3340 9010	98
99	0.4772 4301	0.4221 1305	0.3734 0832	0.3303 7340	99
100	0.4736 9033	0.4184 5159	0.3697 1121	0.3266 9805	100

VI. PRESENT VALUE OF 1

$$v^n = (1 + i)^{-n}$$

n	$1\frac{1}{4}\%$	$1\frac{3}{8}\%$	$1\frac{1}{2}\%$	$1\frac{5}{8}\%$	n
1	0.9876 5432	0.9864 3650	0.9852 2167	0.9840 0984	1
2	0.9754 6106	0.9730 5696	0.9706 6175	0.9682 7537	2
3	0.9634 1833	0.9598 5890	0.9563 1699	0.9527 9249	3
4	0.9515 2428	0.9468 3986	0.9421 8423	0.9375 5718	4
5	0.9397 7706	0.9339 9739	0.9282 6033	0.9225 6549	5
6	0.9281 7488	0.9213 2912	0.9145 4219	0.9078 1352	6
7	0.9167 1593	0.9088 3267	0.9010 2679	0.8932 9744	7
8	0.9053 9845	0.8965 0571	0.8877 1112	0.8790 1347	8
9	0.8942 2069	0.8843 4596	0.8745 9224	0 8649 5791	9
10	0.8831 8093	0.8723 5113	0.8616 6723	0.8511 2709	10
11	0.8722 7746	0.8605 1899	0.8489 3323	0.8375 1743	11
12	0.8615 0860	0.8488 4734	0.8363 8742	0.8241 2539	12
13	0.8508 7269	0.8373 3400	0.8240 2702	0.8109 4750	13
14	0.8403 6809	0.8259 7682	0.8118 4928	0.7979 8032	14
15	0.8299 9318	0.8147 7368	0.7998 5150	0.7852 2048	15
16	0.8197 4635	0.8037 2250	0.7880 3104	0.7726 6468	16
17	0.8096 2602	0.7928 2120	0.7763 8526	0.7603 0965	17
18	0.7996 3064	0.7820 6777	0.7649 1159	0.7481 5218	18
19	0.7897 5866	0.7714 6020	0.7536 0747	0.7361 8911	19
20	0.7800 0855	0.7609 9649	0.7424 7042	0.7244 1732	20
21	0.7703 7881	0.7506 7472	0.7314 9795	0.7128 3378	21
22	0.7608 6796	0.7404 9294	0.7206 8763	0.7014 3545	22
23	0.7514 7453	0.7304 4926	0.7100 3708	0.6902 1938	23
24	0.7421 9707	0.7205 4181	0.6995 4392	0.6791 8267	24
25	0.7330 3414	0.7107 6874	0.6892 0583	0.6683 2243	25
26	0.7239 8434	0.7011 2823	0.6790 2052	0.6576 3584	26
27	0.7150 4626	0.6916 1847	0.6689 8574	0.6471 2014	27
28	0.7062 1853	0.6822 3771	0.6590 9925	0.6367 7259	28
29	0.6974 9978	0.6729 8417	0.6493 5887	0.6265 9049	29
30	0.6888 8867	0.6638 5615	0.6397 6243	0.6165 7121	30
31	0.6803 8387	0.6548 5194	0.6303 0781	0.6067 1214	31
32	0.6719 8407	0.6459 6985	0.6209 9292	0.5970 1071	32
33	0.6636 8797	0.6372 0824	0.6118 1568	0.5874 6442	33
34	0.6554 9429	0.6285 6546	0.6027 7407	0.5780 7077	34
35	0.6474 0177	0.6200 3991	0.5938 6608	0.5688 2732	35
36	0.6394 0916	0.6116 3000	0.5850 8974	0.5597 3168	36
37	0.6315 1522	0.6033 3416	0.5764 4309	0.5507 8148	37
38	0.6237 1873	0.5951 5083	0.5679 2423	0.5419 7440	38
39	0.6160 1850	0.5870 7850	0.5595 3126	0.5333 0814	39
40	0.6084 1334	0.5791 1566	0.5512 6232	0.5247 8046	40
41	0.6009 0206	0.5712 6083	0.5431 1559	0.5163 8914	41
42	0.5934 8352	0.5635 1253	0.5350 8925	0.5081 3199	42
43	0.5861 5656	0.5558 6933	0.5271 8153	0.5000 0688	43
44	0.5789 2006	0.5483 2979	0.5193 9067	0.4920 1169	44
45	0.5717 7290	0.5408 9252	0.5117 1494	0.4841 4434	45
46	0.5647 1397	0.5335 5612	0.5041 5265	0.4764 0280	46
47	0.5577 4219	0.5263 1923	0.4967 0212	0.4687 8504	47
48	0.5508 5649	0.5191 8050	0.4893 6170	0.4612 8909	48
49	0.5440 5579	0.5121 3860	0.4821 2975	0.4539 1301	49
50	0.5373 3905	0.5051 9220	0.4750 0468	0.4466 5487	50

VI. PRESENT VALUE OF 1

$$v^n = (1 + i)^{-n}$$

n	$1\frac{1}{4}\%$	$1\frac{3}{8}\%$	$1\frac{1}{2}\%$	$1\frac{5}{8}\%$	n
51	0.5307 0524	0.4983 4003	0.4679 8491	0.4395 1278	51
52	0.5241 5332	0.4915 8079	0.4610 6887	0.4324 8490	52
53	0.5176 8229	0.4849 1323	0.4542 5505	0.4255 6940	53
54	0.5112 9115	0.4783 3611	0.4475 4192	0.4187 6448	54
55	0.5049 7892	0.4718 4820	0.4409 2800	0.4120 6837	55
56	0.4987 4461	0.4654 4829	0.4344 1182	0.4054 7933	56
57	0.4925 8727	0.4591 3518	0.4279 9194	0.3989 9565	57
58	0.4865 0594	0.4529 0770	0.4216 6694	0.3926 1564	58
59	0.4804 9970	0.4467 6468	0.4154 3541	0.3863 3766	59
60	0.4745 6760	0.4407 0499	0.4092 9597	0.3801 6006	60
61	0.4687 0874	0.4347 2749	0.4032 4726	0.3740 8124	61
62	0.4629 2222	0.4288 3106	0.3972 8794	0.3680 9962	62
63	0.4572 0713	0.4230 1461	0.3914 1669	0.3622 1365	63
64	0.4515 6259	0.4172 7705	0.3856 3221	0.3564 2179	64
65	0.4459 8775	0.4116 1731	0.3799 3321	0.3507 2255	65
66	0.4404 8173	0.4060 3434	0.3743 1843	0.3451 1444	66
67	0.4350 4368	0.4005 2709	0.3687 8663	0.3395 9601	67
68	0.4296 7277	0.3950 9454	0.3633 3658	0.3341 6581	68
69	0.4243 6817	0.3897 3568	0.3579 6708	0.3288 2245	69
70	0.4191 2905	0.3844 4949	0.3526 7692	0.3235 6452	70
71	0.4139 5462	0.3792 3501	0.3474 6495	0.3183 9067	71
72	0.4088 4407	0.3740 9126	0.3423 3000	0.3132 9956	72
73	0.4037 9661	0.3690 1727	0.3372 7093	0.3082 8985	73
74	0.3988 1147	0.3640 1210	0.3322 8663	0.3033 6024	74
75	0.3938 8787	0.3590 7483	0.3273 7599	0.2985 0946	75
76	0.3890 2506	0.3542 0451	0.3225 3793	0.2937 3625	76
77	0.3842 2228	0.3494 0026	0.3177 7136	0.2890 3936	77
78	0.3794 7879	0.3446 6117	0.3130 7523	0.2844 1757	78
79	0.3747 9387	0.3399 8636	0.3084 4850	0.2798 6969	79
80	0.3701 6679	0.3353 7495	0.3038 9015	0.2753 9453	80
81	0.3655 9683	0.3308 2609	0.2993 9916	0.2709 9093	81
82	0.3610 8329	0.3263 3893	0.2949 7454	0.2666 5774	82
83	0.3566 2547	0.3219 1263	0.2906 1531	0.2623 9384	83
84	0.3522 2268	0.3175 4637	0.2863 2050	0.2581 9812	84
85	0.3478 7426	0.3132 3933	0.2820 8917	0.2540 6949	85
86	0.3435 7951	0.3089 9071	0.2779 2036	0.2500 0688	86
87	0.3393 3779	0.3047 9971	0.2738 1316	0.2460 0923	87
88	0.3351 4843	0.3006 6556	0.2697 6666	0.2420 7550	88
89	0.3310 1080	0.2965 8748	0.2657 7997	0.2382 0468	89
90	0.3269 2425	0.2925 6472	0.2618 5218	0.2343 9575	90
91	0.3228 8814	0.2885 9652	0.2579 8245	0.2306 4772	91
92	0.3189 0187	0.2846 8214	0.2541 6990	0.2269 5963	92
93	0.3149 6481	0.2808 2085	0.2504 1369	0.2233 3051	93
94	0.3110 7636	0.2770 1194	0.2467 1300	0.2197 5942	94
95	0.3072 3591	0.2732 5468	0.2430 6699	0.2162 4543	95
96	0.3034 4287	0.2695 4839	0.2394 7487	0.2127 8763	96
97	0.2996 9666	0.2658 9237	0.2359 3583	0.2093 8512	97
98	0.2959 9670	0.2622 8594	0.2324 4909	0.2060 3702	98
99	0.2923 4242	0.2587 2843	0.2290 1389	0.2027 4245	99
100	0.2887 3326	0.2552 1916	0.2256 2944	0.1995 0057	100

VI. PRESENT VALUE OF 1

$$v^n = (1 + i)^{-n}$$

n	$1\frac{3}{4}\%$	2%	$2\frac{1}{4}\%$	$2\frac{1}{2}\%$	n
1	0.9828 0098	0.9803 9216	0.9779 9511	0.9756 0976	1
2	0.9658 9777	0.9611 6878	0.9564 7444	0.9518 1440	2
3	0.9492 8528	0.9423 2233	0.9354 2732	0.9285 9941	3
4	0.9329 5851	0.9238 4543	0.9148 4335	0.9059 5064	4
5	0.9169 1254	0.9057 3081	0.8947 1232	0.8838 5429	5
6	0.9011 4254	0.8879 7138	0.8750 2427	0.8622 9687	6
7	0.8856 4378	0.8705 6018	0.8557 6946	0.8412 6524	7
8	0.8704 1157	0.8534 9037	0.8369 3835	0.8207 4657	8
9	0.8554 4135	0.8367 5527	0.8185 2161	0.8007 2836	9
10	0.8407 2860	0.8203 4830	0.8005 1013	0.7811 9840	10
11	0.8262 6889	0.8042 6304	0.7828 9499	0.7621 4478	11
12	0.8120 5788	0.7884 9318	0.7656 6748	0.7435 5589	12
13	0.7980 9128	0.7730 3253	0.7488 1905	0.7254 2038	13
14	0.7843 6490	0.7578 7502	0.7323 4137	0.7077 2720	14
15	0.7708 7459	0.7430 1473	0.7162 2628	0.6904 6556	15
16	0.7576 1631	0.7284 4581	0.7004 6580	0.6736 2493	16
17	0.7445 8605	0.7141 6256	0.6850 5212	0.6571 9506	17
18	0.7317 7990	0.7001 5937	0.6699 7763	0.6411 6591	18
19	0.7191 9401	0.6864 3076	0.6552 3484	0.6255 2772	19
20	0.7068 2458	0.6729 7133	0.6408 1647	0.6102 7094	20
21	0.6946 6789	0.6597 7582	0.6267 1538	0.5953 8629	21
22	0.6827 2028	0.6468 3904	0.6129 2457	0.5808 6467	22
23	0.6709 7817	0.6341 5592	0.5994 3724	0.5666 9724	23
24	0.6594 3800	0.6217 2149	0.5862 4668	0.5528 7535	24
25	0.6480 9632	0.6095 3087	0.5733 4639	0.5393 9059	25
26	0.6369 4970	0.5975 7928	0.5607 2997	0.5262 3472	26
27	0.6259 9479	0.5858 6204	0.5483 9117	0.5133 9973	27
28	0.6152 2829	0.5743 7455	0.5363 2388	0.5008 7778	28
29	0.6046 4697	0.5631 1231	0.5245 2213	0.4886 6125	29
30	0.5942 4764	0.5520 7089	0.5129 8008	0.4767 4269	30
31	0.5840 2716	0.5412 4597	0.5016 9201	0.4651 1481	31
32	0.5739 8247	0.5306 3330	0.4906 5233	0.4537 7055	32
33	0.5641 1053	0.5202 2873	0.4798 5558	0.4427 0298	33
34	0.5544 0839	0.5100 2817	0.4692 9641	0.4319 0534	34
35	0.5448 7311	0.5000 2761	0.4589 6960	0.4213 7107	35
36	0.5355 0183	0.4902 2315	0.4488 7002	0.4110 9372	36
37	0.5262 9172	0.4806 1093	0.4389 9268	0.4010 6705	37
38	0.5172 4002	0.4711 8719	0.4293 3270	0.3912 8492	38
39	0.5083 4400	0.4619 4822	0.4198 8528	0.3817 4139	39
40	0.4996 0098	0.4528 9042	0.4106 4575	0.3724 3062	40
41	0.4910 0834	0.4440 1021	0.4016 0954	0.3633 4695	41
42	0.4825 6348	0.4353 0413	0.3927 7216	0.3544 8483	42
43	0.4742 6386	0.4267 6875	0.3841 2925	0.3458 3886	43
44	0.4661 0699	0.4184 0074	0.3756 7653	0.3374 0376	44
45	0.4580 9040	0.4101 9680	0.3674 0981	0.3291 7440	45
46	0.4502 1170	0.4021 5373	0.3593 2500	0.3211 4576	46
47	0.4424 6850	0.3942 6836	0.3514 1809	0.3133 1294	47
48	0.4348 5848	0.3865 3761	0.3436 8518	0.3056 7116	48
49	0.4273 7934	0.3789 5844	0.3361 2242	0.2982 1576	49
50	0.4200 2883	0.3715 2788	0.3287 2608	0.2909 4221	50

VI. PRESENT VALUE OF 1

$$v^n = (1 + i)^{-n}$$

n	1¾%	2%	2¼%	2½%	n
51	0.4128 0475	0.3642 4302	0.3214 9250	0.2838 4606	51
52	0.4057 0492	0.3571 0100	0.3144 1810	0.2769 2298	52
53	0.3987 2719	0.3500 9902	0.3074 9936	0.2701 6876	53
54	0.3918 6947	0.3432 3433	0.3007 3287	0.2635 7928	54
55	0.3851 2970	0.3365 0425	0.2941 1528	0.2571 5052	55
56	0.3785 0585	0.3299 0613	0.2876 4330	0.2508 7855	56
57	0.3719 9592	0.3234 3738	0.2813 1374	0.2447 5956	57
58	0.3655 9796	0.3170 9547	0.2751 2347	0.2387 8982	58
59	0.3593 1003	0.3108 7791	0.2690 6940	0.2329 6568	59
60	0.3531 3025	0.3047 8227	0.2631 4856	0.2272 8359	60
61	0.3470 5676	0.2988 0614	0.2573 5801	0.2217 4009	61
62	0.3410 8772	0.2929 4720	0.2516 9487	0.2163 3179	62
63	0.3352 2135	0.2872 0314	0.2461 5635	0.2110 5541	63
64	0.3294 5587	0.2815 7170	0.2407 3971	0.2059 0771	64
65	0.3237 8956	0.2760 5069	0.2354 4226	0.2008 8557	65
66	0.3182 2069	0.2706 3793	0.2302 6138	0.1959 8593	66
67	0.3127 4761	0.2653 3130	0.2251 9450	0.1912 0578	67
68	0.3073 6866	0.2601 2873	0.2202 3912	0.1865 4223	68
69	0.3020 8222	0.2550 2817	0.2153 9278	0.1819 9241	69
70	0.2968 8670	0.2500 2761	0.2106 5309	0.1775 5358	70
71	0.2917 8054	0.2451 2511	0.2060 1769	0.1732 2300	71
72	0.2867 6221	0.2403 1874	0.2014 8429	0.1689 9805	72
73	0.2818 3018	0.2356 0661	0.1970 5065	0.1648 7615	73
74	0.2769 8298	0.2309 8687	0.1927 1458	0.1608 5478	74
75	0.2722 1914	0.2264 5771	0.1884 7391	0.1569 3149	75
76	0.2675 3724	0.2220 1737	0.1843 2657	0.1531 0389	76
77	0.2629 3586	0.2176 6408	0.1802 7048	0.1493 6965	77
78	0.2584 1362	0.2133 9616	0.1763 0365	0.1457 2649	78
79	0.2539 6916	0.2092 1192	0.1724 2411	0.1421 7218	79
80	0.2496 0114	0.2051 0973	0.1686 2993	0.1387 0457	80
81	0.2453 0825	0.2010 8797	0.1649 1925	0.1353 2153	81
82	0.2410 8919	0.1971 4507	0.1612 9022	0.1320 2101	82
83	0.2369 4269	0.1932 7948	0.1577 4105	0.1288 0098	83
84	0.2328 6751	0.1894 8968	0.1542 6997	0.1256 5949	84
85	0.2288 6242	0.1857 7420	0.1508 7528	0.1225 9463	85
86	0.2249 2621	0.1821 3157	0.1475 5528	0.1196 0452	86
87	0.2210 5770	0.1785 6036	0.1443 0835	0.1166 8733	87
88	0.2172 5572	0.1750 5918	0.1411 3286	0.1138 4130	88
89	0.2135 1914	0.1716 2665	0.1380 2724	0.1110 6468	89
90	0.2098 4682	0.1682 6142	0.1349 8997	0.1083 5579	90
91	0.2062 3766	0.1649 6217	0.1320 1953	0.1057 1296	91
92	0.2026 9057	0.1617 2762	0.1291 1445	0.1031 3460	92
93	0.1992 0450	0.1585 5649	0.1262 7331	0.1006 1912	93
94	0.1957 7837	0.1554 4754	0.1234 9468	0.0981 6500	94
95	0.1924 1118	0.1523 9955	0.1207 7719	0.0957 7073	95
96	0.1891 0190	0.1494 1132	0.1181 1950	0.0934 3486	96
97	0.1858 4953	0.1464 8169	0.1155 2029	0.0911 5596	97
98	0.1826 5310	0.1436 0950	0.1129 7828	0.0889 3264	98
99	0.1795 1165	0.1407 9363	0.1104 9221	0.0867 6355	99
100	0.1764 2422	0.1380 3297	0.1080 6084	0.0846 4737	100

VI. PRESENT VALUE OF 1

$$v^n = (1 + i)^{-n}$$

n	$2\frac{3}{4}\%$	3%	$3\frac{1}{4}\%$	$3\frac{1}{2}\%$	n
1	0.9732 3601	0.9708 7379	0.9685 2300	0.9661 8357	1
2	0.9471 8833	0.9425 9591	0.9380 3681	0.9335 1070	2
3	0.9218 3779	0.9151 4166	0.9085 1022	0.9019 4271	3
4	0.8971 6573	0.8884 8705	0.8799 1305	0.8714 4223	4
5	0.8731 5400	0.8626 0878	0.8522 1603	0.8419 7317	5
6	0.8497 8491	0.8374 8426	0.8253 9083	0.8135 0064	6
7	0.8270 4128	0.8130 9151	0.7994 1000	0.7859 9096	7
8	0.8049 0635	0.7894 0923	0.7742 4698	0.7594 1156	8
9	0.7833 6385	0.7664 1673	0.7498 7601	0.7337 3097	9
10	0.7623 9791	0.7440 9391	0.7262 7216	0.7089 1881	10
11	0.7419 9310	0.7224 2128	0.7034 1129	0.6849 4571	11
12	0.7221 3440	0.7013 7988	0.6812 7002	0.6617 8330	12
13	0.7028 0720	0.6809 5134	0.6598 2568	0.6394 0415	13
14	0.6839 9728	0.6611 1781	0.6390 5635	0.6177 8179	14
15	0.6656 9078	0.6418 6195	0.6189 4078	0.5968 9062	15
16	0.6478 7424	0.6231 6694	0.5994 5838	0.5767 0591	16
17	0.6305 3454	0.6050 1645	0.5805 8923	0.5572 0378	17
18	0.6136 5892	0.5873 9461	0.5623 1402	0.5383 6114	18
19	0.5972 3496	0.5702 8603	0.5446 1407	0.5201 5569	19
20	0.5812 5057	0.5536 7575	0.5274 7125	0.5025 6588	20
21	0.5656 9398	0.5375 4928	0.5108 6804	0.4855 7090	21
22	0.5505 5375	0.5218 9250	0.4947 8745	0.4691 5063	22
23	0.5358 1874	0.5066 9175	0.4792 1302	0.4532 8563	23
24	0.5214 7809	0.4919 3374	0.4641 2884	0.4379 5713	24
25	0.5075 2126	0.4776 0557	0.4495 1945	0.4231 4699	25
26	0.4939 3796	0.4636 9473	0.4353 6993	0.4088 3767	26
27	0.4807 1821	0.4501 8906	0.4216 6579	0.3950 1224	27
28	0.4678 5227	0.4370 7675	0.4083 9302	0.3816 5434	28
29	0.4553 3068	0.4243 4636	0.3955 3803	0.3687 4815	29
30	0.4431 4421	0.4119 8676	0.3830 8768	0.3562 7841	30
31	0.4312 8391	0.3999 8715	0.3710 2923	0.3442 3035	31
32	0.4197 4103	0.3883 3703	0.3593 5035	0.3325 8971	32
33	0.4085 0708	0.3770 2625	0.3480 3908	0.3213 4271	33
34	0.3975 7380	0.3660 4490	0.3370 8385	0.3104 7605	34
35	0.3869 3314	0.3553 8340	0.3264 7346	0.2999 7686	35
36	0.3765 7727	0.3450 3243	0.3161 9706	0.2898 3272	36
37	0.3664 9856	0.3349 8294	0.3062 4413	0.2800 3161	37
38	0.3566 8959	0.3252 2615	0.2966 0448	0.2705 6194	38
39	0.3471 4316	0.3157 5355	0.2872 6826	0.2614 1250	39
40	0.3378 5222	0.3065 5684	0.2782 2592	0.2525 7247	40
41	0.3288 0995	0.2976 2800	0.2694 6820	0.2440 3137	41
42	0.3200 0968	0.2889 5922	0.2609 8615	0.2357 7910	42
43	0.3114 4495	0.2805 4294	0.2527 7109	0.2278 0590	43
44	0.3031 0944	0.2723 7178	0.2448 1462	0.2201 0231	44
45	0.2949 9702	0.2644 3862	0.2371 0859	0.2126 5924	45
46	0.2871 0172	0.2567 3653	0.2296 4512	0.2054 6787	46
47	0.2794 1773	0.2492 5876	0.2224 1658	0.1985 1968	47
48	0.2719 3940	0.2419 9880	0.2154 1558	0.1918 0645	48
49	0.2646 6122	0.2349 5029	0.2086 3494	0.1853 2024	49
50	0.2575 7783	0.2281 0708	0.2020 6774	0.1790 5337	50

VI. PRESENT VALUE OF 1

$$v^n = (1 + i)^{-n}$$

n	$2\frac{3}{4}\%$	3%	$3\frac{1}{4}\%$	$3\frac{1}{2}\%$	n
51	0.2506 8402	0.2214 6318	0.1957 0725	0.1729 9843	51
52	0.2439 7471	0.2150 1280	0.1895 4698	0.1671 4824	52
53	0.2374 4497	0.2087 5029	0.1835 8061	0.1614 9589	53
54	0.2310 9000	0.2026 7019	0.1778 0204	0.1560 3467	54
55	0.2249 0511	0.1967 6717	0.1722 0537	0.1507 5814	55
56	0.2188 8575	0.1910 3609	0.1667 8486	0.1456 6004	56
57	0.2130 2749	0.1854 7193	0.1615 3497	0.1407 3433	57
58	0.2073 2603	0.1800 6984	0.1564 5034	0.1359 7520	58
59	0.2017 7716	0.1748 2508	0.1515 2575	0.1313 7701	59
60	0.1963 7679	0.1697 3309	0.1467 5617	0.1269 3431	60
61	0.1911 2097	0.1647 8941	0.1421 3673	0.1226 4184	61
62	0.1860 0581	0.1599 8972	0.1376 6269	0.1184 9453	62
63	0.1810 2755	0.1553 2982	0.1333 2948	0.1144 8747	63
64	0.1761 8253	0.1508 0565	0.1291 3267	0.1106 1591	64
65	0.1714 6718	0.1464 1325	0.1250 6796	0.1068 7528	65
66	0.1668 7804	0.1421 4879	0.1211 3120	0.1032 6114	66
67	0.1624 1172	0.1380 0853	0.1173 1835	0.0997 6922	67
68	0.1580 6493	0.1339 8887	0.1136 2552	0.0963 9538	68
69	0.1538 3448	0.1300 8628	0.1100 4893	0.0931 3563	69
70	0.1497 1726	0:1262 9736	0.1065 8492	0.0899 8612	70
71	0.1457 1023	0.1226 1880	0.1032 2995	0.0869 4311	71
72	0.1418 1044	0.1190 4737	0.0999 8058	0.0840 0300	72
73	0.1380 1503	0.1155 7998	0.0968 3349	0.0811 6232	73
74	0.1343 2119	0.1122 1357	0.0937 8546	0.0784 1770	74
75	0.1307 2622	0.1089 4521	0.0908 3338	0.0757 6590	75
76	0.1272 2747	0.1057 7205	0.0879 7422	0.0732 0376	76
77	0.1238 2235	0.1026 9131	0.0852 0505	0.0707 2827	77
78	0.1205 0837	0.0997 0030	0.0825 2305	0.0683 2650	78
79	0.1172 8309	0.0967 9641	0.0799 2548	0.0660 2560	79
80	0.1141 4412	0.0939 7710	0.0774 0966	0.0637 9285	80
81	0.1110 8917	0.0912 3990	0.0749 7304	0.0616 3561	81
82	0.1081 1598	0.0885 8243	0.0726 1311	0.0595 5131	82
83	0.1052 2237	0.0860 0236	0.0703 2747	0.0575 3750	[83
84	0.1024 0620	0.0834 9743	0.0681 1377	0.0555 9178	84
85	0.0996 6540	0.0810 6547	0.0659 6976	0.0537 1187	85
86	0.0969 9795	0.0787 0434	0.0638 9323	0.0518 9553	86
87	0.0944 0190	0.0764 1198	0.0618 8206	0.0501 4060	87
88	0.0918 7533	0.0741 8639	0.0599 3420	0.0484 4503	88
89	0.0894 1638	0.0720 2562	0.0580 4765	0.0468 0679	89
90	0.0870 2324	0.0699 2779	0.0562 2048	0.0452 2395	90
91	0.0846 9415	0.0678 9105	0.0544 5083	0.0436 9464	91
92	0.0824 2740	0.0659 1364	0.0527 3688	0.0422 1704	92
93	0.0802 2131	0.0639 9383	0.0510 7688	0.0407 8941	93
94	0.0780 7427	0.0621 2993	0.0494 6914	0.0394 1006	94
95	0.0759 8469	0.0603 2032	0.0479 1200	0.0380 7735	95
96	0.0739 5104	0.0585 6342	0.0464 0387	0.0367 8971	96
97	0.0719 7181	0.0568 5769	0.0449 4322	0.0355 4562	97
98	0.0700 4556	0.0552 0164	0.0435 2854	0.0343 4359	98
99	0.0681 7086	0.0535 9383	0.0421 5839	0.0331 8221	99
100	0.0663 4634	0.0520 3284	0.0408 3137	0.0320 6011	100

$$v^n = (1 + i)^{-n}$$

n	4%	$4\frac{1}{2}\%$	5%	$5\frac{1}{2}\%$	n
1	0.9615 3846	0.9569 3780	0.9523 8095	0.9478 6730	1
2	0.9245 5621	0.9157 2995	0.9070 2948	0.8984 5242	2
3	0.8889 9636	0.8762 9660	0.8638 3760	0.8516 1366	3
4	0.8548 0419	0.8385 6134	0.8227 0247	0.8072 1674	4
5	0.8219 2711	0.8024 5105	0.7835 2617	0.7651 3435	5
6	0.7903 1453	0.7678 9574	0.7462 1540	0.7252 4583	6
7	0.7599 1781	0.7348 2846	0.7106 8133	0.6874 3681	7
8	0.7306 9021	0.7031 8513	0.6768 3936	0.6515 9887	8
9	0.7025 8674	0.6729 0443	0.6446 0892	0.6176 2926	9
10	0.6755 6417	0.6439 2768	0.6139 1325	0.5854 3058	10
11	0.6495 8093	0.6161 9874	0.5846 7929	0.5549 1050	11
12	0.6245 9705	0.5896 6386	0.5568 3742	0.5259 8152	12
13	0.6005 7409	0.5642 7164	0.5303 2135	0.4985 6068	13
14	0.5774 7508	0.5399 7286	0.5050 6795	0.4725 6937	14
15	0.5552 6450	0.5167 2044	0.4810 1710	0.4479 3305	15
16	0.5339 0818	0.4944 6932	0.4581 1152	0.4245 8109	16
17	0.5133 7325	0.4731 7639	0.4362 9669	0.4024 4653	17
18	0.4936 2812	0.4528 0037	0.4155 2065	0.3814 6590	18
19	0.4746 4242	0.4333 0179	0.3957 3396	0.3615 7906	19
20	0.4563 8695	0.4146 4286	0.3768 8948	0.3427 2896	20
21	0.4388 3360	0.3967 8743	0.3589 4236	0.3248 6158	21
22	0.4219 5539	0.3797 0089	0.3418 4987	0.3079 2567	22
23	0.4057 2633	0.3633 5013	0.3255 7131	0.2918 7267	23
24	0.3901 2147	0.3477 0347	0.3100 6791	0.2766 5656	24
25	0.3751 1680	0.3327 3060	0.2953 0277	0.2622 3370	25
26	0.3606 8923	0.3184 0248	0.2812 4073	0.2485 6275	26
27	0.3468 1657	0.3046 9137	0.2678 4832	0.2356 0450	27
28	0.3334 7747	0.2915 7069	0.2550 9364	0.2233 2181	28
29	0.3206 5141	0.2790 1502	0.2429 4632	0.2116 7944	29
30	0.3083 1867	0.2670 0002	0.2313 7745	0.2006 4402	30
31	0.2964 6026	0.2555 0241	0.2203 5947	0.1901 8390	31
32	0.2850 5794	0.2444 9991	0.2098 6617	0.1802 6910	32
33	0.2740 9417	0.2339 7121	0.1998 7254	0.1708 7119	33
34	0.2635 5209	0.2238 9589	0.1903 5480	0.1619 6321	34
35	0.2534 1547	0.2142 5444	0.1812 9029	0.1535 1963	35
36	0.2436 6872	0.2050 2817	0.1726 5741	0.1455 1624	36
37	0.2342 9685	0.1961 9921	0.1644 3563	0.1379 3008	37
38	0.2252 8543	0.1877 5044	0.1566 0536	0.1307 3941	38
39	0.2166 2061	0.1796 6549	0.1491 4797	0.1239 2362	39
40	0.2082 8904	0.1719 2870	0.1420 4568	0.1174 6314	40
41	0.2002 7793	0.1645 2507	0.1352 8160	0.1113 3947	41
42	0.1925 7493	0.1574 4026	0.1288 3962	0.1055 3504	42
43	0.1851 6820	0.1506 6054	0.1227 0440	0.1000 3322	43
44	0.1780 4635	0.1441 7276	0.1168 6133	0.0948 1822	44
45	0.1711 9841	0.1379 6437	0.1112 9651	0.0898 7509	45
46	0.1646 1386	0.1320 2332	0.1059 9668	0.0851 8965	46
47	0.1582 8256	0.1263 3810	0.1009 4921	0.0807 4849	47
48	0.1521 9476	0.1208 9771	0.0961 4211	0.0765 3885	48
49	0.1463 4112	0.1156 9158	0.0915 6391	0.0725 4867	49
50	0.1407 1262	0.1107 0965	0.0872 0373	0.0687 6652	50

VI. PRESENT VALUE OF 1

$$v^n = (1 + i)^{-n}$$

n	6%	$6\frac{1}{2}\%$	7%	8%	n
1	0.9433 9623	0.9389 6714	0.9345 7944	0.9259 2593	1
2	0.8899 9644	0.8816 5928	0.8734 3873	0.8573 3882	2
3	0.8396 1928	0.8278 4909	0.8162 9788	0.7938 3224	3
4	0.7920 9366	0.7773 2309	0.7628 9521	0.7350 2985	4
5	0.7472 5817	0.7298 8084	0.7129 8618	0.6805 8320	5
6	0.7049 6054	0.6853 3412	0.6663 4222	0.6301 6963	6
7	0.6650 5711	0.6435 0621	0.6227 4974	0.5834 9040	7
8	0.6274 1237	0.6042 3119	0.5820 0910	0.5402 6888	8
9	0.5918 9846	0.5673 5323	0.5439 3374	0.5002 4897	9
10	0.5583 9478	0.5327 2604	0.5083 4929	0.4631 9349	10
11	0.5267 8753	0.5002 1224	0.4750 9280	0.4288 8286	11
12	0.4969 6936	0.4696 8285	0.4440 1196	0.3971 1376	12
13	0.4688 3902	0.4410 1676	0.4149 6445	0.3676 9792	13
14	0.4423 0096	0.4141 0025	0.3878 1724	0.3404 6104	14
15	0.4172 6506	0.3888 2652	0.3624 4602	0.3152 4170	15
16	0.3936 4628	0.3650 9533	0.3387 3460	0.2918 9047	16
17	0.3713 6442	0.3428 1251	0.3165 7439	0.2702 6895	17
18	0.3503 4379	0.3218 8969	0.2958 6392	0.2502 4903	18
19	0.3305 1301	0.3022 4384	0.2765 0833	0.2317 1206	19
20	0.3118 0473	0.2837 9703	0.2584 1900	0.2145 4821	20
21	0.2941 5540	0.2664 7608	0.2415 1309	0.1986 5575	21
22	0.2775 0510	0.2502 1228	0.2257 1317	0.1839 4051	22
23	0.2617 9726	0.2349 4111	0.2109 4688	0.1703 1528	23
24	0.2469 7855	0.2206 0198	0.1971 4662	0.1576 9934	24
25	0.2329 9863	0.2071 3801	0.1842 4918	0.1460 1790	25
26	0.2198 1003	0.1944 9579	0.1721 9549	0.1352 0176	26
27	0.2073 6795	0.1826 2515	0.1609 3037	0.1251 8682	27
28	0.1956 3014	0.1714 7902	0.1504 0221	0.1159 1372	28
29	0.1845 5674	0.1610 1316	0.1405 6282	0.1073 2752	29
30	0.1741 1013	0.1511 8607	0.1313 6712	0.0993 7733	30
31	0.1642 5484	0.1419 5875	0.1227 7301	0.0920 1605	31
32	0.1549 5740	0.1332 9460	0.1147 4113	0.0852 0005	32
33	0.1461 8622	0.1251 5925	0.1072 3470	0.0788 8893	33
34	0.1379 1153	0.1175 2042	0.1002 1934	0.0730 4531	34
35	0.1301 0522	0.1103 4781	0.0936 6294	0.0676 3454	35
36	0.1227 4077	0.1036 1297	0.0875 3546	0.0626 2458	36
37	0.1157 9318	0.0972 8917	0.0818 0884	0.0579 8572	37
38	0.1092 3885	0.0913 5134	0.0764 5686	0.0536 9048	38
39	0.1030 5552	0.0857 7590	0.0714 5501	0.0497 1341	39
40	0.0972 2219	0.0805 4075	0.0667 8038	0.0460 3093	40
41	0.0917 1905	0.0756 2512	0.0624 1157	0.0426 2123	41
42	0.0865 2740	0.0710 0950	0.0583 2857	0.0394 6411	42
43	0.0816 2962	0.0666 7559	0.0545 1268	0.0365 4084	43
44	0.0770 0908	0.0626 0619	0.0509 4643	0.0338 3411	44
45	0.0726 5007	0.0587 8515	0.0476 1349	0.0313 2788	45
46	0.0685 3781	0.0551 9733	0.0444 9859	0.0290 0730	46
47	0.0646 5831	0.0518 2848	0.0415 8747	0.0268 5861	47
48	0.0609 9840	0.0486 6524	0.0388 6679	0.0248 6908	48
49	0.0575 4566	0.0456 9506	0.0363 2410	0.0230 2693	49
50	0.0542 8836	0.0429 0616	0.0339 4776	0.0213 2123	50

$$s_{\overline{n}|i} = \frac{(1+i)^n - 1}{i}$$

n	$\frac{1}{4}\%$	$\frac{7}{24}\%$	$\frac{1}{3}\%$	$\frac{3}{8}\%$	n
1	1.0000 0000	1.0000 0000	1.0000 0000	1.0000 0000	1
2	2.0025 0000	2.0029 1667	2.0033 3333	2.0037 5000	2
3	3.0075 0625	3.0087 5851	3.0100 1111	3.0112 6406	3
4	4.0150 2502	4.0175 3405	4.0200 4448	4.0225 5630	4
5	5.0250 6258	5.0292 5186	5.0334 4463	5.0376 4089	5
6	6.0376 2523	6.0439 2051	6.0502 2278	6.0565 3204	6
7	7.0527 1930	7.0615 4861	7.0703 9019	7.0792 4404	7
8	8.0703 5110	8.0821 4480	8.0939 5816	8.1057 9120	8
9	9.0905 2697	9.1057 1772	9.1209 3802	9.1361 8792	9
10	10.1132 5329	10.1322 7606	10.1513 4114	10.1704 4862	10
11	11.1385 3642	11.1618 2853	11.1851 7895	11.2085 8781	11
12	12.1663 8277	12.1943 8387	12.2224 6288	12.2506 2001	12
13	13.1967 9872	13.2299 5082	13.2632 0442	13.2965 5984	13
14	14.2297 9072	14.2685 3818	14.3074 1510	14.3464 2194	14
15	15.2653 6520	15.3101 5475	15.3551 0648	15.4002 2102	15
16	16.3035 2861	16.3548 0936	16.4062 9017	16.4579 7185	16
17	17.3442 8743	17.4025 1089	17.4609 7781	17.5196 8924	17
18	18.3876 4815	18.4532 6822	18.5191 8107	18.5853 8808	18
19	19.4336 1727	19.5070 9025	19.5809 1167	19.6550 8328	19
20	20.4822 0131	20.5639 8593	20.6461 8137	20.7287 8984	20
21	21.5334 0682	21.6239 6422	21.7150 0198	21.8065 2280	21
22	22.5872 4033	22.6870 3412	22.7873 8532	22.8882 9727	22
23	23.6437 0843	23.7532 0463	23.8633 4327	23.9741 2838	23
24	24.7028 1770	24.8224 8481	24.9428 8775	25.0640 3136	24
25	25.7645 7475	25.8948 8373	26.0260 3071	26.1580 2148	25
26	26.8289 8619	26.9704 1047	27.1127 8414	27.2561 1406	26
27	27.8960 5865	28.0490 7417	28.2031 6009	28.3583 2449	27
28	28.9657 9880	29.1308 8397	29.2971 7062	29.4646 6820	28
29	30.0382 1330	30.2158 4904	30.3948 2786	30.5751 6071	29
30	31.1133 0883	31.3039 7860	31.4961 4395	31.6898 1756	30
31	32.1910 9210	32.3952 8188	32.6011 3110	32.8086 5438	31
32	33.2715 6983	33.4897 6811	33.7098 0154	33.9316 8683	32
33	34.3547 4876	34.5874 4660	34.8221 6754	35.0589 3066	33
34	35.4406 3563	35.6883 2666	35.9382 4143	36.1904 0165	34
35	36.5292 3722	36.7924 1761	37.0580 3557	37.3261 1565	35
36	37.6205 6031	37.8997 2883	38.1815 6236	38.4660 8859	36
37	38.7146 1171	39.0102 6970	39.3088 3423	39.6103 3642	37
38	39.8113 9824	40.1240 4966	40.4398 6368	40.7588 7518	38
39	40.9109 2673	41.2410 7814	41.5746 6322	41.9117 2096	39
40	42.0132 0405	42.3613 6461	42.7132 4543	43.0688 8992	40
41	43.1182 3706	43.4849 1859	43.8556 2292	44.2303 9825	41
42	44.2260 3265	44.6117 4961	45.0018 0833	45.3962 6225	42
43	45.3365 9774	45.7418 6721	46.1518 1436	46.5664 9823	43
44	46.4499 3923	46.8752 8099	47.3056 5374	47.7411 2260	44
45	47.5660 6408	48.0120 0056	48.4633 3925	48.9201 5181	45
46	48.6849 7924	49.1520 3556	49.6248 8371	50.1036 0238	46
47	49.8066 9169	50.2953 9566	50.7902 9999	51.2914 9089	47
48	50.9312 0842	51.4420 9057	51.9596 0099	52.4838 3398	48
49	52.0585 3644	52.5921 3000	53.1327 9966	53.6806 4836	49
50	53.1886 8278	53.7455 2371	54.3099 0899	54.8819 5079	50

VII. AMOUNT OF ANNUITY OF 1 PER PERIOD

$$s_{\overline{n}|i} = \frac{(1 + i)^n - 1}{i}$$

n	$\frac{1}{4}\%$	$\frac{7}{24}\%$	$\frac{1}{3}\%$	$\frac{3}{8}\%$	n
51	54.3216 5449	54.9022 8149	55.4909 4202	56.0877 5810	51
52	55.4574 5862	56.0624 1314	56.6759 1183	57.2980 8720	52
53	56.5961 0227	57.2259 2851	57.8648 3154	58.5129 5502	53
54	57.7375 9252	58.3928 3747	59.0577 1431	59.7323 7860	54
55	58.8819 3650	59.5631 4991	60.2545 7336	60.9563 7502	55
56	60.0291 4135	60.7368 7577	61.4554 2194	62.1849 6143	56
57	61.1792 1420	61.9140 2499	62.6602 7334	63.4181 5504	57
58	62.3321 6223	63.0946 0756	63.8691 4092	64.6559 7312	58
59	63.4879 9264	64.2786 3350	65.0820 3806	65.8984 3302	59
60	64.6467 1262	65.4661 1285	66.2989 7818	67.1455 5214	60
61	65.8083 2940	66.6570 5568	67.5199 7478	68.3973 4796	61
62	66.9728 5023	67.8514 7209	68.7450 4136	69.6538 3802	62
63	68.1402 8235	69.0493 7222	69.9741 9150	70.9150 3991	63
64	69.3106 3306	70.2507 6622	71.2074 3880	72.1809 7131	64
65	70.4839 0964	71.4556 6429	72.4447 9693	73.4516 4995	65
66	71.6601 1942	72.6640 7664	73.6862 7959	74.7270 9364	66
67	72.8392 6971	73.8760 1353	74.9319 0052	76.0073 2024	67
68	74.0213 6789	75.0914 8524	76.1816 7352	77.2923 4769	68
69	75.2064 2131	76.3105 0207	77.4356 1243	78.5821 9399	69
70	76.3944 3736	77.5330 7437	78.6937 3114	79.8768 7722	70
71	77.5854 2345	78.7592 1250	79.9560 4358	81.1764 1551	71
72	78.7793 8701	79.9889 2687	81.2225 6372	82.4808 2707	72
73	79.9763 3548	81.2222 2791	82.4933 0560	83.7901 3017	73
74	81.1762 7632	82.4591 2607	83.7682 8329	85.1043 4316	74
75	82.3792 1701	83.6996 3186	85.0475 1090	86.4234 8444	75
76	83.5851 6505	84.9437 5578	86.3310 0260	87.7475 7251	76
77	84.7941 2797	86.1915 0840	87.6187 7261	89.0766 2591	77
78	86.0061 1329	87.4429 0030	88.9108 3519	90.4106 6326	78
79	87.2211 2857	88.6979 4210	90.2072 0464	91.7497 0324	79
80	88.4391 8139	89.9566 4443	91.5078 9532	93.0937 6463	80
81	89.6602 7934	91.2190 1797	92.8129 2164	94.4428 6625	81
82	90.8844 3004	92.4850 7344	94.1222 9804	95.7970 2700	82
83	92.1116 4112	93.7548 2157	95.4360 3904	97.1562 6585	83
84	93.3419 2022	95.0282 7314	96.7541 5917	98.5206 0184	84
85	94.5752 7502	96.3054 3893	98.0766 7303	99.8900 5410	85
86	95.8117 1321	97.5863 2980	99.4035 9527	101.2646 4180	86
87	97.0512 4249	98.8709 5659	100.7349 4059	102.6443 8421	87
88	98.2938 7060	100.1593 3022	102.0707 2373	104.0293 0065	88
89	99.5396 0527	101.4514 6160	103.4109 5947	105.4194 1053	89
90	100.7884 5429	102.7473 6169	104.7556 6267	106.8147 3332	90
91	102.0404 2542	104.0470 4150	106.1048 4821	108.2152 8857	91
92	103.2955 2649	105.3505 1203	107.4585 3104	109.6210 9590	92
93	104.5537 6530	106.6577 8436	108.8167 2614	111.0321 7501	93
94	105.8151 4972	107.9688 6957	110.1794 4856	112.4485 4567	94
95	107.0796 8759	109.2837 7877	111.5467 1339	113.8702 2771	95
96	108.3473 8681	110.6025 2312	112.9185 3577	115.2972 4107	96
97	109.6182 5528	111.9251 1382	114.2949 3089	116.7296 0572	97
98	110.8923 0091	113.2515 6206	115.6759 1399	118.1673 4174	98
99	112.1695 3167	114.5818 7912	117.0615 0037	119.6104 6927	99
100	113.4499 5550	115.9160 7627	118.4517 0537	121.0590 0853	100

VII. AMOUNT OF ANNUITY OF 1 PER PERIOD

$$s_{\overline{n}|i} = \frac{(1 + i)^n - 1}{i}$$

n	$\frac{1}{4}\%$	$\frac{7}{24}\%$	$\frac{1}{3}\%$	$\frac{3}{8}\%$	n
101	114.7335 8038	117.2541 6482	119.8465 4439	122.5129 7981	101
102	116.0204 1434	118.5961 5614	121.2460 3287	123.9724 0349	102
103	117.3104 6537	119.9420 6159	122.6501 8632	125.4373 0000	103
104	118.6037 4153	121.2918 9261	124.0590 2027	126.9076 8988	104
105	119.9002 5089	122.6456 6063	125.4725 5034	128.3835 9371	105
106	121.2000 0152	124.0033 7714	126.8907 9217	129.8650 3219	106
107	122.5030 0152	125.3650 5365	128.3137 6148	131.3520 2606	107
108	123.8092 5902	126.7307 0173	129.7414 7402	132.8445 9616	108
109	125.1187 8217	128.1003 3294	131.1739 4560	134.3427 6339	109
110	126.4315 7913	129.4739 5891	132.6111 9208	135.8465 4876	110
111	127.7476 5807	130.8515 9129	134.0532 2939	137.3559 7332	111
112	129.0670 2722	132.2332 4177	135.5000 7349	138.8710 5822	112
113	130.3896 9479	133.6189 2205	136.9517 4040	140.3918 2468	113
114	131.7156 6902	135.0086 4391	138.4082 4620	141.9182 9403	114
115	133.0449 5820	136.4024 1912	139.8696 0702	143.4504 8763	115
116	134.3775 7059	137.8002 5951	141.3358 3904	144.9884 2696	116
117	135.7135 1452	139.2021 7693	142.8069 5851	146.5321 3356	117
118	137.0527 9830	140.6081 8328	144.2829 8170	148.0816 2906	118
119	138.3954 3030	142.0182 9048	145.7639 2498	149.6369 3517	119
120	139.7414 1888	143.4325 1050	147.2498 0473	151.1980 7368	120
121	141.0907 7242	144.8508 5532	148.7406 3741	152.7650 6645	121
122	142.4434 9935	146.2733 3698	150.2364 3953	154.3379 3545	122
123	143.7996 0810	147.6999 6755	151.7372 2766	155.9167 0271	123
124	145.1591 0712	149.1307 5912	153.2430 1842	157.5013 9034	124
125	146.5220 0489	150.5657 2383	154.7538 2848	159.0920 2056	125
126	147.8883 0990	152.0048 7386	156.2696 7458	160.6886 1563	126
127	149.2580 3068	153.4482 2141	157.7905 7349	162.2911 9794	127
128	150.6311 7575	154.8957 7872	159.3165 4207	163.8997 8994	128
129	152.0077 5369	156.3475 5808	160.8475 9721	165.5144 1415	129
130	153.3877 7308	157.8035 7179	162.3837 5587	167.1350 9320	130
131	154.7712 4251	159.2638 3221	163.9250 3506	168.7618 4980	131
132	156.1581 7062	160.7283 5172	165.4714 5184	170.3947 0674	132
133	157.5485 6604	162.1971 4274	167.0230 2335	172.0336 8689	133
134	158.9424 3746	163.6702 1774	168.5797 6676	173.6788 1321	134
135	160.3397 9355	165.1475 8920	170.1416 9931	175.3301 0876	135
136	161.7406 4304	166.6292 6968	171.7088 3831	176.9875 9667	136
137	163.1449 9464	168.1152 7172	173.2812 0111	178.6513 0016	137
138	164.5528 5713	169.6056 0793	174.8588 0511	180.3212 4253	138
139	165.9642 3927	171.1002 9095	176.4416 6779	181.9974 4719	139
140	167.3791 4987	172.5993 3346	178.0298 0669	183.6799 3762	140
141	168.7975 9775	174.1027 4819	179.6232 3937	185.3687 3739	141
142	170.2195 9174	175.6105 4787	181.2219 8351	187.0638 7015	142
143	171.6451 4072	177.1227 4530	182.8260 5678	188.7653 5966	143
144	173.0742 5357	178.6393 5331	184.4354 7697	190.4732 2976	144
145	174.5069 3921	180.1603 8475	186.0502 6190	192.1875 0437	145
146	175.9432 0655	181.6858 5254	187.6704 2944	193.9082 0752	146
147	177.3830 6457	183.2157 6961	189.2959 9753	195.6353 6329	147
148	178.8265 2223	184.7501 4894	190.9269 8419	197.3689 9591	148
149	180.2735 8854	186.2890 0354	192.5634 0747	199.1091 2964	149
150	181.7242 7251	187.8323 4647	194.2052 8550	200.8557 8888	150

VII. AMOUNT OF ANNUITY OF 1 PER PERIOD

$$s_{\overline{n}|i} = \frac{(1 + i)^n - 1}{i}$$

n	$\frac{1}{4}\%$	$\frac{7}{24}\%$	$\frac{1}{3}\%$	$\frac{3}{8}\%$	n
151	183.1785 8319	189.3801 9081	195.8526 3645	202.6089 9809	151
152	184.6365 2965	190.9325 4970	197.5054 7857	204.3687 8183	152
153	186.0981 2097	192.4894 3631	199.1638 3017	206.1351 6476	153
154	187.5633 6627	194.0508 6383	200.8277 0960	207.9081 7163	154
155	189.0322 7469	195.6168 4551	202.4971 3530	209.6878 2727	155
156	190.5048 5538	197.1873 9465	204.1721 2575	211.4741 5662	156
157	191.9811 1752	198.7625 2455	205.8526 9950	213.2671 8471	157
158	193.4610 7031	200.3422 4858	207.5388 7517	215 0669 3665	158
159	194.9447 2298	201.9265 8014	209.2306 7142	216.8734 3767	159
160	196.4320 8479	203.5155 3266	210.9281 0700	218.6867 1306	160
161	197.9231 6500	205.1091 1963	212.6312 0068	220.5067 8823	161
162	199.4179 7292	206.7073 5456	214.3399 7135	222.3336 8869	162
163	200.9165 1785	208.3102 5102	216.0544 3792	224.1674 4002	163
164	202.4188 0914	209.9178 2258	217.7746 1938	226.0080 6792	164
165	203.9248 5617	211.5300 8290	219.5005 3478	227.8555 9818	165
166	205.4346 6831	213.1470 4564	221.2322 0323	229.7100 5667	166
167	206.9482 5498	214.7687 2452	222.9696 4390	231.5714 6938	167
168	208.4656 2562	216.3951 3330	224.7128 7605	233.4398 6239	168
169	209.9867 8968	218.0262 8577	226.4619 1897	235.3152 6188	169
170	211.5117 5665	219.6621 9577	228.2167 9203	237.1976 9411	170
171	213.0405 3605	221.3028 7718	229.9775 1467	239.0871 8546	171
172	214.5731 3739	222.9483 4390	231.7441 0639	240.9837 6241	172
173	216.1095 7023	224.5986 0991	233.5165 8674	242.8874 5151	173
174	217.6498 4415	226.2536 8919	235.2949 7537	244.7982 7946	174
175	219.1939 6876	227.9135 9578	237.0792 9195	246.7162 7301	175
176	220.7419 5369	229.5783 4377	238.8695 5626	248.6414 5903	176
177	222.2938 0857	231.2479 4727	240.6657 8811	250.5738 6450	177
178	223.8495 4309	232.9224 2045	242.4680 0741	252.5135 1649	178
179	225.4091 6695	234.6017 7751	244.2762 3410	254.4604 4218	179
180	226.9726 8987	236.2860 3269	246.0904 8821	256.4146 6884	180
181	228.5401 2159	237.9752 0029	247.9107 8984	258.3762 2385	181
182	230.1114 7190	239.6692 9462	249.7371 5914	260.3451 3469	182
183	231.6867 5058	241.3683 3007	251.5696 1634	262.3214 2894	183
184	233.2659 6745	243.0723 2103	253.4081 8172	264.3051 3430	184
185	234.8491 3237	244.7812 8196	255.2528 7566	266.2962 7855	185
186	236.4362 5520	246.4952 2737	257.1037 1858	268.2948 8960	186
187	238.0273 4584	248.2141 7178	258.9607 3098	270.3009 9543	187
188	239.6224 1420	249.9381 2978	260.8239 3341	272.3146 2417	188
189	241.2214 7024	251.6671 1600	262.6933 4652	274.3358 0401	189
190	242.8245 2392	253.4011 4508	264.5689 9101	276.3645 6327	190
191	244.4315 8523	255.1402 3176	266.4508 8765	278.4009 3038	191
192	246.0426 6419	256.8843 9077	268.3390 5727	280.4449 3387	192
193	247.6577 7085	258.6336 3691	270.2335 2080	282.4966 0237	193
194	249.2769 1528	260.3879 8501	272.1342 9920	284.5559 6463	194
195	250.9001 0756	262.1474 4997	274.0414 1353	286.6230 4950	195
196	252.5273 5783	263.9120 4670	275.9548 8491	288.6978 8594	196
197	254.1586 7623	265.6817 9017	277.8747 3453	290.7805 0301	197
198	255.7940 7292	267.4566 9539	279.8009 8364	292.8709 2990	198
199	257.4335 5810	269.2367 7742	281.7336 5359	294.9691 9588	199
200	259.0771 4200	271.0220 5135	283.6727 6577	297.0753 3037	200

VII. AMOUNT OF ANNUITY OF 1 PER PERIOD

$$s_{\overline{n}|i} = \frac{(1 + i)^n - 1}{i}$$

n	$\frac{1}{4}\%$	$\frac{7}{24}\%$	$\frac{1}{3}\%$	$\frac{3}{8}\%$	n
201	260.7248 3485	272.8125 3234	285.6183 4165	299.1893 6286	201
202	262.3766 4694	274.6082 3556	287.5704 0279	301.3113 2297	202
203	264.0325 8855	276.4091 7624	289.5289 7080	303.4412 4043	203
204	265.6926 7003	278.2153 6967	291.4940 6737	305.5791 4508	204
205	267.3569 0170	280.0268 3117	293.4657 1426	307.7250 6687	205
206	269.0252 9396	281.8435 7609	295.4439 3331	309.8790 3587	206
207	270.6978 5719	283.6656 1986	297.4287 4642	312.0410 8226	207
208	272.3746 0183	285.4929 7791	299.4201 7557	314.2112 3632	208
209	274.0555 3834	287.3256 6577	301.4182 4283	316.3895 2845	209
210	275.7406 7718	289.1636 9896	303.4229 7030	318.5759 8918	210
211	277.4300 2888	291.0070 9308	305.4343 8020	320.7706 4914	211
212	279.1236 0395	292.8558 6377	307.4524 9480	322.9735 3908	212
213	280.8214 1296	294.7100 2670	309.4773 3645	325.1846 8985	213
214	282.5234 6649	296.5695 9761	311.5089 2757	327.4041 3244	214
215	284.2297 7516	298.4345 9227	313.5472 9067	329.6318 9793	215
216	285.9403 4960	300.3050 2650	315.5924 4830	331.8680 1755	216
217	287.6552 0047	302.1809 1616	317.6444 2313	334.1125 2262	217
218	289.3743 3847	304.0622 7717	319.7032 3787	336.3654 4458	218
219	291.0977 7432	305.9491 2548	321.7689 1533	338.6268 1499	219
220	292.8255 1875	307.8414 7709	323.8414 7838	340.8966 6555	220
221	294.5575 8255	309.7393 4807	325.9209 4998	343.1750 2805	221
222	296.2939 7651	311.6427 5450	328.0073 5315	345.4619 3440	222
223	298.0347 1145	313.5517 1253	330.1007 1099	347.7574 1666	223
224	299.7797 9823	315.4662 3836	332.2010 4669	350.0615 0697	224
225	301.5292 4772	317.3863 4822	334.3083 8351	352.3742 3762	225
226	303.2830 7084	319.3120 5841	336.4227 4479	354.6956 4101	226
227	305.0412 7852	321.2433 8524	338.5441 5394	357.0257 4966	227
228	306.8038 8171	323.1803 4512	340.6726 3446	359.3645 9622	228
229	308.5708 9142	325.1229 5446	342.8082 0990	361.7122 1346	229
230	310.3423 1865	327.0712 2974	344.9509 0394	364.0686 3426	230
231	312.1181 7444	329.0251 8749	347.1007 4028	366.4338 9164	231
232	313.8984 6988	330.9848 4429	349.2577 4275	368.8080 1873	232
233	315.6832 1605	332.9502 1675	351.4219 3523	371.1910 4880	233
234	317.4724 2409	334.9213 2155	353.5933 4168	373.5830 1524	234
235	319.2661 0515	336.8981 7541	355.7719 8615	375.9839 5154	235
236	321.0642 7042	338.8807 9508	357.9578 9277	378.3938 9136	236
237	322.8669 3109	340.8691 9740	360.1510 8575	380.8128 6845	237
238	324.6740 9842	342.8633 9923	362.3515 8937	383.2409 1671	238
239	326.4857 8367	344.8634 1748	364.5594 2800	385.6780 7015	239
240	328.3019 9813	346.8692 6911	366.7746 2609	388.1243 6291	240
241	330.1227 5312	348.8809 7115	368.9972 0818	390.5798 2927	241
242	331.9480 6000	350.8985 4065	371.2271 9887	393.0445 0363	242
243	333.7779 3015	352.9219 9472	373.4646 2287	395.5184 2052	243
244	335.6123 7498	354.9513 5054	375.7095 0494	398.0016 1460	244
245	337.4514 0592	356.9866 2531	377.9618 6996	400.4941 2065	245
246	339.2950 3443	359.0278 3630	380.2217 4286	402.9959 7361	246
247	341.1432 7202	361.0750 0083	382.4891 4867	405.5072 0851	247
248	342.9961 3020	363.1281 3624	384.7641 1250	408.0278 6054	248
249	344.8536 2052	365.1872 5998	387.0466 5954	410.5579 6502	249
250	346.7157 5458	367.2523 8948	389.3368 1507	413.0975 5738	250

VII. AMOUNT OF ANNUITY OF 1 PER PERIOD

$$s_{\overline{n}|i} = \frac{(1 + i)^n - 1}{i}$$

n	$\frac{5}{12}\%$	$\frac{1}{2}\%$	$\frac{7}{12}\%$	$\frac{5}{8}\%$	n
1	1.0000 0000	1.0000 0000	1.0000 0000	1.0000 0000	1
2	2.0041 6667	2.0050 0000	2.0058 3333	2.0062 5000	2
3	3.0125 1736	3.0150 2500	3.0175 3403	3.0187 8906	3
4	4.0250 6952	4.0301 0013	4.0351 3631	4.0376 5649	4
5	5.0418 4064	5.0502 5063	5.0586 7460	5.0628 9185	5
6	6.0628 4831	6.0755 0188	6.0881 8354	6.0945 3492	6
7	7.0881 1018	7.1058 7939	7.1236 9794	7.1326 2576	7
8	8.1176 4397	8.1414 0879	8.1652 5285	8.1772 0468	8
9	9.1514 6749	9.1821 1583	9.2128 8349	9.2283 1220	9
10	10.1895 9860	10.2280 2641	10.2666 2531	10.2859 8916	10
11	11.2320 5526	11.2791 6654	11.3265 1396	11.3502 7659	11
12	12.2788 5549	12.3355 6237	12.3925 8529	12.4212 1582	12
13	13.3300 1739	13.3972 4018	13.4648 7537	13.4988 4842	13
14	14.3855 5913	14.4642 2639	14.5434 2048	14.5832 1622	14
15	15.4454 9896	15.5365 4752	15.6282 5710	15.6743 6132	15
16	16.5098 5520	16.6142 3026	16.7194 2193	16.7723 2608	16
17	17.5786 4627	17.6973 0141	17.8169 5189	17.8771 5312	17
18	18.6518 9063	18.7857 8791	18.9208 8411	18.9888 8532	18
19	19.7296 0684	19.8797 1685	20.0312 5593	20.1075 6586	19
20	20.8118 1353	20.9791 1544	21.1481 0493	21.2332 3814	20
21	21.8985 2942	22.0840 1101	22.2714 6887	22.3659 4588	21
22	22.9897 7330	23.1944 3107	23.4013 8577	23.5057 3304	22
23	24.0855 6402	24.3104 0322	24.5378 9386	24.6526 4387	23
24	25.1859 2053	25.4319 5524	25.6810 3157	25.8067 2290	24
25	26.2908 6187	26.5591 1502	26.8308 3759	26.9680 1492	25
26	27.4004 0713	27.6919 1059	27.9873 5081	28.1365 6501	26
27	28.5145 7549	28.8303 7015	29.1506 1035	29.3124 1854	27
28	29.6333 8622	29.9745 2200	30.3206 5558	30.4956 2116	28
29	30.7568 5866	31.1243 9461	31.4975 2607	31.6862 1879	29
30	31.8850 1224	32.2800 1658	32.6812 6164	32.8842 5766	30
31	33.0178 6646	33.4414 1666	33.8719 0233	34.0897 8427	31
32	34.1554 4090	34.6086 2375	35.0694 8843	35.3028 4542	32
33	35.2977 5524	35.7816 6686	36.2740 6045	36.5234 8820	33
34	36.4448 2922	36.9605 7520	37.4856 5913	37.7517 6000	34
35	37.5966 8268	38.1453 7807	38.7043 2548	38.9877 0850	35
36	38.7533 3552	39.3361 0496	39.9301 0071	40.2313 8168	36
37	39.9148 0775	40.5327 8549	41.1630 2630	41.4828 2782	37
38	41.0811 1945	41.7354 4942	42.4031 4395	42.7420 9549	38
39	42.2522 9078	42.9441 2666	43.6504 9562	44.0092 3359	39
40	43.4283 4199	44.1588 4730	44.9051 2352	45.2842 9130	40
41	44.6092 9342	45.3796 4153	46.1670 7007	46.5673 1812	41
42	45.7951 6547	46.6065 3974	47.4363 7798	47.8583 6386	42
43	46.9859 7866	47.8395 7244	48.7130 9018	49.1574 7863	43
44	48.1817 5357	49.0787 7030	49.9972 4988	50.4647 1287	44
45	49.3825 1088	50.3241 6415	51.2889 0050	51.7801 1733	45
46	50.5882 7134	51.5757 8497	52.5880 8575	53.1037 4306	46
47	51.7990 5581	52.8336 6390	53.8948 4959	54.4356 4146	47
48	53.0148 8521	54.0978 3222	55.2092 3621	55.7758 6421	48
49	54.2357 8056	55.3683 2138	56.5312 9009	57.1244 6337	49
50	55.4617 6298	56.6451 6299	57.8610 5595	58.4814 9126	50

$$s_{\overline{n}|i} = \frac{(1 + i)^n - 1}{i}$$

n	$\frac{5}{12}\%$	$\frac{1}{2}\%$	$\frac{7}{12}\%$	$\frac{5}{8}\%$	n
51	56.6928 5366	57.9283 8880	59.1985 7877	59.8470 0058	51
52	57.9290 7388	59.2180 3075	60.5439 0381	61.2210 4434	52
53	59.1704 4502	60.5141 2090	61.8970 7659	62.6036 7586	53
54	60.4169 8854	61.8166 9150	63.2581 4287	63.9949 4884	54
55	61.6687 2600	63.1257 7496	64.6271 4870	65.3949 1727	55
56	62.9256 7902	64.4414 0384	66.0041 4040	66.8036 3550	56
57	64.1878 6935	65.7636 1086	67.3891 6455	68.2211 5822	57
58	65.4553 1881	67.0924 2891	68.7822 6801	69.6475 4046	58
59	66.7280 4930	68.4278 9105	70.1834 9791	71.0828 3759	59
60	68.0060 8284	69.7700 3051	71.5929 0165	72.5271 0532	60
61	69.2894 4152	71.1188 8066	73.0105 2691	73.9803 9973	61
62	70.5781 4753	72.4744 7507	74.4364 2165	75.4427 7723	62
63	71.8722 2314	73.8368 4744	75.8706 3411	76.9142 9459	63
64	73.1716 9074	75.2060 3168	77.3132 1281	78.3950 0893	64
65	74.4765 7278	76.5820 6184	78.7642 0655	79.8849 7774	65
66	75.7868 9183	77.9649 7215	80.2236 6442	81.3842 5885	66
67	77.1026 7055	79.3547 9701	81.6916 3580	82.8929 1046	67
68	78.4239 3168	80.7515 7099	83.1681 7034	84.4109 9115	68
69	79.7506 9806	82.1553 2885	84.6533 1800	85.9385 5985	69
70	81.0829 9264	83.5661 0549	86.1471 2902	87.4756 7585	70
71	82.4208 3844	84.9839 3602	87.6496 5394	89.0223 9882	71
72	83.7642 5860	86.4088 5570	89.1609 4359	90.5787 8882	72
73	85.1132 7634	87.8408 9998	90.6810 4909	92.1449 0625	73
74	86.4679 1499	89.2801 0448	92.2100 2188	93.7208 1191	74
75	87.8281 9797	90.7265 0500	93.7479 1367	95.3065 6698	75
76	89.1941 4880	92.1801 3752	95.2947 7650	96.9022 3303	76
77	90.5657 9108	93.6410 3821	96.8506 6270	98.5078 7198	77
78	91.9431 4855	95.1092 4340	98.4156 2490	100.1235 4618	78
79	93.3262 4500	96.5847 8962	99.9897 1604	101.7493 1835	79
80	94.7151 0435	98.0677 1357	101.5729 8939	103.3852 5159	80
81	96.1097 5062	99.5580 5214	103.1654 9849	105.0314 0941	81
82	97.5102 0792	101.0558 4240	104.7672 9723	106.6878 5572	82
83	98.9165 0045	102.5611 2161	106.3784 3980	108.3546 5482	83
84	100.3286 5253	104.0739 2722	107.9989 8070	110.0318 7141	84
85	101.7466 8859	105.5942 9685	109.6289 7475	111.7195 7061	85
86	103.1706 3312	107.1222 6834	111.2684 7710	113.4178 1792	86
87	104.6005 1076	108.6578 7968	112.9175 4322	115.1266 7928	87
88	106.0363 4622	110.2011 6908	114.5762 2889	116.8462 2103	88
89	107.4781 6433	111.7521 7492	116.2445 9022	118.5765 0991	89
90	108.9259 9002	113.3109 3580	117.9226 8367	120.3176 1310	90
91	110.3798 4831	114.8774 9048	119.6105 6599	122.0695 9818	91
92	111.8397 6434	116.4518 7793	121.3082 9429	123.8325 3317	92
93	113.3057 6336	118.0341 3732	123.0159 2601	125.6064 8650	93
94	114.7778 7071	119.6243 0800	124.7335 1891	127.3915 2704	94
95	116.2561 1184	121.2224 2954	126.4611 3110	129.1877 2408	95
96	117.7405 1230	122.8285 4169	128.1988 2103	130.9951 4736	96
97	119.2310 9777	124.4426 8440	129.9466 4749	132.8138 6703	97
98	120.7278 9401	126.0648 9782	131.7046 6960	134.6439 5370	98
99	122.2309 2690	127.6952 2231	133.4729 4684	136.4854 7841	99
100	123.7402 2243	129.3336 9842	135.2515 3903	138.3385 1265	100

$$s_{\overline{n}|i} = \frac{(1 + i)^n - 1}{i}$$

n	$\frac{5}{12}\%$	$\frac{1}{2}\%$	$\frac{7}{12}\%$	$\frac{5}{8}\%$	n
101	125.2558 0669	130.9803 6692	137.0405 0634	140.2031 2836	101
102	126.7777 0589	132.6352 6875	138.8399 0929	142.0793 9791	102
103	128.3059 4633	134.2984 4509	140.6498 0877	143.9673 9414	103
104	129.8405 5444	135.9699 3732	142.4702 6598	145.8671 9036	104
105	131.3815 5675	137.6497 8701	144.3013 4253	147.7788 6030	105
106	132.9289 7990	139.3380 3594	146.1431 0037	149.7024 7817	106
107	134.4828 5065	141.0347 2612	147.9956 0178	151.6381 1866	107
108	136.0431 9586	142.7398 9975	149.8589 0946	153.5858 5690	108
109	137.6100 4251	144.4535 9925	151.7330 8643	155.5457 6851	109
110	139.1834 1769	146.1758 6725	153.6181 9610	157.5179 2956	110
111	140.7633 4859	147.9067 4658	155.5143 0225	159.5024 1662	111
112	142.3498 6255	149.6462 8032	157.4214 6901	161.4993 0673	112
113	143.9429 8697	151.3945 1172	159.3397 6091	163.5086 7739	113
114	145.5427 4942	153.1514 8428	161.2692 4285	165.5306 0663	114
115	147.1491 7754	154.9172 4170	163.2099 8010	167.5651 7292	115
116	148.7622 9911	156.6918 2791	165.1620 3832	169.6124 5525	116
117	150.3821 4203	158.4752 8704	167.1254 8354	171.6725 3310	117
118	152.0087 3429	160.2676 6348	169.1003 8220	173.7454 8643	118
119	153.6421 0401	162.0690 0180	171.0868 0109	175.8313 9572	119
120	155.2822 7945	163.8793 4681	173.0848 0743	177.9303 4194	120
121	156.9292 8894	165.6987 4354	175.0944 6881	180.0424 0658	121
122	158.5831 6098	167.5272 3726	177.1158 5321	182.1676 7162	122
123	160.2439 2415	169.3648 7344	179.1490 2902	184.3062 1957	123
124	161.9116 0717	171.2116 9781	181.1940 6502	186.4581 3344	124
125	163.5862 3887	173.0677 5630	183.2510 3040	188.6234 9677	125
126	165.2678 4819	174.9330 9508	185.3199 9475	190.8023 9363	126
127	166.9564 6423	176.8077 6056	187.4010 2805	192.9949 0859	127
128	168.6521 1616	178.6917 9936	189.4942 0071	195.2011 2677	128
129	170.3548 3331	180.5852 5836	191.5995 8355	197.4211 3381	129
130	172.0646 4512	182.4881 8465	193.7172 4779	199.6550 1589	130
131	173.7815 8114	184.4006 2557	195.8472 6507	201.9028 5974	131
132	175.5056 7106	186.3226 2870	197.9897 0745	204.1647 5262	132
133	177.2369 4469	188.2542 4184	200.1446 4741	206.4407 8232	133
134	178.9754 3196	190.1955 1305	202.3121 5785	208.7310 3721	134
135	180.7211 6293	192.1464 9062	204.4923 1210	211.0356 0619	135
136	182.4741 6777	194.1072 2307	206.6851 8393	213.3545 7873	136
137	184.2344 7680	196.0777 5919	208.8908 4750	215.6880 4485	137
138	186.0021 2046	198.0581 4798	211.1093 7744	218.0360 9513	138
139	187.7771 2929	200.0484 3872	213.3408 4881	220.3988 2072	139
140	189.5595 3400	202.0486 8092	215.5853 3710	222.7763 1335	140
141	191.3493 6539	204.0589 2432	217.8429 1823	225.1686 6531	141
142	193.1466 5441	206.0792 1894	220.1136 6858	227.5759 6947	142
143	194.9514 3214	208.1096 1504	222.3976 6498	229.9983 1928	143
144	196.7637 2977	210.1501 6311	224.6949 8470	232.4358 0878	144
145	198.5835 7865	212.2009 1393	227.0057 0544	234.8885 3258	145
146	200.4110 1023	214.2619 1850	229.3299 0539	237.3565 8591	146
147	202.2460 5610	216.3332 2809	231.6676 6317	239.8400 6457	147
148	204.0887 4800	218.4148 9423	234.0190 5787	242.3390 6497	148
149	205.9391 1778	220.5069 6870	236.3841 6904	244.8536 8413	149
150	207.7971 9744	222.6095 0354	238.7630 7670	247.3840 1966	150

VII. AMOUNT OF ANNUITY OF 1 PER PERIOD

$$s_{\overline{n}|i} = \frac{(1+i)^n - 1}{i}$$

n	$\frac{5}{12}\%$	$\frac{1}{2}\%$	$\frac{7}{12}\%$	$\frac{5}{8}\%$	n
151	209.6630 1910	224.7225 5106	241.1558 6131	249.9301 6978	151
152	211.5366 1501	226.8461 6382	243.5626 0383	252.4922 3334	152
153	213.4180 1757	228.9803 9464	245.9833 8569	255.0703 0980	153
154	215.3072 5931	231.1252 9661	248.4182 8877	257.6644 9923	154
155	217.2043 7289	233.2809 2309	250.8673 9546	260.2749 0235	155
156	219.1093 9111	235.4473 2771	253.3307 8860	262.9016 2049	156
157	221.0223 4691	237.6245 6435	255.8085 5153	265.5447 5562	157
158	222.9432 7336	239.8126 8717	258.3007 6808	268.2044 1035	158
159	224.8722 0366	242.0117 5060	260.8075 2256	270.8806 8791	159
160	226.8091 7118	244.2218 0936	263.3288 9978	273.5736 9221	160
161	228.7542 0939	246.4429 1840	265.8649 8503	276.2835 2779	161
162	230.7073 5193	248.6751 3300	268.4158 6411	279.0102 9983	162
163	232.6686 3256	250.9185 0866	270.9816 2331	281.7541 1421	163
164	234.6380 8520	253.1731 0121	273.5623 4945	284.5150 7742	164
165	236.6157 4389	255.4389 6671	276.1581 2982	287.2932 9666	165
166	238.6016 4282	257.7161 6154	278.7690 5225	290.0888 7976	166
167	240.5958 1633	260.0047 4235	281.3952 0505	292.9019 3526	167
168	242.5982 9890	262.3047 6606	284.0366 7708	295.7325 7235	168
169	244.6091 2514	264.6162 8989	286.6935 5770	298.5809 0093	169
170	246.6283 2983	266.9393 7134	289.3659 3678	301.4470 3156	170
171	248.6559 4787	269.2740 6820	292.0539 0475	304.3310 7551	171
172	250.6920 1432	271.6204 3854	294.7575 5252	307.2331 4473	172
173	252.7365 6438	273.9785 4073	297.4769 7158	310.1533 5189	173
174	254.7896 3340	276.3484 3344	300.2122 5392	313.0918 1033	174
175	256.8512 5687	278.7301 7561	302.9634 9206	316.0486 3415	175
176	258.9214 7044	281.1238 2648	305.7307 7910	319.0239 3811	176
177	261.0003 0990	283.5294 4562	308.5142 0864	322.0178 3773	177
178	263.0878 1120	285.9470 9284	311.3138 7486	325.0304 4921	178
179	265.1840 1041	288.3768 2831	314.1298 7247	328.0618 8952	179
180	267.2889 4379	290.8187 1245	316.9622 9672	331.1122 7633	180
181	269.4026 4772	293.2728 0601	319.8112 4345	334.1817 2806	181
182	271.5251 5875	295.7391 7004	322.6768 0904	337.2703 6386	182
183	273.6565 1358	298.2178 6589	325.5590 9042	340.3783 0363	183
184	275.7967 4905	300.7089 5522	328.4581 8512	343.5056 6803	184
185	277.9459 0217	303.2125 0000	331.3741 9120	346.6525 7845	185
186	280.1040 1010	305.7285 6250	334.3072 0731	349.8191 5707	186
187	282.2711 1014	308.2572 0531	337.2573 3269	353.0055 2680	187
188	284.4472 3977	310.7984 9134	340.2246 6713	356.2118 1134	188
189	286.6324 3660	313.3524 8379	343.2093 1102	359.4381 3516	189
190	288.8267 3842	315.9192 4621	346.2113 6534	362.6846 2351	190
191	291.0301 8316	318.4988 4244	349.2309 3163	365.9514 0241	191
192	293.2428 0892	321.0913 3666	352.2681 1207	369.2385 9867	192
193	295.4646 5396	323.6967 9334	355.3230 0939	372.5463 3991	193
194	297.6957 5669	326.3152 7731	358.3957 2694	375.8747 5454	194
195	299.9361 5567	328.9468 5369	361.4863 6868	379.2239 7175	195
196	302.1858 8965	331.5915 8796	364.5950 3917	382.5941 2158	196
197	304.4449 9753	334.2495 4590	367.7218 4356	385.9853 3484	197
198	306.7135 1835	336.9207 9363	370.8668 8765	389.3977 4318	198
199	308.9914 9134	339.6053 9760	374.0302 7783	392.8314 7907	199
200	311.2789 5589	342.3034 2459	377.2121 2112	396.2866 7582	200

VII. AMOUNT OF ANNUITY OF 1 PER PERIOD

$$s_{\overline{n}|i} = \frac{(1+i)^n - 1}{i}$$

n	$\frac{5}{12}\%$	$\frac{1}{2}\%$	$\frac{7}{12}\%$	$\frac{5}{8}\%$	n
201	313.5759 5154	345.0149 4171	380.4125 2516	399.7634 6754	201
202	315.8825 1801	347.7400 1642	383.6315 9822	403.2619 8921	202
203	318.1986 9516	350.4787 1650	386.8694 4921	406.7823 7665	203
204	320.5245 2306	353.2311 1008	390.1261 8766	410.3247 6650	204
205	322.8600 4191	355.9972 6563	393.4019 2376	413.8892 9629	205
206	325.2052 9208	358.7772 5196	396.6967 6831	417.4761 0439	206
207	327.5603 1413	361.5711 3822	400.0108 3280	421.0853 3005	207
208	329.9251 4877	364.3789 9391	403.3442 2932	424.7171 1336	208
209	332.2998 3689	367.2008 8888	406.6970 7066	428.3715 9532	209
210	334.6844 1955	370.0368 9333	410.0694 7024	432.0489 1779	210
211	337.0789 3796	372.8870 7779	413.4615 4215	435.7492 2352	211
212	339.4834 3354	375.7515 1318	416.8734 0114	439.4726 5617	212
213	341.8979 4784	378.6302 7075	420.3051 6265	443.2193 6027	213
214	344.3225 2263	381.5234 2210	423.7569 4276	446.9894 8127	214
215	346.7571 9980	384.4310 3921	427.2228 5826	450.7831 6553	215
216	349.2020 2147	387.3531 9441	430.7210 2660	454.6005 6032	216
217	351.6570 2989	390.2899 6038	434.2335 6593	458.4418 1382	217
218	354.1222 6752	393.2414 1018	437.7665 9506	462.3070 7515	218
219	356.5977 7696	396.2076 1723	441.3202 3353	466.1964 9437	219
220	359.0836 0104	399.1886 5532	444.8946 0156	470.1102 2246	220
221	361.5797 8271	402.1845 9859	448.4898 2007	474.0484 1135	221
222	364.0863 6513	405.1955 2159	452.1060 1069	478.0112 1392	222
223	366.6033 9166	408.2214 9920	455.7432 9575	481.9987 8401	223
224	369.1309 0579	411.2626 0669	459.4017 9831	486.0112 7641	224
225	371.6689 5123	414.3189 1973	463.0816 4213	490.0488 4689	225
226	374.2175 7186	417.3905 1432	466.7829 5171	494.1116 5218	226
227	376.7768 1174	420.4774 6690	470.5058 5226	498.1998 5001	227
228	379.3467 1512	423.5798 5423	474.2504 6973	502.3135 9907	228
229	381.9273 2644	426.6977 5350	478.0169 3081	506.4530 5907	229
230	384.5186 9030	429.8312 4227	481.8053 6290	510.6183 9068	230
231	387.1208 5151	432.9803 9848	485.6158 9419	514.8097 5563	231
232	389.7338 5505	436.1453 0047	489.4486 5357	519.0273 1660	232
233	392.3577 4612	439.3260 2697	493.3037 7071	523.2712 3733	233
234	394.9925 7006	442.5226 5711	497.1813 7604	527.5416 8256	234
235	397.6383 7243	445.7352 7039	501.0816 0074	531.8388 1808	235
236	400.2951 9899	448.9639 4675	505.0045 7674	536.1628 1069	236
237	402.9630 9565	452.2087 6648	508.9504 3677	540.5138 2826	237
238	405.6421 0855	455.4698 1031	512.9193 1432	544.8920 3968	238
239	408.3322 8400	458.7471 5936	516.9113 4365	549.2976 1493	239
240	411.0336 6852	462.0408 9516	520.9266 5983	553.7307 2502	240
241	413.7463 0880	465.3510 9964	524.9653 9867	558.1915 4206	241
242	416.4702 5175	468.6778 5514	529.0276 9683	562.6802 3919	242
243	419.2055 4447	472.0212 4441	533.1136 9173	567.1969 9069	243
244	421.9522 3424	475.3813 5063	537.2235 2160	571.7419 7188	244
245	424.7103 6855	478.7582 5739	541.3573 2548	576.3153 5921	245
246	427.4799 9508	482.1520 4867	545.5152 4321	580.9173 3020	246
247	430.2611 6173	485.5628 0892	549.6974 1546	585.5480 6351	247
248	433.0539 1657	488.9906 2296	553.9039 8372	590.2077 3891	248
249	435.8583 0789	492.4355 7608	558.1350 9029	594.8965 3728	249
250	438.6743 8417	495.8977 5396	562.3908 7832	599.6146 4064	250

VII. AMOUNT OF ANNUITY OF 1 PER PERIOD

$$s_{\overline{n}|i} = \frac{(1 + i)^n - 1}{i}$$

n	$\frac{3}{4}\%$	$\frac{7}{8}\%$	1%	$1\frac{1}{8}\%$	n
1	1.0000 0000	1.0000 0000	1.0000 0000	1.0000 0000	1
2	2.0075 0000	2.0087 5000	2.0100 0000	2.0112 5000	2
3	3.0225 5625	3.0263 2656	3.0301 0000	3.0338 7656	3
4	4.0452 2542	4.0528 0692	4.0604 0100	4.0680 0767	4
5	5.0755 6461	5.0882 6898	5.1010 0501	5.1137 7276	5
6	6.1136 3135	6.1327 9133	6.1520 1506	6.1713 0270	6
7	7.1594 8358	7.1864 5326	7.2135 3521	7.2407 2986	7
8	8.2131 7971	8.2493 3472	8.2856 7056	8.3221 8807	8
9	9.2747 7856	9.3215 1640	9.3685 2727	9.4158 1269	9
10	10.3443 3940	10.4030 7967	10.4622 1254	10.5217 4058	10
11	11.4219 2194	11.4941 0662	11.5668 3467	11.6401 1016	11
12	12.5075 8636	12.5946 8005	12.6825 0301	12.7710 6140	12
13	13.6013 9325	13.7048 8350	13.8093 2804	13.9147 3584	13
14	14.7034 0370	14.8248 0123	14.9474 2132	15.0712 7662	14
15	15.8136 7923	15.9545 1824	16.0968 9554	16.2408 2848	15
16	16.9322 8183	17.0941 2028	17.2578 6449	17.4235 3780	16
17	18.0592 7394	18.2436 9383	18.4304 4314	18.6195 5260	17
18	19.1947 1849	19.4033 2615	19.6147 4757	19.8290 2257	18
19	20.3386 7888	20.5731 0526	20.8108 9504	21.0520 9907	19
20	21.4912 1897	21.7531 1993	22.0190 0399	22.2889 3519	20
21	22.6524 0312	22.9434 5973	23.2391 9403	23.5396 8571	21
22	23.8222 9614	24.1442 1500	24.4715 8598	24.8045 0717	22
23	25.0009 6336	25.3554 7688	25.7163 0183	26.0835 5788	23
24	26.1884 7059	26.5773 3730	26.9734 6485	27.3769 9790	24
25	27.3848 8412	27.8098 8900	28.2431 9950	28.6849 8913	25
26	28.5902 7075	29.0532 2553	29.5256 3150	30.0076 9526	26
27	29.8046 9778	30.3074 4126	30.8208 8781	31.3452 8183	27
28	31.0282 3301	31.5726 3137	32.1290 9669	32.6979 1625	28
29	32.2609 4476	32.8488 9189	33.4503 8766	34.0657 6781	29
30	33.5029 0184	34.1363 1970	34.7848 9153	35.4490 0769	30
31	34.7541 7361	35.4350 1249	36.1327 4045	36.8478 0903	31
32	36.0148 2991	36.7450 6885	37.4940 6785	38.2623 4688	32
33	37.2849 4113	38.0665 8820	38.8690 0853	39.6927 9829	33
34	38.5645 7819	39.3996 7085	40.2576 9862	41.1393 4227	34
35	39.8538 1253	40.7444 1797	41.6602 7560	42.6021 5987	35
36	41.1527 1612	42.1009 3163	43.0768 7836	44.0814 3417	36
37	42.4613 6149	43.4693 1478	44.5076 4714	45.5773 5030	37
38	43.7798 2170	44.8496 7128	45.9527 2361	47.0900 9549	38
39	45.1081 7037	46.2421 0591	47.4122 5085	48.6198 5906	39
40	46.4464 8164	47.6467 2433	48.8863 7336	50.1668 3248	40
41	47.7948 3026	49.0636 3317	50.3752 3709	51.7312 0934	41
42	49.1532 9148	50.4929 3996	51.8789 8946	53.3131 8545	42
43	50.5219 4117	51.9347 5319	53.3977 7936	54.9129 5879	43
44	51.9008 5573	53.3891 8228	54.9317 5715	56.5307 2957	44
45	53.2901 1215	54.8563 3762	56.4810 7472	58.1667 0028	45
46	54.6897 8799	56.3363 3058	58.0458 8547	59.8210 7566	46
47	56.0999 6140	57.8292 7347	59.6263 4432	61.4940 6276	47
48	57.5207 1111	59.3352 7961	61.2226 0777	63.1858 7097	48
49	58.9521 1644	60.8544 6331	62.8348 3385	64.8967 1201	49
50	60.3942 5732	62.3869 3986	64.4631 8218	66.6268 0002	50

$$s_{\overline{n}|i} = \frac{(1 + i)^n - 1}{i}$$

n	$\frac{3}{4}\%$	$\frac{7}{8}\%$	1%	$1\frac{1}{8}\%$	n
51	61.8472 1424	63.9328 2559	66.1078 1401	68.3763 5152	51
52	63.3110 6835	65.4922 3781	67.7688 9215	70.1455 8548	52
53	64.7859 0136	67.0652 9489	69.4465 8107	71.9347 2332	53
54	66.2717 9562	68.6521 1622	71.1410 4688	73.7439 8895	54
55	67.7688 3409	70.2528 2224	72.8524 5735	75.5736 0883	55
56	69.2771 0035	71.8675 3443	74.5809 8192	77.4238 1193	56
57	70.7966 7860	73.4963 7536	76.3267 9174	79.2948 2981	57
58	72.3276 5369	75.1394 6864	78.0900 5966	81.1868 9665	58
59	73.8701 1109	76.7969 3900	79.8709 6025	83.1002 4923	59
60	75.4241 3693	78.4689 1221	81.6696 6986	85.0351 2704	60
61	76.9898 1795	80.1555 1519	83.4863 6655	86.9917 7222	61
62	78.5672 4159	81.8568 7595	85.3212 3022	88.9704 2966	62
63	80.1564 9590	83.5731 2362	87.1744 4252	90.9713 4699	63
64	81.7576 6962	85.3043 8845	89.0461 8695	92.9947 7464	64
65	83.3708 5214	87.0508 0185	90.9366 4882	95.0409 6586	65
66	84.9961 3353	88.8124 9636	92.8460 1531	97.1101 7672	66
67	86.6336 0453	90.5896 0571	94.7744 7546	99.2026 6621	67
68	88.2833 5657	92.3822 6476	96.7222 2021	101.3186 9621	68
69	89.9454 8174	94.1906 0957	98.6894 4242	103.4585 3154	69
70	91.6200 7285	96.0147 7741	100.6763 3684	105.6224 4002	70
71	93.3072 2340	97.8549 0671	102.6831 0021	107.8106 9247	71
72	95.0070 2758	99.7111 3714	104.7099 3121	110.0235 6276	72
73	96.7195 8028	101.5836 0959	106.7570 3052	112.2613 2784	73
74	98.4449 7714	103.4724 6618	108.8246 0083	114.5242 6778	74
75	100.1833 1446	105.3778 5025	110.9128 4684	116.8126 6579	75
76	101.9346 8932	107.2999 0644	113.0219 7530	119.1268 0828	76
77	103.6991 9949	109.2387 8063	115.1521 9506	121.4669 8487	77
78	105.4769 4349	111.1946 1996	117.3037 1701	123.8334 8845	78
79	107.2680 2056	113.1675 7288	119.4767 5418	126.2266 1520	79
80	109.0725 3072	115.1577 8914	121.6715 2172	128.6466 6462	80
81	110.8905 7470	117.1654 1980	123.8882 3694	131.0939 3960	81
82	112.7222 5401	119.1906 1722	126.1271 1931	133.5687 4642	82
83	114.5676 7091	121.2335 3512	128.3883 9050	136.0713 9481	83
84	116.4269 2845	123.2943 2855	130.6722 7440	138.6021 9801	84
85	118.3001 3041	125.3731 5393	132.9789 9715	141.1614 7273	85
86	120.1873 8139	127.4701 6903	135.3087 8712	143.7495 3930	86
87	122.0887 8675	129.5855 3301	137.6618 7499	146.3667 2162	87
88	124.0044 5265	131.7194 0642	140.0384 9374	149.0133 4724	88
89	125.9344 8604	133.8719 5123	142.4388 7868	151.6897 4739	89
90	127.8789 9469	136.0433 3080	144.8632 6746	154.3962 5705	90
91	129.8380 8715	138.2337 0994	147.3119 0014	157.1332 1494	91
92	131.8118 7280	140.4432 5491	149.7850 1914	159.9009 6361	92
93	133.8004 6185	142.6721 3339	152.2828 6933	162.6998 4945	93
94	135.8039 6531	144.9205 1455	154.8056 9803	165.5302 2276	94
95	137.8224 9505	147.1885 6906	157.3537 5501	168.3924 3776	95
96	139.8561 6377	149.4764 6903	159.9272 9256	171.2868 5269	96
97	141.9050 8499	151.7843 8814	162.5265 6549	174.2138 2978	97
98	143.9693 7313	154.1125 0153	165.1518 3114	177.1737 3537	98
99	146.0491 4343	156.4609 8592	167.8033 4945	180.1669 3989	99
100	148.1445 1201	158.8300 1955	170.4813 8294	183.1938 1796	100

VII. AMOUNT OF ANNUITY OF 1 PER PERIOD

$$s_{\overline{n}|i} = \frac{(1 + i)^n - 1}{i}$$

n	$1\frac{1}{4}\%$	$1\frac{3}{8}\%$	$1\frac{1}{2}\%$	$1\frac{5}{8}\%$	n
1	1.0000 0000	1.0000 0000	1.0000 0000	1.0000 0000	1
2	2.0125 0000	2.0137 5000	2.0150 0000	2.0162 5000	2
3	3.0376 5625	3.0414 3906	3.0452 2500	3.0490 1406	3
4	4.0756 2695	4.0832 5885	4.0909 0338	4.0985 6054	4
5	5.1265 7229	5.1394 0366	5.1522 6693	5.1651 6215	5
6	6.1906 5444	6.2100 7046	6.2295 5093	6.2490 9603	6
7	7.2680 3762	7.2954 5893	7.3229 9419	7.3506 4385	7
8	8.3588 8809	8.3957 7149	8.4328 3911	8.4700 9181	8
9	9.4633 7420	9.5112 1335	9.5593 3169	9.6077 3080	9
10	10.5816 6637	10.6419 9253	10.7027 2167	10.7638 5643	10
11	11.7139 3720	11.7883 1993	11.8632 6249	11.9387 6909	11
12	12.8603 6142	12.9504 0933	13.0412 1143	13.1327 7409	12
13	14.0211 1594	14.1284 7745	14.2368 2960	14.3461 8167	13
14	15.1963 7988	15.3227 4402	15.4503 8205	15.5793 0712	14
15	16.3863 3463	16.5334 3175	16.6821 3778	16.8324 7086	15
16	17.5911 6382	17.7607 6644	17.9323 6984	18.1059 9851	16
17	18.8110 5336	19.0049 7697	19.2013 5539	19.4002 2099	17
18	20.0461 9153	20.2662 9541	20.4893 7572	20.7154 7458	18
19	21.2967 6893	21.5449 5697	21.7967 1636	22.0521 0104	19
20	22.5629 7854	22.8412 0013	23.1236 6710	23.4104 4768	20
21	23.8450 1577	24.1552 6663	24.4705 2211	24.7908 6746	21
22	25.1430 7847	25.4874 0155	25.8375 7994	26.1937 1905	22
23	26.4573 6695	26.8378 5332	27.2251 4364	27.6193 6699	23
24	27.7880 8403	28.2068 7380	28.6335 2080	29.0681 8170	24
25	29.1354 3508	29.5947 1832	30.0630 2361	30.5405 3966	25
26	30.4996 2802	31.0016 4569	31.5139 6896	32.0368 2343	26
27	31.8808 7337	32.4279 1832	32.9866 7850	33.5574 2181	27
28	33.2793 8429	33.8738 0220	34.4814 7867	35.1027 2991	28
29	34.6953 7659	35.3395 6698	35.9987 0085	36.6731 4927	29
30	36.1290 6880	36.8254 8602	37.5386 8137	38.2690 8795	30
31	37.5806 8216	38.3318 3646	39.1017 6159	39.8909 6063	31
32	39.0504 4069	39.8588 9921	40.6882 8801	41.5391 8874	32
33	40.5385 7120	41.4069 5907	42.2986 1233	43.2142 0055	33
34	42.0453 0334	42.9763 0476	43.9330 9152	44.9164 3131	34
35	43.5708 6963	44.5672 2895	45.5920 8789	46.6463 2332	35
36	45.1155 0550	46.1800 2835	47.2759 6921	48.4043 2607	36
37	46.6794 4932	47.8150 0374	48.9851 0874	50.1908 9637	37
38	48.2629 4243	49.4724 6004	50.7198 8538	52.0064 9844	38
39	49.8662 2921	51.1527 0636	52.4806 8366	53.8516 0404	39
40	51.4895 5708	52.8560 5608	54.2678 9391	55.7266 9261	40
41	53.1331 7654	54.5828 2685	56.0819 1232	57.6322 5136	41
42	54.7973 4125	56.3333 4072	57.9231 4100	59.5687 7544	42
43	56.4823 0801	58.1079 2415	59.7919 8812	61.5367 6805	43
44	58.1883 3687	59.9069 0811	61.6888 6794	63.5367 4053	44
45	59.9156 9108	61.7306 2810	63.6142 0096	65.5692 1256	45
46	61.6646 3721	63.5794 2423	65.5684 1398	67.6347 1226	46
47	63.4354 4518	65.4536 4131	67.5519 4018	69.7337 7634	47
48	65.2283 8824	67.3536 2888	69.5652 1929	71.8669 5020	48
49	67.0437 4310	69.2797 4128	71.6086 9758	74.0347 8814	49
50	68.8817 8989	71.2323 3772	73.6828 2804	76.2378 5345	50

$$s_{\overline{n}|i} = \frac{(1 + i)^n - 1}{i}$$

n	$1\frac{1}{4}\%$	$1\frac{3}{8}\%$	$1\frac{1}{2}\%$	$1\frac{5}{8}\%$	n
51	70.7428 1226	73.2117 8237	75.7880 7046	78.4767 1857	51
52	72.6270 9741	75.2184 4437	77.9248 9152	80.7519 6525	52
53	74.5349 3613	77.2526 9798	80.0937 6489	83.0641 8468	53
54	76.4666 2283	79.3149 2258	82.2951 7136	85.4139 7768	54
55	78.4224 5562	81.4055 0277	84.5295 9893	87.8019 5482	55
56	80.4027 3631	83.5248 2843	86.7975 4292	90.2287 3659	56
57	82.4077 7052	85.6732 9482	89.0995 0606	92.6949 5356	57
58	84.4378 6765	87.8513 0262	91.4359 9865	95.2012 4655	58
59	86.4933 4099	90.0592 5804	93.8075 3863	97.7482 6681	59
60	88.5745 0776	92.2975 7283	96.2146 5171	100.3366 7614	60
61	90.6816 8910	94.5666 6446	98.6578 7149	102.9671 4713	61
62	92.8152 1022	96.8669 5610	101.1377 3956	105.6403 6327	62
63	94.9754 0034	99.1988 7674	103.6548 0565	108.3570 1918	63
64	97.1625 9285	101.5628 6130	106.2096 2774	111.1178 2074	64
65	99.3771 2526	103.9593 5064	108.8027 7215	113.9234 8532	65
66	101.6193 3933	106.3887 9171	111.4348 1374	116.7747 4196	66
67	103.8895 8107	108.8516 3760	114.1063 3594	119.6723 3152	67
68	106.1882 0083	111.3483 4761	116.8179 3098	122.6170 0690	68
69	108.5155 5334	113.8793 8739	119.5701 9995	125.6095 3327	69
70	110.8719 9776	116.4452 2897	122.3637 5295	128.6506 8818	70
71	113.2578 9773	119.0463 5087	125.1992 0924	131.7412 6186	71
72	115.6736 2145	121.6832 3819	128.0771 9738	134.8820 5737	72
73	118.1195 4172	124.3563 8272	130.9983 5534	138.0738 9080	73
74	120.5960 3599	127.0662 8298	133.9633 3067	141.3175 9153	74
75	123.1034 8644	129.8134 4437	136.9727 8063	144.6140 0239	75
76	125.6422 8002	132.5983 7923	140.0273 7234	147.9639 7993	76
77	128.2128 0852	135.4216 0695	143.1277 8292	151.3683 9460	77
78	130.8154 6863	138.2836 5404	146.2746 9967	154.8281 3102	78
79	133.4506 6199	141.1850 5429	149.4688 2016	158.3440 8814	79
80	136.1187 9526	144.1263 4878	152.7108 5247	161.9171 7958	80
81	138.8202 8020	147.1080 8608	156.0015 1525	165.5483 3374	81
82	141.5555 3370	150.1308 2226	159.3415 3798	169.2384 9417	82
83	144.3249 7787	153.1951 2107	162.7316 6105	172.9886 1970	83
84	147.1290 4010	156.3015 5398	166.1726 3597	176.7996 8477	84
85	149.9681 5310	159.4507 0035	169.6652 2551	180.6726 7965	85
86	152.8427 5501	162.6431 4748	173.2102 0389	184.6086 1069	86
87	155.7532 8945	165.8794 9076	176.8083 5695	188.6085 0061	87
88	158.7002 0557	169.1603 3375	180.4604 8230	192.6733 8875	88
89	161.6839 5814	172.4862 8834	184.1673 8954	196.8043 3132	89
90	164.7050 0762	175.8579 7481	187.9299 0038	201.0024 0170	90
91	167.7638 2021	179.2760 2196	191.7488 4889	205.2686 9073	91
92	170.8608 6796	182.7410 6726	195.6250 8162	209.6043 0695	92
93	173.9966 2881	186.2537 5694	199.5594 5784	214.0103 7694	93
94	177.1715 8667	189.8147 4610	203.5528 4971	218.4880 4557	94
95	180.3862 3151	193.4246 9886	207.6061 4246	223.0384 7631	95
96	183.6410 5940	197.0842 8847	211.7202 3459	227.6628 5155	96
97	186.9365 7264	200.7941 9743	215.8960 3811	232.3623 7288	97
98	190.2732 7980	204.5551 1765	220.1344 7868	237.1382 6144	98
99	193.6516 9580	208.3677 5051	224.4364 9586	241.9917 5819	99
100	197.0723 4200	212.2328 0708	228.8030 4330	246.9241 2426	100

VII. AMOUNT OF ANNUITY OF 1 PER PERIOD

$$s_{\overline{n}|i} = \frac{(1 + i)^n - 1}{i}$$

n	$1\frac{3}{4}\%$	2%	$2\frac{1}{4}\%$	$2\frac{1}{2}\%$	n
1	1.0000 0000	1.0000 0000	1.0000 0000	1.0000 0000	1
2	2.0175 0000	2.0200 0000	2.0225 0000	2.0250 0000	2
3	3.0528 0625	3.0604 0000	3.0680 0625	3.0756 2500	3
4	4.1062 3036	4.1216 0800	4.1370 3639	4.1525 1563	4
5	5.1780 8939	5.2040 4016	5.2301 1971	5.2563 2852	5
6	6.2687 0596	6.3081 2096	6.3477 9740	6.3877 3673	6
7	7.3784 0831	7.4342 8338	7.4906 2284	7.5474 3015	7
8	8.5075 3045	8.5829 6905	8.6591 6186	8.7361 1590	8
9	9.6564 1224	9.7546 2843	9.8539 9300	9.9545 1880	9
10	10.8253 9945	10.9497 2100	11.0757 0784	11.2033 8177	10
11	12.0148 4394	12.1687 1542	12.3249 1127	12.4834 6631	11
12	13.2251 0371	13.4120 8973	13.6022 2177	13.7955 5297	12
13	14.4565 4303	14.6803 3152	14.9082 7176	15.1404 4179	13
14	15.7095 3253	15.9739 3815	16.2437 0788	16.5189 5284	14
15	16.9844 4935	17.2934 1692	17.6091 9130	17.9319 2666	15
16	18.2816 7721	18.6392 8525	19.0053 9811	19.3802 2483	16
17	19.6016 0656	20.0120 7096	20.4330 1957	20.8647 3045	17
18	20.9446 3468	21.4123 1238	21.8927 6251	22.3863 4871	18
19	22.3111 6578	22.8405 5863	23.3853 4966	23.9460 0743	19
20	23.7016 1119	24.2973 6980	24.9115 2003	25.5446 5761	20
21	25.1163 8938	25.7833 1719	26.4720 2923	27.1832 7405	21
22	26.5559 2620	27.2989 8354	28.0676 4989	28.8628 5590	22
23	28.0206 5490	28.8449 6321	29.6991 7201	30.5844 2730	23
24	29.5110 1637	30.4218 6247	31.3674 0338	32.3490 3798	24
25	31.0274 5915	32.0302 9972	33.0731 6996	34.1577 6393	25
26	32.5704 3969	33.6709 0572	34.8173 1628	36.0117 0803	26
27	34.1404 2238	35.3443 2383	36.6007 0590	37.9120 0073	27
28	35.7378 7977	37.0512 1031	38.4242 2178	39.8598 0075	28
29	37.3632 9267	38.7922 3451	40.2887 6677	41.8562 9577	29
30	39.0171 5029	40.5680 7921	42.1952 6402	43.9027 0316	30
31	40.6999 5042	42.3794 4079	44.1446 5746	46.0002 7074	31
32	42.4121 9955	44.2270 2961	46.1379 1226	48.1502 7751	32
33	44.1544 1305	46.1115 7020	48.1760 1528	50.3540 3445	33
34	45.9271 1527	48.0338 0160	50.2599 7563	52.6128 8531	34
35	47.7308 3979	49.9944 7763	52.3908 2508	54.9282 0744	35
36	49.5661 2949	51.9943 6719	54.5696 1864	57.3014 1263	36
37	51.4335 3675	54.0342 5453	56.7974 3506	59.7339 4794	37
38	53.3336 2365	56.1149 3962	59.0753 7735	62.2272 9664	38
39	55.2669 6206	58.2372 3841	61.4045 7334	64.7829 7906	39
40	57.2341 3390	60.4019 8318	63.7861 7624	67.4025 5354	40
41	59.2357 3124	62.6100 2284	66.2213 6521	70.0876 1737	41
42	61.2723 5654	64.8622 2330	68.7113 4592	72.8398 0781	42
43	63.3446 2278	67.1594 6777	71.2573 5121	75.6608 0300	43
44	65.4531 5367	69.5026 5712	73.8606 4161	78.5523 2308	44
45	67.5985 8386	71.8927 1027	76.5225 0605	81.5161 3116	45
46	69.7815 5908	74.3305 6447	79.2442 6243	84.5540 3443	46
47	72.0027 3637	76.8171 7576	82.0272 5834	87.6678 8530	47
48	74.2627 8425	79.3535 1927	84.8728 7165	90.8595 8243	48
49	76.5623 8298	81.9405 8966	87.7825 1126	94.1310 7199	49
50	78.9022 2468	84.5794 0145	90.7576 1776	97.4843 4879	50

$$s_{\overline{n}|i} = \frac{(1 + i)^n - 1}{i}$$

n	$1\frac{3}{4}\%$	2%	$2\frac{1}{4}\%$	$2\frac{1}{2}\%$	n
51	81.2830 1361	87.2709 8948	93.7996 6416	100.9214 5751	51
52	83.7054 6635	90.0164 0927	96.9101 5661	104.4444 9395	52
53	86.1703 1201	92.8167 3746	100.0906 3513	108.0556 0629	53
54	88.6782 9247	95.6730 7221	103.3426 7442	111.7569 9645	54
55	91.2301 6259	98.5865 3365	106.6678 8460	115.5509 2136	55
56	93.8266 9043	101.5582 6432	110.0679 1200	119.4396 9440	56
57	96.4686 5752	104.5894 2961	113.5444 4002	123.4256 8676	57
58	99.1568 5902	107.6812 1820	117.0991 8992	127.5113 2893	58
59	101.8921 0405	110.8348 4257	120.7339 2169	131.6991 1215	59
60	104.6752 1588	114.0515 3942	124.4504 3493	135.9915 8995	60
61	107.5070 3215	117.3325 7021	128.2505 6972	140.3913 7970	61
62	110.3884 0522	120.6792 2161	132.1362 0754	144.9011 6419	62
63	113.3202 0231	124.0928 0604	136.1092 7221	149.5236 9330	63
64	116.3033 0585	127.5746 6216	140.1717 3083	154.2617 8563	64
65	119.3386 1370	131.1261 5541	144.3255 9477	159.1183 3027	65
66	122.4270 3944	134.7486 7852	148.5729 2066	164.0962 8853	66
67	125.5695 1263	138.4436 5209	152.9158 1137	169.1986 9574	67
68	128.7669 7910	142.2125 2513	157.3564 1713	174.4286 6314	68
69	132.0204 0124	146.0567 7563	161.8969 3651	179.7893 7971	69
70	135.3307 5826	149.9779 1114	166.5396 1758	185.2841 1421	70
71	138.6990 4653	153.9774 6937	171.2867 5898	190.9162 1706	71
72	142.1262 7984	158.0570 1875	176.1407 1106	196.6891 2249	72
73	145.6134 8974	162.2181 5913	181.1038 7705	202.6063 5055	73
74	149.1617 2581	166.4625 2231	186.1787 1429	208.6715 0931	74
75	152.7720 5601	170.7917 7276	191.3677 3536	214.8882 9705	75
76	156.4455 6699	175.2076 0821	196.6735 0941	221.2605 0447	76
77	160.1833 6441	179.7117 6038	202.0986 6337	227.7920 1709	77
78	163.9865 7329	184.3059 9558	207.6458 8329	234.4868 1751	78
79	167.8563 3832	188.9921 1549	213.3179 1567	241.3489 8795	79
80	171.7938 2424	193.7719 5780	219.1175 6877	248.3827 1265	80
81	175.8002 1617	198.6473 9696	225.0477 1407	255.5922 8047	81
82	179.8767 1995	203 6203 4490	231.1112 8763	262.9820 8748	82
83	184.0245 6255	208.6927 5180	237.3112 9160	270.5566 3966	83
84	188.2449 9239	213.8666 0683	243.6507 9567	278.3205 5566	84
85	192.5392 7976	219.1439 3897	250.1329 3857	286.2785 6955	85
86	196.9087 1716	224.5268 1775	256.7609 2969	294.4355 3379	86
87	201.3546 1971	230.0173 5411	263.5380 5060	302.7964 2213	87
88	205.8783 2555	235.6177 0119	270.4676 5674	311.3663 3268	88
89	210.4811 9625	241.3300 5521	277.5531 7902	320.1504 9100	89
90	215.1646 1718	247.1566 5632	284.7981 2555	329.1542 5328	90
91	219.9299 9798	253.0997 8944	292.2060 8337	338.3831 0961	91
92	224.7787 7295	259.1617 8523	299.7807 2025	347.8426 8735	92
93	229.7124 0148	265.3450 2094	307.5257 8645	357.5387 5453	93
94	234.7323 6850	271.6519 2135	315.4451 1665	367.4772 2339	94
95	239.8401 8495	278.0849 5978	323.5426 3177	377.6641 5398	95
96	245.0373 8819	284.6466 5898	331.8223 4099	388.1057 5783	96
97	250.3255 4248	291.3395 9216	340.2883 4366	398.8084 0177	97
98	255.7062 3947	298.1663 8400	348.9448 3139	409.7786 1182	98
99	261.1810 9866	305.1297 1168	357.7960 9010	421.0230 7711	99
100	266.7517 6789	312.2323 0591	366.8465 0213	432.5486 5404	100

VII. AMOUNT OF ANNUITY OF 1 PER PERIOD

$$s_{\overline{n}|i} = \frac{(1 + i)^n - 1}{i}$$

n	$2\frac{3}{4}\%$	3%	$3\frac{1}{4}\%$	$3\frac{1}{2}\%$	n
1	1.0000 0000	1.0000 0000	1.0000 0000	1.0000 0000	1
2	2.0275 0000	2.0300 0000	2.0325 0000	2.0350 0000	2
3	3.0832 5625	3.0909 0000	3.0985 5625	3.1062 2500	3
4	4.1680 4580	4.1836 2700	4.1992 5933	4.2149 4288	4
5	5.2826 6706	5.3091 3581	5.3357 3526	5.3624 6588	5
6	6.4279 4040	6.4684 0988	6.5091 4665	6.5501 5218	6
7	7.6047 0876	7.6624 6218	7.7206 9392	7.7794 0751	7
8	8.8138 3825	8.8923 3605	8.9716 1647	9.0516 8677	8
9	10.0562 1880	10.1591 0613	10.2631 9401	10.3684 9581	9
10	11.3327 6482	11.4638 7931	11.5967 4781	11.7313 9316	10
11	12.6444 1585	12.8077 9569	12.9736 4212	13.1419 9192	11
12	13.9921 3729	14.1920 2956	14.3952 8548	14.6019 6164	12
13	15.3769 2107	15.6177 9045	15.8631 3226	16.1130 3030	13
14	16.7997 8639	17.0863 2416	17.3786 8406	17.6769 8636	14
15	18.2617 8052	18.5989 1389	18.9434 9129	19.2956 8088	15
16	19.7639 7948	20.1568 8130	20.5591 5476	20.9710 2971	16
17	21.3074 8892	21.7615 8774	22.2273 2729	22.7050 1575	17
18	22.8934 4487	23.4144 3537	23.9497 1542	24.4996 9130	18
19	24.5230 1460	25.1168 6844	25.7280 8118	26.3571 8050	19
20	26.1973 9750	26.8703 7449	27.5642 4382	28.2796 8181	20
21	27.9178 2593	28.6764 8572	29.4600 8174	30.2694 7068	21
22	29.6855 6615	30.5367 8030	31.4175 3440	32.3289 0215	22
23	31.5019 1921	32.4528 8370	33.4386 0426	34.4604 1373	23
24	33.3682 2199	34.4264 7022	35.5253 5890	36.6665 2821	24
25	35.2858 4810	36.4592 6432	37.6799 3307	38.9498 5669	25
26	37.2562 0892	38.5530 4225	39.9045 3089	41.3131 0168	26
27	39.2807 5467	40.7096 3352	42.2014 2815	43.7590 6024	27
28	41.3609 7542	42.9309 2252	44.5729 7456	46.2906 2734	28
29	43.4984 0224	45.2188 5020	47.0215 9623	48.9107 9930	29
30	45.6946 0830	47.5754 1571	49.5497 9811	51.6226 7728	30
31	47.9512 1003	50.0026 7818	52.1601 6655	54.4294 7098	31
32	50.2698 6831	52.5027 5852	54.8553 7196	57.3345 0247	32
33	52.6522 8969	55.0778 4128	57.6381 7155	60.3412 1005	33
34	55.1002 2765	57.7301 7652	60.5114 1213	63.4531 5240	34
35	57.6154 8391	60.4620 8181	63.4780 3302	66.6740 1274	35
36	60.1999 0972	63.2759 4427	66.5410 6909	70.0076 0318	36
37	62.8554 0724	66.1742 2259	69.7036 5384	73.4578 6930	37
38	65.5839 3094	69.1594 4927	72.9690 2259	77.0288 9472	38
39	68.3874 8904	72.2342 3275	76.3405 1582	80.7249 0604	39
40	71.2681 4499	75.4012 5973	79.8215 8259	84.5502 7775	40
41	74.2280 1898	78.6632 9753	83.4157 8402	88.5095 3747	41
42	77.2692 8950	82.0231 9645	87.1267 9700	92.6073 7128	42
43	80.3941 9496	85.4838 9234	90.9584 1791	96.8486 2928	43
44	83.6050 3532	89.0484 0911	94.9145 6649	101.2383 3130	44
45	86.9041 7379	92.7198 6139	98.9992 8990	105.7816 7290	45
46	90.2940 3857	96.5014 5723	103.2167 6682	110.4840 3145	46
47	93.7771 2463	100.3965 0095	107.5713 1174	115.3509 7255	47
48	97.3559 9556	104.4083 9598	112.0673 7937	120.3882 5659	48
49	101.0332 8544	108.5406 4785	116.7095 6920	125.6018 4557	49
50	104.8117 0079	112.7968 6729	121.5026 3020	130.9979 1016	50

VII. AMOUNT OF ANNUITY OF 1 PER PERIOD

$$s_{\overline{n}|i} = \frac{(1 + i)^n - 1}{i}$$

n	$2\frac{3}{4}\%$	3%	$3\frac{1}{4}\%$	$3\frac{1}{2}\%$	n
51	108.6940 2256	117.1807 7331	126.4514 6568	136.5828 3702	51
52	112.6831 0818	121.6961 9651	131.5611 3832	142.3632 3631	52
53	116.7818 9365	126.3470 8240	136.8368 7531	148.3459 4958	53
54	120.9933 9573	131.1374 9488	142.2840 7366	154.5380 5782	54
55	125.3207 1411	136.0716 1972	147.9083 0616	160.9468 8984	55
56	129.7670 3375	141.1537 6831	153.7153 2611	167.5800 3099	56
57	134.3356 2718	146.3883 8136	159.7110 7421	174.4453 3207	57
58	139.0298 5692	151.7800 3280	165.9016 8412	181.5509 1869	58
59	143.8531 7799	157.3334 3379	172.2934 8885	188.9052 0085	59
60	148.8091 4038	163.0534 3680	178.8930 2724	196.5168 8288	60
61	153.9013 9174	168.9450 3991	185.7070 5063	204.3949 7378	61
62	159.1336 8002	175.0133 9110	192.7425 2977	212.5487 9786	62
63	164.5098 5622	181.2637 9284	200.0066 6199	220.9880 0579	63
64	170.0338 7726	187.7017 0662	207.5068 7850	229.7225 8599	64
65	175.7098 0889	194.3327 5782	215.2508 5205	238.7628 7650	65
66	181.5418 2863	201.1627 4055	223.2465 0475	248.1195 7718	66
67	187.5342 2892	208.1976 2277	231.5020 1615	257.8037 6238	67
68	193.6914 2022	215.4435 5145	240.0258 3168	267.8268 9406	68
69	200.0179 3427	222.9068 5800	248.8266 7120	278.2008 3535	69
70	206.5184 2746	230.5940 6374	257.9135 3802	288.9378 6459	70
71	213.1976 8422	238.5118 8565	267.2957 2800	300.0506 8985	71
72	220.0606 2054	246.6672 4222	276.9828 3916	311.5524 6400	72
73	227.1122 8760	255.0672 5949	286.9847 8144	323.4568 0024	73
74	234.3578 7551	263.7192 7727	297.3117 8683	335.7777 8824	74
75	241.8027 1709	272.6308 5559	307.9744 1991	348.5300 1083	75
76	249.4522 9181	281.8097 8126	318.9835 8855	361.7285 6121	76
77	257.3122 2983	291.2640 7469	330.3505 5518	375.3890 6085	77
78	265.3883 1615	301.0019 9693	342.0869 4822	389.5276 7798	78
79	273.6864 9485	311.0320 5684	354.2047 7404	404.1611 4671	79
80	282.2128 7345	321.3630 1855	366.7164 2920	419.3067 8685	80
81	290.9737 2747	332.0039 0910	379.6347 1315	434.9825 2439	81
82	299.9755 0498	342.9640 2638	392.9728 4132	451.2069 1274	82
83	309.2248 3137	354.2529 4717	406.7444 5867	467.9991 5469	83
84	318.7285 1423	365.8805 3558	420.9636 5357	485.3791 2510	84
85	328.4935 4837	377.8569 5165	435.6449 7232	503.3673 9448	85
86	338.5271 2095	390.1926 6020	450.8034 3392	521.9852 5329	86
87	348.8366 1678	402.8984 4001	466.4545 4552	541.2547 3715	87
88	359.4296 2374	415.9853 9321	482.6143 1825	561.1986 5295	88
89	370.3139 3839	429.4649 5500	499.2992 8359	581.8406 0581	89
90	381.4975 7170	443.3489 0365	516.5265 1031	603.2050 2701	90
91	392.9887 5492	457.6493 7076	534.3136 2189	625.3172 0295	91
92	404.7959 4568	472.3788 5189	552.6788 1460	648.2033 0506	92
93	416.9278 3418	487.5502 1744	571.6408 7608	671.8904 2073	93
94	429.3933 4962	503.1767 2397	591.2192 0455	696.4065 8546	94
95	442.2016 6674	519.2720 2568	611.4338 2870	721.7808 1595	95
96	455.3622 1257	535.8501 8645	632.3054 2813	748.0431 4451	96
97	468.8846 7342	552.9256 9205	653.8553 5455	775.2246 5457	97
98	482.7790 0194	570.5134 6281	676.1056 5357	803.3575 1748	98
99	497.0554 2449	588.6288 6669	699.0790 8731	832.4750 3059	99
100	511.7244 4867	607.2877 3270	722.7991 5765	862.6116 5666	100

VII. AMOUNT OF ANNUITY OF 1 PER PERIOD

$$s_{\overline{n}|i} = \frac{(1 + i)^n - 1}{i}$$

n	4%	$4\frac{1}{2}\%$	5%	$5\frac{1}{2}\%$	n
1	1.0000 0000	1.0000 0000	1.0000 0000	1.0000 0000	1
2	2.0400 0000	2.0450 0000	2.0500 0000	2.0550 0000	2
3	3.1216 0000	3.1370 2500	3.1525 0000	3.1680 2500	3
4	4.2464 6400	4.2781 9113	4.3101 2500	4.3422 6638	4
5	5.4163 2256	5.4707 0973	5.5256 3125	5.5810 9103	5
6	6.6329 7546	6.7168 9166	6.8019 1281	6.8880 5103	6
7	7.8982 9448	8.0191 5179	8.1420 0845	8.2668 9384	7
8	9.2142 2626	9.3800 1362	9.5491 0888	9.7215 7300	8
9	10.5827 9531	10.8021 1423	11.0265 6432	11.2562 5951	9
10	12.0061 0712	12.2882 0937	12.5778 9254	12.8753 5379	10
11	13.4863 5141	13.8411 7879	14.2067 8716	14.5834 9825	11
12	15.0258 0546	15.4640 3184	15.9171 2652	16.3855 9065	12
13	16.6268 3768	17.1599 1327	17.7129 8285	18.2867 9814	13
14	18.2919 1119	18.9321 0937	19.5986 3199	20.2925 7203	14
15	20.0235 8764	20.7840 5429	21.5785 6359	22.4086 6350	15
16	21.8245 3114	22.7193 3673	23.6574 9177	24.6411 3999	16
17	23.6975 1239	24.7417 0689	25.8403 6636	26.9964 0269	17
18	25.6454 1288	26.8550 8370	28.1323 8467	29.4812 0483	18
19	27.6712 2940	29.0635 6246	30.5390 0391	32.1026 7110	19
20	29.7780 7858	31.3714 2277	33.0659 5410	34.8683 1801	20
21	31.9692 0172	33.7831 3680	35.7192 5181	37.7860 7550	21
22	34.2479 6979	36.3033 7795	38.5052 1440	40.8643 0965	22
23	36.6178 8858	38.9370 2996	41.4304 7512	44.1118 4669	23
24	39.0826 0412	41.6891 9631	44.5019 9887	47.5379 9825	24
25	41.6459 0829	44.5652 1015	47.7270 9882	51.1525 8816	25
26	44.3117 4462	47.5706 4460	51.1134 5376	54.9659 8051	26
27	47.0842 1440	50.7113 2361	54.6691 2645	58.9891 0943	27
28	49.9675 8298	53.9933 3317	58.4025 8277	63.2335 1045	28
29	52.9662 8630	57.4230 3316	62.3227 1191	67.7113 5353	29
30	56.0849 3775	61.0070 6966	66.4388 4750	72.4354 7797	30
31	59.3283 3526	64.7523 8779	70.7607 8988	77.4194 2926	31
32	62.7014 6867	68.6662 4524	75.2988 2937	82.6774 9787	32
33	66.2095 2742	72.7562 2628	80.0637 7084	88.2247 6025	33
34	69.8579 0851	77.0302 5646	85.0669 5938	94.0771 2207	34
35	73.6522 2486	81.4966 1800	90.3203 0735	100.2513 6378	35
36	77.5983 1385	86.1639 6581	95.8363 2272	106.7651 8879	36
37	81.7022 4640	91.0413 4427	101.6281 3886	113.6372 7417	37
38	85.9703 3626	96.1382 0476	107.7095 4580	120.8873 2425	38
39	90.4091 4971	101.4644 2398	114.0950 2309	128.5361 2708	39
40	95.0255 1570	107.0303 2306	120.7997 7424	136.6056 1407	40
41	99.8265 3633	112.8466 8760	127.8397 6295	145.1189 2285	41
42	104.8195 9778	118.9247 8854	135.2317 5110	154.1004 6360	42
43	110.0123 8169	125.2764 0402	142.9933 3866	163.5759 8910	43
44	115.4128 7696	131.9138 4220	151.1430 0559	173.5726 6850	44
45	121.0293 9204	138.8499 6510	159.7001 5587	184.1191 6527	45
46	126.8705 6772	146.0982 1353	168.6851 6366	195.2457 1936	46
47	132.9453 9043	153.6726 3314	178.1194 2185	206.9842 3392	47
48	139.2632 0604	161.5879 0163	188.0253 9294	219.3683 6679	48
49	145.8337 3429	169.8593 5720	198.4266 6259	232.4336 2696	49
50	152.6670 8366	178.5030 2828	209.3479 9572	246.2174 7645	50

VII. AMOUNT OF ANNUITY OF 1 PER PERIOD

$$s_{\overline{n}|i} = \frac{(1 + i)^n - 1}{i}$$

n	6%	6½%	7%	8%	n
1	1.0000 0000	1.0000 0000	1.0000 0000	1.0000 0000	1
2	2.0600 0000	2.0650 0000	2.0700 0000	2.0800 0000	2
3	3.1836 0000	3.1992 2500	3.2149 0000	3.2464 0000	3
4	4.3746 1600	4.4071 7463	4.4399 4300	4.5061 1200	4
5	5.6370 9296	5.6936 4098	5.7507 3901	5.8666 0096	5
6	6.9753 1854	7.0637 2764	7.1532 9074	7.3359 2904	6
7	8.3938 3765	8.5228 6994	8.6540 2109	8.9228 0336	7
8	9.8974 6791	10.0768 5648	10.2598 0257	10.6366 2763	8
9	11.4913 1598	11.7318 5215	11.9779 8875	12.4875 5784	9
10	13.1807 9494	13.4944 2254	13.8164 4796	14.4865 6247	10
11	14.9716 4264	15.3715 6001	15.7835 9932	16.6454 8746	11
12	16.8699 4120	17.3707 1141	17.8884 5127	18.9771 2646	12
13	18.8821 3767	19.4998 0765	20.1406 4286	21.4952 9658	13
14	21.0150 6593	21.7672 9515	22.5504 8786	24.2149 2030	14
15	23.2759 6988	24.1821 6933	25.1290 2201	27.1521 1393	15
16	25.6725 2808	26.7540 1034	27.8880 5355	30.3242 8304	16
17	28.2128 7976	29.4930 2101	30.8402 1730	33.7502 2569	17
18	30.9056 5255	32.4100 6738	33.9990 3251	37.4502 4374	18
19	33.7599 9170	35.5167 2176	37.3789 6479	41.4462 6324	19
20	36.7855 9120	38.8253 0867	40.9954 9232	45.7619 6430	20
21	39.9927 2668	42.3489 5373	44.8651 7678	50.4229 2144	21
22	43.3922 9028	46.1016 3573	49.0057 3916	55.4567 5516	22
23	46.9958 2769	50.0982 4205	53.4361 4090	60.8932 9557	23
24	50.8155 7735	54.3546 2778	58.1766 7076	66.7647 5922	24
25	54.8645 1200	58.8876 7859	63.2490 3772	73.1059 3995	25
26	59.1563 8272	63.7153 7769	68.6764 7036	79.9544 1515	26
27	63.7057 6568	68.8568 7725	74.4838 2328	87.3507 6836	27
28	68.5281 1162	74.3325 7427	80.6976 9091	95.3388 2983	28
29	73.6397 9832	80.1641 9159	87.3465 2927	103.9659 3622	29
30	79.0581 8622	86.3748 6405	94.4607 8632	113.2832 1111	30
31	84.8016 7739	92.9892 3021	102.0730 4137	123.3458 6800	31
32	90.8897 7803	100.0335 3017	110.2181 5426	134.2135 3744	32
33	97.3431 6471	107.5357 0963	118.9334 2506	145.9506 2044	33
34	104.1837 5460	115.5255 3076	128.2587 6481	158.6266 7007	34
35	111.4347 7987	124.0346 9026	138.2368 7835	172.3168 0368	35
36	119.1208 6666	133.0969 4513	148.9134 5984	187.1021 4797	36
37	127.2681 1866	142.7482 4656	160.3374 0202	203.0703 1981	37
38	135.9042 0578	153.0268 8259	172.5610 2017	220.3159 4540	38
39	145.0584 5813	163.9736 2996	185.6402 9158	238.9412 2103	39
40	154.7619 6562	175.6319 1590	199.6351 1199	259.0565 1871	40
41	165.0476 8356	188.0479 9044	214.6095 6983	280.7810 4021	41
42	175.9505 4457	201.2711 0981	230.6322 3972	304.2435 2342	42
43	187.5075 7724	215.3537 3195	247.7764 9650	329.5830 0530	43
44	199.7580 3188	230.3517 2453	266.1208 5125	356.9496 4572	44
45	212.7435 1379	246.3245 8662	285.7493 1084	386.5056 1738	45
46	226.5081 2462	263.3356 8475	306.7517 6260	418.4260 6677	46
47	241.0986 1210	281.4525 0426	329.2243 8598	452.9001 5211	47
48	256.5645 2882	300.7469 1704	353.2700 9300	490.1321 6428	48
49	272.9584 0055	321.2954 6665	378.9989 9951	530.3427 3742	49
50	290.3359 0458	343.1796 7198	406.5289 2947	573.7701 5642	50

VIII. PRESENT VALUE OF ANNUITY OF 1 PER PERIOD

$$a_{\overline{n}|i} = \frac{1 - (1 + i)^{-n}}{i}$$

n	$\frac{1}{4}\%$	$\frac{7}{24}\%$	$\frac{1}{3}\%$	$\frac{3}{8}\%$	n
1	0.9975 0623	0.9970 9182	0.9966 7774	0.9962 6401	1
2	1.9925 2492	1.9912 8390	1.9900 4426	1.9888 0599	2
3	2.9850 6227	2.9825 8470	2.9801 1056	2.9776 3984	3
4	3.9751 2446	3.9710 0261	3.9668 8760	3.9627 7942	4
5	4.9627 1766	4.9565 4602	4.9503 8631	4.9442 3852	5
6	5.9478 4804	5.9392 2328	5.9306 1759	5.9220 3090	6
7	6.9305 2174	6.9190 4274	6.9075 9228	6.8961 7027	7
8	7.9107 4487	7.8960 1270	7.8813 2121	7.8666 7025	8
9	8.8885 2357	8.8701 4146	8.8518 1516	8.8335 4446	9
10	9.8638 6391	9.8414 3726	9.8190 8487	9.7968 0644	10
11	10.8367 7198	10.8099 0836	10.7831 4107	10.7564 6968	11
12	11.8072 5384	11.7755 6297	11.7439 9442	11.7125 4762	12
13	12.7753 1555	12.7384 0928	12.7016 5557	12.6650 5367	13
14	13.7409 6314	13.6984 5545	13.6561 3512	13.6140 0117	14
15	14.7042 0264	14.6557 0963	14.6074 4364	14.5594 0340	15
16	15.6650 4004	15.6101 7994	15.5555 9167	15.5012 7363	16
17	16.6234 8133	16.5618 7447	16.5005 8970	16.4396 2503	17
18	17.5795 3250	17.5108 0130	17.4424 4821	17.3744 7077	18
19	18.5331 9950	18.4569 6848	18.3811 7762	18.3058 2393	19
20	19.4844 8828	19.4003 8402	19.3167 8832	19.2336 9756	20
21	20.4334 0477	20.3410 5594	20.2492 9069	20.1581 0467	21
22	21.3799 5488	21.2789 9222	21.1786 9504	21.0790 5820	22
23	22.3241 4452	22.2142 0080	22.1050 1167	21.9965 7106	23
24	23.2659 7957	23.1466 8962	23.0282 5083	22.9106 5610	24
25	24.2054 6591	24.0764 6659	23.9484 2275	23.8213 2613	25
26	25.1426 0939	25.0035 3960	24.8655 3763	24.7285 9390	26
27	26.0774 1585	25.9279 1651	25.7796 0561	25.6324 7213	27
28	27.0098 9112	26.8496 0516	26.6906 3682	26.5329 7348	28
29	27.9400 4102	27.7686 1337	27.5986 4135	27.4301 1056	29
30	28.8678 7134	28.6849 4894	28.5036 2925	28.3238 9595	30
31	29.7933 8787	29.5986 1963	29.4056 1055	29.2143 4217	31
32	30.7165 9638	30.5096 3320	30.3045 9523	30.1014 6169	32
33	31.6375 0262	31.4179 9738	31.2005 9325	30.9852 6694	33
34	32.5561 1234	32.3237 1986	32.0936 1454	31.8657 7030	34
35	33.4724 3126	33.2268 0834	32.9836 6898	32.7429 8411	35
36	34.3864 6510	34.1272 7046	33.8707 6642	33.6169 2066	36
37	35.2982 1955	35.0251 1388	34.7549 1670	34.4875 9219	37
38	36.2077 0030	35.9203 4621	35.6361 2960	35.3550 1090	38
39	37.1149 1302	36.8129 7503	36.5144 1488	36.2191 8894	39
40	38.0198 6336	37.7030 0792	37.3897 8228	37.0801 3842	40
41	38.9225 5697	38.5904 5244	38.2622 4147	37.9378 7140	41
42	39.8229 9947	39.4753 1610	39.1318 0213	38.7923 9990	42
43	40.7211 9648	40.3576 0641	39.9984 7389	39.6437 3589	43
44	41.6171 5359	41.2373 3086	40.8622 6633	40.4918 9130	44
45	42.5108 7640	42.1144 9691	41.7231 8903	41.3368 7801	45
46	43.4023 7047	42.9891 1200	42.5812 5153	42.1787 0785	46
47	44.2916 4137	43.8611 8355	43.4364 6332	43.0173 9263	47
48	45.1786 9463	44.7307 1895	44.2888 3387	43.8529 4409	48
49	46.0635 3580	45.5977 2559	45.1383 7263	44.6853 7394	49
50	46.9461 7037	46.4622 1081	45.9850 8900	45.5146 9383	50

$$a_{\overline{n}|i} = \frac{1 - (1 + i)^{-n}}{i}$$

n	$\frac{1}{4}\%$	$\frac{7}{24}\%$	$\frac{1}{3}\%$	$\frac{3}{8}\%$	n
51	47.8266 0386	47.3241 8194	46.8289 9236	46.3409 1540	51
52	48.7048 4176	48.1836 4631	47.6700 9205	47.1640 5021	52
53	49.5808 8953	49.0406 1119	48.5083 9739	47.9841 0980	53
54	50.4547 5265	49.8950 8386	49.3439 1767	48.8011 0566	54
55	51.3264 3656	50.7470 7157	50.1766 6213	49.6150 4922	55
56	52.1959 4669	51.5965 8154	51.0066 3999	50.4259 5190	56
57	53.0632 8847	52.4436 2098	51.8338 6046	51.2338 2506	57
58	53.9284 6730	53.2881 9707	52.6583 3268	52.0386 8001	58
59	54.7914 8858	54.1303 1698	53.4800 6580	52.8405 2803	59
60	55.6523 5769	54.9699 8785	54.2990 6890	53.6393 8035	60
61	56.5110 7999	55.8072 1680	55.1153 5106	54.4352 4817	61
62	57.3676 6083	56.6420 1094	55.9289 2133	55.2281 4264	62
63	58.2221 0557	57.4743 7734	56.7397 8870	56.0180 7485	63
64	59.0744 1952	58.3043 2306	57.5479 6216	56.8050 5590	64
65	59.9246 0800	59.1318 5515	58.3534 5065	57.5890 9678	65
66	60.7726 7631	59.9569 8062	59.1562 6311	58.3702 0850	66
67	61.6186 2974	60.7797 0648	59.9564 0842	59.1484 0199	67
68	62.4624 7355	61.6000 3970	60.7538 9543	59.9236 8816	68
69	63.3042 1302	62.4179 8723	61.5487 3299	60.6960 7787	69
70	64.1438 5339	63.2335 5603	62.3409 2989	61.4655 8194	70
71	64.9813 9989	64.0467 5300	63.1304 9491	62.2322 1115	71
72	65.8168 5774	64.8575 8504	63.9174 3678	62.9959 7624	72
73	66.6502 3216	65.6660 5904	64.7017 6424	63.7568 8790	73
74	67.4815 2834	66.4721 8184	65.4834 8595	64.5149 5682	74
75	68.3107 5146	67.2759 6029	66.2626 1058	65.2701 9359	75
76	69.1379 0670	68.0774 0120	67.0391 4676	66.0226 0881	76
77	69.9629 9920	68.8765 1138	67.8131 0308	66.7722 1301	77
78	70.7860 3411	69.6732 9759	68.5844 8812	67.5190 1670	78
79	71.6070 1657	70.4677 6661	69.3533 1042	68.2630 3033	79
80	72.4259 5169	71.2599 2516	70.1195 7849	69.0042 6434	80
81	73.2428 4458	72.0497 7997	70.8833 0082	69.7427 2911	81
82	74.0577 0033	72.8373 3773	71.6444 8587	70.4784 3498	82
83	74.8705 2402	73.6226 0513	72.4031 4206	71.2113 9226	83
84	75.6813 2072	74.4055 8883	73.1592 7780	71.9416 1121	84
85	76.4900 9548	75.1862 9547	73.9129 0146	72.6691 0208	85
86	77.2968 5335	75.9647 3167	74.6640 2139	73.3938 7505	86
87	78.1015 9935	76.7409 0403	75.4126 4591	74.1159 4027	87
88	78.9043 3850	77.5148 1914	76.1587 8330	74.8353 0787	88
89	79.7050 7581	78.2864 8357	76.9024 4182	75.5519 8791	89
90	80.5038 1627	79.0559 0385	77.6436 2972	76.2659 9045	90
91	81.3005 6486	79.8230 8651	78.3823 5521	76.9773 2548	91
92	82.0953 2654	80.5880 3807	79.1186 2645	77.6860 0297	92
93	82.8881 0628	81.3507 6500	79.8524 5161	78.3920 3284	93
94	83.6789 0900	82.1112 7379	80.5838 3882	79.0954 2500	94
95	84.4677 3966	82.8695 7087	81.3127 9616	79.7961 8929	95
96	85.2546 0315	83.6256 6269	82.0393 3172	80.4943 3553	96
97	86.0395 0439	84.3795 5565	82.7634 5355	81.1898 7351	97
98	86.8224 4827	85.1312 5616	83.4851 6965	81.8828 1296	98
99	87.6034 3967	85.8807 7057	84.2044 8802	82.5731 6359	99
100	88.3824 8346	86.6281 0527	84.9214 1663	83.2609 3509	100

$$a_{\overline{n}|i} = \frac{1 - (1 + i)^{-n}}{i}$$

n	$\frac{1}{4}\%$	$\frac{7}{24}\%$	$\frac{1}{3}\%$	$\frac{3}{8}\%$	n
101	89.1595 8450	87.3732 6657	85.6359 6342	83.9461 3708	101
102	89.9347 4763	88.1162 6081	86.3481 3630	84.6287 7915	102
103	90.7079 7768	88.8570 9429	87.0579 4315	85.3088 7089	103
104	91.4792 7948	89.5957 7328	87.7653 9185	85.9864 2181	104
105	92.2486 5784	90.3323 0406	88.4704 9021	86.6614 4140	105
106	93.0161 1755	91.0666 9287	89.1732 4606	87.3339 3913	106
107	93.7816 6339	91.7989 4595	89.8736 6717	88.0039 2441	107
108	94.5453 0014	92.5290 6950	90.5717 6130	88.6714 0664	108
109	95.3070 3256	93.2570 6971	91.2675 3618	89.3363 9516	109
110	96.0668 6539	93.9829 5276	91.9609 9951	89.9988 9928	110
111	96.8248 0338	94.7067 2482	92.6521 5898	90.6589 2830	111
112	97.5808 5126	95.4283 9201	93.3410 2224	91.3164 9146	112
113	98.3350 1372	96.1479 6046	94.0275 9692	91.9715 9797	113
114	99.0872 9548	96.8654 3627	94.7118 9062	92.6242 5700	114
115	99.8377 0123	97.5808 2553	95.3939 1092	93.2744 7771	115
116	100.5862 3564	98.2941 3430	96.0736 6536	93.9222 6920	116
117	101.3329 0338	99.0053 6864	96.7511 6149	94.5676 4055	117
118	102.0777 0911	99.7145 3458	97.4264 0680	95.2106 0080	118
119	102.8206 5747	100.4216 3814	98.0994 0877	95.8511 5895	119
120	103.5617 5308	101.1266 8531	98.7701 7486	96.4893 2399	120
121	104.3010 0058	101.8296 8207	99.4387 1248	97.1251 0484	121
122	105.0384 0457	102.5306 3438	100.1050 2905	97.7585 1043	122
123	105.7739 6965	103.2295 4820	100.7691 3195	98.3895 4962	123
124	106.5077 0040	103.9264 2945	101.4310 2852	99.0182 3125	124
125	107.2396 0139	104.6212 8404	102.0907 2610	99.6445 6414	125
126	107.9696 7720	105.3141 1786	102.7482 3199	100.2685 5705	126
127	108.6979 3237	106.0049 3679	103.4035 5348	100.8902 1873	127
128	109.4243 7144	106.6937 4670	104.0566 9782	101.5095 5788	128
129	110.1489 9894	107.3805 5342	104.7076 7225	102.1265 8320	129
130	110.8718 1939	108.0653 6278	105.3564 8397	102.7413 0331	130
131	111.5928 3730	108.7481 8058	106.0031 4016	103.3537 2683	131
132	112.3120 5716	109.4290 1263	106.6476 4800	103.9638 6235	132
133	113.0294 8345	110.1078 6469	107.2900 1462	104.5717 1841	133
134	113.7451 2065	110.7847 4253	107.9302 4713	105.1773 0352	134
135	114.4589 7321	111.4596 5187	108.5683 5262	105.7806 2617	135
136	115.1710 4560	112.1325 9846	109.2043 3816	106.3816 9481	136
137	115.8813 4224	112.8035 8800	109.8382 1079	106.9805 1787	137
138	116.5898 6758	113.4726 2617	110.4699 7754	107.5771 0373	138
139	117.2966 2601	114.1397 1866	111.0996 4538	108.1714 6076	139
140	118.0016 2196	114.8048 7112	111.7272 2131	108.7635 9727	140
141	118.7048 5981	115.4680 8919	112.3527 1227	109.3535 2156	141
142	119.4063 4395	116.1293 7850	112.9761 2519	109.9412 4190	142
143	120.1060 7875	116.7887 4466	113.5974 6696	110.5267 6653	143
144	120.8040 6858	117.4461 9327	114.2167 4448	111.1101 0364	144
145	121.5003 1778	118.1017 2989	114.8339 6460	111.6912 6141	145
146	122.1948 3071	118.7553 6009	115.4491 3415	112.2702 4798	146
147	122.8876 1168	119.4070 8941	116.0622 5995	112.8470 7146	147
148	123.5786 6502	120.0569 2338	116.6733 4879	113.4217 3994	148
149	124.2679 9503	120.7048 6752	117.2824 0743	113.9942 6146	149
150	124.9556 0601	121.3509 2732	117.8894 4262	114.5646 4404	150

VIII. PRESENT VALUE OF ANNUITY OF 1 PER PERIOD

$$a_{\overline{n}|i} = \frac{1 - (1 + i)^{-n}}{i}$$

n	$\frac{1}{4}\%$	$\frac{7}{24}\%$	$\frac{1}{3}\%$	$\frac{3}{8}\%$	n
151	125.6415 0226	121.9951 0825	118.4944 6109	115.1328 9568	151
152	126.3256 8804	122.6374 1579	119.0974 6952	115.6990 2434	152
153	127.0081 6762	123.2778 5538	119.6984 7461	116.2630 3795	153
154	127.6889 4525	123.9164 3245	120.2974 8300	116.8249 4441	154
155	128.3680 2519	124.5531 5242	120.8945 0133	117.3847 5159	155
156	129.0454 1166	125.1880 2069	121.4895 3621	117.9424 6734	156
157	129.7211 0889	125.8210 4265	122.0825 9422	118.4980 9946	157
158	130.3951 2109	126.4522 2367	122.6736 8195	119.0516 5575	158
159	131.0674 5246	127.0815 6909	123.2628 0593	119.6031 4396	159
160	131.7381 0719	127.7090 8426	123.8499 7269	120.1525 7182	160
161	132.4070 8946	128.3347 7450	124.4351 8873	120.6999 4702	161
162	133.0744 0346	128.9586 4512	125.0184 6053	121.2452 7723	162
163	133.7400 5332	129.5807 0141	125.5997 9454	121.7885 7009	163
164	134.4040 4321	130.2009 4864	126.1791 9722	122.3298 3322	164
165	135.0663 7727	130.8193 9208	126.7566 7497	122.8690 7419	165
166	135.7270 5962	131.4360 3697	127.3322 3419	123.4063 0056	166
167	136.3860 9439	132.0508 8855	127.9058 8125	123.9415 1986	167
168	137.0434 8567	132.6639 5202	128.4776 2251	124.4747 3959	168
169	137.6992 3758	133.2752 3259	129.0474 6430	125.0059 6721	169
170	138.3533 5419	133.8847 3545	129.6154 1292	125.5352 1017	170
171	139.0058 3959	134.4924 6576	130.1814 7467	126.0624 7589	171
172	139.6566 9785	135.0984 2867	130.7456 5582	126.5877 7174	172
173	140.3059 3302	135.7026 2934	131.3079 6261	127.1111 0510	173
174	140.9535 4914	136.3050 7287	131.8684 0127	127.6324 8329	174
175	141.5995 5027	136.9057 6439	132.4269 7801	128.1519 1361	175
176	142.2439 4042	137.5047 0899	132.9837 9901	128.6694 0335	176
177	142.8867 2361	138.1019 1175	133.5385 7045	129.1849 5975	177
178	143.5279 0385	138.6973 7773	134.0915 9845	129.6985 9004	178
179	144.1674 8514	139.2911 1199	134.6427 8915	130.2103 0141	179
180	144.8054 7146	139.8831 1956	135.1921 4866	130.7201 0103	180
181	145.4418 6679	140.4734 0546	135.7396 8305	131.2279 9604	181
182	146.0766 7510	141.0619 7470	136.2853 9839	131.7339 9357	182
183	146.7099 0035	141.6488 3227	136.8293 0072	132.2381 0069	183
184	147.3415 4649	142.2339 8315	137.3713 9606	132.7403 2447	184
185	147.9716 1744	142.8174 3231	137.9116 9043	133.2406 7195	185
186	148.6001 1715	143.3991 8469	138.4501 8980	133.7391 5014	186
187	149.2270 4952	143.9792 4522	138.9869 0013	134.2357 6602	187
188	149.8524 1848	144.5576 1883	139.5218 2737	134.7305 2654	188
189	150.4762 2791	145.1343 1043	140.0549 7745	135.2234 3865	189
190	151.0984 8170	145.7093 2490	140.5863 5626	135.7145 0924	190
191	151.7191 8375	146.2826 6712	141.1159 6969	136.2037 4519	191
192	152.3383 3790	146.8543 4195	141.6438 2362	136.6911 5337	192
193	152.9559 4803	147.4243 5425	142.1699 2387	137.1767 4059	193
194	153.5720 1799	147.9927 0885	142.6942 7628	137.6605 1367	194
195	154.1865 5161	148.5594 1057	143.2168 8666	138.1424 7937	195
196	154.7995 5272	149.1244 6422	143.7377 6079	138.6226 4445	196
197	155.4110 2516	149.6878 7458	144.2569 0444	139.1010 1564	197
198	156.0209 7273	150.2496 4645	144.7743 2336	139.5775 9964	198
199	156.6293 9923	150.8097 8458	145.2900 2339	140.0524 0313	199
200	157.2363 0846	151.3682 9372	145.8040 0992	140.5254 3276	200

VIII. PRESENT VALUE OF ANNUITY OF 1 PER PERIOD

$$a_{\overline{n}|i} = \frac{1 - (1 + i)^{-n}}{i}$$

n	$\frac{1}{4}\%$	$\frac{7}{24}\%$	$\frac{1}{3}\%$	$\frac{3}{8}\%$	n
201	157.8417 0420	151.9251 7862	146.3162 8896	140.9966 9515	201
202	158.4455 9022	152.4804 4399	146.8268 6607	141.4661 9691	202
203	159.0479 7030	153.0340 9455	147.3357 4691	141.9339 4462	203
204	159.6488 4818	153.5861 3499	147.8429 3712	142.3999 4483	204
205	160.2482 2761	154.1365 6999	148.3484 4232	142.8642 0406	205
206	160.8461 1233	154.6854 0423	148.8522 6809	143.3267 2883	206
207	161.4425 0606	155.2326 4235	149.3544 2002	143.7875 2561	207
208	162.0374 1253	155.7782 8901	149.8549 0368	144.2466 0086	208
209	162.6308 3544	156.3223 4883	150.3537 2459	144.7039 6100	209
210	163.2227 7850	156.8648 2642	150.8508 8830	145.1596 1246	210
211	163.8132 4538	157.4057 2638	151.3464 0030	145.6135 6160	211
212	164.4022 3978	157.9450 5331	151.8402 6608	146.0658 1479	212
213	164.9897 6537	158.4828 1177	152.3324 9111	146.5163 7838	213
214	165.5758 2581	159.0190 0634	152.8230 8084	146.9652 5866	214
215	166.1604 2474	159.5536 4155	153.3120 4070	147.4124 6192	215
216	166.7435 6583	160.0867 2195	153.7993 7612	147.8579 9444	216
217	167.3252 5270	160.6182 5204	154.2850 9247	148.3018 6246	217
218	167.9054 8898	161.1482 3635	154.7691 9516	148.7440 7219	218
219	168.4842 7828	161.6766 7937	155.2516 8953	149.1846 2983	219
220	169 0616 2422	162.2035 8558	155.7325 8092	149.6235 4155	220
221	169.6375 3039	162.7289 5945	156.2118 7467	150.0608 1350	221
222	170.2120 0039	163.2528 0543	156.6895 7609	150.4964 5180	222
223	170.7850 3780	163.7751 2798	157.1656 9045	150.9304 6257	223
224	171.3566 4618	164.2959 3151	157.6402 2304	151.3628 5187	224
225	171.9268 2911	164.8152 2045	158 1131 7911	151.7936 2578	225
226	172.4955 9013	165.3329 9920	158.5845 6390	152.2227 9031	226
227	173.0629 3280	165.8492 7216	159.0543 8262	152.6503 5149	227
228	173.6288 6065	166.3640 4370	159.5226 4049	153.0763 1531	228
229	174.1933 7721	166.8773 1819	159.9893 4268	153.5006 8773	229
230	174.7564 8599	167.3890 9998	160.4544 9436	153.9234 7470	230
231	175.3181 9052	167.8993 9341	160.9181 0070	154.3446 8214	231
232	175.8784 9428	168.4082 0282	161.3801 6681	154.7643 1596	232
233	176.4374 0078	168.9155 3252	161.8406 9781	155.1823 8203	233
234	176.9949 1350	169.4213 8681	162.2996 9882	155.5988 8620	234
235	177.5510 3591	169.9257 6998	162.7571 7490	156.0138 3432	235
236	178.1057 7148	170.4286 8631	163.2131 3113	156.4272 3220	236
237	178.6591 2367	170.9301 4007	163.6675 7256	156.8390 8563	237
238	179.2110 9593	171.4301 3551	164.1205 0421	157.2494 0038	238
239	179.7616 9170	171.9286 7687	164.5719 3110	157.6581 8220	239
240	180.3109 1441	172.4257 6838	165.0218 5824	158.0654 3681	240
241	180.8587 6749	172.9214 1425	165.4702 9061	158.4711 6992	241
242	181.4052 5436	173.4156 1870	165.9172 3316	158.8753 8722	242
243	181.9503 7841	173.9083 8590	166.3626 9086	159.2780 9437	243
244	182.4941 4305	174.3997 2005	166.8066 6863	159.6792 9700	244
245	183.0365 5168	174.8896 2531	167.2491 7139	160.0790 0075	245
246	183.5776 0766	175.3781 0584	167.6902 0405	160.4772 1121	246
247	184.1173 1437	175.8651 6577	168.1297 7148	160.8739 3396	247
248	184.6556 7518	176.3508 0924	168.5678 7855	161.2691 7455	248
249	185.1926 9345	176.8350 4038	169.0045 3011	161.6629 3853	249
250	185.7283 7252	177.3178 6327	169.4397 3101	162.0552 3141	250

VIII. PRESENT VALUE OF ANNUITY OF 1 PER PERIOD

$$a_{\overline{n}|i} = \frac{1 - (1 + i)^{-n}}{i}$$

n	$\frac{5}{12}\%$	$\frac{1}{2}\%$	$\frac{7}{12}\%$	$\frac{5}{8}\%$	n
1	0.9958 5062	0.9950 2488	0.9942 0050	0.9937 8882	1
2	1.9875 6908	1.9850 9938	1.9826 3513	1.9814 0504	2
3	2.9751 7253	2.9702 4814	2.9653 3732	2.9628 8699	3
4	3.9586 7804	3.9504 9566	3.9423 4034	3.9382 7279	4
5	4.9381 0261	4.9258 6633	4.9136 7722	4.9076 0029	5
6	5.9134 6318	5.8963 8441	5.8793 8083	5.8709 0712	6
7	6.8847 7661	6.8620 7404	6.8394 8384	6.8282 3068	7
8	7.8520 5970	7.8229 5924	7.7940 1874	7.7796 0813	8
9	8.8153 2916	8.7790 6392	8.7430 1780	8.7250 7640	9
10	9.7746 0165	9.7304 1186	9.6865 1314	9.6646 7220	10
11	10.7298 9376	10.6770 2673	10.6245 3667	10.5984 3200	11
12	11.6812 2200	11.6189 3207	11.5571 2014	11.5263 9205	12
13	12.6286 0283	12.5561 5131	12.4842 9509	12.4485 8837	13
14	13.5720 5261	13.4887 0777	13.4060 9288	13.3650 5676	14
15	14.5115 8766	14.4166 2465	14.3225 4470	14.2758 3281	15
16	15.4472 2422	15.3399 2502	15.2336 8156	15.1809 5186	16
17	16.3789 7848	16.2586 3186	16.1395 3427	16.0804 4905	17
18	17.3068 6654	17.1727 6802	17.0401 3350	16.9743 5931	18
19	18.2309 0443	18.0823 5624	17.9355 0969	17.8627 1733	19
20	19.1511 0815	18.9874 1915	18.8256 9315	18.7455 5759	20
21	20.0674 9359	19.8879 7925	19.7107 1398	19.6229 1438	21
22	20.9800 7661	20.7840 5896	20.5906 0213	20.4948 2174	22
23	21.8888 7297	21.6756 8055	21.4653 8738	21.3613 1353	23
24	22.7938 9839	22.5628 6622	22.3350 9930	22.2224 2338	24
25	23.6951 6853	23.4456 3803	23.1997 6732	23.0781 8473	25
26	24.5926 9895	24.3240 1794	24.0594 2070	23.9286 3079	26
27	25.4865 0517	25.1980 2780	24.9140 8852	24.7737 9457	27
28	26.3766 0266	26.0676 8936	25.7637 9968	25.6137 0889	28
29	27.2630 0680	26.9330 2423	26.6085 8295	26.4484 0635	29
30	28.1457 3291	27.7940 5397	27.4484 6689	27.2779 1935	30
31	29.0247 9626	28.6507 9997	28.2834 7993	28.1022 8010	31
32	29.9002 1205	29.5032 8355	29.1136 5030	28.9215 2060	32
33	30.7719 9540	30.3515 2592	29.9390 0610	29.7356 7265	33
34	31.6401 6139	31.1955 4818	30.7595 7524	30.5447 6785	34
35	32.5047 2504	32.0353 7132	31.5753 8549	31.3488 3761	35
36	33.3657 0128	32.8710 1624	32.3864 6445	32.1479 1315	36
37	34.2231 0501	33.7025 0372	33.1928 3955	32.9420 2550	37
38	35.0769 5105	34.5298 5445	33.9945 3808	33.7312 0546	38
39	35.9272 5416	35.3530 8900	34.7915 8716	34.5154 8369	39
40	36.7740 2904	36.1722 2786	35.5840 1374	35.2948 9062	40
41	37.6172 9033	36.9872 9141	36.3718 4465	36.0694 5652	41
42	38.4570 5261	37.7982 9991	37.1551 0653	36.8392 1145	42
43	39.2933 3040	38.6052 7354	37.9338 2588	37.6041 8529	43
44	40.1261 3816	39.4082 3238	38.7080 2904	38.3644 0774	44
45	40.9554 9028	40.2071 9640	39.4777 4221	39.1199 0831	45
46	41.7814 0111	41.0021 8547	40.2429 9143	39.8707 1634	46
47	42.6038 8492	41.7932 1937	41.0038 0258	40.6168 6096	47
48	43.4229 5594	42.5803 1778	41.7602 0141	41.3583 7114	48
49	44.2386 2832	43.3635 0028	42.5122 1349	42.0952 7566	49
50	45.0509 1617	44.1427 8635	43.2598 6428	42.8276 0314	50

VIII. PRESENT VALUE OF ANNUITY OF 1 PER PERIOD

$$a_{\overline{n}|i} = \frac{1 - (1 + i)^{-n}}{i}$$

n	$\frac{5}{12}\%$	$\frac{1}{2}\%$	$\frac{7}{12}\%$	$\frac{5}{8}\%$	n
51	45.8598 3353	44.9181 9537	44.0031 7907	43.5553 8201	51
52	46.6653 9439	45.6897 4664	44.7421 8301	44.2786 4050	52
53	47.4676 1267	46.4574 5934	45.4769 0108	44.9974 0671	53
54	48.2665 0224	47.2213 5258	46.2073 5816	45.7117 0853	54
55	49.0620 7692	47.9814 4535	46.9335 7995	46.4215 7370	55
56	49.8543 5046	48.7377 5657	47.6555 8802	47.1270 2976	56
57	50.6433 3656	49.4903 0505	48.3734 0980	47.8281 0410	57
58	51.4290 4885	50.2391 0950	49.0870 6856	48.5248 2396	58
59	52.2115 0093	50.9841 8855	49.7965 8846	49.2172 1636	59
60	52.9907 0632	51.7255 6075	50.5019 9350	49.9053 0818	60
61	53.7666 7850	52.4632 4453	51.2033 0754	50.5891 2614	61
62	54.5394 3087	53.1972 5824	51.9005 5431	51.2686 9679	62
63	55.3089 7680	53.9276 2014	52.5937 5739	51.9440 4650	63
64	56.0753 2959	54.6543 4839	53.2829 4024	52.6152 0149	64
65	56.8385 0250	55.3774 6109	53.9681 2617	53.2821 8781	65
66	57.5985 0871	56.0969 7621	54.6493 3836	53.9450 3137	66
67	58.3553 6137	56.8129 1165	55.3265 9986	54.6037 5788	67
68	59.1090 7357	57.5252 8522	55.9999 3358	55.2583 9293	68
69	59.8596 5832	58.2341 1465	56.6693 6230	55.9089 6191	69
70	60.6071 2862	58.9394 1756	57.3349 0867	56.5554 9010	70
71	61.3514 9738	59.6412 1151	57.9965 9520	57.1980 0258	71
72	62.0927 7748	60.3395 1394	58.6544 4427	57.8365 2431	72
73	62.8309 8172	61.0343 4222	59.3084 7815	58.4710 8006	73
74	63.5661 2287	61.7257 1366	59.9587 1896	59.1016 9447	74
75	64.2982 1365	62.4136 4543	60.6051 8869	59.7283 9201	75
76	65.0272 6670	63.0981 5466	61.2479 0922	60.3511 9703	76
77	65.7532 9464	63.7792 5836	61.8869 0229	60.9701 3370	77
78	66.4763 1002	64.4569 7349	62.5221 8952	61.5852 2604	78
79	67.1963 2533	65.1313 1691	63.1537 9239	62.1964 9792	79
80	67.9133 5303	65.8023 0538	63.7817 3229	62.8039 7309	80
81	68.6274 0550	66.4699 5561	64.4060 3044	63.4076 7512	81
82	69.3384 9511	67.1342 8419	65.0267 0798	64.0076 2745	82
83	70.0466 3413	67.7953 0765	65.6437 8590	64.6038 5337	83
84	70.7518 3482	68.4530 4244	66.2572 8507	65.1963 7602	84
85	71.4541 0936	69.1075 0491	66.8672 2625	65.7852 1840	85
86	72.1534 6991	69.7587 1135	67.4736 3007	66.3704 0338	86
87	72.8499 2854	70.4066 7796	68.0765 1706	66.9519 5367	87
88	73.5434 9730	71.0514 2086	68.6759 0759	67.5298 9185	88
89	74.2341 8818	71.6929 5608	69.2718 2197	68.1042 4034	89
90	74.9220 1313	72.3312 9958	69.8642 8033	68.6750 2146	90
91	75.6069 8403	72.9664 6725	70.4533 0273	69.2422 5735	91
92	76.2891 1272	73.5984 7487	71.0389 0910	69.8059 7004	92
93	76.9684 1101	74.2273 3818	71.6211 1923	70.3661 8141	93
94	77.6448 9063	74.8530 7282	72.1999 5284	70.9229 1320	94
95	78.3185 6329	75.4756 9434	72.7754 2950	71.4761 8703	95
96	78.9894 4062	76.0952 1825	73.3475 6869	72.0260 2438	96
97	79.6575 3422	76.7116 5995	73.9163 8975	72.5724 4658	97
98	80.3228 5566	77.3250 3478	74.4819 1193	73.1154 7487	98
99	80.9854 1642	77.9353 5799	75.0441 5436	73.6551 3030	99
100	81.6452 2797	78.5426 4477	75.6031 3606	74.1914 3384	100

$$a_{\overline{n}|i} = \frac{1 - (1 + i)^{-n}}{i}$$

n	$\frac{5}{12}\%$	$\frac{1}{2}\%$	$\frac{7}{12}\%$	$\frac{5}{8}\%$	n
101	82.3023 0172	79.1469 1021	76.1588 7596	74.7244 0630	101
102	82.9566 4901	79.7481 6937	76.7113 9283	75.2540 6838	102
103	83.6082 8117	80.3464 3718	77.2607 0538	75.7804 4062	103
104	84.2572 0947	80.9417 2854	77.8068 3219	76.3035 4348	104
105	84.9034 4511	81.5340 5825	78.3497 9174	76.8233 9724	105
106	85.5469 9928	82.1234 4104	78.8896 0240	77.3400 2210	106
107	86.1878 8310	82.7098 9158	79.4262 8241	77.8534 3812	107
108	86.8261 0765	83.2934 2446	79.9598 4996	78.3636 6521	108
109	87.4616 8397	83.8740 5419	80.4903 2307	78.8707 2319	109
110	88.0946 2304	84.4517 9522	81.0177 1971	79.3746 3174	110
111	88.7249 3581	85.0266 6191	81.5420 5770	79.8754 1043	111
112	89.3526 3317	85.5986 6856	82.0633 5480	80.3730 7868	112
113	89.9777 2598	86.1678 2942	82.5816 2863	80.8676 5583	113
114	90.6002 2504	86.7341 5862	83.0968 9674	81.3591 6108	114
115	91.2201 4112	87.2976 7027	83.6091 7654	81.8476 1349	115
116	91.8374 8493	87.8583 7838	84.1184 8537	82.3330 3204	116
117	92.4522 6715	88.4162 9690	84.6248 4047	82.8154 3557	117
118	93.0644 9841	88.9714 3970	85.1282 5896	83.2948 4280	118
119	93.6741 8929	89.5238 2059	85.6287 5787	83.7712 7235	119
120	94.2813 5033	90.0734 5333	86.1263 5414	84.2447 4271	120
121	94.8859 9203	90.6203 5157	86.6210 6460	84.7152 7226	121
122	95.4881 2484	91.1645 2892	87.1129 0598	85.1828 7926	122
123	96.0877 5918	91.7059 9893	87.6018 9493	85.6475 8188	123
124	96.6849 0541	92.2447 7505	88.0880 4798	86.1093 9814	124
125	97.2795 7385	92.7808 7070	88.5713 8159	86.5683 4597	125
126	97.8717 7479	93.3142 9921	89.0519 1210	87.0244 4320	126
127	98.4615 1846	93.8450 7384	89.5296 5577	87.4777 0753	127
128	99.0488 1506	94.3732 0780	90.0046 2877	87.9281 5655	128
129	99.6336 7475	94.8987 1423	90.4768 4716	88.3758 0776	129
130	100.2161 0764	95.4216 0619	90.9463 2692	88.8206 7852	130
131	100.7961 2379	95.9418 9671	91.4130 8393	89.2627 8610	131
132	101.3737 3323	96.4595 9872	91.8771 3399	89.7021 4768	132
133	101.9489 4596	96.9747 2509	92.3384 9278	90.1387 8030	133
134	102.5217 7191	97.4872 8865	92.7971 7592	90.5727 0092	134
135	103.0922 2099	97.9973 0214	93.2531 9893	91.0039 2638	135
136	103.6603 0306	98.5047 7825	93.7065 7722	91.4324 7342	136
137	104.2260 2794	99.0097 2960	94.1573 2616	91.8583 5868	137
138	104.7894 0542	99.5121 6876	94.6054 6097	92.2815 9869	138
139	105.3504 4523	100.0121 0821	95.0509 9682	92.7022 0988	139
140	105.9091 5708	100.5095 6041	95.4939 4878	93.1202 0857	140
141	106.4655 5061	101.0045 3772	95.9343 3185	93.5356 1100	141
142	107.0196 3547	101.4970 5246	96.3721 6091	93.9484 3330	142
143	107.5714 2121	101.9871 1688	96.8074 5078	94.3586 9148	143
144	108.1209 1739	102.4747 4316	97.2402 1619	94.7664 0147	144
145	108.6681 3350	102.9599 4344	97.6704 7177	95.1715 7910	145
146	109.2130 7900	103.4427 2979	98.0982 3208	95.5742 4010	146
147	109.7557 6332	103.9231 1422	98.5235 1160	95.9744 0010	147
148	110.2961 9584	104.4011 0868	98.9463 2470	96.3720 7463	148
149	110.8343 8590	104.8767 2506	99.3666 8570	96.7672 7913	149
150	111.3703 4280	105.3499 7518	99.7846 0882	97.1600 2895	150

$$a_{\overline{n}|i} = \frac{1 - (1 + i)^{-n}}{i}$$

n	$\frac{5}{12}\%$	$\frac{1}{2}\%$	$\frac{7}{12}\%$	$\frac{5}{8}\%$	n
151	111.9040 7582	105.8208 7083	100.2001 0819	97.5503 3933	151
152	112.4355 9418	106.2894 2371	100.6131 9786	97.9382 2542	152
153	112.9649 0707	106.7556 4548	101.0238 9183	98.3237 0228	153
154	113.4920 2364	107.2195 4774	101.4322 0397	98.7067 8488	154
155	114.0169 5300	107.6811 4203	101.8381 4811	99.0874 8808	155
156	114.5397 0423	108.1404 3983	102.2417 3797	99.4658 2666	156
157	115.0602 8637	108.5974 5257	102.6429 8721	99.8418 1532	157
158	115.5787 0842	109.0521 9161	103.0419 0941	100.2154 6864	158
159	116.0949 7934	109.5046 6827	103.4385 1805	100.5868 0113	159
160	116.6091 0805	109.9548 9380	103.8328 2656	100.9558 2721	160
161	117.1211 0346	110.4028 7940	104.2248 4828	101.3225 6120	161
162	117.6309 7440	110.8486 3622	104.6145 9647	101.6870 1734	162
163	118.1387 2969	111.2921 7535	105.0020 8431	102.0492 0978	163
164	118.6443 7811	111.7335 0781	105.3873 2491	102.4091 5258	164
165	119.1479 2841	112.1726 4458	105.7703 3132	102.7668 5971	165
166	119.6493 8929	112.6095 9660	106.1511 1647	103.1223 4505	166
167	120.1487 6942	113.0443 7473	106.5296 9326	103.4756 2241	167
168	120.6460 7743	113.4769 8978	106.9060 7449	103.8267 0550	168
169	121.1413 2192	113.9074 5252	107.2802 7290	104.1756 0795	169
170	121.6345 1146	114.3357 7365	107.6523 0114	104.5223 4330	170
171	122.1256 5456	114.7619 6383	108.0221 7181	104.8669 2502	171
172	122.6147 5973	115.1860 3366	108.3898 9741	105.2093 6648	172]
173	123.1018 3542	115.6079 9369	108.7554 9038	105.5496 8098	173
174	123.5868 9004	116.0278 5442	109.1189 6309	105.8878 8172	174
175	124.0699 3199	116.4456 2629	109.4803 2785	106.2239 8183	175
176	124.5509 6962	116.8613 1969	109.8395 9687	106.5579 9436	176
177	125.0300 1124	117.2749 4496	110.1967 8230	106.8899 3229	177
178	125.5070 6513	117.6865 1240	110.5518 9624	107.2198 0848	178
179	125.9821 3955	118.0960 3224	110.9049 5070	107.5476 3576	179
180	126.4552 4271	118.5035 1467	111.2559 5761	107.8734 2684	180
181	126.9263 8278	118.9089 6982	111.6049 2886	108.1971 9438	181
182	127.3955 6791	119.3124 0778	111.9518 7625	108.5189 5094	182
183	127.8628 0622	119.7138 3859	112.2968 1151	108.8387 0900	183
184	128.3281 0578	120.1132 7223	112.6397 4633	109.1564 8100	184
185	128.7914 7463	120.5107 1863	112.9806 9229	109.4722 7925	185
186	129.2529 2080	120.9061 8769	113.3196 6093	109.7861 1603	186
187	129.7124 5225	121.2996 8925	113.6566 6373	110.0980 0351	187
188	130.1700 7693	121.6912 3308	113.9917 1207	110.4079 5379	188
189	130.6258 0275	122.0808 2894	114.3248 1731	110.7159 7893	189
190	131.0796 3759	122.4684 8651	114.6559 9069	111.0220 9086	190
191	131.5315 8930	122.8542 1543	114.9852 4344	111.3263 0147	191
192	131.9816 6570	123.2380 2530	115.3125 8668	111.6286 2258	192
193	132.4298 7455	123.6199 2567	115.6380 3150	111.9290 6592	193
194	132.8762 2362	123.9999 2604	115.9615 8890	112.2276 4315	194
195	133.3207 2062	124.3780 3586	116.2832 6982	112.5243 6586	195
196	133.7633 7323	124.7542 6454	116.6030 8516	112.8192 4558	196
197	134.2041 8911	125.1286 2143	116.9210 4573	113.1122 9374	197
198	134.6431 7587	125.5011 1585	117.2371 6228	113.4035 2173	198
199	135.0803 4112	125.8717 5707	117.5514 4552	113.6929 4085	199
200	135.5156 9240	126.2405 5430	117.8639 0606	113.9805 6234	200

$$a_{\overline{n}|i} = \frac{1 - (1 + i)^{-n}}{i}$$

n	$\frac{5}{12}\%$	$\frac{1}{2}\%$	$\frac{7}{12}\%$	$\frac{5}{8}\%$	n
201	135.9492 3725	126.6075 1671	118.1745 5450	114.2663 9735	201
202	136.3809 8315	126.9726 5345	118.4834 0132	114.5504 5700	202
203	136.8109 3758	127.3359 7358	118.7904 5699	114.8327 5230	203
204	137.2391 0796	127.6974 8615	119.0957 3189	115.1132 9421	204
205	137.6655 0170	128.0572 0015	119.3992 3634	115.3920 9362	205
206	138.0901 2618	128.4151 2452	119.7009 8062	115.6691 6136	206
207	138.5129 8872	128.7712 6818	120.0009 7493	115.9445 0819	207
208	138.9340 9665	129.1256 3998	120.2992 2943	116.2181 4478	208
209	139.3534 5725	129.4782 4874	120.5957 5420	116.4900 8177	209
210	139.7710 7776	129.8291 0322	120.8905 5927	116.7603 2971	210
211	140.1869 6540	130.1782 1216	121.1836 5461	117.0288 9909	211
212	140.6011 2737	130.5255 8424	121.4750 5016	117.2958 0034	212
213	141.0135 7083	130.8712 2810	121.7647 5575	117.5610 4382	213
214	141.4243 0290	131.2151 5234	122.0527 8119	117.8246 3982	214
215	141.8333 3069	131.5573 6551	122.3391 3623	118.0865 9858	215
216	142.2406 6127	131.8978 7613	122.6238 3055	118.3469 3026	216
217	142.6463 0167	132.2366 9267	122.9068 7379	118.6056 4498	217
218	143.0502 5893	132.5738 2355	123.1882 7551	118.8627 5278	218
219	143.4525 4001	132.9092 7716	123.4680 4525	119.1182 6363	219
220	143.8531 5188	133.2430 6186	123.7461 9246	119.3721 8746	220
221	144.2521 0146	133.5751 8593	124.0227 2655	119.6245 3412	221
222	144.6493 9564	133.9056 5764	124.2976 5689	119.8753 1341	222
223	145.0450 4130	134.2344 8521	124.5709 9276	120.1245 3507	223
224	145.4390 4528	134.5616 7683	124.8427 4343	120.3722 0876	224
225	145.8314 1439	134.8872 4062	125.1129 1807	120.6183 4411	225
226	146.2221 5541	135.2111 8470	125.3815 2584	120.8629 5067	226
227	146.6112 7509	135.5335 1712	125.6485 7581	121.1060 3793	227
228	146.9987 8018	135.8542 4589	125.9140 7703	121.3476 1534	228
229	147.3846 7735	136.1733 7899	126.1780 3847	121.5876 9226	229
230	147.7689 7330	136.4909 2437	126.4404 6907	121.8262 7802	230
231	148.1516 7465	136.8068 8992	126.7013 7770	122.0633 8188	231
232	148.5327 8804	137.1212 8350	126.9607 7319	122.2990 1305	232
233	148.9123 2004	137.4341 1294	127.2186 6431	122.5331 8067	233
234	149.2902 7722	137.7453 8601	127.4750 5980	122.7658 9384	234
235	149.6666 6611	138.0551 1045	127.7299 6832	122.9971 6158	235
236	150.0414 9322	138.3632 9398	127.9833 9849	123.2269 9287	236
237	150.4147 6503	138.6699 4426	128.2353 5890	123.4553 9664	237
238	150.7864 8800	138.9750 6892	128.4858 5806	123.6823 8176	238
239	151.1566 6855	139.2786 7554	128.7349 0445	123.9079 5703	239
240	151.5253 1307	139.5807 7168	128.9825 0650	124.1321 3121	240
241	151.8924 2796	139.8813 6486	129.2286 7257	124.3549 1300	241
242	152.2580 1954	140.1804 6255	129.4734 1101	124.5763 1105	242
243	152.6220 9415	140.4780 7218	129.7167 3008	124.7963 3397	243
244	152.9846 5808	140.7742 0118	129.9586 3803	125.0149 9028	244
245	153.3457 1759	141.0688 5689	130.1991 4303	125.2322 8848	245
246	153.7052 7892	141.3620 4666	130.4382 5322	125.4482 3699	246
247	154.0633 4831	141.6537 7777	130.6759 7669	125.6628 4422	247
248	154.4199 3192	141.9440 5748	130.9123 2148	125.8761 1848	248
249	154.7750 3594	142.2328 9302	131.1472 9559	126.0880 6805	249
250	155.1286 6650	142.5202 9156	131.3809 0696	126.2987 0117	250

$$a_{\overline{n}|i} = \frac{1 - (1 + i)^{-n}}{i}$$

n	$\frac{3}{4}\%$	$\frac{7}{8}\%$	1%	$1\frac{1}{8}\%$	n
1	0.9925 5583	0.9913 2590	0.9900 9901	0.9888 7515	1
2	1.9777 2291	1.9740 5294	1.9703 9506	1.9667 4923	2
3	2.9555 5624	2.9482 5570	2.9409 8521	2.9337 4460	3
4	3.9261 1041	3.9140 0813	3.9019 6555	3.8899 8230	4
5	4.8894 3961	4.8713 8352	4.8534 3124	4.8355 8200	5
6	5.8455 9763	5.8204 5454	5.7954 7647	5.7706 6205	6
7	6.7946 3785	6.7612 9323	6.7281 9453	6.6953 3948	7
8	7.7366 1325	7.6939 7098	7.6516 7775	7.6097 3002	8
9	8.6715 7642	8.6185 5859	8.5660 1758	8.5139 4810	9
10	9.5995 7958	9.5351 2624	9.4713 0453	9.4081 0690	10
11	10.5206 7452	10.4437 4348	10.3676 2825	10.2923 1832	11
12	11.4349 1267	11.3444 7929	11.2550 7747	11.1666 9302	12
13	12.3423 4508	12.2374 0202	12.1337 4007	12.0313 4044	13
14	13.2430 2242	13.1225 7945	13.0037 0304	12.8863 6880	14
15	14.1369 9495	14.0000 7876	13.8650 5252	13.7318 8509	15
16	15.0243 1261	14.8699 6656	14.7178 7378	14.5679 9514	16
17	15.9050 2492	15.7323 0885	15.5622 5127	15.3948 0360	17
18	16.7791 8107	16.5871 7111	16.3982 6858	16.2124 1395	18
19	17.6468 2984	17.4346 1820	17.2260 0850	17.0209 2850	19
20	18.5080 1969	18.2747 1445	18.0455 5297	17.8204 4845	20
21	19.3627 9870	19.1075 2361	18.8569 8313	18.6110 7387	21
22	20.2112 1459	19.9331 0891	19.6603 7934	19.3929 0371	22
23	21.0533 1473	20.7515 3300	20.4558 2113	20.1660 3580	23
24	21.8891 4614	21.5628 5799	21.2433 8726	20.9305 6693	24
25	22.7187 5547	22.3671 4547	22.0231 5570	21.6865 9276	25
26	23.5421 8905	23.1644 5647	22.7952 0366	22.4342 0792	26
27	24.3594 9286	23.9548 5152	23.5596 0759	23.1735 0598	27
28	25.1707 1251	24.7383 9060	24.3164 4316	23.9045 7946	28
29	25.9758 9331	25.5151 3319	25.0657 8530	24.6275 1986	29
30	26.7750 8021	26.2851 3823	25.8077 0822	25.3424 1766	30
31	27.5683 1783	27.0484 6417	26.5422 8537	26.0493 6233	31
32	28.3556 5045	27.8051 6894	27.2695 8947	26.7484 4236	32
33	29.1371 2203	28.5553 0998	27.9896 9255	27.4397 4522	33
34	29.9127 7621	29.2989 4422	28.7026 6589	28.1233 5745	34
35	30.6826 5629	30.0361 2809	29.4085 8009	28.7993 6460	35
36	31.4468 0525	30.7669 1757	30.1075 0504	29.4678 5127	36
37	32.2052 6576	31.4913 6810	30.7995 0994	30.1289 0114	37
38	32.9580 8016	32.2095 3467	31.4846 6330	30.7825 9692	38
39	33.7052 9048	32.9214 7179	32.1630 3298	31.4290 2044	39
40	34.4469 3844	33.6272 3350	32.8346 8611	32.0682 5260	40
41	35.1830 6545	34.3268 7335	33.4996 8922	32.7903 7340	41
42	35.9137 1260	35.0204 4446	34.1581 0814	33.3254 6195	42
43	36.6389 2070	35.7079 9947	34.8100 0806	33.9435 9649	43
44	37.3587 3022	36.3895 9055	35.4554 5352	34.5548 5438	44
45	38.0731 8136	37.0652 6944	36.0945 0844	35.1593 1212	45
46	38.7823 1401	37.7350 8743	36.7272 3608	35.7570 4536	46
47	39.4861 6775	38.3990 9535	37.3536 9909	36.3481 2891	47
48	40.1847 8189	39.0573 4359	37.9739 5949	36.9326 3674	48
49	40.8781 9542	39.7098 8212	38.5880 7871	37.5106 4202	49
50	41.5664 4707	40.3567 6047	39.1961 1753	38.0822 1708	50

$$a_{\overline{n}|i} = \frac{1 - (1 + i)^{-n}}{i}$$

n	$\frac{3}{4}\%$	$\frac{7}{8}\%$	1%	$1\frac{1}{8}\%$	n
51	42.2495 7525	40.9980 2772	39.7981 3617	38.6474 3345	51
52	42.9276 1812	41.6337 3256	40.3941 9423	39.2063 6188	52
53	43.6006 1351	42.2639 2324	40.9843 5072	39.7590 7232	53
54	44.2685 9902	42.8886 4757	41.5686 6408	40.3056 3394	54
55	44.9316 1193	43.5079 5298	42.1471 9216	40.8461 1514	55
56	45.5896 8926	44.1218 8647	42.7199 9224	41.3805 8358	56
57	46.2428 6776	44.7304 9465	43.2871 2102	41.9091 0613	57
58	46.8911 8388	45.3338 2369	43.8486 3468	42.4317 4896	58
59	47.5346 7382	45.9319 1939	44.4045 8879	42.9485 7746	59
60	48.1733 7352	46.5248 2716	44.9550 3841	43.4596 5633	60
61	48.8073 1863	47.1125 9198	45.5000 3803	43.9650 4952	61
62	49.4365 4455	47.6952 5846	46.0396 4161	44.4648 2029	62
63	50.0610 8640	48.2728 7084	46.5739 0258	44.9590 3119	63
64	50.6809 7906	48.8454 7296	47.1028 7385	45.4477 4407	64
65	51.2962 5713	49.4131 0826	47.6266 0777	45.9310 2009	65
66	51.9069 5497	49.9758 1984	48.1451 5621	46.4089 1975	66
67	52.5131 0667	50.5336 5039	48.6585 7050	46.8815 0284	67
68	53.1147 4607	51.0866 4227	49.1669 0149	47.3488 2852	68
69	53.7119 0677	51.6348 3745	49.6701 9949	47.8109 5527	69
70	54.3046 2210	52.1782 7752	50.1685 1435	48.2679 4094	70
71	54.8929 2516	52.7170 0374	50.6618 9539	48.7198 4270	71
72	55.4768 4880	53.2510 5699	51.1503 9148	49.1667 1714	72
73	56.0564 2561	53.7804 7781	51.6340 5097	49.6086 2016	73
74	56.6316 8795	54.3053 0638	52.1129 2175	50.0456 0708	74
75	57.2026 6794	54.8255 8253	52.5870 5124	50.4777 3259	75
76	57.7693 9746	55.3413 4575	53.0564 8638	50.9050 5077	76
77	58.3319 0815	55.8526 3520	53.5212 7364	51.3276 1510	77
78	58.8902 3141	56.3594 8966	53.9814 5905	51.7454 7847	78
79	59.4443 9842	56.8619 4762	54.4370 8817	52.1586 9317	79
80	59.9944 4012	57.3600 4721	54.8882 0611	52.5673 1092	80
81	60.5403 8722	57.8538 2623	55.3348 5753	52.9713 8286	81
82	61.0822 7019	58.3433 2216	55.7770 8666	53.3709 5957	82
83	61.6201 1930	58.8285 7215	56.2149 3729	53.7660 9104	83
84	62.1539 6456	59.3096 1304	56.6484 5276	54.1568 2674	84
85	62.6838 3579	59.7864 8133	57.0776 7600	54.5432 1557	85
86	63.2097 6257	60.2592 1321	57.5026 4951	54.9253 0588	86
87	63.7317 7427	60.7278 4457	57.9234 1535	55.3031 4549	87
88	64.2499 0002	61.1924 1097	58.3400 1520	55.6767 8169	88
89	64.7641 6875	61.6529 4768	58.7524 9030	56.0462 6126	89
90	65.2746 0918	62.1094 8965	59.1608 8148	56.4116 3041	90
91	65.7812 4981	62.5620 7152	59.5652 2919	56.7729 3490	91
92	66.2841 1892	63.0107 2765	59.9655 7346	57.1302 1992	92
93	66.7832 4458	63.4554 9210	60.3619 5392	57.4835 3021	93
94	67.2786 5467	63.8963 9861	60.7544 0982	57.8329 0997	94
95	67.7703 7685	64.3334 8066	61.1429 8002	58.1784 0294	95
96	68.2584 3856	64.7667 7141	61.5277 0299	58.5200 5235	96
97	68.7428 6705	65.1963 0375	61.9086 1682	58.8579 0096	97
98	69.2236 8938	65.6221 1028	62.2857 5923	59.1919 9106	98
99	69.7009 3239	66.0442 2333	62.6591 6755	59.5223 6446	99
100	70.1746 2272	66.4626 7492	63.0288 7877	59.8490 6251	100

VIII. PRESENT VALUE OF ANNUITY OF 1 PER PERIOD

$$a_{\overline{n}|i} = \frac{1 - (1 + i)^{-n}}{i}$$

n	$1\frac{1}{4}\%$	$1\frac{3}{8}\%$	$1\frac{1}{2}\%$	$1\frac{5}{8}\%$	n
1	0.9876 5432	0.9864 3650	0.9852 2167	0.9840 0984	1
2	1.9631 1538	1.9594 9346	1.9558 8342	1.9522 8521	2
3	2.9265 3371	2.9193 5237	2.9122 0042	2.9050 7769	3
4	3.8780 5798	3.8661 9222	3.8543 8465	3.8426 3488	4
5	4.8178 3504	4.8001 8962	4.7826 4497	4.7652 0037	5
6	5.7460 0992	5.7215 1874	5.6971 8717	5.6730 1389	6
7	6.6627 2585	6.6303 5140	6.5982 1396	6.5663 1134	7
8	7.5681 2429	7.5268 5712	7.4859 2508	7.4453 2481	8
9	8.4623 4498	8.4112 0308	8.3605 1732	8.3102 8271	9
10	9.3455 2591	9.2835 5421	9.2221 8455	9.1614 0980	10
11	10.2178 0337	10.1440 7320	10.0711 1779	9.9989 2724	11
12	11.0793 1197	10.9929 2054	10.9075 0521	10.8230 5263	12
13	11.9301 8466	11.8302 5454	11.7315 3222	11.6340 0013	13
14	12.7705 5275	12.6562 3136	12.5433 8150	12.4319 8045	14
15	13.6005 4592	13.4710 0504	13.3432 3301	13.2172 0093	15
16	14.4202 9227	14.2747 2754	14.1312 6405	13.9898 6562	16
17	15.2299 1829	15.0675 4874	14.9076 4931	14.7501 7527	17
18	16.0295 4893	15.8496 1651	15.6725 6089	15.4983 2745	18
19	16.8193 0759	16.6210 7671	16.4261 6837	16.2345 1655	19
20	17.5993 1613	17.3820 7320	17.1686 3879	16.9589 3388	20
21	18.3696 9495	18.1327 4792	17.9001 3673	17.6717 6765	21
22	19.1305 6291	18.8732 4086	18.6208 2437	18.3732 0310	22
23	19.8820 3744	19.6036 9012	19.3308 6145	19.0634 2249	23
24	20.6242 3451	20.3242 3193	20.0304 0537	19.7426 0515	24
25	21.3572 6865	21.0350 0067	20.7196 1120	20.4109 2758	25
26	22.0812 5299	21.7361 2890	21.3986 3172	21.0685 6342	26
27	22.7962 9925	22.4277 4737	22.0676 1746	21.7156 8357	27
28	23.5025 1778	23.1099 8508	22.7267 1671	22.3524 5615	28
29	24.2000 1756	23.7829 6925	23.3760 7558	22.9790 4665	29
30	24.8889 0623	24.4468 2540	24.0158 3801	23.5956 1786	30
31	25.5692 9010	25.1016 7734	24.6461 4582	24.2023 2999	31
32	26.2412 7418	25.7476 4719	25.2671 3874	24.7993 4071	32
33	26.9049 6215	26.3848 5543	25.8789 5442	25.3868 0512	33
34	27.5604 5644	27.0134 2089	26.4817 2849	25.9648 7589	34
35	28.2078 5822	27.6334 6080	27.0755 9458	26.5337 0321	35
36	28.8472 6737	28.2450 9080	27.6606 8431	27.0934 3490	36
37	29.4787 8259	28.8484 2496	28.2371 2740	27.6442 1638	37
38	30.1025 0133	29.4435 7579	28.8050 5163	28.1861 9078	38
39	30.7185 1983	30.0306 5430	29.3645 8288	28.7194 9892	39
40	31.3269 3316	30.6097 6996	29.9158 4520	29.2442 7938	40
41	31.9278 3522	31.1810 3079	30.4589 6079	29.7606 6852	41
42	32.5213 1874	31.7445 4332	30.9940 5004	30.2688 0051	42
43	33.1074 7530	32.3004 1264	31.5212 3157	30.7688 0739	43
44	33.6863 9536	32.8487 4243	32.0406 2223	31.2608 1908	44
45	34.2581 6825	33.3896 3495	32.5523 3718	31.7449 6342	45
46	34.8228 8222	33.9231 9108	33.0564 8983	32.2213 6622	46
47	35.3806 2442	34.4495 1031	33.5531 9195	32.6901 5127	47
48	35.9314 8091	34.9686 9081	34.0425 0365	33.1514 4036	48
49	36.4755 3670	35.4808 2941	34.5246 8339	33.6053 5337	49
50	37.0128 7575	35.9860 2161	34.9996 8807	34.0520 0823	50

VIII. PRESENT VALUE OF ANNUITY OF 1 PER PERIOD

$$a_{\overline{n}|i} = \frac{1 - (1 + i)^{-n}}{i}$$

n	$1\frac{1}{4}\%$	$1\frac{3}{8}\%$	$1\frac{1}{2}\%$	$1\frac{5}{8}\%$	n
51	37.5435 8099	36.4843 6164	35.4676 7298	34.4915 2102	51
52	38.0677 3431	36.9759 4243	35.9287 4185	34.9240 0592	52
53	38.5854 1660	37.4608 5566	36.3829 9690	35.3495 7532	53
54	39.0967 0776	37.9391 9178	36.8305 3882	35.7683 3980	54
55	39.6016 8667	38.4110 3998	37.2714 6681	36.1804 0817	55
56	40.1004 3128	38.8764 8826	37.7058 7863	36.5858 8750	56
57	40.5930 1855	39.3356 2344	38.1338 7058	36.9848 8314	57
58	41.0795 2449	39.7885 3114	38.5555 3751	37.3774 9879	58
59	41.5600 2419	40.2352 9582	38.9709 7292	37.7638 3645	59
60	42.0345 9179	40.6760 0081	39.3802 6889	38.1439 9650	60
61	42.5033 0054	41.1107 2829	39.7835 1614	38.5180 7774	61
62	42.9662 2275	41.5395 5935	40.1808 0408	38.8861 7736	62
63	43.4234 2988	41.9625 7396	40.5722 2077	39.2483 9100	63
64	43.8749 9247	42.3798 5101	40.9578 5298	39.6048 1280	64
65	44.3209 8022	42.7914 6832	41.3377 8618	39.9555 3535	65
66	44.7614 6195	43.1975 0266	41.7121 0461	40.3006 4979	66
67	45.1965 0563	43.5980 2975	42.0808 9125	40.6402 4579	67
68	45.6261 7840	43.9931 2429	42.4442 2783	40.9744 1161	68
69	46.0505 4656	44.3828 5997	42.8021 9490	41.3032 3405	69
70	46.4696 7562	44.7673 0946	43.1548 7183	41.6267 9858	70
71	46.8836 3024	45.1465 4448	43.5023 3678	41.9451 8925	71
72	47.2924 7431	45.5206 3573	43.8446 6677	42.2584 8881	72
73	47.6962 7093	45.8896 5300	44.1819 3771	42.5667 7865	73
74	48.0950 8240	46.2536 6511	44.5142 2434	42.8701 3890	74
75	48.4889 7027	46.6127 3994	44.8416 0034	43.1686 4836	75
76	48.8779 9533	46.9669 4445	45.1641 3826	43.4623 8461	76
77	49.2622 1761	47.3163 4471	45.4819 0962	43.7514 2397	77
78	49.6416 9640	47.6610 0588	45.7949 8485	44.0358 4155	78
79	50.0164 9027	48.0009 9224	46.1034 3335	44.3157 1124	79
80	50.3866 5706	48.3363 6719	46.4073 2349	44.5911 0577	80
81	50.7522 5389	48.6671 9328	46.7067 2265	44.8620 9670	81
82	51.1133 3717	48.9935 3221	47.0016 9720	45.1287 5444	82
83	51.4699 6264	49.3154 4484	47.2923 1251	45.3911 4828	83
84	51.8221 8532	49.6329 9122	47.5786 3301	45.6493 4640	84
85	52.1700 5958	49.9462 3055	47.8607 2218	45.9034 1589	85
86	52.5136 3909	50.2552 2125	48.1386 4254	46.1534 2277	86
87	52.8529 7688	50.5600 2096	48.4124 5571	46.3994 3200	87
88	53.1881 2531	50.8606 8653	48.6822 2237	46.6415 0750	88
89	53.5191 3611	51.1572 7401	48.9480 0234	46.8797 1218	89
90	53.8460 6035	51.4498 3873	49.2098 5452	47.1141 0793	90
91	54.1689 4850	51.7384 3524	49.4678 3696	47.3447 5565	91
92	54.4878 5037	52.0231 1738	49.7220 0686	47.5717 1528	92
93	54.8028 1518	52.3039 3823	49.9724 2055	47.7950 4578	93
94	55.1138 9154	52.5809 5016	50.2191 3355	48.0148 0520	94
95	55.4211 2744	52.8542 0484	50.4622 0054	48.2310 5062	95
96	55.7245 7031	53.1237 5324	50.7016 7541	48.4438 3825	96
97	56.0242 6698	53.3896 4561	50.9376 1124	48.6532 2337	97
98	56.3202 6368	53.6519 3155	51.1700 6034	48.8592 6039	98
99	56.6126 0610	53.9106 5998	51.3990 7422	49.0620 0285	99
100	56.9013 3936	54.1658 7914	51.6247 0367	49.2615 0341	100

VIII. PRESENT VALUE OF ANNUITY OF 1 PER PERIOD

$$a_{\overline{n}|i} = \frac{1 - (1 + i)^{-n}}{i}$$

n	$1\frac{3}{4}\%$	2%	$2\frac{1}{4}\%$	$2\frac{1}{2}\%$	n
1	0.9828 0098	0.9803 9216	0.9779 9511	0.9756 0976	1
2	1.9486 9875	1.9415 6094	1.9344 6955	1.9274 2415	2
3	2.8979 8403	2.8838 8327	2.8698 9687	2.8560 2356	3
4	3.8309 4254	3.8077 2870	3.7847 4021	3.7619 7421	4
5	4.7478 5508	4.7134 5951	4.6794 5253	4.6458 2850	5
6	5.6489 9762	5.6014 3089	5.5544 7680	5.5081 2536	6
7	6.5346 4139	6.4719 9107	6.4102 4626	6.3493 9060	7
8	7.4050 5297	7.3254 8144	7.2471 8461	7.1701 3717	8
9	8.2604 9432	8.1622 3671	8.0657 0622	7.9708 6553	9
10	9.1012 2291	8.9825 8501	8.8662 1635	8.7520 6393	10
11	9.9274 9181	9.7868 4805	9.6491 1134	9.5142 0871	11
12	10.7395 4969	10.5753 4122	10.4147 7882	10.2577 6460	12
13	11.5376 4097	11.3483 7375	11.1635 9787	10.9831 8497	13
14	12.3220 0587	12.1062 4877	11.8959 3924	11.6909 1217	14
15	13.0928 8046	12.8492 6350	12.6121 6551	12.3813 7773	15
16	13.8504 9677	13.5777 0931	13.3126 3131	13.0550 0266	16
17	14.5950 8282	14.2918 7188	13.9976 8343	13.7121 9772	17
18	15.3268 6272	14.9920 3125	14.6676 6106	14.3533 6363	18
19	16.0460 5673	15.6784 6201	15.3228 9590	14.9788 9134	19
20	16.7528 8130	16.3514 3334	15.9637 1237	15.5891 6229	20
21	17.4475 4919	17.0112 0916	16.5904 2775	16.1845 4857	21
22	18.1302 6948	17.6580 4820	17.2033 5232	16.7654 1324	22
23	18.8012 4764	18.2922 0412	17.8027 8955	17.3321 1048	23
24	19.4606 8565	18.9139 2560	18.3890 3624	17.8849 8583	24
25	20.1087 8196	19.5234 5647	18.9623 8263	18.4243 7642	25
26	20.7457 3166	20.1210 3576	19.5231 1260	18.9506 1114	26
27	21.3717 2644	20.7068 9780	20.0715 0376	19.4640 1087	27
28	21.9869 5474	21.2812 7236	20.6078 2764	19.9648 8866	28
29	22.5916 0171	21.8443 8466	21.1323 4977	20.4535 4991	29
30	23.1858 4934	22.3964 5555	21.6453 2985	20.9302 9259	30
31	23.7698 7650	22.9377 0152	22.1470 2186	21.3954 0741	31
32	24.3438 5897	23.4683 3482	22.6376 7419	21.8491 7796	32
33	24.9079 6951	23.9885 6355	23.1175 2977	22.2918 8094	33
34	25.4623 7789	24.4985 9172	23.5868 2618	22.7237 8628	34
35	26.0072 5100	24.9986 1933	24.0457 9577	23.1451 5734	35
36	26.5427 5283	25.4888 4248	24.4946 6579	23.5562 5107	36
37	27.0690 4455	25.9694 5341	24.9336 5848	23.9573 1812	37
38	27.5862 8457	26.4406 4060	25.3629 9118	24.3486 0304	38
39	28.0946 2857	26.9025 8883	25.7828 7646	24.7303 4443	39
40	28.5942 2955	27.3554 7924	26.1935 2221	25.1027 7505	40
41	29.0852 3789	27.7994 8945	26.5951 3174	25.4661 2200	41
42	29.5678 0135	28.2347 9358	26.9879 0390	25.8206 0683	42
43	30.0420 6522	28.6615 6233	27.3720 3316	26.1664 4569	43
44	30.5081 7221	29.0799 6307	27.7477 0969	26.5038 4945	44
45	30.9662 6261	29.4901 5987	28.1151 1950	26.8330 2386	45
46	31.4164 7431	29.8923 1360	28.4744 4450	27.1541 6962	46
47	31.8589 4281	30.2865 8196	28.8258 6259	27.4674 8255	47
48	32.2938 0129	30.6731 1957	29.1695 4777	27.7731 5371	48
49	32.7211 8063	31.0520 7801	29.5056 7019	28.0713 6947	49
50	33.1412 0946	31.4236 0589	29.8343 9627	28.3623 1168	50

$$a_{\overline{n}|i} = \frac{1 - (1 + i)^{-n}}{i}$$

n	$1\frac{3}{4}\%$	2%	$2\frac{1}{4}\%$	$2\frac{1}{2}\%$	n
51	33.5540 1421	31.7878 4892	30.1558 8877	28.6461 5774	51
52	33.9597 1913	32.1449 4992	30.4703 0687	28.9230 8072	52
53	34.3584 4632	32.4950 4894	30.7778 0623	29.1932 4948	53
54	34.7503 1579	32.8382 8327	31.0785 3910	29.4568 2876	54
55	35.1354 4550	33.1747 8752	31.3726 5438	29.7139 7928	55
56	35.5139 5135	33.5046 9365	31.6602 9768	29.9648 5784	56
57	35.8859 4727	33.8281 3103	31.9416 1142	30.2096 1740	57
58	36.2515 4523	34.1452 2650	32.2167 3489	30.4484 0722	58
59	36.6108 5526	34.4561 0441	32.4858 0429	30.6813 7290	59
60	36.9639 8552	34.7608 8668	32.7489 5285	30.9086 5649	60
61	37.3110 4228	35.0596 9282	33.0063 1086	31.1303 9657	61
62	37.6521 3000	35.3526 4002	33.2580 0573	31.3467 2836	62
63	37.9873 5135	35.6398 4316	33.5041 6208	31.5577 8377	63
64	38.3168 0723	35.9214 1486	33.7449 0179	31.7636 9148	64
65	38.6405 9678	36.1974 6555	33.9803 4405	31.9645 7705	65
66	38.9588 1748	36.4681 0348	34.2106 0543	32.1605 6298	66
67	39.2715 6509	36.7334 3478	34.4357 9993	32.3517 6876	67
68	39.5789 3375	36.9935 6351	34.6560 3905	32.5383 1099	68
69	39.8810 1597	37.2485 9168	34.8714 3183	32.7203 0340	69
70	40.1779 0267	37.4986 1929	35.0820 8492	32.8978 5698	70
71	40.4696 8321	37.7437 4441	35.2881 0261	33.0710 7998	71
72	40.7564 4542	37.9840 6314	35.4895 8691	33.2400 7803	72
73	41.0382 7560	38.2196 6975	35.6866 3756	33.4049 5417	73
74	41.3152 5857	38.4506 5662	35.8793 5214	33.5658 0895	74
75	41.5874 7771	38.6771 1433	36.0678 2605	33.7227 4044	75
76	41.8550 1495	38.8991 3170	36.2521 5262	33.8758 4433	76
77	42.1179 5081	39.1167 9578	36.4324 2310	34.0252 1398	77
78	42.3763 6443	39.3301 9194	36.6087 2675	34.1709 4047	78
79	42.6303 3359	39.5394 0386	36.7811 5085	34.3131 1265	79
80	42.8799 3474	39.7445 1359	36.9497 8079	34.4518 1722	80
81	43.1252 4298	39.9456 0156	37.1147 0004	34.5871 3875	81
82	43.3663 3217	40.1427 4663	37.2759 9026	34.7191 5976	82
83	43.6032 7486	40.3360 2611	37.4337 3130	34.8479 6074	83
84	43.8361 4237	40.5255 1579	37.5880 0127	34.9736 2023	84
85	44.0650 0479	40.7112 8999	37.7388 7655	35.0962 1486	85
86	44.2899 3099	40.8934 2156	37.8864 3183	35.2158 1938	86
87	44.5109 8869	41.0719 8192	38.0307 4018	35.3325 0671	87
88	44.7282 4441	41.2470 4110	38.1718 7304	35.4463 4801	88
89	44.9417 6355	41.4186 6774	38.3099 0028	35.5574 1269	89
90	45.1516 1037	41.5869 2916	38.4448 9025	35.6657 6848	90
91	45.3578 4803	41.7518 9133	38.5769 0978	35.7714 8144	91
92	45.5605 3861	41.9136 1895	38.7060 2423	35.8746 1604	92
93	45.7597 4310	42.0721 7545	38.8322 9754	35.9752 3516	93
94	45.9555 2147	42.2276 2299	38.9557 9221	36.0734 0016	94
95	46.1479 3265	42.3800 2254	39.0765 6940	36.1691 7089	95
96	46.3370 3455	42.5294 3386	39.1946 8890	36.2626 0574	96
97	46.5228 8408	42.6759 1555	39.3102 0920	36.3537 6170	97
98	46.7055 3718	42.8195 2505	39.4231 8748	36.4426 9434	98
99	46.8850 4882	42.9603 1867	39.5336 7968	36.5294 5790	99
100	47.0614 7304	43.0983 5164	39.6417 4052	36.6141 0526	100

VIII. PRESENT VALUE OF ANNUITY OF 1 PER PERIOD

$$a_{\overline{n}|i} = \frac{1 - (1 + i)^{-n}}{i}$$

n	$2\frac{3}{4}\%$	3%	$3\frac{1}{4}\%$	$3\frac{1}{2}\%$	n
1	0.9732 3601	0.9708 7379	0.9685 2300	0.9661 8357	1
2	1.9204 2434	1.9134 6970	1.9065 5981	1.8996 9428	2
3	2.8422 6213	2.8286 1135	2.8150 7003	2.8016 3698	3
4	3.7394 2787	3.7170 9840	3.6949 8308	3.6730 7921	4
5	4.6125 8186	4.5797 0719	4.5471 9911	4.5150 5238	5
6	5.4623 6678	5.4171 9144	5.3725 8994	5.3285 5302	6
7	6.2894 0806	6.2302 8296	6.1719 9994	6.1145 4398	7
8	7.0943 1441	7.0196 9219	6.9462 4692	6.8739 5554	8
9	7.8776 7826	7.7861 0892	7.6961 2292	7.6076 8651	9
10	8.6400 7616	8.5302 0284	8.4223 9508	8.3166 0532	10
11	9.3820 6926	9.2526 2411	9.1258 0637	9.0015 5104	11
12	10.1042 0366	9.9540 0399	9.8070 7639	9.6633 3433	12
13	10.8070 1086	10.6349 5533	10.4669 0207	10.3027 3849	13
14	11.4910 0814	11.2960 7314	11.1059 5842	10.9205 2028	14
15	12.1566 9892	11.9379 3509	11.7248 9920	11.5174 1090	15
16	12.8045 7315	12.5611 0203	12.3243 5758	12.0941 1681	16
17	13.4351 0769	13.1661 1847	12.9049 4681	12.6513 2059	17
18	14.0487 6661	13.7535 1308	13.4672 6083	13.1896 8173	18
19	14.6460 0157	14.3237 9911	14.0118 7490	13.7098 3742	19
20	15.2272 5213	14.8774 7486	14.5393 4615	14.2124 0330	20
21	15.7929 4612	15.4150 2414	15.0502 1419	14.6979 7420	21
22	16.3434 9987	15.9369 1664	15.5450 0163	15.1671 2484	22
23	16.8793 1861	16.4436 0839	16.0242 1466	15.6204 1047	23
24	17.4007 9670	16.9355 4212	16.4883 4349	16.0583 6760	24
25	17.9083 1795	17.4131 4769	16.9378 6295	16.4815 1459	25
26	18.4022 5592	17.8768 4242	17.3732 3288	16.8903 5226	26
27	18.8829 7413	18.3270 3147	17.7948 9867	17.2853 6451	27
28	19.3508 2640	18.7641 0823	18.2032 9169	17.6670 1885	28
29	19.8061 5708	19.1884 5459	18.5988 2973	18.0357 6700	29
30	20.2493 0130	19.6004 4135	18.9819 1741	18.3920 4541	30
31	20.6805 8520	20.0004 2849	19.3529 4664	18.7362 7576	31
32	21.1003 2623	20.3887 6553	19.7122 9699	19.0688 6547	32
33	21.5088 3332	20.7657 9178	20.0603 3607	19.3902 0818	33
34	21.9064 0712	21.1318 3668	20.3974 1992	19.7006 8423	34
35	22.2933 4026	21.4872 2007	20.7238 9339	20.0006 6110	35
36	22.6699 1753	21.8322 5250	21.0400 9045	20.2904 9381	36
37	23.0364 1609	22.1672 3544	21.3463 3457	20.5705 2542	37
38	23.3931 0568	22.4924 6159	21.6429 3905	20.8410 8736	38
39	23.7402 4884	22.8082 1513	21.9302 0732	21.1024 9987	39
40	24.0781 0106	23.1147 7197	22.2084 3324	21.3550 7234	40
41	24.4069 1101	23.4123 9997	22.4779 0144	21.5991 0371	41
42	24.7269 2069	23.7013 5920	22.7388 8759	21.8348 8281	42
43	25.0383 6563	23.9819 0213	22.9916 5869	22.0626 8870	43
44	25.3414 7507	24.2542 7392	23.2364 7330	22.2827 9102	44
45	25.6364 7209	24.5187 1254	23.4735 8189	22.4954 5026	45
46	25.9235 7381	24.7754 4907	23.7032 2701	22.7009 1813	46
47	26.2029 9154	25.0247 0783	23.9256 4360	22.8994 3780	47
48	26.4749 3094	25.2667 0664	24.1410 5917	23.0912 4425	48
49	26.7395 9215	25.5016 5693	24.3496 9412	23.2765 6450	49
50	26.9971 6998	25.7297 6401	24.5517 6185	23.4556 1787	50

VIII. PRESENT VALUE OF ANNUITY OF 1 PER PERIOD

$$a_{\overline{n}|i} = \frac{1 - (1 + i)^{-n}}{i}$$

n	$2\frac{3}{4}\%$	3%	$3\frac{1}{4}\%$	$3\frac{1}{2}\%$	n
51	27.2478 5400	25.9512 2719	24.7474 6911	23.6286 1630	51
52	27.4918 2871	26.1662 3999	24.9370 1609	23.7957 6454	52
53	27.7292 7368	26.3749 9028	25.1205 9669	23.9572 6043	53
54	27.9603 6368	26.5776 6047	25.2983 9873	24.1132 9510	54
55	28.1852 6879	26.7744 2764	25.4706 0410	24.2640 5323	55
56	28.4041 5454	26.9654 6373	25.6373 8896	24.4097 1327	56
57	28.6171 8203	27.1509 3566	25.7989 2393	24.5504 4760	57
58	28.8245 0806	27.3310 0549	25.9553 7427	24.6864 2281	58
59	29.0262 8522	27.5058 3058	26.1069 0002	24.8177 9981	59
60	29.2226 6201	27.6755 6367	26.2536 5619	24.9447 3412	60
61	29.4137 8298	27.8403 5307	26.3957 9292	25.0673 7596	61
62	29.5997 8879	28.0003 4279	26.5334 5561	25.1858 7049	62
63	29.7808 1634	28.1556 7261	26.6667 8510	25.3003 5796	63
64	29.9569 9887	28.3064 7826	26.7959 1777	25.4109 7388	64
65	30.1284 6605	28.4528 9152	26.9209 8573	25.5178 4916	65
66	30.2953 4409	28.5950 4031	27.0421 1693	25.6211 1030	66
67	30.4577 5581	28.7330 4884	27.1594 3529	25.7208 7951	67
68	30.6158 2074	28.8670 3771	27.2730 6081	25.8172 7489	68
69	30.7696 5522	28.9971 2399	27.3831 0974	25.9104 1052	69
70	30.9193 7247	29.1234 2135	27.4896 9467	26.0003 9664	70
71	31.0650 8270	29.2460 4015	27.5929 2462	26.0873 3975	71
72	31.2068 9314	29.3650 8752	27.6929 0520	26.1713 4275	72
73	31.3449 0816	29.4806 6750	27.7897 3869	26.2525 0508	73
74	31.4792 2936	29.5928 8107	27.8835 2416	26.3309 2278	74
75	31.6099 5558	29.7018 2628	27.9743 5754	26.4066 8868	75
76	31.7371 8304	29.8075 9833	28.0623 3175	26.4798 9244	76
77	31.8610 0540	29.9102 8964	28.1475 3681	26.5506 2072	77
78	31.9815 1377	30.0099 8994	28.2300 5986	26.6189 5721	78
79	32.0987 9685	30.1067 8635	28.3099 8534	26.6849 8281	79
80	32.2129 4098	30.2007 6345	28.3873 9500	26.7487 7567	80
81	32.3240 3015	30.2920 0335	28.4623 6804	26.8104 1127	81
82	32.4321 4613	30.3805 8577	28.5349 8115	26.8699·6258	82
83	32.5373 6850	30.4665 8813	28.6053 0862	26.9275 0008	83
84	32.6397 7469	30.5500 8556	28.6734 2239	26.9830 9186	84
85	32.7394 4009	30.6311 5103	28.7393 9215	27.0368 0373	85
86	32.8364 3804	30.7098 5537	28.8032 8537	27.0886 9926	86
87	32.9308 3994	30.7862 6735	28.8651 6743	27.1388 3986	87
88	33.0227 1527	30.8604 5374	28.9251 0163	27.1872 8489	88
89	33.1121 3165	30.9324 7936	28.9831 4928	27.2340 9168	89
90	33.1991 5489	31.0024 0714	29.0393 6976	27.2793 1564	90
91	33.2838 4905	31.0702 9820	29.0938 2059	27.3230 1028	91
92	33.3662 7644	31.1362 1184	29.1465 5747	27.3652 2732	92
93	33.4464 9776	31.2002 0567	29.1976 3436	27.4060 1673	93
94	33.5245 7202	31.2623 3560	29.2471 0349	27.4454 2680	94
95	33.6005 5671	31.3226 5592	29.2950 1549	27.4835 0415	95
96	33.6745 0775	31.3812 1934	29.3414 1936	27.5202 9387	96
97	33.7464 7956	31.4380 7703	29.3863 6258	27.5558 3948	97
98	33.8165 2512	31.4932 7867	29.4298 9112	27.5901 8308	98
99	33.8846 9598	31.5468 7250	29.4720 4951	27.6233 6529	99
100	33.9510 4232	31.5989 0534	29.5128 8088	27.6554 2540	100

VIII. PRESENT VALUE OF ANNUITY OF 1 PER PERIOD

$$a_{\overline{n}|i} = \frac{1 - (1 + i)^{-n}}{i}$$

n	4%	4½%	5%	5½%	n
1	0.9615 3846	0.9569 3780	0.9523 8095	0.9478 6730	1
2	1.8860 9467	1.8726 6775	1.8594 1043	1.8463 1971	2
3	2.7750 9103	2.7489 6435	2.7232 4803	2.6979 3338	3
4	3.6298 9522	3.5875 2570	3.5459 5050	3.5051 5012	4
5	4.4518 2233	4.3899 7674	4.3294 7667	4.2702 8448	5
6	5.2421 3686	5.1578 7248	5.0756 9207	4.9955 3031	6
7	6.0020 5467	5.8927 0094	5.7863 7340	5.6829 6712	7
8	6.7327 4487	6.5958 8607	6.4632 1276	6.3345 6599	8
9	7.4353 3161	7.2687 9050	7.1078 2168	6.9521 9525	9
10	8.1108 9578	7.9127 1818	7.7217 3493	7.5376 2583	10
11	8.7604 7671	8.5289 1692	8.3064 1422	8.0925 3633	11
12	9.3850 7376	9.1185 8078	8.8632 5164	8.6185 1785	12
13	9.9856 4785	9.6828 5242	9.3935 7299	9.1170 7853	13
14	10.5631 2293	10.2228 2528	9.8986 4094	9.5896 4790	14
15	11.1183 8743	10.7395 4573	10.3796 5804	10.0375 8094	15
16	11.6522 9561	11.2340 1505	10.8377 6956	10.4621 6203	16
17	12.1656 6885	11.7071 9143	11.2740 6625	10.8646 0856	17
18	12.6592 9697	12.1599 9180	11.6895 8690	11.2460 7447	18
19	13.1339 3940	12.5932 9359	12.0853 2086	11.6076 5352	19
20	13.5903 2634	13.0079 3645	12.4622 1034	11.9503 8248	20
21	14.0291 5995	13.4047 2388	12.8211 5271	12.2752 4406	21
22	14.4511 1533	13.7844 2476	13.1630 0258	12.5831 6973	22
23	14.8568 4167	14.1477 7489	13.4885 7388	12.8750 4239	23
24	15.2469 6314	14.4954 7837	13.7986 4179	13.1516 9895	24
25	15.6220 7994	14.8282 0896	14.0939 4457	13.4139 3266	25
26	15.9827 6918	15.1466 1145	14.3751 8530	13.6624 9541	26
27	16.3295 8575	15.4513 0282	14.6430 3362	13.8980 9991	27
28	16.6630 6322	15.7428 7351	14.8981 2726	14.1214 2172	28
29	16.9837 1463	16.0218 8853	15.1410 7358	14.3331 0116	29
30	17.2920 3330	16.2888 8854	15.3724 5103	14.5337 4517	30
31	17.5884 9356	16.5443 9095	15.5928 1050	14.7239 2907	31
32	17.8735 5150	16.7888 9086	15.8026 7667	14.9041 9817	32
33	18.1476 4567	17.0228 6207	16.0025 4921	15.0750 6936	33
34	18.4111 9776	17.2467 5796	16.1929 0401	15.2370 3257	34
35	18.6646 1323	17.4610 1240	16.3741 9429	15.3905 5220	35
36	18.9082 8195	17.6660 4058	16.5468 5171	15.5360 6843	36
37	19.1425 7880	17.8622 3979	16.7112 8734	15.6739 9851	37
38	19.3678 6423	18.0499 9023	16.8678 9271	15.8047 3793	38
39	19.5844 8484	18.2296 5572	17.0170 4067	15.9286 6154	39
40	19.7927 7388	18.4015 8442	17.1590 8635	16.0461 2469	40
41	19.9930 5181	18.5661 0949	17.2943 6796	16.1574 6416	41
42	20.1856 2674	18.7235 4975	17.4232 0758	16.2629 9920	42
43	20.3707 9494	18.8742 1029	17.5459 1198	16.3630 3242	43
44	20.5488 4129	19.0183 8305	17.6627 7331	16.4578 5063	44
45	20.7200 3970	19.1563 4742	17.7740 6982	16.5477 2572	45
46	20.8846 5356	19.2883 7074	17.8800 6650	16.6329 1537	46
47	21.0429 3612	19.4147 0884	17.9810 1571	16.7136 6386	47
48	21.1951 3088	19.5356 0654	18.0771 5782	16.7902 0271	48
49	21.3414 7200	19.6512 9813	18.1687 2173	16.8627 5139	49
50	21.4821 8462	19.7620 0778	18.2559 2546	16.9315 1790	50

VIII. PRESENT VALUE OF ANNUITY OF 1 PER PERIOD

$$a_{\overline{n}|i} = \frac{1 - (1 + i)^{-n}}{i}$$

n	6%	6½%	7%	8%	n
1	0.9433 9623	0.9389 6714	0.9345 7944	0.9259 2593	1
2	1.8333 9267	1.8206 2642	1.8080 1817	1.7832 6475	2
3	2.6730 1195	2.6484 7551	2.6243 1604	2.5770 9699	3
4	3.4651 0561	3.4257 9860	3.3872 1126	3.3121 2684	4
5	4.2123 6379	4.1556 7944	4.1001 9744	3.9927 1004	5
6	4.9173 2433	4.8410 1356	4.7665 3966	4.6228 7966	6
7	5.5823 8144	5.4845 1977	5.3892 8940	5.2063 7006	7
8	6.2097 9381	6.0887 5096	5.9712 9851	5.7466 3894	8
9	6.8016 9227	6.6561 0419	6.5152 3225	6.2468 8791	9
10	7.3600 8705	7.1888 3022	7.0235 8154	6.7100 8140	10
11	7.8868 7458	7.6890 4246	7.4986 7434	7.1389 6426	11
12	8.3838 4394	8.1587 2532	7.9426 8630	7.5360 7802	12
13	8.8526 8296	8.5997 4208	8.3576 5074	7.9037 7594	13
14	9.2949 8393	9.0138 4233	8.7454 6799	8.2442 3698	14
15	9.7122 4899	9.4026 6885	9.1079 1401	8.5594 7869	15
16	10.1058 9527	9.7677 6418	9.4466 4860	8.8513 6916	16
17	10.4772 5969	10.1105 7670	9.7632 2299	9.1216 3811	17
18	10.8276 0348	10.4324 6638	10.0590 8691	9.3718 8714	18
19	11.1581 1649	10.7347 1022	10.3355 9524	9.6035 9920	19
20	11.4699 2122	11.0185 0725	10.5940 1425	9.8181 4741	20
21	11.7640 7662	11.2849 8333	10.8355 2733	10.0168 0316	21
22	12.0415 8172	11.5351 9562	11.0612 4050	10.2007 4366	22
23	12.3033 7898	11.7701 3673	11.2721 8738	10.3710 5895	23
24	12.5503 5753	11.9907 3871	11.4693 3400	10.5287 5828	24
25	12.7833 5616	12.1978 7673	11.6535 8318	10.6747 7619	25
26	13.0031 6619	12.3923 7251	11.8257 7867	10.8099 7795	26
27	13.2105 3414	12.5749 9766	11.9867 0904	10.9351 6477	27
28	13.4061 6428	12.7464 7668	12.1371 1125	11.0510 7849	28
29	13.5907 2102	12.9074 8984	12.2776 7407	11.1584 0601	29
30	13.7648 3115	13.0586 7591	12.4090 4118	11.2577 8334	30
31	13.9290 8599	13.2006 3465	12.5318 1419	11.3497 9939	31
32	14.0840 4339	13.3339 2925	12.6465 5532	11.4349 9944	32
33	14.2302 2961	13.4590 8850	12.7537 9002	11.5138 8837	33
34	14.3681 4114	13.5766 0892	12.8540 0936	11.5869 3367	34
35	14.4982 4636	13.6869 5673	12.9476 7230	11.6545 6822	35
36	14.6209 8713	13.7905 6970	13.0352 0776	11.7171 9279	36
37	14.7367 8031	13.8878 5887	13.1170 1660	11.7751 7851	37
38	14.8460 1916	13.9792 1021	13.1934 7345	11.8288 6899	38
39	14.9490 7468	14.0649 8611	13.2649 2846	11.8785 8240	39
40	15.0462 9687	14.1455 2687	13.3317 0884	11.9246 1333	40
41	15.1380 1592	14.2211 5199	13.3941 2041	11.9672 3457	41
42	15.2245 4332	14.2921 6149	13.4524 4898	12.0066 9867	42
43	15.3061 7294	14.3588 3708	13.5069 6167	12.0432 3951	43
44	15.3831 8202	14.4214 4327	13.5579 0810	12.0770 7362	44
45	15.4558 3209	14.4802 2842	13.6055 2159	12.1084 0150	45
46	15.5243 6990	14.5354 2575	13.6500 2018	12.1374 0880	46
47	15.5890 2821	14.5872 5422	13.6916 0764	12.1642 6741	47
48	15.6500 2661	14.6359 1946	13.7304 7443	12.1891 3649	48
49	15.7075 7227	14.6816 1451	13.7667 9853	12.2121 6341	49
50	15.7618 6064	14.7245 2067	13.8007 4629	12.2334 8464	50

IX. ANNUITY WHOSE PRESENT VALUE IS 1

$$\frac{1}{a_{\overline{n}|i}} = \frac{i}{1 - (1 + i)^{-n}} = i + \frac{1}{s_{\overline{n}|i}}$$

n	$\frac{1}{4}\%$	$\frac{7}{24}\%$	$\frac{1}{3}\%$	$\frac{3}{8}\%$	n
1	1.0025 0000	1.0029 1667	1.0033 3333	1.0037 5000	1
2	0.5018 7578	0.5021 8856	0.5025 0139	0.5028 1425	2
3	0.3350 0139	0.3352 7967	0.3355 5802	0.3358 3645	3
4	0.2515 6445	0.2518 2557	0.2520 8680	0.2523 4814	4
5	0.2015 0250	0.2017 5340	0.2020 0444	0.2022 5561	5
6	0.1681 2803	0.1683 7218	0.1686 1650	0.1688 6099	6
7	0.1442 8928	0.1445 2866	0.1447 6824	0.1450 0802	7
8	0.1264 1035	0.1266 4620	0.1268 8228	0.1271 1859	8
9	0.1125 0462	0.1127 3777	0.1129 7118	0.1132 0484	9
10	0.1013 8015	0.1016 1117	0.1018 4248	0.1020 7408	10
11	0.0922 7840	0.0925 0772	0.0927 3736	0.0929 6731	11
12	0.0846 9370	0.0849 2163	0.0851 4990	0.0853 7852	12
13	0.0782 7595	0.0785 0274	0.0787 2989	0.0789 5742	13
14	0.0727 7510	0.0730 0093	0.0732 2716	0.0734 5379	14
15	0.0680 0777	0.0682 3279	0.0684 5825	0.0686 8413	15
16	0.0638 3642	0.0640 6076	0.0642 8557	0.0645 1083	16
17	0.0601 5587	0.0603 7964	0.0606 0389	0.0608 2864	17
18	0.0568 8433	0.0571 0761	0.0573 3140	0.0575 5571	18
19	0.0539 5722	0.0541 8008	0.0544 0348	0.0546 2742	19
20	0.0513 2288	0.0515 4537	0.0517 6844	0.0519 9208	20
21	0.0489 3947	0.0491 6166	0.0493 8445	0.0496 0784	21
22	0.0467 7278	0.0469 9471	0.0472 1726	0.0474 4045	22
23	0.0447 9455	0.0450 1625	0.0452 3861	0.0454 6163	23
24	0.0429 8121	0.0432 0272	0.0434 2492	0.0436 4781	24
25	0.0413 1298	0.0415 3433	0.0417 5640	0.0419 7919	25
26	0.0397 7312	0.0399 9434	0.0402 1630	0.0404 3902	26
27	0.0383 4736	0.0385 6847	0.0387 9035	0.0390 1301	27
28	0.0370 2347	0.0372 4450	0.0374 6632	0.0376 8895	28
29	0.0357 9093	0.0360 1188	0.0362 3367	0.0364 5629	29
30	0.0346 4059	0.0348 6149	0.0350 8325	0.0353 0588	30
31	0.0335 6449	0.0337 8536	0.0340 0712	0.0342 2976	31
32	0.0325 5569	0.0327 7653	0.0329 9830	0.0332 2098	32
33	0.0316 0806	0.0318 2889	0.0320 5067	0.0322 7340	33
34	0.0307 1620	0.0309 3703	0.0311 5885	0.0313 8164	34
35	0.0298 7533	0.0300 9618	0.0303 1803	0.0305 4089	35
36	0.0290 8121	0.0293 0208	0.0295 2399	0.0297 4692	36
37	0.0283 3004	0.0285 5094	0.0287 7291	0.0289 9594	37
38	0.0276 1843	0.0278 3938	0.0280 6141	0.0282 8453	38
39	0.0269 4335	0.0271 6434	0.0273 8644	0.0276 0967	39
40	0.0263 0204	0.0265 2308	0.0267 4527	0.0269 6862	40
41	0.0256 9204	0.0259 1315	0.0261 3543	0.0263 5889	41
42	0.0251 1112	0.0253 3229	0.0255 5466	0.0257 7825	42
43	0.0245 5724	0.0247 7848	0.0250 0095	0.0252 2467	43
44	0.0240 2855	0.0242 4987	0.0244 7246	0.0246 9630	44
45	0.0235 2339	0.0237 4479	0.0239 6749	0.0241 9147	45
46	0.0230 4022	0.0232 6170	0.0234 8451	0.0237 0864	46
47	0.0225 7762	0.0227 9920	0.0230 2213	0.0232 4641	47
48	0.0221 3433	0.0223 5600	0.0225 7905	0.0228 0349	48
49	0.0217 0915	0.0219 3092	0.0221 5410	0.0223 7869	49
50	0.0213 0099	0.0215 2287	0.0217 4618	0.0219 7093	50

IX. ANNUITY WHOSE PRESENT VALUE IS 1

$$\frac{1}{a_{\overline{n}|i}} = \frac{i}{1 - (1 + i)^{-n}} = i + \frac{1}{s_{\overline{n}|i}}$$

n	$\frac{1}{4}\%$	$\frac{7}{24}\%$	$\frac{1}{3}\%$	$\frac{3}{8}\%$	n
51	0.0209 0886	0.0211 3085	0.0213 5429	0.0215 7920	51
52	0.0205 3184	0.0207 5393	0.0209 7751	0.0212 0259	52
53	0.0201 6906	0.0203 9126	0.0206 1499	0.0208 4023	53
54	0.0198 1974	0.0200 4205	0.0202 6592	0.0204 9134	54
55	0.0194 8314	0.0197 0557	0.0199 2958	0.0201 5518	55
56	0.0191 5858	0.0193 8113	0.0196 0529	0.0198 3106	56
57	0.0188 4542	0.0190 6810	0.0192 9241	0.0195 1836	57
58	0.0185 4308	0.0187 6589	0.0189 9035	0.0192 1648	58
59	0.0182 5101	0.0184 7394	0.0186 9856	0.0189 2487	59
60	0.0179 6869	0.0181 9175	0.0184 1652	0.0186 4302	60
61	0.0176 9564	0.0179 1883	0.0181 4377	0.0183 7045	61
62	0.0174 3142	0.0176 5474	0.0178 7984	0.0181 0671	62
63	0.0171 7561	0.0173 9906	0.0176 2432	0.0178 5138	63
64	0.0169 2780	0.0171 5139	0.0173 7681	0.0176 0407	64
65	0.0166 8764	0.0169 1136	0.0171 3695	0.0173 6440	65
66	0.0164 5476	0.0166 7863	0.0169 0438	0.0171 3203	66
67	0.0162 2886	0.0164 5286	0.0166 7878	0.0169 0663	67
68	0.0160 0961	0.0162 3376	0.0164 5985	0.0166 8789	68
69	0.0157 9674	0.0160 2102	0.0162 4729	0.0164 7553	69
70	0.0155 8996	0.0158 1439	0.0160 4083	0.0162 6927	70
71	0.0153 8902	0.0156 1359	0.0158 4021	0.0160 6885	71
72	0.0151 9368	0.0154 1840	0.0156 4518	0.0158 7403	72
73	0.0150 0370	0.0152 2857	0.0154 5553	0.0156 8458	73
74	0.0148 1887	0.0150 4389	0.0152 7103	0.0155 0028	74
75	0.0146 3898	0.0148 6415	0.0150 9147	0.0153 2093	75
76	0.0144 6385	0.0146 8916	0.0149 1666	0.0151 4633	76
77	0.0142 9327	0.0145 1874	0.0147 4641	0.0149 7629	77
78	0.0141 2708	0.0143 5270	0.0145 8056	0.0148 1064	78
79	0.0139 6511	0.0141 9089	0.0144 1892	0.0146 4922	79
80	0.0138 0721	0.0140 3313	0.0142 6135	0.0144 9186	80
81	0.0136 5321	0.0138 7929	0.0141 0770	0.0143 3841	81
82	0.0135 0298	0.0137 2922	0.0139 5781	0.0141 8874	82
83	0.0133 5639	0.0135 8278	0.0138 1156	0.0140 4270	83
84	0.0132 1330	0.0134 3985	0.0136 6881	0.0139 0016	84
85	0.0130 7359	0.0133 0030	0.0135 2944	0.0137 6101	85
86	0.0129 3714	0.0131 6400	0.0133 9333	0.0136 2512	86
87	0.0128 0384	0.0130 3086	0.0132 6038	0.0134 9237	87
88	0.0126 7357	0.0129 0076	0.0131 3046	0.0133 6268	88
89	0.0125 4625	0.0127 7360	0.0130 0349	0.0132 3592	89
90	0.0124 2177	0.0126 4928	0.0128 7936	0.0131 1200	90
91	0.0123 0004	0.0125 2770	0.0127 5797	0.0129 9084	91
92	0.0121 8096	0.0124 0879	0.0126 3925	0.0128 7233	92
93	0.0120 6446	0.0122 9245	0.0125 2310	0.0127 5640	93
94	0.0119 5044	0.0121 7860	0.0124 0944	0.0126 4296	94
95	0.0118 3884	0.0120 6716	0.0122 9819	0.0125 3193	95
96	0.0117 2957	0.0119 5805	0.0121 8928	0.0124 2323	96
97	0.0116 2257	0.0118 5121	0.0120 8263	0.0123 1681	97
98	0.0115 1776	0.0117 4657	0.0119 7818	0.0122 1258	98
99	0.0114 1508	0.0116 4405	0.0118 7585	0.0121 1047	99
100	0.0113 1446	0.0115 4360	0.0117 7559	0.0120 1043	100

IX. ANNUITY WHOSE PRESENT VALUE IS 1

$$\frac{1}{a_{\overline{n}|i}} = \frac{i}{1 - (1 + i)^{-n}} = i + \frac{1}{s_{\overline{n}|i}}$$

n	$\frac{1}{4}\%$	$\frac{7}{24}\%$	$\frac{1}{3}\%$	$\frac{3}{8}\%$	n
101	0.0112 1584	0.0114 4515	0.0116 7734	0.0119 1240	101
102	0.0111 1917	0.0113 4864	0.0115 8103	0.0118 1631	102
103	0.0110 2439	0.0112 5403	0.0114 8660	0.0117 2211	103
104	0.0109 3144	0.0111 6124	0.0113 9401	0.0116 2974	104
105	0.0108 4027	0.0110 7024	0.0113 0320	0.0115 3916	105
106	0.0107 5083	0.0109 8096	0.0112 1413	0.0114 5030	106
107	0.0106 6307	0.0108 9337	0.0111 2673	0.0113 6313	107
108	0.0105 7694	0.0108 0741	0.0110 4097	0.0112 7759	108
109	0.0104 9241	0.0107 2305	0.0109 5680	0.0111 9364	109
110	0.0104 0942	0.0106 4023	0.0108 7417	0.0111 1125	110
111	0.0103 2793	0.0105 5891	0.0107 9306	0.0110 3035	111
112	0.0102 4791	0.0104 7906	0.0107 1340	0.0109 5092	112
113	0.0101 6932	0.0104 0064	0.0106 3518	0.0108 7292	113
114	0.0100 9211	0.0103 2360	0.0105 5834	0.0107 9631	114
115	0.0100 1626	0.0102 4791	0.0104 8285	0.0107 2105	115
116	0.0099 4172	0.0101 7355	0.0104 0868	0.0106 4710	116
117	0.0098 6846	0.0101 0046	0.0103 3579	0.0105 7444	117
118	0.0097 9646	0.0100 2863	0.0102 6416	0.0105 0303	118
119	0.0097 2567	0.0099 5801	0.0101 9374	0.0104 3284	119
120	0.0096 5607	0.0098 8859	0.0101 2451	0.0103 6384	120
121	0.0095 8764	0.0098 2032	0.0100 5645	0.0102 9600	121
122	0.0095 2033	0.0097 5318	0.0099 8951	0.0102 2929	122
123	0.0094 5412	0.0096 8715	0.0099 2367	0.0101 6368	123
124	0.0093 8899	0.0096 2219	0.0098 5892	0.0100 9915	124
125	0.0093 2491	0.0095 5828	0.0097 9521	0.0100 3567	125
126	0.0092 6186	0.0094 9540	0.0097 3253	0.0099 7322	126
127	0.0091 9981	0.0094 3352	0.0096 7085	0.0099 1176	127
128	0.0091 3873	0.0093 7262	0.0096 1015	0.0098 5129	128
129	0.0090 7861	0.0093 1267	0.0095 5040	0.0097 9177	129
130	0.0090 1942	0.0092 5366	0.0094 9158	0.0097 3318	130
131	0.0089 6115	0.0091 9556	0.0094 3368	0.0096 7551	131
132	0.0089 0376	0.0091 3834	0.0093 7667	0.0096 1873	132
133	0.0088 4725	0.0090 8200	0.0093 2053	0.0095 6281	133
134	0.0087 9159	0.0090 2651	0.0092 6524	0.0095 0775	134
135	0.0087 3675	0.0089 7186	0.0092 1079	0.0094 5353	135
136	0.0086 8274	0.0089 1801	0.0091 5715	0.0094 0011	136
137	0.0086 2952	0.0088 6497	0.0091 0430	0.0093 4750	137
138	0.0085 7707	0.0088 1270	0.0090 5223	0.0092 9566	138
139	0.0085 2539	0.0087 6119	0.0090 0093	0.0092 4458	139
140	0.0084 7446	0.0087 1043	0.0089 5037	0.0091 9425	140
141	0.0084 2425	0.0086 6040	0.0089 0054	0.0091 4465	141
142	0.0083 7476	0.0086 1109	0.0088 5143	0.0090 9577	142
143	0.0083 2597	0.0085 6247	0.0088 0301	0.0090 4758	143
144	0.0082 7787	0.0085 1454	0.0087 5528	0.0090 0008	144
145	0.0082 3043	0.0084 6728	0.0087 0822	0.0089 5325	145
146	0.0081 8365	0.0084 2067	0.0086 6182	0.0089 0708	146
147	0.0081 3752	0.0083 7471	0.0086 1607	0.0088 6155	147
148	0.0080 9201	0.0083 2938	0.0085 7094	0.0088 1665	148
149	0.0080 4712	0.0082 8467	0.0085 2643	0.0087 7237	149
150	0.0080 0284	0.0082 4056	0.0084 8253	0.0087 2870	150

IX. ANNUITY WHOSE PRESENT VALUE IS 1

$$\frac{1}{a_{\overline{n}|i}} = \frac{i}{1 - (1 + i)^{-n}} = i + \frac{1}{s_{\overline{n}|i}}$$

n	$\frac{1}{4}\%$	$\frac{7}{24}\%$	$\frac{1}{3}\%$	$\frac{3}{8}\%$	n
151	0.0079 5915	0.0081 9705	0.0084 3921	0.0086 8561	151
152	0.0079 1605	0.0081 5412	0.0083 9648	0.0086 4311	152
153	0.0078 7351	0.0081 1176	0.0083 5433	0.0086 0119	153
154	0.0078 3153	0.0080 6995	0.0083 1273	0.0085 5982	154
155	0.0077 9010	0.0080 2870	0.0082 7167	0.0085 1899	155
156	0.0077 4921	0.0079 8798	0.0082 3116	0.0084 7871	156
157	0.0077 0885	0.0079 4780	0.0081 9118	0.0084 3895	157
158	0.0076 6900	0.0079 0813	0.0081 5171	0.0083 9972	158
159	0.0076 2966	0.0078 6896	0.0081 1275	0.0083 6099	159
160	0.0075 9082	0.0078 3030	0.0080 7429	0.0083 2275	160
161	0.0075 5247	0.0077 9212	0.0080 3631	0.0082 8501	161
162	0.0075 1459	0.0077 5442	0.0079 9882	0.0082 4774	162
163	0.0074 7719	0.0077 1720	0.0079 6180	0.0082 1095	163
164	0.0074 4025	0.0076 8044	0.0079 2524	0.0081 7462	164
165	0.0074 0377	0.0076 4413	0.0078 8913	0.0081 3874	165
166	0.0073 6773	0.0076 0826	0.0078 5347	0.0081 0331	166
167	0.0073 3213	0.0075 7284	0.0078 1825	0.0080 6832	167
168	0.0072 9695	0.0075 3784	0.0077 8346	0.0080 3376	168
169	0.0072 6220	0.0075 0327	0.0077 4909	0.0079 9962	169
170	0.0072 2787	0.0074 6911	0.0077 1513	0.0079 6589	170
171	0.0071 9394	0.0074 3536	0.0076 8158	0.0079 3257	171
172	0.0071 6042	0.0074 0201	0.0076 4844	0.0078 9966	172
173	0.0071 2728	0.0073 6905	0.0076 1568	0.0078 6713	173
174	0.0070 9454	0.0073 3648	0.0075 8332	0.0078 3500	174
175	0.0070 6217	0.0073 0429	0.0075 5133	0.0078 0324	175
176	0.0070 3018	0.0072 7248	0.0075 1972	0.0077 7186	176
177	0.0069 9855	0.0072 4103	0.0074 8847	0.0077 4084	177
178	0.0069 6729	0.0072 0994	0.0074 5759	0.0077 1018	178
179	0.0069 3638	0.0071 7921	0.0074 2706	0.0076 7988	179
180	0.0069 0582	0.0071 4883	0.0073 9688	0.0076 4993	180
181	0.0068 7560	0.0071 1879	0.0073 6704	0.0076 2033	181
182	0.0068 4572	0.0070 8908	0.0073 3754	0.0075 9106	182
183	0.0068 1617	0.0070 5971	0.0073 0838	0.0075 6212	183
184	0.0067 8695	0.0070 3067	0.0072 7954	0.0075 3351	184
185	0.0067 5805	0.0070 0195	0.0072 5102	0.0075 0522	185
186	0.0067 2947	0.0069 7354	0.0072 2281	0.0074 7724	186
187	0.0067 0120	0.0069 4545	0.0071 9492	0.0074 4958	187
188	0.0066 7323	0.0069 1766	0.0071 6734	0.0074 2222	188
189	0.0066 4557	0.0068 9017	0.0071 4005	0.0073 9517	189
190	0.0066 1820	0.0068 6298	0.0071 1307	0.0073 6841	190
191	0.0065 9112	0.0068 3608	0.0070 8637	0.0073 4194	191
192	0.0065 6434	0.0068 0947	0.0070 5996	0.0073 1576	192
193	0.0065 3783	0.0067 8314	0.0070 3384	0.0072 8987	193
194	0.0065 1160	0.0067 5709	0.0070 0799	0.0072 6425	194
195	0.0064 8565	0.0067 3131	0.0069 8242	0.0072 3890	195
196	0.0064 5997	0.0067 0581	0.0069 5711	0.0072 1383	196
197	0.0064 3455	0.0066 8057	0.0069 3208	0.0071 8902	197
198	0.0064 0939	0.0066 5559	0.0069 0730	0.0071 6447	198
199	0.0063 8450	0.0066 3087	0.0068 8279	0.0071 4018	199
200	0.0063 5985	0.0066 0640	0.0068 5852	0.0071 1615	200

$$\frac{1}{a_{\overline{n}|i}} = \frac{i}{1 - (1 + i)^{-n}} = i + \frac{1}{s_{\overline{n}|}}$$

n	$\frac{1}{4}\%$	$\frac{7}{24}\%$	$\frac{1}{3}\%$	$\frac{3}{8}\%$	n
201	0.0063 3546	0.0065 8219	0.0068 3451	0.0070 9236	201
202	0.0063 1131	0.0065 5822	0.0068 1074	0.0070 6883	202
203	0.0062 8741	0.0065 3449	0.0067 8722	0.0070 4553	203
204	0.0062 6375	0.0065 1100	0.0067 6393	0.0070 2247	204
205	0.0062 4032	0.0064 8775	0.0067 4089	0.0069 9965	205
206	0.0062 1712	0.0064 6473	0.0067 1807	0.0069 7707	206
207	0.0061 9416	0.0064 4194	0.0066 9548	0.0069 5471	207
208	0.0061 7141	0.0064 1938	0.0066 7312	0.0069 3257	208
209	0.0061 4890	0.0063 9704	0.0066 5098	0.0069 1066	209
210	0.0061 2660	0.0063 7492	0.0066 2906	0.0068 8897	210
211	0.0061 0451	0.0063 5301	0.0066 0736	0.0068 6749	211
212	0.0060 8264	0.0063 3132	0.0065 8587	0.0068 4623	212
213	0.0060 6098	0.0063 0983	0.0065 6459	0.0068 2518	213
214	0.0060 3953	0.0062 8856	0.0065 4351	0.0068 0433	214
215	0.0060 1828	0.0062 6748	0.0065 2264	0.0067 8369	215
216	0.0059 9723	0.0062 4661	0.0065 0198	0.0067 6325	216
217	0.0059 7638	0.0062 2594	0.0064 8151	0.0067 4300	217
218	0.0059 5573	0.0062 0547	0.0064 6123	0.0067 2296	218
219	0.0059 3527	0.0061 8518	0.0064 4115	0.0067 0310	219
220	0.0059 1500	0.0061 6509	0.0064 2126	0.0066 8344	220
221	0.0058 9492	0.0061 4519	0.0064 0156	0.0066 6396	221
222	0.0058 7503	0.0061 2547	0.0063 8205	0.0066 4467	222
223	0.0058 5531	0.0061 0593	0.0063 6271	0.0066 2557	223
224	0.0058 3578	0.0060 8658	0.0063 4356	0.0066 0664	224
225	0.0058 1643	0.0060 6740	0.0063 2458	0.0065 8789	225
226	0.0057 9725	0.0060 4840	0.0063 0578	0.0065 6932	226
227	0.0057 7824	0.0060 2957	0.0062 8716	0.0065 5092	227
228	0.0057 5941	0.0060 1091	0.0062 6870	0.0065 3269	228
229	0.0057 4075	0.0059 9243	0.0062 5042	0.0065 1463	229
230	0.0057 2225	0.0059 7410	0.0062 3230	0.0064 9673	230
231	0.0057 0391	0.0059 5595	0.0062 1434	0.0064 7901	231
232	0.0056 8574	0.0059 3795	0.0061 9655	0.0064 6144	232
233	0.0056 6773	0.0059 2012	0.0061 7892	0.0064 4403	233
234	0.0056 4988	0.0059 0244	0.0061 6144	0.0064 2678	234
235	0.0056 3218	0.0058 8492	0.0061 4412	0.0064 0969	235
236	0.0056 1464	0.0058 6756	0.0061 2696	0.0063 9275	236
237	0.0055 9725	0.0058 5034	0.0061 0995	0.0063 7596	237
238	0.0055 8001	0.0058 3328	0.0060 9308	0.0063 5932	238
239	0.0055 6292	0.0058 1637	0.0060 7637	0.0063 4284	239
240	0.0055 4598	0.0057 9960	0.0060 5980	0.0063 2649	240
241	0.0055 2918	0.0057 8297	0.0060 4338	0.0063 1030	241
242	0.0055 1252	0.0057 6649	0.0060 2710	0.0062 9424	242
243	0.0054 9600	0.0057 5015	0.0060 1096	0.0062 7833	243
244	0.0054 7963	0.0057 3395	0.0059 9496	0.0062 6255	244
245	0.0054 6339	0.0057 1789	0.0059 7910	0.0062 4692	245
246	0.0054 4729	0.0057 0197	0.0059 6338	0.0062 3141	246
247	0.0054 3132	0.0056 8617	0.0059 4779	0.0062 1605	247
248	0.0054 1548	0.0056 7052	0.0059 3233	0.0062 0081	248
249	0.0053 9978	0.0056 5499	0.0059 1700	0.0061 8571	249
250	0.0053 8421	0.0056 3959	0.0059 0180	0.0061 7074	250

IX. ANNUITY WHOSE PRESENT VALUE IS 1

$$\frac{1}{a_{\overline{n}|i}} = \frac{i}{1 - (1 + i)^{-n}} = i + \frac{1}{s_{\overline{n}|i}}$$

n	$\frac{5}{12}\%$	$\frac{1}{2}\%$	$\frac{7}{12}\%$	$\frac{5}{8}\%$	n
1	1.0041 6667	1.0050 0000	1.0058 3333	1.0062 5000	1
2	0.5031 2717	0.5037 5312	0.5043 7924	0.5046 9237	2
3	0.3361 1496	0.3366 7221	0.3372 2976	0.3375 0865	3
4	0.2526 0958	0.2531 3279	0.2536 5644	0.2539 1842	4
5	0.2025 0693	0.2030 0997	0.2035 1357	0.2037 6558	5
6	0.1691 0564	0.1695 9546	0.1700 8594	0.1703 3143	6
7	0.1452 4800	0.1457 2854	0.1462 0986	0.1464 5082	7
8	0.1273 5512	0.1278 2886	0.1283 0351	0.1285 4118	8
9	0.1134 3876	0.1139 0736	0.1143 7698	0.1146 1218	9
10	0.1023 0596	0.1027 7057	0.1032 3632	0.1034 6963	10
11	0.0931 9757	0.0936 5903	0.0941 2175	0.0943 5358	11
12	0.0856 0748	0.0860 6643	0.0865 2675	0.0867 5742	12
13	0.0791 8532	0.0796 4224	0.0801 0064	0.0803 3039	13
14	0.0736 8082	0.0741 3609	0.0745 9295	0.0748 2198	14
15	0.0689 1045	0.0693 6436	0.0698 1999	0.0700 4845	15
16	0.0647 3655	0.0651 8937	0.0656 4401	0.0658 7202	16
17	0.0610 5387	0.0615 0579	0.0619 5966	0.0621 8732	17
18	0.0577 8053	0.0582 3173	0.0586 8499	0.0589 1239	18
19	0.0548 5191	0.0553 0253	0.0557 5532	0.0559 8252	19
20	0.0522 1630	0.0526 6645	0.0531 1889	0.0533 4597	20
21	0.0498 3183	0.0502 8163	0.0507 3383	0.0509 6083	21
22	0.0476 6427	0.0481 1380	0.0485 6585	0.0487 9281	22
23	0.0456 8531	0.0461 3465	0.0465 8663	0.0468 1360	23
24	0.0438 7139	0.0443 2061	0.0447 7258	0.0449 9959	24
25	0.0422 0270	0.0426 5186	0.0431 0388	0.0433 3096	25
26	0.0406 6247	0.0411 1163	0.0415 6376	0.0417 9094	26
27	0.0392 3645	0.0396 8565	0.0401 3793	0.0403 6523	27
28	0.0379 1239	0.0383 6167	0.0388 1415	0.0390 4159	28
29	0.0366 7974	0.0371 2914	0.0375 8186	0.0378 0946	29
30	0.0355 2936	0.0359 7892	0.0364 3191	0.0366 5969	30
31	0.0344 5330	0.0349 0304	0.0353 5633	0.0355 8430	31
32	0.0334 4458	0.0338 9453	0.0343 4815	0.0345 7633	32
33	0.0324 9708	0.0329 4727	0.0334 0124	0.0336 2964	33
34	0.0316 0540	0.0320 5586	0.0325 1020	0.0327 3883	34
35	0.0307 6476	0.0312 1550	0.0316 7024	0.0318 9911	35
36	0.0299 7090	0.0304 2194	0.0308 7710	0.0311 0622	36
37	0.0292 2003	0.0296 7139	0.0301 2698	0.0303 5636	37
38	0.0285 0875	0.0289 6045	0.0294 1649	0.0296 4614	38
39	0.0278 3402	0.0282 8607	0.0287 4258	0.0289 7250	39
40	0.0271 9310	0.0276 4552	0.0281 0251	0.0283 3271	40
41	0.0265 8352	0.0270 3631	0.0274 9379	0.0277 2429	41
42	0.0260 0303	0.0264 5622	0.0269 1420	0.0271 4499	42
43	0.0254 4961	0.0259 0320	0.0263 6170	0.0265 9278	43
44	0.0249 2141	0.0253 7541	0.0258 3443	0.0260 6583	44
45	0.0244 1675	0.0248 7117	0.0253 3073	0.0255 6243	45
46	0.0239 3409	0.0243 8894	0.0248 4905	0.0250 8106	46
47	0.0234 7204	0.0239 2733	0.0243 8798	0.0246 2032	47
48	0.0230 2929	0.0234 8503	0.0239 4624	0.0241 7890	48
49	0.0226 0468	0.0230 6087	0.0235 2265	0.0237 5563	49
50	0.0221 9711	0.0226 5376	0.0231 1612	0.0233 4943	50

IX. ANNUITY WHOSE PRESENT VALUE IS 1

$$\frac{1}{a_{\overline{n}|i}} = \frac{i}{1 - (1+i)^{-n}} = i + \frac{1}{s_{\overline{n}|i}}$$

n	$\frac{5}{12}\%$	$\frac{1}{2}\%$	$\frac{7}{12}\%$	$\frac{5}{8}\%$	n
51	0.0218 0557	0.0222 6269	0.0227 2563	0.0229 5928	51
52	0.0214 2916	0.0218 8675	0.0223 5027	0.0225 8425	52
53	0.0210 6700	0.0215 2507	0.0219 8919	0.0222 2350	53
54	0.0207 1830	0.0211 7686	0.0216 4157	0.0218 7623	54
55	0.0203 8234	0.0208 4139	0.0213 0671	0.0215 4171	55
56	0.0200 5843	0.0205 1797	0.0209 8390	0.0212 1925	56
57	0.0197 4593	0.0202 0598	0.0206 7251	0.0209 0821	57
58	0.0194 4426	0.0199 0481	0.0203 7196	0.0206 0801	58
59	0.0191 5287	0.0196 1392	0.0200 8170	0.0203 1809	59
60	0.0188 7123	0.0193 3280	0.0198 0120	0.0200 3795	60
61	0.0185 9888	0.0190 6096	0.0195 2999	0.0197 6709	61
62	0.0183 3536	0.0187 9796	0.0192 6762	0.0195 0508	62
63	0.0180 8025	0.0185 4337	0.0190 1366	0.0192 5148	63
64	0.0178 3315	0.0182 9681	0.0187 6773	0.0190 0591	64
65	0.0175 9371	0.0180 5789	0.0185 2946	0.0187 6800	65
66	0.0173 6156	0.0178 2627	0.0182 9848	0.0185 3739	66
67	0.0171 3639	0.0176 0163	0.0180 7449	0.0183 1376	67
68	0.0169 1788	0.0173 8366	0.0178 5716	0.0180 9680	68
69	0.0167 0574	0.0171 7206	0.0176 4622	0.0178 8622	69
70	0.0164 9971	0.0169 6657	0.0174 4138	0.0176 8175	70
71	0.0162 9952	0.0167 6693	0.0172 4239	0.0174 8313	71
72	0.0161 0493	0.0165 7289	0.0170 4901	0.0172 9011	72
73	0.0159 1572	0.0163 8422	0.0168 6100	0.0171 0247	73
74	0.0157 3165	0.0162 0070	0.0166 7814	0.0169 1999	74
75	0.0155 5253	0.0160 2214	0.0165 0024	0.0167 4246	75
76	0.0153 7816	0.0158 4832	0.0163 2709	0.0165 6968	76
77	0.0152 0836	0.0156 7908	0.0161 5851	0.0164 0147	77
78	0.0150 4295	0.0155 1423	0.0159 9432	0.0162 3766	78
79	0.0148 8177	0.0153 5360	0.0158 3436	0.0160 7808	79
80	0.0147 2464	0.0151 9704	0.0156 7847	0.0159 2256	80
81	0.0145 7144	0.0150 4439	0.0155 2650	0.0157 7096	81
82	0.0144 2200	0.0148 9552	0.0153 7830	0.0156 2314	82
83	0.0142 7620	0.0147 5028	0.0152 3373	0.0154 7895	83
84	0.0141 3391	0.0146 0855	0.0150 9268	0.0153 3828	84
85	0.0139 9500	0.0144 7021	0.0149 5501	0.0152 0098	85
86	0.0138 5935	0.0143 3513	0.0148 2060	0.0150 6696	86
87	0.0137 2685	0.0142 0320	0.0146 8935	0.0149 3608	87
88	0.0135 9740	0.0140 7431	0.0145 6115	0.0148 0826	88
89	0.0134 7088	0.0139 4837	0.0144 3588	0.0146 8337	89
90	0.0133 4721	0.0138 2527	0.0143 1347	0.0145 6134	90
91	0.0132 2629	0.0137 0493	0.0141 9380	0.0144 4205	91
92	0.0131 0803	0.0135 8724	0.0140 7679	0.0143 2542	92
93	0.0129 9234	0.0134 7213	0.0139 6236	0.0142 1137	93
94	0.0128 7915	0.0133 5950	0.0138 5042	0.0140 9982	94
95	0.0127 6837	0.0132 4930	0.0137 4090	0.0139 9067	95
96	0.0126 5992	0.0131 4143	0.0136 3372	0.0138 8387	96
97	0.0125 5374	0.0130 3583	0.0135 2880	0.0137 7933	97
98	0.0124 4976	0.0129 3242	0.0134 2608	0.0136 7700	98
99	0.0123 4790	0.0128 3115	0.0133 2549	0.0135 7679	99
100	0.0122 4811	0.0127 3194	0.0132 2696	0.0134 7865	100

$$\frac{1}{a_{\overline{n}|i}} = \frac{i}{1 - (1 + i)^{-n}} = i + \frac{1}{s_{\overline{n}|i}}$$

n	$\frac{5}{12}\%$	$\frac{1}{2}\%$	$\frac{7}{12}\%$	$\frac{5}{8}\%$	n
101	0.0121 5033	0.0126 3473	0.0131 3045	0.0133 8251	101
102	0.0120 5449	0.0125 3947	0.0130 3587	0.0132 8832	102
103	0.0119 6054	0.0124 4610	0.0129 4319	0.0131 9602	103
104	0.0118 6842	0.0123 5457	0.0128 5234	0.0131 0555	104
105	0.0117 7809	0.0122 6481	0.0127 6328	0.0130 1687	105
106	0.0116 8948	0.0121 7679	0.0126 7594	0.0129 2992	106
107	0.0116 0256	0.0120 9045	0.0125 9029	0.0128 4465	107
108	0.0115 1727	0.0120 0575	0.0125 0628	0.0127 6102	108
109	0.0114 3358	0.0119 2264	0.0124 2385	0.0126 7897	109
110	0.0113 5143	0.0118 4107	0.0123 4298	0.0125 9848	110
111	0.0112 7079	0.0117 6102	0.0122 6361	0.0125 1950	111
112	0.0111 9161	0.0116 8242	0.0121 8571	0.0124 4198	112
113	0.0111 1386	0.0116 0526	0.0121 0923	0.0123 6588	113
114	0.0110 3750	0.0115 2948	0.0120 3414	0.0122 9118	114
115	0.0109 6249	0.0114 5506	0.0119 6041	0.0122 1783	115
116	0.0108 8880	0.0113 8195	0.0118 8799	0.0121 4579	116
117	0.0108 1639	0.0113 1013	0.0118 1686	0.0120 7504	117
118	0.0107 4524	0.0112 3956	0.0117 4698	0.0120 0555	118
119	0.0106 7530	0.0111 7021	0.0116 7832	0.0119 3727	119
120	0.0106 0655	0.0111 0205	0.0116 1085	0.0118 7018	120
121	0.0105 3896	0.0110 3505	0.0115 4454	0.0118 0425	121
122	0.0104 7251	0.0109 6918	0.0114 7936	0.0117 3945	122
123	0.0104 0715	0.0109 0441	0.0114 1528	0.0116 7575	123
124	0.0103 4288	0.0108 4072	0.0113 5228	0.0116 1314	124
125	0.0102 7965	0.0107 7808	0.0112 9033	0.0115 5157	125
126	0.0102 1745	0.0107 1647	0.0112 2941	0.0114 9102	126
127	0.0101 5625	0.0106 5586	0.0111 6948	0.0114 3148	127
128	0.0100 9603	0.0105 9623	0.0111 1054	0.0113 7292	128
129	0.0100 3677	0.0105 3755	0.0110 5255	0.0113 1531	129
130	0.0099 7844	0.0104 7981	0.0109 9550	0.0112 5864	130
131	0.0099 2102	0.0104 2298	0.0109 3935	0.0112 0288	131
132	0.0098 6449	0.0103 6703	0.0108 8410	0.0111 4800	132
133	0.0098 0883	0.0103 1197	0.0108 2972	0.0110 9400	133
134	0.0097 5403	0.0102 5775	0.0107 7619	0.0110 4086	134
135	0.0097 0005	0.0102 0436	0.0107 2349	0.0109 8854	135
136	0.0096 4689	0.0101 5179	0.0106 7161	0.0109 3703	136
137	0.0095 9453	0.0101 0002	0.0106 2052	0.0108 8633	137
138	0.0095 4295	0.0100 4902	0.0105 7021	0.0108 3640	138
139	0.0094 9213	0.0099 9879	0.0105 2067	0.0107 8723	139
140	0.0094 4205	0.0099 4930	0.0104 7187	0.0107 3881	140
141	0.0093 9271	0.0099 0055	0.0104 2380	0.0106 9111	141
142	0.0093 4408	0.0098 5250	0.0103 7644	0.0106 4414	142
143	0.0092 9615	0.0098 0516	0.0103 2978	0.0105 9786	143
144	0.0092 4890	0.0097 5850	0.0102 8381	0.0105 5226	144
145	0.0092 0233	0.0097 1252	0.0102 3851	0.0105 0734	145
146	0.0091 5641	0.0096 6718	0.0101 9386	0.0104 6307	146
147	0.0091 1114	0.0096 2250	0.0101 4986	0.0104 1944	147
148	0.0090 6650	0.0095 7844	0.0101 0649	0.0103 7645	148
149	0.0090 2247	0.0095 3500	0.0100 6374	0.0103 3407	149
150	0.0089 7905	0.0094 9217	0.0100 2159	0.0102 9230	150

IX. ANNUITY WHOSE PRESENT VALUE IS 1

$$\frac{1}{a_{\overline{n}|i}} = \frac{i}{1 - (1 + i)^{-n}} = i + \frac{1}{s_{\overline{n}|i}}$$

n	$\frac{5}{12}\%$	$\frac{1}{2}\%$	$\frac{7}{12}\%$	$\frac{5}{8}\%$	n
151	0.0089 3623	0.0094 4993	0.0099 8003	0.0102 5112	151
152	0.0088 9398	0.0094 0827	0.0099 3905	0.0102 1052	152
153	0.0088 5231	0.0093 6719	0.0098 9865	0.0101 7049	153
154	0.0088 1119	0.0093 2666	0.0098 5880	0.0101 3102	154
155	0.0087 7063	0.0092 8668	0.0098 1950	0.0100 9209	155
156	0.0087 3060	0.0092 4723	0.0097 8074	0.0100 5370	156
157	0.0086 9110	0.0092 0832	0.0097 4251	0.0100 1584	157
158	0.0086 5211	0.0091 6992	0.0097 0479	0.0099 7850	158
159	0.0086 1364	0.0091 3203	0.0096 6758	0.0099 4166	159
160	0.0085 7566	0.0090 9464	0.0096 3087	0.0099 0532	160
161	0.0085 3817	0.0090 5773	0.0095 9464	0.0098 6947	161
162	0.0085 0116	0.0090 2131	0.0095 5890	0.0098 3410	162
163	0.0084 6462	0.0089 8536	0.0095 2362	0.0097 9919	163
164	0.0084 2855	0.0089 4987	0.0094 8881	0.0097 6475	164
165	0.0083 9293	0.0089 1483	0.0094 5445	0.0097 3076	165
166	0.0083 5775	0.0088 8024	0.0094 2053	0.0096 9722	166
167	0.0083 2302	0.0088 4608	0.0093 8705	0.0096 6411	167
168	0.0082 8871	0.0088 1236	0.0093 5401	0.0096 3143	168
169	0.0082 5482	0.0087 7906	0.0093 2138	0.0095 9918	169
170	0.0082 2135	0.0087 4617	0.0092 8917	0.0095 6733	170
171	0.0081 8829	0.0087 1369	0.0092 5736	0.0095 3589	171
172	0.0081 5563	0.0086 8161	0.0092 2595	0.0095 0486	172
173	0.0081 2336	0.0086 4992	0.0091 9494	0.0094 7421	173
174	0.0080 9147	0.0086 1862	0.0091 6431	0.0094 4395	174
175	0.0080 5997	0.0085 8770	0.0091 3406	0.0094 1407	175
176	0.0080 2884	0.0085 5715	0.0091 0418	0.0093 8456	176
177	0.0079 9808	0.0085 2697	0.0090 7468	0.0093 5542	177
178	0.0079 6768	0.0084 9715	0.0090 4553	0.0093 2664	178
179	0.0079 3763	0.0084 6769	0.0090 1673	0.0092 9821	179
180	0.0079 0794	0.0084 3857	0.0089 8828	0.0092 7012	180
181	0.0078 7858	0.0084 0979	0.0089 6018	0.0092 4238	181
182	0.0078 4957	0.0083 8136	0.0089 3241	0.0092 1498	182
183	0.0078 2088	0.0083 5325	0.0089 0497	0.0091 8791	183
184	0.0077 9253	0.0083 2547	0.0088 7786	0.0091 6116	184
185	0.0077 6449	0.0082 9802	0.0088 5107	0.0091 3473	185
186	0.0077 3677	0.0082 7088	0.0088 2459	0.0091 0862	186
187	0.0077 0936	0.0082 4404	0.0087 9843	0.0090 8282	187
188	0.0076 8226	0.0082 1752	0.0087 7257	0.0090 5732	188
189	0.0076 5546	0.0081 9129	0.0087 4701	0.0090 3212	189
190	0.0076 2895	0.0081 6537	0.0087 2174	0.0090 0722	190
191	0.0076 0274	0.0081 3973	0.0086 9677	0.0089 8260	191
192	0.0075 7681	0.0081 1438	0.0086 7208	0.0089 5828	192
193	0.0075 5117	0.0080 8931	0.0086 4767	0.0089 3423	193
194	0.0075 2580	0.0080 6452	0.0086 2355	0.0089 1046	194
195	0.0075 0071	0.0080 4000	0.0085 9969	0.0088 8696	195
196	0.0074 7589	0.0080 1576	0.0085 7610	0.0088 6374	196
197	0.0074 5133	0.0079 9178	0.0085 5278	0.0088 4077	197
198	0.0074 2704	0.0079 6806	0.0085 2972	0.0088 1807	198
199	0.0074 0300	0.0079 4459	0.0085 0691	0.0087 9502	199
200	0.0073 7922	0.0079 2138	0.0084 8436	0.0087 7343	200

IX. ANNUITY WHOSE PRESENT VALUE IS 1

$$\frac{1}{a_{\overline{n}|i}} = \frac{i}{1 - (1 + i)^{-n}} = i + \frac{1}{s_{\overline{n}|i}}$$

n	$\frac{5}{12}\%$	$\frac{1}{2}\%$	$\frac{7}{12}\%$	$\frac{5}{8}\%$	n
201	0.0073 5569	0.0078 9843	0.0084 6206	0.0087 5148	201
202	0.0073 3240	0.0078 7571	0.0084 4000	0.0087 2978	202
203	0.0073 0936	0.0078 5324	0.0084 1818	0.0087 0832	203
204	0.0072 8655	0.0078 3101	0.0083 9661	0.0086 8709	204
205	0.0072 6398	0.0078 0901	0.0083 7526	0.0086 6610	205
206	0.0072 4165	0.0077 8724	0.0083 5415	0.0086 4535	206
207	0.0072 1954	0.0077 6571	0.0083 3327	0.0086 2482	207
208	0.0071 9766	0.0077 4440	0.0083 1261	0.0086 0451	208
209	0.0071 7600	0.0077 2330	0.0082 9217	0.0085 8442	209
210	0.0071 5456	0.0077 0243	0.0082 7194	0.0085 6455	210
211	0.0071 3333	0.0076 8178	0.0082 5194	0.0085 4490	211
212	0.0071 1232	0.0076 6133	0.0082 3214	0.0085 2545	212
213	0.0070 9152	0.0076 4110	0.0082 1256	0.0085 0622	213
214	0.0070 7092	0.0076 2107	0.0081 9318	0.0084 8719	214
215	0.0070 5053	0.0076 0125	0.0081 7400	0.0084 6836	215
216	0.0070 3034	0.0075 8162	0.0081 5502	0.0084 4973	216
217	0.0070 1035	0.0075 6220	0.0081 3624	0.0084 3130	217
218	0.0069 9055	0.0075 4297	0.0081 1766	0.0084 1306	218
219	0.0069 7095	0.0075 2393	0.0080 9926	0.0083 9502	219
220	0.0069 5153	0.0075 0508	0.0080 8106	0.0083 7716	220
221	0.0069 3231	0.0074 8642	0.0080 6304	0.0083 5949	221
222	0.0069 1327	0.0074 6794	0.0080 4520	0.0083 4200	222
223	0.0068 9441	0.0074 4965	0.0080 2755	0.0083 2469	223
224	0.0068 7573	0.0074 3154	0.0080 1008	0.0083 0757	224
225	0.0068 5723	0.0074 1360	0.0079 9278	0.0082 9061	225
226	0.0068 3891	0.0073 9584	0.0079 7566	0.0082 7383	226
227	0.0068 2076	0.0073 7825	0.0079 5871	0.0082 5723	227
228	0.0068 0278	0.0073 6083	0.0079 4192	0.0082 4079	328
229	0.0067 8497	0.0073 4358	0.0079 2531	0.0082 2452	229
230	0.0067 6732	0.0073 2649	0.0079 0886	0.0082 0841	230
231	0.0067 4984	0.0073 0957	0.0078 9257	0.0081 9247	231
232	0.0067 3252	0.0072 9281	0.0078 7645	0.0081 7668	232
233	0.0067 1536	0.0072 7621	0.0078 6048	0.0081 6105	233
234	0.0066 9836	0.0072 5977	0.0078 4467	0.0081 4558	234
235	0.0066 8151	0.0072 4348	0.0078 2902	0.0081 3027	235
236	0.0066 6482	0.0072 2735	0.0078 1351	0.0081 1511	236
237	0.0066 4828	0.0072 1137	0.0077 9816	0.0081 0009	237
238	0.0066 3189	0.0071 9554	0.0077 8296	0.0080 8523	238
239	0.0066 1565	0.0071 7985	0.0077 6790	0.0080 7051	239
240	0.0065 9956	0.0071 6431	0.0077 5299	0.0080 5593	240
241	0.0065 8361	0.0071 4892	0.0077 3822	0.0080 4150	241
242	0.0065 6780	0.0071 3366	0.0077 2359	0.0080 2721	242
243	0.0065 5213	0.0071 1855	0.0077 0911	0.0080 1306	243
244	0.0065 3660	0.0071 0357	0.0076 9476	0.0079 9904	244
245	0.0065 2121	0.0070 8874	0.0076 8054	0.0079 8516	245
246	0.0065 0596	0.0070 7403	0.0076 6646	0.0079 7142	246
247	0.0064 9084	0.0070 5947	0.0076 5252	0.0079 5780	247
248	0.0064 7585	0.0070 4503	0.0076 3870	0.0079 4432	248
249	0.0064 6099	0.0070 3072	0.0076 2501	0.0079 3096	249
250	0.0064 4626	0.0070 1654	0.0076 1146	0.0079 1774	250

IX. ANNUITY WHOSE PRESENT VALUE IS 1

$$\frac{1}{a_{\overline{n}|i}} = \frac{i}{1 - (1 + i)^{-n}} = i + \frac{1}{s_{\overline{n}|i}}$$

n	$\frac{3}{4}\%$	$\frac{7}{8}\%$	1%	$1\frac{1}{8}\%$	n
1	1.0075 0000	1.0087 5000	1.0100 0000	1.0112 5000	1
2	0.5056 3201	0.5065 7203	0.5075 1244	0.5084 5323	2
3	0.3383 4579	0.3391 8361	0.3400 2211	0.3408 6130	3
4	0.2547 0501	0.2554 9257	0.2562 8109	0.2570 7058	4
5	0.2045 2242	0.2052 8049	0.2060 3980	0.2068 0034	5
6	0.1710 6891	0.1718 0789	0.1725 4837	0.1732 9034	6
7	0.1471 7488	0.1479 0070	0.1486 2828	0.1493 5762	7
8	0.1292 5552	0.1299 7190	0.1306 9029	0.1314 1071	8
9	0.1153 1929	0.1160 2868	0.1167 4036	0.1174 5432	9
10	0.1041 7123	0.1048 7538	0.1055 8208	0.1062 9131	10
11	0.0950 5094	0.0957 5111	0.0964 5408	0.0971 5984	11
12	0.0874 5148	0.0881 4860	0.0888 4879	0.0895 5203	12
13	0.0810 2188	0.0817 1669	0.0824 1482	0.0831 1626	13
14	0.0755 1146	0.0762 0453	0.0769 0117	0.0776 0138	14
15	0.0707 3639	0.0714 2817	0.0721 2378	0.0728 2321	15
16	0.0665 5879	0.0672 4965	0.0679 4460	0.0686 4363	16
17	0.0628 7321	0.0635 6346	0.0642 5806	0.0649 5698	17
18	0.0595 9766	0.0602 8756	0.0609 8205	0.0616 8113	18
19	0.0566 6740	0.0573 5715	0.0580 5175	0.0587 5120	19
20	0.0540 3063	0.0547 2042	0.0554 1531	0.0561 1531	20
21	0.0516 4543	0.0523 3541	0.0530 3075	0.0537 3145	21
22	0.0494 7748	0.0501 6779	0.0508 6372	0.0515 6525	22
23	0.0474 9846	0.0481 8921	0.0488 8584	0.0495 8833	23
24	0.0456 8474	0.0463 7604	0.0470 7347	0.0477 7701	24
25	0.0440 1650	0.0447 0843	0.0454 0675	0.0461 1144	25
26	0.0424 7693	0.0431 6959	0.0438 6888	0.0445 7479	26
27	0.0410 5176	0.0417 4520	0.0424 4553	0.0431 5273	27
28	0.0397 2871	0.0404 2300	0.0411 2444	0.0418 3299	28
29	0.0384 9723	0.0391 9243	0.0398 9502	0.0406 0498	29
30	0.0373 4816	0.0380 4431	0.0387 4811	0.0394 5953	30
31	0.0362 7352	0.0369 7068	0.0376 7573	0.0383 8866	31
32	0.0352 6634	0.0359 6454	0.0366 7089	0.0373 8535	32
33	0.0343 2048	0.0350 1976	0.0357 2744	0.0364 4349	33
34	0.0334 3053	0.0341 3092	0.0348 3997	0.0355 5763	34
35	0.0325 9170	0.0332 9324	0.0340 0368	0.0347 2299	35
36	0.0317 9973	0.0325 0244	0.0332 1431	0.0339 3529	36
37	0.0310 5082	0.0317 5473	0.0324 6805	0.0331 9072	37
38	0.0303 4157	0.0310 4671	0.0317 6150	0.0324 8589	38
39	0.0296 6893	0.0303 7531	0.0310 9160	0.0318 1773	39
40	0.0290 3016	0.0297 3780	0.0304 5560	0.0311 8349	40
41	0.0284 2276	0.0291 3169	0.0298 5102	0.0305 8069	41
42	0.0278 4452	0.0285 5475	0.0292 7563	0.0300 0709	42
43	0.0272 9338	0.0280 0493	0.0287 2737	0.0294 6064	43
44	0.0267 6751	0.0274 8039	0.0282 0441	0.0289 3949	44
45	0.0262 6521	0.0269 7943	0.0277 0505	0.0284 4197	45
46	0.0257 8495	0.0265 0053	0.0272 2775	0.0279 6652	46
47	0.0253 2532	0.0260 4228	0.0267 7111	0.0275 1173	47
48	0.0248 8504	0.0256 0338	0.0263 3384	0.0270 7632	48
49	0.0244 6292	0.0251 8265	0.0259 1474	0.0266 5910	49
50	0.0240 5787	0.0247 7900	0.0255 1273	0.0262 5898	50

IX. ANNUITY WHOSE PRESENT VALUE IS 1

$$\frac{1}{a_{\overline{n}|i}} = \frac{i}{1 - (1 + i)^{-n}} = i + \frac{1}{s_{\overline{n}|i}}$$

n	$\frac{3}{4}\%$	$\frac{7}{8}\%$	1%	$1\frac{1}{8}\%$	n
51	0.0236 6888	0.0243 9142	0.0251 2680	0.0258 7494	51
52	0.0232 9503	0.0240 1899	0.0247 5603	0.0255 0606	52
53	0.0229 3546	0.0236 6084	0.0243 9956	0.0251 5149	53
54	0.0225 8938	0.0233 1619	0.0240 5658	0.0248 1043	54
55	0.0222 5605	0.0229 8430	0.0237 2637	0.0244 8213	55
56	0.0219 3478	0.0226 6449	0.0234 0824	0.0241 6592	56
57	0.0216 2496	0.0223 5611	0.0231 0156	0.0238 6116	57
58	0.0213 2597	0.0220 5858	0.0228 0573	0.0235 6726	58
59	0.0210 3727	0.0217 7135	0.0225 2020	0.0232 8366	59
60	0.0207 5836	0.0214 9390	0.0222 4445	0.0230 0985	60
61	0.0204 8873	0.0212 2575	0.0219 7800	0.0227 4534	61
62	0.0202 2795	0.0209 6644	0.0217 2041	0.0224 8969	62
63	0.0199 7560	0.0207 1557	0.0214 7125	0.0222 4247	63
64	0.0197 3127	0.0204 7273	0.0212 3013	0.0220 0329	64
65	0.0194 9460	0.0202 3754	0.0209 9667	0.0217 7178	65
66	0.0192 6524	0.0200 0968	0.0207 7052	0.0215 4758	66
67	0.0190 4286	0.0197 8879	0.0205 5136	0.0213 3037	67
68	0.0188 2716	0.0195 7459	0.0203 3889	0.0211 1985	68
69	0.0186 1785	0.0193 6677	0.0201 3280	0.0209 1571	69
70	0.0184 1464	0.0191 6506	0.0199 3282	0.0207 1769	70
71	0.0182 1728	0.0189 6921	0.0197 3870	0.0205 2552	71
72	0.0180 2554	0.0187 7897	0.0195 5019	0.0203 3896	72
73	0.0178 3917	0.0185 9411	0.0193 6706	0.0201 5779	73
74	0.0176 5796	0.0184 1441	0.0191 8910	0.0199 8177	74
75	0.0174 8170	0.0182 3966	0.0190 1609	0.0198 1072	75
76	0.0173 1020	0.0180 6967	0.0188 4784	0.0196 4442	76
77	0.0171 4328	0.0179 0426	0.0186 8416	0.0194 8269	77
78	0.0169 8074	0.0177 4324	0.0185 2488	0.0193 2536	78
79	0.0168 2244	0.0175 8645	0.0183 6983	0.0191 7226	79
80	0.0166 6821	0.0174 3374	0.0182 1885	0.0190 2323	80
81	0.0165 1790	0.0172 8494	0.0180 7179	0.0188 7812	81
82	0.0163 7136	0.0171 3992	0.0179 2851	0.0187 3678	82
83	0.0162 2847	0.0169 9854	0.0177 8887	0.0185 9908	83
84	0.0160 8908	0.0168 6067	0.0176 5273	0.0184 6489	84
85	0.0159 5308	0.0167 2619	0.0175 1998	0.0183 3409	85
86	0.0158 2034	0.0165 9497	0.0173 9050	0.0182 0654	86
87	0.0156 9076	0.0164 6691	0.0172 6418	0.0180 8215	87
88	0.0155 6423	0.0163 4190	0.0171 4089	0.0179 6081	88
89	0.0154 4064	0.0162 1982	0.0170 2056	0.0178 4240	89
90	0.0153 1989	0.0161 0060	0.0169 0306	0.0177 2684	90
91	0.0152 0190	0.0159 8413	0.0167 8832	0.0176 1403	91
92	0.0150 8657	0.0158 7031	0.0166 7624	0.0175 0387	92
93	0.0149 7382	0.0157 5908	0.0165 6673	0.0173 9629	93
94	0.0148 6356	0.0156 5033	0.0164 5971	0.0172 9119	94
95	0.0147 5571	0.0155 4401	0.0163 5511	0.0171 8851	95
96	0.0146 5020	0.0154 4002	0.0162 5284	0.0170 8816	96
97	0.0145 4696	0.0153 3829	0.0161 5284	0.0169 9007	97
98	0.0144 4592	0.0152 3877	0.0160 5503	0.0168 9418	98
99	0.0143 4701	0.0151 4137	0.0159 5936	0.0168 0041	99
100	0.0142 5017	0.0150 4604	0.0158 6574	0.0167 0870	100

IX. ANNUITY WHOSE PRESENT VALUE IS 1

$$\frac{1}{a_{\overline{n}|i}} = \frac{i}{1 - (1 + i)^{-n}} = i + \frac{1}{s_{\overline{n}|i}}$$

n	$1\frac{1}{4}\%$	$1\frac{3}{8}\%$	$1\frac{1}{2}\%$	$1\frac{5}{8}\%$	n
1	1.0125 0000	1.0137 5000	1.0150 0000	1.0162 5000	1
2	0.5093 9441	0.5103 3597	0.5112 7792	0.5122 2024	2
3	0.3417 0117	0.3425 4173	0.3433 8296	0.3442 2487	3
4	0.2578 6102	0.2586 5243	0.2594 4479	0.2602 3810	4
5	0.2075 6211	0.2083 2510	0.2090 8932	0.2098 5476	5
6	0.1740 3381	0.1747 7877	0.1755 2521	0.1762 7314	6
7	0.1500 8872	0.1508 2157	0.1515 5616	0.1522 9250	7
8	0.1321 3314	0.1328 5758	0.1335 8402	0.1343 1247	8
9	0.1181 7055	0.1188 8906	0.1196 0982	0.1203 3285	9
10	0.1070 0307	0.1077 1737	0.1084 3418	0.1091 5351	10
11	0.0978 6839	0.0985 7973	0.0992 9384	0.1000 1073	11
12	0.0902 5831	0.0909 6764	0.0916 7999	0.0923 9537	12
13	0.0838 2100	0.0845 2903	0.0852 4036	0.0859 5496	13
14	0.0783 0515	0.0790 1246	0.0797 2332	0.0804 3771	14
15	0.0735 2646	0.0742 3351	0.0749 4436	0.0756 5898	15
16	0.0693 4672	0.0700 5388	0.0707 6508	0.0714 8031	16
17	0.0656 6023	0.0663 6780	0.0670 7966	0.0677 9580	17
18	0.0623 8479	0.0630 9301	0.0638 0578	0.0645 2309	18
19	0.0594 5548	0.0601 6457	0.0608 7847	0.0615 9715	19
20	0.0568 2039	0.0575 3054	0.0582 4574	0.0589 6597	20
21	0.0544 3749	0.0551 4884	0.0558 6550	0.0565 8743	21
22	0.0522 7238	0.0529 8507	0.0537 0332	0.0544 2709	22
23	0.0502 9666	0.0510 1080	0.0517 3075	0.0524 5648	23
24	0.0484 8665	0.0492 0235	0.0499 2410	0.0506 5188	24
25	0.0468 2247	0.0475 3981	0.0482 6345	0.0489 9336	25
26	0.0452 8729	0.0460 0635	0.0467 3196	0.0474 6408	26
27	0.0438 4677	0.0445 8763	0.0453 1527	0.0460 4967	27
28	0.0425 4863	0.0432 7134	0.0440 0108	0.0447 3781	28
29	0.0413 2228	0.0420 4689	0.0427 7878	0.0435 1791	29
30	0.0401 7854	0.0409 0511	0.0416 3919	0.0423 8075	30
31	0.0391 0942	0.0398 3798	0.0405 7430	0.0413 1834	31
32	0.0381 0791	0.0388 3850	0.0395 7710	0.0403 2365	32
33	0.0371 6786	0.0379 0053	0.0386 4144	0.0393 9054	33
34	0.0362 8387	0.0370 1864	0.0377 6189	0.0385 1357	34
35	0.0354 5111	0.0361 8801	0.0369 3363	0.0376 8792	35
36	0.0346 6533	0.0354 0438	0.0361 5240	0.0369 0931	36
37	0.0339 2270	0.0346 6394	0.0354 1437	0.0361 7393	37
38	0.0332 1983	0.0339 6327	0.0347 1613	0.0354 7837	38
39	0.0325 5365	0.0332 9931	0.0340 5463	0.0348 1955	39
40	0.0319 2141	0.0326 6931	0.0334 2710	0.0341 9472	40
41	0.0313 2063	0.0320 7078	0.0328 3106	0.0336 0140	41
42	0.0307 4906	0.0315 0148	0.0322 6426	0.0330 3732	42
43	0.0302 0466	0.0309 5936	0.0317 2465	0.0325 0045	43
44	0.0296 8557	9.0304 4257	0.0312 1038	0.0319 8893	44
45	0.0291 9012	0.0299 4941	0.0307 1976	0.0315 0106	45
46	0.0287 1675	0.0294 7836	0.0302 5125	0.0310 3531	46
47	0.0282 6406	0.0290 2799	0.0298 0342	0.0305 9025	47
48	0.0278 3075	0.0285 9701	0.0293 7500	0.0301 6460	48
49	0.0274 1563	0.0281 8423	0.0289 6478	0.0297 5716	49
50	0.0270 1763	0.0277 8857	0.0285 7168	0.0293 6684	50

$$\frac{1}{a_{\overline{n}|i}} = \frac{i}{1 - (1 + i)^{-n}} = i + \frac{1}{s_{\overline{n}|i}}$$

n	$1\frac{1}{4}\%$	$1\frac{3}{8}\%$	$1\frac{1}{2}\%$	$1\frac{5}{8}\%$	n
51	0.0266 3571	0.0274 0900	0.0281 9469	0.0289 9263	51
52	0.0262 6897	0.0270 4461	0.0278 3287	0.0286 3360	52
53	0.0259 1653	0.0266 9453	0.0274 8537	0.0282 8888	53
54	0.0255 7760	0.0263 5797	0.0271 5138	0.0279 5769	54
55	0.0252 5145	0.0260 3418	0.0268 3018	0.0276 3927	55
56	0.0249 3739	0.0257 2249	0.0265 2106	0.0273 3294	56
57	0.0246 3478	0.0254 2225	0.0262 2341	0.0270 3807	57
58	0.0243 4303	0.0251 3287	0.0259 3661	0.0267 5406	58
59	0.0240 6158	0.0248 5380	0.0256 6012	0.0264 8036	59
60	0.0237 8993	0.0245 8452	0.0253 9343	0.0262 1645	60
61	0.0235 2758	0.0243 2455	0.0251 3604	0.0259 6184	61
62	0.0232 7410	0.0240 7344	0.0248 8751	0.0257 1608	62
63	0.0230 2904	0.0238 3076	0.0246 4741	0.0254 7875	63
64	0.0227 9203	0.0235 9612	0.0244 1534	0.0252 4946	64
65	0.0225 6268	0.0233 6914	0.0241 9094	0.0250 2782	65
66	0.0223 4065	0.0231 4949	0.0239 7386	0.0248 1350	66
67	0.0221 2560	0.0229 3682	0.0237 6376	0.0246 0615	67
68	0.0219 1724	0.0227 3082	0.0235 6033	0.0244 0548	68
69	0.0217 1527	0.0225 3122	0.0233 6329	0.0242 1118	69
70	0.0215 1941	0.0223 3773	0.0231 7235	0.0240 2299	70
71	0.0213 2941	0.0221 5009	0.0229 8727	0.0238 4064	71
72	0.0211 4501	0.0219 6806	0.0228 0779	0.0236 6388	72
73	0.0209 6600	0.0217 9140	0.0226 3368	0.0234 9250	73
74	0.0207 9215	0.0216 1991	0.0224 6473	0.0233 2626	74
75	0.0206 2325	0.0214 5336	0.0223 0072	0.0231 6496	75
76	0.0204 5910	0.0212 9157	0.0221 4146	0.0230 0840	76
77	0.0202 9953	0.0211 3435	0.0219 8676	0.0228 5640	77
78	0.0201 4436	0.0209 8151	0.0218 3645	0.0227 0877	78
79	0.0199 9341	0.0208 3290	0.0216 9036	0.0225 6536	79
80	0.0198 4652	0.0206 8836	0.0215 4832	0.0224 2600	80
81	0.0197 0356	0.0205 4772	0.0214 1019	0.0222 9053	81
82	0.0195 6437	0.0204 1086	0.0212 7583	0.0221 5882	82
83	0.0194 2881	0.0202 7762	0.0211 4509	0.0220 3073	83
84	0.0192 9675	0.0201 4789	0.0210 1784	0.0219 0612	84
85	0.0191 6808	0.0200 2153	0.0208 9396	0.0217 8487	85
86	0.0190 4267	0.0198 9843	0.0207 7333	0.0216 6687	86
87	0.0189 2041	0.0197 7847	0.0206 5584	0.0215 5199	87
88	0.0188 0119	0.0196 6155	0.0205 4138	0.0214 4013	88
89	0.0186 8491	0.0195 4756	0.0204 2984	0.0213 3119	89
90	0.0185 7146	0.0194 3641	0.0203 2113	0.0212 2506	90
91	0.0184 6076	0.0193 2799	0.0202 1516	0.0211 2166	91
92	0.0183 5272	0.0192 2222	0.0201 1182	0.0210 2089	92
93	0.0182 4724	0.0191 1902	0.0200 1104	0.0209 2267	93
94	0.0181 4425	0.0190 1829	0.0199 1273	0.0208 2691	94
95	0.0180 4366	0.0189 1997	0.0198 1681	0.0207 3353	95
96	0.0179 4541	0.0188 2397	0.0197 2321	0.0206 4246	96
97	0.0178 4941	0.0187 3022	0.0196 3186	0.0205 5362	97
98	0.0177 5560	0.0186 3866	0.0195 4268	0.0204 6695	98
99	0.0176 6391	0.0185 4921	0.0194 5560	0.0203 8237	99
100	0.0175 7428	0.0184 6181	0.0193 7057	0.0202 9983	100

IX. ANNUITY WHOSE PRESENT VALUE IS 1

$$\frac{1}{a_{\overline{n}|i}} = \frac{i}{1 - (1 + i)^{-n}} = i + \frac{1}{s_{\overline{n}|i}}$$

n	$1\frac{3}{4}\%$	2%	$2\frac{1}{4}\%$	$2\frac{1}{2}\%$	n
1	1.0175 0000	1.0200 0000	1.0225 0000	1.0250 0000	1
2	0.5131 6295	0.5150 4950	0.5169 3758	0.5188 2716	2
3	0.3450 6746	0.3467 5467	0.3484 4458	0.3501 3717	3
4	0.2610 3237	0.2626 2375	0.2642 1893	0.2658 1788	4
5	0.2106 2142	0.2121 5839	0.2137 0021	0.2152 4686	5
6	0.1770 2256	0.1785 2581	0.1800 3496	0.1815 4997	6
7	0.1530 3059	0.1545 1196	0.1560 0025	0.1574 9543	7
8	0.1350 4292	0.1365 0980	0.1379 8462	0.1394 6735	8
9	0.1210 5813	0.1225 1544	0.1239 8170	0.1254 5689	9
10	0.1098 7534	0.1113 2653	0.1127 8768	0.1142 5876	10
11	0.1007 3038	0.1021 7794	0.1036 3649	0.1051 0596	11
12	0.0931 1377	0.0945 5960	0.0960 1740	0.0974 8713	12
13	0.0866 7283	0.0881 1835	0.0895 7686	0.0910 4827	13
14	0.0811 5562	0.0826 0197	0.0840 6230	0.0855 3652	14
15	0.0763 7739	0.0778 2547	0.0792 8852	0.0807 6646	15
16	0.0721 9958	0.0736 5013	0.0751 1663	0.0765 9899	16
17	0.0685 1623	0.0699 6984	0.0714 4039	0.0729 2777	17
18	0.0652 4492	0.0667 0210	0.0681 7720	0.0696 7008	18
19	0.0623 2061	0.0637 8177	0.0652 6182	0.0667 6062	19
20	0.0596 9122	0.0611 5672	0.0626 4207	0.0641 4713	20
21	0.0573 1464	0.0587 8477	0.0602 7572	0.0617 8733	21
22	0.0551 5638	0.0566 3140	0.0581 2821	0.0596 4661	22
23	0.0531 8796	0.0546 6810	0.0561 7097	0.0576 9638	23
24	0.0513 8565	0.0528 7110	0.0543 8023	0.0559 1282	24
25	0.0497 2952	0.0512 2044	0.0527 3599	0.0542 7592	25
26	0.0482 0269	0.0496 9923	0.0512 2134	0.0527 6875	26
27	0.0467 9079	0.0482 9309	0.0498 2188	0.0513 7687	27
28	0.0454 8151	0.0469 8967	0.0485 2525	0.0500 8793	28
29	0.0442 6424	0.0457 7836	0.0473 2081	0.0488 9127	29
30	0.0431 2975	0.0446 4992	0.0461 9934	0.0477 7764	30
31	0.0420 7005	0.0435 9635	0.0451 5280	0.0467 3900	31
32	0.0410 7812	0.0426 1061	0.0441 7415	0.0457 6831	32
33	0.0401 4779	0.0416 8653	0.0432 5722	0.0448 5938	33
34	0.0392 7363	0.0408 1867	0.0423 9655	0.0440 0675	34
35	0.0384 5082	0.0400 0221	0.0415 8731	0.0432 0558	35
36	0.0376 7507	0.0392 3285	0.0408 2522	0.0424 5158	36
37	0.0369 4257	0.0385 0678	0.0401 0643	0.0417 4090	37
38	0.0362 4990	0.0378 2057	0.0394 2753	0.0410 7012	38
39	0.0355 9399	0.0371 7114	0.0387 8543	0.0404 3615	39
40	0.0349 7209	0.0365 5575	0.0381 7738	0.0398 3623	40
41	0.0343 8170	0.0359 7188	0.0376 0087	0.0392 6786	41
42	0.0338 2057	0.0354 1729	0.0370 5364	0.0387 2876	42
43	0.0332 8666	0.0348 8993	0.0365 3364	0.0382 1688	43
44	0.0327 7810	0.0343 8794	0.0360 3901	0.0377 3037	44
45	0.0322 9321	0.0339 0962	0.0355 6805	0.0372 6751	45
46	0.0318 3043	0.0334 5342	0.0351 1921	0.0368 2676	46
47	0.0313 8836	0.0330 1792	0.0346 9107	0.0364 0669	47
48	0.0309 6569	0.0326 0184	0.0342 8233	0.0360 0599	48
49	0.0305 6124	0.0322 0396	0.0338 9179	0.0356 2348	49
50	0.0301 7391	0.0318 2321	0.0335 1836	0.0352 5806	50

IX. ANNUITY WHOSE PRESENT VALUE IS 1

$$\frac{1}{a_{\overline{n}|i}} = \frac{i}{1 - (1 + i)^{-n}} = i + \frac{1}{s_{\overline{n}|i}}$$

n	$1\frac{3}{4}\%$	2%	$2\frac{1}{4}\%$	$2\frac{1}{2}\%$	n
51	0.0298 0269	0.0314 5856	0.0331 6102	0.0349 0870	51
52	0.0294 4665	0.0311 0909	0.0328 1884	0.0345 7446	52
53	0.0291 0492	0.0307 7392	0.0324 9094	0.0342 5449	53
54	0.0287 7672	0.0304 5226	0.0321 7654	0.0339 4799	54
55	0.0284 6129	0.0301 4337	0.0318 7489	0.0336 5419	55
56	0.0281 5795	0.0298 4656	0.0315 8530	0.0333 7243	56
57	0.0278 6606	0.0295 6120	0.0313 0712	0.0331 0204	57
58	0.0275 8503	0.0292 8667	0.0310 3977	0.0328 4244	58
59	0.0273 1430	0.0290 2243	0.0307 8268	0.0325 9307	59
60	0.0270 5336	0.0287 6797	0.0305 3533	0.0323 5340	60
61	0.0268 0172	0.0285 2278	0.0302 9724	0.0321 2294	61
62	0.0265 5892	0.0282 8643	0.0300 6795	0.0319 0126	62
63	0.0263 2455	0.0280 5848	0.0298 4704	0.0316 8790	63
64	0.0260 9821	0.0278 3855	0.0296 3411	0.0314 8249	64
65	0.0258 7952	0.0276 2624	0.0294 2878	0.0312 8463	65
66	0.0256 6813	0.0274 2122	0.0292 3070	0.0310 9398	66
67	0.0254 6372	0.0272 2316	0.0290 3955	0.0309 1021	67
68	0.0252 6597	9.0270 3173	0.0288 5500	0.0307 3300	68
69	0.0250 7459	0.0268 4665	0.0286 7677	0.0305 6206	69
70	0.0248 8930	0.0266 6765	0.0285 0458	0.0303 9712	70
71	0.0247 0985	0.0264 9446	0.0283 3816	0.0302 3790	71
72	0.0245 3600	0.0263 2683	0.0281 7728	0.0300 8417	72
73	0.0243 6750	0.0261 6454	0.0280 2169	0.0299 3568	73
74	0.0242 0413	0.0260 0736	0.0278 7118	0.0297 9222	74
75	0.0240 4570	0.0258 5508	0.0277 2554	0.0296 5358	75
76	0.0238 9200	0.0257 0751	0.0275 8457	0.0295 1956	76
77	0.0237 4285	0.0255 6447	0.0274 4808	0.0293 8997	77
78	0.0235 9806	0.0254 2576	0.0273 1589	0.0292 6463	78
79	0.0234 5748	0.0252 9123	0.0271 8784	0.0291 4338	79
80	0.0233 2093	0.0251 6071	0.0270 6376	0.0290 2605	80
81	0.0231 8828	0.0250 3405	0.0269 4350	0.0289 1248	81
82	0.0230 5936	0.0249 1110	0.0268 2692	0.0288 0254	82
83	0.0229 3406	0.0247 9173	0.0267 1387	0.0286 9608	83
84	0.0228 1223	0.0246 7581	0.0266 0423	0.0285 9298	84
85	0.0226 9375	0.0245 6321	0.0264 9787	0.0284 9310	85
86	0.0225 7850	0.0244 5381	0.0263 9467	0.0283 9633	86
87	0.0224 6636	0.0243 4750	0.0262 9452	0.0283 0255	87
88	0.0223 5724	0.0242 4416	0.0261 9730	0.0282 1165	88
89	0.0222 5102	0.0241 4370	0.0261 0291	0.0281 2353	89
90	0.0221 4760	0.0240 4602	0.0260 1126	0.0280 3809	90
91	0.0220 4690	0.0239 5101	0.0259 2224	0.0279 5523	91
92	0.0219 4882	0.0238 5859	0.0258 3577	0.0278 7486	92
93	0.0218 5327	0.0237 6868	0.0257 5176	0.0277 9690	93
94	0.0217 6017	0.0236 8118	0.0256 7012	0.0277 2126	94
95	0.0216 6944	0.0235 9602	0.0255 9078	0.0276 4786	95
96	0.0215 8101	0.0235 1313	0.0255 1366	0.0275 7662	96
97	0.0214 9480	0.0234 3242	0.0254 3868	0.0275 0747	97
98	0.0214 1074	0.0233 5383	0.0253 6578	0.0274 4034	98
99	0.0213 2876	0.0232 7729	0.0252 9489	0.0273 7517	99
100	0.0212 4880	0.0232 0274	0.0252 2594	0.0273 1188	100

IX. ANNUITY WHOSE PRESENT VALUE IS 1

$$\frac{1}{a_{\overline{n}|i}} = \frac{i}{1 - (1 + i)^{-n}} = i + \frac{1}{s_{\overline{n}|i}}$$

n	$2\frac{3}{4}\%$	3%	$3\frac{1}{4}\%$	$3\frac{1}{2}\%$	n
1	1.0275 0000	1.0300 0000	1.0325 0000	1.0350 0000	1
2	0.5207 1825	0.5226 1084	0.5245 0492	0.5264 0049	2
3	0.3518 3243	0.3535 3036	0.3552 3095	0.3569 3418	3
4	0.2674 2059	0.2690 2705	0.2706 3723	0.2722 5114	4
5	0.2167 9832	0.2183 5457	0.2199 1560	0.2214 8137	5
6	0.1830 7083	0.1845 9750	0.1861 2997	0.1876 6821	6
7	0.1589 9747	0.1605 0635	0.1620 2204	0.1635 4449	7
8	0.1409 5795	0.1424 5639	0.1439 6263	0.1454 7665	8
9	0.1269 4095	0.1284 3386	0.1299 3555	0.1314 4601	9
10	0.1157 3972	0.1172 3051	0.1187 3107	0.1202 4137	10
11	0.1065 8629	0.1080 7745	0.1095 7936	0.1110 9197	11
12	0.0989 6871	0.1004 6209	0.1019 6719	0.1034 8395	12
13	0.0925 3252	0.0940 2954	0.0955 3925	0.0970 6157	13
14	0.0870 2457	0.0885 2634	0.0900 4176	0.0915 7073	14
15	0.0822 5917	0.0837 6658	0.0852 8858	0.0868 2507	15
16	0.0780 9710	0.0796 1085	0.0811 4013	0.0826 8483	16
17	0.0744 3186	0.0759 5253	0.0774 8966	0.0790 4313	17
18	0.0711 8063	0.0727 0870	0.0742 5415	0.0758 1684	18
19	0.0682 7802	0.0698 1388	0.0713 6804	0.0729 4033	19
20	0.0656 7173	0.0672 1571	0.0687 7888	0.0703 6108	20
21	0.0633 1941	0.0648 7178	0.0664 4424	0.0680 3659	21
22	0.0611 8640	0.0627 4739	0.0643 2936	0.0659 3207	22
23	0.0592 4410	0.0608 1390	0.0624 0555	0.0640 1880	23
24	0.0574 6863	0.0590 4742	0.0606 4891	0.0622 7283	24
25	0.0558 3997	0.0574 2787	0.0590 3933	0.0606 7404	25
26	0.0543 4116	0.0559 3829	0.0575 5981	0.0592 0540	26
27	0.0529 5776	0.0545 6421	0.0561 9588	0.0578 5241	27
28	0.0516 7738	0.0532 9323	0.0549 3512	0.0566 0265	28
29	0.0504 8935	0.0521 1467	0.0537 6682	0.0554 4538	29
30	0.0493 8442	0.0510 1926	0.0526 8172	0.0543 7133	30
31	0.0483 5453	0.0499 9893	0.0516 7172	0.0533 7240	31
32	0.0473 9263	0.0490 4662	0.0507 2976	0.0524 4150	32
33	0.0464 9253	0.0481 5612	0.0498 4961	0.0515 7242	33
34	0.0456 4875	0.0473 2196	0.0490 2581	0.0507 5966	34
35	0.0448 5645	0.0465 3929	0.0482 5348	0.0499 9835	35
36	0.0441 1132	0.0458 0379	0.0475 2831	0.0492 8416	36
37	0.0434 0953	0.0451 1162	0.0468 4645	0.0486 1325	37
38	0.0427 4764	0.0444 5934	0.0462 0445	0.0479 8214	38
39	0.0421 2256	0.0438 4385	0.0455 9920	0.0473 8775	39
40	0.0415 3151	0.0432 6238	0.0450 2794	0.0468 2728	40
41	0.0409 7200	0.0427 1241	0.0444 8814	0.0462 9822	41
42	0.0404 4175	0.0421 9167	0.0439 7753	0.0457 9828	42
43	0.0399 3871	0.0416 9811	0.0434 9403	0.0453 2539	43
44	0.0394 6100	0.0412 2985	0.0430 3579	0.0448 7768	44
45	0.0390 0693	0.0407 8518	0.0426 0108	0.0444 5343	45
46	0.0385 7493	0.0403 6254	0.0421 8835	0.0440 5108	46
47	0.0381 6358	0.0399 6051	0.0417 9616	0.0436 C919	47
48	0.0377 7158	0.0395 7777	0.0414 2320	0.0433 0646	48
49	0.0373 9773	0.0392 1314	0.0410 6828	0.0429 6167	49
50	0.0370 4092	0.0388 6549	0.0407 3027	0.0426 3371	50

IX. ANNUITY WHOSE PRESENT VALUE IS 1

$$\frac{1}{a_{\overline{n}|i}} = \frac{i}{1 - (1 + i)^{-n}} = i + \frac{1}{s_{\overline{n}|i}}$$

n	$2\frac{3}{4}\%$	3%	$3\frac{1}{4}\%$	$3\frac{1}{2}\%$	n
51	0.0367 0014	0.0385 3382	0.0404 0817	0.0423 2156	51
52	0.0363 7444	0.0382 1718	0.0401 0103	0.0420 2429	52
53	0.0360 6297	0.0379 1471	0.0398 0797	0.0417 4100	53
54	0.0357 6491	0.0376 2558	0.0395 2819	0.0414 7090	54
55	0.0354 7953	0.0373 4907	0.0392 6095	0.0412 1323	55
56	0.0352 0612	0.0370 8447	0.0390 0553	0.0409 6730	56
57	0.0349 4404	0.0368 3114	0.0387 6131	0.0407 3245	57
58	0.0346 9270	0.0365 8848	0.0385 2767	0.0405 0810	58
59	0.0344 5153	0.0363 5593	0.0383 0405	0.0402 9366	59
60	0.0342 2002	0.0361 3296	0.0380 8993	0.0400 8862	60
61	0.0339 9767	0.0359 1908	0.0378 8483	0.0398 9249	61
62	0.0337 8402	0.0357 1385	0.0376 8827	0.0397 0480	62
63	0.0335 7866	0.0355 1682	0.0374 9983	0.0395 2513	63
64	0.0333 8118	0.0353 2760	0.0373 1912	0.0393 5308	64
65	0.0331 9120	0.0351 4581	0.0371 4574	0.0391 8826	65
66	0.0330 0837	0.0349 7110	0.0369 7935	0.0390 3031	66
67	0.0328 3236	0.0348 0313	0.0368 1962	0.0388 7892	67
68	0.0326 6285	0.0346 4159	0.0366 6622	0.0387 3375	68
69	0.0324 9955	0.0344 8618	0.0365 1886	0.0385 9453	69
70	0.0323 4218	0.0343 3663	0.0363 7727	0.0384 6095	70
71	0.0321 9048	0.0341 9266	0.0362 4117	0.0383 3277	71
72	0.0320 4420	0.0340 5404	0.0361 1033	0.0382 0973	72
73	0.0319 0311	0.0339 2053	0.0359 8451	0.0380 9160	73
74	0.0317 6698	0.0337 9191	0.0358 6347	0.0379 7816	74
75	0.0316 3560	0.0336 6796	0.0357 4702	0.0378 6919	75
76	0.0315 0878	0.0335 4849	0.0356 3496	0.0377 6450	76
77	0.0313 8633	0.9334 3331	0.0355 2709	0.0376 6390	77
78	0.0312 6806	0.0333 2224	0.0354 2323	0.0375 6721	78
79	0.0311 5382	0.0332 1510	0.0353 2323	0.0374 7426	79
80	0.0310 4342	0.0331 1175	0.0352 2690	0.0373 8489	80
81	0.0309 3674	0.0330 1201	0.0351 3411	0.0372 9894	81
82	0.0308 3361	0.0329 1576	0.0350 4471	0.0372 1628	82
83	0.0307 3389	0.0328 2284	0.0349 5855	0.0371 3676	83
84	0.0306 3747	0.0327 3313	0.0348 7550	0.0370 6025	84
85	0.0305 4420	0.0326 4650	0.0347 9545	0.0369 8662	85
86	0.0304 5397	0.0325 6284	0.0347 1826	0.0369 1576	86
87	0.0303 6667	0.0324 8202	0.0346 4383	0.0368 4756	87
88	0.0302 8219	0.0324 0393	0.0345 7205	0.0367 8190	88
89	0.0302 0041	0.0323 2848	0.0345 0281	0.0367 1868	89
90	0.0301 2125	0.0322 5556	0.0344 3601	0.0366 5781	90
91	0.0300 4460	0.0321 8508	0.0343 7156	0.0365 9919	91
92	0.0299 7038	0.0321 1694	0.0343 0937	0.0365 4273	92
93	0.0298 9850	0.0320 5107	0.0342 4935	0.0364 8834	93
94	0.0298 2887	0.0319 8737	0.0341 9142	0.0364 3594	94
95	0.0297 6141	0.0319 2577	0.0341 3550	0.0363 8546	95
96	0.0296 9605	0.0318 6619	0.0340 8152	0.0363 3682	96
97	0.0296 3272	0.0318 0856	0.0340 2939	0.0362 8995	97
98	0.0295 7134	0.0317 5281	0.0339 7906	0.0362 4478	98
99	0.0295 1185	0.0316 9886	0.0339 3045	0.0362 0124	99
100	0.0294 5418	0.0316 4667	0.0338 8351	0.0361 5927	100

IX. ANNUITY WHOSE PRESENT VALUE IS 1

$$\frac{1}{a_{\overline{n}|i}} = \frac{i}{1 - (1 + i)^{-n}} = i + \frac{1}{s_{\overline{n}|i}}$$

n	4%	4½%	5%	5½%	n
1	1.0400 0000	1.0450 0000	1.0500 0000	1.0550 0000	1
2	0.5301 9608	0.5339 9756	0.5378 0488	0.5416 1800	2
3	0.3603 4854	0.3637 7336	0.3672 0856	0.3706 5407	3
4	0.2754 9005	0.2787 4365	0.2820 1183	0.2852 9449	4
5	0.2246 2711	0.2277 9164	0.2309 7480	0.2341 7644	5
6	0.1907 6190	0.1938 7839	0.1970 1747	0.2001 7895	6
7	0.1666 0961	0.1697 0147	0.1728 1982	0.1759 6442	7
8	0.1485 2783	0.1516 0965	0.1547 2181	0.1578 6401	8
9	0.1344 9299	0.1375 7447	0.1406 9008	0.1438 3946	9
10	0.1232 9094	0.1263 7882	0.1295 0458	0.1326 6777	10
11	0.1141 4904	0.1172 4818	0.1203 8889	0.1235 7065	11
12	0.1065 5217	0.1096 6619	0.1128 2541	0.1160 2923	12
13	0.1001 4373	0.1032 7535	0.1064 5577	0.1096 8426	13
14	0.0946 6897	0.0978 2032	0.1010 2397	0.1042 7912	14
15	0.0899 4110	0.0931 1381	0.0963 4229	0.0996 2560	15
16	0.0858 2000	0.0890 1537	0.0922 6991	0.0955 8254	16
17	0.0821 9852	0.0854 1758	0.0886 9914	0.0920 4197	17
18	0.0789 9333	0.0822 3690	0.0855 4622	0.0889 1992	18
19	0.0761 3862	0.0794 0734	0.0827 4501	0.0861 5006	19
20	0.0735 8175	0.0768 7614	0.0802 4259	0.0836 7933	20
21	0.0712 8011	0.0746 0057	0.0779 9611	0.0814 6478	21
22	0.0691 9881	0.0725 4565	0.0759 7051	0.0794 7123	22
23	0.0673 0906	0.0706 8249	0.0741 3682	0.0776 6965	23
24	0.0655 8683	0.0689 8703	0.0724 7090	0.0760 3580	24
25	0.0640 1196	0.0674 3903	0.0709 5246	0.0745 4935	25
26	0.0625 6738	0.0660 2137	0.0695 6432	0.0731 9307	26
27	0.0612 3854	0.0647 1946	0.0682 9186	0.0719 5228	27
28	0.0600 1298	0.0635 2081	0.0671 2253	0.0708 1440	28
29	0.0588 7993	0.0624 1461	0.0660 4551	0.0697 6857	29
30	0.0578 3010	0.0613 9154	0.0650 5144	0.0688 0539	30
31	0.0568 5535	0.0604 4345	0.0641 3212	0.0679 1665	31
32	0.0559 4859	0.0595 6320	0.0632 8042	0.0670 9519	32
33	0.0551 0357	0.0587 4453	0.0624 9004	0.0663 3469	33
34	0.0543 1477	0.0579 8191	0.0617 5545	0.0656 2958	34
35	0.0535 7732	0.0572 7045	0.0610 7171	0.0649 7493	35
36	0.0528 8688	0.0566 0578	0.0604 3446	0.0643 6635	36
37	0.0522 3957	0.0559 8402	0.0598 3979	0.0637 9993	37
38	0.0516 3192	0.0554 0169	0.0592 8423	0.0632 7217	38
39	0.0510 6083	0.0548 5567	0.0587 6462	0.0627 7991	39
40	0.0505 2349	0.0543 4315	0.0582 7816	0.0623 2034	40
41	0.0500 1738	0.0538 6158	0.0578 2229	0.0618 9090	41
42	0.0495 4020	0.0534 0868	0.0573 9471	0.0614 8927	42
43	0.0490 8990	0.0529 8235	0.0569 9333	0.0611 1337	43
44	0.0486 6454	0.0525 8071	0.0566 1625	0.0607 6128	44
45	0.0482 6246	0.0522 0202	0.0562 6173	0.0604 3127	45
46	0.0478 8205	0.0518 4471	0.0559 2820	0.0601 2175	46
47	0.0475 2189	0.0515 0734	0.0556 1421	0.0598 3129	47
48	0.0471 8065	0.0511 8858	0.0553 1843	0.0595 5854	48
49	0.0468 5712	0.0508 8722	0.0550 3965	0.0593 0230	49
50	0.0465 5020	0.0506 0215	0.0547 7674	0.0590 6145	50

IX. ANNUITY WHOSE PRESENT VALUE IS 1

$$\frac{1}{a_{\overline{n}|i}} = \frac{i}{1 - (1 + i)^{-n}} = i + \frac{1}{s_{\overline{n}|i}}$$

n	6%	6½%	7%	8%	n
1	1.0600 0000	1.0650 0000	1.0700 0000	1.0800 0000	1
2	0.5454 3689	0.5492 6150	0.5530 9179	0.5607 6923	2
3	0.3741 0981	0.3775 7570	0.3810 5167	0.3880 3351	3
4	0.2885 9149	0.2919 0274	0.2952 2812	0.3019 2080	4
5	0.2373 9640	0.2406 3454	0.2438 9069	0.2504 5645	5
6	0.2033 6263	0.2065 6831	0.2097 9580	0.2163 1539	6
7	0.1791 3502	0.1823 3137	0.1855 5322	0.1920 7240	7
8	0.1610 3594	0.1642 3730	0.1674 6776	0.1740 1476	8
9	0.1470 2224	0.1502 3803	0.1534 8647	0.1600 7971	9
10	0.1358 6796	0.1391 0469	0.1423 7750	0.1490 2949	10
11	0.1267 9294	0.1300 5521	0.1333 5690	0.1400 7634	11
12	0.1192 7703	0.1225 6817	0.1259 0199	0.1326 9502	12
13	0.1129 6011	0.1162 8256	0.1196 5085	0.1265 2181	13
14	0.1075 8491	0.1109 4048	0.1143 4494	0.1212 9685	14
15	0.1029 6276	0.1063 5278	0.1097 9462	0.1168 2954	15
16	0.0989 5214	0.1023 7757	0.1058 5765	0.1129 7687	16
17	0.0954 4480	0.0989 0633	0.1024 2519	0.1096 2943	17
18	0.0923 5654	0.0958 5461	0.0994 1260	0.1067 0210	18
19	0.0896 2086	0.0931 5575	0.0967 5301	0.1041 2763	19
20	0.0871 8456	0.0907 5640	0.0943 9293	0.1018 5221	20
21	0.0850 0455	0.0886 1333	0.0922 8900	0.0998 3225	21
22	0.0830 4557	0.0866 9120	0.0904 0577	0.0980 3207	22
23	0.0812 7848	0.0849 6078	0.0887 1393	0.0964 2217	23
24	0.0796 7900	0.0833 9770	0.0871 8902	0.0949 7796	24
25	0.0782 2672	0.0819 8148	0.0858 1052	0.0936 7878	25
26	0.0769 0435	0.0806 9480	0.0845 6103	0.0925 0713	26
27	0.0756 9717	0.0795 2288	0.0834 2573	0.0914 4810	27
28	0.0745 9255	0.0784 5305	0.0823 9193	0.0904 8891	28
29	0.0735 7961	0.0774 7440	0.0814 4865	0.0896 1854	29
30	0.0726 4891	0.0765 7744	0.0805 8640	0.0888 2743	30
31	0.0717 9222	0.0757 5393	0.0797 9691	0.0881 0728	31
32	0.0710 0234	0.0749 9665	0.0790 7292	0.0874 5081	32
33	0.0702 7293	0.0742 9924	0.0784 0807	0.0868 5163	33
34	0.0695 9843	0.0736 5610	0.0777 9674	0.0863 0411	34
35	0.0689 7386	0.0730 6226	0.0772 3396	0.0858 0326	35
36	0.0683 9483	0.0725 1332	0.0767 1531	0.0853 4467	36
37	0.0678 5743	0.0720 0534	0.0762 3685	0.0849 2440	37
38	0.0673 5812	0.0715 3480	0.0757 9505	0.0845 3894	38
39	0.0668 9377	0.0710 9854	0.0753 8676	0.0841 8513	39
40	0.0664 6154	0.0706 9373	0.0750 0914	0.0838 6016	40
41	0.0660 5886	0.0703 1779	0.0746 5962	0.0835 6149	41
42	0.0656 8342	0.0699 6842	0.0743 3591	0.0832 8684	42
43	0.0653 3312	0.0696 4352	0.0740 3590	0.0830 3414	43
44	0.0650 0606	0.0693 4119	0.0737 5769	0.0828 0152	44
45	0.0647 0050	0.0690 5968	0.0734 9957	0.0825 8728	45
46	0.0644 1485	0.0687 9743	0.0732 5996	0.0823 8991	46
47	0.0641 4768	0.0685 5300	0.0730 3744	0.0822 0799	47
48	0.0638 9765	0.0683 2505	0.0728 3070	0.0820 4027	48
49	0.0636 6356	0.0681 1240	0.0726 3853	0.0818 8557	49
50	0.0634 4429	0.0679 1393	0.0724 5985	0.0817 4286	50

X. VALUES OF

$$a_{\overline{k}|i} = \frac{1 - (1 + i)^{-k}}{i}, \quad k = \frac{1}{p}$$

k	$\frac{1}{4}\%$	$\frac{7}{24}\%$	$\frac{1}{3}\%$	$\frac{3}{8}\%$	k
1/3	.3327 7886	.3326 8665	.3325 9451	.3325 0242	1/3
k	$\frac{5}{12}\%$	$\frac{1}{2}\%$	$\frac{7}{12}\%$	$\frac{5}{8}\%$	k
1/3	.3324 1040	.3322 2653	.3320 4289	.3319 5116	1/3
k	$\frac{3}{4}\%$	$\frac{7}{8}\%$	1%	$1\frac{1}{8}\%$	k
1/2	.4972 0496	.4967 4249	.4962 8098	.4958 2042	1/2
1/3	.3316 7633	.3314 0203	.3311 2825	.3308 5501	1/3
1/6	.1659 4143	.1658 2131	.1657 0141	.1655 8172	1/6
k	$1\frac{1}{4}\%$	$1\frac{3}{8}\%$	$1\frac{1}{2}\%$	$1\frac{5}{8}\%$	k
1/2	.4953 6080	.4949 0213	.4944 4440	.4939 8761	1/2
1/3	.3305 8228	.3303 1009	.3300 3841	.3297 6725	1/3
1/4	.2480 6500	.2478 7347	.2476 8230	.2474 9148	1/4
1/6	.1654 6225	.1653 4299	.1652 2395	.1651 0511	1/6
1/12	.0827 7395	.0827 1854	.0826 6322	.0826 0800	1/12
k	$1\frac{3}{4}\%$	2%	$2\frac{1}{4}\%$	$2\frac{1}{2}\%$	k
1/2	.4935 3176	.4926 2285	.4917 1765	.4908 1613	1/2
1/3	.3294 9662	.3289 5689	.3284 1922	.3278 8360	1/3
1/4	.2473 0101	.2469 2113	.2465 4264	.2461 6554	1/4
1/6	.1649 8649	.1647 4987	.1645 1409	.1642 7915	1/6
1/12	.0825 5287	.0824 4290	.0823 3331	.0822 2408	1/12
k	$2\frac{3}{4}\%$	3%	$3\frac{1}{4}\%$	$3\frac{1}{2}\%$	k
1/2	.4899 1828	.4890 2406	.4881 3346	.4872 4645	1/2
1/3	.3273 5001	.3268 1843	.3262 8886	.3257 6129	1/3
1/4	.2457 8981	.2454 1546	.2450 4247	.2446 7084	1/4
1/6	.1640 4503	.1638 1173	.1635 7925	.1633 4759	1/6
1/12	.0821 1523	.0820 0674	.0818 9862	.0817 9086	1/12
k	4%	$4\frac{1}{2}\%$	5%	$5\frac{1}{2}\%$	k
1/2	.4854 8311	.4837 3386	.4819 9854	.4802 7696	1/2
1/3	.3247 1208	.3236 7070	.3226 3706	.3216 1108	1/3
1/4	.2439 3161	.2431 9770	.2424 6905	.2417 4561	1/4
1/6	.1628 8668	.1624 2897	.1619 7442	.1615 2300	1/6
1/12	.0815 7643	.0813 6344	.0811 5185	.0809 4167	1/12
k	6%	$6\frac{1}{2}\%$	7%	8%	k
1/2	.4785 6896	.4768 7437	.4751 9301	.4718 6939	1/2
1/3	.3205 9265	.3195 8169	.3185 7811	.3165 9276	1/3
1/4	.2410 2731	.2403 1409	.2396 0589	.2382 0435	1/4
1/6	.1610 7468	.1606 2940	.1601 8715	.1593 1159	1/6
1/12	.0807 3287	.0805 2544	.0803 1937	.0799 1123	1/12

XI. VALUES OF

$$s_{\overline{k}|i} = \frac{(1 + i)^k - 1}{i}, \quad k = \frac{1}{p}$$

k	$\frac{1}{4}\%$	$\frac{7}{24}\%$	$\frac{1}{3}\%$	$\frac{3}{8}\%$	k
1/3	.3330 5594	.3330 0978	.3329 6365	.3329 1753	1/3

k	$\frac{5}{12}\%$	$\frac{1}{2}\%$	$\frac{7}{12}\%$	$\frac{5}{8}\%$	k
1/3	.3328 7144	.3327 7932	.3326 8728	.3326 4129	1/3

k	$\frac{3}{4}\%$	$\frac{7}{8}\%$	1%	$1\frac{1}{8}\%$	k
1/2	.4990 6600	.4989 1101	.4987 5621	.4986 0160	1/2
1/3	.3325 0345	.3323 6581	.3322 2835	.3320 9109	1/3
1/6	.1661 4821	.1660 6226	.1659 7644	.1658 9075	1/6

k	$1\frac{1}{4}\%$	$1\frac{3}{8}\%$	$1\frac{1}{2}\%$	$1\frac{5}{8}\%$	k
1/2	.4984 4719	.4982 9297	.4981 3893	.4979 8509	1/2
1/3	.3319 5401	.3318 1712	.3316 8042	.3315 4390	1/3
1/4	.2488 3660	.2487 2118	.2486 0593	.2484 9084	1/4
1/6	.1658 0518	.1657 1975	.1656 3445	.1655 4927	1/6
1/12	.0828 5968	.0828 1273	.0827 6585	.0827 1904	1/12

k	$1\frac{3}{4}\%$	2%	$2\frac{1}{4}\%$	$2\frac{1}{2}\%$	k
1/2	.4978 3143	.4975 2469	.4972 1870	.4969 1346	1/2
1/3	.3314 0758	.3311 3548	.3308 6412	.3305 9350	1/3
1/4	.2483 7592	.2481 4658	.2479 1789	.2476 8985	1/4
1/6	.1654 6423	.1652 9452	.1651 2531	.1649 5662	1/6
1/12	.0826 7231	.0825 7907	.0824 8611	.0823 9345	1/12

k	$2\frac{3}{4}\%$	3%	$3\frac{1}{4}\%$	$3\frac{1}{2}\%$	k
1/2	.4966 0897	.4963 0522	.4960 0220	.4956 9993	1/2
1/3	.3303 2362	.3300 5447	.3297 8604	.3295 1834	1/3
1/4	.2474 6247	.2472 3573	.2470 0963	.2467 8417	1/4
1/6	.1647 8843	.1646 2073	.1644 5354	.1642 8684	1/6
1/12	.0823 0108	.0822 0899	.0821 1719	.0820 2568	1/12

k	4%	$4\frac{1}{2}\%$	5%	$5\frac{1}{2}\%$	k
1/2	.4950 9757	.4944 9811	.4939 0153	.4933 0780	1/2
1/3	.3289 8510	.3284 5470	.3279 2714	.3274 0237	1/3
1/4	.2463 3516	.2458 8868	.2454 4469	.2450 0317	1/4
1/6	.1639 5492	.1636 2496	.1632 9692	.1629 7080	1/6
1/12	.0818 4349	.0816 6243	.0814 8248	.0813 0362	1/12

k	6%	$6\frac{1}{2}\%$	7%	8%	k
1/2	.4927 1690	.4921 2880	.4915 4348	.4903 8106	1/2
1/3	.3268 8037	.3263 6112	.3258 4460	.3248 1960	1/3
1/4	.2445 6410	.2441 2746	.2436 9321	.2428 3184	1/4
1/6	.1626 4657	.1623 2422	.1620 0372	.1613 6821	1/6
1/12	.0811 2584	.0809 4914	.0807 7351	.0804 2538	1/12

XII. VALUES OF

$$\frac{1}{s_{\overline{k}|i}} = s_{\overline{k}|i}^{-1} = \frac{i}{(1+i)^k - 1}, \quad where \quad k = \frac{1}{p}; \quad \frac{1}{a_{\overline{k}|i}} = \frac{1}{s_{\overline{k}|i}} + i$$

k	$\frac{1}{4}\%$	$\frac{7}{24}\%$	$\frac{1}{3}\%$	$\frac{3}{8}\%$	k
1/3	3.0024 9861	3.0029 1478	3.0033 3087	3.0037 4688	1/3
k	$\frac{5}{12}\%$	$\frac{1}{2}\%$	$\frac{7}{12}\%$	$\frac{5}{8}\%$	k
1/3	3.0041 6282	3.0049 9446	3.0058 2579	3.0062 4135	1/3
k	$\frac{3}{4}\%$	$\frac{7}{8}\%$	1%	$1\frac{1}{8}\%$	k
1/2	2.0037 4299	2.0043 6547	2.0049 8756	2.0056 0927	1/2
1/3	3.0074 8755	3.0087 3306	3.0099 7789	3.0112 2203	1/3
1/6	6.0187 2276	6.0218 3794	6.0249 5163	6.0280 6382	1/6
k	$1\frac{1}{4}\%$	$1\frac{3}{8}\%$	$1\frac{1}{2}\%$	$1\frac{5}{8}\%$	k
1/2	2.0062 3059	2.0068 5153	2.0074 7208	2.0080 9226	1/2
1/3	3.0124 6549	3.0137 0827	3.0149 5037	3.0161 9179	1/3
1/4	4.0187 0147	4.0205 6632	4.0224 3021	4.0242 9314	1/4
1/6	6.0311 7452	6.0342 8372	6.0373 9144	6.0404 9767	1/6
1/12	12.0685 9580	12.0754 3853	12.0822 7822	12.0891 1488	1/12
k	$1\frac{3}{4}\%$	2%	$2\frac{1}{4}\%$	$2\frac{1}{2}\%$	k
1/2	2.0087 1205	2.0099 5049	2.0111 8742	2.0124 2284	1/2
1/3	3.0174 3253	3.0199 1199	3.0223 8875	3.0248 6282	1/3
1/4	4.0261 5513	4.0298 7623	4.0335 9355	4.0373 0709	1/4
1/6	6.0436 0242	6.0498 0748	6.0560 0664	6.0621 9992	1/6
1/12	12.0959 4851	12.1096 0670	12.1232 5284	12.1368 8698	1/12
k	$2\frac{3}{4}\%$	3%	$3\frac{1}{4}\%$	$3\frac{1}{2}\%$	k
1/2	2.0136 5675	2.0148 8916	2.0161 2007	2.0173 4950	1/2
1/3	3.0273 3422	3.0298 0294	3.0322 6902	3.0347 3244	1/3
1/4	4.0410 1687	4.0447 2289	4.0484 2518	4.0521 2374	1/4
1/6	6.0683 8735	6.0745 6894	6.0807 4472	6.0869 1471	1/6
1/12	12.1505 0915	12.1641 1941	12.1777 1779	12.1913 0434	1/12
k	4%	$4\frac{1}{2}\%$	5%	$5\frac{1}{2}\%$	k
1/2	2.0198 0390	2.0222 5241	2.0246 9508	2.0271 3193	1/2
1/3	3.0396 5138	3.0445 5985	3.0494 5791	3.0543 4565	1/3
1/4	4.0595 0975	4.0668 8103	4.0742 3769	4.0815 7981	1/4
1/6	6.0992 3740	6.1115 3716	6.1238 1418	6.1360 6860	1/6
1/12	12.2184 4211	12.2455 3306	12.2725 7753	12.2995 7585	1/12
k	6%	$6\frac{1}{2}\%$	7%	8%	k
1/2	2.0295 6301	2.0319 8837	2.0344 0804	2.0392 3048	1/2
1/3	3.0592 2313	3.0640 9043	3.0689 4762	3.0786 3195	1/3
1/4	4.0889 0752	4.0962 2091	4.1035 2009	4.1180 7618	1/4
1/6	6.1483 0059	6.1605 1031	6.1726 9791	6.1970 0737	1/6
1/12	12.3265 2834	12.3534 3533	12.3802 9715	12.4338 8648	1/12

XIII. VALUES OF

$$j_p = p[(1 + i)^{\frac{1}{p}} - 1]$$

p	$\frac{1}{4}\%$	$\frac{7}{24}\%$	$\frac{1}{3}\%$	$\frac{3}{8}\%$	p
3	.0024 9792	.0029 1384	.0033 2964	.0037 4532	3
1/3	.0025 0626	.0029 2518	.0033 4446	.0037 6408	1/3
1/6	.0025 1568	.0029 3802	.0033 6123	.0037 8533	1/6
1/12	.0025 3466	.0029 6391	.0033 9513	.0038 2832	1/12

p	$\frac{5}{12}\%$	$\frac{1}{2}\%$	$\frac{7}{12}\%$	$\frac{5}{8}\%$	p
2	.0041 6234	.0049 9377	.0058 2485	.0062 4026	2
3	.0041 6089	.0049 9169	.0058 2203	.0062 3702	3
4	.0041 6017	.0049 9065	.0058 2062	.0062 3540	4
6	.0041 5945	.0049 8962	.0058 1921	.0062 3379	6
12	.0041 5873	.0049 8858	.0058 1780	.0062 3217	12
1/2	.0041 7535	.0050 1250	.0058 5035	.0062 6953	1/2
1/3	.0041 8405	.0050 2504	.0058 6743	.0062 8914	1/3
1/4	.0041 9278	.0050 3763	.0058 8457	.0063 0884	1/4
1/6	.0042 1031	.0050 6292	.0059 1907	.0063 4847	1/6
1/12	.0042 6349	.0051 3982	.0060 2417	.0064 6938	1/12

p	$\frac{3}{4}\%$	$\frac{7}{8}\%$	1%	$1\frac{1}{8}\%$	p
2	.0074 8599	.0087 3094	.0099 7512	.0112 1854	2
3	.0074 8133	.0087 2460	.0099 6685	.0112 0807	3
4	.0074 7900	.0087 2143	.0099 6272	.0112 0285	4
6	.0074 7667	.0087 1827	.0099 5859	.0111 9763	6
12	.0074 7434	.0087 1510	.0099 5446	.0111 9241	12
1/2	.0075 2812	.0087 8828	.0100 5000	.0113 1328	1/2
1/4	.0075 8480	.0088 6552	.0101 5100	.0114 4127	1/4

p	$1\frac{1}{4}\%$	$1\frac{3}{8}\%$	$1\frac{1}{2}\%$	$1\frac{5}{8}\%$	p
2	.0124 6118	.0137 0306	.0149 4417	.0161 8452	2
3	.0124 4828	.0136 8746	.0149 2562	.0161 6277	3
4	.0124 4183	.0136 7966	.0149 1636	.0161 7182	4
6	.0124 3539	.0136 7188	.0149 0710	.0161 4105	6
12	.0124 2895	.0136 6410	.0148 9785	.0161 3021	12
1/2	.0125 7812	.0138 4453	.0151 1250	.0163 8203	1/2
1/4	.0127 3633	.0140 3620	.0153 4089	.0166 5040	1/4

XIII. VALUES OF

$$j_p = p[(1 + i)^{\frac{1}{p}} - 1]$$

p	$1\frac{3}{4}\%$	2%	$2\frac{1}{4}\%$	$2\frac{1}{2}\%$	p
2	.0174 2410	.0199 0099	.0223 7484	.0248 4567	2
3	.0173 9890	.0198 6813	.0223 3333	.0247 9451	3
4	.0173 8631	.0198 5173	.0223 1261	.0247 6899	4
6	.0173 7374	.0198 3534	.0222 9192	.0247 4349	6
12	.0173 6119	.0198 1898	.0222 7125	.0247 1804	12
1/2	.0176 5312	.0202 0000	.0227 5312	.0253 1250	1/2
1/4	.0179 6476	.0206 0804	.0232 7083	.0259 5322	1/4
p	$2\frac{3}{4}\%$	3%	$3\frac{1}{4}\%$	$3\frac{1}{2}\%$	p
2	.0273 1349	.0297 7831	.0322 4014	.0346 9899	2
3	.0272 5170	.0297 0490	.0321 5414	.0345 9943	3
4	.0272 2087	.0296 6829	.0321 1125	.0345 4978	4
6	.0271 9009	.0296 3173	.0320 6844	.0345 0024	6
12	.0271 5936	.0295 9524	.0320 2571	.0344 5078	12
1/2	.0278 7812	.0304 5000	.0330 2812	.0356 1250	1/2
1/4	.0286 5531	.0313 7720	.0341 1898	.0368 8075	1/4
p	4%	$4\frac{1}{2}\%$	5%	$5\frac{1}{2}\%$	p
2	.0396 0781	.0445 0483	.0493 9015	.0542 6386	2
3	.0394 7821	.0443 4138	.0491 8907	.0540 2139	3
4	.0394 1363	.0442 5996	.0490 8894	.0539 0070	4
6	.0393 4918	.0441 7874	.0489 8908	.0537 8036	6
12	.0392 8488	.0440 9771	.0488 8949	.0536 6039	12
1/2	.0408 0000	.0460 1250	.0512 5000	.0565 1250	1/2
p	6%	$6\frac{1}{2}\%$	7%	8%	p
2	.0591 2603	.0639 7674	.0688 1609	.0784 6097	2
3	.0588 3847	.0636 4042	.0684 2737	.0779 5670	3
4	.0586 9538	.0634 7314	.0682 3410	.0777 0619	4
6	.0585 5277	.0633 0644	.0680 4156	.0774 5674	6
12	.0584 1061	.0631 4033	.0678 4974	.0772 0836	12
1/2	.0618 0000	.0671 1250	.0724 5000	.0832 0000	1/2

XIV. VALUES OF $(1 + i)^{\frac{1}{p}}$

p	$\frac{1}{4}\%$	$\frac{7}{24}\%$	$\frac{1}{3}\%$	$\frac{3}{8}\%$	p
3	1.0008 3264	1.0009 7128	1.0011 0988	1.0012 4844	3

p	$\frac{5}{12}\%$	$\frac{1}{2}\%$	$\frac{7}{12}\%$	$\frac{5}{8}\%$	p
3	1.0013 8696	1.0016 6390	1.0019 4068	1.0020 7901	3

p	$\frac{3}{4}\%$	$\frac{7}{8}\%$	1%	$1\frac{1}{8}\%$	p
2	1.0037 4299	1.0043 6547	1.0049 8756	1.0056 0927	2
3	1.0024 9378	1.0029 0820	1.0033 2228	1.0037 3602	3
6	1.0012 4611	1.0014 5304	1.0016 5976	1.0018 6627	6

p	$1\frac{1}{4}\%$	$1\frac{3}{8}\%$	$1\frac{1}{2}\%$	$1\frac{5}{8}\%$	p
2	1.0062 3059	1.0068 5153	1.0074 7208	1.0080 9226	2
3	1.0041 4943	1.0045 6249	1.0049 7521	1.0053 8759	3
4	1.0031 1046	1.0034 1947	1.0037 2909	1.0040 3798	4
6	1.0020 7256	1.0022 7865	1.0024 8452	1.0026 9018	6
12	1.0010 3575	1.0011 3868	1.0012 4149	1.0013 4418	12

p	$1\frac{3}{4}\%$	2%	$2\frac{1}{4}\%$	$2\frac{1}{2}\%$	p
2	1.0087 1205	1.0099 5049	1.0111 8742	1.0124 2284	2
3	1.0057 9963	1.0066 2271	1.0074 4444	1.0082 6484	3
4	1.0043 4658	1.0049 6293	1.0055 7815	1.0061 9225	4
6	1.0028 9562	1.0033 0589	1.0037 1532	1.0041 2392	6
12	1.0014 4677	1.0016 5158	1.0018 5594	1.0020 5984	12

p	$2\frac{3}{4}\%$	3%	$3\frac{1}{4}\%$	$3\frac{1}{2}\%$	p
2	1.0136 5675	1.0148 8916	1.0161 2007	1.0173 4950	2
3	1.0090 8390	1.0099 0163	1.0107 1805	1.0115 3314	3
4	1.0068 0522	1.0074 1707	1.0080 2781	1.0086 3745	4
6	1.0045 3168	1.0049 3862	1.0053 4474	1.0057 5004	6
12	1.0022 6328	1.0024 6627	1.0026 6881	1.0028 7090	12

p	4%	$4\frac{1}{2}\%$	5%	$5\frac{1}{2}\%$	p
2	1.0198 0390	1.0222 5242	1.0246 9508	1.0271 3193	2
3	1.0131 5941	1.0147 8046	1.0163 9636	1.0180 0713	3
4	1.0098 5340	1.0110 6499	1.0122 7223	1.0134 7517	4
6	1.0065 5820	1.6073 6312	1.0081 6485	1.0089 6339	6
12	1.0032 7374	1.0036 7481	1.0040 7412	1.0044 7170	12

p	6%	$6\frac{1}{2}\%$	7%	8%	p
2	1.0295 6301	1.0319 8837	1.0344 0804	1.0392 3048	2
3	1.0196 1282	1.0212 1347	1.0228 0912	1.0259 8557	3
4	1.0146 7385	1.0158 6828	1.0170 5853	1.0194 2655	4
6	1.0097 5879	1.0105 5107	1.0113 4026	1.0129 0946	6
12	1.0048 6755	1.0052 6169	1.0056 5415	1.0064 3403	12

Selected Actuarial Tables

XV. COMMISSIONERS' 1958 STANDARD ORDINARY
MORTALITY TABLE FOR MALES

Age x	Number Living l_x	Number Dying d_x	Rate of Mortality q_x	Expectation of Life $\overset{\circ}{e}_x$
0	10 000 000	70 800	.007 08	68.30
1	9 929 200	17 475	.001 76	67.78
2	9 911 725	15 066	.001 52	66.90
3	9 896 659	14 449	.001 46	66.00
4	9 882 210	13 835	.001 40	65.10
5	9 868 375	13 322	.001 35	64.19
6	9 855 053	12 812	.001 30	63.27
7	9 842 241	12 401	.001 26	62.35
8	9 829 840	12 091	.001 23	61.43
9	9 817 749	11 879	.001 21	60.51
10	9 805 870	11 865	.001 21	59.58
11	9 794 005	12 047	.001 23	58.65
12	9 781 958	12 325	.001 26	57.72
13	9 769 633	12 896	.001 32	56.80
14	9 756 737	13 562	.001 39	55.87
15	9 743 175	14 225	.001 46	54.95
16	9 728 950	14 983	.001 54	54.03
17	9 713 967	15 737	.001 62	53.11
18	9 698 230	16 390	.001 69	52.19
19	9 681 840	16 846	.001 74	51.28
20	9 664 994	17 300	.001 79	50.37
21	9 647 694	17 655	.001 83	49.46
22	9 630 039	17 912	.001 86	48.55
23	9 612 127	18 167	.001 89	47.64
24	9 593 960	18 324	.001 91	46.73
25	9 575 636	18 481	.001 93	45.82
26	9 557 155	18 732	.001 96	44.90
27	9 538 423	18 981	.001 99	43.99
28	9 519 442	19 324	.002 03	43.08
29	9 500 118	19 760	.002 08	42.16
30	9 480 358	20 193	.002 13	41.25
31	9 460 165	20 718	.002 19	40.34
32	9 439 447	21 239	.002 25	39.43
33	9 418 208	21 850	.002 32	38.51
34	9 396 358	22 551	.002 40	37.60
35	9 373 807	23 528	.002 51	36.69
36	9 350 279	24 685	.002 64	35.78
37	9 325 594	26 112	.002 80	34.88
38	9 299 482	27 991	.003 01	33.97
39	9 271 491	30 132	.003 25	33.07
40	9 241 359	32 622	.003 53	32.18
41	9 208 737	35 362	.003 84	31.29
42	9 173 375	38 253	.004 17	30.41
43	9 135 122	41 382	.004 53	29.54
44	9 093 740	44 741	.004 92	28.67
45	9 048 999	48 412	.005 35	27.81
46	9 000 587	52 473	.005 83	26.95
47	8 948 114	56 910	.006 36	26.11
48	8 891 204	61 794	.006 95	25.27
49	8 829 410	67 104	.007 60	24.45

XV. COMMISSIONERS' 1958 STANDARD ORDINARY MORTALITY TABLE FOR MALES

Age x	Number Living l_x	Number Dying d_x	Rate of Mortality q_x	Expectation of Life $\mathring{e}_x$
50	8 762 306	72 902	.008 32	23.63
51	8 689 404	79 160	.009 11	22.82
52	8 610 244	85 758	.009 96	22.03
53	8 524 486	92 832	.010 89	21.25
54	8 431 654	100 337	.011 90	20.47
55	8 331 317	108 307	.013 00	19.71
56	8 223 010	116 849	.014 21	18.97
57	8 106 161	125 970	.015 54	18.23
58	7 980 191	135 663	.017 00	17.51
59	7 844 528	145 830	.018 59	16.81
60	7 698 698	156 592	.020 34	16.12
61	7 542 106	167 736	.022 24	15.44
62	7 374 370	179 271	.024 31	14.78
63	7 195 099	191 174	.026 57	14.14
64	7 003 925	203 394	.029 04	13.51
65	6 800 531	215 917	.031 75	12.90
66	6 584 614	228 749	.034 74	12.31
67	6 355 865	241 777	.038 04	11.73
68	6 114 088	254 835	.041 68	11.17
69	5 859 253	267 241	.045 61	10.64
70	5 592 012	278 426	.049 79	10.12
71	5 313 586	287 731	.054 15	9.63
72	5 025 855	294 766	.058 65	9.15
73	4 731 089	299 289	.063 26	8.69
74	4 431 800	301 894	.068 12	8.24
75	4 129 906	303 011	.073 37	7.81
76	3 826 895	303 014	.079 18	7.39
77	3 523 881	301 997	.085 70	6.98
78	3 221 884	299 829	.093 06	6.59
79	2 922 055	295 683	.101 19	6.21
80	2 626 372	288 848	.109 98	5.85
81	2 337 524	278 983	.119 35	5.51
82	2 058 541	265 902	.129 17	5.19
83	1 792 639	249 858	.139 38	4.89
84	1 542 781	231 433	.150 01	4.60
85	1 311 348	211 311	.161 14	4.32
86	1 100 037	190 108	.172 82	4.06
87	909 929	168 455	.185 13	3.80
88	741 474	146 997	.198 25	3.55
89	594 477	126 303	.212 46	3.31
90	468 174	106 809	.228 14	3.06
91	361 365	88 813	.245 77	2.82
92	272 552	72 480	.265 93	2.58
93	200 072	57 881	.289 30	2.33
94	142 191	45 026	.316 66	2.07
95	97 165	34 128	.351 24	1.80
96	63 037	25 250	.400 56	1.51
97	37 787	18 456	.488 42	1.18
98	19 331	12 916	.668 15	.83
99	6 415	6 415	1.000 00	.50

XVI. COMMUTATION COLUMNS: CSO AT 3%

Age x	D_x	N_x	C_x	M_x
0	10 000 000.0	288 963 016.7	68 737.864	1 583 601.456
1	9 640 000.0	278 963 016.7	16 471.864	1 514 863.592
2	9 342 751.4	269 323 016.7	13 787.524	1 498 391.728
3	9 056 844.9	259 980 265.3	12 837.749	1 484 604.204
4	8 780 215.6	250 923 420.4	11 934.192	1 471 766.455
5	8 512 546.9	242 143 204.8	11 156.965	1 459 832.263
6	8 253 451.8	233 630 657.9	10 417.328	1 448 675.298
7	8 002 642.6	225 377 206.1	9 789.464	1 438 257.970
8	7 759 766.4	217 374 563.5	9 266.745	1 428 468.506
9	7 524 487.1	209 614 797.1	8 839.092	1 419 201.761
10	7 296 488.1	202 090 310.0	8 571.528	1 410 362.669
11	7 075 397.6	194 793 821.9	8 449.523	1 401 791.141
12	6 860 868.5	187 718 424.3	8 392.725	1 393 341.618
13	6 652 644.7	180 857 555.8	8 525.775	1 384 948.893
14	6 450 352.6	174 204 911.1	8 704.932	1 376 423.118
15	6 253 773.3	167 754 558.5	8 864.550	1 367 718.186
16	6 062 760.0	161 500 785.2	9 064.961	1 358 853.636
17	5 877 109.8	155 438 025.2	9 243.829	1 349 788.675
18	5 696 688.0	149 560 915.4	9 346.988	1 340 544.846
19	5 521 418.1	143 864 227.4	9 327.222	1 331 197.858
20	5 351 272.8	138 342 809.3	9 299.603	1 321 870.636
21	5 186 111.0	132 991 536.5	9 214.012	1 312 571.033
22	5 025 845.1	127 805 425.5	9 075.863	1 303 357.021
23	4 870 385.5	122 779 580.4	8 936.960	1 294 281.158
24	4 719 592.6	117 909 194.9	8 751.644	1 285 344.198
25	4 573 377.1	113 189 602.3	8 569.542	1 276 592.554
26	4 431 602.4	108 616 225.2	8 432.941	1 268 023.012
27	4 294 093.7	104 184 622.8	8 296.154	1 259 590.071
28	4 160 726.8	99 890 529.1	8 200.069	1 251 293.917
29	4 031 340.5	95 729 802.3	8 140.858	1 243 093.848
30	3 905 782.0	91 698 461.8	8 076.941	1 234 952.990
31	3 783 944.4	87 792 679.8	8 045.567	1 226 876.049
32	3 665 686.8	84 008 735.4	8 007.661	1 218 830.482
33	3 550 911.6	80 343 048.6	7 998.081	1 210 822.821
34	3 439 488.9	76 792 137.0	8 014.251	1 202 824.740
35	3 331 295.4	73 352 648.1	8 117.923	1 194 810.489
36	3 226 149.5	70 021 352.7	8 269.054	1 186 692.566
37	3 123 914.9	66 795 203.2	8 492.305	1 178 423.512
38	3 024 434.7	63 671 288.3	8 838.258	1 169 931.207
39	2 927 506.2	60 646 853.6	9 237.171	1 161 092.949
40	2 833 001.8	57 719 347.4	9 709.221	1 151 855.778
41	2 740 778.0	54 886 345.6	10 218.176	1 142 146.557
42	2 650 731.3	52 145 567.6	10 731.609	1 131 928.381
43	2 562 794.0	49 494 836.3	11 271.289	1 121 196.772
44	2 476 878.2	46 932 042.3	11 831.248	1 109 925.483
45	2 392 904.8	44 455 164.1	12 429.129	1 098 094.235
46	2 310 779.5	42 062 259.3	13 079.355	1 085 665.106
47	2 230 395.8	39 751 479.8	13 772.152	1 072 585.751
48	2 151 660.7	37 521 084.0	14 518.518	1 058 813.599
49	2 074 472.4	35 369 423.3	15 306.897	1 044 295.081

XVI. COMMUTATION COLUMNS: CSO AT 3%

Age x	D_x	N_x	C_x	M_x
50	1 998 744.0	33 294 950.9	16 145.109	1 028 988.184
51	1 924 383.0	31 296 206.9	17 020.413	1 012 843.075
52	1 851 312.7	29 371 823.9	17 902.007	995 822.662
53	1 779 488.9	27 520 511.2	18 814.279	977 920.655
54	1 708 844.9	25 741 022.3	19 743.028	959 106.376
55	1 639 329.7	24 032 177.4	20 690.546	939 363.348
56	1 570 891.7	22 392 847.7	21 672.210	918 672.802
57	1 503 465.3	20 821 956.0	22 683.398	897 000.592
58	1 436 991.7	19 318 490.7	23 777.295	874 317.194
59	1 371 420.2	17 881 499.0	24 752.177	850 599.899
60	1 306 723.8	16 510 078.8	25 804.703	825 847.722
61	1 242 859.2	15 203 355.0	26 836.036	800 043.019
62	1 179 823.4	13 960 495.8	27 846.132	773 206.983
63	1 117 613.4	12 780 672.4	28 830.119	745 360.851
64	1 056 231.5	11 663 059.0	29 779.577	716 530.732
65	995 687.8	10 606 827.5	30 692.340	686 751.155
66	935 994.9	9 611 139.7	31 569.313	656 058.815
67	877 163.6	8 675 144.8	32 395.427	624 489.502
68	819 219.7	7 797 981.2	33 150.537	592 094.075
69	762 208.4	6 978 761.5	33 751.833	558 943.538
70	706 256.4	6 216 553.1	34 140.262	525 191.705
71	651 545.5	5 510 296.7	34 253.619	491 051.443
72	598 314.8	4 858 751.2	34 069.048	456 797.824
73	546 819.2	4 260 436.4	33 584.287	422 728.776
74	497 308.1	3 713 617.2	32 889.905	389 144.489
75	449 933.5	3 216 309.1	32 050.095	356 254.584
76	404 778.5	2 766 375.6	31 116.905	324 204.489
77	361 872.0	2 361 597.1	30 109.191	293 087.584
78	321 222.8	1 999 725.1	29 022.371	262 978.393
79	282 844.4	1 678 502.3	27 787.431	233 956.022
80	246 818.8	1 395 657.9	26 354.463	206 168.591
81	213 275.5	1 148 839.1	24 712.922	179 814.128
82	182 350.6	935 563.6	22 868.200	155 101.136
83	154 171.2	753 213.0	20 862.501	132 232.936
84	128 818.2	599 041.8	18 761.225	111 370.435
85	106 305.0	470 223.6	16 631.093	92 609.210
86	86 577.7	363 918.6	14 526.529	75 978.117
87	69 529.5	‑277 340.9	12 497.068	61 451.588
88	55 007.3	207 811.4	10 587.550	48 954.520
89	42 817.6	152 804.1	8 832.090	38 366.970
90	32 738.4	109 986.5	7 251.375	29 534.880
91	24 533.4	77 248.1	5 853.988	22 283.505
92	17 964.9	52 714.7	4 638.273	16 429.517
93	12 803.4	34 749.8	3 596.142	11 791.244
94	8 834.3	21 946.4	2 715.983	8 195.102
95	5 861.0	13 112.1	1 998.652	5 479.119
96	3 691.7	7 251.1	1 435.657	3 480.467
97	2 148.5	3 559.4	1 018.801	2 044.810
98	1 067.1	1 410.9	692.218	1 026.009
99	343.8	343.8	333.791	333.791

XVII. SQUARES, SQUARE ROOTS, AND RECIPROCALS

N	N^2	$\sqrt{N}$	$1/N$	N	N^2	$\sqrt{N}$	$1/N$
0	0	0	————	50	2500	7.071	.020 000
1	1	1.000	1.000 000	51	2601	7.141	.019 608
2	4	1.414	.500 000	52	2704	7.211	.019 231
3	9	1.732	.333 333	53	2809	7.280	.018 868
4	16	2.000	.250 000	54	2916	7.348	.018 519
5	25	2.236	.200 000	55	3025	7.416	.018 182
6	36	2.449	.166 667	56	3136	7.483	.017 857
7	49	2.646	.142 857	57	3249	7.550	.017 544
8	64	2.828	.125 000	58	3364	7.616	.017 241
9	81	3.000	.111 111	59	3481	7.681	.016 949
10	100	3.162	.100 000	60	3600	7.746	.016 667
11	121	3.317	.090 909	61	3721	7.810	.016 393
12	144	3.464	.083 333	62	3844	7.874	.016 129
13	169	3.606	.076 923	63	3969	7.937	.015 873
14	196	3.742	.071 429	64	4096	8.000	.015 625
15	225	3.873	.066 667	65	4225	8.062	.015 385
16	256	4.000	.062 500	66	4356	8.124	.015 152
17	289	4.123	.058 824	67	4489	8.185	.014 925
18	324	4.243	.055 556	68	4624	8.246	.014 706
19	361	4.359	.052 632	69	4761	8.307	.014 493
20	400	4.472	.050 000	70	4900	8.367	.014 286
21	441	4.583	.047 619	71	5041	8.426	.014 085
22	484	4.690	.045 455	72	5184	8.485	.013 889
23	529	4.796	.043 478	73	5329	8.544	.013 699
24	576	4.899	.041 667	74	5476	8.602	.013 514
25	625	5.000	.040 000	75	5625	8.660	.013 333
26	676	5.009	.038 462	76	5776	8.718	.013 158
27	729	5.196	.037 037	77	5929	8.775	.012 987
28	784	5.291	.035 714	78	6084	8.832	.012 821
29	841	5.385	.034 483	79	6241	8.888	.012 658
30	900	5.477	.033 333	80	6400	8.944	.012 500
31	961	5.568	.032 258	81	6561	9.000	.012 346
32	1024	5.657	.031 250	82	6724	9.055	.012 195
33	1089	5.745	.030 303	83	6889	9.110	.012 048
34	1156	5.831	.029 412	84	7056	9.165	.011 905
35	1225	5.916	.028 571	85	7225	9.220	.011 765
36	1296	6.000	.027 778	86	7396	9.274	.011 628
37	1369	6.083	.027 027	87	7569	9.327	.011 494
38	1444	6.164	.026 316	88	7744	9.381	.011 364
39	1521	6.245	.025 641	89	7921	9.434	.011 236
40	1600	6.325	.025 000	90	8100	9.487	.011 111
41	1681	6.403	.024 390	91	8281	9.539	.010 989
42	1764	6.481	.023 810	92	8464	9.592	.010 870
43	1849	6.557	.023 256	93	8649	9.644	.010 753
44	1936	6.633	.022 727	94	8836	9.695	.010 638
45	2025	6.708	.022 222	95	9025	9.747	.010 526
46	2116	6.782	.021 739	96	9216	9.798	.010 417
47	2209	6.856	.021 277	97	9409	9.849	.010 309
48	2304	6.928	.020 833	98	9604	9.899	.010 204
49	2401	7.000	.020 408	99	9801	9.950	.010 101
50	2500	7.071	.020 000	100	10000	10.000	.010 000

1 2 3 4 5 6 7 8 9 0